Also by the Editors of Cook's Illustrated,
Home of America's Test Kitchen

The Best Recipe
The Best Recipe: American Classics
The Best Recipe: Italian Classics
The Best Recipe: Grilling and Barbecue
The Best Recipe: Soups and Stews
The Quick Recipe

The America's Test Kitchen Cookbook
Here in America's Test Kitchen

The Best Kitchen Quick Tips

The Complete Book of Pasta and Noodles
The Cook's Illustrated Complete Book of Poultry

How to Barbecue and Roast on the Grill
How to Cook Chicken Breasts
How to Cook Chinese Favorites
How to Cook Garden Vegetables
How to Cook Shrimp and Other Shellfish
How to Grill
How to Make an American Layer Cake
How to Make Cookie Jar Favorites
How to Make Ice Cream
How to Make Muffins, Biscuits, and Scones
How to Make Pasta Sauces
How to Make Pot Pies and Casseroles
How to Make Salad
How to Make Sauces and Gravies
How to Make Simple Fruit Desserts
How to Make Soup
How to Make Stew
How to Sauté

RESTAURANT FAVORITES AT HOME

A BEST RECIPE CLASSIC

A BEST RECIPE CLASSIC

RESTAURANT FAVORITES *at Home*

BY THE EDITORS OF

COOK'S ILLUSTRATED

PHOTOGRAPHY BY KELLER & KELLER AND DANIEL VAN ACKERE

FRONT COVER PHOTOGRAPH BY CHRISTOPHER HIRSHEIMER

ILLUSTRATIONS BY JOHN BURGOYNE

BROOKLINE, MASSACHUSETTS

America's Test Kitchen

17 Station Street

Brookline, MA, 02445

Library of Congress Cataloging-in-Publication Data
The Editors of *Cook's Illustrated*
Restaurant Favorites at Home—Would you like to cook restaurant recipes at home? We exhaustively tested more than 700 of America's best restaurant dishes to bring you 150 streamlined and foolproof recipes that capture all the genius and drama of four-star cooking.
1st Edition

ISBN 0-936184-67-1 (hardcover): $29.95
I. Cooking. I. Title
2003

10 9 8 7 6 5 4 3 2 1

Manufactured in the United States of America

Distributed by America's Test Kitchen, 17 Station Street, Brookline, MA, 02445

Designed by Robin Gilmore-Barnes

Edited by Lori Galvin-Frost

Recipe credits:

For Crab and Asparagus Egg Drop Soup:

From: *Patricia Yeo: Cooking from A to Z* by Patricia Yeo

Reprinted by permission of St. Martin's Press, LLC

For Roasted Sea Scallops with Bean Fricassee and Pistou:

Adapted from *Chef Daniel Boulud: Cooking in New York City* (Assouline 2002)

For Brown Sugar Shortbread:

Recipe Courtesy of Emeril Lagasse

Pictured on front of jacket: Caramelized Pears with Blue Cheese and Black Pepper–Caramel Sauce (page 391)

Pictured on back of jacket: Crab Towers with Avocado and Gazpacho Salsas (page 58),

Salmon Confit with Lemon Grass Broth and Spring Vegetables (page 277), and

Individual German Chocolate Cakes (page 349)

Contents

Preface

LIKE MANY OF US WHO GREW UP IN THE 1950s and 1960s, my experience with restaurant food was limited to third-rate Chinese restaurants and second-rate French establishments, the sort that specialized in dishes like duck à l'orange and desserts like Grand Marnier soufflé, which had to be ordered along with the main course. It wasn't until 1967 that I experienced a transcendent restaurant meal. I was in Paris and, at the ripe age of 16, had managed to ditch the family for the better part of the day. I ended up at a small bistro on the Left Bank and, in my grade-school French, managed to order roast chicken, a half-bottle of cheap Beaujolais, and a simple dessert of jewel-like fraises des bois. The revelation—that something so simple could be so good—was transformative. Ever since that day, I have not only appreciated the possibilities of restaurant cooking but felt that it is usually best left to restaurants. As a cook who even goes so far as to raise his own chickens and grow his own strawberries, I have yet to be able to recreate that simple meal at home.

Since then, of course, I have had my share of fancy restaurant food, some of it pretentious and some of it extraordinary. Every time I have thought about trying to prepare this food for my family, I am reminded of the couple I once met on a book tour. The husband professed a unique ability: reproducing virtually any restaurant meal at home. Out of earshot, his wife confided that his versions of restaurant classics were, at best, disappointing. There's the rub. Restaurant recipes are as different from home cooking as the Major Leagues are from Little League. None of us has six prep cooks, a grill station, a saucier, a pastry chef, a sous chef, and three dishwashers. Which member of your family is going to make the veal stock, finely dice a half-dozen tomatoes, braise the endive, bone two chickens, and make a dessert requiring caramel sauce, génoise, pastry cream, and curls of dark chocolate?

Yet restaurant chefs have a lot to offer, if not actual recipes, then ideas: flavor combinations, contrasts in texture, and four-star presentation. This is a book, then, about ideas, about thinking about food from the point of view of a chef, not a cook, and then translating these ideas into recipes that work at home. This may lead to something as simple as pan-roasting mussels (from Restaurant LuLu in San Francisco) to something as explosive as Chocolate Volcano Cakes with Espresso Ice Cream (from Ixora in Whitehouse Station, New Jersey.

What this book really has to offer, beyond culinary imagination, is our extensive, if not obsessive, approach to recipe testing. Each recipe has been tested, retested, and then tested again to make sure that any decent home cook can turn out restaurant-style food at home. And for those of you who read cookbooks more than you cook from them, this book is full of ideas. Who knew that Dixie cups could be used in place of individual charlotte molds, that broiled corn tastes as good as grilled, and that already-grilled meat can be marinated for only 15 minutes for even better flavor than if it had been marinated well ahead of time?

I admit that this project was more work than I had expected. When that last recipe was finally tested and edited, it reminded me of haying on a hot July day. When the last bale is thrown into the barn and your neck and arms are red and pricked with small stems of timothy, someone always says, "That's the one we've been looking for." The "one," of course, is the last bale, the end of the job. It was hard work, but there is nothing like a barn full of hay or a book full of well-tested recipes to make it all worthwhile.

That, of course, goes to the heart of this book. These are not quick, four-ingredient recipes, but they are worth the time and trouble because they really do let you make restaurant favorites—successfully—at home. This is not a hollow promise. We've made all of the food in this book over and over again in America's Test Kitchen, and you should find the recipes not only dependable but occasionally inspirational. It is my hope that more than a few of these recipes will turn out meals as good as the one I ate in Paris more than 35 years ago. We'll know that we have succeeded if you taste one of these recipes, stop, and say, "Now, that's the one I've been looking for!"

Christopher Kimball
Founder and Editor
Cook's Illustrated

Acknowledgments

During our search for great restaurant recipes, we relied on food editors at newspapers across the country to identify possible candidates for inclusion in this book. Thank you to all of these editors for their insights about local restaurants and chefs:

Wanda Adams of the *Honolulu Advertiser*
Susan Alai of *The Star-Ledger* (Newark, New Jersey)
Sylvia Carter of *Newsday*
Danielle Centoni of the *Oakland Tribune*
Hsiao-Ching Chou of the *Seattle Post-Intelligencer*
Judith Evans of the *St. Louis Post-Dispatch*
Teresa Farney of the *Colorado Springs Gazette*
Dennis Getto of the *Milwaukee Journal Sentinel*
Peter Gianotti of *Newsday*
Linda Gordon of the *Naples Daily News*
Carol Haddix of the *Chicago Tribune*
Ann Haigh of *Pittsburgh Magazine*
Karen Haram of the *San Antonio Express-News*
Debby Hartz of the *Ft. Lauderdale Sun Sentinel*
Ann Heller of the *Dayton Daily News*
David Holloway of the *Mobile Register*
Kathie Jenkins of the *Pioneer Press* (St. Paul, Minnesota)
Elizabeth Johnson of *The Journal News* (White Plains, New York)
Carolyn Jung of the *San Jose Mercury News*
Nancy Leson of the *Seattle Times*
Dan Macdonald of *The Florida Times-Union*
Louis Mahoney of the *Richmond Times-Dispatch*
Jo-Ellen O'Hara of *The Birmingham News*
Joan Reminick of *Newsday*
Judith A. Rollman of the *Reading Eagle* (Reading, Pennsylvania)
Anne Rutter of the *Cedar Rapids Gazette*
Bill St. John of the *Denver Post*
Betty Shimabukuro of the *Honolulu Star-Bulletin*
Jill Silva of the *Kansas City Star*
Tommy C. Simmons of *The Advocate* (Baton Rouge, Louisiana)
Kathleen Stebbins of the *Reno Gazette-Journal*
Nancy Stohs of the *Milwaukee Journal Sentinel*
Ann Strosnider of *The News Tribune* (Tacoma, Washington)
Joe Stumpe of the *Wichita Eagle*
Robin Swartz of the *Lansing State Journal*
Karin A. Welzel of the *Pittsburgh Tribune-Review*
Virginia Wood of *The Austin Chronicle*

We also thank all our colleagues and friends who made recipe recommendations. And we could not have undertaken this book if it had not been for all the restaurants, chefs, and kitchen staff who not only contributed recipes, but also took the time to answer questions from our test kitchen.

All of the projects undertaken at *Cook's Illustrated* are collective efforts, the combined experience and work of editors, test cooks, and writers, all joining in the search for the best cooking methods. Lori Galvin-Frost spearheaded this project with Rebecca Hays. Julia Collin oversaw recipe development and along with Matthew Card, Keith Dresser, Diane Mahoney, and Susan Light wrote the essays to accompany the recipes. Nina West and Garth Clingingsmith assisted in the kitchen.

Amy Klee created the design for the Best Recipe series, and Robin Gilmore-Barnes was responsible for the art direction of this book. Christopher Hirsheimer photographed the front cover image. Keller & Keller captured the color images that appear in the book and Mary Jane Sawyer styled all the food for photography. Daniel van Ackere took photographs of the equipment and ingredients throughout the book, and John Burgoyne drew all the illustrations. Jessica Sherman copyedited the manuscript, Jayne Yaffe Kemp proofread the pages, and Cathy Dorsey compiled the index.

The following individuals on the editorial, production, circulation, customer service, and office staffs also worked on the book: Ron Bilodeau, Jack Bishop, Barbara Bourassa, Rich Cassidy, Sharyn Chabot, Mary Connelly, Bob Connolly, Larisa Greiner, India Koopman, Jim McCormack, Jennifer McCreary, Henrietta Murray, Jessica Lindheimer Quirk, Mandy Shito, Aaron Shuman, Tadashi Tezuka, and Elizabeth Wray. And without help from members of the marketing staff, readers might never find our books. Special thanks to Deborah Broide, Steven Browall, Shekinah Cohn, Connie Forbes, Julie Gardner, Jason Geller, David Mack, Steven Sussman, Jacqui Valerio, and Jonathan Venier. All contributed to our marketing and distribution efforts.

Making Sense of Restaurant Recipes

WHY PREPARE RESTAURANT FOOD AT HOME? After all, isn't dining out about not having to do the cooking or the dishes? But anyone who's ever caught a television cooking show or flipped through a glossy food magazine knows that restaurant chefs have become a cultural phenomenon. Much of their creative genius might be out of place (and a bit silly) in a home kitchen, but surely some of those inventive combinations and techniques could elevate a home-cooked meal from good to great.

Our goal for this book was simple: Figure out which restaurant ideas are most valuable for the home cook and then write clear, precise recipes that show how to reproduce these dishes.

First, we needed to identify noteworthy recipes. We started by sending letters to 175 newspaper food editors, requesting the names of the local restaurant dishes they'd most like to prepare at home. We also reviewed "best restaurant" lists from all available media and quizzed dozens of industry colleagues. We followed these leads to the restaurants and chefs, who generously shared their recipes. After this initial research, we carefully reviewed each recipe and chose those which could be best adapted to the home kitchen.

In adapting these recipes, we set out to capture the magic of the recipes without the madness of their execution. We put these recipes through our usual rigorous development and testing process to turn out recipes that would both maintain the spirit and essence of the original dishes and be approachable to the home cook. We began by addressing the problems that usually befall restaurant recipes when attempted at home (as follows).

➢ LENGTHY INGREDIENT LISTS AND COMPLEX PREPARATION We trimmed these recipes to their essentials, without compromising flavor or visual appeal, to get at the heart of the dish. In Tuna Tartare with Sweet Potato Crisps (page 40), we nixed the time-consuming roasted tomato garnish and replaced the fussy tuiles with sweet potato chips (you could even use store-bought). In the end, we had a dish with sophisticated flavor, wonderful contrasts in texture, and elegant visual appeal, but the workload was now manageable. We eliminated the eight-hour marinating step in the Grilled Skirt Steak Tacos (page 180) to turn an all-day affair into a weeknight supper. How? We found that allowing the grilled meat to rest in the marinade for just 10 minutes packed the same flavor punch as the original technique.

Restaurants, which employ dishwashers, needn't worry about piles of dirty pots and pans—not so for the home cook. Both Creamed Spinach (page 310) and Chicken-Fried Oysters with Warm Spinach, Apple, and Bacon Salad (page 113) originally called for four pans. We were able to use just two pans to prepare each recipe.

➢ EXPENSIVE OR HARD-TO-FIND INGREDIENTS We looked for substitutions, keeping convenience and economy in mind. For example, we found that a combination of chicken and beef broths with a little added tomato paste produced a worthy stand-in for veal stock. The Sane Truffle Soup (page 93) originally seemed insane to us: Between the mushrooms, truffle oil, and truffles, the recipe set us back more than $100 for eight servings. To reduce costs, we sweated the mushrooms to extract as much flavor from them as possible and reserved the pricey truffles and truffle oil for a garnish, where a little of these luxuries could go a long way.

We also looked for ways to use high-quality prepared foods to stand in for home-made. We mixed freshly grated ginger juice into premium vanilla ice cream to make Ginger Ice Cream (page 383), transforming a restaurant staple that requires an ice cream machine and many hours into a low-tech, 10-minute recipe.

➢ EXPENSIVE OR HARD-TO-FIND TOOLS We used what we had on hand—relying on biscuit cutters instead of metal timbale rings (which no one has at home) to make Crab Towers with Avocado and Gazpacho Salsas (page 58). And we fashioned our own charlotte molds—from paper Dixie cups—to make the garnishes for Carrot Soup with Root Vegetable Charlotte (page 71).

➢ RESTAURANT-STYLE OVENS In adapting the baked goods in this book, we were initially perplexed by our unsuccessful results. When we spoke with pastry chefs, we realized that these recipes were developed for convection ovens, which are equipped with fans to circulate heat evenly around the foods and thus speed up the cooking process. We tested (and tested and tested) cooking times and temperatures in regular ovens until we got things right.

Most restaurant kitchens are equipped with grills. But could home cooks, especially those in colder climates, achieve grilled flavor without the grill? For Roasted Corn Bisque (page 81), we compensated by high-roasting fresh corn under the broiler to achieve a similar smoky flavor. We found the technique equally successful when broiling the eggplant slices in the Eggplant Rolls with Smoked Mozzarella (page 12).

➢ ABUNDANT QUANTITIES Restaurants often prepare huge batches of food at a time, so we needed to rework many recipes to feed 4 rather than 40. This isn't as easy as it might sound. Many recipes, especially those that involve baking, cannot be scaled back using basic arithmetic—the revised proportions just don't work without some tinkering. Again, trial-and-error was employed until our persistence paid off.

➢ VAGUE INSTRUCTIONS Many restaurant recipes are written in kitchen shorthand, which may be comprehensible to everyone working on the line but reads like a foreign language to anyone else. To make sure that the home cook wouldn't be left guessing, we were careful to provide clear instructions and accurate timing information, all reinforced with visual cues.

This book contains all of the usual *Cook's Illustrated* food tastings and equipment tests. We covered basics, such as olive oil and chicken broth, as well as ingredients not usually part of our repertoire, such as wasabi (which comes closer to fresh, the powder or the paste?) and truffle oil (is there a difference between white truffle oil and black truffle oil?). We wondered if it was necessary to invest in a fancy stainless-steel mandoline ($169), a prized tool many chefs use to cut vegetables such as potatoes and carrots into paper-thin slices. Or would a plastic V-slicer ($8.99) do just fine at home? In addition, we offer detailed explanations of terms and techniques commonly used by chefs—including frying, flambéing, plating, and garnishing.

As a result of our test kitchen's work, this book isn't your typical restaurant cookbook. We like to think it has more allure—clearly written, inventive recipes that any cook (even one without a culinary degree) can reproduce at home. We hope you enjoy them.

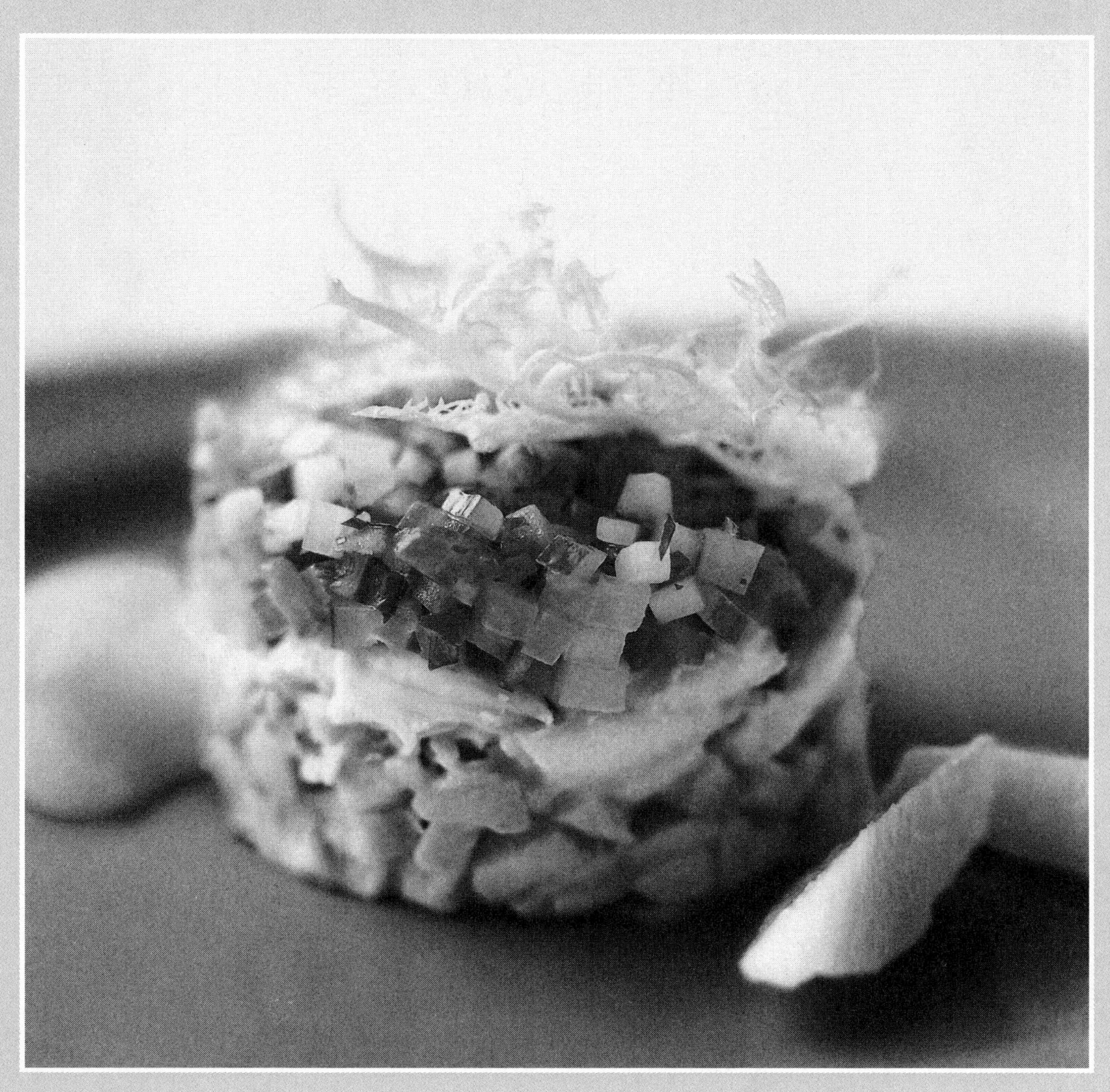

1 FIRST COURSES

First Courses

Appetizers

Soups

Salads

Mediterranean-Style Deviled Eggs

Adapted from Deviled Eggs with Tuna, Black Olives, and Tomato

OLEANA, CAMBRIDGE, MASSACHUSETTS

OLEANA HAS A REPUTATION FOR INSPIRED, Mediterranean-style food, and this recipe for deviled eggs is a case in point. The humble deviled egg, a stalwart of the backyard barbecue circuit, is reinvented with the addition of fresh tuna, celery, olives, and tomato. Ostensibly repackaged tuna salad, the filling is a crowd-pleaser and couldn't be easier to make, requiring no specialized equipment and no exotic ingredients. We found the secret to success lay in perfectly cooked eggs (easier said than done) and the best tuna—by no means would workaday canned tuna do in this dish.

The best deviled egg starts off with the perfect hard-cooked egg, which, by our definition, possesses a tender white and bright yellow yolk just barely set solid—a far cry from the usual rubbery white and green-tinged yolk. Because the recipe didn't specify cooking instructions for hard-cooked eggs, we followed our own method developed in the test kitchen.

In researching how to hard-cook an egg, we found two predominant schools of thought: starting in cold water and bringing to a boil, or adding eggs to already boiling water. For each method, timing ranged widely—hard to believe, all things considered. Both methods produced eggs that we were not fully satisfied with, since they were hard and rubbery, sulfurous, or undercooked. There had to be a better way.

Flummoxed, we called the experts. The American Egg Board recommended an entirely different method from those we had tried. It started the eggs in cold water and then, once the water had come to a boil, removed the pot from the heat and allowed the eggs to steep in the hot water for 15 minutes. The method yielded almost perfect eggs, but they were tainted by a slightly green yolk. We decided to shorten the steeping period and found that 10 minutes was ideal, resulting in perfectly tender whites and sulfur-free, bright yellow yolks.

Perfect hard-cooked eggs in hand, we were prepared to tackle the rest of Oleana's recipe. The most striking ingredient in the egg's filling is minced fresh tuna. The tuna is briefly sautéed before being folded into the filling. The amount required was a scant four ounces—easy for a restaurant to compile from trimmed scraps, but an amount many fishmongers are hesitant to provide. We thought high-quality, oil-packed tuna, available in small amounts, might serve as a suitable substitution, and our intuition proved correct. In a side-by-side taste test, we found the differences were slight between fresh and canned, so we chose canned for our recipe.

Oil-packed tuna is available in a variety of forms. After a recent taste test, we have our favorites (see page 6). Any of the Ortiz-brand tunas tasted great in the deviled eggs, although the first-place "Ventresca" tuna is very expensive for such an application—it's best appreciated on its own, as in a niçoise salad. If you can't find Ortiz-brand tuna, try another brand of high-quality, imported oil-packed tuna. Conventional water-packed tuna is not a suitable substitution, since its flavor pales in comparison and its wet texture has a negative impact on the filling's creaminess.

To round out the filling's flavor, Oleana includes sautéed celery and scallion, a pinch of curry powder (basic Madras), and mayonnaise. Briefly sautéing the celery and scallion tempers their assertive flavors, which would have been overwhelming otherwise. Homemade mayonnaise is the best choice in this dish, but we found that good-quality prepared mayonnaise was perfectly acceptable and much more convenient for the home cook. The original recipe included a full cup of mayonnaise for the filling, but tasters much preferred it scaled back to three-quarters cup—less fat allowed the tuna flavor to shine.

Oleana garnishes its deviled eggs with finely diced tomato and a whole pitted olive. The olive type was unspecified, so we chose the widely available Kalamata for convenience. However, a whole Kalamata olive easily overpowered the subtly flavored filling, so we opted for a sprinkle of chopped olives, which tasted mellower and was also aesthetically pleasing—always important for appetizers.

Mediterranean-Style Deviled Eggs

MAKES 16

Make sure the sautéed celery mixture is thoroughly cooled before adding it to the eggs and mayonnaise. For more information about buying tuna packed in oil, see page 6.

PREPARING HARD-COOKED EGGS

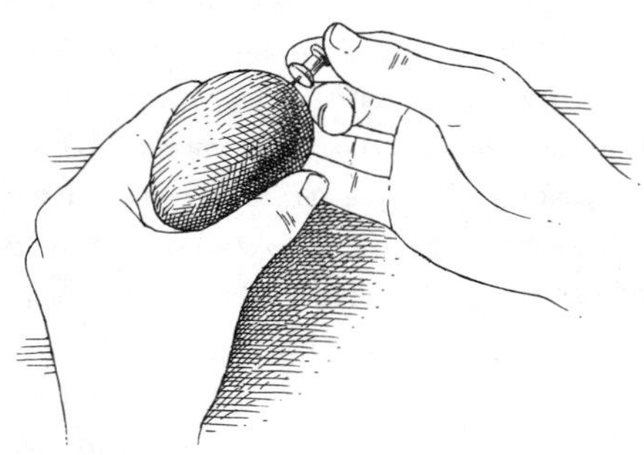

1. Prick a tiny air hole in the large end of the egg using a common pushpin or tack. Cook the eggs.

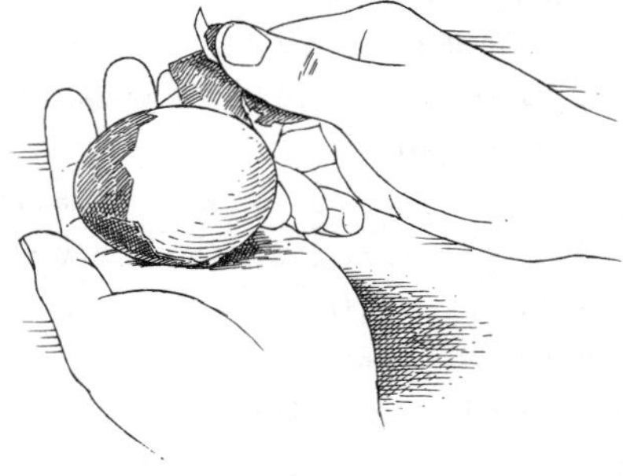

2. Remove the eggs from the hot water with a slotted spoon and plunge them into ice water. When the eggs are chilled thoroughly, their shells will peel right off.

- 8 large eggs, pricked with a pushpin (see the illustration on page 5)
- 1 tablespoon extra-virgin olive oil
- 2 small celery ribs, minced (about ½ cup)
- 1 medium scallion, minced (about 2 tablespoons)
- Pinch Madras curry powder
- Salt
- ¾ cup mayonnaise
- 1 tablespoon minced fresh parsley leaves
- 4 ounces canned oil-packed tuna, well drained and chopped fine (about 1 cup)
- Ground black pepper
- 1 medium plum tomato, cored, seeded, and chopped fine
- 8 Kalamata olives, pitted and chopped fine

1. Place the eggs in a large saucepan, cover with 1 inch of water, and bring to a boil over high heat. Remove the pan from the heat, cover, and let stand for 10 minutes. Meanwhile, fill a medium bowl with ice water. Transfer the eggs to the ice-water bath with a slotted spoon and let stand for 5 minutes. Peel the eggs (see the illustration on page 5) and cut in half lengthwise. Scoop out the yolks into a small bowl and set aside.

2. While the eggs cook, prepare the filling. Heat the olive oil in a medium skillet over medium-high heat until shimmering. Add the celery, scallion, curry powder, and ¼ teaspoon salt. Cook, stirring frequently, until the celery has just begun to soften, about 1½ minutes. Transfer the mixture to a plate and refrigerate to cool.

3. Mash the egg yolks with a fork and stir in the mayonnaise, parsley, and cooled celery mixture. Add the tuna to the mixture and stir to combine. Adjust the seasonings with salt and pepper. Divide the filling equally among the egg-white halves and garnish with the tomato and olives. Serve immediately or refrigerate for up to 1 day before serving (if storing, reserve the garnish until just before serving).

INGREDIENTS: Tuna Packed in Olive Oil

We wondered if all brands of oil-packed tuna are created equal. The six we found in grocery stores fell into three categories: light (made from bluefin, yellowfin, or skipjack tuna, or a mixture thereof), white (made from albacore tuna), and imported "white tuna" (made from bonito tuna).

As we found in an earlier tasting of tunas packed in water, our panel of tasters did not care for light tuna. The representative brands, Cento Solid Pack Light Tuna and Pastene Fancy Light Tuna, were thought to have "potent" and "metallic" flavors with a "bitter finish," as well as "chewed" and "unpleasant" textures. Surprisingly, our albacore contender, Dave's Albacore Fillets, came in dead last. "It's like eating nothing" was the comment that summed up all others.

The three best-tasting tunas were made by Ortiz, a small Spanish company. Ortiz cans primarily northern bonito white tuna fished off the coast of Spain, a tuna not used by American packers. Europeans consider this tuna to be of the highest quality because of its extremely white meat, tender texture, and full, clean flavor. Although each of the three Ortiz tunas consists of the same ingredients—bonito del norte, olive oil, and salt—they have markedly different textures. Ortiz Bonito del Norte "Ventresca" ($9.95 for a 3.88-ounce can) boasts a silky texture and fresh flavor. Ventresca refers to the underside of the fish where fat is more concentrated; the Ortiz Bonito del Norte (tinned) ($3.99 for a 3.95-ounce can) had a flaky, tender, and pleasant texture; and the Ortiz Bonito del Norte (jarred) ($7.99 for a 7.76-ounce jar) contained large, dense chunks of tuna that were somewhat "dry," but the flavor was great "light," "clean," and "mild."

Olivia's Onion Strings *with* Blue Cheese

Adapted from Olivia's Onion Strings with Maytag Blue Cheese
Olivia's, Dayton, Ohio

SOME OF THE TASTIEST DISHES ON A RESTAURANT menu have humble beginnings. For example, concocted as a last-minute kitchen-staff snack, this pairing of onion strings and blue cheese was such a hit among the staff that the restaurant put it on the menu. Although the combination of fried onion and blue cheese is simple, we found the success of this appetizer depends on using onion rings of the right thickness and employing the frying method recommended by the restaurant.

Finding that one large yellow onion made plenty of rings to serve six people, we noted that slicing it very thinly, as Chef McCarthy had instructed, was important. Determining that one-sixteenth-inch-thick slices yielded the best strings—crisp exterior with a tender, onion-flavored center—we quickly realized that cutting an onion this thin was another matter. Slicing them by hand is nearly impossible, yet we had some success using a food processor fitted with the slicing blade. Although the food processor was able to slice the onions thin enough, it had some trouble with uniformity, depending on the orientation of the onion in the feed tube (which changes slightly with every blade rotation). What worked best, however, was a mandoline. Able to adjust the thickness of the onion slice to the slightest fraction, the mandoline offered the ultimate control and absolutely uniform slices (see page 8 for information about buying a mandoline). Luckily, this recipe requires only one onion so that the actual time spent slicing is minimal.

Tossing the sliced onion with salt, pepper, and flour was the next step, and again Chef McCarthy offered some valuable tips. In the restaurant, he fries the onion in a deep-fryer using large, wire-mesh baskets. The onion is tossed liberally with a seasoned flour mixture in a basket, and then the basket is set over a sink and whacked several times against the edge to knock off any excess. In lieu of using wire-mesh fry baskets, we found a large strainer (or colander) worked perfectly. After tossing the onion with seasoned flour, we transferred it to a strainer set over a sink or large bowl and shook it vigorously. This not only minimized mess, but ensured that the onion received a thin, even coat of flour.

Because commercial deep-fryers are quite big, they can accommodate large batches of food at a time. Yet in a home kitchen, frying is a different story. To start, we noted that it's best to fry in a 12-inch-wide Dutch oven. Not only do the 5-inch-high sides of this size pot prevent some of the oil from splattering,

EQUIPMENT: Mandolines

What's cheaper than a food processor and faster (if not also sharper) than a chef's knife? A mandoline. This hand-operated slicing machine comes in two basic styles—the classic stainless steel model, supported by legs, and the plastic hand-held model, often called a V-slicer. We put both types of machines—ranging in price from $8.99 to $169—to the test. To determine the winners, we sliced melons, cut carrots into julienne (matchstick pieces), cut potatoes into batonette (long, skinny french fry pieces), and sliced potatoes into thin rounds. Then we evaluated three aspects of the mandolines: ease of use, including degree of effort, adjustment ease, grip/handle comfort, and safety; quality, including sturdiness and uniformity/cleanliness of slices; and cleanup.

The Progressive Mandoline Multi Slicer ($8.99) is a plastic V-slicer. Testers gave this model high marks for safety, handle comfort, and blade sharpness, which helped them whip through melon and potato slices. An interchangeable blade platform cut respectable batonette and julienne, though these cuts required more effort on the part of testers.

The two other V-slicers tested were the Börner V-Slicer Plus ($34.95) and the Joyce Chen Asian Mandoline Plus ($49.95). The latter produced flawless melon slices, carrot julienne, and potato batonette but got low marks for its small, ineffective safety mechanism and tricky blade adjustment. Testers also downgraded the poorly designed and not very sturdy base. The Börner unit sliced melons and carrots with little effort, but the potato slices were inconsistent and required more effort to produce. The Börner's well-designed safety guard, however, kept hands away from blades, and its adjustments were quick and easy to make. In the end, testers preferred the cheaper V-slicers made by Progressive and Target to either of these more expensive options.

We also tested two classic stainless steel mandolines. The deBuyer mandoline from Williams-Sonoma ($169) was controversial. Shorter testers had difficulty gaining leverage to cut consistently; some melon slices were one eighth inch thicker on one side. However, the safety mechanism, sturdiness, and adjustment mechanism were lauded by taller testers. With some practice, all testers were able to produce perfect slices, julienne, and batonette with the Bron Coucke mandoline ($99). This machine has fewer parts to clean and switch out than its plastic counterparts and requires less effort to operate once the user becomes familiar with it. Still, the quality comes at an awfully high price.

THE BEST CLASSIC MANDOLINE

Of the two stainless steel mandolines tested, we preferred the model made by Bron Coucke. Note, however, that it costs 10 times more than a good V-slicer.

THE BEST V-SLICER

Plastic mandolines (also called V-slicers) may not be as sturdy as stainless steel versions, but their quality far exceeds the minimal dollar investment. Among the four models tested, we liked the Progressive.

but they are low enough to offer easy access to the food as it cooks. Striking a balance between enough oil to fry the onion strings properly and economy, we found the onion required about three-quarters inch of vegetable oil (roughly four cups). We often find it necessary to fry in batches to prevent the oil from cooling off too much, but were surprised to find that these onion strings could actually be fried all at once. We brought the oil to an initial temperature of 350 degrees (using a candy/deep-fat thermometer or instant-read thermometer that registers high temperatures) and then simply added all of the floured onion strings and cooked them to a golden crisp in just four to five minutes. The key here to prevent the rings from fusing together is to agitate them (using a spider or long-handled slotted spoon) while they are in the oil. As a final touch to this snack, we found that the one-quarter cup of strong blue cheese sprinkled over the top was just enough to impart flavor without overpowering the onion.

EQUIPMENT: Spider

More often referred to as a mesh skimmer or strainer, this piece of equipment is invaluable when it comes to working with boiling water or hot oil. Compared with a slotted spoon, which generally retrieves only a few food items from the water or oil at a time, this not so itsy-bitsy spider has a wide basket made of open webbed (hence the name) mesh that can cradle food and allow excess water or oil to drain away quickly.

Olivia's Onion Strings with Blue Cheese

SERVES 4 TO 6

Serve these dressed-up onion rings with plenty of napkins at your next Super Bowl party.

- **1 quart vegetable oil, for frying**
- **1 cup all-purpose flour**
- **Salt and ground black pepper**
- **1 medium-large onion (about 10 ounces)**
- **1 1/2 ounces assertive blue cheese, crumbled (a heaping 1/4 cup)**

1. Heat the oil in a Dutch oven over medium-high heat until it reaches 350 degrees. (Use an instant-read thermometer that registers high temperatures or clip a candy/deep-fat thermometer onto the side of the pan before turning on the heat.) Meanwhile, mix the flour, 1 tablespoon salt, and 1 teaspoon pepper together in a large bowl.

2. Cut the onion in half through the root, peel, and cut into 1/16-inch-thick slices using a mandoline or food processor fitted with a slicing disk.

3. Add the onion to the flour mixture and toss to coat. Transfer the floured onion to a large strainer set over the sink or another large bowl, and shake vigorously to remove the excess flour. Add all the onion strings to the oil and fry until golden brown, 4 to 5 minutes, adjusting the heat as necessary to maintain the cooking temperature. Remove the onion from the oil using a metal spider or slotted spoon, tapping the handle several times on the rim of the pot to drain any excess oil, then transfer to a rimmed baking sheet lined with several layers of paper towels. Season with salt and pepper and transfer to a large serving plate. Sprinkle the blue cheese over the onion strings and serve immediately.

TECHNIQUE: Frying

FRYING WORKSTATION

While most restaurants have dedicated frying workstations (Fry-o-lators and extra-large stainless cooling racks), deep-frying in a home kitchen is a different matter. Cramped space, spattering oil, and inappropriate equipment all conspire to take the fun out of the job. But it needn't be an onerous task: With a bit of organization and some basic working knowledge, frying at home can be both fun and rewarding—your french fries will rival those of the most authentic bistro, and those wontons and dumplings will put the local carryout to shame.

You may already own most of the equipment you need. For a cooking vessel, we favor a large heavy-bottomed Dutch oven, since the pot's tall sides contain the spattering oil and its heavy weight maintains an even temperature. In testing at *Cook's Illustrated,* we have favored All-Clad and Le Creuset Dutch ovens for their even heating and solid construction. For a more economical model (at one third the price of its competitors), the traditional Lodge cast-iron Dutch oven performed quite well, but its extreme weight—a whopping 17 pounds—can make it cumbersome for all but the most robust cook.

Proper oil temperature is crucial to success when deep-frying, so a thermometer is an essential piece of equipment. We favor instant-read thermometers for their accuracy and rapid response, but a candy thermometer works just as well—at a lower price (though we heartily endorse instant-read thermometers for a wide variety of kitchen purposes).

If you will be breading or battering items prior to frying (such as the Crispy Chicken Dumplings with Sweet-and-

Sour Sauce, page 30, or the Coconut Shrimp with Mango Chutney, page 48), a trio of cake pans keeps each step of the procedure neat and tidy. Inexpensive cake pans or eight-inch square Pyrex baking dishes work equally well.

Proper breading is more than just tossing the items in flour, egg wash, and crumbs. Each layer must be applied judiciously, or the coating will be uneven, leading to poor results. After each step, shake off any excess coating, be it flour, egg wash, or bread crumbs. We like to use tongs for breading to keep our hands clean—it's all too easy to build up a thick layer of messy goo on your hands. Long-handled tongs are also handy for separating items in the cooking oil that may have fused together.

For cooking oil, we almost universally fry in vegetable oil, since it possesses a high smoke point and is flavorless. We have tested a wide variety of oils and fats—including such exotica as goose fat—and none possesses the attributes of vegetable oil. In some instances (like Hand-Cut Fries with Whole-Grain Mustard Aïoli, page 318), however, we favor peanut oil for its light flavor.

Properly equipped, you're now ready for the nitty-gritty of frying. First and foremost is to understand the importance of oil temperature. Food cooks sequentially when deep-fried; the outer breading or coating is cooked by the oil and then the foodstuff inside the coating steams in its own moisture. If the oil temperature is too low, the coating won't cook properly and the oil can penetrate to the interior to make things greasy-tasting and oil-sodden. If the oil temperature is too high, the outer coating will burn long before the interior is cooked, and this can be dangerous if cooking foods like pork or chicken that must be cooked to the proper temperature for safe consumption. If you have any doubt, you can also insert an instant-read thermometer directly into the fried food.

That said, there are two key ways to maintain proper temperature. First, adjust the burner's temperature as needed. The oil temperature will plummet when food is added, so it's likely that you will need to increase the temperature to reflect the change. And second, never overcrowd the pan—a sure way to drop the oil temperature precipitously low. Fry items in batches as the recipe indicates; trying to hasten cooking time by doubling up will only lead to soggy, improperly browned food.

For removing items from the hot oil, we favor spiders—open-meshed strainers on long handles (see the illustration on page 9). We prefer spiders with fairly small heads, since they are more maneuverable than larger models, making it easier to fish out small foodstuffs. While there are a variety of deluxe models on the market, there's no need to get too fancy: they all do pretty much the same job. If you don't own or can't find a spider, a slotted metal spoon can work in a pinch; so, too, can long-handled tongs.

To keep freshly fried food crisp and light, it's imperative to remove any clinging oil as quickly as possible. Our tried-and-true method employs common kitchen equipment: paper toweling, a wire cooling rack, and a rimmed baking sheet. The paper towels trap excess oil, and the rack allows air to circulate freely beneath the foodstuffs. The baking sheet on the bottom catches any crumbs or oil not trapped by the toweling.

And while the food rests on the rack, go ahead and give it a final seasoning; extra salt will remain behind on the rack instead of on the serving platter.

WHAT TO DO WITH THE OIL AFTER FRYING

If you've just fried a few things, the oil may be filtered and reused—though you must store it in the refrigerator to prevent rancidity. Never reuse oil used for frying fish.

To dispose of spent oil, we allow it to cool entirely and then pour it into several leftover plastic grocery bags placed inside one another. It's helpful to have someone hold the bag open if you have a significant quantity of oil. Tie the handles tightly before discarding.

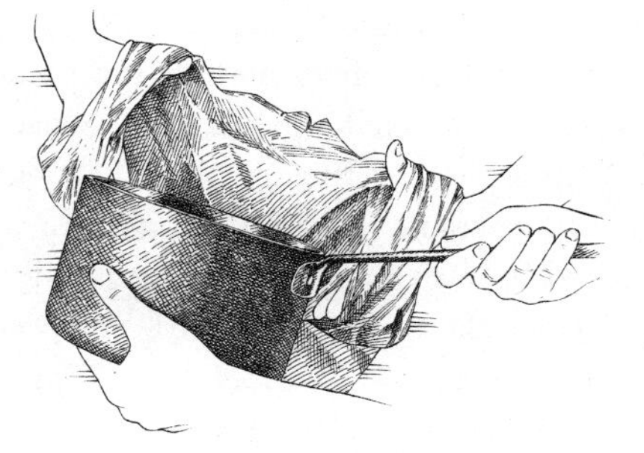

Eggplant Rolls *with* Smoked Mozzarella

Adapted from Il Mito's Smoked Mozzarella Wrapped in Eggplant

Il Mito, Milwaukee, Wisconsin

EGGPLANT SHOWS UP ON RESTAURANT menus in many guises, but most often breaded and fried, parmigiana-style. Il Mito takes a more refined approach. Its preparation is similar to the antipasto that one often encounters in southern Italy. It consists of creamy fresh mozzarella wrapped with thin slices of smoky grilled eggplant, punctuated by sweet, fresh basil. Normally served at room temperature, Il Mito's version takes a different course. Incorporating smoked mozzarella and roasted red peppers, this dish is then baked in a tomato sauce, creating a more substantial result. We enjoyed this variation so much that we felt there was little to modify for the home cook.

We started with the eggplant, which forms the base of this dish. The original recipe calls for brushing the eggplant slices with olive oil and then grilling them until tender. Although we liked the smokiness that the grill imparted to the eggplant, setting up the grill at home just to cook eggplant slices seemed excessive and unnecessary. This led us to search for an alternative method to cook the eggplant without sacrificing flavor. Our first thought was to use a cast-iron grill pan, which often can achieve the same results as a charcoal grill. While we liked the flavor of the eggplant cooked this way, we found that we could fit only two slices of eggplant in the pan at one time, resulting in a significant commitment of time to cook the whole vegetable—not very practical for the home cook. We then turned to our broiler. Laying the eggplant slices on a baking sheet and then placing them under the broiler enabled us to cook all the eggplant at once. Importantly, the intense heat of the broiler browned the eggplant, bringing out its sweetness.

The recipe did not specify whether to use freshly roasted red bell peppers or jarred roasted red bell peppers. Among ourselves, we questioned whether there would be a noticeable taste difference between the two, knowing that jarred peppers would more than halve the preparation time. After preparing the dish with both fresh and jarred peppers and tasting each side by side, very few of the tasters could discern the difference. Pleasantly surprised, we opted to used the jarred peppers.

The question of tomato sauce and baking time were the only two items left for development. The recipe instructed us to bake the eggplant rolls in a homemade tomato sauce. We prepared our own simple, quick, chunky

ASSEMBLING EGGPLANT ROLLS

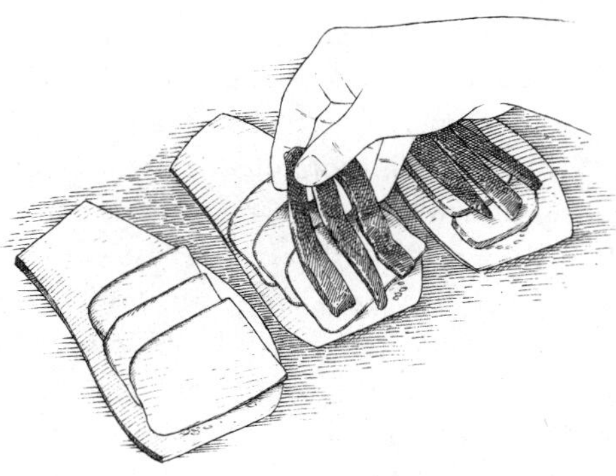

1. Lay the eggplant slices on a clean, flat surface and shingle 3 mozzarella slices over the bottom two thirds of each eggplant slice. Lay 3 strips of red pepper on top of the mozzarella and sprinkle with a scant teaspoon chopped basil.

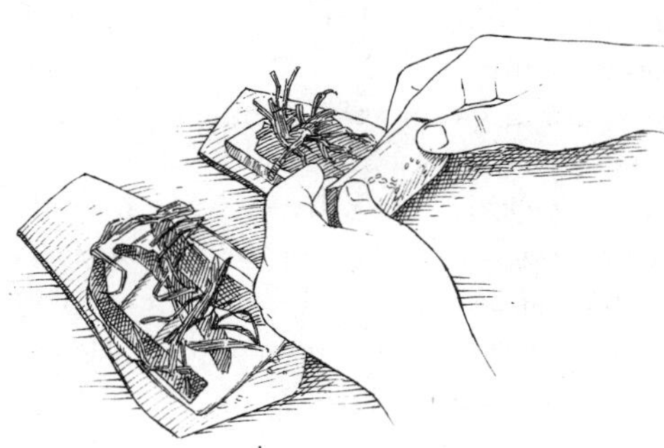

2. Starting at the cheese-filled end, gently roll the eggplant into a cylinder.

3. Transfer the rolls seam-side down to an 8-inch square baking dish filled with half of the tomato sauce.

tomato sauce and then our longer-cooked, smoother sauce. Almost unanimously, the tasters agreed that the chunkier, quick sauce was fresher tasting and melded better with the other flavors of the dish. A quick sauce also meant that we could prepare the sauce within the short time it took to prepare the other elements of the dish. And after baking the mozzarella for just 20 minutes in the oven, we found that it had melted, imparting just the right amount of its smokiness to the tomato sauce and mingling all the flavors.

Each serving consists of two eggplant rolls, and we found they looked most attractive arranged one stacked crosswise over the other. Spoon a pool of tomato sauce around each serving and add a sprinkle of Parmesan cheese as a final touch.

Eggplant Rolls with Smoked Mozzarella

SERVES 4

A sharp knife is an invaluable tool when slicing the eggplant for this recipe. Look for smoked mozzarella in the cheese case of your supermarket, near the regular mozzarella. You can turn this hearty first course into a main course with the accompaniment of a mixed green salad and crusty bread.

SIMPLE TOMATO SAUCE

- **3 tablespoons unsalted butter**
- **1 small onion, minced**
- **1 medium carrot, peeled and minced**
- **1 (28-ounce) can diced tomatoes with their juice**
- **Salt**
- **2 tablespoons minced fresh basil or fresh parsley leaves**

EGGPLANT ROLLS

- 1 medium eggplant (about 1 pound), sliced lengthwise 1/4 inch thick (8 slices)
- 3 tablespoons extra-virgin olive oil
- Salt and ground black pepper
- 6 ounces smoked mozzarella, cut into 1/8-inch-thick slices (24 slices)
- 6 ounces jarred roasted red bell peppers, rinsed and cut into 3 by 1/2-inch strips (24 strips)
- 2 tablespoons chopped fresh basil
- 1/4 cup plus 2 tablespoons grated Parmesan (about 2 ounces)

1. FOR THE SAUCE: Melt the butter in a medium saucepan. Add the onion and carrot; cook over medium heat until the vegetables soften but are not browned, about 10 minutes. Stir in the tomatoes and ½ teaspoon salt; simmer until thickened slightly, about 10 minutes. Stir in the basil and adjust the seasonings.

2. FOR THE EGGPLANT ROLLS: Adjust an oven rack so it is 6 inches away from the broiler element and heat the broiler. Place the eggplant slices on a wire rack set in a rimmed baking sheet. Brush both sides of the eggplant slices with the oil and season with salt and pepper. Broil the eggplant until tender and browned, 3 to 4 minutes on each side. Transfer to a plate to cool. Adjust an oven rack to the middle position and reduce the oven temperature to 425 degrees.

3. Cover the bottom of an 8-inch square baking dish with half of the tomato sauce. Place the eggplant slices on a flat surface, with the short sides facing you. Following the illustrations on page 13, place 3 slices smoked mozzarella on the bottom two thirds of each eggplant slice, followed by 3 strips red pepper and a scant teaspoon basil. Gently roll up the eggplant and place seam-side down in the tomato sauce. Cover with the remaining tomato sauce and sprinkle with ¼ cup Parmesan. Bake until the cheese is melted and the sauce is bubbling, about 20 minutes.

4. Using spoons, transfer 2 eggplant rolls to the center of each of 4 warmed appetizer plates, stacking one roll crosswise over the other. Spoon a portion of the tomato sauce around each serving and sprinkle each with ½ tablespoon of the remaining Parmesan cheese. Serve immediately.

Fried Green Tomatoes *with* Goat Cheese

Adapted from Fried Green Tomatoes with Goat Cheese and Red Pepper Coulis

South City Kitchen, Atlanta, Georgia

TAKING FRIED GREEN TOMATOES A STEP higher, South City Kitchen cooks up this southern favorite with a smear of goat cheese underneath the breading and accompanies it with a red bell pepper sauce and a garnish of fried dandelion greens. We found that with just a few minor adjustments, this stellar recipe is a cinch to reproduce at home.

For the tomatoes, we discarded the awkward, outermost slices off the top and bottom, which made cutting the tomato into perfectly round slices a breeze. We then followed the restaurant's instructions to spread a thin layer of goat cheese over one side of each slice, and dip the slices in eggs, flour, and Japanese-style bread crumbs, called panko. (See more about panko on page 17.) This bound-bread coating, when fried, renders the crust a crisp golden brown, while inside the tomato becomes soft and the goat cheese warm. The restaurant refrigerates the breaded tomatoes ahead. At home, you can bread the tomatoes and keep them refrigerated until you're ready to cook, but we recommend that you do this no more than a few hours in advance. (While green tomatoes are not as juicy as their ripe counterparts, they still exude juices that can gum up the breading.) At the restaurant, the tomatoes are fried to order, just two at a time, but for the home cook, who needs to fry several slices at once, we found a 12-inch-wide Dutch oven essential. You'll also need to fry the slices in two batches to prevent overcrowding in the pan.

Coulis is simply another word for sauce, and in this case it's made from red bell peppers. We made no changes to the recipe beyond paring down the ingredients by half for six servings of tomatoes.

The fried dandelion green garnish is the type of restaurant flourish that rarely gets reproduced in the home kitchen. Finding the dandelion greens was no easy task. But of more concern to us was cooking the greens. Adding them to hot oil turned out to be like throwing firecrackers into a fire—loud, scary, and a bit dangerous. The splatter and sputter of hot oil across the stove (after you've jumped backward) is a not-so-subtle reminder of why it's nice to go out for dinner. We tried a few ways to reproduce the funky fried garnish without the hassle and mess, but came up short. In the end, we decided it best to substitute similarly flavored fresh arugula (also easier to find than dandelion greens), and we took a risk-free approach by lightly dressing the arugula with olive oil and salt, preserving both the pepper-flavored punch and the presentation.

Fried Green Tomatoes with Goat Cheese

SERVES 6

You won't find green tomatoes in the supermarket, so seek them out at your local farmers market in early fall, just before the chill sets in.

RED PEPPER COULIS

- 1 tablespoon olive oil
- 2 red bell peppers, cored, seeded, and cut into 1-inch pieces
- 1/2 small onion, cut into 1/2-inch pieces (about 1/3 cup)
- 1 medium garlic clove, minced or pressed through a garlic press (about 1 teaspoon)
- 2 tablespoons sugar
- 1 sprig fresh thyme
- 3 fresh basil leaves
- 1 cup low-sodium chicken broth
- 2 tablespoons dry white wine
- Salt and ground black pepper
- Tabasco sauce

FRIED GREEN TOMATOES

- 3 medium green tomatoes, cored, tops and bottoms discarded, each tomato sliced crosswise into 4 rounds, 1/4 inch thick
- Salt and ground black pepper
- 6 ounces goat cheese, at room temperature (about 3/4 cup)
- 1/2 cup all-purpose flour
- 3 large eggs
- 2 cups panko (Japanese-style bread crumbs) or Homemade Panko (page 17)
- 3 cups vegetable oil
- 1 1/2 ounces arugula (about 3 cups lightly packed), washed and dried
- 1 tablespoon olive oil
- Salt

1. For the coulis: Heat the olive oil in a medium saucepan over medium-high heat until shimmering. Add the bell peppers and onion and sauté until the peppers have softened, 5 to 6 minutes. Add the garlic and sauté until fragrant, about 30 seconds. Add the sugar, thyme, basil, chicken broth, and wine; simmer until the flavors have melded and the peppers are completely soft, 10 to 13 minutes. Transfer the mixture to a blender and process until smooth, about 30 seconds. Pour the mixture into a medium bowl and season to taste with salt, pepper, and Tabasco; set aside. The sauce can be served either warm or at room temperature. The sauce can be made up to 3 days ahead and refrigerated in an airtight container. (Be sure to heat slightly to take off the chill before serving.)

2. For the tomatoes: Lay the tomato slices in a single layer on a rimmed baking sheet lined with several layers of paper towels. Season the tomato slices liberally with salt and pepper. Spread 1 tablespoon goat cheese evenly over one cut side of each tomato slice.

3. Spread the flour in a shallow dish or pie plate. Lightly whisk the eggs together in a separate shallow dish. Spread the panko in a third dish. Working with several slices of tomato at a time, drop them into the flour and gently shake the dish back and forth to coat. Shake the excess flour from each piece, then, using tongs, dip the tomato slices into the egg mixture, turning to coat well, and allow the excess to drip off. Drop the tomato slices into the panko, and press the crumbs lightly to adhere. Shake off any excess crumbs and place the breaded tomatoes on a wire rack set over a rimmed baking sheet. Repeat with the remaining tomato slices. (The breaded tomato slices can be refrigerated for up to 2 hours.)

4. Heat the vegetable oil in a large Dutch oven over medium-high heat until the

temperature reaches 350 degrees. (Use an instant-read thermometer that registers high temperatures or clip a candy/deep-fat thermometer onto the side of the pan before turning on the heat.) Using tongs, gently place 6 breaded tomato slices into the oil, being careful not to overlap them, or they'll stick together. Fry until golden brown on one side, 2 to 2½ minutes, adjusting the heat as necessary to maintain the cooking temperature. Flip the slices over and fry on the second side until golden, 2 to 2½ minutes longer. Transfer the fried tomatoes to a baking sheet lined with paper towels, and repeat with the remaining tomato slices.

5. Toss the arugula with the olive oil in a medium bowl and season with salt. Stack 2 fried tomatoes in the center of each of 6 individual plates and top each serving with about ½ cup of the arugula. Drizzle each portion with 3 tablespoons of the red pepper coulis and serve immediately.

Homemade Panko

MAKES 1 CUP

5 slices high-quality white bread (such as Pepperidge Farm), crusts removed, quartered

Adjust an oven rack to the middle position and heat the oven to 300 degrees. Process the bread through a food processor fitted with the shredding disk, using only the weight of the feed-tube guard to press the bread against the disk. Transfer the crumbs to a rimmed baking sheet and bake, shaking the pan occasionally, until the crumbs are dry and crisp but not toasted, about 6 minutes. Transfer the baking sheet to a wire rack. Panko can be stored in a zipper-lock bag at room temperature for up to 2 weeks.

INGREDIENTS: Panko

After tasting numerous brands and styles of bread crumbs in a side-by-side test, we determined that Japanese-style bread crumbs, called panko, were absolutely the best. They have a light, flaky texture that fries to a clean-tasting, perfectly golden crisp unlike any other. Panko can be found in restaurant supply stores, Asian markets, and sometimes the international food aisle at the supermarket, although depending on where you live you might have to resort to mail order.

For those times when panko can't be found, we decided to find a way to make a panko substitute. Using a good-quality, sliced white bread and a food processor, we began by testing the difference between processing the bread with the blade versus the shredding disk. Finding that the blade produced even and round crumbs, we preferred the large, airy texture of crumbs made with the shredding disk. Next we tested the difference among shredded fresh, frozen, dried, and toasted bread. Toasted and dried bread were the losers of the bunch because their stiffness kept them from processing evenly into large flakes. Frozen bread also didn't work well, since the shredding disk turned the bread into long, shredded pieces. Fresh bread, however, worked perfectly. We quartered the slices of bread so that they fit easily into the feed tube. The only trick we learned was not to press too hard on the feed-tube guard. Rather, we found the weight of the feed-tube guard alone pressed the bread against the shredding disk to just the right degree.

Wanting to dry the crumbs quickly in the oven without toasting them, we tried various oven temperatures and landed on 300 degrees. Higher temperatures wound up turning the crumbs golden, while lower temperatures took longer. Lastly, we found it important to remove the crusts from the bread before processing so that its toasted flavor and golden color wouldn't mar the otherwise perfectly dry crumbs—just like panko.

Goat Cheese Wontons

Adapted from Goat Cheese Wontons with Sweet-and-Sour Dipping Sauce

Indigo, Honolulu, Hawaii

ONE OF THE MOST POPULAR APPETIZERS at Honolulu's Indigo, these goat cheese wontons are an uptown riff on the pupu-platter staple crab Rangoon (deep-fried wontons stuffed with a cream cheese–crabmeat mixture). By definition, wontons are small dumplings flavored with any number of assertive fillings. Indigo's unique takeoff is filled with a mixture of fresh, creamy goat cheese, diced bell pepper, sun-dried tomato, and chives—an East-meets-West success story. We found them to be perfect for home entertaining since they can be prepared well ahead of time and can even be frozen before frying. However, the dipping sauce, a fruit-vinegar concoction, proved problematic since it required hard-to-find ingredients. We decided to develop a simple sauce with the same sweet-and-sour flavor profile, but made from common ingredients.

Our first inclination was to streamline the recipe's ingredients, but there was little we could do; the ingredient list was surprisingly spare. From the filling, we found we could omit green bell pepper in favor of using all red pepper (Indigo mixes the two, undoubtedly for color) without having a negative impact on the filling's flavor, but that was it. Each of the remaining ingredients—mild goat cheese, sun-dried tomatoes, and chives—were integral. For sun-dried tomatoes, we preferred the hydrated tomatoes jarred in oil over the leathery dehydrated tomatoes since their flavor was more intense and they required less preparation. Before chopping, it's important to drain the tomatoes of any oil, which would mar the filling's texture and flavor.

Wonton wrappers are available in most grocery stores, often alongside fresh noodles. They are made from wheat flour, salt, and water, not unlike pasta dough, and measure about two to three inches square. To prevent the wontons from drying and cracking, we discovered it was imperative to keep them covered with a damp paper towel or plastic wrap.

Admittedly, we were daunted by folding the wontons. We've eaten enough wontons to know that some involve pretty intricate folding. The perfect wonton looks similar to a paper crown; the points and edges crisply folded and tightly sealed. Our first few attempts yielded wontons that exploded when fried. After a few more batches, our wontons finally began to resemble little crowns. The secret to our success? We found it important to squeeze out as much air as possible from the center and seal the wontons tightly to prevent oil from seeping in. A slick of egg wash brushed on the wrapper helped to glue the wonton firmly shut.

Deep-frying at home can be an intimidating endeavor. A potful of bubbling oil can rattle the nerves of the most confident cook.

Over the years, we have developed what we believe to be a fairly foolproof system. For equipment, the essentials are a large heavy-bottomed Dutch oven and an instant-read or basic candy thermometer. The heavy-bottomed pot retains heat well, resulting in less fluctuation of oil temperature and more consistent frying. (See more about frying on page 10.) If the heat was too low, the wontons soaked up the oil and tasted greasy; when too high, the wrapper cooked too quickly and burned long before the filling was heated through. Indigo's recipe specified 360 degrees as the ideal temperature, but we had slightly more consistent results at 350 degrees, no doubt because we were frying multiple batches.

Wontons fried, we tackled the dipping sauce. Indigo serves the wontons with an exotically flavored "four-fruit sauce" made from several fruit vinegars (red currant, blackberry, and blueberry), as well as pickled ginger juice—all of which we found quite difficult to source. As a replacement, we devised a quick sweet-and-sour "duck" sauce of sorts, admittedly ersatz, but complementary to the filling and traditional—wontons are commonly paired with duck sauce. Traditional duck sauce, sometimes called plum sauce, is a long-simmered mix of plums, apricots, vinegar, sugar, and seasonings. To keep the ingredient list short, we opted to exclude the plums and rely on apricot jam (or preserves) for both fruitiness and sweetness. Rice vinegar provided the requisite sourness, and a few coins of ginger and pinch of red pepper flakes the spice. Briefly simmered and strained of solids, the sauce proved a piquant foil to the wontons.

For presentation, Indigo plates the wontons with a garnish of grated carrot and zucchini. While this looks great, we preferred a simpler sprinkling of chives since they were already required for the filling and we had plenty of leftovers. They can be left in longish lengths or finely minced and scattered about.

The wontons are at their best freshly fried, so we recommend serving them as soon as possible. For family-style presentation, we placed the wontons in a napkin-lined shallow bowl, but use your imagination: try Chinese paper takeout containers (available at paper goods or party stores), for example, or lace the wontons onto wooden skewers.

FOLDING WONTONS

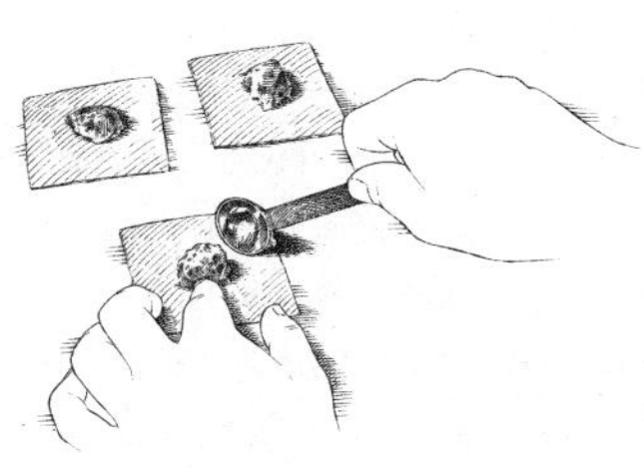

1. Place ½ teaspoon filling in the center of each wrapper.

2. Fold the square diagonally in half to make a triangle, and use your fingers to squeeze the air out of the center. Brush the two corners at either end of the sealed edge with the egg wash.

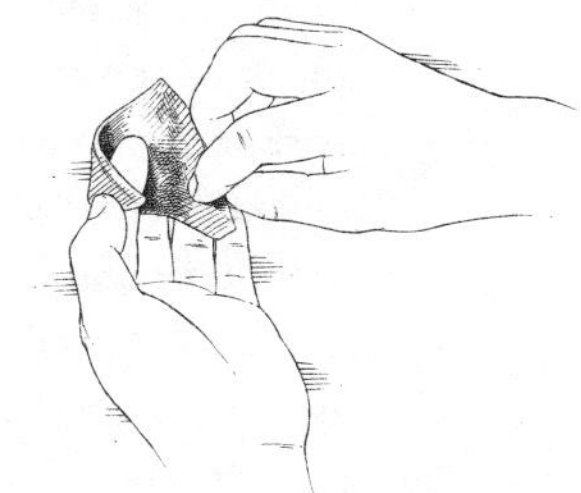

3. Lift the filled triangle from the counter and wrap the back of the triangle around the top of the your index finger, sealing the corners together.

Goat Cheese Wontons

MAKES 25 WONTONS

Most wonton wrappers come in packages of 50; this recipe employs only half, but the remainder can be wrapped tightly in plastic wrap and frozen. Filled but not cooked wontons also freeze well. You can fry them directly from the freezer, but only a few at a time to maintain proper frying temperature. If time is tight, feel free to use a prepared dipping sauce, such as duck or plum sauce, commonly found in the international food aisle of most supermarkets.

SPICY SWEET-AND-SOUR DUCK SAUCE

- 1/2 cup rice vinegar
- 1/2 cup apricot jam or preserves
- 1 (1-inch) piece fresh ginger, cut into 4 coins
- 1 tablespoon light brown sugar
- Pinch red pepper flakes
- Salt and ground black pepper

WONTONS

- 4 ounces goat cheese (about 1/2 cup), softened
- 1/2 small red bell pepper, diced fine (about 1/4 cup)
- 1 tablespoon finely chopped oil-packed sun-dried tomatoes
- 1/2 teaspoon minced fresh chives, plus additional for garnish
- Salt and ground white pepper
- 25 square wonton wrappers
- 1 large egg, lightly beaten
- 1 quart vegetable oil, for frying

1. FOR THE DUCK SAUCE: Bring the rice vinegar, jam, ginger, brown sugar, and red pepper flakes to a boil in a small saucepan over medium-high heat. Reduce the heat to low and simmer for 15 minutes. Strain the mixture through a fine-mesh sieve into a bowl, pressing on the solids to extract as much liquid as possible. Season with salt and pepper to taste and set aside. (The sauce can be made up to 1 week ahead and refrigerated in an airtight container.)

2. FOR THE WONTONS: Thoroughly combine the goat cheese, bell pepper, sun-dried tomatoes, and chives in a medium bowl. Season with salt and white pepper to taste. Place 5 wonton wrappers on a work surface (keeping the other wrappers covered with plastic wrap so they don't dry out), and place ½ teaspoon filling in the center of a wonton wrapper. Following the illustrations on page 19, fold the square diagonally in half to make a triangle, and use your fingers to squeeze the air out of the center. Brush the two corners at either end of the sealed edge with the egg wash. Lift the filled triangle from the counter and wrap the back of the triangle around the top of the your index finger. Squeeze the two egg-washed corners of the triangle together. Place the finished wontons on a plate and cover with plastic wrap to keep them from drying out. Repeat the process until completed.

3. Heat the vegetable oil in a Dutch oven over medium-high heat until it reaches 350 degrees. (Use an instant-read thermometer that registers high temperatures or clip a candy/deep-fat thermometer onto the side of the pan before turning on the heat.) Add half the wontons and fry, stirring frequently to prevent sticking, until light golden brown, 1½ to 2 minutes, adjusting the heat as necessary to maintain the cooking temperature. Using a slotted spoon, spider (see page 9), or tongs, transfer the wontons to a rimmed baking sheet lined with several layers of paper towels, and repeat the process with the remaining wontons. Serve immediately, accompanied by the dipping sauce.

Baked Brie *with* Candied Nuts

Adapted from Baked Brie en Croute with Candied Hazelnuts

Adagio, Iowa City, Iowa

WITH ITS GLOSSY, GOLDEN PASTRY EXTERIOR and rich, unctuous interior, baked Brie en croute became a cocktail-party favorite in the 1980s. It was a dish that satisfied all cravings, since the cheesy filling often contained a sweet element like fruit chutney or sweet pepper jam. Adagio's version updates this crowd pleaser by replacing the jam with a handful of sweetened nuts. It's not as sweet as the original, and not as cloying, either.

The first component we developed was the caramelized nut topping. The original recipe's procedure for candying the nuts required first melting butter and then adding the nuts and sugar. This combination was cooked further until the sugar was caramelized and the nuts were toasted. While this method worked, we occasionally had problems fully dissolving the sugar, resulting in patches of crystallized sugar with an off-putting texture. No doubt restaurant cooks familiar with candying have spent many hours mastering the craft. But for the home cook, we thought there might be an easier, foolproof way to prepare the candied nuts. We also weren't able to toast the nuts evenly using this method, costing us the benefit of the nuts' fullest flavor. We tackled the problem by first toasting the nuts in the oven. Toasting before adding the sugar allowed us more control and avoided the issue of spotty browning. Next, we found that if we brought the butter and the sugar to a boil together with a little water we could ensure that the sugar would fully dissolve. After the sugar had caramelized slightly, we added the fully toasted nuts and continued to cook until all the water had evaporated and the nuts were coated with the remaining syrup and appeared glossy. This technique yielded beautifully and evenly glazed nuts that remained crisp but did not become too hard when cooled.

CHOPPING NUTS QUICKLY

Place the nuts on a cutting board and hold two chef's knives parallel to each other in one hand and chop. Use the other hand to guide the knives through the nuts.

We were hit with an unexpected twist when moving on to the cheese. In the past when using Brie, we always recommended a cheese that was pliant to the touch and whose edges have started to brown ever so slightly. In this stage, the Brie should be a little runny and at its peak flavor. We assumed that this would be the best Brie to use for Brie en croute. We were wrong. After baking the encased Brie at this stage of ripeness, we found that when we cut into the cheese, it ran into a shallow, oily pool around a hollow shell of puff pastry. Wondering if the cheese was too ripe, we attempted the same recipe with a less-mature piece of cheese that was a little firmer in the center and had a snow white exterior, with no hint of coloration. The result of this test was what we expected, a molten center of cheese that was spreadable but didn't run like melted butter once baked. We were also curious to determine whether the type of Brie had any effect on the outcome of this dish. After trying cheeses from Vermont, Wisconsin, and France, we found that there was very little difference in flavor, although the Wisconsin Brie was the richest tasting.

After we addressed the issues regarding the nuts and cheese, we focused on the finer points in the recipe, such as the puff pastry and final baking time. The chef at Adagio recommended using homemade puff pastry as opposed to frozen, though very few restaurants make puff pastry from scratch. While we certainly agree that homemade puff pastry, which is made with 100 percent butter, tastes better than the frozen commercial version, which normally contains all vegetable shortening, we felt that in this case it would be easier and more time efficient for the home cook to use a sheet of frozen puff pastry.

Wrapping the Brie in the pastry proved to be a cinch, no harder than using plastic wrap. However, we did find that if we were not gentle in pulling the puff pastry up around the wheel of cheese, the nuts could puncture the pastry, leaving unsightly holes.

Just as with pie dough, it's important when baking puff pastry to preheat the oven and to make sure your temperature gauge is accurate. The water contained in the dough must steam so that the dough separates into delicate, flaky layers. If the temperature is too low, the pastry won't have enough lift, and you won't achieve those flaky layers; if it's too hot, the outer layers of the puff pastry overcook before the inside cooks through. Preheating the oven to 425 degrees provided just enough heat for the maximum "puff" and the proper browning.

With a few adjustments we had an impressive hors d'oeuvre that any home cook could prepare with a modicum of time and effort. Serve the wheel on a platter surrounded by crackers or slices from a crispy baguette.

Baked Brie with Candied Nuts

SERVES 6 TO 8

This recipe can be prepared with pecans, almonds, or hazelnuts. If using hazelnuts, be sure to remove their skins after toasting (see the illustrations on page 306). Leftover puff pastry can be cut into decorative pieces that can be used to garnish the top of the cheese. When choosing a wheel of Brie, select one that is slightly underripe; its exterior should be snow white and when pressed in the center it should be firm but yielding.

- **1/2 cup roughly chopped pecans, almonds, or hazelnuts**
- **2 tablespoons light brown sugar**
- **1 tablespoon unsalted butter**
- **1 (9 1/2 by 9-inch) sheet frozen commercial puff pastry, thawed on the counter for 10 minutes**

1 (8-ounce) wheel Brie (about 4 inches in diameter)
1 large egg, beaten with 1 teaspoon water
Crackers or slices from a crispy baguette, for accompaniment

1. Adjust an oven rack to the middle position and heat the oven to 350 degrees. Line a rimmed baking sheet with parchment paper and spread the nuts in an even layer. Toast for 4 minutes, then rotate the pan and toast until the nuts are fragrant and the color deepens, about 4 minutes longer. Transfer the baking sheet to a wire rack. Increase the oven temperature to 425 degrees.

2. Bring the sugar, butter, and 2 tablespoons water to a boil in a small saucepan over medium-high heat, stirring constantly. Stir in the nuts and cook, stirring constantly with a wooden spoon, until the nuts are shiny and almost all the liquid has evaporated, about 1 to 2 minutes. Return the glazed nuts to the parchment-lined baking sheet and cool.

3. Place the puff pastry on a lightly floured surface. Cut into a circle with a diameter of 7 inches, reserving the leftover puff pastry to garnish the top, if desired. Place the cooled nuts in the center, in a circle roughly the diameter of the wheel of Brie. Place the Brie on top of the nuts. Following the illustrations at right, pull the edges of the puff pastry up and around the Brie, sealing it with the egg wash.

4. Place the wrapped Brie seam-side down on a rimmed baking sheet lined with parchment paper. Brush with the remaining egg wash. Bake, turning once, until the crust is a deep golden brown, about 20 minutes. Transfer to a serving platter and let stand for 10 minutes before serving with the crackers or baguette slices.

WRAPPING BRIE IN PUFF PASTRY

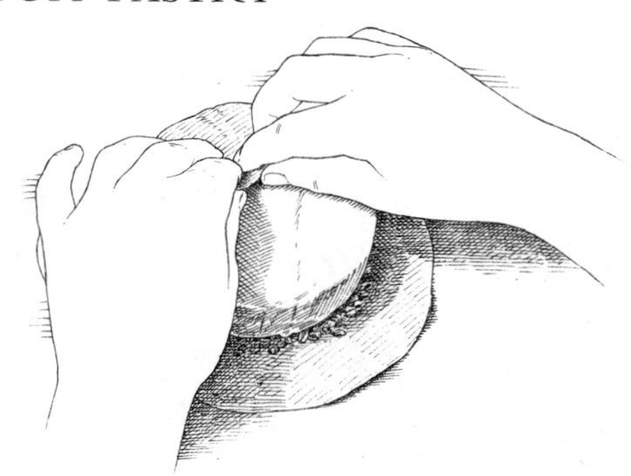

1. After arranging the nuts and wheel of Brie in the center of the pastry, gently pull a fold of pastry up over the Brie.

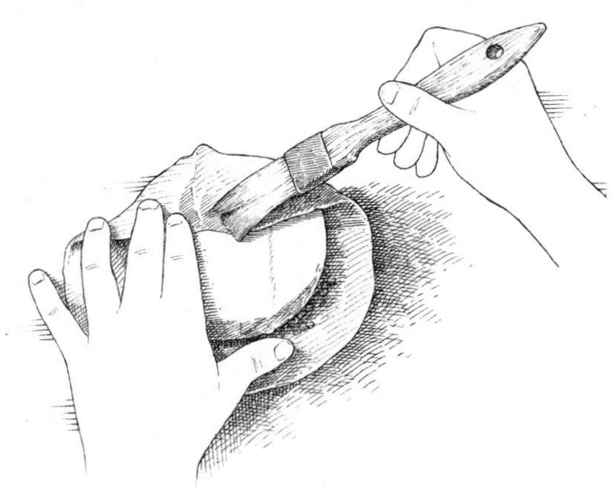

2. Brush the edge of the fold with the egg wash to help seal it.

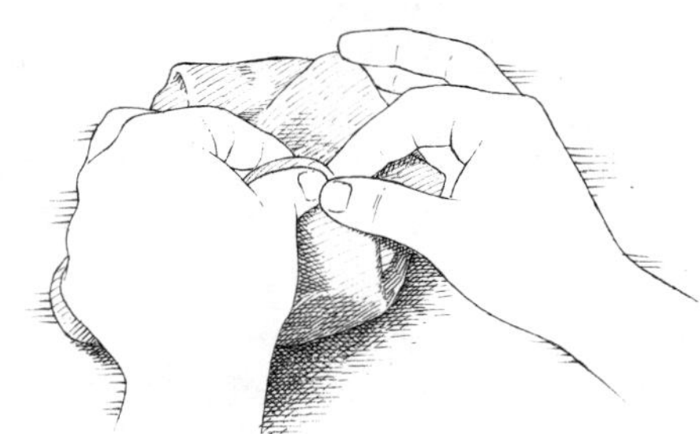

3. Continue to fold the pastry up around the Brie, sealing the folds as you go, until the cheese is completely covered.

Swiss-Blend Fondue

Adapted from Swiss-Blend Fondue

Artisanal, New York, New York

TERRANCE BRENNAN'S NEW YORK BISTRO Artisanal is all about the cheese. At any one time, there are well over 100 varieties on hand in the custom-built, state-of-the-art cheese cave. What better way to highlight superior cheese than with fondue, Switzerland's most notable culinary export? Literally translated from the French as "melted sauce," fondue is little more than that: a blend of cheeses melted into seasoned wine and eaten with cubes of bread and a wide variety of other accompaniments. While suitable as an appetizer (as it's served at Artisanal), fondue is traditionally served as a main course with a hearty array of cured or dried meats and vegetables. Artisanal serves several varieties of fondue, though a Swiss cheese–based fondue—the classic—is the most popular. This simple recipe needed little work to make it home-kitchen friendly, although we did make minor adjustments to the ratio of ingredients and cooking time for a slightly thinner, more manageable consistency.

Successful fondue lies in the quality of the ingredients and the fine balancing of flavor. The sharpness of the wine and lemon juice cuts the cheeses' richness. At the restaurant, Brennan uses fruity kirschwasser (a German cherry-flavored brandy) to intensify the cheeses' nuttiness. The mildest hints of garlic and nutmeg round out the edges. The recipe combines Emmentaler (sometimes called Emmental) and Gruyère. Emmentaler is a classic, mild Swiss cheese, possessing a pleasant, nutty flavor and identified by its very large holes (caused by carbon dioxide released as the immature cheese cures). It's produced in the Emmental Valley—sandwiched in the Alps between France and Switzerland—and shaped into enormous rounds weighing well over 100 pounds. Gruyère is fuller-flavored and more pungent than Emmentaler—some say it possesses a toffee-like flavor. It, too, is produced in the Alps close to France, though in smaller wheels than Emmentaler. The many brands of this cheese sold are of varying quality, so it's best to rely on your cheesemonger's wisdom. Artisanal uses cheese from a company called Emmi; this high-grade cheese is widely available.

For wine, a mild, dry white is crucial. Otherwise the wine's flavor may overpower or conflict with the flavor of the cheese. While the recipe doesn't specify a particular varietal, we favored Sauvignon Blanc or Pinot Gris. Oaky or tannic wines like California Chardonnay simply did not work, nor did spicy wines like Gewürztraminer or fruity Viogniers. As for kirschwasser, most liquor stores carry several brands. A moderately priced version is perfectly acceptable since only a scant amount is specified in the recipe.

It takes just minutes to cook fondue. In the recipe, the wine, kirschwasser, and lemon juice are brought to a simmer in a pot that has been rubbed with a halved garlic clove, so that just a bit of the garlic juice is left behind—a quick way to impart just a touch of garlic flavor. Any more garlic and the dish's profile is unpleasantly altered. Once simmering, the cheeses and cornstarch are added and briefly cooked until thickened. The mixture is then transferred to a waiting fondue pot to be consumed at the table. The cornstarch serves two purposes: to thicken the fondue and to prevent the fondue from "breaking"—that is, to keep the fat in the cheese from separating out of the wine-and-cheese mixture and forming a grease slick. For the most part, Artisanal's method is classic, but it diverges in the manner in which the cornstarch is added. Many recipes add the cornstarch in a slurry—a solution of cornstarch dissolved in water—once the wine and cheese are incorporated. Artisanal tosses the cheese with cornstarch prior to adding it to the wine, thereby eliminating any possibility of the fondue breaking while streamlining a step. We found tasters preferred the fondue with less cornstarch than Artisanal specified—a thicker fondue is better suited to the faster pace of restaurant dining. When tasters lingered over batches in the test kitchen (as you would at home), the restaurant's thicker version stiffened too much for easy dipping, despite a hot fondue pot.

We expect most households have a dusty fondue set—a heavy, often enameled pot, rack, dipping forks, and Sterno chafing fuel—tucked way in a closet, but if you don't, there's hope. A standard, heavy-duty saucepan may be kept warm by setting it on a plate warmer or an inexpensive electric heating coil—available from many hardware and kitchen-supply stores. If the coil gets too hot and the fondue begins to brown or stick to the pan's bottom, a heat diffuser may be placed between the coil and the pan. Skewers or long-handled forks may be pressed into service for dipping the bread.

SHREDDING CHEESE NEATLY

Use nonstick cooking spray to coat the coarse side of a box grater lightly, then shred the cheese as usual. The cooking spray will keep cheese from sticking to the surface of the grater.

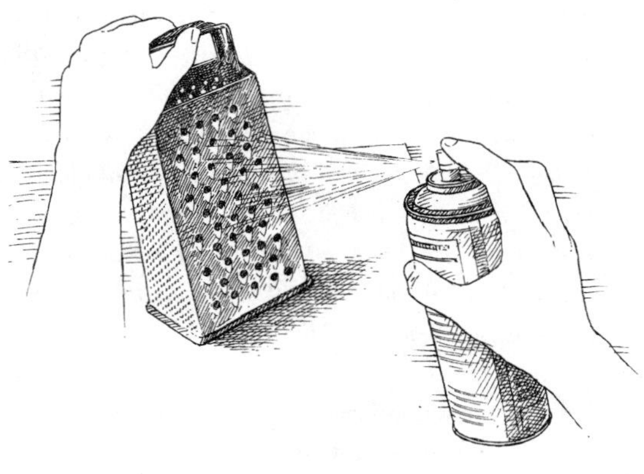

In addition to the classic cubes of baguette, Artisanal serves its fondue with a variety of accompaniments, including boiled fingerling potatoes, pickled carrots and cauliflower, sautéed beef tips, kielbasa, and meats like Bundnerfleisch or bresaola, two European air-dried beef products available at better delis and gourmet stores. Tasters liked all of Artisanal's accompaniments and also suggested gherkins or cornichons.

Swiss-Blend Fondue

SERVES 6 TO 8 AS A FIRST COURSE, 4 TO 6 AS A MAIN COURSE

Try to find the best-quality cheese you can, since it makes a big difference in the fondue's flavor. Ask your cheesemonger for recommendations, because there are many brands of Emmentaler and Gruyère. Many specialty stores carry imported pickled vegetables. If you can't find pickled carrots or cauliflower, there may be other vegetables available that would be an adequate substitute. While a fondue set is very useful for serving fondue (the heat source beneath the fondue pot keeps the cheese hot), you can do without if you make the fondue in a heavy-bottomed pan that retains heat well. If the fondue begins to cool and thicken, return the pan to medium heat until it warms through. You may need to whisk in a tablespoon or two more wine to loosen it. And if you don't have long-handled fondue forks, use kebab skewers. For the accompaniments, we recommend, along with the French bread, choosing one variety of meat and at least two types of vegetables from the list.

- 1 medium garlic clove, peeled and sliced lengthwise in half
- 1 3/4 cups dry white wine
- 1 1/2 tablespoons kirschwasser
- 1 tablespoon juice from 1 lemon
- Salt
- 8 ounces Gruyère cheese, shredded (about 2 cups)
- 8 ounces Emmentaler cheese, shredded (about 2 cups)
- 1 1/2 tablespoons cornstarch
- Large pinch ground nutmeg
- Ground white (or black) pepper

ACCOMPANIMENTS

- 1 baguette, cut into 1-inch cubes
- 1 pound cooked kielbasa
- 1 cup pickled vegetables, such as carrots or cauliflower
- 1 pound boiled fingerling or new potatoes
- 1/2 pound air-dried beef, such as bresaola or Bundnerfleisch
- 1/2 cup cornichons

Thoroughly rub a medium saucepan with the cut sides of the garlic clove; discard the garlic. Add the white wine, kirschwasser, lemon juice, and ½ teaspoon salt to the saucepan and bring to a simmer over medium heat. Meanwhile, in a large bowl, toss together the two cheeses with the cornstarch. While stirring the wine mixture constantly with a whisk, add the cheese by the handful. As it melts, add more cheese until it is fully incorporated. Add the nutmeg and adjust the seasoning with salt and pepper. Transfer to a fondue pot and serve immediately, accompanied by the bread cubes and other chosen accompaniments.

Alsatian Onion & Bacon Tarts

Adapted from Brasserie Jo Classic Tarte Flambé

Brasserie Jo, Chicago, Illinois, and Boston, Massachusetts

TARTE FLAMBÉ, OR FLAMMEKUECHE, IS ONE of the more delectable creations of Alsace. The dish traditionally consists of a thin, crispy dough topped with caramelized onions, bacon, and fromage blanc (a soft, sour cream–like product). More like a pizza than a tart, the dough is made with yeast, as opposed to a butter-enriched dough. As a result, when baked the dough is crisp and chewy, rather than tender and buttery. In turn, the lean dough allows the rich topping to take center stage.

After one trial of the recipe—which makes four tarts, each serving two—we were enamored. While admiring the flavors in this dish, we did find several issues that needed to be addressed to adapt it for the home cook.

The most pressing ingredient to be addressed was the topping. The original recipe called for 12 slices of double-smoked bacon, but a search of our local supermarkets turned up no such product. So we needed a suitable substitute. After purchasing whole-slab bacon, thick-sliced bacon, and regularly sliced bacon, we prepared the recipe with all three to determine which worked best. The slab bacon was the clear favorite for its meatiness, and, since we were able to cut larger pieces, the chunky bacon made the dish more substantial. The thick-sliced bacon lent a similar flavor to the dish, but we missed the bite of the slab bacon, and the regularly sliced bacon seemed to get lost in the onions and other ingredients.

Next we moved on to the topping. Fromage blanc—a key ingredient—is not commonly found in the United States, but we discovered that cottage cheese pureed with sour cream and crème fraîche makes a good substitute. However, given that crème fraîche can sometimes be hard to find, we opted to forgo it and use only cottage cheese and sour cream. The topping was still rich and delicious, but the amount used on each tart seemed too much for the crust to handle, causing it to become a little soggy. It was obvious that we needed to cut the amount of the cottage cheese mixture back from 1 cup to a more suitable measurement. Trying tarts made with one-half, one-third, and one-quarter cup of the cottage cheese mixture, we found that anything over one-quarter cup per tart made the dough soggy. In addition to using less of the cottage cheese mixture, we found it beneficial to change the makeup of the mixture. We increased the amount of cottage cheese in relation to sour cream from equal amounts to 2 parts cottage cheese and 1 part sour cream, which was just enough to reduce the liquidness of the mixture. At this point, we also wondered whether we should parbake the dough before topping it to make the tart even crispier. While this technique did in fact yield a crispier crust, there were several drawbacks to parbaking, one of which was the time expended. We opted to skip this step, feeling that it required too much additional time and effort for a minimal return in the end.

As for the onions, we didn't have any problems with the way that Brasserie Jo prepared them. We did, however, find ways to promote the most onion flavor in the least amount of time. First, we found that onions cut into thin, horizontal, rainbow-like slices (see the illustration below) took much less time to cook than the more traditional vertical slices. Second, we found that a moderate, steady heat provided us with the most flavor and a meltingly tender texture.

Next, we turned to the tart dough. Making the dough was straightforward, much like making a basic pizza dough. Nevertheless, we had a couple of questions about its preparation and the lengthy rise it required. The restaurant lets the dough rest overnight, and we wondered if this had to do with flavor or the fact that most restaurants do a lot of prep work ahead because of the high volume of dishes they're producing. Making two batches of tarts, one with dough that sat for four hours and one with dough that sat overnight, we found we preferred the dough that sat overnight. Tasters felt that the resulting tart was indeed more flavorful and tender. We also found that it was much easier to work with the dough that sat overnight. This long rest allowed the gluten strands to relax, which helped facilitate the rolling process.

With our dough properly rested and rolled out, we now focused on assembly and baking. While this step was not difficult, there were several pieces of equipment that we felt were absolutely critical. The first was a pizza peel, a sort of large wooden spatula just a bit larger than a round of pizza. We found that assembling the tarts and then transferring them to the hot oven was much easier when using the peel. (In a pinch, you can use an inverted baking sheet.) We were also able to work with two tarts at a time, enabling us to cut the time spent cooking the tarts in half. A pizza stone was also an item that we felt we couldn't do without. The stone, which holds the heat, cooked the dough more rapidly and produced a much crispier tart than a baking sheet did. We also found that we could cook all four tarts on the stone in the time it took to bake two tarts on a baking sheet. Last, lining the peel with parchment paper prevented the dough from sticking to the peel and the stone.

We found that the best way to serve the tarts was on a large cutting board. They can be sliced and served straight from the board, so that the hot tarts can be enjoyed as soon as possible.

SLICING ONIONS THIN

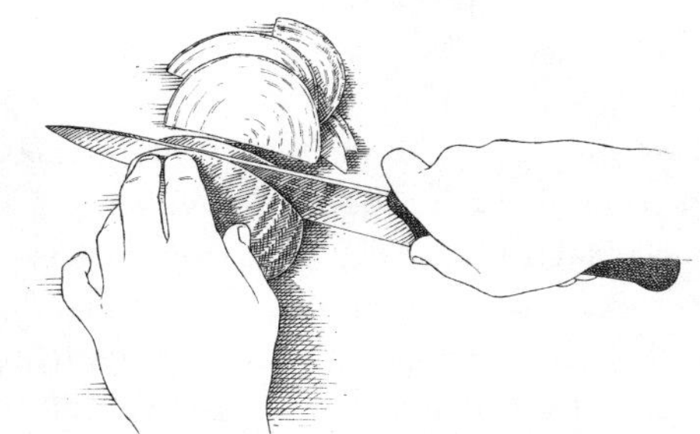

To slice an onion thinly, halve it pole to pole, peel it, set it on a cut side, then slice crosswise.

Alsatian Onion and Bacon Tarts

MAKES 4 TARTS, SERVING 8

Serve a salad with the tart for dinner, or cut it into small pieces for a hearty appetizer. If you cannot find slab bacon, a thick-sliced bacon will do. If you don't have a pizza peel, an inverted rimmed baking sheet also works. But whether you use a peel or a baking sheet, make sure to line it with a sheet of parchment paper to keep the dough from sticking.

TART DOUGH

- 2 cups (10 ounces) unbleached all-purpose flour
- 1 teaspoon instant yeast
- 1 teaspoon salt
- 3/4 cup water, plus 2 tablespoons, at room temperature
- 1 teaspoon canola oil

TOPPING

- 8 ounces slab bacon, cut into 1/4-inch pieces
- 4 medium onions, sliced thin (about 6 cups)
- 2/3 cup cottage cheese
- 1/3 cup sour cream
- 1 teaspoon canola oil
- 1/2 teaspoon salt
- 1/4 teaspoon ground black pepper
- Pinch ground nutmeg

1. For the dough: Mix the flour, yeast, and salt in a large bowl. Add the ¾ cup water and the oil and stir with a wooden spoon until a shaggy dough forms, about 30 seconds. If after 30 seconds there are loose clumps of dough or flour, add more water, 1 tablespoon at a time, until a single ball is formed. Turn the dough out onto a lightly floured work surface and knead until smooth and elastic, about 5 minutes. Place the dough in a 1-quart zipper-lock bag and refrigerate overnight.

2. Adjust an oven rack to the lowest position, set a baking stone on the rack, and heat the oven to 500 degrees. Remove the dough from the refrigerator. Divide it into 4 equal pieces, forming each piece into a ball. Cover the balls with plastic wrap or a dish towel and let rest while you prepare the topping.

3. For the topping: Cook the bacon in a 12-inch nonstick skillet over medium heat until browned and most of the fat has rendered, about 10 minutes. Using a slotted spoon, transfer the bacon to a plate lined with several layers of paper towels; set aside. Add the onions to the pan and cook until tender and lightly browned, about 12 minutes. Remove from the heat, stir in the bacon, and set aside.

4. Puree the cottage cheese in a food processor until almost smooth, about 15 seconds. Transfer the cottage cheese to a medium bowl and stir in the sour cream, oil, salt, pepper, and nutmeg. Set aside.

5. To assemble: On a lightly floured sheet of parchment paper, roll 1 ball of dough into a 12 by 6-inch oblong shape with rounded edges. Transfer the rolled dough (still on the parchment) to a pizza peel or inverted baking sheet. Repeat with another ball of dough; place on the peel alongside the first piece of dough. Top each tart with ¼ cup cottage cheese mixture and spread it to within 1 inch of the edge. Scatter ½ cup of the onion mixture over the cottage cheese mixture. Slide the tarts (still on the parchment) onto the heated stone and bake until the cheese bubbles and the edges of the tart are golden brown, 5 to 6 minutes. Serve immediately, cut into wedges or strips.

6. Repeat step 5 with the 2 remaining balls of dough and the remaining topping.

CRISPY CHICKEN DUMPLINGS *with* SWEET-&-SOUR SAUCE

Adapted from Chicken "Wings"

TSUNAMI, KENMORE, NEW YORK

TSUNAMI'S NAME FOR THIS TASTY APPETIZER may be "chicken wings," but they are actually little pyramid-shaped dumplings made by bundling a ground chicken filling in egg roll wrappers, breading them, then frying. The result is a tender chicken filling and chewy egg roll wrapper enveloped in a crunchy, golden coating that was the hit of the test kitchen when served with Tsunami's famous sweet-and-sour sauce.

The original recipe yielded 40 dumplings, and although we happily ate them, we decided it best to pare the recipe down to make 24, plenty for six to eight people. When we saw that the recipe called for two pounds of chicken wing drumettes to be boned, it became clear how this dish may have gotten its misleading name. Trimming the small amount of meat off chicken wing drumettes is a nifty way for a busy restaurant to turn scraps into profitable tidbits, but for the home cook, boning chicken wings is simply inefficient. We found that substituting inexpensive boneless, skinless chicken thighs eliminated a step, and half a pound of thighs perfectly made 24 dumplings.

To make the filling, the meat is processed in a food processor to a ground consistency, then pulsed briefly with the other ingredients to incorporate them. Fresh garlic and shallot are both key flavors, and although they are processed briefly in the food processor with the meat, it is necessary to mince them first in order to avoid big, overpowering chunks. The original recipe called for both an egg white and heavy cream as binders, but we found we could omit the egg white completely and rely on just a bit of heavy cream to attain a tender, cohesive filling.

The original recipe called for 6-inch-square egg roll wrappers cut into quarters. We substituted the 3-inch-square wrappers that we found in our local supermarket, thus eliminating another step. Filling and folding the dumplings was straightforward, but we found it necessary to fill them in batches to prevent the wrappers from drying out. We also found it best to fry them in two batches, so that each bundle had enough room to brown properly. Last, it is imperative to agitate the dumplings with a spider or long-handled slotted spoon as they fry to ensure even browning—they have a tendency to float point up in the oil. The accompanying sweet-and-sour sauce made with red bell pepper and honey was easy to make; we merely adjusted the yield.

Crispy Chicken Dumplings with Sweet-and-Sour Sauce

SERVES 6 TO 8

If you're pressed for time, commercial Chinese duck sauce can be substituted for the Sweet-and-Sour Sauce.

SWEET-AND-SOUR SAUCE

- 2 tablespoons unsalted butter
- ½ red bell pepper, cored, seeded, and cut into 1-inch pieces
- 1 large garlic clove, minced or pressed through a garlic press (about 2 teaspoons)
- ½ cup red wine vinegar
- ¼ cup honey
- ¼ cup sugar
- 1 teaspoon salt
- 1 teaspoon red pepper flakes

CHICKEN DUMPLINGS

- 2 large eggs
- 1 ½ cups panko (Japanese-style bread crumbs) or Homemade Panko (see page 17)
- ½ pound boneless, skinless chicken thighs, trimmed of excess fat and cut into 1-inch pieces
- 1 small shallot, minced
- 1 small garlic clove, minced or pressed through a garlic press (about 1 teaspoon)
- ½ teaspoon salt
- ⅛ teaspoon red pepper flakes
- Pinch sugar
- 1 tablespoon heavy cream
- 24 (3-inch) square egg roll wrappers
- 1 quart vegetable oil, for frying

1. FOR THE SAUCE: Melt the butter in a small, heavy-bottomed saucepan over medium-high heat. Add the bell pepper and garlic and sauté until tender, about 1½ minutes. Stir in the vinegar, honey, sugar, salt, and red pepper flakes and simmer until the bell pepper is very soft, about 15 minutes. Transfer the mixture to a food processor and process until smooth, about 10 seconds. Transfer to a clean bowl and set aside. Wash the workbowl and blade of the food processor. The sauce may be served either slightly warm or at room temperature.

2. FOR THE DUMPLINGS: Whisk the eggs together in a shallow dish or pie plate. Spread the panko in another shallow dish. Place the chicken in the food processor and process until uniform and smooth, about 10 seconds. Add the shallot, garlic, salt, red pepper flakes, sugar, and heavy cream and process until just combined, about 5 seconds. Transfer the filling to a clean bowl.

3. Place 6 egg roll wrappers on a work surface, keeping the other wrappers covered with plastic wrap so they don't dry out, and, using a pastry brush, brush them lightly with a bit of the beaten eggs. Following the illustrations on page 32, place 1 teaspoon of the filling in the center of each wrapper and fold the wrappers into four-sided, pyramid-shaped bundles. Drop the bundles into the beaten eggs and, using tongs, coat all sides evenly. Allow any excess egg to drip off, then drop the bundles into the panko and gently shake the dish back and forth to coat. Transfer the breaded bundles to a wire rack set over a baking sheet. Repeat with the remaining egg roll wrappers and filling, working with only 6 wrappers at time to avoid drying out the wrappers.

4. Heat the vegetable oil in a Dutch oven over medium-high heat until it reaches 350 degrees. (Use an instant-read thermometer that registers high temperatures or clip a candy/deep-fat thermometer onto the side of

the pan before turning on the heat.) Add half the dumplings and fry, stirring frequently to promote even browning and prevent sticking, until golden brown all over and an instant-read thermometer reads 175 degrees when inserted into the center of a bundle, 3 to 4 minutes. (Adjust the heat as necessary to maintain the cooking temperature.) Using a slotted spoon, spider (see page 9), or tongs, transfer the dumplings to a rimmed baking sheet lined with several layers of paper towels and repeat with the remaining dumplings. Serve immediately, accompanied by the Sweet-and-Sour Sauce.

ASSEMBLING CHICKEN DUMPLINGS

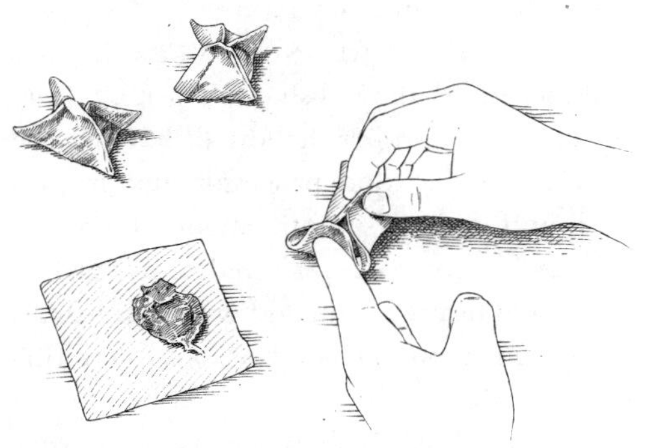

1. Fold the four corners up around the filling and press them together to make a point.

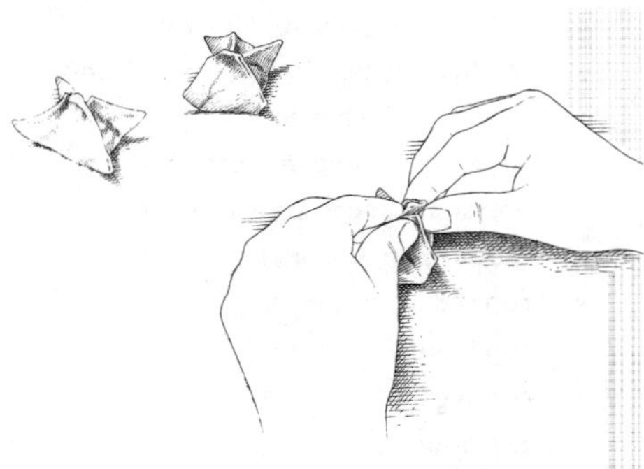

2. Pinch the seams of each dumpling together tightly around the filling to make a four-sided, pyramid-shaped dumpling.

Individual Chicken Liver Flan

Adapted from Chicken Liver Gateau

Le Pichet, Seattle, Washington

THE CHEF OF LE PICHET TOLD US THAT HE received the inspiration for his chicken liver gateau from the superstar French chef Paul Bocuse. While Bocuse and chefs all around France traditionally serve this dish warm with a crayfish sauce, Le Pichet has modified the recipe to be served as a cold appetizer, somewhat akin to chicken liver pâté. However, this dish—as opposed to a traditional pâté—contains a high proportion of eggs and cream in relation to the liver, giving it a pleasant, flan-like consistency.

We made the dish according Le Pichet's recipe and found it to be unique and appetizing. The texture is light, smooth, and creamy and we loved how the sweet nuttiness of the Madeira reduction accentuated the gamy earthiness of the chicken livers. The only drawback of this recipe was that it made enough to serve 16, not very practical for the home cook. Also, the recipe's instructions needed some clarification.

A baked mixture of pureed chicken livers, cream, and eggs flavored with a Madeira reduction, the flan took only minutes to put together. One crucial step that can't be avoided in making the flan is passing the livers through a sieve before baking to remove any tough connective tissue. Omitting this step, as we found by mistake, makes for a grainy and unpleasant texture. Since our priority was to scale down the size of this recipe, we decided to cut the amount of ingredients in half and then went about preparing the flan as we had done originally. By doing so we found that we had a more manageable amount to work with, something more along the lines of what a home cook would find suitable. However, when we cooked this half batch we found that we had lost the deep flavor of the original. Evidently, by halving the recipe we had disturbed the delicate ratio of flavors, so in subsequent tests we found it necessary to leave the full amount of the Madeira reduction and halve the liver mixture in order to ensure the same depth of flavor.

With the amount of flan determined, we could now explore the best method of cooking it, paying attention to cooking times and temperature to find a foolproof method. To approximate the original gateau, which had been baked in a large loaf pan, we had been using small, disposable aluminum loaf pans in our initial tests. While we liked the size of these little loaf pans, we found that the edges of the flan were slightly overcooked. Thinking that the thin aluminum wasn't protecting the edges of the flan, we searched for an alternate cooking vessel and decided on six-ounce ramekins.

It's necessary to bake the flan in a bain-marie (water bath). Dry heat would cause the flan to puff and fall, much like a souffléed omelet, and an unappetizing "skin" would form on top. Simply set the ramekins in a baking pan large enough to accommodate them and pour in enough boiling water to reach halfway up the sides of each ramekin. The water ensures a slow, steady heat.

It was impossible to check the doneness of the flans by visual cue, so we relied on an instant-read thermometer. We proceeded to bake several batches of flan, removing them from the oven at certain internal temperatures. We found that the flan removed from the oven at 155 to 160 degrees were perfectly cooked through, yet still smooth and creamy.

Traditional accompaniments to chicken liver flan include thin slices of baguette, cornichons, and whole-grain mustard.

EQUIPMENT: Kitchen Tongs

Tongs can be used for more than just flipping a steak on the grill or chicken breast in a pan. Professional chefs often use tongs as a more heatsafe extension of their arm, whether for removing ramekins from a hot water bath, as we do here, reaching for an ingredient on a high shelf, or rotating a cake during baking (the tongs can grab onto the lip of the cake pan, whereas a hand clad in a bulky oven mitt risks marring the surface of the cake). Tongs may also be used to remove hot pan lids (for this purpose, a long pair of tongs works best) and to steady a roast or large bird during carving. We prefer 12-inch stainless steel tongs for all-purpose kitchen use.

Individual Chicken Liver Flan

SERVES 6

You will need six 6-ounce ramekins and an instant-read thermometer for this recipe. The flan are more flavorful if refrigerated overnight after baking. You can, if pressed for time, make this dish and serve it the same day. It does, however, need at least 3 hours in the refrigerator to cool completely.

- 1 1/2 cups Madeira
- 1 (2 by 1/2-inch) piece orange peel
- 1 bay leaf
- 15 whole black peppercorns
- 1/2 pound fresh chicken livers, rinsed and patted dry
- 1 1/4 cups heavy cream
- 2 large eggs
- 2 teaspoons salt
- Butter for greasing the ramekins
- Bread or crackers, for accompaniment
- Whole-grain mustard, for accompaniment
- Cornichons, for accompaniment

1. Adjust an oven rack to the middle position and heat the oven to 350 degrees. Bring the Madeira, orange peel, bay leaf, and peppercorns to a boil in a small saucepan

over high heat. Reduce the heat to medium and simmer until ¼ cup remains, about 15 minutes. Remove from the heat and cool completely.

2. Meanwhile, process the livers in a food processor, stopping to scrape down the sides, until smooth, about 15 seconds. Using a rubber spatula, press the livers through a fine-mesh sieve into a large bowl. Process the cream and eggs in the food processor until smooth and well combined, about 5 seconds. Pass this mixture through the sieve into the bowl with the livers. Pass the cooled Madeira through the same sieve into the bowl. Add the salt and stir to combine. (The mixture will be thin, like a pancake batter.)

3. Lightly grease six 6-ounce ramekins. Divide the liver mixture among the ramekins. Place the ramekins in a small roasting pan and place the pan on the oven rack. Fill the pan with boiling water to reach halfway up the sides of the ramekins. Bake until the centers are set and an instant-read thermometer inserted in the middle of a flan registers 155 to 160 degrees, about 25 minutes. Using tongs to avoid burning your fingers, transfer the flan to a wire rack and cool to room temperature. Wrap each loosely with plastic wrap and refrigerate for at least 3 hours or overnight. To serve, set each ramekin on a salad plate, with accompaniments.

TONGS CADDY

The splay of tongs makes them unsuitable for placing on a spoon rest while cooking. We like this space-saving alternative to catch drips and spills. Place the tongs in a heavy beer or coffee mug to keep your stovetop or counter clean.

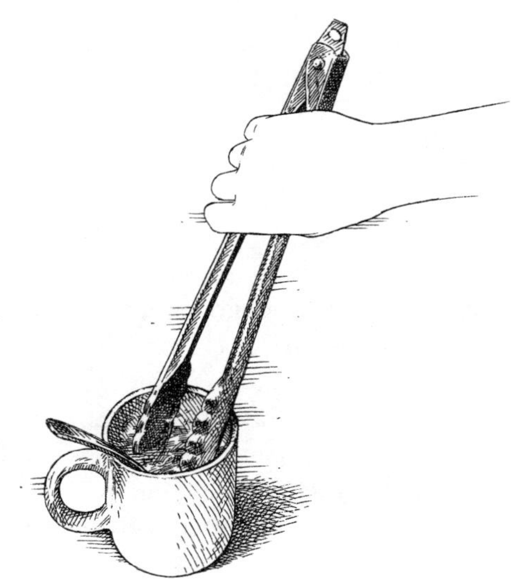

Seared Foie Gras *with* French Toast

Adapted from Sautéed Foie Gras with French Toast, Brûléed Orange, Port Wine Syrup, and Cranberry-Orange Reduction Sauce

Rosemary's at the Rio, Las Vegas, Nevada

FOIE GRAS IS PROBABLY ONE OF THE more decadent (and expensive) ingredients that you'll find on a restaurant menu. It is most commonly found in terrines and pâtés, but it can also be quickly seared and served warm as the main attraction. The fattened liver of a duck or a goose, foie gras contains a very high amount of fat, which translates into a challenge for the home cook, akin to cooking a stick of butter without letting it melt. For this reason, and its high price tag, most home cooks avoid using foie gras. But by following this recipe from Rosemary's at the Rio, the home cook will be able to enjoy a restaurant-quality foie gras appetizer at home without much fuss.

Our initial undertaking of this recipe left a lot of tasters happy. As it stood, this was a sophisticated and multilayered dish. The rich slice of foie gras was set on top of a triangle of custardy French toast perfumed with orange. A sauce of sweet-tart cranberries provided a foil for the foie gras, and the dish was finished with a slice of brûléed orange and a drizzle of fruity port wine syrup. However, we were concerned that its intricacy would be difficult for the home cook to reproduce. So we looked for ways to streamline the preparation while keeping the concept of the original recipe intact.

The first ingredient with which we experimented was the foie gras itself. Getting foie gras proved to be the first hurdle—unlike a restaurant, we didn't have a wholesale meat purveyor to call. We checked several high-end meat markets and found that they didn't carry foie gras, or that the foie gras they did have came in a jar. We then turned to the Internet, and here found our solution. D'Artagnan, a catalog- and Internet-based game and meat purveyor, stocked a wide variety of foie gras, and within 24 hours we had it on our doorstep. The original recipe called for cutting a whole lobe of foie gras into 12 individual portions. This is no easy task. The foie gras, which is the size of a small football, has many small veins and pieces of connective tissue that need to be removed before cooking. Oftentimes, these veins run quite deep into the liver, and removing them causes it to fall apart. Trying to butcher slices of the liver that were consistently sized and that remained whole was virtually impossible. After several attempts at simplifying the process, we remembered seeing slices of foie gras being sold by D'Artagnan. We called them back, placed the order, and voilà: sliced foie gras, already cleaned and consistently sized.

From the foie gras, we moved to the French toast. The issue here was not with flavor or cooking technique but with the bread itself. The recipe from Rosemary's called for slices of brioche, an egg-and-butter-enriched white bread. But the brioche we found at our local markets, when we could find it at all, was inconsistently shaped, and often we couldn't get large enough pieces to make the French toast as directed in the recipe. Searching for alternatives, we found that challah worked superbly. The loaves of challah had a flavor and consistency similar to the brioche, were available at almost any store, and were consistently large enough that we could cut thick slices for the French toast.

Now it came time to streamline the sauce preparation while keeping the same flavor components. To do so, we had to figure out how to simplify the port syrup and cranberry preserves so they didn't require an hour's worth of cooking time. Considering that the initial recipe for the cranberry preserves made almost twice the amount called for in the dish, we halved the recipe in order to save some time. We also reduced the amount of sugar in relation to the cranberries, which significantly reduced the amount of time it took for the preserves to reach the proper consistency. In conjunction, these two changes had saved us more than 45 minutes.

Now the question was how to trim the reduction time of the port syrup. As with the preserves, a bottle of port made more syrup than was used in the recipe. But since we had to cook the port so slowly for fear of burning, we were unable to save any significant amount of time by halving the amount of port used. It then occurred to us that perhaps we could forgo the port syrup and incorporate the port into the pan sauce, thereby omitting the long reduction step while maintaining the basic flavors of the original dish. By adding a cup of port to the sauce, we had to extend the sauce's reduction time by several minutes, but compared to the hour devoted to the port reduction before, it was a drop in the bucket.

Topping off the dish were slices of brûléed oranges. Made by sprinkling orange slices with sugar and then placing them under the broiler until they browned, they were an interesting and invaluable addition to the dish. But sensitive to the issue of timing, we

PEELING AND SEGMENTING AN ORANGE

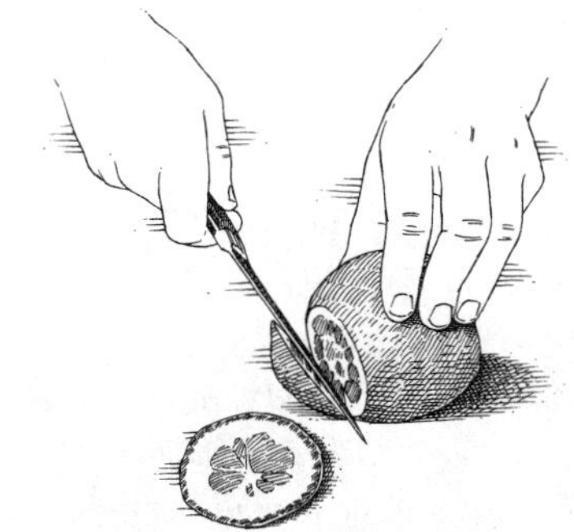

1. Start by slicing off a small section at the top and bottom.

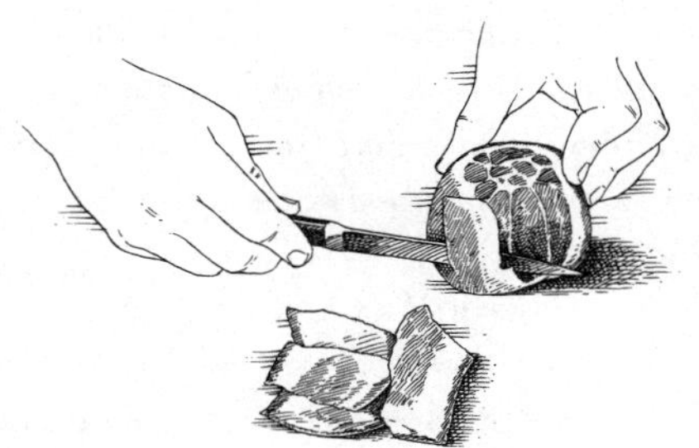

2. Stand the orange on end, and slice off the rind, including the white pith, following the contour of the fruit.

CUTTING CHIVES

To cut chives finely, gather them tightly in one hand and mince finely with the other, turning your fingertips under to shield your fingers from the blade.

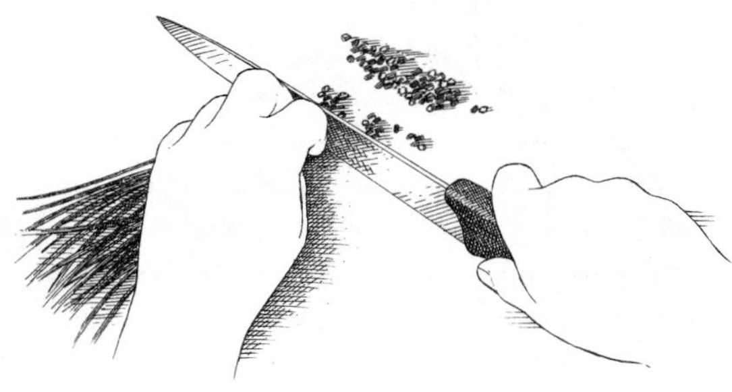

found it necessary to caramelize the oranges in advance, thus simplifying the work to be done during the last crucial steps of the dish. With a few time-saving techniques, we had managed to produce a foie gras appetizer just like those served in fine restaurants—sure to wow your next dinner guests.

Seared Foie Gras with French Toast

SERVES 8

If you cannot easily find brioche or challah, another soft, egg-enriched bread may be substituted. Foie gras can be a challenge to cook. Just keep a couple of things in mind—keep the foie gras refrigerated until you are ready to cook it and do not crowd the pan. If you follow these rules, you can reduce the amount of fat the foie gras renders during cooking. Sliced foie gras can be ordered from D'Artagnan at www.dartagnan.com.

CRANBERRY-ORANGE PRESERVES

- **1 cup cranberries, rinsed and picked over**
- **1/3 cup (2 1/3 ounces) sugar**
- **1/4 cup orange juice from 1 orange**

BRÛLÉED ORANGES

- **2 oranges, peeled (see the illustrations on page 37), and each cut into 4 rounds**
- **2 tablespoons sugar**

FRENCH TOAST

- **3 large eggs**
- **1/3 cup milk**
- **3 tablespoons Grand Marnier (or other orange-flavored liqueur)**
- **1 tablespoon sugar**
- **1 large loaf brioche or challah, cut into eight 3/4-inch-thick rounds**
- **2 tablespoons unsalted butter**

FOIE GRAS

- **8 (2-ounce) pieces sliced foie gras**
- **Salt and ground white pepper**
- **3/4 cup ruby port**
- **1/2 cup low-sodium chicken broth**
- **3 tablespoons minced fresh chives**

1. FOR THE PRESERVES: Bring all the ingredients to a boil in a small saucepan over medium-high heat. Reduce the heat to medium and cook until the mixture is glossy and thickened, about 5 minutes. Set aside.

2. FOR THE ORANGES: Adjust an oven rack so it is 6 inches from the broiler element and heat the broiler. Arrange the orange slices on a wire rack fitted in a rimmed baking sheet. Sprinkle the orange slices with the sugar. Broil the oranges, rotating the pan once, until the slices are spotted with brown and appear glazed, about 10 minutes. Set aside.

3. FOR THE FRENCH TOAST: Adjust an oven rack to the middle position and reduce the oven temperature to 200 degrees. Whisk together the eggs, milk, Grand Marnier, and sugar in a large bowl. Add the bread slices, turn to coat, and let soak for 10 minutes.

4. Melt the butter in a 12-inch nonstick skillet over medium-high heat until the foaming subsides. Remove the bread slices from the liquid, allowing any excess to drain back into the bowl. Place the bread in the skillet and cook until the first side is golden brown, about 1½ minutes. Using a spatula, flip the bread slices and cook until the second side is browned, 1½ minutes longer. Transfer the French toast to a wire rack fitted in a rimmed baking sheet and place in the warm oven. Set 8 serving plates on a separate oven rack to warm.

5. For the foie gras: Heat a 12-inch skillet over medium-high heat for 2 minutes. Season both sides of the foie gras with salt and white pepper. Place it in the skillet and sear until golden brown, about 1 minute. Using tongs, turn the foie gras and cook until the other side is browned, about 1 minute. Transfer to the baking sheet with the French toast and return to the oven.

6. Remove the skillet from the heat and carefully add the Cranberry-Orange Preserves, port, and chicken broth. Bring the mixture to a boil over medium heat, whisking gently, until the sauce is thickened and smooth, about 3 minutes. Season with salt and white pepper to taste.

7. To assemble: Remove the warmed plates from the oven. Pool ¼ cup of the sauce in the center of each plate. Place a piece of French toast on top of the sauce, followed by a piece of foie gras, and stack with a Brûléed Orange. Sprinkle the plate with a portion of the chives. Serve immediately.

Tuna Tartare *with* Sweet Potato Crisps

Adapted from Tuna Tartare with Piquillo Peppers, Roasted Tomatoes, and Spicy Sweet Potato Tuiles

Le Bernardin, New York, New York

THE PERFECT APPETIZER LURES THE DINER into the meal by engaging multiple senses. It will look and smell as good as it tastes—a few finely balanced bites that open the palate to the meal to come. At New York's Le Bernardin, with renowned chef Eric Ripert at the helm, the appetizers are pitch perfect, most notably a rendition of tuna tartare (raw minced fish) that combines the seemingly disparate ingredients of raw tuna, roasted peppers, roasted tomatoes, pickles, capers, and mayonnaise with a curry-spiced sweet potato tuile (a light, crisp cookie made savory with spices). It's a gamble of a dish that pays off: the flavors and textures pair beautifully—sweet and spicy, silky and crunchy, all artfully complementing one another.

Not surprisingly, we found this ambitious dish to be difficult for the home cook. From exotic ingredients to expensive equipment and a day's worth of labor, this was a restaurant recipe through and through, and in need of serious adjustment for the home kitchen. After some trial and error, we altered the tartare a little and excluded the tomato, but made major changes to the tuile.

This dish is dependent on the availability of ultra-fresh tuna. Many markets carry "sushi-grade" tuna, which is nothing more than a marketing term for ultra-fresh tuna (therefore suitable for raw consumption). But not every market labels its freshest tuna "sushi-grade" even though it might qualify as such (and the label doesn't guarantee anything). We've had good luck with unlabeled tuna from several local markets. So how do you recognize really fresh tuna? It should be ruby red, shiny, and smell oceanic but far from fishy. If it's the least bit dull or brown or off-smelling, try a different market or wait until fresh tuna arrives. If you can't find fresh tuna at all, it's best to wait until you can to make this dish.

Le Bernardin recommends yellowfin tuna for this recipe, and we could find no reason to suggest anything else. Luckily, it is the most readily available tuna—most markets we visited regularly carried it. Bluefin is the next best choice and is also widely available, though its assertive flavor and high moisture content can affect the quality of the tartare.

Mincing tuna is easier said than done; we found the soft flesh tended to mush when cut with anything but the sharpest blade (explaining the long, thin knives employed by sushi chefs). The fish's texture and appearance (precise, tiny cubes) are crucial to the appetizer's charm, so this was an important step to investigate. After trying several techniques, we had the best luck with a method we use to slice boneless cuts of pork and poultry thinly: we partially froze the tuna. After about a half hour in the freezer, the tuna had firmed up enough so that a knife could easily slice through without damaging the tender flesh. We cut the tuna into planks (see the illustrations on page 42), then into thin strips, which could be diced into precise cubes. A very sharp knife is still important, so use a freshly honed, long-bladed knife. Long, smooth cuts provide the best result: a jagged, sawing motion will damage the tuna.

The minced tuna and accompaniments—red onion, capers, cornichons (the French name for gherkins), and chives—are bound in a puree of roasted peppers, jalapeño, and mayonnaise, reminiscent of rouille, the Provençal sauce often served with fish dishes. Le Bernardin's recipe specifies piquillo peppers, a unique variety of small, mildly spicy, but sweet red bell peppers grown only in northern Spain. They are sold canned or jarred, roasted and packed in their own juices. Many specialty stores carry them and they are worth seeking out, but if they prove too elusive, roasted red bell peppers, either freshly roasted or jarred, come in a close second. If you choose jarred, pick a high-quality pepper like Divina-brand Florina peppers (imported from Greece and a recent taste-test winner in the test kitchen) since the flavor difference is easily noticed. While Le Bernardin uses homemade mayonnaise, we found good-quality prepared mayonnaise a fine substitute. To puree the mixture, a blender is the best bet since it produces the smoothest texture, though a food processor will do in a pinch.

The only ingredient we excluded from the tartare mixture was lemon oil. Tasters disliked the floral note of the commercial oil we found, certainly of an inferior quality to that which Le Bernardin employs. A spritz of lemon juice and a minor increase in the amount of mayonnaise (for fat content) adequately filled the void.

The sweet potato tuile that Le Bernardin serves with the tartare proved problematic because it was difficult to prepare—requiring many steps (including boiling the sweet potato, ricing it, and making a batter), exotic ingredients, and specialized equipment—and yielded a much larger amount than needed. We decided to reduce the tuile to its base elements: a crisp sweet potato chip spiced with curry powder and cayenne pepper (the prime flavors of the tuile). The crisp texture and flavors were essentially the same, but with a quarter of the effort.

Since sweet potatoes have a much higher moisture content than potatoes, frying them crisp took some experimentation. After trying a variety of thicknesses, we found the thinner the slice, the crisper the chip. One sixteenth of an inch—easily achievable with a mandoline—yielded the crispest chip. If you don't own a mandoline, the thinnest slicing blade of a food processor will work adequately, although the thicker slices won't be as crisp. A knife, however, won't do: even with the steadiest hand and sharpest knife, we could not slice the sweet potatoes thin enough. There are a variety of mandolines on the market, and in a recent testing, we found that the low-end models can hold their own against the expensive ones. One of our favorites retails for less than $10 (see page 8).

For presentation, the appetizer lends itself well to a variety of arrangements. We favored austere towers of tartare (gently spooned into place—molding seemed too fussy) and carefully stacked chips, encircled by a drizzle of

DICING FRESH TUNA

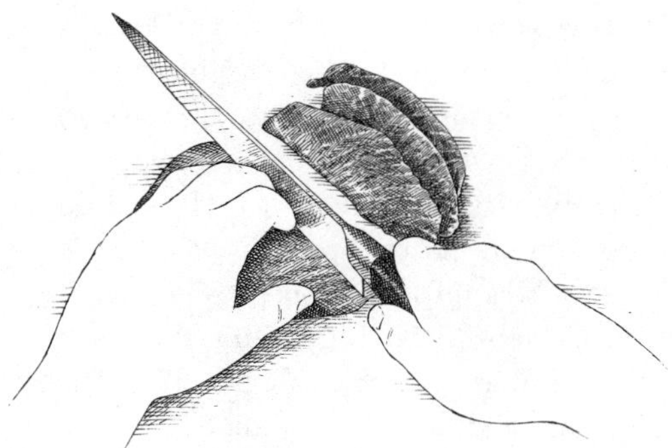

1. Using a steady slicing motion, cut the partially frozen tuna block into 1/8-inch-thick planks.

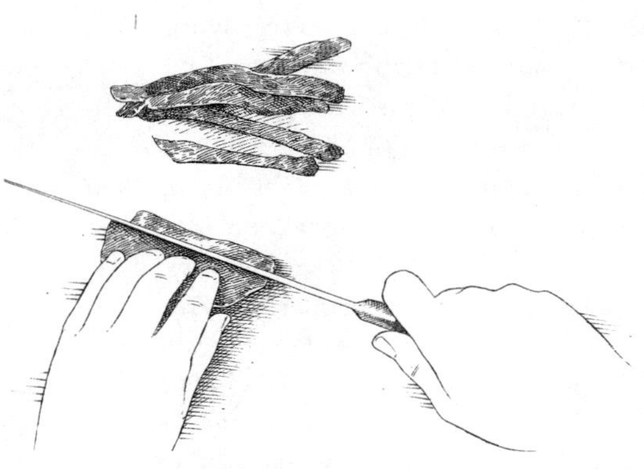

2. Slice each plank into 1/8-inch-thick strips.

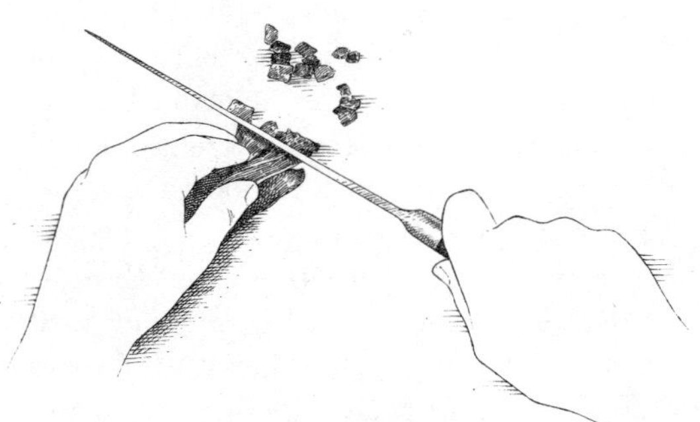

3. Slice the strips crosswise into 1/8-inch cubes.

extra-virgin olive oil for luster and color. We also liked the addition of a small pile (no more than a few tablespoons) of baby greens, such as mâche; admittedly not part of the original recipe, the greens looked great and provided a contrast to the tartare's texture and flavor.

Tuna Tartare with Sweet Potato Crisps

SERVES 4 TO 6

If the tuna at your market is not labeled "sushi-grade," ask your fishmonger; his standard tuna may be perfectly acceptable. Make sure that your chef's knife is quite sharp prior to cutting the tuna; otherwise it will be difficult to cut cleanly. If time is too tight to make the sweet potato crisps, store-bought sweet potato chips, like Terra Chips, can work, but you'll need to sprinkle them with curry powder and cayenne before serving—they should be salty enough.

SWEET POTATO CRISPS

- 1/2 teaspoon salt
- 1/4 teaspoon curry powder
- 1/8 teaspoon cayenne pepper
- 3 cups vegetable oil, for frying
- 1 small sweet potato (about 3/4 pound), peeled and sliced very thin crosswise (about 1/16 inch) with a mandoline

TUNA TARTARE

- 1/2 cup roughly chopped roasted piquillo peppers or best-quality jarred roasted red bell peppers
- 1 small jalapeño pepper, seeded, ribs removed, and diced fine
- 2 tablespoons mayonnaise
- 1/2 teaspoon lemon juice from 1 lemon
- 3/4 pound sushi-grade tuna, chilled for 30 minutes in the freezer and diced fine (see the illustrations at left)

- 3 **tablespoons finely minced red onion**
- 3 **tablespoons chopped cornichons**
- 3 **tablespoons chopped fresh chives**
- 2 **tablespoons chopped capers**
- **Salt and ground black pepper**

MÂCHE

- 1 ½ **cups fresh mâche or other baby greens, washed and dried**
- 2 **teaspoons extra-virgin olive oil**

1. FOR THE CRISPS: Combine the salt, curry powder, and cayenne pepper in a small bowl and set aside. Heat the vegetable oil in a Dutch oven over medium-high heat until it reaches 350 degrees. (Use an instant-read thermometer that registers high temperatures or clip a candy/deep-fat thermometer onto the side of the pan before turning on the heat.) Add roughly one quarter of the sweet potato slices and cook until lightly browned on the bottom, about 1½ minutes, adjusting the heat as necessary to maintain the cooking temperature. Using a slotted spoon, spider (see page 9), or tongs, flip the chips and cook until the second side has lightly browned, about 1 minute longer. Transfer the chips to a rimmed baking sheet lined with several layers of paper towels and dust with some of the spice mixture. Repeat with the remaining sweet potato slices and spice mixture.

2. FOR THE TARTARE: Puree the red peppers, jalapeño, mayonnaise, and lemon juice in a blender until smooth, about 30 seconds, scraping down the sides of the jar as necessary. Transfer to a medium bowl. Add the tuna, red onion, cornichons, chives, and capers, and gently mix together with a rubber spatula. Season with salt and pepper to taste.

3. FOR THE MÂCHE: In a large mixing bowl, drizzle the mâche with the olive oil.

4. Divide the tartare among 4 serving plates. Serve immediately, accompanied by the sweet potato crisps and garnished with mâche.

Pan-Roasted Mussels *with* Garlic Butter

Adapted from Restaurant LuLu's Iron Skillet–Roasted Mussels

RESTAURANT LULU, SAN FRANCISCO, CALIFORNIA

THERE ARE CERTAIN DISHES THAT YOU CAN bet will be prepared in a similar fashion in most restaurants. Hamburgers are often grilled. Calamari is usually fried. It's not that these dishes can't be prepared other ways, it's just that these classic preparations are the comfortable and desired default. Mussels are the same way. If you order mussels in a restaurant, most likely you will receive a bowl full of steamed shellfish bathed in a fragrant and flavorful broth. Every once in a while, though, a restaurant will surprise you. A chef will prepare a dish that runs contrary to tradition, oftentimes developing new and unique flavors. The skillet-roasted mussels from LuLu's fit this description.

The premise behind LuLu's recipe is to cook mussels on the stovetop in a cast-iron skillet that has been heated for six minutes. The intense heat of the pan "roasts" the mussels, lending them a smoky, charred flavor. While this technique of roasting over a burner may seem slightly unorthodox, it's as quick and easy as steaming. This method, however, does not create a flavorful broth (the liquor that results after steaming the mussels). To make up for this lack of moisture, LuLu's serves the mussels with a savory clarified butter infused with garlic, thyme, and black pepper—a perfect pairing with the roasted mussels. The only problem we had with this recipe was that we felt the procedure for the clarified butter took too long for the home cook. Perhaps this method is suited for a busy kitchen clarifying ten pounds of butter at once, but it seemed foolish to spend an hour clarifying butter to serve as a dipping sauce. Especially considering that mussels are a quick-cooking item, we felt that the sauce too should be relatively quick to prepare.

When clarifying butter, several things happen. First, the milk solids separate from the butterfat and fall to the bottom of the pan and the water contained in the butter evaporates. Then the proteins in the butter, along with other impurities, float to the top, forming a white foam. After removing the milk solids and the white foam, you are left with pure butterfat, a rich, flavorful liquid with a slightly nutty undertone.

In the recipe from LuLu's, the procedure for clarifying butter required slowly cooking the butter in a double boiler over low heat for an hour until clarified. Wanting to save time, we tried to create a similar dipping sauce in less time. In our first attempt, we simply heated butter slowly until melted and then allowed it to sit for five minutes. This was obviously too short a cooking time, since the milk solids did not separate from the fat and the foam did not coagulate on top. Next we tried cooking the butter over a higher heat for several minutes followed by a short resting time. This, too, left us with inferior results. While the foam formed on the surface and was easily removed, the bubbling of the butter kept the milk solids and the fat from separating fully. In a subsequent test, we tried cooking the butter over very low heat, so it would not bubble, for 10 minutes, and then allowed the butter to settle for 5 minutes. This seemed to work. The foam formed on the top and was easily removed, and the milk solids and the fat were clearly separated. This left us with a "quick" clarification: the elegance and taste we were looking for in a much shorter amount of time.

Pan-Roasted Mussels with Garlic Butter

SERVES 4

In order to protect your table from being burned by the hot skillet, serve the mussels on a heatproof trivet. If you don't own a cast-iron skillet, you can still prepare this recipe using a traditional skillet. However, do not attempt this with a nonstick skillet. The intense heat required will ruin the pan. When cleaning the live mussels, throw out any that won't close after being gently tapped or that have broken shells.

- **16 tablespoons (2 sticks) unsalted butter, cut into 16 pieces**
- **2 medium garlic cloves, lightly crushed**
- **1 sprig fresh thyme**
- **1 bay leaf**
- **1 teaspoon whole black peppercorns**
- **2 tablespoons juice from 1 lemon**
- **2 pounds mussels, scrubbed and debearded (see the illustration below)**
- **Salt and ground black pepper**
- **1 lemon, cut into wedges**

1. Melt the butter with the garlic, thyme, bay leaf, and peppercorns in a small saucepan over low heat. Cook the butter, without stirring or letting it bubble, until a white foam appears on the top and the butterfat appears clear, about 10 minutes. Remove the pan from the heat and let stand for 5 minutes. Skim the foam from the surface with a spoon. Slowly pour the butter through a fine-mesh sieve into a small serving bowl, leaving the milky white residue in the bottom of the pan. Stir in the lemon juice. Set aside in a warm place.

2. Heat a 12-inch cast-iron skillet over medium heat for 6 minutes. Add the mussels, spreading them in an even layer. Increase the heat to high and cook, uncovered, until all the mussels open, 3 to 4 minutes. Very carefully remove the pan from the heat (the entire pan, including the handle, will be hot) and season the mussels with salt and pepper. Serve the mussels immediately in the pan, with the garlic butter and lemon wedges.

DEBEARDING MUSSELS

Trap the beard between the side of a small knife and your thumb and pull to remove it. The flat surface of the knife gives you some leverage to extract the pesky beard.

Thai-Style Steamed Mussels

Adapted from Sister-in-Law Mussels

Flying Fish, Seattle, Washington

WITH WILD SEAFOOD BECOMING MORE expensive and less available, farm-raised seafood is fulfilling diners' desire for fish and shellfish and chefs' needs for an economical seafood menu item. Mussels have become the darling of aquaculture. Farmers have perfected the growing of mussels and can produce clean, plump, mildly flavored mussels without any of the unsavory characteristic of wild mussels. Now that the grittiness and sometimes strong flavors of the mussels are things of the past, they have become a consumer favorite, both when dining out and when cooking at home.

Mussels are also a favorite of chefs, their mildness providing a base for many different styles of preparation, from French to Spanish to—like this recipe from Flying Fish—Thai. Here we find briny mussels served in a wonderfully perfumed broth, flavored with lemon grass, lime leaves, and ginger. The mussels are also served with a dipping sauce made with lime juice, fish sauce, and chiles.

The dipping sauce gives the dish a spicy-tart character that was welcome, but we thought it might also be a little overpowering to most American palates. Looking at the ingredients in the sauce, we searched for ways to tone down the flavors. A consistent comment from the tasters was that the sauce was too fiery. In light of the fact that the recipe called for six Thai chiles, we were not surprised. By halving the amount of chiles, we achieved a better balance—still some spiciness, but not so much that all you tasted were chiles.

We also looked at the combination of the lime juice and fish sauce, thinking that if we reduced the amount of salty fish sauce we could diminish the strength of the sauce. However, reducing the amount of fish sauce only made the lime juice stand out, making the sauce overall less strong but bracingly tart. We then thought that if we added a sweet component to the sauce we could round out the salty-tart combination of the lime juice and fish sauce. By adding a tablespoon of brown sugar to the sauce, we found we could achieve a less potent sauce, but it still was not mild enough. In addition to adding brown sugar, we thinned the sauce with a little bit of the broth from cooking the mussels. This worked very well. Not only did the mussel liquor reduce the intensity of the sauce, but it also drew out the ginger and lime flavors, rounding out the sauce and finishing the dish.

Thai-Style Steamed Mussels

SERVES 4

If you desire a less spicy dipping sauce, use only two Thai chiles. (For more information on Thai chiles, see page 161.) While lemon grass can usually be found in well-stocked markets, kaffir lime leaves are more difficult to locate. If you cannot find lime leaves, it is possible to use a teaspoon of lime zest in their place, although the flavor won't be quite the same. When cleaning the live mussels, throw out any that won't close after being gently tapped or that have broken shells.

- **1/4 cup lime juice from 2 limes**
- **1/4 cup fish sauce**
- **3 Thai chiles, cut into thin rings**
- **1 tablespoon light brown sugar**
- **1 medium garlic clove, minced or pressed through a garlic press (about 1 teaspoon)**
- **1 (2-inch) piece fresh ginger, peeled, cut in half lengthwise, then sliced thin on the bias**
- **1/2 stalk lemon grass, minced (see the illustrations below)**
- **2 kaffir lime leaves, torn into 1/4-inch pieces**
- **2 pounds mussels, scrubbed and debearded (see the illustration on page 45)**

1. Mix the lime juice, fish sauce, chiles, sugar, and garlic in a small bowl. Set aside.

2. Bring ½ cup water, ginger, lemon grass, and lime leaves to a simmer in a Dutch oven over medium heat. Add the mussels, increase the heat to medium-high, and cover. Cook, stirring once, until the mussels are fully open, about 4 minutes.

3. Transfer the mussels, with any liquid, to a serving bowl. Thin out the dipping sauce with 3 tablespoons of the mussel liquor. Serve immediately, accompanied by the dipping sauce.

MINCING LEMON GRASS

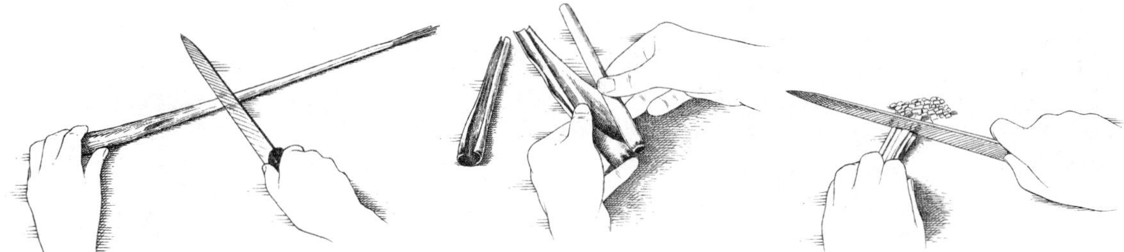

1. Trim all but the bottom 3 to 4 inches of the lemon grass stalk.

2. Remove the tough outer sheath from the trimmed lemon grass. If the lemon grass is particularly thick or tough, you may need to remove several layers to reveal the tender inner portion of the stalk.

3. Cut the trimmed and peeled lemon grass in half lengthwise, then mince finely.

Coconut Shrimp *with* Mango Chutney

Adapted from Rapscallion Cajun Coconut Prawns with Coco Prawn Sauce

Rapscallion, Reno, Nevada

THIS RECIPE FROM RAPSCALLION PRODUCED the quintessential example of coconut shrimp: plump juicy shrimp with a crunchy, golden exterior punctuated by spices like paprika and cayenne. There were, however, several issues that we felt needed to be addressed in order to translate this restaurant recipe into one for the home cook.

The first issue we examined was how to bread the shrimp. The original recipe called for making a seasoned flour, which was used both to dredge the shrimp and as the base of a batter in which the shrimp would later be coated before being rolled in coconut and fried. We felt this method had a couple of drawbacks. While we liked the use of the seasoned flour to dredge the shrimp because it added flavor, we felt that the batter, which was made by adding eggs and beer to a portion of the seasoned flour, was counterproductive because it inhibited the coating from sticking to the shrimp. Looking to simplify the process, we decided to use only eggs. And to our surprise, we ended up with a coating that was lighter and slightly crispier than before. Another issue we struggled with was how to keep the coconut shrimp crisp after frying. Although the shrimp tasted delicious just after they were fried, those left sitting while we waited for the whole batch to be cooked failed to retain their crispiness. A restaurant doesn't have to worry about this problem, but at home, where we fry in batches, we needed a solution. To counter the sogginess and improve the crunch, we added a cup of panko (Japanese-style bread crumbs) to the coconut, thus ensuring that the first batch

DEVEINING SHRIMP

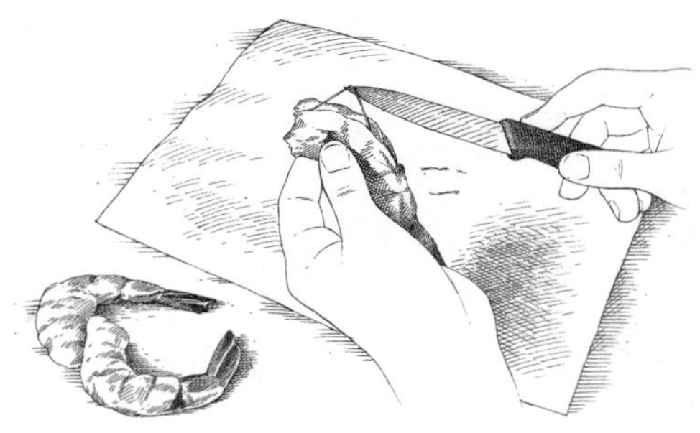

Hold the shelled shrimp between thumb and forefinger and cut down the length of its back, about $\frac{1}{8}$ to $\frac{1}{4}$ inch deep, with a sharp paring knife. If the shrimp has a vein, it will be exposed and can be pulled out easily. Once you have freed the vein with the tip of a paring knife, just touch the knife to a paper towel and the vein will slip off the knife and stick to the towel.

would stay crunchy while we fried the rest.

We also sought to improve the dipping sauce for the home cook. Considering that a home cook is going to be focused on breading and frying the shrimp, we felt that a sauce with the least number of ingredients and amount of preparation would be crucial in this recipe. While we felt that perhaps Rapscallion's sauce was a little too ingredient intensive, we did like the flavor that the mango chutney contributed to the sauce. In our next test, we decided simply to serve the shrimp with just the mango chutney. To our surprise, the mango chutney, which contains a wide array of ingredients, made a sauce that had varied and effusive flavors—along with a spritz of lime, it was all that was needed to serve with the shrimp. More importantly, the use of the mango chutney on its own was a significant time-saver for the home cook.

Coconut Shrimp with Mango Chutney

SERVES 4 TO 6

Panko can be found in the international food aisle at most supermarkets, or see our recipe for Homemade Panko on page 17.

- 1 cup all-purpose flour
- 1/2 teaspoon paprika
- 1/2 teaspoon ground white pepper
- 1/4 teaspoon cayenne pepper
- 1/4 teaspoon salt
- 1/4 teaspoon sugar
- 2 large eggs
- 1 cup unsweetened shredded coconut
- 1 cup panko (Japanese-style bread crumbs) or Homemade Panko (page 17)
- 1 (9-ounce) jar high-quality mango chutney, such as Major Grey's (about 1 cup)

INGREDIENTS: Shrimp

Shrimp are sold by size (small, medium, large, and so on) as well as by the number needed to make one pound, usually given in a range. Choosing shrimp by the numerical rating is more accurate than choosing by a size label, which varies from store to store. Here's how the two systems line up.

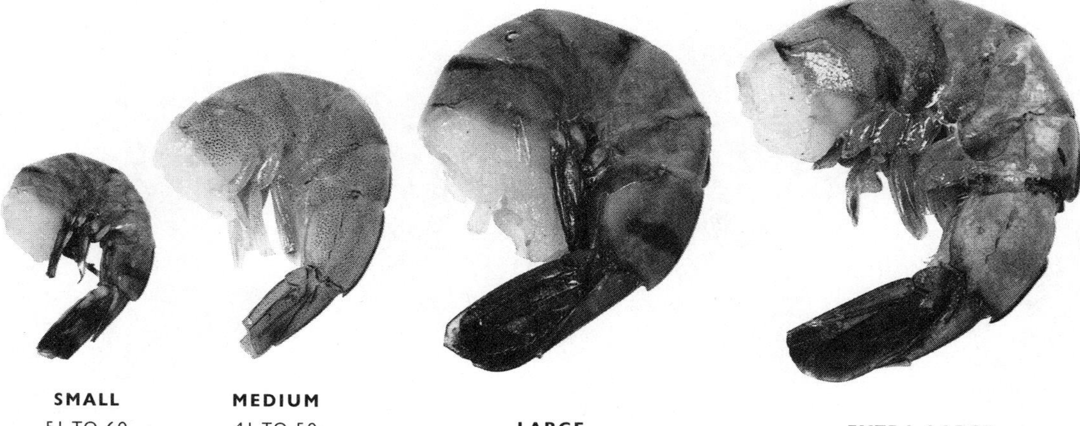

SMALL 51 TO 60 PER POUND

MEDIUM 41 TO 50 PER POUND

LARGE 31 TO 40 PER POUND

EXTRA-LARGE 21 TO 25 PER POUND

- 1 pound extra-large (21–25 per pound) shrimp, peeled and deveined
- 3–4 cups vegetable oil, for frying
- 1 lime, cut into wedges

1. Adjust an oven rack to the middle position and heat the oven to 200 degrees. Combine the flour, spices, salt, and sugar in a shallow dish or pie plate. Lightly beat the eggs with 1 tablespoon water in another shallow dish. Combine the coconut and panko in a third shallow dish. Puree the chutney in a food processor until almost smooth, ten 1-second pulses. Transfer the pureed chutney to a medium serving bowl and set aside.

2. Working with several shrimp at a time, drop them into the flour mixture and gently shake the dish back and forth to coat. Shake the excess flour from each shrimp. Then, using tongs, dip the shrimp into the eggs, turning to coat well, and allow the excess to drip off. Drop the shrimp into the coconut-panko mixture, and press the coconut lightly to adhere. Shake off any excess coconut and place the shrimp on a wire rack set over a rimmed baking sheet. Repeat with the remaining shrimp.

3. Meanwhile, heat the vegetable oil in a Dutch oven over medium-high heat until it reaches 350 degrees. (Use an instant-read thermometer that registers high temperatures or clip a candy/deep-fat thermometer onto the side of the pan before turning on the heat.) Gently place half of the shrimp in the oil and fry, stirring frequently to prevent sticking, until golden, about 2½ minutes. Using a slotted spoon, spider (see page 9), or tongs, transfer the shrimp to a rimmed baking sheet lined with several layers of paper towels and repeat with the remaining shrimp. Serve immediately, accompanied by the mango chutney and lime wedges.

Crisp Jumbo-Shrimp Rolls

Adapted from Crisp Jumbo-Prawn Rolls with Roasted Corn Salsa, Heart of Palm, and Mâche Salad with Cactus Pear Vinaigrette

The Morrison Clark Inn, Washington, D.C.

DAZZLING TO THE EYE AND BURSTING with remarkable textural and flavor contrasts, this dish from the Morrison Clark Inn will shatter your notion of the ubiquitous egg roll, which is most often filled with an unidentifiable compost of cabbage and pork. In this upscale version, extra-large shrimp are encased in an egg roll wrapper with scallions and fried until crisp and golden. The wrapper protects these giants from the drying effects of high heat, keeping them tender and succulent. A roasted corn salsa, mâche salad, and piquant cactus pear vinaigrette complement the simplicity of the shrimp filling.

To facilitate the preparation of this appetizer for the home cook, we broke the recipe down into three components: the corn salsa, the cactus pear vinaigrette, and the shrimp rolls. We then took the quantities of both the corn salsa and the cactus pear vinaigrette to a fraction of the original to keep to our goal of six servings.

Though not difficult, the corn salsa seemed to be the place to start, requiring more ingredients and advance preparation. The original recipe called for four roasted ears of corn. We found roasting too time consuming and opted to test the faster, more intense heat of the broiler. Broiling for 15 minutes resulted in kernels that were nicely browned and delicately flavored—any longer and the kernels began to shrivel. Both red onion and scallions were called for, but our desire to pare down the list of ingredients prompted us to eliminate the red onion. We also cut back on the quantity of oil and settled on 2 tablespoons of cilantro leaves for maximum flavor.

We then set upon the cactus pear vinaigrette. Native to Mexico, the cactus pear (also known as prickly pear or Indian fig) is a barrel-shaped berry with loads of tiny black seeds. Either medium green or dark magenta, the skin of this berry sports spines that need to be removed prior to peeling. The flesh of this prickly fruit can range from crimson to orange to a startling fuchsia, with a delicate, melon-like flavor. Available sporadically from summer through early spring, cactus pear can be a tough fruit to find, making this an impractical choice for the home cook. We experimented with several options that were more readily available, settling on cranberry juice concentrate for its vibrant color and fruity flavor. While you can whisk the vinaigrette ingredients in a medium bowl, we found that mixing in a blender yielded a smoother, more emulsified dressing.

Finally, we turned to the shrimp rolls. The original recipe called for eight U8 shrimp (about the size of a small lobster tail). Shrimp are sold by size as well as by the number needed to make one pound, usually given in a range (see page 49). In this case, U8 (the U denoting "under") means that there are eight shrimp or under per pound. This size isn't very common in the United States, so we settled on the largest available from our local market, frozen shrimp labeled "extra-large, 21–25 per pound." The bottom line is, use 12 of the biggest shrimp you can find (two per roll) and lightly pound the thicker end after butterflying to keep the roll even and reduce the cooking time. Originally, wasabi paste was spread on the shrimp prior to sealing it in its wrapper. While the wasabi added a pungent, fiery flavor to the original recipe, we found it difficult to achieve consistent heat owing to the variations in potency of the wasabi powders we tested. Some contained fillers such as cornstarch; others had added dyes or even the microalga spirulina to the mix. We opted to let the clean, briny flavor of the shrimp shine through on its own.

That settled, the choice of wrapper became the next challenge. The term "spring roll wrapper" translates into a diverse array of choices depending on the type of cuisine, including Vietnamese spring roll wrappers made from rice flour and water and egg roll (sometimes called spring roll) wrappers made from a wheat flour and water batter similar to noodle dough. The shrimp fried in the delicate rice paper wrapper instantly curled up when added to the hot oil, leaving them naked on one side of the pot, their covering shriveled and wan nearby. We did find success with the widely available egg roll wrapper. It proved to be an encasement sturdy enough to prevent the gargantuan shrimp from escaping their enclosure, frying up to a crisp golden brown.

Grown hydroponically year-round, mâche (also known as lamb's lettuce) is a tender, dark green leaf that adds to the vibrant colors and subtle flavors of this dish. A suitable replacement would be any tender baby field lettuce available.

A far cry from the egg rolls you're used to, this appetizer features large, tender pink shrimp with a crispy exterior, perched atop a fresh corn salsa and garnished with delicate green mâche. We suggest serving this dish on a plain white plate to allow the vibrant colors to take center stage.

INGREDIENTS: Prawns

We were curious about the difference (or similarity) between prawns and shrimp. It became apparent that there were wide-ranging differences between the scientific definition and the culinary meaning of this crustacean. After consulting several sources, a call to the owner of a local wholesale seafood distributor revealed a trade secret. Although technically a species of its own, in the United States the term "prawn" is often imprecisely used to describe any extra-large shrimp and, depending on the region of the country, with or without the head.

Crisp Jumbo-Shrimp Rolls

SERVES 6

To butterfly shrimp, simply lay a shrimp flat on a cutting board and slice partway but not all the way through the back of the shrimp. The corn salsa and vinaigrette may be prepared up to a day in advance; the rolls are best prepared as close to cooking time as possible.

ROASTED CORN SALSA

- **2 ears corn, husks and silk removed**
- **1 small red bell pepper, seeded and cut into 1/2-inch dice (about 3/4 cup)**

- 3 scallions, both green and white parts, minced
- 2 tablespoons minced fresh cilantro leaves
- 2 tablespoons extra-virgin olive oil
- 1 tablespoon plus 2 teaspoons rice vinegar
- Salt and ground black pepper

CRANBERRY VINAIGRETTE

- 1/3 cup frozen cranberry juice concentrate, thawed
- 2 tablespoons whole-grain mustard
- 1/4 cup rice vinegar
- 2 tablespoons extra-virgin olive oil
- 1 tablespoon honey
- Salt and ground black pepper

SHRIMP ROLLS

- 12 extra-large shrimp, peeled and patted dry with paper towels (about 1/2 to 3/4 pound)
- 6 (6 1/2-inch square) egg roll wrappers
- Salt and ground black pepper
- 3 scallions, green parts only, cut into twelve 2 1/2-inch lengths
- 4 cups vegetable oil
- 3 cups mâche or other tender baby leaf lettuce, washed and dried

1. FOR THE ROASTED CORN SALSA: Adjust an oven rack so it is 6 inches from the broiler element and heat the broiler. Place the corn on a rimmed baking sheet. Broil until the kernels are lightly browned, about 15 minutes, turning the corn every couple of minutes. Transfer the corn to a large bowl and cool. Working with one ear at a time, stand it on end inside the bowl and, using a paring knife, cut the kernels off the cob. Toss the corn with the remaining ingredients except the salt and pepper. Season with salt and pepper. Set aside.

2. FOR THE CRANBERRY VINAIGRETTE: Process all the ingredients except the salt and pepper in a blender until emulsified, about 30 seconds. Season with salt and pepper. Set aside.

3. FOR THE SHRIMP ROLLS: Butterfly the shrimp and discard the veins. Using a meat pounder or rubber mallet, lightly flatten the ends of the shrimp.

4. Working with one wrapper at a time, and keeping the other wrappers covered with plastic wrap so they don't dry out, place 1 shrimp cut-side up in the center of the wrapper. Season the shrimp with salt and pepper. Lay 2 pieces of scallion on top of the shrimp and, following the illustrations on page 54, place another shrimp directly on top of the first, with the tail facing the opposite direction. Using a pastry brush, moisten the edges of the wrapper with water. Fold the left, then the right side of the wrapper over the shrimp and press the edges to seal. Brush the ends of the wrapper once more with water. Fold up the bottom of the wrapper to cover the shrimp, then fold down the top and press to seal. Repeat with remaining wrappers and shrimp.

5. Heat the vegetable oil in a Dutch oven over medium-high heat until it reaches 350 degrees. (Use an instant-read thermometer that registers high temperatures or clip a candy/deep-fat thermometer onto the side of the pan before turning on the heat.) Fry the shrimp rolls until golden, turning them over halfway through the cooking time, about 4 minutes, and adjusting the heat as necessary to maintain the cooking temperature. Using a slotted spoon, spider (see page 9), or tongs, transfer the rolls to a plate lined with several layers of paper towels to drain, about 1 minute. Transfer the shrimp rolls to a cutting board and, using a serrated knife, cut them in half on the bias. Return the halves cut-side down to the paper towel–lined plate to drain off any excess liquid that may have been

exuded from the shrimp.

6. To serve, place ¼ cup of the corn salsa in the center of each of 6 individual plates. Arrange ½ cup of the mâche on top of the salsa and place 2 shrimp roll halves next to the salad. Drizzle 2 tablespoons of the vinaigrette around the shrimp roll and serve immediately.

ASSEMBLING SHRIMP ROLLS

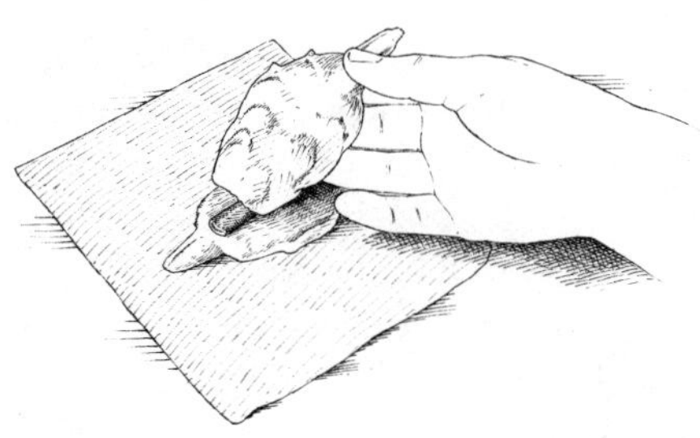

1. Working with one wrapper at a time, lay a shrimp cut side up, in the center of the wrapper. Season the shrimp with salt and pepper and lay 2 pieces of scallion down the center groove of the shrimp. Lay a second shrimp directly on top, with the tail pointing in the opposite direction of the first shrimp.

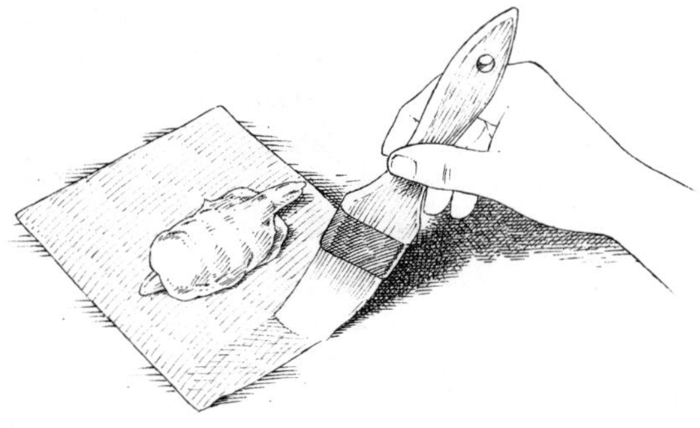

2. Using a pastry brush, moisten the edges of the wrapper with water.

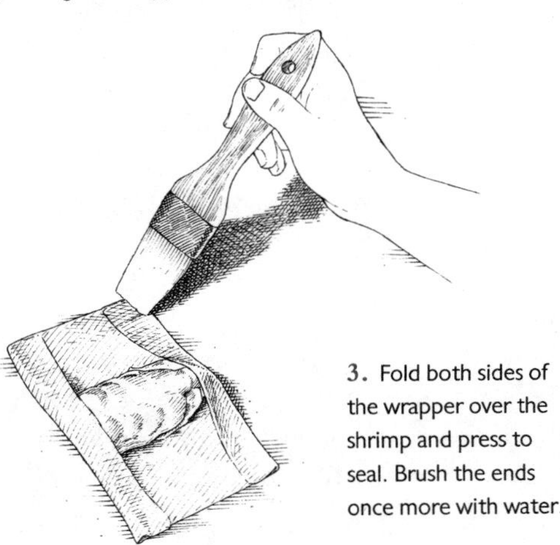

3. Fold both sides of the wrapper over the shrimp and press to seal. Brush the ends once more with water.

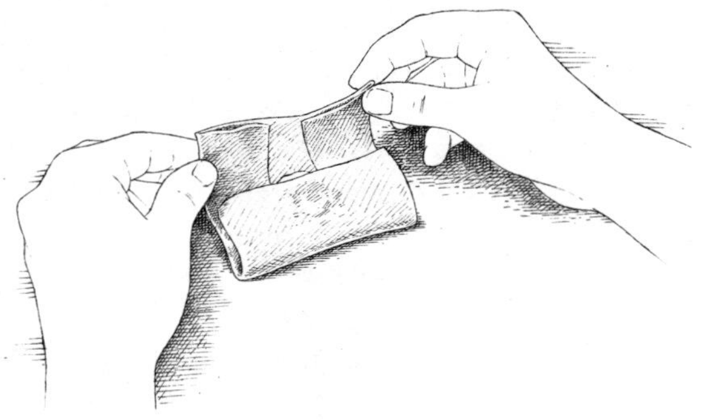

4. Fold the bottom of the wrapper up to cover the shrimp, pressing tightly to seal, then fold the top of the wrapper over the shrimp and press to seal.

Crab Cakes *with* Rémoulade Sauce

Adapted from Juban's Crab Cakes

Juban's, Baton Rouge, Louisiana

THE IDEAL CRAB CAKE CONTAINS LITTLE more than large chunks of crab, the lightest veil of binding, and a whisper of seasoning. Juban's—in the heart of Cajun country—makes stellar crab cakes that come close to this paradigm. Barely bound with mayonnaise and bread crumbs and subtly flavored with scallions and mustard, Juban's crab cakes consist almost entirely of sweet chunks of crabmeat, galvanized by a quick turn in a skillet. We could do little to improve Juban's recipe outside of applying our known experience with crabs and the mechanics of cooking crab cakes.

Almost by definition, crab cakes are made from Atlantic blue crabs. Found along the Atlantic seaboard from Florida to Cape Cod—most notably in the Chesapeake Bay region—they possess very sweet, rich-tasting meat. Atlantic blue crabmeat is always sold cooked and is available in four grades: lump, backfin, special, and claw. Lump meat is of the highest quality and is nothing but large chunks of meat removed from the body. Backfin is slightly lower in quality and is composed of smaller pieces and some lump meat. Special and claw round out the grading and are best reserved for soups or dips. Both lump meat and backfin can cost a pretty penny, especially during the winter months, but they are well worth it for the flavor and texture. Juban's specifies lump meat in its recipe, but we found that backfin worked just as well. At the time of testing, lump meat was almost twice as expensive as backfin—a premium we found hard to justify. Fresh crabmeat is found in tins or plastic containers in the fish department. It's often sold pasteurized (at a slightly lower price), though we found that the pasteurization process has a negative impact on the meat's flavor. And as far as the cans you find next to the canned tuna, don't bother; we found their contents inedible.

Crabmeat must be thoroughly sorted—though never rinsed—to remove bits of shell and cartilage. A mouthful of shell will ruin even the best crab cake. Our favorite technique for picking through the meat is placing it in a large bowl or on a large plate and carefully running our fingers through it. Any detritus will quickly become evident among the tender pieces of meat. Be careful not to break up any of the large chunks—those are the fat pieces for which you're paying a premium.

Crab cakes need just enough binder to hold them together, but not enough to impair the crabmeat's flavor or delicate texture.

The binding is most commonly a mixture of mayonnaise, eggs, and bread crumbs or cracker crumbs, a standard from which Juban's doesn't deviate. For bread crumbs, the restaurant specifies panko (Japanese-style bread crumbs), a unique style of bread crumbs that are lighter in both flavor and texture than conventional crumbs. They are available in most markets, often in the international aisle. If you have trouble finding them, see our recipe for Homemade Panko on page 17. For mayonnaise, we preferred a high-quality, neutrally flavored prepared mayonnaise. Refrigerating the crab cakes briefly before cooking gives the ingredients a chance to set, ensuring that they don't fall to pieces in the pan.

For seasoning, Juban's employs a simple mixture of garlic, scallions, and dried mustard. The trio worked well, especially the dried mustard, which lent flavor without the acid kick of prepared mustard. For spice, Juban's uses ground white pepper—a Cajun staple that has a flavor distinct from black pepper. If you don't have white pepper, black pepper is perfectly acceptable.

Since the crabmeat is already cooked, frying the crab cakes is strictly to tighten the binding and to create a light crust; overcooking will rob the crabmeat of its delicate texture and sweet flavor. That said, Juban's is right on the money. The chefs pan-fry the cakes for about two minutes per side, or just enough for a bit of color and firming of the cake. We found vegetable oil to be the best cooking medium because its neutral flavor and light mouthfeel did not affect the crab cakes' flavor.

In Louisiana, crab cakes are commonly served with rémoulade sauce, a mayonnaise-based concoction flavored with gherkins, capers, anchovies, hot pepper sauce, and a variety of herbs. It's based on the classic French sauce of the same name, but reinterpreted Creole style. The sauce's piquancy intensifies the crab's sweet, mild flavor. We created a quick version of rémoulade. We based it on good-quality, prepared mayonnaise to save time (and it is used in the crab cake) and flavored it with the usual suspects. Each component rounded out the flavor so that the resulting sauce was sweet, spicy, and tart—the perfect accompaniment to the mildly sweet crab.

MINCING GARLIC TO A PASTE

1. Mince the garlic as you normally would on a cutting board. Sprinkle the minced garlic with salt.

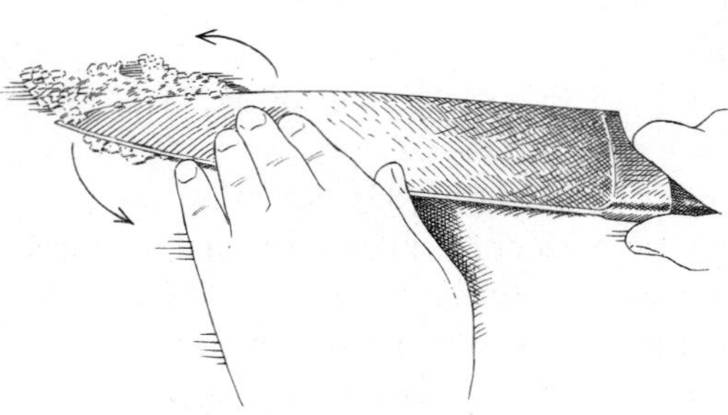

2. Drag the side of a chef's knife over the garlic-salt mixture to form a fine puree. Continue to mince and drag the knife as necessary until the puree is smooth.

Crab Cakes with Rémoulade Sauce

SERVES 4

Do your best to find top-quality crabmeat, since the success of the crab cakes depends on it. If you have trouble finding blue crabmeat, your fishmonger should be able to special-order it or you can search the Internet. There are numerous companies online that sell crabmeat.

RÉMOULADE SAUCE

- 1/2 cup mayonnaise
- 1/2 teaspoon capers
- 1/2 teaspoon Dijon mustard
- 1 anchovy fillet, chopped coarse
- 1 very small garlic clove, chopped coarse
- 1 1/2 teaspoons sweet pickle relish, or 1 gherkin, chopped
- 1 teaspoon hot pepper sauce, such as Tabasco
- 1 teaspoon juice from 1 lemon
- 1 teaspoon finely minced fresh parsley leaves
- Salt and ground black pepper

CRAB CAKES

- 1 large egg, lightly beaten
- 1/4 cup mayonnaise
- 2 medium scallions, both white and green parts, sliced thin (about 1/4 cup)
- 2 medium garlic cloves, minced to a paste (see the illustrations on page 56)
- 1 1/2 teaspoons dry mustard powder
- 1/4 teaspoon salt
- 1/4 teaspoon ground white pepper
- 1 pound lump or backfin Atlantic blue crabmeat, carefully picked over for shell fragments
- 1/2 cup panko (Japanese-style bread crumbs) or Homemade Panko (page 17)
- 2 tablespoons vegetable oil

1. FOR THE RÉMOULADE: Pulse all the ingredients except the salt and pepper in a food processor until well combined but not smooth, about ten 1-second pulses. Season with salt and pepper to taste. Transfer to a serving bowl. The rémoulade can be made up to 3 days ahead and refrigerated in an airtight container.

2. FOR THE CRAB CAKES: Combine the egg, mayonnaise, scallions, garlic, mustard powder, salt, and pepper in a large bowl. Using a rubber spatula, fold in the crabmeat and bread crumbs until just combined. Divide the mixture into 8 portions and gently pat into fat, round cakes. Arrange on a large plate or baking sheet, cover with plastic wrap, and refrigerate for at least 20 minutes and up to 8 hours before cooking.

3. Adjust an oven rack to the middle position and heat the oven to 200 degrees. Heat the vegetable oil in a large skillet over medium heat until shimmering. Gently place 4 crab cakes in the skillet and cook until lightly browned, about 2 minutes. Using a spatula, gently turn the cakes and cook the second side until lightly browned, 1½ to 2 minutes longer. Transfer the crab cakes to an ovensafe plate and set in the oven to keep warm. Repeat the process with the remaining crab cakes. Serve immediately on warm plates, 2 per person, accompanied by the Rémoulade Sauce.

Crab Towers *with* Avocado & Gazpacho Salsas

Adapted from Crab Tower Timbale

Mayflower Park Hotel, Seattle, Washington

DEVELOPING A MENU FOR A LARGE HOTEL restaurant allows you abundant freedom that you won't find in a standard restaurant—access to endless ingredients and many able hands to prepare them. A hotel kitchen wouldn't break a sweat preparing multi-component appetizers using over 35 ingredients. The Crab Tower at the Mayflower Park Hotel is a prime example of such hotel kitchen exuberance. It is a tidy, striated tower composed of three salads—an avocado–hearts of palm salsa, a crab salad, and a gazpacho salsa—garnished with frisée lightly dressed in a champagne vinaigrette, pea tendrils, grapefruit segments, and minced chives. Although replicating this dish sounds like a huge undertaking, we found a few ways to simplify the recipe without losing either its flavor or its impressive appearance.

Breaking the plate down into its various components, we focused on each component separately before combining them on the plate. All in all, the focus of this dish is on the crab, so we began with the crab salad. In the test kitchen, we prefer Atlantic blue crabmeat. Sold in both lump and backfin forms, the lump offers tender pieces of crab while the backfin has a more shredded texture. Both types work in this recipe, although tasters preferred the bite-size pieces of lump over the shredded backfin. The cost, however, may make the decision between the two for you—lump can cost up to twice as much as backfin.

To make the crab salad, the Mayflower mixes the crabmeat with a little mayonnaise and a champagne vinaigrette. When preparing the crabmeat, do not rinse it, but rather spread it out on a plate and check for small pieces of shell. Finding that 12 ounces of crabmeat was plenty for six plates, we tossed it with two tablespoons of mayonnaise and three tablespoons of vinaigrette to produce a flavorful, well-bound salad that highlights crabmeat's naturally sweet flavor.

Next, we focused our attention on the champagne vinaigrette. Made in bulk at the hotel, it makes sense that the chefs use it as a flavoring in the crab salad, as well as to dress the frisée garnish. Figuring that we needed a total of four tablespoons of vinaigrette, we pared down the Mayflower's eight-cup recipe, which called for two types of oil; we simplified the ingredients to include only olive oil. Other ingredients we included were champagne vinegar, lemon zest, Dijon mustard, salt, and pepper.

Moving on to the avocado–hearts of palm salsa, we figured that our six plates would require a total of three cups of salsa. Having a hard time finding decent-tasting hearts of palm with any regularity, we decided to omit them, using three avocados and an appropriate amount of the recipe's original seasonings—lime and coriander. Tasters liked the clean, streamlined avocado flavor in combination with the array of other ingredients.

We next turned our attention to the gazpacho salsa, which contained sixteen ingredients (eight of which are time-consumingly cut into ⅛-inch dice). We simplified the recipe, which yielded three times more than we needed, by cutting both ingredients and amounts. Although it called for both yellow and red bell peppers, we decided to use just yellow, which contrasts nicely with the red tomato and green cucumber. We also omitted the ⅛-inch dice of lime and orange segments. Not only were they difficult to cut in a tidy fashion, but their juice turned the gazpacho unnecessarily wet. Keeping the sherry vinegar and olive oil, we omitted the other seasonings, including lemon juice, celery salt, and sugar. The result was a crisp, clean flavor and colorful presentation that the tasters liked just as well as the original.

Addressing the last few ingredients used to garnish the plate—dressed frisée, grapefruit segments, pea tendrils, and chives—we omitted both the chives and the hard-to-find, sweet-tasting pea tendrils. On their own, the grapefruit segments tasted a bit too tart, so we substituted orange segments, a flavor that we had omitted from the gazpacho salsa.

At the hotel, tall, open-ended metal rings, called timbale rings, are used to build the tall towers of crab and avocado and gazpacho salsas. However, we found that a round biscuit cutter worked just as well after accommodating for its lack of depth (see the illustrations on page 61). Although it sounds a bit fussy, layering the salad into a tall-towered presentation is a simple way to bring the hotel dining experience to the kitchen table.

Crab Towers with Avocado and Gazpacho Salsas

SERVES 6

You can prepare the crabmeat salad and gazpacho salsa several hours ahead of serving, but the avocado salsa should be prepared just before assembly.

CRABMEAT SALAD

- 3 tablespoons extra-virgin olive oil
- 1 tablespoon champagne vinegar
- 1 teaspoon minced or grated lemon zest
- ½ teaspoon Dijon mustard
- ½ teaspoon salt
- ⅛ teaspoon ground black pepper
- 2 tablespoons mayonnaise
- 12 ounces lump or backfin Atlantic blue crabmeat, carefully picked over for shell fragments

GAZPACHO SALSA

- 1 small yellow bell pepper, cored, seeded, and cut into ⅛-inch pieces (about ½ cup)
- ½ small cucumber, peeled if desired, seeded, and cut into ⅛-inch pieces (about ½ cup)
- 1 medium plum tomato, cored, seeded, and cut into ⅛-inch pieces (about ½ cup)
- 1 small celery rib, cut into ⅛-inch pieces (about ½ cup)
- ½ small red onion, minced (about ¼ cup)
- ½ small jalapeño pepper, minced
- 1 tablespoon minced fresh cilantro leaves
- ¾ teaspoon salt

- 1/4 teaspoon ground black pepper
- 2 tablespoons extra-virgin olive oil
- 1 tablespoon sherry vinegar

AVOCADO SALSA

- 3 ripe avocados, cut into 1/4-inch dice
- 1/4 teaspoon ground coriander
- 1/2 teaspoon salt
- 1/8 teaspoon ground black pepper
- 2 tablespoons juice from 1 lime

- 1 cup frisée
- 2 oranges, peeled using a paring knife and segmented (following illustrations on page 37), optional

1. For the crabmeat salad: Whisk the olive oil, champagne vinegar, lemon zest, mustard, salt, and pepper together in a small bowl. Measure 3 tablespoons of the vinaigrette into a medium bowl and mix with the mayonnaise. Add the crabmeat to the mayonnaise mixture and toss to coat. Cover with plastic wrap and refrigerate until needed. Set the remaining vinaigrette aside.

2. For the gazpacho salsa: Toss the yellow bell pepper, cucumber, tomato, celery, red onion, jalapeño, cilantro, salt, pepper, olive oil, and sherry vinegar in a medium bowl and set aside.

3. For the avocado salsa: Toss the avocado, coriander, salt, pepper, and lime juice in a medium bowl and set aside.

4. To assemble, place a 3-inch-wide round biscuit cutter in the center of an individual plate. Following the illustrations on page 61, use a slotted spoon to press ⅓ cup of the Avocado Salsa into the bottom of the cutter using the back of a soup spoon. Lift the cutter off the plate slightly to reveal some but not all of the avocado. Holding the cutter aloft, press ⅓ cup of the crab mixture evenly into the cutter on top of the avocado. Lift the cutter further to reveal some but not all of the crab salad. Holding the cutter aloft, use a slotted spoon to press ⅓ cup of Gazpacho Salsa evenly into the cutter on top of the crab. Gently lift the cutter up and away from the plate to reveal the crab tower. Repeat the procedure five more times with the remaining ingredients.

5. Dress the frisée with the remaining champagne vinaigrette. Place a few sprigs of the dressed frisée on top of each crab tower and arrange the orange segments, if using, around the towers. Serve immediately.

DICING AN AVOCADO

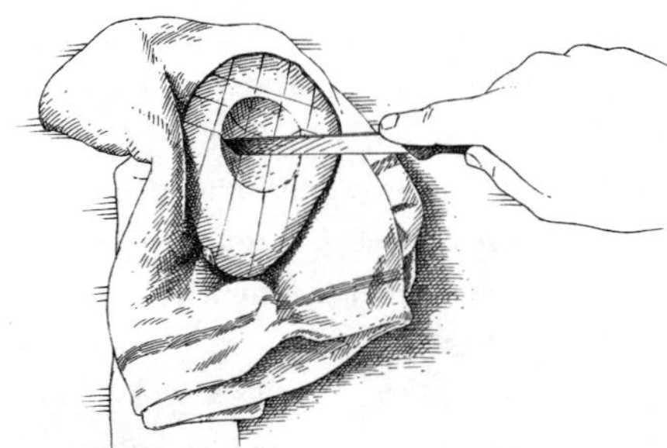

1. Halve and pit the avocado. Hold one half steady in a dish towel. Make 1/4-inch crosshatch incisions in the flesh with a dinner knife, cutting down to but not through the skin.

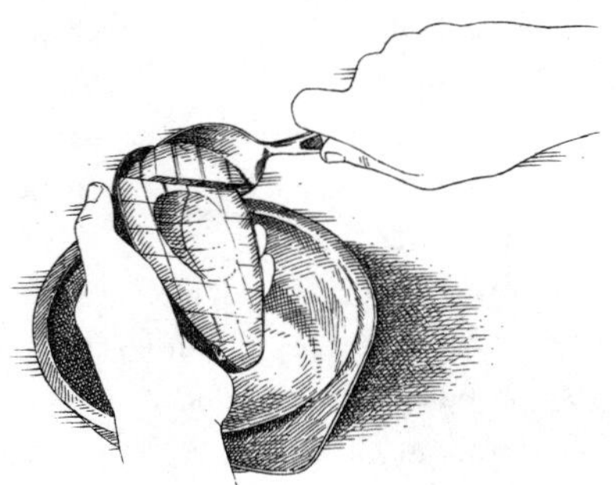

2. Separate the diced flesh from the skin by inserting a soup spoon or rubber spatula between the skin and flesh, gently scooping out the diced avocado.

ASSEMBLING CRAB TOWERS

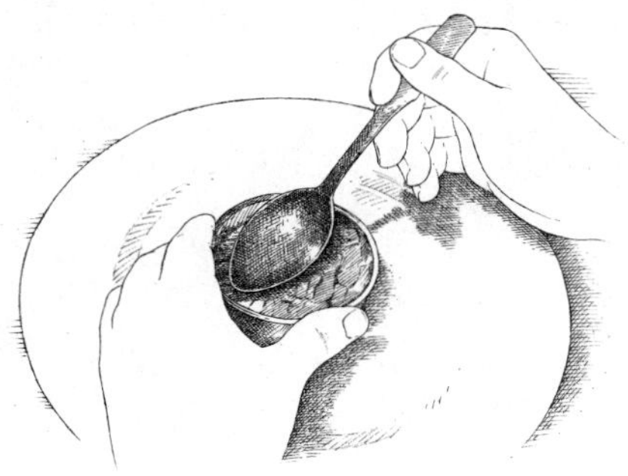

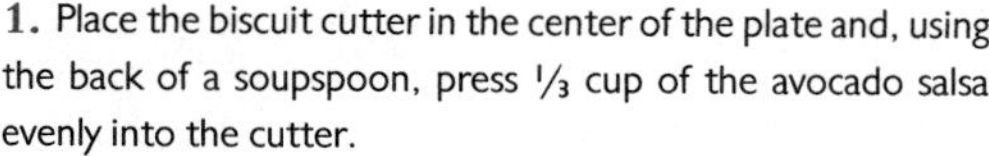

1. Place the biscuit cutter in the center of the plate and, using the back of a soupspoon, press 1/3 cup of the avocado salsa evenly into the cutter.

2. Lift the cutter off the plate slightly to reveal some but not all of the avocado.

3. Holding the cutter aloft, press 1/3 cup of the crab salad evenly into the cutter, on top of the avocado.

4. Lift the cutter farther off the plate to reveal some but not all of the crab mixture, and press 1/3 cup of the gazpacho salsa evenly into the cutter, on top of the crab.

5. Gently lift the cutter up and away from the plate to reveal the crab tower.

Seared Scallops *with* Fennel Compote & Curry Sauce

Adapted from Seared Scallops with Fennel Compote and Curry Sauce

Le Bec-Fin, Philadelphia, Pennsylvania

REFINED, SUAVE, AUSTERE—ALL APT DESCRIPTORS for this elegant appetizer of seared scallops on a bed of fennel "compote" napped with a buttery curry sauce. The fennel's sweet anise flavor amplifies the scallops' natural sweetness, and the hint of Madras curry powder adds a rich and exotic aroma, effectively bridging French and Southeast Asian cuisine. Surprisingly, such a fine dish comes together with little effort: each component of the appetizer may be fully realized at home without any special equipment or skills, unusual for a dish from such a high-end restaurant. Our easy task was to finesse the ingredient list and make the recipe as foolproof as possible.

There are three components to this appetizer: fennel compote, curry sauce, and sautéed scallops. The compote is the most time-consuming, so it was the natural point to commence testing. By definition, compote is fruit slowly simmered in sugar syrup until soft. Clearly, Le Bec-Fin stretches the definition by using fennel—a vegetable—but the result tastes great, so why split hairs? The fennel bulb is sliced thinly (once the thick core is excised), sautéed until soft, then simmered in chicken stock seasoned with sugar and lemon juice. Le Bec-Fin's instructions proved impeccable, and tasters felt the flavors and texture were perfect—sweet with a fleeting tartness, and tender but toothsome—the perfect foil to the silky scallops.

For the curry sauce, clam juice is flavored with a variety of ingredients, including shallots, mushrooms, curry powder, and two types of wine (dry white wine and dry vermouth), concentrated, and enriched with a prodigious amount of butter. Unsurprisingly for Le Bec-Fin, the recipe employs classic French procedure: everything is combined in a saucepan, brought to a simmer, then slowly reduced over low heat. Once the liquid has reduced dramatically, the sauce is strained of the now flavorless, mushy solids and further reduced after the addition of heavy cream. Straightforward in technique and finely flavored, this recipe presented little room for change. We did try to trim down the ingredient list, but to no avail. The mushrooms initially seemed expendable, but the sauce tasted thin without their presence. Shallots, too, were crucial. In the end, the only exclusion we could make was the white wine by increasing the amount of vermouth. Any alterations to the sauce's flavor went unnoticed by tasters.

Finishing a sauce with butter, called "mounting" in cooking patois, is a bit of kitchen alchemy. The butter turns an otherwise homely sauce thick and lustrous and amplifies the flavor. If you have never mounted a sauce, however, it can be intimidating. How can so much butter be added to so little liquid without turning into a greasy oil slick? The butterfat and liquid emulsify, much like oil and vinegar in a vinaigrette. If the butter is added recklessly, the sauce will break, just like a vinaigrette that has sat too long. After experimenting with a variety of mounting techniques, we admit the classic method is still the best. The butter must be added in small amounts to the liquid—no more than a tablespoon at a time—and steadily whisked over low heat. Only after each piece of butter is incorporated may more be added. The finished sauce may be covered to keep warm, but too much heat will encourage the sauce to break.

Half the charm of scallops is their silky, supple texture, yet they often come to the table leathery and tough. By our reckoning, they are easily the most overcooked shellfish, though they needn't be. Le Bec-Fin offered sketchy instruction in its recipe, so we applied our own technique. After searing pounds of scallops, we discovered that the secret to perfect scallops lay in single-side cooking. In the time it took for the scallops to develop a golden-brown crust on one side over medium-high heat, they were virtually cooked. A few seconds on the second side finished them off, leaving the interior buttery soft and tender. Tongs (with a gentle hand) were the best tool for maneuvering the cooked scallops.

For presentation, we favored making a small mound of the compote in the center of the plate and spacing the scallops around the perimeter. We then spooned a drizzle of sauce around the scallops—the sauce is intense and a little goes a long way. A sprinkling of the feathery fennel tops—lightly chopped—makes an attractive additional garnish, picking up the yellowish green hue of the sauce.

Seared Scallops with Fennel Compote and Curry Sauce

SERVES 4 TO 6

If you don't have dry vermouth, substitute a dry white wine, such as Sauvignon Blanc. Avoid Chardonnay or any wine with heavy tannins, since the flavor will overpower the delicate sauce. Larger scallops are the easiest to cook and look most dramatic, though not all fishmongers carry them. See the illustrations on page 64 for tips on coring fennel.

FENNEL COMPOTE

- **9 tablespoons (1 stick plus 1 tablespoon) unsalted butter**
- **3 medium fennel bulbs (about 2 pounds), cored and sliced thin, plus 2 tablespoons chopped fronds (if any)**
- **Salt**
- **3 tablespoons sugar**
- **1 cup low-sodium chicken broth**
- **3 tablespoons lemon juice from 1 lemon**
- **Ground black pepper**

CURRY SAUCE

- **1 1/2 cups bottled clam juice**
- **6 tablespoons dry vermouth**
- **2 large white mushrooms, sliced thin**
- **1 medium shallot, sliced thin crosswise**
- **1 teaspoon Madras curry powder**
- **1/4 cup heavy cream**
- **7 tablespoons (1 stick minus 1 tablespoon) unsalted butter, chilled and cut into 7 pieces**
- **Salt and ground black pepper**

SCALLOPS
- 1 tablespoon vegetable oil
- 1 pound sea scallops, tendons removed (see the illustration below)
- Salt and ground black pepper

1. FOR THE COMPOTE: Melt the butter in a large skillet over medium heat until the foaming subsides. Add the fennel bulbs and ¾ teaspoon salt and cook, stirring occasionally, until tender, about 15 minutes. Stir in the sugar, chicken broth, and lemon juice and cook, stirring occasionally, until the fennel is very tender and the liquid has almost completely evaporated, 16 to 18 minutes. Remove the skillet from the heat, adjust the seasoning with salt and pepper, and cover to keep warm.

2. FOR THE SAUCE: Bring the clam juice, vermouth, mushrooms, shallot, and curry powder to a boil in a medium saucepan over medium-high heat. Reduce the heat to medium and simmer until reduced to roughly ¾ cup, about 15 minutes. Strain the sauce through a fine-mesh strainer into a small saucepan, lightly pressing on the solids to extract the liquid. Add the cream and cook until reduced to ¾ cup, about 5 minutes. Over low heat, slowly whisk the butter into the sauce, one piece at a time, until incorporated. Remove from the heat, adjust the seasoning with salt and pepper, and cover to keep warm.

3. FOR THE SCALLOPS: Heat the vegetable oil in a 12-inch skillet over medium-high heat until smoking. Meanwhile, pat the scallops dry and season them on both sides with salt and pepper. Add the scallops flat-side down in the pan and cook until well browned, about

REMOVING SCALLOP TENDONS

The small, rough-textured, crescent-shaped muscle that attaches the scallop to the shell often is not removed during processing. It will toughen if heated and should be removed before cooking.

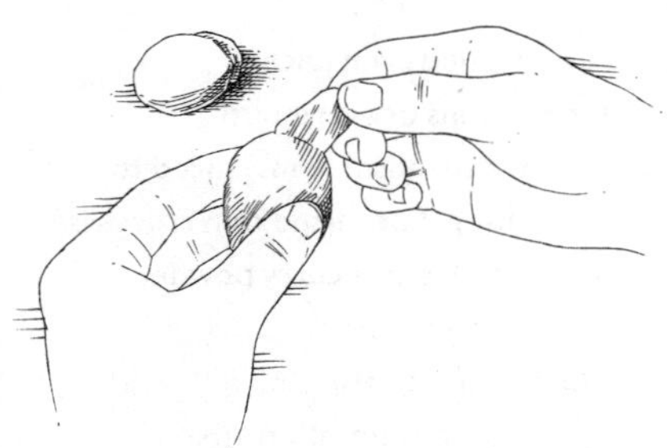

With your fingertips, gently peel away a single tendon from the side of each scallop.

CORING FENNEL

1. Cut off the stems and feathery fronds.

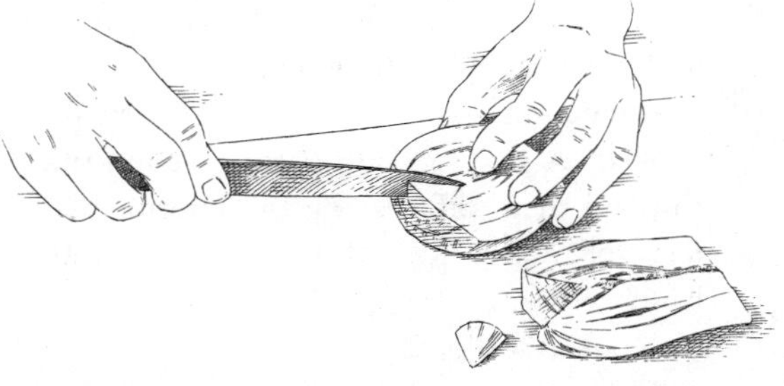

2. Trim a thin slice from the base of the bulb and remove any tough or blemished outer layers of the bulb. Cut the bulb in half through the base and use a paring knife to cut out the pyramid-shaped piece of the core in each half.

2½ minutes. Using tongs, turn the scallops over, one at a time. Cook until medium-rare (the sides have firmed up and all but the middle third of the scallop is opaque), about 30 seconds longer. Immediately transfer the scallops to a large plate.

4. Place a small portion of the Fennel Compote in the center of each plate and divide the scallops in a circle around the compote. Drizzle the sauce around the scallops, garnish with the fennel fronds (if using), and serve immediately.

INGREDIENTS: Vermouth

Though it's often used in cooking, and even more often in martinis, dry vermouth is a potable that is paid very little attention. Imagine our surprise, then, when we did a little research and turned up nearly a dozen different brands. We pared them down to eight and tasted the vermouths straight, chilled, and in simple pan sauces for chicken (containing only shallots, chicken stock, and butter in addition to the vermouth).

First, a quick description of what dry vermouth is. Its base is a white wine, presumably not of particularly high quality as evidenced by the relatively low prices of most vermouths. The wine is fortified with neutral grape spirits, which hike the alcohol level up a few percentage points to 16 to 18 percent, and it is "aromatized," or infused with botanicals, such as herbs, spices, and fruits. Dry vermouth, also called extra-dry vermouth, is imported from France and Italy (Italian vermouths being most common in the United States) and is made domestically in California.

Two vermouths found their way into the top three in both tastings: Gallo Extra Dry (California; $5 for 750 ml) and Noilly Prat Original French Dry (France; $6.79 for 750 ml). Tasters described the nose of the Gallo vermouth as sweet, floral, and "bubblegummy." Tasted straight, many agreed that it was fruity ("bizarrely" so, according to one)—in particular, melons and apples were detected. It was further characterized as fresh, refreshing, and simple, even water-like. It made the favorite pan sauce, which was called "balanced, complex, smooth," and "round. "

Noilly Prat had a more elusive nose. To one taster it was reminiscent of apple juice; others found it sweet, honeyed, earthy, herbaceous (thyme was mentioned), and "calming" (aromatherapy, anyone?). Its flavor was described as smooth, woodsy, with very faint anise notes. Several tasters noted a light acidity, a slight bitterness, and a lingering finish. The pan sauce made with Noilly Prat tasted fresh and balanced; one dissenter called it weak and bland, while one enthusiast declared it rich-tasting, with the chicken and wine flavors in perfect accord.

Tasted plain, Boissiere (Italy; $6.99 for 1 liter) was one of the three favorites. It was described as fresh, floral, fruity, and sweet, with a faint sherry-like finish. But in the sauce, it wound up seventh—old, stale, and as sweet as sugar water were criticisms. Martini & Rossi Extra Dry (Italy; $6.79 for 750 ml) made it into the pan sauce top three. Balanced, bright, and lively with sweet-and-sour notes was how the sauce was characterized. But tasted plain, it landed in seventh place, receiving low marks for tasting medicinal and harsh.

Other contenders, but not notable finishers, were Cinzano Extra Dry (Italy; $6.79 for 750 ml); Stock Extra Dry (Italy; $6.79 for 1 liter); Tribuno Extra Dry (California; $4.99 for 1 liter); and Vya Extra Dry (California; $19.99 for 750 ml).

FRIED CALAMARI *with* GARLIC BUTTER & HOT CHERRY PEPPERS

Adapted from Frank & Sheri's Special Calamari

FRANK & SHERI'S, MORRISTOWN, NEW JERSEY

BY ADDING SPICY, TANGY PEPPER RINGS and a garlic and herb butter to your basic calamari, Frank & Sheri's has created a dish bursting with unique and varied flavors. There were, however, some elements we felt could be simplified in order for the home cook to enjoy this restaurant classic.

The original recipe called for a pound of butter to form the base of this sauce. Since we felt that most home cooks would find this excessive, we decided to reduce the amount of butter so it merely coated the squid and distributed the other flavors without becoming too greasy. To the next batch of fried calamari, we added the melted butter mixture two tablespoons at a time until we had achieved a good balance. Six tablespoons did the trick.

Turning our attention to the other ingredients in the sauce, we considered the roasted garlic in the original recipe. While roasted garlic is a common ingredient in a restaurant, it provides a challenge for the home cook because of the lengthy roasting time. In light of this, we tried the sauce made with melted butter and minced garlic. To be sure, we lost the mellow sweetness that the roasted garlic contributed, but the minced garlic was a suitable substitute and was certainly more feasible for the home cook.

With a flavorful sauce to add to our calamari, we now moved on to the cooking process. The recipe from Frank & Sheri's called for frying the squid at a temperature of 350 degrees for two minutes. While this might work in a commercial deep fryer that uses a large volume of oil and regulates the temperature evenly, we had problems frying our calamari using only home-kitchen tools. Using a Dutch oven filled with two inches of oil (about six cups) we found that at 350 degrees, by the time the calamari had browned, it had become very tough and chewy. By increasing the oil's temperature to 380 degrees, we found that the pieces of squid browned very quickly without becoming little rubber bands. It also tasted slightly less greasy than the squid cooked in the 350-degree oil.

In perfecting the cooking method, however, an issue arose with the prescribed breading of the calamari. The recipe instructed us to dredge the squid in seasoned flour. We found this method troublesome for several reasons. First, we found that with nothing to bind the flour to the squid, a lot of loose flour ended up in the bottom of the pot, which ended up toasting and flavoring the oil. By the time we had fried the last batches of squid, they all had a slightly burnt flavor. Second, we found that the flour coating didn't keep the calamari crispy after the seafood sat for several minutes. We tried breading the squid in a more traditional manner with flour, eggs, and then bread crumbs, but found this too heavy for the squid. We next tried dipping the squid in egg whites before coating it with the flour. This procedure provided the best results. The egg whites acted as glue and helped the flour stick to the squid, promoting the development of a thin, crisp exterior that didn't become soggy after the squid sat awhile.

Fried Calamari with Garlic Butter and Hot Cherry Peppers

SERVES 6 TO 8

If you want a little more spice, you can increase the amount of cherry peppers to 1 cup.

GARLIC BUTTER AND HOT CHERRY PEPPERS

- **6** **tablespoons unsalted butter**
- **4** **medium garlic cloves, minced or pressed through a garlic press (about 4 teaspoons)**
- **3/4** **cup jarred hot cherry peppers, drained and cut into thin rings**
- **Salt and ground black pepper**

CALAMARI

- **2** **cups unbleached all-purpose flour**
- **Salt**
- **1/2** **teaspoon ground black pepper**
- **3** **large egg whites**
- **2 1/2** **pounds cleaned squid, tubes cut into 1/2-inch rings, large tentacles cut in half**
- **5–6** **cups vegetable oil, for frying**
- **2** **tablespoons chopped fresh parsley leaves**

1. FOR THE BUTTER AND PEPPERS: Bring the butter and garlic to a simmer in a small saucepan over medium-low heat. Simmer for 2 minutes. Remove from the heat, stir in the pepper rings, and season with salt and pepper. Set aside.

2. FOR THE CALAMARI: Combine the flour, ½ teaspoon salt, and pepper in a medium bowl. In another medium bowl, whisk the egg whites until frothy, about 10 seconds. Add half the squid to the egg whites, toss to coat, and remove with a slotted spoon or your hands, allowing the excess egg whites to drip back into the bowl. Add the squid to the seasoned flour and, using your hands or a large rubber spatula, toss to coat. Place the coated squid in a single layer on a wire rack set over a rimmed baking sheet, allowing the excess flour to fall free of the squid. Repeat the process with the remaining squid.

3. Meanwhile, heat 2 inches of vegetable oil in a Dutch oven over medium-high heat until it reaches 380 degrees. (Use an instant-read thermometer that registers high temperatures or clip a candy/deep-fat thermometer onto the side of the pan before turning on the heat.) Add one quarter of the squid and fry until light golden, about 1½ minutes, adjusting the heat as necessary to maintain the cooking temperature. Using a slotted spoon, spider (see page 9), or tongs, transfer the fried squid to a clean rimmed baking sheet lined with several layers of paper towels. Repeat with the remaining batches of squid and add them to the baking sheet.

4. Transfer the fried squid to a large bowl, toss it with the butter mixture and the parsley, and adjust the seasoning with salt. Transfer the calamari to a serving platter and serve immediately.

Traditional Andalusian Gazpacho

Adapted from Traditional Andalusian Gazpacho

Jaleo, Washington, D.C.

GAZPACHO, THE TRADITIONAL SOUP FROM Andalusia in southern Spain, is made from the ripest red tomatoes, fresh cucumbers, bell peppers, and a touch of garlic and finished with Spanish extra-virgin olive oil and sherry vinegar. A cross between an iced summer drink and a garden salad, this uncooked vegetable soup is as nourishing as it is refreshing. Gazpacho originated as a simple peasant dish whose humble beginnings were stale bread, water, and olive oil. Ingredients indigenous to the New World, such as the tomato, were later added, resulting in the vibrant, flavorful soup known today.

There are as many versions of gazpacho as there are people who make them. What differentiates Andalusian gazpacho from others is the inclusion of bread as a thickener, in deference to tradition. This version features a pureed base, minimally thickened with rustic bread and finished with diced fresh vegetables and crisp croutons that add body and intensify the fresh flavors.

As with any fresh tomato dish, only the ripest tomatoes produced a soup worth eating. While Spain is known for its tomatoes, our winter plum tomatoes produced a pale soup with little tomato flavor. The amount of bread used as a thickener seemed to overpower what little tomato flavor was there. We cut back on the bread and tried the tiny pear tomatoes that are available in markets year-round, with great improvement. The bottom line seemed to be to base the recipe on the weight of the tomato rather than the type. Choose the ripest tomatoes available, regardless of size or variety.

We then moved on to the olive oil and the sherry vinegar, both of which are key components of gazpacho. With Spain being one of the largest producers of olive oil in the world, it stands to reason that a traditional recipe would specify Spanish olive oil, and only extra-virgin will do. We tested soups made with both Spanish and Italian olive oils, and found both acceptable. Some tasters preferred the pungency of the Spanish oil, but any high-quality extra-virgin oil worked in providing the soup with both flavor and mouthfeel. In addition to being a leader in olive oil production, southern Spain is renowned for its superior-quality sherries made from Palomino Fino grapes. We tasted sherry vinegar along with champagne, red wine, and white wine vinegars. The sherry vinegar proved to be the clear favorite, adding not only acidity but a unique, well-balanced flavor. The runner-up was white wine vinegar, which can be substituted in a pinch.

Gazpachos can be thick and chunky, smooth and silky, or anywhere in between, with tomato juice or water used to blend the soup. What we liked about this recipe was that it had the best of both worlds. The base is smooth and flavorful, while the garnish adds texture and multiplies the flavors achieved in the base. Andalusian gazpacho includes only the juice from the ripe tomatoes and enough water to process the soup, creating a clean, fresh flavor unmasked by bottled tomato juice. Originally, the ingredients were pounded vigorously with a mortar and pestle until the desired consistency was reached. These days, a blender or food processor serves as the workhorse, and we wondered about the differences between the two. Our industrial-strength blender produced a smooth, incredibly creamy base that was without texture; it had an almost foamy feel. We preferred the texture achieved by the food processor, which left chunky bits of vegetables, some of which are later strained out. Jaleo's recipe instructed us to strain the soup through a colander, which initially left us stumped (wouldn't everything simply fall through the holes?). We strained our first batch through a fine-mesh sieve and all of the "good stuff" was left in the strainer, leaving a watery liquid. We then tried one of our medium-mesh colanders and found it worked perfectly, eliminating the fibrous tomato skins and seeds but allowing tiny bits of vegetable to fall through the holes.

Presenting this soup is the fun part: the flavorful array of vegetables that are pureed into the base reappear as the colorful, crunchy garnish. The loaf of bread that is used as a thickener in the soup doubles as crisp garlic croutons. All of the flavors in the foundation of the soup are punctuated by the garnish. A drizzle of extra-virgin olive oil finishes the soup, creating a reviving appetizer true to the flavors and traditions of Andalusia.

Traditional Andalusian Gazpacho

SERVES 6

Use the ripest tomatoes you can find and serve the gazpacho in ice-cold bowls. See page 70 for tips on neatly dicing the peppers, tomatoes, and cucumber for the garnish.

GAZPACHO

- 1 slice country white bread (about 1 1/2 ounces), torn into small pieces
- 2 pounds very ripe tomatoes, diced
- 1 medium garlic clove, minced or pressed through a garlic press
- 1 medium cucumber, peeled, seeded, and diced
- 1 medium green bell pepper, stemmed, seeded, and diced
- 1/4 cup Spanish extra-virgin olive oil (or any good-quality extra-virgin olive oil)
- 2 tablespoons sherry vinegar
- Salt and ground black pepper

GARNISHES

- 3 medium green bell peppers, cut into 1/4-inch dice
- 4–5 medium plum tomatoes, cut into 1/4-inch dice (about 1 1/2 cups)
- 1 medium cucumber, peeled, seeded, and cut into 1/4-inch dice
- 8 tablespoons Spanish extra-virgin olive oil (or any good-quality extra-virgin olive oil)
- 6 garlic cloves, crushed
- 3 cups 1/2-inch country white bread cubes (day-old or dried in the oven)

1. FOR THE GAZPACHO: Place the bread in a small bowl and soak with cold water to cover, then squeeze it dry and place in a large bowl. Add the remaining gazpacho ingredients to the bowl except salt and pepper. Stir to combine. Working in batches, puree the vegetables in a food processor until very smooth, adding up to 1½ cups water to achieve the desired consistency. Strain through a medium-mesh strainer. Season the soup with salt and pepper to taste. Refrigerate to blend the flavors, at least 4 and up to 8 hours. Place 6 individual bowls in the freezer to chill.

2. FOR THE GARNISHES: Place the peppers, tomatoes, and cucumber in individual bowls, cover, and refrigerate.

3. Heat 6 tablespoons of the oil with the garlic cloves in a 12-inch nonstick skillet over medium heat until the garlic is golden and fragrant, about 2 minutes. Turn the garlic cloves over and cook for 1 to 2 minutes, or until golden on the second side. Discard the garlic. Add the bread cubes to the hot oil and cook until golden and crispy, 4 to 5 minutes, stirring frequently. Transfer to a rimmed baking sheet lined with paper towels and set aside.

4. TO SERVE: Remove the bowls from the freezer and the soup and vegetable garnishes from the refrigerator. Season the soup with salt and pepper to taste. Divide the soup among the bowls. Spoon 3 to 4 tablespoons of each vegetable garnish into each portion, top with 2 tablespoons croutons, and drizzle with 1 teaspoon of the remaining olive oil. (Alternatively, place the garnishes on the table and allow diners to garnish their own bowls.) Serve immediately.

DICING THE VEGETABLES FOR GAZPACHO

TOMATOES

1. Core the tomatoes, halve them pole to pole, and, working over a bowl to catch all the juices, scoop out the inner pulp and seeds. Chop the tomato pulp into ¼-inch cubes.
2. Cut the tomato halves into ¼-inch slices, then cut again into ¼-inch cubes.

PEPPERS

1. Slice a ¾-inch section off both the tip and stem ends of the peppers. Make one slit in the trimmed shells, place skin-side down, and open the flesh.
2. Scrape off the seeds and membranes. Cut flesh into ¼-inch strips, then cut again into ¼-inch cubes.

CUCUMBERS

1. Cut a ¾-inch section off both ends of the cucumbers. Halve the cucumbers lengthwise and scoop out the seeds with a spoon. Cut each seeded half lengthwise into ¼-inch strips,
2. Cut the cucumber strips crosswise into ¼-inch cubes.

Carrot Soup *with* Root Vegetable Charlotte

Adapted from Carrot Soup with Carrot Charlotte with Diced Parsnip and Celery Root

The Ryland Inn, Whitehouse, New Jersey

THIS ELEGANT, TWO-PART SOUP IS A CLEAN-tasting puree of carrots and aromatics (shallots and leek) encircling a root vegetable "charlotte"—a molded tower of braised baby carrots surrounding a puree of celery root and diced parsnip. It may be a stretch to call this structure a charlotte—typically a dessert composed of cake or bread and cooked fruit packed into a mold—but it's stunning and has a flavor to match. Despite its high-class looks, we found that with a few alterations the soup was entirely feasible for the home cook to assemble.

The charlotte was the most daunting portion of the recipe. Each of the ingredients—carrots, celery root, and parsnips—must be cooked separately, tedious but important nonetheless to ensure that each vegetable retains its own flavor. The carrots are blanched in a mixture of carrot juice and extra-virgin olive oil. The recipe specifies fresh-from-the-garden, pinkie-thin baby carrots, which are halved lengthwise after braising and trimmed to the height of the mold in which the charlotte is formed. This process took longer than we liked, so we found an easier route by employing the bagged "baby" carrots so prevalent. Misleadingly named, these carrots are far from "baby": they are actually full-sized carrots trimmed down to their stubby size. They required no prep work prior to braising and no trimming since, for the most part, they are all the same size.

Both the celery root and parsnips cook quickly—the celery root until soft enough to puree and the diced parsnips until tender but toothsome. We didn't relish cooking each vegetable in separate pans, as the recipe specified—why dirty another pan if we could avoid it?—so we simply used one pan. First, we cooked the celery root in salted water, then scooped it out and blanched the parsnips in the same water. The celery root is then pureed with a little butter, and the parsnips are folded into the puree.

Assembling the charlottes was simple. The Ryland Inn's recipe specified ring molds to form the charlottes, but we came up with a convenient alternative: eight-ounce, microwave-safe, disposable cups. Trimmed to the height of the carrots (about two inches), the cups were almost identical in size to the inn's specified mold. We found that nonstick cooking spray or a wipe of olive oil helped cement the carrots to the cups' sides. Once the carrots were fully lining the cups,

PREPARING THE CHARLOTTES

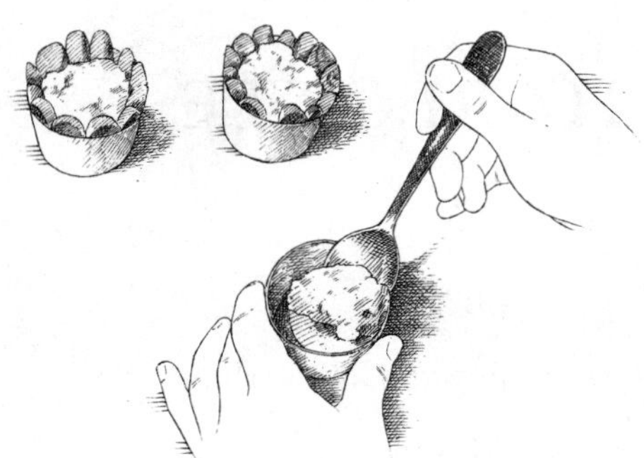

1. Using a soupspoon, drop a small dollop of the celery root and parsnip mixture into the bottom of each cup.

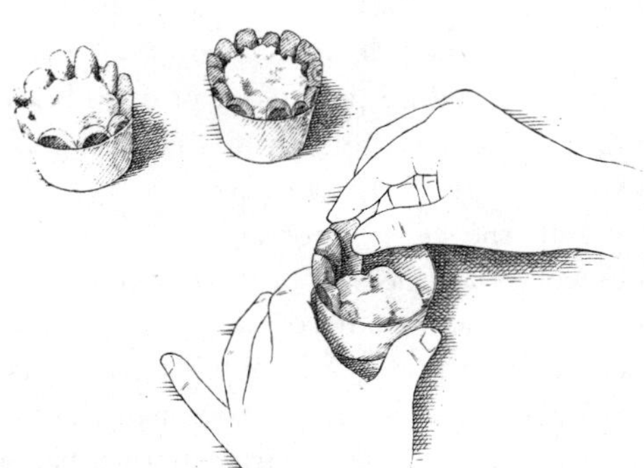

2. Line the circumference of each cup with halved carrots, cut-side facing outward.

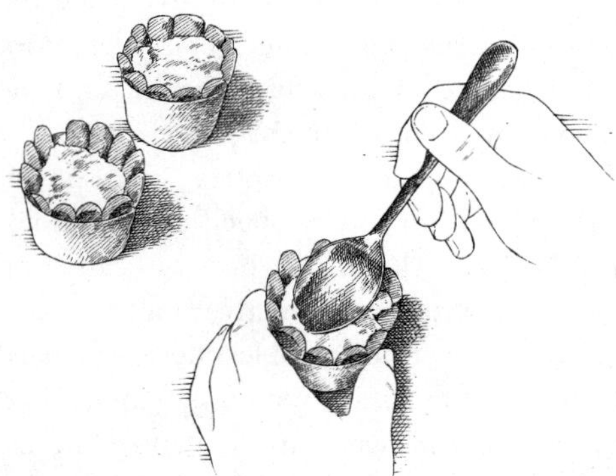

3. Fill the cup with more celery root and parsnip mixture, using the back of the spoon to tamp it down gently into the cup.

we filled them with the celery root and parsnip filling, gently packing it in with the back of a spoon. We found that the charlottes kept well in the refrigerator for up to one day. To warm them through, we popped them in the microwave.

The soup itself couldn't have been any easier to make—it's little more than leek, shallots, carrots, and carrot juice. The aromatics are "sweated," or cooked slowly until quite soft but not browned, before the carrots are added. The inn replaces the usual stock with carrot juice, which lends the soup a surprisingly pure carrot flavor.

Once the carrots are tender, the soup is ready for a quick spin in the blender and then the soup bowl. The charlotte sits in the center of a wide, shallow bowl, and the soup encircles it—a deep or narrow bowl reduces the visual appeal. We found the easiest, most accurate way to pour the soup was from a measuring cup with a pouring spout, though a medium ladle works almost as well. Just be careful to not splash soup on the charlotte. At the inn, the chefs finish the dish with either salad burnet or pimpernel—two herbs rare to most markets. As a substitute, tasters most liked a sprinkling of chopped tarragon, since its anise-like bite intensified the inherent sweetness of the carrots.

Carrot Soup with Root Vegetable Charlotte

SERVES 6

Unsweetened carrot juice can be purchased in natural food stores and many supermarkets. Use a blender for pureeing the soup; it produces a smoother puree than a food processor. Both the soup and the charlottes may be made a day ahead and reheated prior to serving. A microwave is the best way to reheat the charlottes, since they may be heated in the disposable cup "molds."

- **3 cups carrot juice**
- **3 tablespoons extra-virgin olive oil**
- **8 ounces baby carrots, halved lengthwise**
- **Salt and ground black pepper**
- **4 medium shallots, chopped rough (about 1 cup)**
- **1 medium leek, white part only, halved lengthwise and cut into 1/4-inch slices, well rinsed**
- **4 medium carrots (about 3/4 pound), peeled and cut into 1/2-inch-thick slices**
- **1 small celery root (about 1/2 pound), peeled and cut into medium dice**
- **1 tablespoon unsalted butter**
- **4 medium parsnips (about 1/2 pound), peeled and cut into fine dice**
- **1 tablespoon chopped fresh tarragon leaves**

1. Bring 1 cup of the carrot juice, 2 tablespoons of the olive oil, the baby carrots, ¼ teaspoon salt, and a pinch of pepper to a simmer in a medium saucepan over medium-high heat. Reduce the heat to medium-low and cook, stirring occasionally, until the carrots are just tender and can be pierced with the tip of a knife, about 7 minutes. Gently strain the carrots, reserving the liquid. Return the carrots to the pan, cover, and keep warm.

2. Add the remaining 1 tablespoon olive oil, shallots, leek, and ½ teaspoon salt to a large saucepan over medium heat and cook, stirring occasionally, until the shallots are translucent and tender, about 15 minutes (if the vegetables begin to brown or stick, add 1 tablespoon water). Add the raw carrots, the remaining 2 cups carrot juice, the baby carrot–braising liquid, and 1 cup water. Increase the heat to medium-high and bring to a simmer. Reduce the heat to medium-low and cook until the carrots are tender, about 15 minutes. Transfer the mixture to a blender (in batches, if necessary) and process until smooth, about 1 minute. Return the soup to the pan, adjust the seasoning with salt and pepper, cover, and keep warm.

3. Bring 4 cups water, the celery root, and 1 teaspoon salt to a boil in a medium saucepan over medium-high heat. Simmer until the celery root can be easily pierced with a knife, 7 to 8 minutes. Using a wire skimmer or slotted spoon, transfer the celery root to a food processor and add the butter. Process until smooth, about 1 minute, scraping down the sides of the workbowl as necessary.

4. Add the parsnips to the hot water and simmer until tender, 4 to 5 minutes. Transfer the celery root to a large bowl. Gently fold in the parsnips. Adjust the seasoning with salt and pepper.

5. Using scissors, trim 6 microwave-safe, 3-inch-wide disposable cups to a height of 2 inches (the average length of the baby carrots) and spray with nonstick cooking spray or rub with a thin layer of olive oil. Following the illustrations on page 72, drop a small dollop of the celery root and parsnip mixture into the bottom of each cup. Line the circumference of each cup with the braised carrots, cut-side facing outward. Use a spoon to fill the centers with the celery root and parsnip mixture, gently packing it down. If the charlottes are cool to the touch, microwave them until warm.

6. Invert a charlotte cup in the center of each of 6 warmed, shallow soup bowls, pressing slightly on the sides of cup so that the charlotte slides out freely. Gently pour the soup from a measuring cup or ladle around the charlotte, being careful not to splash the charlotte. Garnish with the chopped tarragon and serve immediately.

SPICED CARROT SOUP *with* SHRIMP

Adapted from Spiced New Carrot Soup with Shrimp

CAFÉ BOULUD, NEW YORK, NEW YORK

CARROT SOUPS APPEAR ON MANY A RESTAURANT menu, but few we have come across are as refined in flavor and concept as this one from the famed Café Boulud: a smooth, velvety puree redolent of sweet carrots, with coconut milk providing richness and an exotic flair, all punctuated by the warm spiciness of curry and ginger. Poached pink shrimp provide a visual contrast with the orange soup, making for a stunning presentation. But what we liked most about this recipe was the fact that it was finished with carrot juice. This technique—of adding "raw" flavor to a dish at the very end of cooking—is employed by many chefs to heighten flavors. It gave the soup a bright, sweet carrot flavor, without any heaviness. This recipe was easy to prepare, but we did want to fill in a couple of holes for the home cook to clarify the process.

Obviously, the most important ingredient to clarify was the carrots. The original recipe called for two bunches of new carrots, one to be used in the base of the soup, the other to be juiced, to be used in finishing the soup. Considering that most people don't have a juicer at home, we opted to go with the chef's other suggestion, which was to use store-bought carrot juice. Carrot juice can be found in natural food stores and many supermarkets. We also questioned the use of "new" carrots, assuming that true "new" carrots (small, young carrots that are freshly dug) would be available to the home cook for a only brief period every summer, if at all. With this in mind, we prepared the soup with regular bagged carrots. However, we found that the base of the soup was slightly less sweet than when we used new carrots. But, as it turned out, after adding the fresh

---

INGREDIENTS: Coconut Milk

Coconut milk lends a creamy richness and unmistakable Southeast Asian flavor to this soup. We wondered if it mattered which brand we chose.

We went to a local Asian market and purchased several brands recommended in Southeast Asian cookbooks, including Chao Koh and Mae Ploy. We also purchased Thai Kitchen, Kame, and A Taste of Thai brands, all of which are sold in supermarkets and natural food stores. With one exception, we found that all of these brands had a nice thick layer of solid coconut cream on top. The only brand we don't recommend is A Taste of Thai. The coconut cream in this can was not solid (the texture was akin to crème fraîche) and less plentiful—⅔ cup, not the ¾ to 1 full cup of thick, almost solid cream we found in other cans the same size.

---

carrot juice at the end, there was no difference between the two.

The only other issue that needed further attention was the shrimp that garnished the soup. Since the recipe called just for "cooked shrimp," without distinguishing the preferred cooking method, we opted to poach them because we felt that pink poached shrimp would be attractive with the orange soup. To avoid overcooked and tough shrimp, which can easily result from poaching, we took an even gentler approach. We brought the poaching liquid to a boil, added the shrimp, covered the pot, then turned off the heat. With this technique, the shrimp gently cook in the water for six minutes. Without direct heat, there is no danger of overcooking.

The presentation of the soup was straightforward—a mound of shrimp placed in the center of shallow soup bowls, with the soup gently ladled around it. Without any other garnishes, the soup had a minimalist feel, but considering its simple and unassuming flavors, it felt just right.

PUREEING SOUP SAFELY

Pureeing soups in a blender creates a smooth texture. Because hot soup can be dangerous, though, don't fill the blender jar more than halfway and hold the lid in place with a folded kitchen towel.

Spiced Carrot Soup with Shrimp

SERVES 4

We found that smaller carrots (at least 6 per pound) were better for this soup. While using larger carrots might save time when it comes to peeling and chopping, we found that larger carrots usually were less sweet than their younger and thinner counterparts.

- **2 tablespoons extra-virgin olive oil**
- **1 small onion, sliced (about 1 cup)**
- **1 pound (about 6 medium) carrots, trimmed and peeled, halved lengthwise, and sliced thin**
- **1 (½-inch) piece fresh ginger, peeled and sliced thin**
- **1 large garlic clove, peeled and sliced thin**
- **1 teaspoon curry powder**
- **Salt and ground white pepper**
- **2½ cups Quick Chicken Stock (page 77) or low-sodium chicken broth**
- **¾ cup canned unsweetened coconut milk**
- **2 tablespoons juice from 1 lemon**
- **16 extra-large shrimp (about ¾ pound), peeled and deveined**
- **½ cup carrot juice**

1. Heat the olive oil in a large saucepan over medium heat until shimmering. Add the onion and cook, stirring occasionally, until translucent and tender, about 6 minutes. Add the carrots, ginger, garlic, curry powder, ½ teaspoon salt, and ¼ teaspoon white pepper. Cook until the garlic and curry are fragrant, about 1½ minutes. Add the stock and

INGREDIENTS: Commercial Chicken Broth

Few of the commercial broths in our tasting came close to the full-bodied consistency of a successful homemade stock. Many lacked even a hint of chicken flavor. Interestingly, the four broths we rated best were all products of the Campbell Soup Company, of which Swanson is a subsidiary. In order, they were Swanson Chicken Broth, Campbell's Chicken Broth, Swanson Natural Goodness Chicken Broth (with 33 percent less sodium than regular Swanson chicken broth), and Campbell's Healthy Request Chicken Broth (with 30 percent less sodium than regular Campbell's chicken broth). The remaining broths were decidedly inferior and hard to recommend.

We tried to find out why Campbell's broths are superior to so many others, but the giant soup company declined to respond to questions, explaining that its recipes and cooking techniques are considered proprietary information. Many of the answers, however, could be found on the products' ingredient labels. As it turned out, the top two broths happened to contain the highest levels of sodium. Salt has been used for years in the food industry to make foods with less than optimum flavor tastier. The top two products also contained the controversial monosodium glutamate (MSG), an effective flavor enhancer.

Sadly, most of the products that had lower levels of salt and did not have the benefit of other food industry flavor enhancers simply tasted like dishwater. Their labels did indicate that their ingredients included "chicken broth" or "chicken stock," sometimes both. But calls to the U.S. Food and Drug Administration and the U.S. Department of Agriculture revealed that there are no standards that define chicken broth or stock, so an ingredient label indicating that the contents include chicken broth or chicken stock may mean anything as long as some chicken is used.

Ingredients aside, we found one more important explanation for why most commercial broths simply cannot replicate the full flavor and body of homemade stock. Most broths are sold canned, which entails an extended heating process carried out to ensure a sterilized product. The immediate disadvantage of this processing is that heat breaks down naturally present flavor enhancers found in chicken protein. Further, as it destroys other volatile flavors, the prolonged heating concentrates flavor components that are not volatile, such as salt.

A few national brands of chicken broth have begun to offer their products in aseptic packaging (cartons rather than cans). Compared with traditional canning, in which products are heated in the can for up to nearly an hour to ensure sterilization, the process of aseptic packaging entails a flash heating and cooling process that is said to help products better retain both their nutritional value and their flavor.

We decided to hold another tasting to see if we could detect more flavor in the products sold in aseptic packaging. Of the recommended broths in the tasting, only Swanson broths are available in aseptic packaging. We tasted Swanson's traditional and Natural Goodness chicken broths sold in cans and in aseptic packages. The results fell clearly in favor of the aseptically packaged broths; both tasted cleaner and more chickeny than their canned counterparts. So if you are truly seeking the best of the best in commercial broths, choose one of the two Swanson broths sold in aseptic packaging. An opened aseptic package will keep in the refrigerator for up to two weeks (broth from a can keeps, refrigerated, for only a few days).

THE BEST CHICKEN BROTHS
Swanson Chicken Broth (right) and its reduced-sodium counterpart, Swanson Natural Goodness Chicken Broth (center), are our top choices in the test kitchen. In testing, we've found that broth packaged in aseptic cartons (left) tastes better than canned broth.

coconut milk and bring to a boil. Reduce the heat to medium-low, cover, and simmer until the carrots are very tender, about 20 minutes.

2. Bring 2 cups water, the lemon juice, and 1 teaspoon salt to a boil in a medium saucepan over medium-high heat. Add the shrimp, cover, and remove the pan from the heat. Let stand for 6 minutes. Remove the shrimp from the liquid and halve them lengthwise. Set aside.

3. Meanwhile, puree the carrot mixture in batches in a blender until very smooth. Return the soup to a large, clean saucepan, add the carrot juice, and cook over low heat until just warmed through. Adjust the seasoning with salt and white pepper.

4. Arrange 8 shrimp halves in a pile in the center of each of 4 shallow soup bowls. Ladle the soup around the shrimp, trying to keep as much of the shrimp exposed as possible. Serve immediately.

Quick Chicken Stock

MAKES ABOUT 2 QUARTS

Chicken pieces are sautéed and then sweated before being cooked in water for a rich but very quick stock. This is our favorite all-purpose stock. It takes about an hour to prepare.

- **1 tablespoon vegetable oil**
- **1 medium onion, chopped medium**
- **4 pounds whole chicken legs or backs and wing tips, cut into 2-inch pieces**
- **2 quarts boiling water**
- **2 teaspoons salt**
- **2 bay leaves**

1. Heat the oil in a large stockpot or Dutch oven over medium-high heat. Add the onion; sauté until colored and softened slightly, 2 to 3 minutes. Transfer the onion to a large bowl.

2. Add half of the chicken pieces to the pot; sauté both sides until lightly browned, 4 to 5 minutes. Transfer the cooked chicken to the bowl with the onions. Sauté the remaining chicken pieces. Return the onions and chicken pieces to the pot. Reduce the heat to low, cover, and cook until the chicken releases its juices, about 20 minutes.

3. Increase the heat to high; add the boiling water, salt, and bay leaves. Return to a simmer, then cover and barely simmer until the stock is rich and flavorful, about 20 minutes.

4. Strain the stock; discard the solids. Before using, defat the stock. The stock can be refrigerated in an airtight container for up to 2 days or frozen for several months.

Spring Pea Soup *with* Potato Gnocchi

Adapted from Spring Pea Soup with Potato Gnocchi

Stone Creek Inn, Quogue, New York

THIS SOUP FROM THE STONE CREEK INN features multidimensional flavors from fresh fennel and basil along with sweet English peas. Potato gnocchi float like pillows in the soup's refreshingly clean, balanced broth.

The star of this soup is the English pea, also known as the common garden pea. While fresh or frozen peas can be used here, we found frozen peas to be reliably sweeter, more tender, and less dry than fresh. (Fresh peas tend to deteriorate within 24 hours of being picked, so their sugars break down into starch, resulting in a bland, dry legume.) Frozen peas are picked, sorted, and frozen within hours of harvest, preserving their delicate sugars, subtle flavor, and fresh texture. A 15-minute defrost allows you to add the peas at the very end of the cooking time, which preserves their brilliant green color, preventing an overcooked, army green soup. While some fresh pea soups rely on potato, flour, or cream for body, this healthful version utilizes pureed peas to lend body to the soup. We found that pureeing the soup in a blender produced a velvety texture superior to soup pureed in a food processor. The blender broth was silky smooth, with enough structure to support the potato gnocchi.

Playing supporting roles in this soup are fresh fennel and fresh basil leaves, both distinctly Italian ingredients. Fennel bulbs are pale green, with celery-like stems and a flavor that has been likened to licorice, but much more subtle. Fresh basil adds yet another flavor dimension as well as contributing to the overall appearance of the soup as a garnish.

Where many restaurants would throw a few croutons on top for garnish and call it a day, the Stone Creek Inn floats delicate potato gnocchi on the soup, an attractive garnish that may sound a bit intimidating, but is actually uncomplicated to prepare. Gnocchi are Italian dumplings that are formed, poached, then lightly sautéed in butter before being added to the soup. These gnocchi start with a base that is easily made from high-starch (we use russets) potatoes boiled in their jackets. The potatoes are then peeled, mashed, and combined with the remaining ingredients by hand to form a smooth dough. While it would be more convenient to peel cooled potatoes, we found that the potato skin lifts and separates from the flesh more easily when hot. The tip of a paring knife made light work of peeling the hot potato, with the help of an oven mitt.

Knowing that the key to a smooth gnocchi dough lies in the preparation of the potato, we set about to find the best method to make the smoothest mash possible. We tested a potato masher, a food processor, a potato ricer, and a food mill for the job and found that the potato masher left lumps and the food processor produced potato glue. Only the food mill and the potato ricer provided a smooth mash that could be easily incorporated into the flour.

We experimented with different methods of mixing the gnocchi dough, striving for a light, tender dumpling. The food processor yielded an overmixed, gummy dough, resulting in tough gnocchi that sank in our soup. Mixing the dough as little as possible proved to be crucial in creating the ethereal dumpling we were looking for; we found the best tool for the job was our hands, giving us better control over the mixing process. Traditionally rolled into ropes, cut, and then imprinted with ridges (to trap sauces), forming gnocchi can be a time-consuming proposition. However, this recipe eliminates the imprinting step, saving a great deal of time. We soon discovered that cooking the gnocchi in rapidly boiling water (as you would pasta) made it difficult to determine whether the gnocchi were floating (an indication of doneness) or simply bobbing around in the boiling water. A gentle simmer allowed us to gauge when the gnocchi were floating and perfectly cooked.

Using an eight-ounce ladle or one-cup measuring cup to portion the soup makes for speedy service (restaurant style) and guarantees equal portions for all. The gnocchi are lightly sautéed in butter, perched atop the hot soup and, using a trick often employed by restaurant chefs, garnished with a whole basil leaf rubbed with olive oil for an attractive sheen and eye-catching presentation.

Spring Pea Soup with Potato Gnocchi

SERVES 8

This delicately flavored soup would make a perfect prelude to a hearty salad for lunch, or a simple grilled or broiled fish (such as halibut or bass) for dinner. If you're short on time, use good-quality packaged gnocchi in place of homemade.

POTATO GNOCCHI

- 1 pound russet potatoes (about 2 medium)
- 1 large egg yolk
- 1/2 cup (2 1/2 ounces) unbleached all-purpose flour
- 1/8 teaspoon ground nutmeg
- Salt and ground black pepper
- Olive oil for greasing the baking sheet
- 2 tablespoons unsalted butter, for sautéing the gnocchi

SPRING PEA SOUP

- 4 tablespoons unsalted butter
- 1 medium onion, cut into 1/2 inch dice (about 1 cup)
- 1 medium fennel bulb, fronds removed, cored, and cut into 1/4-inch dice
- 1 bay leaf
- 1/2 teaspoon dried thyme
- 1/4 teaspoon dried rosemary
- 4 cups Quick Chicken Stock (page 77) or low-sodium chicken broth
- 1 pound frozen peas (about 3 1/2 cups), partially thawed at room temperature for 15 minutes
- 15 fresh basil leaves, washed and dried
- Salt and ground black pepper
- 1 teaspoon olive oil

1. For the gnocchi: Place the potatoes in a large pot and cover with water. Bring to a boil and cook the potatoes until a metal

skewer slides easily through them, about 30 minutes. Drain the potatoes.

2. Peel the potatoes and rice the peeled potatoes into a large bowl. Cool the potatoes at room temperature for 15 minutes. Add the egg yolk, flour, nutmeg, and salt and pepper to taste and gently work the ingredients together with your hands, handling the dough as little as possible.

3. Divide the dough into 4 pieces. With your hands, roll each piece on a lightly floured work surface into ¾-inch-diameter ropes, about 12 inches long. Cut each rope into 1-inch lengths and transfer to a parchment-lined rimmed baking sheet in a single layer. (The gnocchi can be refrigerated on the baking sheet for several hours or the gnocchi may be frozen in a plastic bag or airtight container for up to 1 month.)

4. Bring 4 quarts water to a low boil in a large pot with 2 teaspoons salt or to taste. Add half of the gnocchi and cook until they float, about 1 minute. Using a slotted spoon, transfer the gnocchi to a rimmed baking sheet coated with olive oil. Repeat with the remaining gnocchi.

5. For the soup: Melt the butter in a Dutch oven over medium heat until the foaming subsides. Add the onion and fennel, cover, reduce the heat to low, and cook until translucent, about 15 minutes. Add the bay leaf, thyme, rosemary, and chicken stock, increase the heat to high, and bring to a simmer. Reduce the heat to medium-low and simmer until the fennel is soft, about 15 minutes. Stir in the peas and 7 of the basil leaves and simmer until the peas are heated through, 3 to 4 minutes.

6. Puree the soup in batches in a blender until smooth. Return the pureed soup to a clean pot set over low heat and season with salt and pepper to taste. (Do not boil the soup or the striking green color will be lost.)

7. Adjust an oven rack to the middle position and heat the oven to its lowest setting. Place 8 ovenproof soup bowls on the rack to warm. Melt the 2 tablespoons butter in a nonstick 12-inch skillet over medium heat. Add the gnocchi to the pan and sauté, stirring frequently, until heated through.

8. Remove the soup bowls from the oven. Ladle 1 cup of soup into each bowl. Place 6 gnocchi in the center of each bowl. Rub the olive oil onto the remaining 8 basil leaves. Garnish each bowl with a basil leaf and serve immediately.

Roasted Corn Bisque

Adapted from Grilled Corn Bisque

Dué, Garden City, New York

THIS BISQUE IS SMOOTH AND SUPPLE, with a creamy, sweet flavor lightly perfumed by smoke from the grill. Garnished with small bites of corn and a flourish of fried leeks, the soup is also a breeze to make.

In a restaurant kitchen, an indoor grill fueled either by gas or wood is a common piece of equipment. Because most home kitchens don't have indoor grills (and firing up an outdoor grill for this recipe seemed a bit much), we began by looking for a way to "grill" the corn indoors. Roasting the corn on top of a gas burner worked well, but was impossible to do on an electric stove. Broiling the corn turned out to be our answer. Laying the corn in a single layer on a rimmed baking sheet, we broiled it until toasted. The extent to which the corn was broiled, however, made all the difference. When the corn was fully toasted, the soup tasted dry and dull. The corn's flavor and moisture evaporated under the intense heat of the broiler. Lightly toasting the kernels was just enough. It imparted a light, roasted flavor without drying out the cobs completely. We then cut the kernels off the cobs.

Rounding out the flavor of the bisque are leek, onion, garlic, and thyme, while a potato is used as a thickener. Not surprisingly, we found it necessary to use more vegetables than the original recipe did. Restaurants generally make their own stocks, which are far more flavorful than any of the canned versions found in the supermarket. But if you want to avoid extra hours in the kitchen to make your own stock, use canned low-sodium chicken broth (see the results of our tasting on page 76).

After the soup has finished cooking it is removed from the heat and allowed to sit for 15 minutes. As it sits, the flavors meld and balance, resulting in a far more complex flavor than in a batch fresh off the stove. We found that a pinch of sugar in addition to the salt and pepper did wonders in bringing out the flavor of even the blandest corn.

Last, the soup is garnished with reserved corn kernels and fried leeks, adding both flavor and texture. Restaurants commonly use fried leeks as a tasty garnish because an extra leek and hot deep fryer are always on hand.

REMOVING KERNELS FROM CORN COBS

Hold the cob on end inside a large, wide bowl and cut off the kernels using a paring knife.

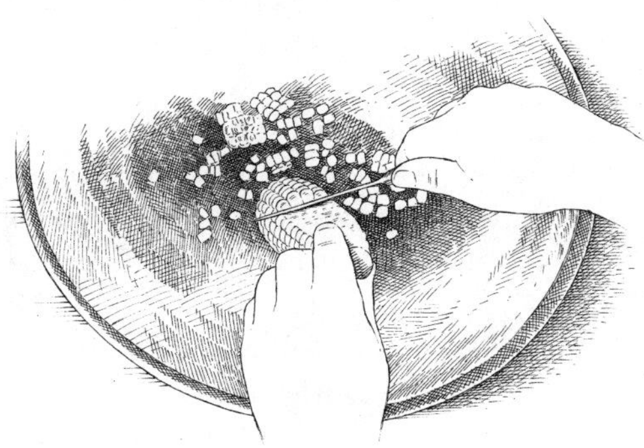

Slice the white and light green parts of the leek thinly, toss them with some flour seasoned with salt and pepper, and fry them until they are golden and crunchy.

Roasted Corn Bisque

SERVES 6 TO 8

The leeks can be fried several hours ahead of time and stored between layers of paper towels to help keep them crisp.

BISQUE

- **8** **ears corn, husks and silk removed**
- **2** **tablespoons unsalted butter**
- **1** **medium russet potato (about 8 ounces) peeled, quartered, and sliced thin**
- **3/4** **large leek (about 8 ounces), white part only, cut into 1-inch pieces**
- **1** **small onion, cut into 1/2-inch pieces**
- **2** **garlic cloves, crushed and peeled**
- **Salt**
- **6** **cups Quick Chicken Stock (page 77) or low-sodium chicken broth**
- **3** **sprigs fresh thyme**
- **Ground black pepper**
- **1/2** **cup heavy cream**
- **Sugar**

FRIED LEEKS

- **1 1/2** **cups vegetable oil**
- **1/4** **large leek, white part only, sliced very thin**
- **2** **tablespoons all-purpose flour**
- **1** **teaspoon salt**

1. FOR THE BISQUE: Adjust an oven rack so it is 6 inches from the broiler element and heat the broiler. Place the corn on a rimmed baking sheet. Broil until the kernels are lightly browned, about 15 minutes, turning the corn every couple of minutes. Transfer the corn to a large bowl and cool. Working with one ear at a time, stand it on end inside the bowl and, using a paring knife, cut the kernels off the cob (see the illustration on page 81). Transfer 1 cup of the corn kernels to a separate bowl and set aside.

2. Meanwhile, melt the butter in a Dutch oven over medium-high heat until the foaming subsides. Add the potato, leek, onion, garlic, and ½ teaspoon salt and sauté until the leeks are wilted, about 5 minutes. Add the chicken stock and bring to a simmer. Reduce the heat to medium and simmer until the potato is cooked through, 15 to 20 minutes. Add the corn kernels, thyme, and ⅛ teaspoon pepper and simmer until the broth tastes of corn, about 10 minutes. Remove the pot from the heat, cover, and let stand to meld the flavors, about 15 minutes. Discard the thyme. Puree the soup in batches in a blender until smooth. Return the pureed soup to a clean pot set over medium heat. Add the cream and the reserved 1 cup corn kernels and bring to a simmer. Immediately remove the pot from the heat. Season with salt, pepper, and sugar to taste.

3. FOR THE FRIED LEEKS: Heat the vegetable oil in a Dutch oven over medium-high heat until it reaches 350 degrees. (Use an instant-read thermometer that registers high temperatures or clip a candy/deep-fat thermometer onto the side of the pan before turning on the heat.) Meanwhile, toss the leek, flour, and salt together in a small bowl. Transfer the floured leek to a wire-mesh strainer (or colander) set over another bowl (or the sink) and shake to remove the excess flour. Fry the leek until golden brown, 2 to 3 minutes, adjusting the heat as needed to maintain the cooking temperature. Using a slotted spoon or spider (see page 9), transfer the fried leeks to a plate lined with several layers of paper towels and cool.

4. TO SERVE: Ladle the soup into bowls and garnish with the fried leeks. Serve.

Tortilla Soup

Adapted from Tortilla Soup

Inn of the Anasazi, Santa Fe, New Mexico

WITH ITS ROOTS IN MEXICAN COOKING, tortilla soup has grown to encompass many different styles and variations. Most commonly, tortilla soup is a broth-based soup thickened with flour or corn tortillas, highly seasoned with chiles and spices such as cumin and coriander, and finished with a wide array of garnishes. This recipe from Inn of the Anasazi is an exemplary version.

Anasazi's recipe produced a soup that was hearty and satisfying with a warm, toasty chile flavor. To round out the soup's flavors, a touch of tomato is added for acidity and a healthy amount of cilantro for freshness. Topped with rich, tangy cheddar and crunchy tortilla chips, we found this soup very pleasing. We nevertheless found some issues that needed addressing. Given that a restaurant makes gallons of soup at one time, we had to scale down the recipe for the size of a family. As is frequently the case when scaling down recipes, this process was tricky.

The first component of the soup we considered was the vegetable base. This consisted of onions, garlic, and tomatoes that were roasted in the oven before being added to the soup. While we liked the depth of flavor this method added, we wondered if it was necessary. In order to test this variable, we made the soup without roasting the vegetables, but instead caramelized them in the pot before adding the other ingredients. The results were striking. The soup prepared in this fashion didn't have nearly the depth of flavor that the original soup had. We then considered using the broiler to roast the vegetables, hoping that we could coax out the same flavor with less time and effort. This turned out to be the ideal option for two reasons. First, the soup made with these vegetables tasted virtually the same as the original. Second, by using the broiler, we could at the same time roast the ears of corn, which were also used in the soup, essentially compressing two steps into one.

Next, we turned our attention to the tortillas in the soup. The original recipe for the soup called for eight cups of corn tortillas. The soup produced from this many tortillas was very flavorful, but also so thick that it no longer had a soup-like consistency. Feeling that this soup should have some body, but not be stew-like, we tried varying the amount of tortillas added to the soup. After several batches, we found that three cups of tortillas provided just the degree of thickness we wanted.

In addition to the amount of tortillas, we also looked at the method used to incorporate them into the soup. The restaurant's recipe called for frying the chiles and tortillas together in a small amount of oil until crispy, and then adding the other components. However, we had a hard time getting the tortillas crispy in such a small amount of oil, and they had a tendency to stick to the sides of the pot. It occurred to us that if we could use store-bought chips instead, we could eliminate the time and mess involved in frying tortillas. We prepared the soup using good-quality chips, and, surprisingly, the results were as tasty as when we had fried our own chips.

The only remaining ingredient left to address was the liquid used in the soup. The chef called for using either vegetable stock or water. Curious as to which produced a better soup, we prepared two batches—one with vegetable stock and one with water. We immediately dismissed the water because it produced a thin, bland soup. Clearly, vegetable stock was a better option. We also wanted to try using chicken stock in place of the vegetable stock, wondering whether it would add more richness to the soup. Indeed this was the case, but tasters agreed that both versions were good.

Tortilla Soup

SERVES 8 TO 10

The soup can be served with other garnishes in addition to the cheddar and tortilla chips, such as sour cream, diced avocado, and sliced jalapeños. Our favorite brand of white corn chips is Miguel's.

- **2** medium onions, cut into ½-inch dice
- **10** medium garlic cloves, peeled
- **1** (14.5-ounce) can diced tomatoes, drained
- **3** tablespoons vegetable oil
- **2** ears corn, husks and silk removed
- **5** ancho chiles (about 2 ½ ounces), stems removed, seeded, and torn into ½-inch pieces
- **2** tablespoons ground cumin
- **1** tablespoon ground coriander
- **4 ½** cups lightly crushed, high-quality white corn tortilla chips
- **8** cups Quick Chicken Stock (page 77) or low-sodium chicken broth
- **1** cup tomato juice
- **2** cups cilantro leaves from 1 bunch
- **2** tablespoons lime juice from 1 lime
- Salt and ground black pepper
- **1** cup grated cheddar cheese (about 4 ounces)

1. Adjust an oven rack so it is 6 inches away from the broiler element and heat the broiler. Toss the onions, garlic, and tomatoes with 1 tablespoon of the vegetable oil in a medium bowl, then spread on a rimmed baking sheet. Place the corn alongside the other vegetables. Broil, stirring the vegetables and turning the corn every few minutes, until lightly browned, 15 to 20 minutes. Transfer the vegetables and corn to two separate medium bowls and cool. Working with one ear of corn at a time, stand it on end inside the bowl and, using a paring knife, cut the kernels off the cob (see the illustration on page 81). Set aside.

2. Heat the remaining 2 tablespoons oil and ancho chiles in a Dutch oven over medium-high heat. Cook, stirring occasionally, until the chiles are fragrant and toasted, about 2½ minutes. Add the cumin and coriander and cook for 30 seconds longer. Add 3 cups of the tortilla chips, roasted vegetables, chicken stock, and tomato juice and bring to a boil. Reduce the heat to medium-low and simmer for 30 minutes.

3. Puree the soup in batches in a food processor with the cilantro until smooth and uniformly textured. Transfer to a clean pot and add the lime juice and corn kernels. Season with salt and pepper to taste. Serve immediately, garnished with the cheddar and the remaining 1½ cups tortilla chips.

Pasta e Fagioli

Adapted from Pasta e Fagioli

Jasper's Restaurant, Kansas City, Missouri

PASTA E FAGIOLI—OR PASTA FEZOOL, as they call it in earshot of New Jersey—is a homey stew of slow-cooked beans, vegetables, and pasta finished with fruity extra-virgin olive oil. Traditionally from the Veneto region of Italy, it has also become a cornerstone of Italian-American cooking, served as a *primi piatti* (first course) at tiny neighborhood trattorias and mega-chain red sauce joints alike. At Jasper's in Kansas City, the chef makes a pasta e fagioli that cleaves closely to tradition—nothing newfangled or exotic, just a well-executed classic that needed little input from us to bring it into the home kitchen.

For superior pasta e fagioli, the beans and pasta should be of relatively equal proportion, the broth ample, and the vegetables flavorful. On each count, Jasper's succeeds. Classically, the dish starts with soffrito, a slow-cooked blend of aromatic vegetables and olive oil. The vegetables are cooked until dramatically reduced in volume and lightly browned—concentrated to their very essence. Jasper's soffrito includes diced yellow onion, garlic, celery, carrot, and pancetta—all traditional ingredients. For those who have never tasted pancetta, it's the closest thing Italians have to bacon. Pancetta is the same cut of meat as bacon, though it is unsmoked and cured with salt and spices—usually including at least black pepper and cloves—and rolled up like a jelly roll and packed into a casing. It adds the same richness to a dish as bacon, but without the smokiness that can compete with other flavors.

Along with the soffrito, Jasper's pasta e fagioli is flavored with red pepper flakes, bay leaves, chicken stock, and tomato. While canned tomatoes aren't the center of attention—as too many mediocre versions of pasta e fagioli suggest—they are important to the overall flavor. We found it important to drain the tomatoes of excess juices thoroughly before adding them to the soup; otherwise the tomato flavor became too prominent. Jasper's specifies six to eight tomatoes, roughly the contents of a 28-ounce can.

While pasta e fagioli is not wedded to any particular variety of beans, it is most commonly made with cannellini beans (sometimes called white kidney beans) or great Northern beans. These beans share a similar mild flavor and creamy texture; Jasper's recommends either. The recipe specifies dried beans, since canned beans lack the structure and flavor necessary for long-cooked soups. The beans are soaked overnight to hydrate them and to expedite cooking—soaked beans take less time to cook than those left unsoaked.

Jasper's stews the beans and vegetables in chicken stock at the barest bubble, well below the rapid simmer more typical of this dish. At this low simmer, the beans retain their discrete shape and develop a creamy, unctuous texture. We tried a few batches cooked at higher temperatures, but met with little success. Clearly, slow and low cooking had its merits.

Once the beans are tender, the soup is ready for the addition of the pasta. At Jasper's, the chefs employ tiny tubular ditali (or ditalini), cooked separately from the beans to ensure evenly cooked, flavorful pasta. When we cooked the pasta in the soup, as many pasta e fagioli recipes suggest, we found that it lost its identity, soaking up the flavor and color of the broth. For the best-textured pasta, pasta e fagioli should be served as soon as possible after the pasta is added; otherwise the pasta will continue to soak up broth and balloon in size.

The soup has such rich flavor that garnishes (outside of a drizzle of olive oil) would be overkill. This is the time to break out the expensive, high-grade extra-virgin olive oil, since its full flavor and lush mouthfeel will suffuse the soup.

Pasta e Fagioli

SERVES 6 TO 8

You will need to soak the beans overnight before beginning this recipe. If ditali pasta is hard to find, any small pasta shape will do, though the cooking time listed may not be accurate. Consult the instructions on the package. If you wish, the soup base (without the pasta) can be prepared up to three days ahead and refrigerated in an airtight container. The pasta should be cooked at the last minute.

- **1/4 cup extra-virgin olive oil, plus more for drizzling**
- **2 medium carrots, cut into medium dice**
- **1 medium onion, cut into medium dice**
- **1 large celery rib, cut into medium dice**
- **4 ounces pancetta, cut into medium dice**
- **1/2 teaspoon red pepper flakes**
- **2 bay leaves**
- **2 medium garlic cloves, minced or pressed through a garlic press (about 2 teaspoons)**
- **8 ounces (about 1 1/4 cups) dried great Northern or cannellini beans, picked over, soaked overnight, and drained**
- **1 28-ounce can whole tomatoes packed in juice, drained and chopped coarse**
- **6 cups Quick Chicken Stock (page 77) or low-sodium chicken broth**
- **1 cup ditali (or ditalini) pasta**
- **Salt and ground black pepper**

1. Heat the olive oil in a Dutch oven over medium-high heat until shimmering. Add the carrots, onion, celery, pancetta, red pepper flakes, and bay leaves and cook, stirring occasionally, until softened and lightly browned, about 10 minutes. Add the garlic and cook until aromatic, about 30 seconds. Add the beans, tomatoes, and chicken stock and bring to a simmer. Reduce the heat to the barest simmer and cook until the beans are tender, 2 to 2¼ hours. (Add up to 1½ cups water if necessary to keep the beans submerged.)

2. Bring 2 quarts water and 1½ teaspoons salt to a boil in a medium saucepan. Add the pasta and cook, stirring occasionally, until tender but still firm, about 7 minutes. Drain the pasta and add to the beans. Cook over medium-low heat until the pasta is tender, 3 to 4 minutes. Season with salt and pepper to taste. Serve immediately in warmed bowls, drizzled with extra-virgin olive oil.

Lamb & Barley Soup

Adapted from Lamb and Barley Soup

Fire, Cleveland, Ohio

BORDERING ON A STEW, THIS HEARTY barley soup from the restaurant Fire is dotted with tender pieces of lamb and Swiss chard and tastes surprisingly light and fresh. Far more interesting than the standard beef and barley soup, we found the original recipe tasted great and that its technique could be easily streamlined to accommodate a smaller batch.

At the restaurant, the chefs use two large pots to get the soup started, merging them later in the process. Although this dual-pot method is a great way to speed up the cooking of a huge batch, it is unnecessary when making just two quarts. Originally, the recipe cooked four pounds of lamb in one pot, while two gallons of vegetables were softened with lots of butter in another. Reducing the amounts of lamb and vegetables to one pound and six cups respectively, we found it easy to sear the lamb first, then remove it from the pot so that the vegetables could be sautéed in the flavorful lamb drippings, eliminating the need for butter altogether.

After the vegetables have begun to soften, the seared lamb, stock, and some herbs are added to the pot to simmer. The barley is added partway through the simmering time, since it requires only 30 minutes to cook while the lamb requires a full hour to turn tender. We preferred the flavor and color of the Swiss chard when allowed to wilt into the soup just before serving.

Last, we noted that the original recipe adds both freshly chopped rosemary and sage to the soup to finish. For a restaurant this makes sense, but not for the home cook. Both of these tough herbs require some time in the hot soup for their flavors to meld. At the restaurant, the soup is probably made a few hours before opening, so these herbs would have considerable time to mellow. At home, however, soups are usually served immediately, making the rosemary and sage taste raw and overwhelmingly medicinal. Adding the herbs to the pot along with the stock and letting them simmer worked perfectly to soften their flavors. This soup looks most attractive when served in a large, wide soup bowl accompanied by crusty bread.

Lamb and Barley Soup

SERVES 6 TO 8

If you can't find boneless lamb shoulder, you can substitute about 2 ½ pounds of lamb shoulder steaks and trim the meat from around the bones. For extra flavor, simmer the bones in the soup, but be sure to remove them before serving.

- **1 pound boneless lamb shoulder, cut into 1-inch pieces**
- **Salt and ground black pepper**
- **1 tablespoon vegetable oil**

- 4 small onions, cut into 1/4-inch dice (about 3 cups)
- 3 celery ribs, cut into 1/4-inch dice (about 1 1/2 cups)
- 4 medium carrots, cut into 1/4-inch dice (about 1 1/2 cups)
- 8 cups Quick Chicken Stock (page 77) or low-sodium chicken broth
- 3 bay leaves
- 1 sprig fresh rosemary
- 3 large fresh sage leaves, chopped coarse
- 3/4 cup pearl barley, rinsed and picked over
- 3 ounces Swiss chard, stems discarded, leaves cut into 1-inch pieces (about 3 cups)

1. Season the lamb liberally with salt and pepper. Heat the oil in a Dutch oven over medium-high heat until smoking. Add the lamb and cook until browned on all sides, 4 to 6 minutes. Remove the pot from heat and, using a slotted spoon, transfer the browned lamb to a clean bowl and set aside. Return the pot along with the lamb drippings to medium heat and stir in the onions, celery, carrots, and ½ teaspoon salt. Cook until slightly softened, about 5 minutes. Add the chicken stock, bay leaves, rosemary, sage, and browned lamb. Bring to a simmer, scraping the browned bits off the bottom of the pot. Reduce the heat to medium-low and simmer until the lamb is almost tender, about 30 minutes.

2. Stir in the barley and simmer until the barley is completely tender, about 30 minutes. Remove the pot from the heat, and discard the bay leaves and rosemary. Stir in the Swiss chard and allow it to wilt, about 5 minutes. Adjust the seasoning with salt and pepper and serve immediately in shallow soup bowls.

PREPARING SWISS CHARD

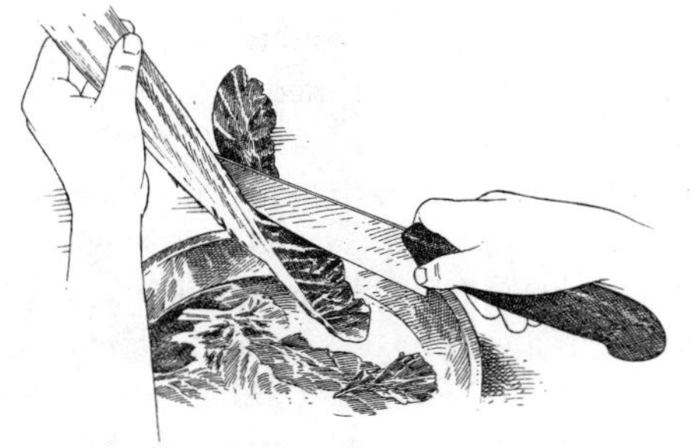

Hold each leaf at the base of the stem over a bowl filled with water and use a sharp knife to slash the leafy portion from either side of the thick stem.

CRAB & ASPARAGUS EGG DROP SOUP

Adapted from Crab and Asparagus Egg Drop Soup

AZ, NEW YORK, NEW YORK

TRADITIONALLY, EGG DROP SOUP IS A simple combination of thin ribbons of egg suspended in a flavorful, thickened chicken broth. This interpretation from AZ in New York, which sports chunks of sweet lump crabmeat, slivers of crisp asparagus, and tender strands of egg, bears little resemblance to its Chinese-American restaurant counterpart.

To start, we focused our attention on the stock. Homemade stock is essential in a restaurant kitchen, and most chefs make their own. AZ is no exception, but the home cook has the option of using doctored canned broth. Canned broth alone did not yield the richness needed to support this soup, so we fortified the broth with the addition of vegetables and herbs; shallots and garlic added to the Asian influence. After a simmer, the solids are strained out, but their rich flavor remains. In place of the traditional soy sauce, AZ uses fish sauce (also known as *nam pla* or *nuoc nam*) in the soup. It not only contributes salty flavor, but adds a hint of the sea, helping to accentuate the delicate crab flavor. Although not a Chinese condiment, it works well in this soup.

Next, we turned our attention to the asparagus. We soon discovered that if not diligently timed by an eagle-eyed restaurant chef, cooking the asparagus directly in the soup could easily lead to an overcooked vegetable. We opted for blanching the asparagus before adding it to the soup, finding it easier to avoid overcooking it.

Crabmeat is sold in different varieties and different forms, with the top of the line being fresh Atlantic blue crab. You can purchase both lump and backfin blue crab. For this recipe we prefer lump, because its firmer texture holds its shape well in the soup.

Adding the egg to the soup is the trickiest part of this recipe. Our goal was to create long ribbons of egg that were fully cooked but still tender. While some egg drop soup recipes instructed us to whisk the egg into the hot soup, we found this produced tiny bits of egg rather than the characteristic ribbons we were looking for. AZ instructed us to stir two tablespoons of the hot stock into the eggs before adding them to the soup. The purpose of this step is to help break down the proteins of the egg, and we found that it did help the egg form nice, long ribbons. We found that stirring the soup in a circle and slowly drizzling in the eggs produced the delicate strands we wanted.

Crab and Asparagus Egg Drop Soup

SERVES 6

This delicate soup will not hold long, so be sure to serve it as soon as it's ready.

- 2 celery ribs, cut into 1/2-inch pieces
- 1 medium onion, cut into 1/2-inch pieces
- 1 carrot, cut into 1/4-inch rounds
- 2 teaspoons whole black peppercorns
- 1 bay leaf
- 8 cups low-sodium chicken broth
- Salt
- 1/2 pound asparagus, tough ends trimmed and sliced thin on the bias
- 2 tablespoons vegetable oil
- 6 large shallots, sliced thin (about 3/4 cup)
- 12 garlic cloves, sliced thin (about 1/4 cup)
- 3 tablespoons minced fresh cilantro leaves
- 4 teaspoons fish sauce
- Ground black pepper
- 2 large eggs, beaten
- 1 pound lump Atlantic blue crabmeat, carefully picked over for shell fragments
- 4 scallions, both white and green parts, sliced thin

1. Bring the celery, onion, carrot, peppercorns, bay leaf, and chicken broth to a simmer in a Dutch oven over medium-high heat. Simmer until the vegetables are soft, about 15 minutes. Strain the broth through a fine-mesh strainer into a clean pot and set aside.

2. Bring 2 quarts water to a boil in a large saucepan. Have ready a large bowl of ice water. Stir ½ teaspoon salt and the asparagus into the boiling water and cook until crisp-tender, about 45 seconds. Drain the asparagus and immediately transfer it to the bowl of ice water to cool completely, about 1 minute. Transfer the asparagus to a plate lined with several layers of paper towel and set aside to drain.

3. Heat the vegetable oil in a Dutch oven over medium-high heat until shimmering. Add the shallots and sauté until softened, about 5 minutes. Add the garlic and sauté, stirring constantly, until the garlic is softened and golden, about 2 minutes. Add the broth and bring to a simmer. Simmer until the shallots are softened, about 10 minutes. Add the asparagus, cilantro, and fish sauce. Adjust the seasoning with salt and pepper.

4. Whisk the eggs together in a small bowl. Stir 2 tablespoons of the hot broth into the eggs. Stir the soup so that it is moving in a circle. Following the illustration below, continue to stir the soup while adding the eggs in a slow, steady stream, forming ribbons of coagulated egg, about 1 minute. Let the eggs stand in the soup without mixing until they are set, about 1 minute.

5. Divide the crabmeat among 6 individual bowls. Ladle some hot soup into each bowl on top of the crab and garnish with the sliced scallions. Serve immediately.

MAKING EGG DROP SOUP

Stir the soup with a wooden spoon so that it is moving in a circle. Keep stirring as you pour the eggs into the stock in a slow, steady stream so that ribbons of coagulated egg form, about 1 minute.

Oyster Chowder *with* Spinach

Adapted from Oyster Chowder

TJ's (Hotel Jefferson), Richmond, Virginia

THE NAME "CHOWDER" CONJURES IMAGES of a thick, creamy soup with a smoky flavor and lots of potatoes. At TJ's, however, the oyster chowder is far more elegant. The barely thickened, cream-based soup skips the potatoes and has small bits of carrot, celery, and onion as well as country ham, spinach, and an ample amount of perfectly cooked oysters. And the soup takes only 15 minutes to make, to boot.

With an incredibly straightforward procedure, we found the most difficult part of this recipe was the shopping. Finding shucked oysters took a bit of calling around, and we weren't able to get our hands on just a small amount of Smithfield country ham. Smithfield ham is cured and smoked and has an intense, salty flavor. Although buying just a slice or two of such ham is common in Virginia and other parts of the South, we found that here in the Northeast, we would have to buy an entire 12-pound ham, to the tune of $60. Not wanting to break the bank, we looked for a substitution. We tried cooking the soup with diced prosciutto (which is cured but not smoked), but it was far too chewy, and its potent, cured flavor made the broth taste awful and barnyardy. Trying Black Forest deli ham, we found its texture far better, but it lacked the good, smoky flavor of Smithfield ham, so we added a slice of bacon to the soup in addition to the ham. Chopping the bacon into small pieces, we added it the pot in the beginning with the butter.

The key to the success of this soup is in *not* overcooking the oysters. After bringing the soup base to a simmer, the oysters are stirred in and allowed to cook for only 30 seconds before the pot is removed from the heat. With such a short simmering time, it is necessary to add the oysters' natural juices (known as oyster liquor) to amplify the oyster flavor. The spinach is also given only this 30-second simmering time, which wilts it just slightly. Made with 3 cups of cream, the final soup is deceptively light and clean, with a graceful oyster flavor that is neither overpowering nor frail.

Oyster Chowder with Spinach

SERVES 6 TO 8

If the oysters do not yield ¾ cup of oyster liquor (their natural juice), augment it with an appropriate amount of bottled clam juice or low-sodium chicken broth. If Smithfield ham is available, substitute it for the deli ham and omit the bacon.

- 1 tablespoon unsalted butter
- 1 slice bacon, minced
- 1 celery rib, cut into 1/4-inch pieces
- 1/2 medium onion, cut into 1/4-inch pieces
- 1 small carrot, peeled, cut into 1/4-inch pieces
- Salt
- 1/2 cup 1/4-inch pieces good-quality smoked deli ham, such as Black Forest
- 3 cups heavy cream
- 1 pint shucked oysters, with 3/4 cup reserved oyster liquor
- 1 1/2 ounces flat-leaf spinach, stems trimmed, torn into 1-inch pieces (about 1 1/2 cups packed)
- Ground black pepper

1. Melt the butter with the bacon in a medium saucepan over medium heat. Cook until the bacon has rendered its fat but is not crisp, 2 to 3 minutes. Add the celery, onion, carrot, and ¼ teaspoon salt and sauté until very soft, 8 to 10 minutes. Add the ham and sauté until aromatic, about 2 minutes.

2. Add the cream and bring to a simmer. Add the oysters, oyster liquor, and spinach. Cook until the edges of the oysters begin to curl, about 30 seconds. Remove from the heat and adjust the seasoning with salt and pepper. Ladle the chowder into individual bowls and serve immediately.

Sane Truffle Soup

Adapted from Insane Truffle Soup

Tru, Chicago, Illinois

THE CHEFS AT TRU PROBABLY CALL THIS SOUP "insane" because it is insanely expensive. The original recipe, which yields 1 gallon, calls for 1 cup chopped truffles and ½ cup white truffle oil, which would cost over $200. Making a batch to serve eight people would therefore cost over $100. Insane indeed. Our goal was simple: capture the perfumed essence of truffle in a Tru-style soup without blowing the budget.

The original recipe was fairly straightforward. Aromatics (celery, onion, and garlic) are first sautéed in white truffle oil, then combined with chopped portobello mushrooms, mushroom stock, and heavy cream and simmered for several hours. The soup is then pureed, strained of any residual, offensively fibrous texture, and finished with both butter and chopped truffles. At Tru, the soup is served in elegant coffee cups and garnished with scalded milk froth—like a cappuccino.

Wanting to eke out even more flavor and save a few bucks, we decided to substitute butter for the truffle oil ($35 a bottle) when sautéing the aromatics. (We saved the truffle oil for finishing the soup, where its flavor would have the most impact.) After sautéing the aromatics, the portobello caps, with their dark underbelly gills, are added to the pot. The original recipe gives them just a minute to heat through. To maximize their flavor, we cut them into small pieces and cooked them under a lid without adding any stock for 20 minutes. Underneath the lid, the portobellos released most of their liquid and flavor into the pot, resulting in a more intense mushroom flavor.

Then it was time to add the stock. At Tru the chefs use mushroom stock, but we found we could substitute low-sodium chicken broth fortified with dried porcini mushrooms, garlic, fresh thyme, and bay leaves. Dried porcini (available in most supermarkets) are small, intensely flavored mushrooms that when rehydrated add a deep mushroom flavor to any dish. The soup required only 30 minutes of simmering to incorporate all the flavors. After pureeing the soup in a blender and straining it through a fine-mesh sieve into a clean pot, we finished the soup with cream, preferring its fresh, clean flavor to that of cream that has been simmered in the soup. Seasoned with salt and pepper, the mushroom soup was delicious and could only get better with the addition of the truffles.

Finishing the soup with lots of chopped truffles is what the original recipe requests, but this doesn't make sense in terms of budget. Rather than hide this incredibly expensive ingredient in the thick, dark soup, we preferred to use it as a garnish. Using an ample amount of chopped truffles per serving, so that when stirred in they will flavor the soup, we still managed to use a lot less than the original recipe—¼ ounce as opposed to the original 2 ¾ ounces. The only trouble with the chopped truffle garnish was its tough, crunchy texture. To soften the truffles slightly and bring out their flavor, we tossed them with a tablespoon of white truffle oil and heated them in a microwave on half power for 20 seconds.

Last, we found the dollop of cappuccino-like milk froth added both good texture and color to the soup. Most cappuccino machines have a steaming wand for frothing milk, but if you don't have one, we found it easy just to heat some milk on the stove and whisk it vigorously. Be sure to use nonfat or low-fat milk, since it is easier to bring to a froth than whole milk. The fragrant yet fleeting aroma of white truffle oil, saved for last, delivered maximum impact when drizzled onto the soup just before serving (it also looked stunning). Our version of truffle soup not only tastes authentic, but costs only a fraction of the original soup's "insane" price.

INGREDIENTS: Black Truffles

Foraged with the help of either an aroused pig or a well-trained dog, truffles are among the most expensive ingredients in the world. Although truffles are harvested in both the summer and winter months, winter truffles are traditionally preferred for their intense flavor and heady aroma. Summer truffles, on the other hand, are harvested when they are immature and suffer dramatically in terms of flavor and fragrance. Fresh, black winter truffles can be found in gourmet food markets from December through March; both jarred and canned versions, packed either in water or in oil, are available year-round.

There are three species of black truffles, and choosing the right one will make all the difference. Look for the variety called Périgord (French), Tricastin (Spanish), or Norcia (Umbrian). The other two varieties—the musky truffle and the Chinese truffle—are inferior in aroma and flavor and cost much less. Like most produce, the longer a truffle is kept, the less potent and aromatic it will taste, so use it within a few days or so of purchasing.

Sane Truffle Soup

SERVES 6

When buying fresh truffles, make sure they are winter truffles, usually called Périgord, Tricastin, or Norcia, which are firm to the touch with a pungent aroma. Use a fresh truffle within a day or so of purchasing. To clean, brush off the dirt using a dry mushroom brush or toothbrush, using a toothpick for deep crevices. To read more about truffle oil, see page 95.

- 4 tablespoons unsalted butter
- 1 celery rib, chopped fine
- 1 medium onion, chopped fine
- Salt
- 2 garlic cloves, minced or pressed through a garlic press (about 2 teaspoons)
- 1 pound portobello mushroom caps (about 12 medium caps), chopped fine
- 8 cups Quick Chicken Stock (page 77) or low-sodium chicken broth
- ½ ounce dried porcini, rinsed well
- 2 bay leaves
- 2 sprigs fresh thyme
- ¼ ounce fresh or canned black truffles, chopped fine
- 3 tablespoons white truffle oil
- 1 cup heavy cream
- Ground black pepper
- ½ cup low-fat or nonfat milk

1. Melt the butter in a Dutch oven over medium heat until the foaming subsides. Add the celery, onion, and ½ teaspoon salt and sauté until softened, about 10 minutes. Stir in the garlic and sauté until aromatic, about 30 seconds. Stir in the portobellos and

INGREDIENTS: Truffle Oil

With designer bottles and hefty price tags, we wondered why all the fuss over black and white truffle oils? After buying more than 13 bottles of truffle oil (spending just shy of $400), we tasted them side by side to determine if they were worth all the hype. To start, we learned that there are three basic techniques for making truffle oil—both black and white. The most costly is called aromatization, which scatters fresh truffles around a small enclosed room filled with pans of oil. The aroma fills the space and, after a daily stir, the oil absorbs the truffle aroma in about six months. The second, more cost-effective method is to steep the truffles in oil (either olive or safflower), allowing their aroma to permeate the oil. The third, most offensive way is to soak the truffles in some form of solvent, which is then added to the oil. We concluded that it was difficult to determine exactly which method had been used based on the unregulated wording in the list of ingredients. On the bottles we tested, we found everything from just olive oil and truffles, to oil, natural flavoring, aroma, and artificial flavoring. Also, we found that three types of oil are generally used when making truffle oil: olive, extra-virgin olive, and safflower.

We began by tasting six black truffle oils, and although we determined a winner, almost all tasted of toxic chemicals with noxious aromas; some tasters could not even finish the tasting. The most expensive sample, Boscovivo, containing extra-virgin olive oil and aroma, had an overpowering, bitter flavor of cheap extra-virgin olive oil. The most offensive and inedible of the lot was a French oil, Huile d'Olive à la Truffe, purchased from Dean & DeLuca. Containing olive oil, winter truffle, and flavoring, this sample had tasters gagging. The only palatable oil in the bunch was Fondo di Alba, an Italian oil listing only olive oil and black truffles. Ranging in price from $3.14 to $6.84 per ounce, black truffle oil is not worth the expense.

Moving on to white truffle oils, we were pleased with their pleasant, earthy, rich aromas—unlike the foul aromas of their black counterparts. Again, the Boscovivo brand, listing extra-virgin olive oil and white truffle flavoring, tasted only of the overpowering oil; it received low scores from all tasters. The all-out loser, though, was the Williams-Sonoma brand, Tartufolio. Including natural and artificial white truffle flavors as ingredients, tasters described this oil as "plasticky" with "an odd alcohol aroma." The winner of the tasting, Fondo di Alba, is an Italian oil with olive oil and white truffles. It garnered remarks such as "well balanced," "incredibly fragrant," and "this is what truffle oil should taste like." Fondo di Alba can be purchased at Sid Wainer and Son (www.sidwainer.com).

When all was said and tasted, we determined that fancy bottles and exorbitant price tags don't necessarily mark the difference between good and bad truffle oils. Rather, look for a white truffle oil that lists truffles and either olive oil or safflower oil as the only ingredients.

heat through, about 1 minute. Cover, reduce the heat to medium-low, and cook until the portobellos release all their juices, about 20 minutes. Add the stock, dried porcini, bay leaves, and thyme, and bring to a simmer uncovered. Simmer until the stock tastes of mushrooms, about 30 minutes.

2. Meanwhile, combine the chopped truffles and 1 tablespoon of the truffle oil in a small, microwave-safe bowl, cover tightly with plastic wrap, and poke several steam vents using the tip of a paring knife. Microwave the mixture on half power until the truffles are slightly softened, about 20 seconds. Set aside, covered.

3. Puree the soup in batches in a blender until smooth. Strain the soup through a fine-mesh sieve into a clean pot and set over low heat. Stir in the cream and adjust the seasoning with salt and pepper. Keep warm.

4. Scald the milk in a small saucepan over high heat, whisking vigorously until foamy, about 2 minutes. Remove from the heat. (Alternatively, froth the milk using the steam wand of an espresso maker or other milk-frothing gadget.) Ladle the soup into coffee cups and garnish each serving with some milk froth, 1 teaspoon of the remaining truffle oil, and some chopped truffles. Serve immediately.

Coconut–Lime Leaf Soup *with* Chicken

Adapted from Coconut–Lime Leaf Soup

Peter Pratt's Inn, Yorktown, New York

COCONUT SOUPS, INDIGENOUS TO SOUTHeast Asia, and in particular Thailand, are rich and luscious, and serve as the perfect canvas for a myriad of ingredients, leaving the choice of colors and flavors up to the artist. Consisting of a rich broth infused with the clean flavors of lime leaf, lemon grass, coconut, and chiles, this recipe from Peter Pratt's Inn will transport the flavors and aromas of Thailand into your kitchen with ease. Although there are some unusual ingredients in this soup, if you are able to root them out your search will be well rewarded with an authentic replication of a true Thai classic. However, we did test ingredients that could serve as alternatives to the traditional Asian ingredients.

Many Thai restaurants feature a version of this soup. What makes this coconut soup stand above the rest is the unique inclusion of both red curry paste and masaman curry paste. These intense blends of chiles and herbal ingredients add an amazing depth of flavor and color to the broth. We found that of the many varieties of curry pastes used in Thai cooking, red curry is the most widely used. Almost all curry pastes contain lemon grass, chiles, shallots, garlic, and shrimp paste, but the intensity varies depending on the proportion and type of chile used. The classic red curry paste (considered one of the hottest) contains the deep flavors of both dried long, red chiles and dried Japanese chiles. The highly spiced masaman curry paste, which gets its name from the Muslims of southern Thailand, also contains long, red chiles with the addition of fragrant spices such as cinnamon, coriander seeds, and cardamom pods. The resulting combination lends an exotic perfume to the soup, tempering the heat of the red curry paste.

While red curry paste seemed to be relatively easy to find, we decided to try to find an alternative for the masaman curry paste, which proved to be a bit difficult to locate. Curious about the heat level of green curry paste, we replaced the masaman with equal amounts of green curry paste in one of our tests. Green curry paste turns out to be one of the hottest around, gaining its heat from the deceptively small serrano chile. Imparting a completely different spectrum of flavors, this innocent-looking jade green paste produced a soup that made some tasters' eyes water while others appreciated the heat. We concluded that green curry paste can be used in this soup, although the finished dish will be significantly spicier.

The next ingredient on our list was the creamy, rich coconut milk. Made by steaming and pressing fresh coconut meat, the milk that is extracted is silky and has a texture similar to that of heavy cream, with a taste all its own. It is readily available, canned, in most supermarkets, but be sure to buy unsweetened coconut milk, not be confused with canned cream of coconut, a sweetened concoction intended for cocktails and some desserts. Fish sauce (made from salted, fermented fish) is a salty brown sauce indispensable in Thai cuisine. Although its aroma may be a bit off-putting, it adds a unique depth of flavor to Thai dishes. The fresh lime juice offsets the saltiness of the fish sauce and adds a tanginess to balance the richness of the coconut milk.

The next somewhat unusual ingredient in this soup is fresh lemon grass, a tall lemon-scented grass grown in warm climates with a distinctly refreshing flavor. Bruising the stalks of the lemon grass releases the intense, lemony flavor. We found that substituting 2 or 3 strips of lemon zest adds a similar, though not identical, flavor to the soup. Another unusual ingredient called for is kaffir lime leaves. These fragrant leaves are used in many Southeast Asian cuisines and give a citrusy perfume to the soup. Grated lime zest is a viable substitute if the leaves are unavailable. The sweetener originally called for was palm sugar. Made from the boiled-down sap of the coconut palm, this golden sugar has a flavor and aroma similar to maple sugar. Though there is no identical counterpart, we found that substituting equal parts of light brown sugar and pure maple syrup yielded a reasonable flavor likeness.

At the restaurant, this soup is prepared with boneless chicken breast. However, the chef offers unconventional variations with shrimp or tofu, which were both successful in our tests. Thinly sliced snow white mushrooms, tiny slivers of bright green scallion, and delicate, fresh cilantro leaves complete this soup, creating an aromatic appetizer to rival the most authentic of Thai restaurants.

Coconut–Lime Leaf Soup with Chicken

SERVES 8

For a spicier version of this soup, substitute green curry paste for the masaman curry paste.

- **3** tablespoons peanut or vegetable oil
- **3** garlic cloves, sliced
- **5** teaspoons (about 1 ounce) masaman curry paste
- **5** teaspoons (about 1 ounce) red curry paste
- **4** cups canned unsweetened coconut milk
- **2** cups Quick Chicken Stock (page 77) or low-sodium chicken broth
- **½** cup juice from 3–4 limes
- **¼** cup fish sauce
- **2** stalks fresh lemon grass, smashed (see the illustration on page 99)
- **4** kaffir lime leaves or 1 tablespoon grated lime zest from 2 limes
- **2** tablespoons palm sugar or 1 tablespoon light brown sugar plus 1 tablespoon pure maple syrup
- **½** cup loosely packed fresh basil leaves
- **2** tablespoons minced fresh cilantro leaves
- **1** pound skinless boneless chicken breasts, sliced thin into bite-sized pieces
- **1** pound small white mushrooms, sliced thin
- **3** scallions, both white and green parts, sliced thin
- **8** sprigs fresh cilantro

1. Heat the peanut oil in a Dutch oven over medium-high heat until shimmering. Add the garlic and sauté until light golden, 30 seconds to 1 minute. Remove the garlic from the pan using a slotted spoon and set aside in a bowl. Add the curry pastes and stir until they soften and blend with the oil, about 2 minutes. Add the coconut milk, chicken stock, 2 cups water, lime juice, and fish sauce and bring to a simmer. Add the lemon grass, lime leaves, palm sugar, and garlic and simmer for 10 minutes. Remove the pan from the heat and add the basil and cilantro. Let the soup steep for 5 minutes, then strain through a fine-mesh sieve into a large bowl.

2. Bring the strained soup to a simmer in a medium saucepan over medium-high heat. Add the chicken, separating the pieces with a spoon so they don't stick together, and simmer until the chicken is cooked through, 3 to 5 minutes. Remove the chicken from the soup and divide it equally among 8 individual soup bowls.

3. To serve, ladle 1 cup soup over the chicken in each bowl and garnish with the mushrooms, scallions, and cilantro sprigs.

VARIATIONS

Coconut–Lime Leaf Soup with Tofu

Before beginning the soup, prepare the tofu. Slice 1 pound firm tofu in half horizontally. Place the tofu on a large plate lined with several layers of paper towels, and cover with several more layers of paper towels. Place another plate on top and weigh the plate down with several large cans, such as tomato or soup cans. Refrigerate for 30 minutes to 1 hour. Remove the tofu from the refrigerator, discard the paper towels, and cut the tofu into ¼-inch-thick slices. In step 2, omit the chicken and proceed to step 3. To serve, divide the tofu evenly among the soup bowls, ladle 1 cup soup over the tofu in each bowl, and garnish with the mushrooms, scallions, and cilantro.

Coconut–Lime Leaf Soup with Shrimp

Follow the recipe for Coconut–Lime Leaf Soup with Chicken, replacing the chicken in step 2 with 24 extra-large shrimp (about 1 pound), peeled and deveined, patted dry with paper towels. Proceed with step 3 to finish the soup.

BRUISING LEMON GRASS

Smack the stalk with the back of a large chef's knife and use immediately.

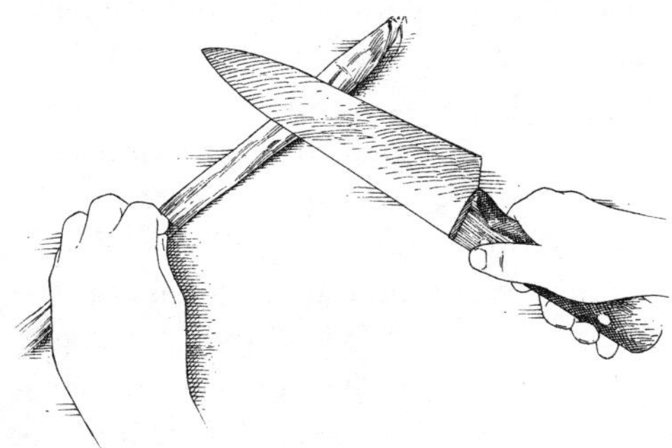

Greek Salad

Adapted from Greek Salad

Byblos Restaurant, Wichita, Kansas

FOR MANY OF US IN THE TEST KITCHEN, memories of delicious Greek salads are just that—memories. We trade stories on the difficulties of finding superb restaurant Greek salads and recount endless versions of flavorless iceberg lettuce topped with unpalatable and cumbersome chunks of green pepper, tomato, and red onion, a lonely olive, and a few cubes of feta cheese lost in the mix. We approached this recipe with trepidation born from years of disappointment. Once we made the recipe and tasted the result, however, we were delighted. It revives Greek salad by unburdening it of the chunks of bell pepper and onion and brightening the flavors with slivers of fresh mint. Choosing fresh, flavorful ingredients and following a couple of simple techniques will ensure the success of this recipe.

Like most American versions of the traditional Greek salad, lettuce forms the foundation of this recipe. The chef at Byblos Restaurant gave the option of using romaine or iceberg lettuce. We found that owing to the abundance of water in its leaves, iceberg lettuce tends to contribute more crunch than flavor to salads. Testers hands-down preferred the texture and flavor of romaine lettuce in the Greek salad and were happy to leave the crunch to the cucumber.

Because the season for flavorful, fresh, local tomatoes is sadly short, look for vine-ripened versions when making this salad during the rest of the year. We found the cool, delicate flavor of the cucumber was less important than a firm texture. Look for firm cucumbers with unblemished skin. However, even the most flavorful tomatoes and crisp cucumbers can mar the salad if left unseeded. Unseeded tomatoes and cucumbers leach water and slippery seeds into the salad and leave an unpalatable, sloppy texture.

Rather than using large chunks of red onion, whose pleasing color is too often overpowered by a caustic bite, this recipe calls for scallions and radishes. The combination retains the color and pungency of the red onions while omitting their unwelcome heat.

Choose the best feta cheese you can find for this recipe. The ideal feta is creamy, tangy, supple, and moist. Having too often unwittingly purchased dry and chalky feta, we conducted a tasting of supermarket versions as well as artisanal brands. We learned that most supermarket feta cheese is made by large producers that use pasteurized cow's milk. Producers of artisanal brands, on the other hand, generally continue the Greek tradition of making feta from sheep's milk or a mixture of sheep's and goat's milk. After testing, we found that the type of milk used in the production of the cheese was less important than the method of packaging. Packaging feta with some of the brine is the key to a moist texture. Look for feta cheese in vacuum-sealed packaging or plastic tubs that retain some of the brine. Avoid feta cheese that sits on a Styrofoam tray and is wrapped in plastic.

This recipe originally called for dried mint in the vinaigrette. Because fresh mint is readily available and dried mint quickly grows dull in the back of the herb and spice cabinet, we decided to try adding fresh mint leaves, sliced into thin strips, to the vinaigrette. We found that the vinaigrette coated the mint and dulled its flavor. We then tried sprinkling the fresh mint strips over the top of the dressed salad. The result was perfect. The fresh mint complemented the heat of the radishes and added a refreshing brightness to the salad.

Once you have assembled the fresh and flavorful ingredients, whisk together the vinaigrette components and then separately toss the prepared vegetables and the lettuce with the dressing before combining. We found that if the vegetables and lettuce are tossed together, the heavier vegetables invariably end up on the bottom of the salad bowl and the lighter greens stay on top. To more evenly disperse the vegetables among the romaine leaves, toss the greens with half of the dressing in a medium bowl. Toss the prepared vegetables with the remaining vinaigrette in another medium bowl. Arrange the greens on a serving platter or individual plates and then spoon the dressed vegetable mixture over the greens. Finish by sprinkling the salad with crumbled feta, quartered black olives, and slivered mint leaves. The result is a colorful, crisp, and brightly flavored Greek salad.

Greek Salad

SERVES 6

Look for feta cheese in vacuum-sealed packaging or plastic tubs that retain some of the brine. Avoid feta cheese that sits on a Styrofoam tray and is wrapped in plastic—its flavor pales in comparison.

- **1/3 cup red wine vinegar**
- **1/2 cup extra-virgin olive oil**
- **2 garlic cloves, minced or pressed through a garlic press (about 2 teaspoons)**
- **1/2 teaspoon salt**
- **1/8 teaspoon ground black pepper**
- **1 head romaine lettuce, washed, dried, and torn into 1 1/2-inch pieces (about 12 cups)**
- **3 large vine-ripened tomatoes, cored, seeded, and cut into 1-inch-thick wedges**
- **1 medium cucumber, peeled, halved lengthwise, seeded, and cut into 1/8-inch-thick slices**
- **2 radishes, halved and sliced thin**
- **2 scallions, both green and white parts, sliced thin**
- **5 ounces feta cheese, crumbled (about 1 1/4 cups)**
- **20 large Kalamata olives, pitted and quartered lengthwise**
- **10 medium mint leaves, sliced thin**

Whisk the vinegar, oil, garlic, salt, and pepper together in a small bowl. Toss the romaine with half the dressing in a medium bowl. Toss the tomatoes, cucumber, radishes, and scallions with the remaining dressing in another medium bowl. Arrange the romaine on a serving platter or individual plates. Spoon the tomato mixture over the romaine. Sprinkle with the feta, Kalamata olives, and mint. Serve immediately.

INGREDIENTS: Red Wine Vinegar

The source of that notable edge you taste when sampling any red wine vinegar is acetic acid, the chief flavor component in all vinegar and the by-product of the bacterium *Acetobacter aceti*, which feeds on the alcohol in wine. The process of converting red wine to vinegar once took months, if not years, but now, with the help of an acetator (a machine that speeds the metabolism of the ***Acetobacter aceti***), red wine vinegar can be made in less than 24 hours.

Does this faster, cheaper method—the one used to make most supermarket brands—produce inferior red wine vinegar? Or is this a case in which modern technology trumps Old World craftsmanship, which is still employed by makers of the more expensive red wine vinegars? To find out, we included in our tasting vinegars made using the fast process (acetator) and the slow process (often called the Orleans method, after the city in France where it was developed).

We first tasted 10 nationally available supermarket brands in two ways: by dipping sugar cubes in each brand and sucking out the vinegar (a method professionals use to cut down on palate fatigue) and by making a simple vinaigrette with each and tasting it on iceberg lettuce. We then pitted the winners of the supermarket tasting against four high-end red wine vinegars.

Although no single grape variety is thought to make the best red wine vinegar, we were curious to find out if our tasters were unwittingly fond of vinegars made from the same grape. We sent the vinegars to a food lab for an anthocyanin pigment profile, a test that can detect the 10 common pigments found in red grapes. Although the lab was unable to distinguish specific grape varieties (Cabernet, Merlot, Pinot Noir, Zinfandel, and the like), it did provide us with an interesting piece of information: Some of the vinegars weren't made with wine grapes (known as ***Vitus vinifera***) but with less expensive Concord-type grapes, the kind used to make Welch's grape juice.

Did the vinegars made with grape juice fare poorly, as might be expected? Far from it. The taste-test results were both shocking and unambiguous: Concord-type grapes not only do just fine when it comes to making vinegar but may also be a key element in the success of the top-rated brands in our tasting. Spectrum, our overall winner, is made from a mix of wine grapes and Concord grapes. Pompeian, which came in second among the supermarket brands, is made entirely of Concord-type grapes.

What else might contribute to the flavor of these vinegars? One possibility, we thought, was the way in which the acetic acid is developed. Manufacturers that mass-produce vinegar generally prefer not to use the Orleans method, because it's slow and expensive. Spectrum red wine vinegar is produced with the Orleans method, but Pompeian is made in an acetator in less than 24 hours.

What, then, can explain why Spectrum and Pompeian won the supermarket tasting and beat the gourmet vinegars? Oddly enough, for a food that defines ***sourness***, the answer seems to lie in its sweetness. It turns out that Americans like their vinegar sweet (think balsamic vinegar).

The production of Spectrum is outsourced to a small manufacturer in Modena, Italy, that makes generous use of the Trebbiano grape, the same grape used to make balsamic vinegar. The Trebbiano, which is a white wine grape, gives Spectrum the sweetness our tasters admired. Pompeian vinegar is finished with a touch of sherry vinegar, added to give the red vinegar a more fruity, well-rounded flavor. Also significant to our results may be that both Spectrum and Pompeian start with wines containing Concord grapes, which are sweet enough to be a common choice when making jams and jellies.

When pitted against gourmet vinegars, Spectrum and Pompeian still came out on top. Which red wine vinegar should you buy? Skip the specialty shop and head to the supermarket.

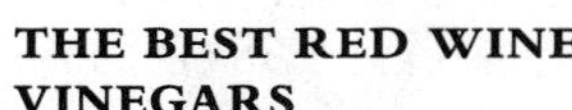

THE BEST RED WINE VINEGARS

Spectrum vinegar (left) and Pompeian vinegar (right) are available in supermarkets and bested gourmet brands costing 8 times as much.

Frisée Salad *with* Cranberry-Bacon Vinaigrette & Blue Cheese Pastries

Adapted from Frisée Salad with Cranberry-Bacon Vinaigrette and Blue Cheese Pastries

L'Étoile, Madison, Wisconsin

THERE ARE FEW SALADS THAT ARE elegant enough to take your breath away, but this one from L'Étoile fits the bill. An ideal accompaniment to pork or duck, this flavorful salad unites strong flavors to harmonious effect. The warm, salty-sweet, slightly acidic vinaigrette mellows the bitterness of the frisée and tenderizes its characteristically tough leaves. Topped with a small puff pastry surrounding warm, soft blue cheese, the salad appears to be complicated. In fact, the most difficult step in preparing the salad is not making the puff pastry—easy-to-use, store-bought puff pastry replaces the time-consuming and laborious steps involved in making puff pastry at home—but is, instead, identifying frisée in your local market or supermarket.

Frisée is a tough, bitter-leafed vegetable with spiky green leaves that extend loosely outward from a pale base. It is often marketed as curly endive, curly chicory, chicory, or chicorée frisée. Often used in combination with other greens, frisée adds a pleasant bitterness and sturdy texture to salads. Its spiky texture requires blanching or wilting with a warm dressing as called for in this recipe.

We added an extra tablespoon of balsamic

INGREDIENTS: Blue Cheese

We sampled eight blue cheeses on their own and in a salad. Eaten plain, each cheese had its fans, but tasters agreed that the milder cheeses were better in the salad.

THE BEST MILD BLUE CHEESES

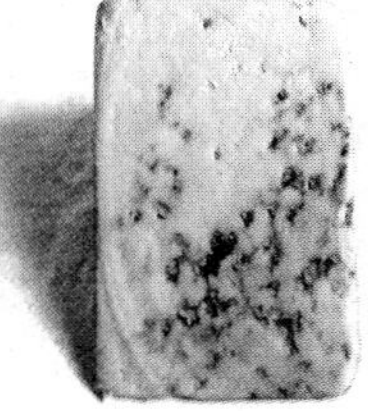

DANISH BLUE, DENMARK
$11.95 per pound
Danish blue is straightforward and cheddar-like. It has a strong, salty, and tangy presence, is slightly crumbly in texture, and is spotted with silvery blue pockets.

STELLA BLUE, WISCONSIN
$6.29 per pound
This supermarket brand was very crumbly and almost feta-like in texture. Tasters who preferred mild blue cheese liked this one.

vinegar to boost the dressing's acidity, a necessary contrast to the sweetness of the port and the tartness of the cranberries. We reduced the bacon from 9 to 6 slices and, instead of chopping them, cut them into thin slivers that cook more evenly. In kitchen tests, we discovered that reducing the port mixture too much left insufficient warm liquid to coat and wilt the frisée properly. Reducing the liquid by half left the right amount to coat the greens. Once coated with the warm vinaigrette, the greens are divided among salad plates, sprinkled with the bacon slivers, and topped with a delicate blue cheese pastry, resulting in a pleasing arrangement of complementary flavors and textures.

Frisée Salad with Cranberry-Bacon Vinaigrette and Blue Cheese Pastries

SERVES 6

The baked but unfilled puff pastries may be prepared up to 8 hours ahead and stored in an airtight container at room temperature. When ready to serve, simply spoon some cheese into each pastry and warm the pastries in the oven until the cheese is softened and the pastry is crisp.

- **2 medium heads frisée, cored and cut into bite-size pieces (about 9 cups)**
- **1 (9 1/2 by 9-inch) sheet frozen commercial puff pastry, thawed on the counter for 30 minutes and unfolded**
- **1 large egg, beaten**
- **3 ounces blue cheese, crumbled (about 3/4 cup)**
- **6 slices bacon, cut into 1/4-inch thick slivers**
- **2 small shallots, minced (about 1/3 cup)**
- **1 cup ruby port (or fruity red wine mixed with 1/2 teaspoon sugar)**
- **Ground black pepper**
- **1/2 cup dried cranberries**
- **2 tablespoons balsamic vinegar**

1. Adjust an oven rack to the upper-middle position and heat the oven to 425 degrees. Place the frisée in a large bowl and set aside. Unfold the puff pastry and lay on a floured surface. Following the illustrations on page 105 and using the beaten egg, cut and assemble the pastries. Bake the pastries on a parchment-lined baking sheet until puffed and golden, 12 to 15 minutes. Remove the pastries from the oven and reduce the oven temperature to 325 degrees. Spoon 2 tablespoons of the crumbled blue cheese in the center of each pastry. Return the pastries to the oven until the cheese is warm and the pastry is recrisped, about 6 minutes.

2. Meanwhile, cook the bacon, stirring occasionally, in a 10-inch skillet over medium-high heat until crisp. Remove the pan from the heat. Using a slotted spoon, transfer the bacon to a plate lined with several layers of paper towels to drain. Pour all but 1 teaspoon of the bacon fat into a small bowl and set aside.

3. Return the pan to medium-high heat until the bacon fat shimmers. Add the shallots and sauté until tender, about 3 minutes. Add the port, ¼ teaspoon pepper, and the cranberries and simmer, scraping up any browned bits from the bottom of the pan, until the cranberries are soft and the liquid is reduced by half, about 6 to 8 minutes. Stir 3 tablespoons of the reserved bacon fat into the port mixture and heat through, 10 to 20 seconds. Remove the pan from the heat and whisk in the balsamic vinegar. Immediately pour the dressing over the frisée and toss to coat. Divide the frisée among individual plates and sprinkle with the bacon. Arrange a warm blue cheese pastry on top of each salad. Serve immediately.

PREPARING THE BLUE CHEESE PASTRIES

1. Using a 2-inch-wide, scalloped cookie cutter or round biscuit cutter, cut out 12 rounds by pressing the cutter straight down through the pastry and then lifting it straight up. Do not twist the cutter to loosen the pastry. Dip the cutter in flour as needed to prevent the dough from sticking.

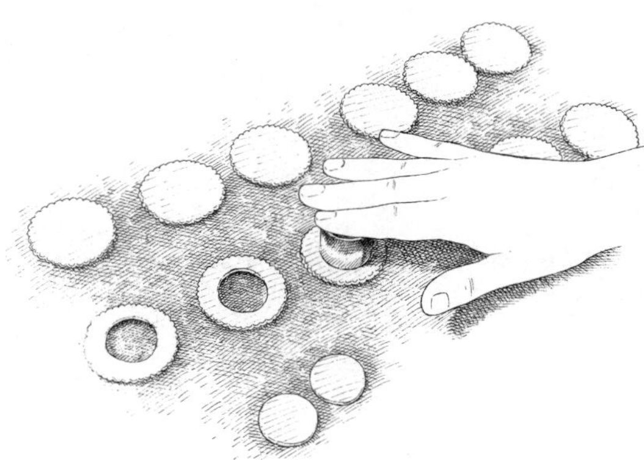

2. Using a 1-inch-wide cookie or biscuit cutter, remove the centers from 6 of the rounds. Discard the centers and reserve the rings.

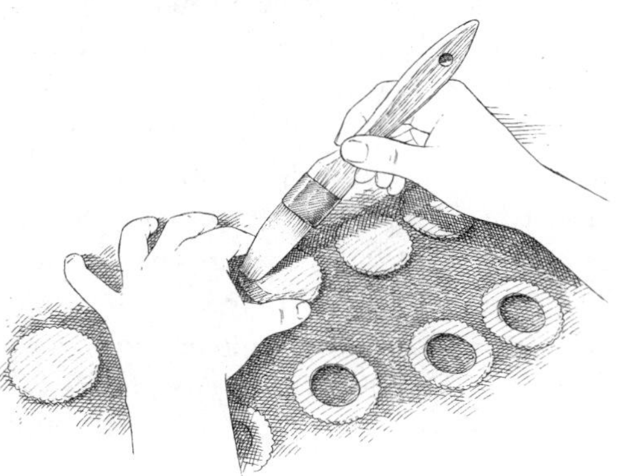

3. Using a small pastry brush, coat the circumference of the rounds with the egg wash, taking care not to drip it down the sides of the pastry.

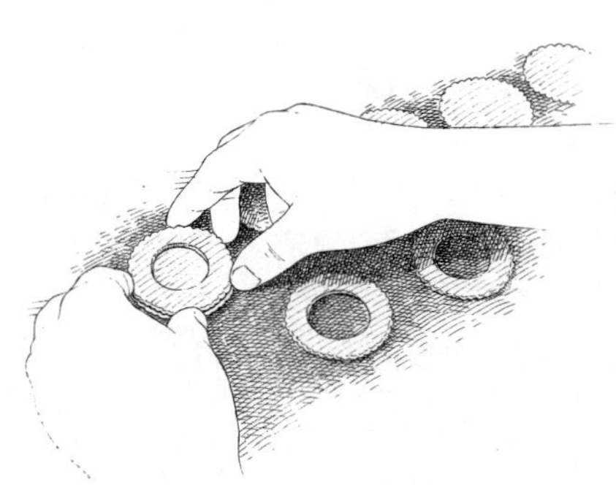

4. Top the rounds with the pastry rings and press gently to adhere.

Summer Farmers Salad *with* Smoked Trout

Adapted from Summer Farmers Salad with Lemon, Thyme, and Mint Vinaigrette

Lucia's Restaurant and Wine Bar, Minneapolis, Minnesota

LUCIA'S RESTAURANT AND WINE BAR prides itself on using seasonal vegetables as much as possible, and its Summer Farmers Salad is the ideal showcase for perfect, farm-fresh produce. Stretched across a bed of mixed greens and herbs, tomatoes, corn, carrots, snow peas, and smoked trout all add their own particular flavor and character to the salad. It is simple, delicious, and easy to prepare.

While each of the vegetables plays an important role, the vinaigrette is really the star of the show. A potent blend of fresh mint, thyme, garlic, and lemon juice and zest energizes the salad and unifies the seemingly disparate mix of greens, vegetables, and other herbs. Admittedly, we were at first shocked by the large volume of herbs in the vinaigrette: one-quarter cup minced herbs to a scant three-quarters cup vinaigrette seemed excessive. Tasted on its own, the vinaigrette was indeed very strong—both herby and sharp. On the salad, however, the flavor was tempered by the vegetables and greens. The mint added lightness and the thyme brought earthy depth to the vegetables. The combination of lemon juice and lemon zest is responsible for the acidity and full citrus flavor. Lucia's recipe specified neutral-tasting vegetable oil, but mild olive oil also tasted fine. Extra-virgin olive oil, however, was unpleasant in this vinaigrette since it competed with the vinaigrette's herbiness.

For greens, the recipe includes a small amount of each of several different types, though we found that a good-quality mesclun mix (sometimes called spring mix) was an easy substitution. Most markets carry either bagged greens or a loose mix. While we can't vouch for the loose greens, we have tasted nationally sold bagged blends and found that some are definitely better than others in both freshness and variety of greens. Lucia's augments the greens with a handful of different herbs, including sorrel, basil, chervil, and chives. Sometimes referred to as spinach dock, sorrel is a bright green, broad-leafed herb with a potent, lemony tartness. While we liked it in the salad, we found it hard to find and so opted to exclude it (if you can find it, feel free to add it). Likewise, we excluded chervil because of its rarity, though its mild, anise flavor lent depth. Basil and chives we included—they're easy to find and a flavorful addition to the greens.

As a general rule, we recommend two tablespoons dressing per quart of greens. We have found that this amply coats the greens without weighing them down. In this case, the dressing coats both the greens and the vegetables arranged on top. We tossed the greens with the appropriate amount of dressing—four tablespoons for the two quarts—and drizzled the remaining half cup over the top of the vegetables. At first, we were concerned that it was too much dressing, but after consuming several batches, we realized the amount was appropriate.

With the vinaigrette blended and the greens picked, all that was left was to prepare the vegetables. It would be hard to imagine a summer vegetable salad without corn and tomatoes, but snow peas and carrots? However odd they seemed, we found the carrots and snow peas lent a crisp sweetness important to the salad's success. Lucia's blanches the vegetables, cooking them in salted boiling water until tender. The brief cooking does well by both: their flavor and color is improved. Part and parcel of blanching is "shocking," or plunging the vegetables into ice water once tender to curtail any further cooking. Otherwise, they will keep cooking and turn mushy and lose their vibrant hues.

Following the recipe, we added very fresh raw corn to the salad—fine if the corn is impeccably fresh; otherwise the cobs should be briefly blanched. Removing the kernels from the cob can be a messy proposition, but we have found a hassle-free method, involving only a short, sharp knife and a large bowl. We rest the bottom of the cob in the center of the bowl and shave downward. The kernels are confined to the bowl.

The recipe specifies heirloom tomatoes, which are those knobby sorts that come in all shades of the rainbow. Heirlooms are not one particular variety; it's a catchall category for any number of tomatoes grown from old-stock seeds. They generally possess more flavor than the average market sort, which has been genetically engineered to be glossy, red, symmetrical, and sturdy, with little regard for flavor. If you have trouble finding flavorful tomatoes, try cherry tomatoes since they are almost always sweet and flavorful.

The final touch to the salad is a garnish of flaked, smoked trout. What sounds unusual makes a great deal of sense: its richness and chewy texture added a new dimension to the otherwise lean salad. Available at most seafood counters, smoked trout often comes packaged as a whole fish, or sometimes in fillets. Strewn across the salad in small flakes, the fish nestled into the vegetables and greens, adding a mildly briny, smoky flavor that surprisingly sharpened the vegetables' freshness.

Summer Farmers Salad with Smoked Trout

SERVES 6 TO 8

While this salad may easily be served on individual plates, we liked it best served "family-style," laid out on a large platter. Cherry tomatoes, halved lengthwise, are a good substitute for the larger tomatoes. If your corn is very fresh, it can be used raw. As with all salads, make sure your plates are chilled before serving—a restaurant touch that ensures crisp greens.

VINAIGRETTE

- 1/2 cup vegetable oil or mild olive oil
- 1/4 cup juice from 2 lemons, plus 1 teaspoon grated lemon zest
- 2 tablespoons chopped fresh thyme leaves
- 2 tablespoons chopped fresh mint leaves
- 1 medium garlic clove, minced or pressed through a garlic press (about 1 teaspoon)
- 1 teaspoon sugar
- Salt and ground black pepper

SALAD

- Salt
- 1 cup snow peas, trimmed
- 1 cup baby carrots, halved lengthwise
- 2 ears corn, husks and silk removed
- 2 quarts loosely packed mixed mesclun greens
- 1 tablespoon coarsely chopped fresh basil leaves
- 1 tablespoon chopped fresh chives
- 2 medium ripe tomatoes, cored and sliced thin
- ½ pound smoked trout, flaked with a fork

1. FOR THE VINAIGRETTE: Process all of the vinaigrette ingredients except the salt and pepper in a blender until smooth, about 30 seconds. Season with salt and pepper to taste and set aside.

2. FOR THE SALAD: Bring 3 quarts of water and 2½ teaspoons salt to a boil in a large saucepan. Fill a large bowl with ice water. Add the snow peas to the boiling water and cook until tender, 1 to 1½ minutes. Using a wire skimmer, transfer the snow peas to the ice bath and cool completely, about 30 seconds. Transfer the snow peas to a paper towel–lined baking sheet; blot to dry. Add the carrots to the pan and cook until tender, 4 to 5 minutes. Transfer to the ice bath and cool completely, about 30 seconds. Transfer the carrots to the same baking sheet, lined with more paper towels and blot to dry. Add the corn to the pan and cook until tender, about 4 minutes. Add the corn to the ice bath and cool completely, about 2 minutes. Working with one ear at a time, stand it on end inside a large bowl and, using a paring knife, cut the kernels off the cob (see the illustration on page 81).

3. Whisk the vinaigrette to recombine. In another large bowl, toss the greens, basil, and chives with ¼ cup of the vinaigrette until lightly coated. Spread the greens on a large platter. Arrange the snow peas, baby carrots, corn kernels, and tomatoes in rows across the top of the greens. Drizzle the remaining vinaigrette over the vegetables and scatter the trout evenly over the top. Serve immediately.

Roasted Beet Salad *with* Toasted Pine Nuts & Arugula

Adapted from Roasted Beet Salad with Toasted Pine Nuts and Arugula

Acacia, Richmond, Virginia

A SALAD COMPOSED OF ROASTED BEETS, arugula, and pine nuts is typical of Acacia's Mediterranean-inspired menu—clean, simple dishes highlighting top-notch, seasonal ingredients. It's a felicitous combination of flavors and textures: the sweet, earthy flavor of the cumin-scented beets is accented by the peppery arugula, acid-sharp vinaigrette, and rich pine nuts. Such an uncomplicated salad required little input from us outside of streamlining the method.

Beets come in a variety of shapes, sizes, and colors, but the basic red beet is the best choice for this recipe since its assertive flavor stands up to arugula's potent bite. Try to purchase them with the greens still attached because the health of the greens is an accurate indication of the beets' age. Loose beets are often older beets from which the wilted greens have been trimmed. We have found little difference in flavor or texture between small and medium beets, though large beets can be tough in texture. They also take a good deal longer to cook. That said, we prefer medium-size beets (two to three inches in diameter) for this recipe, since they cook within an hour and require less preparation than smaller beets.

Roasting is the best method for cooking beets, since the high heat intensifies their sweetness. At Acacia, the chefs wrap the beets individually in aluminum foil and roast them at 400 degrees until they can easily be pierced with a knife—a sure sign of doneness. Prior to roasting, Acacia seasons the beets with olive oil, salt, and cumin seeds. We were skeptical that the flavors would penetrate the beets' skins, but they did: the beets were suffused with a mild hint of cumin. Fresh from the oven (the beets were tender within the hour), we removed the foil and cooled them to the point at which they could be comfortably peeled. And peeling couldn't be easier—the skins slipped right off.

The vinaigrette is a blend of sherry and balsamic vinegars, olive oil, mustard, and shallot. The recipe yielded a particularly tart vinaigrette, but when tasted with the greens and beets, the acidity was tamed. We found the balsamic and sherry vinegar combination unusual, but it paid off. The sweetness of the balsamic mellowed the sherry vinegar's sharpness, making it taste like a fine, aged sherry vinegar—but at a much more modest price. Acacia specifies regular olive oil for its mild flavor, and we agreed after tasting an unbalanced, bitter dressing made with extra-virgin olive oil. A small amount of mustard rounded out the dressing, lending piquancy and sweetness. While we found it wasn't imperative to make the dressing in a blender, it did provide the most thorough emulsification.

For the salad greens, we found that young, mild arugula was the most complementary choice, accenting the beets' sweet flavor without overpowering them. Young arugula can be found prewashed and bagged in some markets, though it's more often found bundled with the roots still attached. Because of its sandy growing medium, it's important to soak and rinse arugula thoroughly.

For serving, we tossed the arugula with the dressing and placed small mounds on each plate. We then added the wedges of beets in a tidy pile and garnished the salad with the pine nuts.

Roasted Beet Salad with Toasted Pine Nuts and Arugula

SERVES 4 TO 6

Pay close attention to the pine nuts as they toast: their high fat content means that they can burn quickly. The beets and vinaigrette can be prepared up to a day ahead of time and stored in an airtight container in the refrigerator. Toss the beets with the vinaigrette just before serving; otherwise the sharp vinaigrette will overpower the beets' subtle flavor.

- **2 pounds medium red beets, tops and bottoms trimmed**
- **1 teaspoon cumin seeds**
- **Salt**
- **7 tablespoons olive oil (not extra-virgin)**
- **1/3 cup pine nuts**
- **2 tablespoons sherry vinegar**
- **1 1/2 teaspoons balsamic vinegar**
- **1 teaspoon Dijon mustard**
- **Ground black pepper**
- **1 tablespoon minced shallot**
- **3 quarts loosely packed arugula, stems trimmed (about 10 ounces)**

1. Adjust an oven rack to the middle position and heat the oven to 400 degrees. Toss together the beets, cumin seeds, 1 teaspoon salt, and 1 tablespoon olive oil in a large bowl. Wrap each beet separately in aluminum foil and place on a rimmed baking sheet. Cook the beets until soft and easily pierced with a paring knife or skewer, about 1 hour. Once the beets are cool enough to handle, peel them by rubbing them with a paper towel—the skin should slide right off. Cut each beet into 6 or 8 wedges.

2. Toast the pine nuts in a large skillet over medium heat, stirring frequently, until light golden, 5 to 6 minutes. Transfer the nuts to a small bowl and set aside.

3. Process the remaining 6 tablespoons olive oil, sherry vinegar, balsamic vinegar, mustard, ¼ teaspoon salt, and a pinch of pepper in a blender until fully emulsified, 20 to 30 seconds. Stir in the shallot and adjust the seasoning with salt and pepper. Toss the beets with 2 tablespoons of the vinaigrette in a medium bowl.

4. Toss the arugula with the remaining vinaigrette in a large bowl. Divide the arugula equally among chilled salad plates and top with the beets. Sprinkle with the pine nuts and serve immediately.

WINTER SALAD *with* BLUE CHEESE & CANDIED PECANS

Adapted from Fore Street's 2002–2003 Winter Salad

FORE STREET RESTAURANT, PORTLAND, MAINE

THIS RECIPE WON RAVE REVIEWS AMONG our tasters in the test kitchen. Perfect for the winter months, as its name implies, this salad combines the complementary colors and textures of Belgian endive and radicchio with a bright vinaigrette, lightly spiced pecans, sliced apple, and creamy blue cheese. The recipe's elegant flavor and pleasing appearance belie its ease of preparation. The chef, Sam Hayward, specified difficult-to-find ingredients. We tried the recipe using produce and cheese found at the supermarket and found the outcome just as tempting.

The two lettuces called for in this recipe, Belgian endive and radicchio, are the most commonly available members of their related plant families, *Cichorium intybus* and *C. endivia,* respectively. Given his relationship with growers and distributors, Chef Hayward is able to use varieties of these plants not commonly available to the home cook.

The recipe originally called for two varieties of these greens, Rosa di Treviso and Magdeburg. Unable to locate these specific varieties in our local supermarket, we selected the readily available round radicchio and pale green and white Belgian endive. Both worked very well and imparted the intended flavors and textures of their reclusive relatives. Our tasters, who sampled the salad in January, agreed with Chef Hayward, who chooses the endive and radicchio for their "certain 'tonic' quality from which the New England temperament benefits in cold weather." Perfect for a winter salad!

Hayward also specified Berkshire Blue, a blue-veined cheese made from Jersey cow's milk in the Great Barrington area of Massachusetts. Because this cheese is difficult to find and quite expensive, he also recommended other, more widely available, artisanal brands, such as Maytag Blue and Great Hill Blue. In the test kitchen, we tried the salad with these, and other less expensive brands. Although Maytag Blue was among our favorites, we found the salad delicious with any number of blue cheeses.

For making the candied pecans, the restaurant calls for simple syrup, a boiled mixture of sugar and water that restaurants invariably have on hand and use in any number of savory and sweet applications. Since the home cook generally does not keep a supply of simple syrup at the ready, we devised a method in the test kitchen for preparing the exact amount of the mixture required for the spicy pecans. Combining 1 tablespoon of sugar with the same amount of water and bringing the mixture to a boil in the microwave produces just enough syrup to coat the pecans perfectly.

The crostini are baguette slices toasted in the oven until lightly crisp, then brushed with extra-virgin olive oil. For serving, the dressed salad is placed on top of the crostini, allowing some of the vinaigrette to flavor the toast.

Winter Salad with Blue Cheese and Candied Pecans

SERVES 6

The pecans and croutons can be made ahead and stored in an airtight container at room temperature (for the pecans, up to 5 days; the croutons, up to 1 day). This colorful, flavorful salad is perfect for the winter holidays.

- **8 ounces (about 2 cups) pecans**
- **1 tablespoon sugar**
- **7 tablespoons extra-virgin olive oil**
- **Salt and ground black pepper**
- **1/8 teaspoon ground allspice**
- **1 French baguette, cut into twelve 1/2-inch-thick slices on the bias**
- **1 small McIntosh apple**
- **3 medium heads Belgian endive, root ends trimmed and leaves separated**
- **2 heads radicchio, root ends trimmed and leaves separated**
- **1 tablespoon cider vinegar**
- **1 teaspoon sherry vinegar**
- **2 ounces mild blue cheese, crumbled (about 1/2 cup)**

1. Adjust an oven rack to the middle position and heat the oven to 350 degrees. Place the pecans in a medium bowl and set aside. Combine the sugar with 1 tablespoon water in a small, microwave-proof bowl. Microwave on high until the sugar mixture comes to a boil, about 15 seconds. Stir and continue to microwave on high until the sugar is completely dissolved, 15 to 30 seconds longer. Pour the hot sugar mixture over the pecans and toss to combine. Pour 2 tablespoons of the olive oil, ¼ teaspoon salt, ⅛ teaspoon pepper, and the allspice over the pecans and toss to combine. Spread the pecans on a rimmed baking sheet in a single layer. Toast until the pecans are fragrant and begin to brown, 5 to 10 minutes. Remove the pecans from the oven and cool.

2. Increase the oven temperature to 400 degrees. Arrange the baguette slices in a single layer on another baking sheet and bake until dry and crisp, about 10 minutes, turning the bread slices over halfway through the cooking time. Remove the baguette slices from the oven, drizzle with 2 tablespoons of the remaining olive oil, and set aside.

3. Quarter and core the unpeeled apple. Cut each quarter into ⅛-inch-thick slices. Toss the apple with the endive and radicchio in a large bowl. Whisk the remaining 3 tablespoons olive oil, cider vinegar, sherry vinegar, ½ teaspoon salt, and ⅛ teaspoon pepper together in a small bowl. Pour the dressing over the endive mixture and toss thoroughly to coat.

4. To serve, fan two toasted baguette slices, just off center, on individual plates. Arrange the endive salad in tall piles on top of the toasts in the center of the plates, leaving the ends of the toasts exposed. Sprinkle the salads with the pecans and blue cheese. Serve immediately.

Chicken-Fried Oysters *with* Warm Spinach, Apple, & Bacon Salad

Adapted from Chicken-Fried Oysters with Applewood-Smoked Bacon and Hollandaise Sauce

Silo Elevated Cuisine, San Antonio, Texas

IF IT'S TRUE WHAT THEY SAY ABOUT Texas—that everything is bigger there—then this appetizer of "chicken-fried" oysters with applewood bacon, sautéed apples, wilted spinach, and mustardy hollandaise sauce from San Antonio's Silo Elevated Cuisine is right at home. It is a spectacle of an appetizer, packed with complex flavors: the mild, oceanic flavor of the oysters is sharpened by tart, seared apple and smoky bacon bits, and the mineraly spinach further deepens the oysters' iodine edge. Buttery hollandaise finishes the dish with a creamy lushness and mustardy tang. With its multiple components and laborious prep work, this is the sort of appetizer best left to the professionals in a fully staffed kitchen. However, we created a pared-down version, true to the original flavors but simpler in preparation. We didn't alter the oysters—the star of the dish—but transformed the wilted spinach into a spinach salad garnished with bacon bits and apple and the hollandaise sauce into a warm, mustard-flavored vinaigrette.

The French term *mise en place* means a lot of things to restaurant chefs, but the overarching concept is that of readiness and organization. Be prepared for what you are about to cook. A dish like this appetizer, with its various components and steps, requires careful mise en place. Our first step, then, was to identify the ingredients and cooking times of each component of the appetizer. Once we had the facts straight, we could get down to the nitty-gritty of prep work and cooking. Our reinterpretation of Silo's appetizer has three components: the chicken-fried oysters; the salad of spinach, bacon, and sautéed apple; and the warm vinaigrette. The oysters needed to be hot and crisp, so we decided they would be the last item cooked (though the coating could be assembled early); the salad ingredients would be first.

In Silo's recipe, the bacon and apple are sautéed together, the bacon turning crisp and the apples browning. We found we had better control over each ingredient when we cooked them separately. Cooking the bacon first rendered plenty of fat in which the apples could be browned (and the bacon fat lent the apples great flavor). Silo's recipe specifies applewood bacon, a mildly smoked bacon that is widely available. If it's inaccessible in your area, standard bacon is acceptable (Oscar Mayer was the winner in a *Cook's Illustrated* tasting several years back). Briefly freezing bacon—10 to 15 minutes—firms it up and enables clean slicing. For apples, Granny Smiths are the best choice for their crisp texture and tart flavor. For spinach, tasters favored bagged baby spinach because it's convenient and has a delicate flavor and texture.

We employed the same ingredients for the vinaigrette that flavor the hollandaise sauce (namely champagne vinegar and mustard), but replaced the butter—for obvious reasons—with neutral-tasting canola oil. Warming the vinaigrette in the skillet in which the bacon and apple were cooked served two purposes: the hot vinaigrette would slightly soften the spinach and the liquid would release any *fond* (flavorful browned bits) left from the apples.

"Chicken-fried" refers to the method in which the oysters are coated in seasoned flour and fried. Silo seasons the flour mixture with ground bay leaves, celery seeds, cayenne, and black pepper, lending the oysters the unmistakable flavor of a certain fast-food fried chicken. If you can't find ground bay leaves, whole bay leaves can be ground in a spice mill. However, it's important to sift them through a fine-mesh strainer to remove any large pieces—a big bite of bay leaf is an unpleasant surprise.

Shucked oysters can be found in fish markets and some supermarkets, but we suggest you call before making the trip. Silo's recipe specifies pan-frying the oysters, but we found it much safer and easier to deep-fry them in a tall Dutch oven. In a shallow skillet, the oysters sputtered in the hot oil and made a greasy mess—much less of an issue in a professional kitchen with someone else cleaning up the mess. Conventionally, we deep-fry between 350 and 360 degrees, but from experience we knew oysters are a special case. Because of their delicate texture and high moisture content, an extremely high oil temperature is necessary to brown the crust before the oyster overcooks. Silo's recipe specified 375 degrees, but we had better results with 400 degrees. In less than two minutes, the exterior crust was lightly browned and the interior oyster was firmed, yet still juicy and tender.

With all of the components hot and ready to eat, it was just a matter of plating. At Silo, the chefs arrange the oysters on top of the salad and drizzle the hollandaise sauce over them. We found that we preferred dressing the salad first, then arranging the oysters over the top. Silo also scatters chives over the finished dish, which tasters found superfluous in our reinterpretation.

Chicken-Fried Oysters with Warm Spinach, Apple, and Bacon Salad

SERVES 6 TO 8

If you prefer to shuck your own oysters, feel free: you will need two dozen. If you use small Olympia or Kumamoto oysters, you will need to increase the volume by half. We found a spider (see page 9) adept at retrieving fried oysters from the Dutch oven, since the thin wire doesn't hold oil. Otherwise, use a long-handled, slotted spoon or tongs. Because of the oysters' high moisture content, they do not stay crisp for long once fried and are best served immediately.

OYSTERS

- 1 ½ cups unbleached all-purpose flour
- 1 teaspoon cayenne pepper
- 1 teaspoon ground bay leaf or 4 whole bay leaves, ground in a spice grinder, unprocessed pieces removed

- 1 teaspoon celery seeds
- Salt and ground black pepper
- 2 pints shucked oysters, drained
- 1 cup buttermilk

- 4 cups canola oil, for frying the oysters

SPINACH SALAD

- 1 tablespoon whole-grain Dijon mustard
- 5 tablespoons canola oil
- 2 tablespoons champagne vinegar
- 2 teaspoons mild-flavored honey
- 4 dashes Tabasco sauce
- Salt and ground black pepper
- 4 slices bacon (about 4 ounces), diced
- 2 medium Granny Smith apples, peeled, cored, and diced medium (about 2 cups)
- 1 (10-ounce) bag baby spinach, washed and dried

1. FOR THE OYSTERS: Combine the flour, cayenne pepper, bay leaf, celery seeds, 1 teaspoon salt, and 1 teaspoon pepper in a medium bowl. Set aside. In a medium bowl, combine the oysters and buttermilk, then cover and refrigerate for at least 30 minutes and up to 1 hour.

2. FOR THE SALAD: Whisk together the mustard, canola oil, champagne vinegar, honey, and Tabasco sauce in a small bowl until emulsified. Season with salt and pepper to taste and set aside.

3. Cook the bacon in a large, nonstick skillet over medium-high heat, stirring frequently, until the fat is rendered and the bits have browned, about 5 minutes. Using a slotted spoon, transfer the bacon to a plate lined with several layers of paper towels and set aside. Drain all but 1 tablespoon of bacon fat from the skillet, then add the apples to the skillet. Cook the apples until lightly browned, stirring frequently, 3 to 4 minutes. Transfer to a small bowl and set aside. Set the skillet aside—do not wash it.

4. Drain the oysters, shaking off excess buttermilk. Add half of the oysters to the flour mixture and toss to coat. Transfer the oysters to a large, wire-mesh strainer and shake to remove the excess flour. Place the oysters on a wire rack set over a rimmed baking sheet. Repeat with the remaining oysters.

5. Heat the canola oil in a Dutch oven over medium-high heat until it reaches 400 degrees. (Use an instant-read thermometer that registers high temperatures or clip a candy/deep-fat thermometer onto the side of the pan before turning on the heat.) Add half of the oysters and fry, stirring frequently to prevent sticking, until golden brown, 1 to 2 minutes, adjusting the heat as necessary to maintain the cooking temperature. Using a slotted spoon or spider, transfer the oysters to a plate lined with several layers of paper towels and repeat with the remaining oysters.

6. Add the vinaigrette to the reserved skillet and heat over medium-high heat until the vinaigrette is bubbling, scraping up any browned bits from the bottom of the pan, 1 to 2 minutes. Divide the spinach equally among individual salad plates and drizzle with the warm vinaigrette. Sprinkle the bacon bits and sautéed apples over the salads and then divide the oysters equally among the plates. Serve immediately.

INGREDIENTS: Cooking Oils

To keep oils from becoming rancid, buy small quantities that will be used up within a few months. Close the bottles airtight and store them in a cool, dark place. Storing oils in the refrigerator will prolong their freshness.

The term ***cold-pressed*** (or ***expeller-pressed***) means that oil-making ingredients are pressed into a paste using mechanical wheels or hammers and are then kneaded to separate the oil from the fruit, nut, seed, etc. Many commercial oils are not cold-pressed, but rather extracted from raw materials using heat and chemical solvents, which damages their quality—the flavor and aroma of cold-pressed oils are generally superior to those of refined oils. Examine the fine print on labels to determine how an oil has been produced. Manufacturers that use cold-pressing techniques normally indicate so on their labels and in advertising.

VEGETABLE OIL

Loosely speaking, vegetable oil is an edible oil made from any number of "vegetable" (as opposed to "mineral") sources, including nuts, grains, beans, seeds, and olives. In the more narrow confines of recipe writing, it usually refers to one of the more popular brands of cooking oil in the supermarket whose front label reads "Vegetable Oil" in large type. On closer inspection of the small type on the back label, you'll usually find that these generic vegetable oils contain soybean oil. "Vegetable oil" is often the ingredient of choice in recipes that call for an oil with no flavor.

CANOLA OIL

Canola is the commercial name for oil extracted from the seeds of the rapeseed plant, a relative of *Brassica* vegetables (such as cabbage, broccoli, and cauliflower). The popularity of canola oil can be attributed to its very low saturated fat content. The relatively high smoke point of this oil combined with its unremarkable flavor makes it perfect for many cooking applications. If used raw, as for salad dressing, this bland oil is best used to soften a particularly strong nut or seed oil, especially sesame or walnut.

CORN OIL

Corn oil, made from the germ of corn kernels, is a very common all-purpose cooking oil with a high smoke point and a fairly neutral flavor. Corn oil is typically used for sautéing and deep-frying. The primary ingredient in many margarines, corn oil is also used commercially for making salad dressing and mayonnaise.

OLIVE OIL

There are four grades of olive oil: "extra-virgin," "virgin," "pure," and "olive pomace." The label "extra-virgin" denotes the highest-quality olive oil, with the most delicate and prized flavor. To be tagged as extra-virgin, an oil must meet three basic criteria. First, it must contain less than 1 percent oleic free fatty acids per 100 grams of oil. Second, the oil must not have been treated with any solvents or heat. (Heat is used to reduce strong acidity in some non-virgin olive oils to make them palatable.) Third, the oil must pass taste and aroma standards as defined by organizations such as the International Olive Oil Council

(IOOC). The acidity level of "virgin" oil is slightly higher than that of "extra-virgin." "Pure" oil, often labeled simply "olive oil," is the most commonly available—it is made by mixing refined olive oil with virgin olive oil. "Olive pomace" is bland, low-quality oil made by refining pressings left over after making extra-virgin and virgin olive oils. In the test kitchen, we usually cook with either supermarket extra-virgin or pure olive oil, reserving very fine, expensive, extra-virgin olive oil for drizzling over finished dishes or for salad dressings.

What's light olive oil? Despite the misleading name, light olive oils are nutritionally equivalent to regular olive oils. Several years ago, in an attempt to overcome the American perception that olive oil is too heavy and strong for everyday use, Italian companies began bottling a refined pure olive oil that has been stripped of its flavor. Although not sold in Italy, light olive oils were a hit with American consumers looking for oils high in monounsaturated fat but without much taste. Light olive oils can be used in any recipe that calls for a bland vegetable oil.

GRAPESEED OIL

A specialty oil that is becoming more and more popular in this country, grapeseed oil is particularly light in both taste and color and is said to have numerous health benefits. Grapeseed oil is, as its name implies, extracted from grape seeds. The oil's flavor tends to be bland and its smoke point, like most other cooking oils, is well above 400 degrees.

PEANUT OIL

Refined peanut oil has an especially high smoke point, making it ideal for deep-frying. Most peanut oils are refined and therefore have very mild (if any) peanut flavor.

SESAME OIL

There are two types of sesame oil: cold-pressed and roasted (also called toasted). Cold-pressed sesame oil is produced from raw sesame seeds and has a very light color and little aroma or flavor. It may be used interchangeably with other vegetable oils—even to cook foods. Roasted sesame oil, which has a low smoke point (it burns easily),

is not typically used to cook foods but rather as a flavoring agent. Roasted sesame oil is widely used in culinary applications throughout Asia and the Middle East. Generally referred to as dark, or Asian, sesame oil, it is produced from deeply roasted sesame seeds, which give it a dark brown color and rich, perfumed flavor. However, use roasted sesame oil in moderation—more than a tablespoon or two will overwhelm other ingredients.

Because roasted sesame oil is particularly prone to damage from heat and light, it should be purchased only in tinted glass bottles and stored in the refrigerator.

WALNUT OIL

This oil has a warm, nutty flavor that works well in salads with fruits and/or toasted nuts. (Walnut oil is very delicate and we do not recommend it for cooking.) Like other nut oils, walnut oil tends to go rancid quickly and is best stored in the refrigerator. Other popular nut oils include almond, hazelnut, macadamia, and pistachio.

CRAB, JICAMA, & MANGO SALAD *with* LEMON-CURRY VINAIGRETTE

Adapted from Crab, Jicama, and Mango Salad with Lemon-Curry Vinaigrette

JAY'S, DAYTON, OHIO

CRAB AND MANGO ARE TWO INGREDIENTS that draw a lot of eager tasters to the test kitchen. For many of us, crabmeat, like lobster, was a childhood treat to be savored on special occasions, and the giddy enthusiasm when crab is served remains with us still. Mango, once rare in local markets, is now ubiquitous and has won over many fans with its sweet flavor and tender, juicy texture. This delicious salad combines the delicate flavors and succulent textures of crab and mango. Crispy jicama dice and a lightly acidic, warm vinaigrette raise the salad to a new level and make it an impressive, yet simple-to-make addition to a special meal.

This recipe calls for Dungeness crab, a Pacific crab found in waters from Alaska to Baja California. Because only adult males at least 6 ¼ inches long can be harvested, the crabs are particularly meaty and weigh at least 2 pounds and often more. The meat of the crabs, which are in their prime season during the winter, is so rich and firm-textured it is perhaps more akin to Maine lobster than to the blue crab that inhabits the Atlantic and Gulf waters. Because Dungeness crab is not always readily available, we tried the recipe with other kinds of crab. Tuna-style canned crab tasted horrible, while canned, pasteurized crab was both watery and bland. Frozen Alaskan crab was wet and stringy. Fresh Atlantic blue crabmeat tasted the best. For this salad, we preferred the large tender chunks of lump Atlantic blue crabmeat to its backfin form, which has a shredded texture.

While we've all grown to love mangoes and use them regularly in the kitchen, jicama remains underappreciated. A tuberous root vegetable with a crisp, crunchy texture and a taste that lies somewhere between an apple and a potato, jicama is widely used in Latin and Asian cuisines. Its omission in many American kitchens is unfortunate, for jicama can contribute a wonderful crunch and delicate flavor to recipes, as it does here. Even though we welcomed the addition of jicama and thought it worked well with the mango and crab, we found that the one cup of jicama originally called for in the recipe added a little too much crunch, so we reduced the jicama to three quarters cup. The soft texture and subtle sweetness of the mango, on the other hand, were so popular among the tasters that we increased the mango to one cup from the original three quarters cup.

Presentation requires no fancy tricks. The restaurant takes an informal approach and just spoons the crab mixture over the greens.

Crab, Jicama, and Mango Salad with Lemon-Curry Vinaigrette

SERVES 6

To concentrate the flavor of the red bell pepper, cut away the translucent, watery internal membranes as well as the white pith, following the illustrations on page 70. See below and page 120 for tips on dicing the mango and jicama.

- 1/4 cup lemon juice from 1 large lemon
- 1 teaspoon minced lemon zest
- 1 1/2 teaspoons champagne vinegar
- 1/3 cup sour cream
- 1 1/4 teaspoons curry powder
- Ground black pepper
- 1 pound Dungeness or lump Atlantic blue crabmeat, carefully picked over for shell fragments
- 1 large ripe mango, diced (about 1 cup)
- 1 small jicama, peeled and diced (about 3/4 cup)
- 1/4 medium red bell pepper, cored, seeded, inner membrane trimmed, and cut into 1/4-inch pieces (about 1/4 cup)
- 5 tablespoons minced fresh chives
- Salt

PREPARING JICAMA

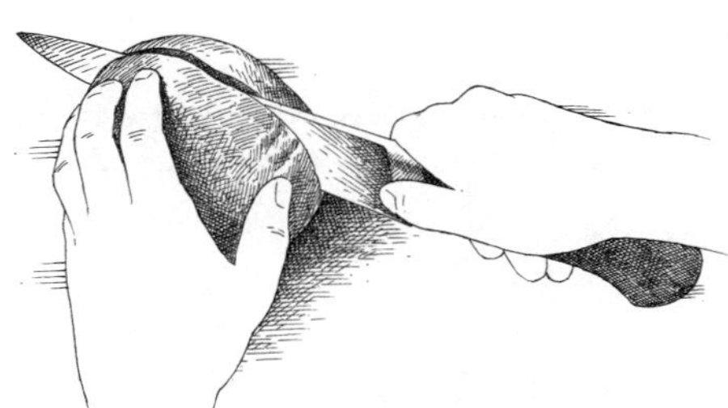

1. Slice the jicama in half through its equator.

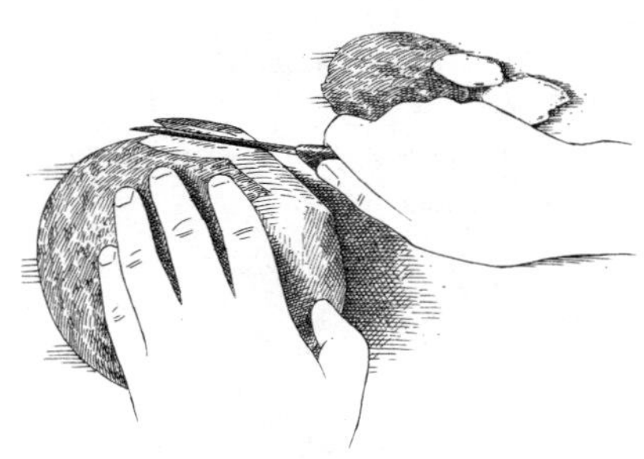

2. Placing the jicama cut-side down on the cutting board, use a paring knife to cut away the brown outer skin.

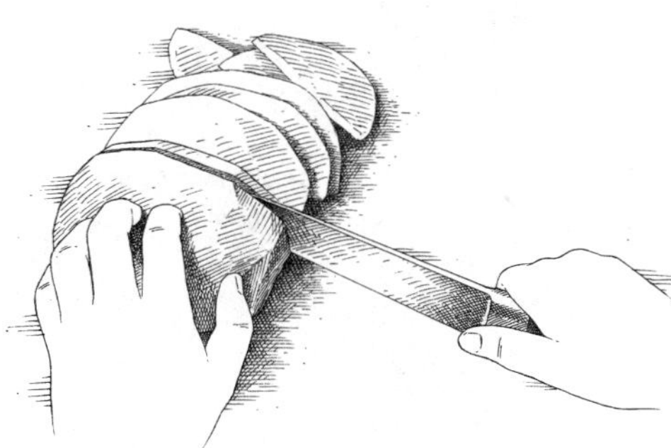

3. Slice the peeled jicama into 1/4-inch-thick disks.

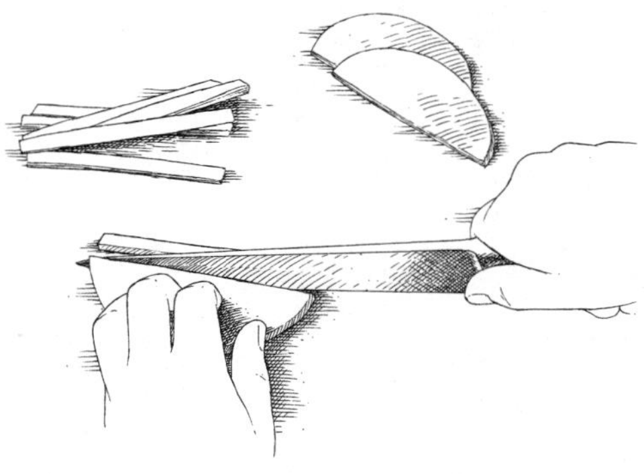

4. Cut each disk into 1/4-inch-thick lengths and dice.

12 cups (6 ounces) lightly packed fresh baby greens
1 lemon, cut into 6 wedges

1. Whisk the lemon juice, lemon zest, champagne vinegar, sour cream, curry powder, and ⅛ teaspoon pepper together in a small bowl and set aside.

2. Gently toss the crab, mango, jicama, red bell pepper, and 2 tablespoons of the minced chives together in a medium bowl. Add the lemon juice mixture to the crab mixture and toss gently to combine. Season with salt and pepper to taste. Cover tightly with plastic wrap and refrigerate until the mixture is well chilled and the flavors have melded, about 2 hours.

3. To serve, divide the baby greens among 6 individual plates. Stir the crab mixture to redistribute the dressing, then spoon 1 cup of the crab salad on top of each plate of greens. Sprinkle the salads with the remaining 3 tablespoons chives. Serve immediately, accompanied by the lemon wedges.

CUTTING MANGOES

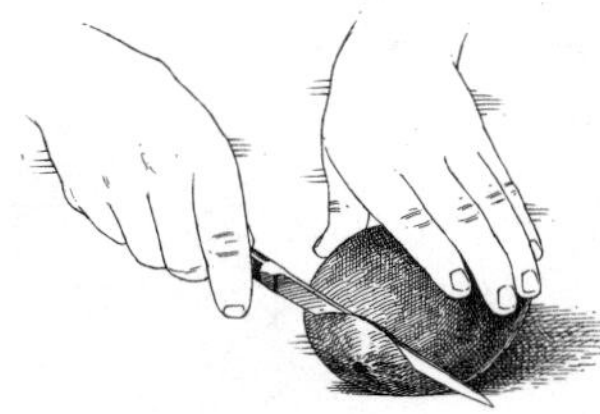

1. Start by removing a thin slice from one end of the mango so that it sits flat on a work surface.

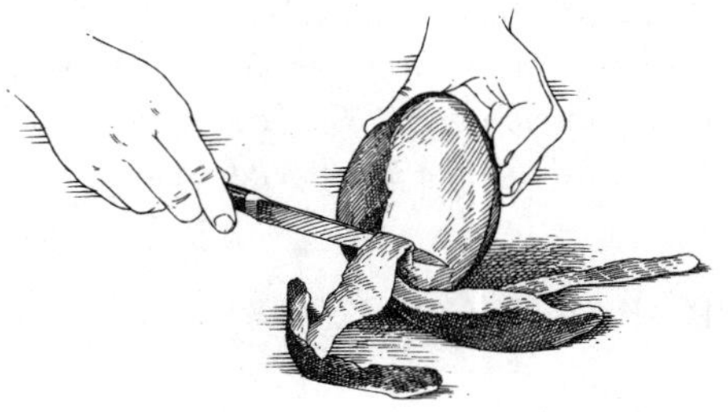

2. Hold the mango cut side down and remove the skin with a sharp paring knife in thin strips, working from top to bottom.

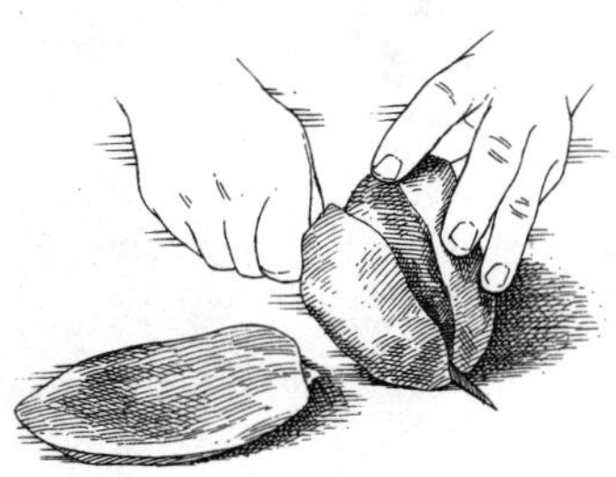

3. Cut down along the side of the flat pit to remove the flesh from one side of the mango. Do the same on the other side of the pit.

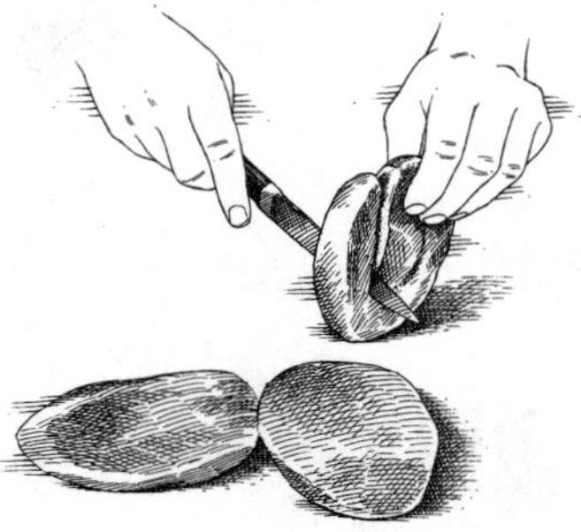

4. Trim around the pit to remove any remaining flesh. The mango flesh can now be chopped or sliced as desired.

2 MAIN COURSES

Main Courses

Pasta, Vegetarian, and Brunch

Poultry

Meat

Fish and Shellfish

Potato Gnocchi *with* Sage Butter & Chives

Adapted from Potato Gnocchi with Sage Butter and Chives

Restaurant Dennis Foy, Point Pleasant Beach, New Jersey

POTATO GNOCCHI ARE CLASSIC ITALIAN dumplings that can be either light and flavorful or bland sinkers in a sea of sauce. This recipe from Dennis Foy yields gnocchi that are tender in the center with a crisp, brown exterior and great potato flavor. Bathed in sage-infused butter and finished with manchego cheese and fresh chives, the resulting dish is simple, yet satisfying.

We found there are a few tricks to making successful gnocchi, the first of which is finding the right potato and the best method for cooking it. Russet potatoes, boiled in their jackets and riced, yielded a mash that retained too much moisture, requiring that more flour be added to the dough. This produced heavier gnocchi than we were looking for—not ideal for a dumpling that is to be sautéed and served in a delicate sauce. Baking the potatoes, then cooling and ricing them, produced the light, fluffy, dry potato base necessary for firm-textured gnocchi. This method required less flour to form a dough that was easy to roll and cut.

Gnocchi are often paired with cheese and herbs, and in this case the cheese of choice is Spain's most famous. Manchego is a semi-hard sheep's milk cheese with a peppery bite, suitable for grating and melting. Manchego is available in most grocery stores, at various stages of ripeness. The youngest cheeses are creamier in texture, the more aged are sharper in flavor and firmer, making them a better choice for grating and for use in this recipe. The addition of some of the cheese to the dough itself lends a distinct creaminess and bite to the gnocchi. If you can't find manchego, a reasonable substitute would be a good-quality sharp cheddar.

Mixing and forming the gnocchi dough can be done by hand or in a standing mixer, as is done at Dennis Foy. We found that mixing the dough with a paddle attachment for a short period of time, just enough to incorporate the flour, did not overdevelop the gluten in the flour, as we had feared. The resulting dough was light and dry and easily formed into ropes with little need for extra flour on the work surface. Adding just enough flour to form a firm dough is crucial, since too much flour will yield heavy dumplings and not enough means the dough will not hold together. The amount of flour added is determined by the moisture in the potato; just watch the dough and stop adding flour when the mixture forms a smooth ball. While some recipes advise creating an indentation or ridges in the gnocchi, both for even cooking and sauce absorption, we found these steps unnecessary since these gnocchi are cut on the diagonal into fairly short pieces and cooked evenly throughout when poached for two to three minutes. After poaching, the gnocchi are immediately transferred to an ice bath (a bowl filled with ice water) to stop them from cooking further, then drained and set on a dish towel to dry while the infused butter is prepared.

To incorporate fresh sage into the recipe without the bitterness of the raw leaves, we fried whole leaves in hot olive oil to a delicate crunch, which infused the oil with the robust flavor of the herb. While the majority of gnocchi recipes heat the dumplings through in butter or oil, Dennis Foy's recipe instructed us to pan-fry the gnocchi in the sage-flavored oil left in the hot pan. This step eliminated the characteristic starchiness and created a crisp, golden shell enclosing a moist, tender interior. Chicken broth and butter are then added to the pan with the gnocchi to form a sauce. The sauce is light and just barely coats the gnocchi so they retain their crisp exterior. The dish is finished with more of the tangy manchego cheese and chopped fresh chives.

Potato Gnocchi with Sage Butter and Chives

SERVES 6 TO 8 AS A MAIN COURSE

For light (as opposed to leaden) gnocchi, be sure to let the potatoes cool before adding the flour and use a light hand when mixing. The dough can be prepared ahead of time and refrigerated. You can double the recipe and freeze half for later use.

4 medium russet potatoes (about 2 pounds), scrubbed and pierced with a fork
6 ounces manchego cheese, grated (about 1 1/2 cups)
3/4–1 cup unbleached all-purpose flour, plus extra for dusting
Salt
3 tablespoons extra-virgin olive oil
18 fresh sage leaves
1/4 cup low-sodium chicken broth
2 tablespoons unsalted butter, cut into 4 pieces
Ground black pepper
2 tablespoons chopped fresh chives

1. Adjust an oven rack to the middle position and heat the oven to 350 degrees. Place the potatoes directly on the oven rack and bake until a paring knife can be inserted into the center of a potato with little resistance, about 1 hour. Transfer the potatoes to a cutting board and slice them in half lengthwise. Cool the potatoes completely, about 30 minutes.

2. Process the cooled potatoes through a food mill or ricer (it's fine if some flecks of peel pass through) into the workbowl of a standing mixer. Add half of the cheese and mix using a paddle attachment until evenly incorporated, about 30 seconds. Add the flour, ¼ cup at a time, until you have a smooth, dry dough (add no less than ¾ cup, no more than 1 cup). Alternatively, you can mix the dough by hand with a wooden spoon.

3. Transfer the dough to a work surface very lightly dusted with flour, form it into a ball, and cut the ball into 8 equal pieces. Roll each piece into a ¾-inch-thick rope 12 inches long. If the rope won't hold together, return all the dough to the bowl and work in a little more flour; let the dough rest for 10 minutes before proceeding.

4. Cut each rope of dough into ¾-inch lengths on the bias (about 16 pieces each) and transfer them to a rimmed baking sheet lightly dusted with flour. (The gnocchi can be placed in a single layer on a baking sheet and refrigerated for several hours. Alternatively, the baking sheet can be placed in the freezer for about 1 hour. For longer storage, transfer the partially frozen gnocchi to a zipper-lock plastic bag or airtight container, seal, and freeze for up to 1 month.)

5. Bring 4 quarts water to a low boil in a large pot with 2 teaspoons salt. Have ready a large bowl or pot filled with ice water. Drop half of the gnocchi into the boiling water and cook until they float, 2 to 3 minutes. Using a slotted spoon, transfer the gnocchi to the ice water to cool for 30 seconds, then transfer to a rimmed baking sheet lined with a clean, dry dish towel. Repeat with the remaining gnocchi.

6. Heat the oil in a 12-inch nonstick skillet over medium-high heat until shimmering. Add the sage leaves and fry until they begin to turn a light golden color, about 2 minutes. Using a slotted spoon, transfer the sage leaves to a plate lined with paper towels and set aside. Add half of the gnocchi to the hot pan and sauté, stirring occasionally, until golden brown on all sides, 5 to 7 minutes. Remove to a dish and keep warm. Repeat with remaining gnocchi. When the second batch is sautéed, return the reserved gnocchi to the skillet. Add the broth and half of the fried sage leaves and simmer until slightly thickened, about 1 minute. Remove from the heat, add the butter, 1 piece at a time, and toss to combine. Season with salt and pepper to taste. Transfer to individual plates or a serving platter and sprinkle with the remaining manchego cheese and the remaining fried sage leaves and chives. Serve immediately.

CUTTING GNOCCHI

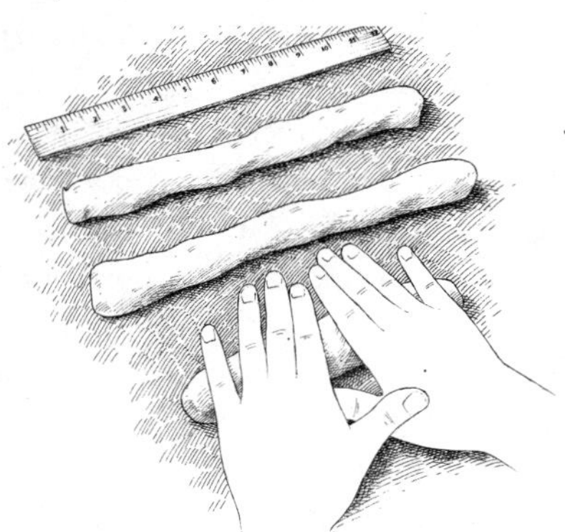

1. Working with one portion at a time, roll each ball of dough into a rope about ¾ inches wide by 12 inches long. Repeat with the remaining portions.

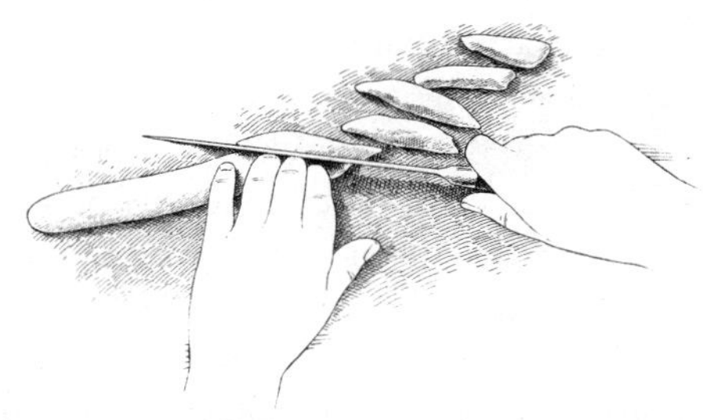

2. Using a sharp knife, cut the ropes into ¾-inch pieces on the bias. Each rope should yield about 16 pieces, for a total of 128 gnocchi.

BAKED RICOTTA-FILLED CRESPELLE *with* TOMATO SAUCE

Adapted from Manicotti (Baked Ricotta-Filled Crespelle with Tomato Sauce)

LIDIA'S, PITTSBURGH, PENNSYLVANIA

IN AN UNEXPECTED TWIST, THIS VERSION of manicotti from Lidia's uses crêpes flavored with lemon zest in place of pasta to lighten this traditional Italian-American comfort food. Easily made, the crêpes, or *crespelle* in Italian, envelop a ricotta, Parmesan, and mozzarella filling. A delicately flavored tomato sauce tops it off. The sauce, filling, and crespelle can be easily prepared in advance and assembled just before baking.

The restaurant adjusts the batter recipe to make the crespelle tender but sturdy enough to hold the cheese filling. It calls for less liquid than standard recipes and omits the traditional step of resting the batter. Less water produces slightly thicker crespelle, creating a formula for crespelle that are still tender, but not so fine that they are overpowered by the robust tomato sauce. It's important to use a nonstick omelet pan or skillet when cooking the crespelle. The crespelle will set and cook in a matter of seconds, so be ready to swirl the pan (immediately after pouring in the batter) so that the batter evenly covers the surface area of the pan.

Each crespelle is filled with a seasoned mixture of ricotta, mozzarella, and Parmesan. We found it best to drain the ricotta overnight in the refrigerator to extract excess liquid and keep the filling from becoming too thin. Place the cheese in a fine-mesh sieve set over a bowl, cover with plastic wrap, and refrigerate overnight. If you don't have time to drain the ricotta overnight, place the cheese in a sieve over a bowl and weigh it down with a plastic-wrapped can of tomatoes, or another heavy object, for 30 minutes. Alternatively, wrap the cheese in cheesecloth and squeeze to extract the excess liquid.

This recipe originally called for fresh tomatoes. We found that out-of-season fresh tomatoes made a sauce inferior to one made with canned tomatoes. Of the canned varieties, we preferred the livelier flavor of canned tomatoes packed in juice, not in puree or sauce. The recipe also called for seeding the tomatoes to produce a smooth sauce, unblemished by flecks of yellowish seeds. Since removing the seeds did not affect the flavor of the sauce, we decided to forgo the extra step. However, should you desire a seedless sauce, pass the tomatoes through a food mill fitted with the fine disk instead of using a food processor. Discard the residual tomato fiber and seeds. The resulting sauce will initially be quite thin but will thicken later over heat.

The tomato sauce cooks for about 40 minutes and reduces to three cups. It can be difficult to determine when the liquid has been reduced to the desired amount. In the test kitchen, we use a surefire method to get an accurate measurement. Before making your sauce, pour three cups of water in a saucepan. Place a clean, metal ruler in the water and note the mark the water reaches. Empty the pan to prepare the sauce. Periodically dip the ruler into the sauce to see if the sauce has been reduced to the right level.

Baked Ricotta-Filled Crespelle with Tomato Sauce

SERVES 6

A nonstick skillet is essential for making the crespelle. To drain the ricotta cheese, place the ricotta in a fine-mesh sieve set over a bowl, cover it with plastic wrap, and refrigerate overnight. If you don't have time to drain the ricotta overnight in the refrigerator, place the cheese in a fine-mesh sieve set over a bowl, cover it with plastic wrap, and weight it down for 30 minutes. Alternatively, wrap the cheese in cheesecloth and squeeze to extract the excess liquid.

TOMATO SAUCE

- **1 (28-ounce) can diced tomatoes packed in juice**
- **1 (14.5-ounce) can diced tomatoes packed in juice**
- **1/4 cup extra-virgin olive oil**
- **1 small onion, chopped fine (about 1/2 cup)**
- **1 small carrot, finely shredded on the small holes of a box grater (about 1/4 cup)**
- **1 small celery rib, chopped fine (about 1/4 cup)**
- **Salt**
- **2 bay leaves**
- **1/4 teaspoon red pepper flakes**

CRESPELLE

- **1 cup (5 ounces) unbleached all-purpose flour**
- **2 1/4 ounces (1 cup plus 2 tablespoons) grated Parmesan cheese**
- **1 teaspoon grated lemon zest from 1 medium lemon**
- **Salt**
- **1 cup whole milk**
- **4 large eggs**
- **2 tablespoons unsalted butter, melted, for coating the pan**
- **2 cups whole milk ricotta cheese, drained overnight (see headnote)**
- **6 ounces fresh mozzarella cheese, cut into 1/4-inch dice (about 1 cup)**
- **1/2 cup minced fresh parsley leaves**
- **1/4 teaspoon ground white pepper**
- **1/4 teaspoon freshly grated nutmeg**

1. FOR THE TOMATO SAUCE: Puree all the tomatoes and their juices in a food processor until smooth, about 8 seconds. Heat the olive oil in a medium, nonreactive saucepan over medium heat until shimmering. Add the onion and cook, stirring occasionally, until soft, about 3 minutes. Stir in the carrot, celery, and ½ teaspoon salt, and cook, stirring occasionally, until the vegetables are golden and lightly caramelized, about 10 minutes. Stir in the pureed tomatoes, bay leaves, and red pepper flakes. Increase the heat to high and bring to a boil. Reduce the heat to medium-low and simmer, stirring occasionally, until the sauce is thickened and reduced to 3 cups, about 40 minutes. Remove and discard the bay leaves. Adjust the seasoning with salt and set aside.

2. FOR THE CRESPELLE: Process the flour, 2 tablespoons of the Parmesan, lemon zest, ½ teaspoon salt, milk, and 2 of the eggs in a blender until smooth, about 5 seconds. Scrape down the sides of the blender jar and

process for 2 to 3 seconds more. Heat an 8-inch nonstick skillet over medium heat until fairly hot. Remove the pan from the heat and, using a pastry brush, lightly brush the pan with some of the melted butter. Pour 2½ tablespoons of the batter into the pan just off center and immediately swirl the pan to coat the bottom with batter. Return the pan to the heat and cook until the top of the crespelle is dry, about 1 minute. Loosen the edge of the crespelle with the tip of a plastic spatula, grab the edge of the crespelle with your fingers, and flip it. Cook on the second side until golden but not brown, about 30 seconds longer. Transfer the crespelle to a large plate and set aside. Repeat with the remaining batter, brushing the pan with melted butter as needed. Insert a square of parchment paper between each crespelle on the plate to prevent sticking. You should have 12 crespelle.

3. Adjust an oven rack to the middle position and heat the oven to 425 degrees. Mix the remaining 2 eggs, ricotta, mozzarella, ½ cup of the remaining Parmesan, parsley, 1 teaspoon salt, white pepper, and nutmeg in a large bowl until smooth.

4. TO ASSEMBLE THE MANICOTTI: Coat the bottom of a 13 by 9-inch baking pan with 1 cup of the tomato sauce. Place a crespelle on a clean, dry work surface. Spoon 3 tablespoons of the cheese filling along the end of the crespelle closest to you and roll it up loosely. Place the manicotti in the pan. Repeat with the remaining crespelle, arranging each seam-side down in the pan, in two rows widthwise, 6 manicotti per side. Spoon the remaining 2 cups tomato sauce on top of the manicotti and sprinkle with the remaining ½ cup Parmesan. Cover with aluminum foil and bake for 15 minutes. Uncover and bake for 15 minutes longer, or until golden. Serve the manicotti from the baking dish at the table.

MAKING CRESPELLE

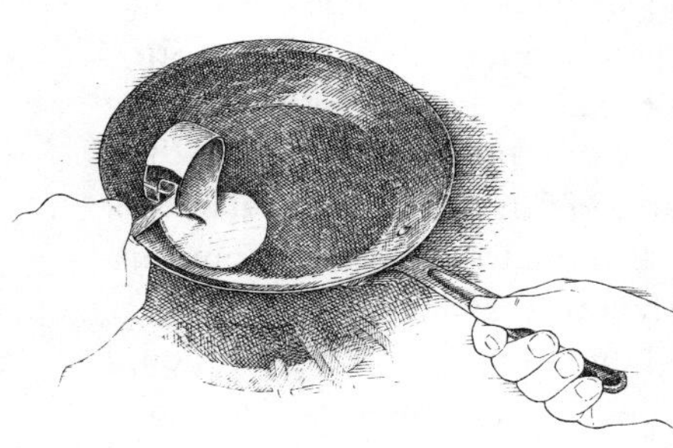

1. Using a ¼-cup measure just over half full, pour 2½ tablespoons of batter just off center in the bottom of an 8-inch nonstick pan.

2. Immediately swirl the pan to coat the bottom with batter.

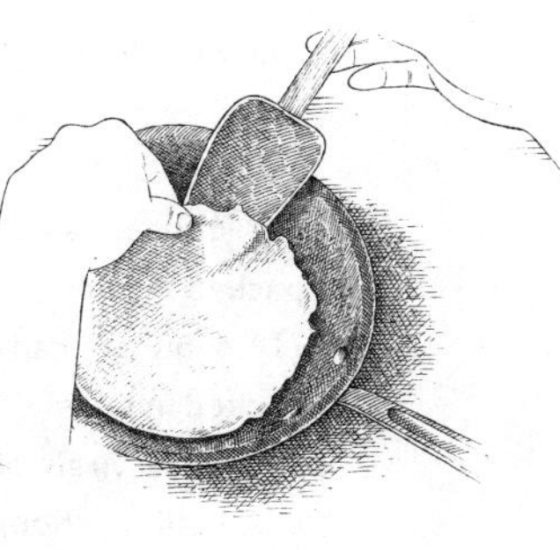

3. After about 1 minute, loosen the edge of the crespelle with a plastic spatula and, using your fingertips, grab the edge of the crespelle and flip it.

White Truffle–Scented Ravioli *with* Mascarpone & Peas

Adapted from White Truffle–Scented Ravioli with Mascarpone and Peas
NAHA, Chicago, Illinois

THE PROCESS OF MAKING RAVIOLI IS A laborious and time-consuming endeavor. In restaurants, there is often a person who spends his or her entire day making hundreds of ravioli for that evening's customers. In some cases, a restaurant might buy ravioli from a company that specializes in pasta. But for the home cook, neither is likely or possible. Moreover, for home cooks committed enough to spend time making ravioli, anything but a superior result can be frustrating. With this recipe from NAHA, however, these problems evaporate.

The flavors that this recipe produced were surprisingly subtle and light. The earthy, truffle-scented pasta blended perfectly with the creamy mascarpone and the sweet peas, while a light cream sauce provided richness without being overly heavy. Although this recipe produced flavorful ravioli, there were several items that needed to be altered before it could be deemed suitable for the home cook.

We started with the filling. The original recipe called for using English peas in the filling, but we opted to use frozen peas in order to maintain uniformity and ensure year-round availability. The peas were blanched and then pureed. This puree, in turn, was mixed with mascarpone to make the filling.

Next, we set to making the pasta itself, which was simple and straightforward. But we did run into problems when it came time to shape and fill the ravioli. Following the instructions in the recipe, we placed a tablespoon of filling within 1½-inch-diameter marks made on one sheet of pasta. This was then covered with another sheet of pasta, and the ravioli were cut out using a round cookie cutter. This procedure left us with many burst raviolis; there was too much filling for the size of the ravioli. We tried decreasing the amount of filling, and while this worked better, we ended up throwing away a lot of unused pasta. Searching for a way to make ravioli that were easier to fill and didn't create as large a quantity, we came upon an old story from a 1993 issue of *Cook's Illustrated,* in which square ravioli were made by folding a single sheet of pasta lengthwise over small piles of filling. The ravioli were then cut into pieces with a fluted pastry wheel, which served to seal them and leave a decorative edge. This method was the solution we were looking for. We were now able to assemble the ravioli in half the time, and since there was little waste we were able to make a larger quantity in this shorter time.

With the pasta prepared and filled, we looked next at the other ingredients that made up this dish. For the sauce, the original recipe called for equal parts of either chicken or vegetable broth and heavy cream to be reduced to "a small amount," into which a small amount of butter was incorporated before serving. Making the sauce with both chicken and vegetable broth, we found that tasters preferred the sauce made with chicken broth because it had a richer flavor, while the sauce made with vegetable broth tasted flat and tinny. We were also unsure just how far to reduce the sauce, so we tried the ravioli with three different sauces reduced to different consistencies. The sauce that was reduced from 3¾ cups to 2 cups provided the most flavor without tasting watery (like the sauce reduced to 3 cups) or becoming cloying (like the sauce reduced to 1 cup).

The garnishes used on the ravioli were the final component to which we turned our attention. The chef of NAHA called for both sautéed pea shoots and baby spinach leaves to be used on the plate. We used both in our initial test of the recipe, but considering that pea shoots can be hard for the home cook to procure and that the added flavor was minimal,

MAKING RAVIOLI

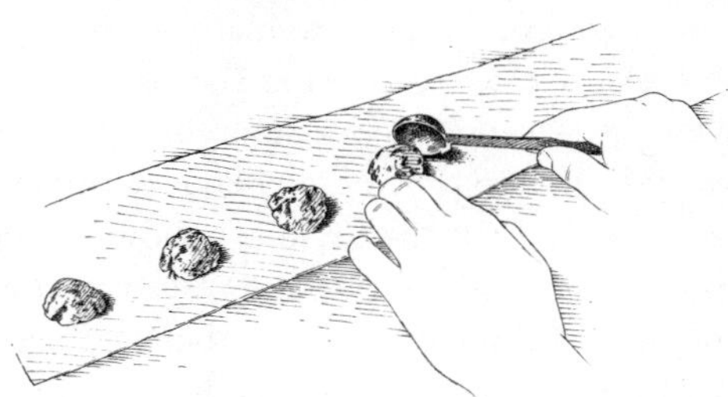

1. Use a pizza wheel or sharp knife to cut pasta sheets into long rectangles measuring 4 inches across. Brush the bottom half of the pasta sheet with the lightly beaten egg. Place about 1 rounded teaspoon in a line 1 inch from the bottom of the pasta sheet. Leave 1 ¼ inches between each ball of filling.

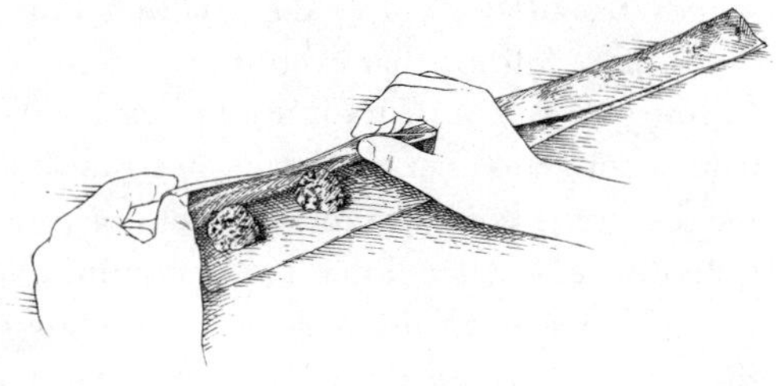

2. Fold over the top of the pasta and line it up with the bottom edge. Seal the bottom and the two open sides with your fingers. Gently press the pasta around the filling to press out any air pockets.

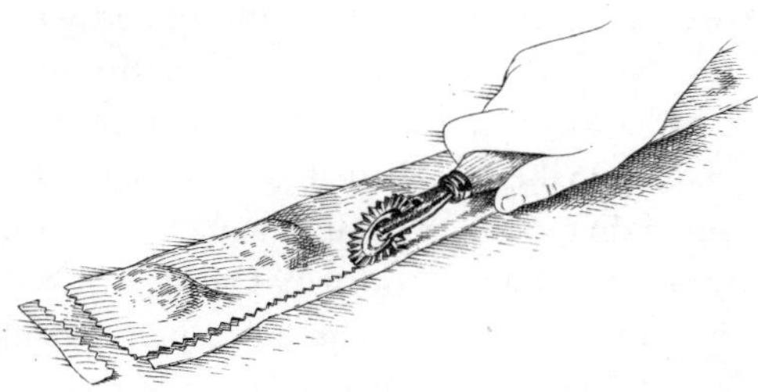

3. Use a fluted pastry wheel to cut along the two sides and bottom of the sealed pasta sheet.

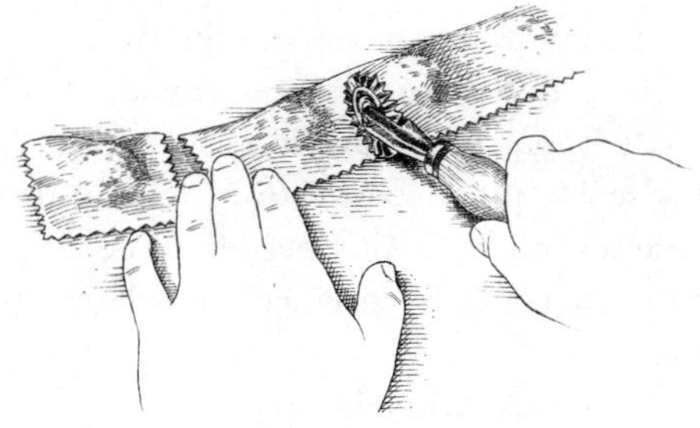

4. Run the pastry wheel between the balls of filling to cut the ravioli.

we decided it was better to stick with the spinach leaves—easier and just as nice. We also decided to forgo the homemade ricotta as a garnish. We found it relatively easy to replicate its flavor and consistency by using store-bought ricotta salata, a smooth, firm sheep's milk cheese, not unlike feta, thus saving time (and a whole gallon of milk).

White Truffle–Scented Ravioli with Mascarpone and Peas

SERVES 6 TO 8

A pasta machine is necessary for rolling the pasta sheets to the proper thinness. Take care to keep the pasta well covered when rolling and filling, because it is nearly impossible to make ravioli with dry pasta. To prevent your ravioli from bursting open when they're placed in the boiling water, press out any air pockets around the filling when sealing the pasta. See the illustrations on page 134 for tips on making pasta dough.

- **2 cups (10 ounces) unbleached all-purpose flour, plus extra for dusting**
- **Salt**
- **3 large eggs, plus 1 large egg, lightly beaten, for sealing the ravioli**
- **1 tablespoon white truffle oil**
- **1 1/2 cups frozen peas**
- **2 1/4 cups heavy cream**
- **1 1/2 cups mascarpone cheese**
- **Ground black pepper**
- **1 3/4 cups low-sodium chicken broth**
- **3 tablespoons unsalted butter, cut into 3 pieces**
- **1 cup baby spinach leaves**
- **3 ounces ricotta salata**

1. Pulse the flour and 1 teaspoon salt in the workbowl of a food processor to distribute evenly and aerate it. Add the eggs and the truffle oil and process until the dough forms a rough ball, about 30 seconds. (If the dough resembles small pebbles, add water, ½ teaspoon at a time; if the dough sticks to the side of the workbowl, add flour, 1 tablespoon at a time, and process until the dough forms a rough ball.)

2. Turn out the dough ball and small bits on a dry work surface; knead until the dough is smooth, 1 to 2 minutes. Form the dough into a flat square, wrap tightly with plastic wrap, and set aside to rest.

3. Bring 5 cups water to a boil in a small saucepan over high heat. Add 2 teaspoons salt and the peas and cook until soft and bright green, about 2 minutes. Drain the peas and immerse immediately in a bowl of ice water to chill. Transfer the peas to a large plate lined with several layers of paper towels and dry thoroughly. Measure ¼ cup of the peas into a small bowl and reserve for a garnish. Process the remaining 1¼ cups peas and ¼ cup of the heavy cream in a food processor until smooth, about twelve 1-second pulses. Transfer the pea mixture to a large bowl and, using a rubber spatula, combine with the mascarpone until uniform. Season with salt and pepper to taste. Cover tightly with plastic wrap and refrigerate until needed.

4. Bring the chicken broth and remaining 2 cups heavy cream to a boil in a medium saucepan over medium-high heat. Reduce the heat to medium and simmer until the mixture is reduced to 2 cups, about 20 minutes. Cover and set aside.

5. Unwrap the dough and cut it into quarters. Working with one piece at a time and keeping the remaining dough covered with plastic wrap so it doesn't dry out, slowly process the dough through a pasta machine, following the manufacturer's instructions (see also the illustrations on page 194), until the

dough is very thin but not translucent. Lay the rolled dough on a lightly floured work surface and cover loosely with plastic wrap. Repeat with the remaining pieces of dough.

6. Following the illustrations on page 132, fill and cut the ravioli from the sheets of pasta. Transfer the ravioli to a rimmed baking sheet dusted with flour. You should have about 50 ravioli.

7. Bring the cream sauce to a simmer and whisk in the butter, 1 tablespoon at a time, until incorporated. Season with salt and pepper to taste and keep warm.

8. Bring 1 gallon of water to a boil in a large pot. Add 1 tablespoon salt and half of the ravioli and cook until the doubled edges of the ravioli are al dente, 3 to 4 minutes. Meanwhile, divide the baby spinach among individual pasta bowls and pour about 2 tablespoons sauce over the top. Using a slotted spoon, transfer the cooked ravioli to the bowls and top with another 2 tablespoons sauce. Repeat the process with the remaining ravioli. Garnish with the reserved ¼ cup peas and shavings of ricotta salata. Serve immediately.

PASTA DOUGH DONE RIGHT

DRY DOUGH
If after 30 seconds of processing, the dough resembles small pebbles, it is too dry. With the motor running, add ½ teaspoon water. Repeat one more time if necessary.

WET DOUGH
If the dough sticks to the sides of the workbowl, it is too wet. Add 1 tablespoon flour at a time until the dough is no longer tacky.

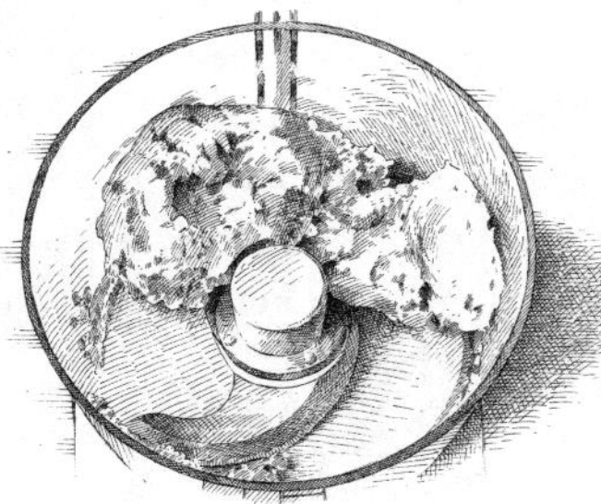

PERFECT DOUGH
Dough that has the right amount of moisture will come together in one large mass. If some small bits remain unincorporated, turn the contents of the workbowl onto a floured surface and knead them together.

Capellini di Mare

Adapted from Capellini di Mare

Biaggi's Ristorante Italiano, Cedar Rapids, Iowa

PASTA WITH SEAFOOD IS STANDARD FARE on many Italian menus. Unfortunately, the featured item in the dish is most often the pasta rather than the seafood. In this version from Biaggi's restaurant, the "fruits of the sea" take center stage, all married in a garlicky, pepper-infused, quick tomato sauce.

Initially, given a recipe intended to serve two, our first challenge was to figure out how best to cook the abundance of seafood required to serve six. While a 12-inch skillet was fine for the two-person recipe, trying to multiply that by three proved to be a disaster. Instead of cooking the seafood in a skillet, we opted for a large Dutch oven to accommodate the four different kinds of seafood. Because of the quantities involved and the individual cooking times of each component, we found it beneficial to cook each separately, then combine them at the last moment to ensure that none became overdone, as is often the case.

We started by selecting marshmallow-size scallops, requesting from our purveyor that they be of similar size to make the cooking times equal. If you find yourself with a jumble of sizes, cut the larger ones in half horizontally to simulate the others. We found that sautéing the scallops well on both sides contributed nice, brown, flavorful bits to the bottom of our pot, setting the foundation for the next ingredient to come, which was the shrimp. Sautéed in the same pot, the shrimp added their delicate flavor to the mix. When we removed the scallops and the shrimp from the Dutch oven, we were left with a base in which we started the quick tomato sauce. We added three tablespoons of oil, which was just enough to brown the garlic slightly and release the flavor from the chili flakes, then added the tomatoes and fresh basil.

Our next task was to figure out when to start cooking the pasta. Because angel hair is so delicate, we needed to be certain that we could easily coordinate finishing the sauce at just about the same time we drained the pasta. We decided that by adding the pasta to the boiling water as soon as the tomato sauce came to a simmer, we would be in sync with the mussels and squid that had yet to cook. As soon as the pasta was dropped into the boiling water, the mussels were added to the Dutch oven, covered, and left to cook until they began to open, about 2 minutes. The next ingredient to contribute to our timing troubles was the squid (or calamari). We've all had rubbery rings of restaurant squid, and we were soon to discover why. Squid needs to be cooked quickly over high heat (one to two minutes) or braised slowly in liquid over low heat (45 to 60 minutes). Anything in between yielded the tough rings we sought to avoid. We added the squid to the pot with the mussels during the last 2 minutes of cooking and were rewarded with tender, not chewy, rings. Off the heat, we stirred the scallops and shrimp into the pot with their juices and let them sit for one minute to let their flavors marry.

Capellini di Mare

SERVES 6 TO 8

One teaspoon of hot red pepper flakes gives the sauce a nice kick; add more to suit your taste. Ask for cleaned squid for this dish, making sure the quill-like cartilage has been removed. Home cooks will find that metal tongs are the best tool for turning the seafood, as restaurant cooks do.

- **5** **tablespoons extra-virgin olive oil**
- **18** **large sea scallops, tendons removed, patted dry with paper towels**
- **Salt and ground black pepper**
- **18** **large shrimp (31–40 per pound), peeled, deveined (see the illustration on page 48), and patted dry with paper towels**
- **6** **garlic cloves, minced or pressed through a garlic press (about 2 tablespoons)**
- **1** **teaspoon red pepper flakes**
- **1** **(28-ounce) can crushed tomatoes**
- **1/4** **cup chopped fresh basil leaves, plus 6–8 whole leaves for garnish**
- **1** **pound capellini or angel hair pasta**
- **36** **mussels, scrubbed and debearded (see the illustration on page 45)**
- **3/4** **pound cleaned squid, sliced crosswise into 1/2-inch rings, tentacles left whole**

1. Bring 4 quarts water to a boil in a large pot. Heat 1 tablespoon of the olive oil in a Dutch oven over medium-high heat until shimmering. Season the scallops with salt and pepper on both sides. Add the scallops flat-side down to the hot pan and cook until well browned, about 2½ minutes. Using tongs, turn the scallops over, one at a time, and cook until medium-rare (the sides have firmed up and all but the middle third of the scallops is opaque), about 30 seconds longer. Transfer the scallops to a rimmed baking sheet and set aside.

2. Add 1 tablespoon more olive oil to the hot Dutch oven. Add the shrimp and quickly spread them in a single layer. Cook, without stirring, until the bottoms of the shrimp turn pink, about 2 minutes. Using tongs, turn the shrimp over, one at a time, and cook until they are opaque, about 2 minutes longer. Transfer the shrimp to the rimmed baking sheet with the scallops and set aside.

3. Reduce the heat to low. Add the 3 remaining tablespoons olive oil to the hot Dutch oven. Stir in the garlic and red pepper flakes and cook until the garlic is sticky and golden, about 1 minute, scraping the bottom of the pot as needed. Stir in the tomatoes and the ¼ cup basil and bring to a simmer. Transfer ½ cup of the tomato sauce to a small bowl and set aside.

4. Add the pasta and 1 tablespoon salt to the boiling water. Stir to separate the pasta and cook until al dente, about 5 minutes. Drain and set aside. As soon as the pasta is added to the boiling water, add the mussels to the Dutch oven. Cover and cook until the mussels begin to open, about 2 minutes. Stir in the squid, cover, and simmer until the mussels are fully opened and the squid is cooked through, 1 to 2 minutes. Discard any mussels that do not open. Stir in the reserved scallops, shrimp, and accumulated juices. Cover, remove from the heat, and set aside for 1 minute. Toss the cooked pasta with the reserved ½ cup tomato sauce, then transfer it to a large platter. Top with the seafood and sauce. Garnish with the remaining basil leaves and serve immediately.

Creole-Style Pasta Alfredo *with* Crawfish

Adapted from Pasta with Crawfish and Tasso Monica

Drayton Place, Mobile, Alabama

THE COMBINATION OF CREAM, BUTTER, Parmesan cheese, and pasta is hard to beat. Most people recognize this combination by its more traditional name, pasta Alfredo. But Drayton Place has put an interesting spin on this classic dish. By adding tasso (a highly spiced cured pork shoulder), crawfish, and a healthy dose of blackening spice (a commercial blend of salt, onion and garlic powders, paprika, cayenne pepper, thyme, and oregano), the chefs have turned this Italian pasta into an innovative Creole creation.

The recipe from Drayton Place was full of bold flavors. The spicy, smoky tasso and the sweet crawfish paired surprisingly well with the rich flavors of the Alfredo sauce. However, we did feel that the thick richness of the sauce, a classic béchamel flavored with Parmesan, might be a little too decadent for some home cooks, so we looked for ways to lighten the sauce and perhaps streamline its preparation.

One way to thin the sauce was to use less roux, a mixture of butter and flour that is used to thicken béchamel. While we found that thinner sauce was somewhat lighter, the overall dish was still a bit heavier than we desired. It then occurred to us that if we omitted the roux-thickened sauce altogether and used straight cream, we might solve our problem.

On the subsequent test, we added straight cream to the pan, allowed it just to heat through, and then removed it from the heat. This sauce was then added to the cooked and drained pasta. The result was exactly what we had been looking for. We were able to keep the rich flavors of the sauce, and it coated the pasta beautifully, without being too heavy or goopy. In addition to making the sauce lighter, we had also omitted the two steps that had required any sort of lengthy cooking time. We were now able to produce the recipe in the time it took to boil the water and cook the pasta.

Other than the sauce, the main concern we had with this dish was the use of tasso and crawfish. Tasso is commonly found in the southern parts of the country, but is a little more difficult to find elsewhere. Although we located tasso in a specialty store, we found that andouille, a commonly available smoked pork sausage, can be substituted. We found the crawfish to be a little more readily available, mostly in the freezer section of the supermarket. But, as with the tasso, we were curious to see if there was a workable substitute. We tried using small "popcorn" shrimp. While they were a reasonable stand-in, their brininess wasn't quite the same as the sweet, delicate flavor provided by their freshwater counterparts. (In short, if you have to go a little out of your way to get crawfish, do so.)

The pasta, best served in wide, shallow pasta bowls, is garnished with a sprinkling of sliced scallions and diced tomatoes. Besides adding a burst of color to the plate, the two garnishes made for a nice contrast in flavor to the rich, creamy pasta. The scallions offered a fresh bite and the tomatoes a bright acidity, which put the finishing touches on an exceptional dish.

Creole-Style Pasta Alfredo with Crawfish

SERVES 4 TO 6

Tasso is a traditional component used often in Creole cooking and can be found in specialty food stores and high-end butcher shops, but andouille sausage can be substituted. Crawfish, another important Creole ingredient, can be found already cooked in the freezer section of many supermarkets and fish markets. Blackening spice is a Cajun spice mixture that can be found in the spice aisle of most supermarkets.

- 3 tablespoons olive oil
- 1 pound tasso, cut into 1/4-inch dice
- 1 pound cooked crawfish tails
- 3 tablespoons unsalted butter
- 2 medium shallots, minced (about 6 tablespoons)
- 1 tablespoon blackening spice, also called Cajun seasoning spice (such as Chef Paul Prudhomme's Blackened Redfish Magic)
- 1/4 teaspoon cayenne pepper
- 1 2/3 cups heavy cream
- 1 pound penne pasta
- Salt
- 1 cup grated Parmesan cheese
- 3 plum tomatoes, seeded and diced
- 2 scallions, both white and green parts, sliced thin

1. Bring 4 quarts water to a boil in a large pot. Heat 2 tablespoons of the olive oil in a 12-inch skillet over medium-high heat until shimmering. Add the tasso and sauté, stirring occasionally, until lightly browned, about 3 minutes. Using a slotted spoon, transfer the tasso to a medium bowl and set aside. Add the remaining 1 tablespoon olive oil and the crawfish to the skillet and sauté, stirring occasionally, until heated through, about 2 minutes. Transfer to the bowl with the tasso and set aside. Reduce the heat to medium, add the butter, shallots, blackening spice, and cayenne to the pan, and sauté, stirring frequently, until the butter has melted and the shallots have softened, about 3 minutes. Add the heavy cream to the pan along with the tasso and crawfish and bring to a bare simmer. Remove from the heat and set aside.

2. When the water comes to a boil, add the pasta and 1 tablespoon salt. Cook until almost al dente. Drain the pasta and return to the pan. Add the sauce, Parmesan, and ½ teaspoon salt. Cook over very low heat, tossing to combine the ingredients, until the sauce is slightly thickened, 1 to 2 minutes. Divide the pasta among warmed pasta bowls. Top each with a portion of tomatoes and scallions. Serve immediately.

Orecchiette *with* Lamb Ragù

Adapted from Orecchiette with Lamb Ragù

Dish, Pittsburgh, Pennsylvania

LAMB RAGÙ APPEARS IN VARIOUS FORMS throughout Italy. At Dish, the chefs use an ample amount of tomatoes and fresh basil. The restaurant follows the classic ragù-making technique—browning the meat, sautéing the aromatics, adding the tomatoes, and simmering for hours until tender and saucy—and their recipe calls for an entire, bone-in leg of lamb along with 9 pounds of tomatoes.

A leg of lamb may make sense when preparing a pasta sauce for 30 people in a restaurant, but not for the home cook. Looking for other, smaller cuts of lamb to replace it, we found loin chops, rib chops, shoulder chops, and "stew meat" readily available at the supermarket. Immediately, we tossed aside the idea of loin or rib chops. Both of these tender and expensive cuts of meat are not meant to be slowly simmered, but rather taste best when cooked to medium-rare. The "stew meat," we realized, could come from any part of the animal and might therefore have inconsistent flavor and texture characteristics, but the shoulder chops looked just about perfect. Not only did they have bones that would help flavor the sauce, but the meat was well marbled (with thin streaks of fat running throughout), ensuring that it would remain tender throughout hours of simmering. We found that 1½ pounds of lamb shoulder chops yielded enough meat to sauce 1 pound of pasta, enough for six people.

Next, we tackled the issue of tomatoes. The recipe called for both diced and crushed tomatoes. Paring the recipe down to accommodate 1 pound of pasta, we required only 28 ounces of tomatoes, total. Although diced tomatoes can be bought in smaller cans, crushed tomatoes cannot. To skirt this

INGREDIENTS: Tomato Paste

We reserve the use of tomato paste for recipes that require a deep tomato flavor, such as cream of tomato soup or a tomato-flavored meat sauce. There is a vast array of tomato pastes out there, and we wondered if it mattered which one we used. To find out, we gathered seven brands for a tasting.

All delivered a big tomato punch, but Amore is the only tomato paste that contains fat, which could account for its bigger flavor. The Amore brand also scored points because of its tube packaging. Just squeeze out what you need and store the rest in the fridge. No fuss, no waste.

issue, we found it easy to grind a can of diced tomatoes ourselves using a food processor. Processing one can to a ground consistency, and leaving the other diced, we were able to achieve the original recipe's consistency.

Last, we found that using shoulder chops (rather than an entire leg) allowed us to cut the sauce's simmer time in half from 3 hours to 1½ hours. After it turned tender, we found it a breeze to shred the meat into bite-size pieces. Although this ragù could be served over several types of small, squiggly pasta, it works very well over orecchiette, since the small pieces of meat nestle perfectly into the pasta's little curves.

Orecchiette with Lamb Ragù

SERVES 6

Remember to reserve some of the cooking water when draining the pasta; it will help distribute the very thick sauce evenly over the noodles.

- **2** **(14.5-ounce) cans diced tomatoes**
- **1 ½** **pounds lamb shoulder chops**
- **Salt and ground black pepper**
- **1** **tablespoon olive oil**
- **3** **carrots, chopped fine**
- **2** **celery ribs, chopped fine**
- **1** **small onion, chopped fine**
- **2** **tablespoons tomato paste**
- **½** **cup dry red wine**
- **3** **sprigs fresh basil, plus 2 tablespoons minced fresh basil leaves, for garnish**
- **1** **pound orecchiette pasta (or medium shells or penne)**
- **⅓** **cup grated pecorino cheese**

1. Process 1 can of the diced tomatoes in a food processor until uniformly ground, about 10 seconds. Transfer to a medium bowl and combine with the remaining can of diced tomatoes. Set aside.

2. Season the lamb liberally with salt and pepper. Heat the olive oil in a 12-inch heavy-bottomed skillet over medium-high heat until just smoking. Brown the chops on all sides, turning them occasionally with tongs, 8 to 10 minutes. Transfer the browned chops to a clean plate and set aside.

3. Pour off all but 1 teaspoon of fat from the skillet and return to medium heat. Add the carrots, celery, onion, and ¼ teaspoon salt and sauté until softened, 2 to 3 minutes. Stir in the tomato paste and cook until aromatic, about 1 minute. Add the wine and simmer, scraping the bottom of the pan with a wooden spoon to loosen any browned bits, until the wine reduces to a glaze, about 2 minutes. Add the browned lamb along with any accumulated juices, tomatoes, and basil sprigs to the skillet and bring to a boil. Reduce the heat to low, cover, and simmer gently, turning the chops several times, until the meat is very tender and falling off the bones, about 1½ hours.

4. Transfer the lamb to a clean plate. When cool enough to handle, remove the meat from bones and shred it with your fingers, discarding the fat and bones. Return the shredded meat to the sauce in the skillet. Bring to a simmer over medium heat and cook, uncovered, until slightly thickened, 5 to 7 minutes. Season with salt and pepper to taste.

5. Bring 4 quarts water to a boil in a large pot. Add the pasta and 1 tablespoon salt and cook until al dente. Drain, reserving ¼ cup of the pasta cooking water. Return the pasta to the empty pot and toss it with the tomato sauce, adding the reserved pasta cooking water as needed to adjust the sauce's consistency. Divide the pasta among warm individual bowls and top with the pecorino and minced basil. Serve immediately.

Raw Pad Thai

Adapted from "Raw" Pad Thai

Roxanne's, Larkspur, California

RAW PAD THAI MAY SOUND LIKE AN OXYmoron, but at Roxanne's, the vanguard of "raw-food" fine dining, it's one of the most popular dishes on the menu. A world apart from greasy carry-out fare, Roxanne's pad thai is composed of julienned vegetables, coconut "noodles," and dueling sauces. Complicated, yes, but with a bit advance preparation, it's an easy and exotic restaurant-style meal for the home cook to master. And it's the perfect summer dish—there's not a lick of heat necessary.

Between the two sauces, the full range of the Thai palette is realized: hot, sour, salty, and sweet. While they are easily prepared, each requires an unusual ingredient or two. Tamarind concentrate is the most exotic ingredient in the tamarind sauce, but it can be found in Asian markets. Tart and tangy, tamarind adds a distinct, fruity sourness that is milder and fuller-tasting than citrus or vinegar. Although maple syrup is hardly associated with Southeast Asian cooking, it does lend the sauce a pleasant sweetness. Almond butter, the base of the almond-chile sauce, is nothing more than almonds ground to a creamy consistency. You're guaranteed to find it at your local natural food store. Soy sauce adds depth and savoriness. For spice, Roxanne's adds a "Thai dragon" chile, a fiery chile that can be easily replaced by the more commonly available serrano chile.

The vegetables for the dish are readily available. We recommend hothouse cucumbers (also called English cucumbers)—the dark green, very long, plastic-wrapped ones—because they are sweet and don't need to be peeled, thus adding a bit more color to the dish. Slicing the vegetables by hand makes for outstanding knife-skill practice, since the vegetables must be thinly julienned (a very sharp chef's knife helps), but a mandoline will make quick work of the task. (See page 8 for information about mandolines.) Cilantro and Thai basil work together to great effect in the dish, lending it a spicy, characteristically Thai aroma.

INGREDIENT:
Tamarind Concentrate

Tamarind concentrate looks more like a scary pomade than a foodstuff. It's black, thick, shiny, and gooey. Its sour-sweet flavor approximates that of tamarind paste, but it's far more convenient than tamarind paste, which must be soaked, boiled, and strained before being used.

Thai basil, however, can be a rare find, and conventional basil is an inadequate substitute. We recommend substituting mint for it or skipping it altogether—the cilantro is delicious by itself.

Something of a culinary "sleight of hand," the rice noodles used in pad thai are replaced with thin strips of "sweet, young" coconut meat. Young coconut, often called Thai or white coconut, is what you want here. The resilient, slightly gelatinous meat plays the role well, and its mild coconut flavor is delicious among the other ingredients. Thai coconuts are fibrous in appearance and are generally trimmed to a chiseled point, sort of like a circus tent. Both Asian and Latin specialty stores usually carry them. Avoid the big, brown coconuts found in standard supermarkets—their older, riper meat is too firm to make the "noodles."

To access the meat, the juice must first be drained, then the coconut can be halved. It's a tough job, one we found best accomplished with a sturdy cleaver and rubber mallet to pound the blade through. To drain the liquid, we first made a notch in the top of the coconut with the heel of a cleaver and then inverted the coconut over a bowl (the liquid can be saved for drinking). Once drained, the coconut can be split in half. The thin, white lining inside is what you're after, ideally removed in large pieces. We found that a large, shallow-bowled spoon was the best tool, slid between the meat and husk and gently worked back and forth to loosen the meat. Once removed, it's easy to slice.

The range in the color and shape of the Pad Thai components make for a very attractive plate. To serve, alternate layers of noodles and vegetables, drizzling each with sauce, and make thin drizzles of sauce on the plate itself.

Raw Pad Thai

SERVES 4

If your local grocery store doesn't have all the ingredients necessary, a trip to an Asian specialty store should prove fruitful. Avoid using "supermarket" coconuts in this dish—their mature meat is too firm. Seek out young coconuts, often called Thai coconuts, which are usually shrink-wrapped and found in Asian or Latin markets. If preparing the coconuts sounds too daunting, the Pad Thai makes a delicious salad or side dish sans "noodles"—just remember to reduce the amount of dressing you use.

TAMARIND SAUCE

- **3 tablespoons tamarind concentrate**
- **1 tablespoon maple syrup**
- **1 1/2 tablespoons soy sauce**
- **1 1/4 teaspoons extra-virgin olive oil**
- **4 medium garlic cloves, minced or pressed through a garlic press**
- **1/4 teaspoon salt**

ALMOND-CHILE SAUCE

- **1/2 cup almond butter**
- **4 medium garlic cloves, minced or pressed through a garlic press**
- **1 (1-inch) piece fresh ginger, peeled and minced (about 1 tablespoon)**
- **1 medium serrano chile, seeded, ribs removed, and minced**
- **2 tablespoons juice from 1 large lemon**
- **1 tablespoon soy sauce**

PAD THAI

- **3 medium carrots, peeled and cut into 1 1/2-inch matchsticks**
- **1/2 hothouse cucumber, seeded and cut into 1 1/2-inch matchsticks**
- **1 medium red bell pepper, seeded, ribs removed, and cut into 1 1/2-inch matchsticks**

- 1 cup mung bean sprouts (about 2 1/2 ounces)
- 1/4 cup coarsely chopped fresh Thai basil (or mint) (optional)
- Salt and ground black pepper
- 1/2 cup coarsely chopped fresh cilantro, plus extra whole sprigs for garnish
- 1/2 cup thinly sliced napa cabbage
- Splash juice from 1 lime
- 3 young Thai coconuts, split lengthwise, scraped clean, and meat julienned following the illustrations below (3–4 cups)

1. FOR THE TAMARIND SAUCE: Thoroughly combine all the ingredients in a small bowl and set aside.

2. FOR THE ALMOND-CHILE SAUCE: Process all the ingredients and 1 tablespoon water in a blender until smooth, about 20 seconds. Transfer to a small bowl and set aside.

3. FOR THE PAD THAI: Combine the carrots, cucumber, bell pepper, bean sprouts, basil, and three-quarters of the almond-chile sauce in a large bowl. Season with salt and pepper to taste. Combine the chopped cilantro, cabbage, lime juice, and ¼ teaspoon salt in a medium bowl.

4. TO SERVE: Divide the cabbage mixture evenly among 4 plates. Top each portion with about ½ cup of the coconut "noodles"; top the noodles with half of the vegetable mixture. Repeat the process with the remaining noodles and vegetables. Drizzle each portion with the tamarind sauce. Drizzle remaining almond-chile sauce around the pad thai and garnish with the cilantro sprigs. Serve immediately.

OPENING A YOUNG COCONUT

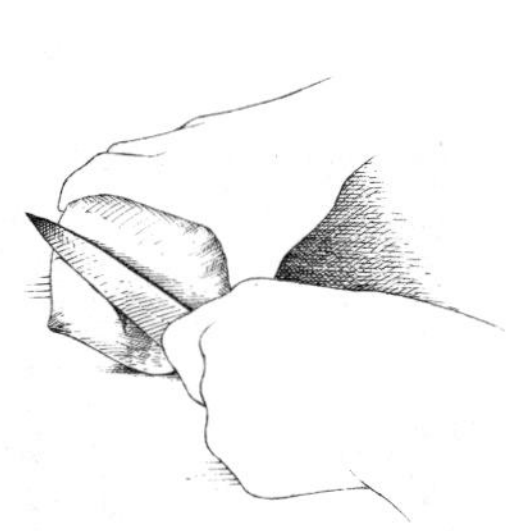

1. Using a heavy-bladed chef's knife, cut off the pointed end of the coconut.

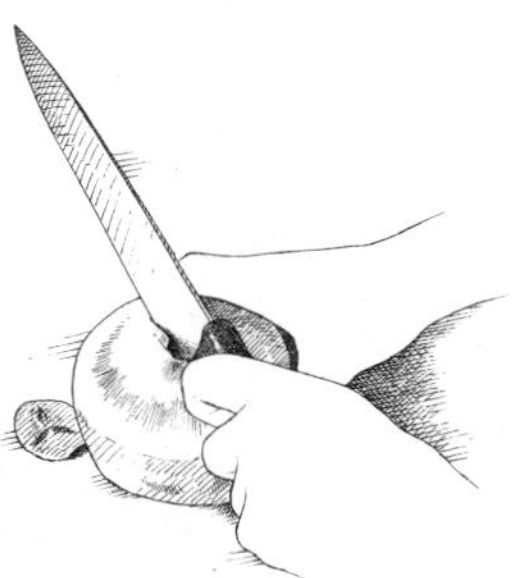

2. Use the heel of the blade to puncture the flesh.

3. Drain all the liquid out of the coconut into a medium bowl (reserve the liquid for another use).

4. With the aid of a rubber mallet, split the coconut in half.

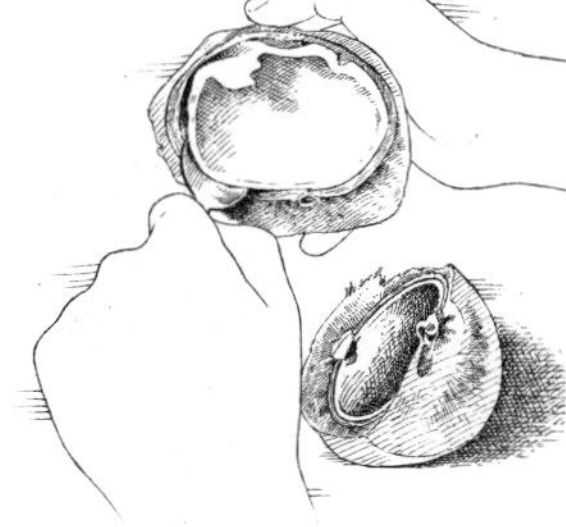

5. Use a large spoon to scrape the white meat from the inside of the coconut. Trim any brown, fibrous membrane from the coconut meat and cut the meat into thin strips.

Black-Eyed Pea Cakes *with* Spicy Tomato-Pepper Sauce

Adapted from Black-Eyed Pea Cakes with Spicy Tomato-Pepper Sauce

Majestic Cafe, Alexandria, Virginia

VEGETARIAN ENTRÉES CAN BE SOME OF THE most challenging dishes for a chef. It is hard to develop intense and interesting flavor combinations without the use of meat, fish, or fowl. But the chef of Majestic Cafe has avoided the bland and the mundane by creating a vegetarian dish that will tempt the most die-hard carnivore.

The Majestic Cafe cooks the intensely earthy black-eyed peas until creamy, flavors them with sweet vegetables and spicy Tabasco, forms them into cakes, and then fries them until their exterior is crisp and crunchy. Served with a zesty tomato-pepper sauce, this dish certainly isn't lacking in flavor. We did, however, find several aspects of the recipe that needed adjustments for home cooks.

The most pressing issue was the frying of the pea cakes themselves. Our initial test of the pea cakes met with disaster. When we tried to fry the cakes, we found that a major portion of the cakes disintegrated before they had browned. We tried everything to rectify this issue, from increasing the amount and temperature of the oil to cooking just a few cakes at a time, but we still had the same results. Even varying the amount of moisture in the cakes made no difference. Restaurants use commercial deep-fryers that contain a large volume of oil and regulate temperatures evenly. After exhausting our options, we found that we had to use a standard breading of flour, eggs, and bread crumbs to provide the pea cakes with an exterior that would protect them from the corrosive action of the hot oil. While this procedure made the recipe a little more complicated, we finally were able to achieve a pea cake with a crunchy exterior and a creamy interior.

Another issue we addressed was the fact that there were two overnight steps in the recipe: one was the soaking of the peas, the other was refrigerating the formed pea cakes. For us, and probably most home cooks, this seemed like a substantial investment of time. We wanted to determine if this dish could be completed in less time.

We first addressed the overnight soaking. We made several different batches of pea cakes using beans that had been soaked overnight, beans that had been quick-soaked (brought to a boil, then soaked for an hour), and beans that had not been soaked at all. Upon completing our test, we found that although there was almost no difference in taste, we did notice a difference in cooking time and texture. The beans that soaked overnight cooked in about 30 minutes and were creamy and evenly cooked. The beans that were quick-soaked didn't take much more time to cook—about 40 minutes—but they were slightly chalky and some of the skins were tough. The peas that we cooked dry took a little over an hour to cook (twice as long as the soaked beans), and they were unevenly cooked, mealy, and slightly raw tasting. For the sake of convenience, we also tried making the cakes using canned black-eyed peas, hoping to forgo the soaking and cooking process. The cakes made with canned peas didn't even taste like peas, but rather like metal. Preferring the beans that were soaked overnight, we knew we would not save any time here.

Unable to reduce the time of the recipe on the soaking end, we explored whether the pea cakes actually had to sit overnight before they were cooked. Preparing two more batches of pea cakes, we let one batch sit overnight and cooked the other batch immediately after we formed them. While the pea cakes that sat overnight had a slightly deeper flavor than the ones we cooked immediately, there was no distinct difference in cooking or texture between the two. As a result, we opted to forgo the step that called for refrigerating the cakes overnight. With this overnight step omitted, the pea cakes became much more manageable for the home cook.

The only question remaining for us was whether we could streamline the making of the sauce. But considering that the sauce was made by sautéing peppers, onions, and tomatoes and then pureeing the trio, there weren't a lot of options for saving time. We did wonder if we could substitute canned tomatoes for fresh. We made the sauce with canned tomatoes and fresh tomatoes and tasted the two side by side. Most tasters preferred the sauce made with fresh tomatoes, explaining that it had a fresher, brighter flavor that paired better with the pea cakes.

Black-Eyed Pea Cakes with Spicy Tomato-Pepper Sauce

SERVES 6 (MAKES 18 CAKES)

Avoid using canned black-eyed peas in this dish, as they won't have the firm texture and earthy flavor of dried. Serve this vegetarian entrée with steamed rice or couscous.

- **4 cups low-sodium vegetable broth**
- **1 pound black-eyed peas, picked over, soaked in cold water overnight, and drained**
- **Salt**
- **6 tablespoons olive oil**
- **2 medium onions, 1 cut into 1/4-inch dice, 1 chopped rough**
- **1 medium carrot, cut into 1/4-inch dice (about 1 cup)**
- **1 celery rib, cut into 1/4-inch dice (about 3/4 cup)**
- **1 teaspoon chopped fresh thyme**
- **Ground black pepper**
- **Hot pepper sauce, such as Tabasco**
- **1 large green bell pepper, chopped rough**
- **2 large tomatoes (about 1 pound), cored and cut into 1/2-inch dice**
- **2 tablespoons Dijon mustard**
- **1 tablespoon unsalted butter**
- **1 cup unbleached all-purpose flour**
- **2 large eggs**
- **1 1/2 cups panko (Japanese-style bread crumbs) or Homemade Panko (page 17)**
- **2 cups vegetable oil, for frying**

1. Bring the vegetable broth and 3 quarts water to a boil in a heavy-bottomed Dutch oven over high heat. Add the peas and 1 tablespoon salt and return to a simmer. Reduce the heat to medium-low and simmer the peas until tender, 30 to 35 minutes.

2. Meanwhile, heat 2 tablespoons of the olive oil in a 12-inch nonstick skillet over medium heat until shimmering. Add the diced onions, carrot, and celery and sauté, stirring occasionally, until the vegetables are tender, about 6 minutes. Transfer to a medium bowl and set aside.

3. Once the peas are tender, drain and transfer them to large bowl. Puree 2 cups of the peas in a food processor until smooth, about twelve 1-second pulses. Mash the remaining peas with the back of a large spoon until most of them are broken. Add the pureed peas, sautéed vegetables, thyme, salt and pepper to taste, and ½ teaspoon hot pepper sauce and mix well. Form the pea mixture into 18 cakes measuring 2 inches in diameter and 1 inch thick. Place the pea cakes on a rimmed baking sheet, cover loosely with plastic wrap, and refrigerate while preparing the sauce.

4. Heat the remaining 4 tablespoons olive oil in a 12-inch skillet over medium heat until shimmering. Add the roughly chopped onion and sauté, stirring frequently, until tender, about 3 minutes. Add the bell pepper and sauté until it starts to soften, about 4 minutes. Add the tomatoes, mustard, and ½ cup water and bring to a simmer. Cook until all the vegetables are tender, about 5 minutes longer. Transfer the sauce to a blender, add the butter, and process until smooth, about 20 seconds. Transfer the sauce back to the clean skillet and season with hot pepper sauce, salt, and pepper to taste.

5. Combine the flour and 1 teaspoon salt in a shallow dish or pie plate. Lightly beat the eggs with 1 tablespoon water in a separate shallow dish. Spread the panko in a third shallow dish.

6. Working with several pea cakes at a time, drop them into the flour and gently shake the dish back and forth to coat. Shake the excess flour from each cake. Then, using tongs, dip the cakes into the egg, turning to coat well, and allow the excess to drip off. Drop the cakes into the panko and press the crumbs lightly to adhere. Shake off any excess crumbs and place the breaded cakes on a wire rack set over a rimmed baking sheet. Repeat with the remaining cakes.

7. Heat the vegetable oil in a Dutch oven over medium-high heat until shimmering. Add half of the cakes and fry until golden brown on the first side, about 3 minutes. Using tongs, carefully turn the cakes and fry until golden brown on the second side, about 2 minutes. Transfer the cakes to a rimmed baking sheet lined with several layers of paper towels. Repeat with the remaining cakes.

8. Meanwhile, reheat the sauce. Place ¼ cup sauce on each of 6 warmed dinner plates, arrange 3 pea cakes on each plate, and top each cake with a small spoonful of sauce. Serve immediately.

Roasted Chile Frittata

Adapted from Roasted Chile Frittata

Border Grill, Santa Monica, California

SOMETIMES, A RECIPE WILL EMPLOY A method so far from what you'd consider correct that you'd think it could never work. This Southwestern-flavored frittata from the Border Grill is a case in point. The restaurant recommends an unusual technique that relies on residual heat for perfectly cooked eggs. You'll be eager to include this amazingly tender and fluffy frittata at your next brunch. Frittatas are the Italian version of the French omelet. Like omelets (and similar egg dishes), special care needs to be taken during the cooking process because once the eggs overcook, there's no going back. But rest assured, with the Border Grill's recipe, overcooking the eggs is staunchly avoided.

To start, we found the ingredients and their amounts easy to scale back for the home kitchen. Red bell peppers and poblano peppers are first roasted and peeled, then sautéed in a skillet with aromatics. Eggs are poured over this flavorful mixture. The eggs are then partially cooked on top of the stove and finished under the broiler. Following our instincts rather than the restaurant's recipe, we cooked and broiled our first frittata until the eggs were done, then let it sit on the counter to cool, as the recipe instructs. Thinking that we had nailed it, we were disappointed to find the eggs rubbery and overdone. Backing off a bit on the cooking, we tried it again, leaving just the center inch or so of the frittata wiggly. But yet again, the frittata was overdone after its 10-minute respite. On our third try, we took the leap of faith required and followed the recipe as instructed. Against all of our instincts, we removed the frittata from the oven when the inner six inches were still wiggly and raw. After its 10-minute rest, the entire frittata was perfectly done and tender. This unusual cooking method is what turns this otherwise tricky egg dish into a guaranteed success.

Roasted Chile Frittata

SERVES 6

This frittata will look very underdone when removed from the broiler, but will set up as it rests.

- 2 small red bell peppers
- 2 poblano peppers
- 12 large eggs
- ½ cup minced fresh cilantro leaves
- 2 teaspoons chili powder
- 1¼ teaspoons salt
- ½ teaspoon ground black pepper
- 1 tablespoon olive oil
- 1 small onion, chopped fine
- 3½ ounces Monterey Jack cheese, shredded (about 1 cup)

1. Adjust an oven rack so it is 6 inches away from the broiler element and heat the broiler. Cut ¼ inch off both the tops and bottoms of the bell and poblano peppers and remove the seeds. Slice through one side of each pepper so they lay flat, and trim away the white ribs. Lay all the peppers skin-side up on a rimmed baking sheet lined with heavy-duty foil and broil until the skin is charred and puffed but the flesh is still firm, 8 to 10 minutes, turning the pan around halfway through. Remove the pan from the oven without turning off the broiler, cover with foil, and allow the peppers to steam for 5 minutes. Peel and discard the skins. Slice the bell peppers into ¼-inch-wide strips and set aside. Cut the poblanos into ¼-inch dice and set aside.

2. Whisk the eggs, cilantro, chili powder, salt, and pepper together in a large bowl until well combined and set aside.

3. Heat the olive oil in a 10-inch oven-proof nonstick skillet over medium heat until shimmering. Add the onion and sauté until softened and slightly golden, 5 to 6 minutes. Stir in the roasted bell and poblano peppers and sauté until fragrant and all the moisture has evaporated, about 2 minutes. Add

ROASTING PEPPERS

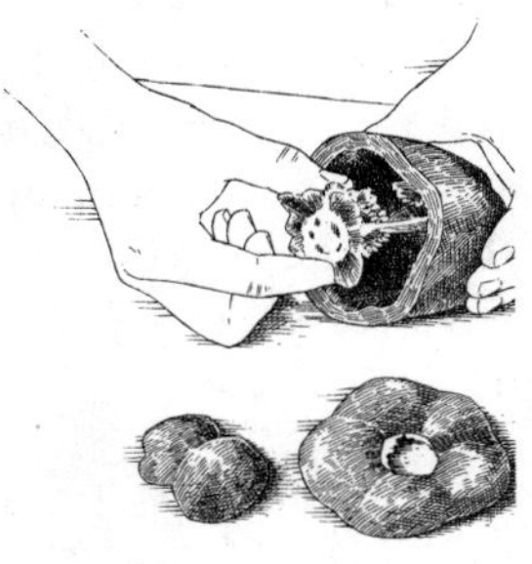

1. Start by removing a ¼-inch-thick slice from the top and bottom of each pepper. Remove the stem from the top lobe. Reach into the pepper and pull out the seeds.

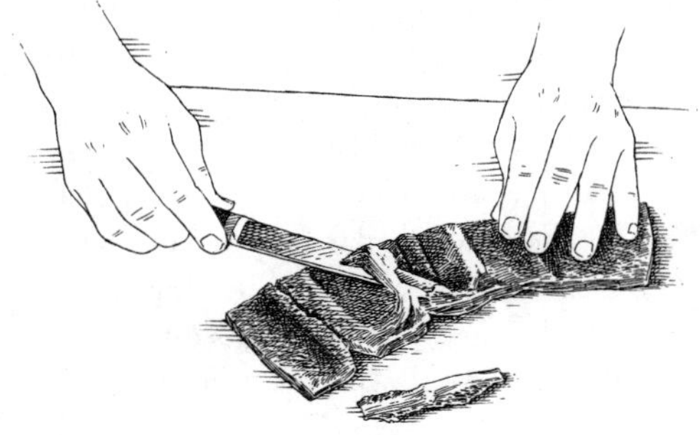

2. Slit through one side of the pepper, then lay it flat, skin-side down. Slide a sharp knife along the inside of the pepper to remove all the white ribs and any remaining seeds.

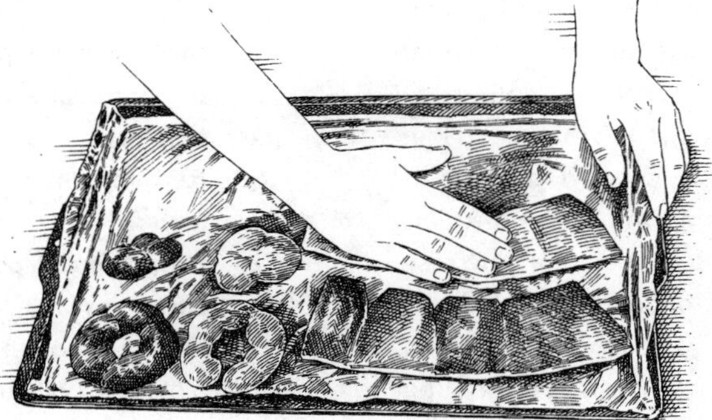

3. Arrange the peppers and the top and bottom pieces skin-side up on a baking sheet lined with foil. Flatten the strips with the palm of your hand. Roast the peppers under the broiler until the skins are charred but the flesh is still firm.

the egg mixture and swirl to coat evenly. Reduce the heat to medium-low, sprinkle evenly with the cheese, and cover. Cook until the eggs have set only about 1 inch in from the rim of the pan, about 5 minutes, shaking the pan occasionally to prevent the frittata from sticking. Remove the lid and place the skillet under the broiler. Broil until the eggs have set roughly 2 inches in from the rim of the pan, about 2 minutes. Using an oven mitt, remove the skillet from the oven and cool on a wire rack until the eggs have set completely, about 10 minutes.

4. Loosen the edges of the frittata using a paring knife. Slide the frittata out onto a serving platter and slice evenly into 6 wedges. Serve the frittata immediately or cool to room temperature before serving.

INGREDIENTS: Egg Sizes

RELATIVE SIZE OF SUPERMARKET EGGS (HALF SCALE)

MEDIUM

LARGE

EXTRA-LARGE

JUMBO

Eggs come in six sizes—jumbo, extra-large, large, medium, small, and peewee. Most markets carry only the top four sizes; small and peewee are generally reserved for commercial use. There's little mystery about size—the bigger or the older the chicken, the bigger the egg. In the test kitchen, we use large eggs, but substitutions are possible in recipes where large quantities of eggs are used. See the egg weight chart (at right) for help in making accurate calculations. For example, 4 jumbo eggs (2.5 ounces each) are equivalent to 5 large eggs (2 ounces each).

Egg Weight Chart

SIZE	WEIGHT
MEDIUM	1.75 ounces
LARGE	2.00 ounces
EXTRA-LARGE	2.25 ounces
JUMBO	2.50 ounces

Ham & Egg Puff Pastry Pockets

Adapted from Ham and Eggs Wrapped in Puff Pastry

Benson's Restaurant, Poulsbo, Washington

FLUFFY, BUTTERY SCRAMBLED EGGS, SMOKY Black Forest ham, and melting cheddar cheese are reason enough to make this dish. Wrap them in a blanket of flaky puff pastry, finish it with a light cream sauce and slivers of scallion, and common breakfast fare is now upscale restaurant "cuisine" in this eye-opener from Benson's Restaurant.

Although it is a skill many restaurant chefs acquired in culinary school, making puff pastry at home can seem a daunting task. Thankfully, puff pastry is widely available frozen, making this dish something that need not be reserved for special occasions. Even with store-bought puff pastry, the recipe was time-consuming in its original form owing to the cutting and assembly of the pastry. One of the most difficult parts of our original tests involved the cutting of 12 circles of puff pastry, 6 inches in diameter (two circles per pastry, serving one person). After 12 circles were cut, we assembled the pastries and found that enclosing the filling with a top circle that was the same size as the bottom was not an easy task. After testing various shapes and sizes and filling and sealing techniques, we found that using a 9-inch plate or cake pan as our template and cutting just one large circle enabled us to make a single crescent-shaped pastry that would yield two servings per sheet of puff pastry. Filling and folding the pastry into a crescent shape was not only easier, but took up less space on our baking sheet as well. Thus, we had reduced the amount of puff pastry from six sheets to three, with an end product that was both efficient and attractive.

With our assembly procedure in place, we turned our attention to the filling. We found that the ham for this pastry needed to have an assertive, smoky flavor. Black Forest ham, with its spicy exterior and strong smokiness, turned out to be the winner when tested against Virginia ham and boiled ham. With a creamy, tangy bite, extra-sharp cheddar tasted the best, pairing well with the ham and holding its own when tasted with the puff pastry and cream sauce.

Benson's suggests baking the pastries for 10 minutes until golden, which in our home-style ovens turned out a pale, undercooked pastry that did not have time to puff. What we suspected was that most restaurant kitchens come equipped with convection ovens that blast the food with high heat in a shorter period of time. Taking this into consideration, we tested oven temperatures ranging from 375 to 450 degrees, finding 400 degrees to be the ideal temperature, allowing for even browning and sufficient time for the steam in the pastry to form the distinct layers we were looking for. Serving suggestions for these pastries included a cream sauce and sliced scallions. While the sauce can be ladled onto individual plates, some tasters preferred the option of having it served on the side.

Ham and Egg Puff Pastry Pockets

SERVES 6

Puff pastry is found in the freezer section of most supermarkets. To prevent the pastry from cracking, be sure to thaw it until pliable; overnight in the refrigerator or 30 to 40 minutes at room temperature. These pastries would be perfect as part of a brunch buffet, or on their own with a fresh fruit salad.

CREAM SAUCE

- **1 cup milk, plus more if needed**
- **3/4 cup half-and-half**
- **2 tablespoons unsalted butter**
- **1 tablespoon unbleached all-purpose flour**
- **2 bay leaves**
- **1/4 teaspoon salt**
- **Pinch ground nutmeg**
- **Ground black pepper**

HAM AND EGG PUFF PASTRY POCKETS

- **7 large eggs**
- **1/2 teaspoon salt**
- **1/8 teaspoon ground black pepper**
- **2 tablespoons unsalted butter**
- **3 (9 1/2 by 9-inch) sheets frozen commercial puff pastry, thawed**
- **Flour for dusting**
- **1 small shallot, minced (about 1 tablespoon)**
- **6 ounces extra-sharp cheddar cheese, shredded (about 1 1/2 cups)**
- **6 slices Black Forest deli ham (about 8 ounces)**
- **4 scallions, sliced thin**

1. FOR THE CREAM SAUCE: Heat the milk and half-and-half together in a medium saucepan over medium heat until hot. (Alternatively heat the milk and half-and-half in a microwave-proof measuring cup in the microwave on high power until hot, about 2 minutes.)

2. Meanwhile, melt the butter in a medium, heavy-bottomed saucepan over medium heat until foaming. Whisk in the flour and cook, whisking constantly, for 2 minutes. Do not let the flour brown. Remove the saucepan from the heat and vigorously whisk in several tablespoons of the hot milk mixture. Repeat, adding a few more tablespoons. Use a wooden spoon to scrape off any flour mixture from the edges of the pan. Return the pan to very low heat and slowly whisk in the remaining milk mixture, scraping any flour from the edges of pan. Increase the heat to medium-low and add the bay leaves and salt. Cook, whisking frequently, until the sauce has the consistency of thick heavy cream, about 10 minutes. Remove the pan from the heat and add the nutmeg and pepper to taste. If necessary, heat and whisk in more milk, 1 tablespoon at a time, until the sauce is thinned to the desired consistency. Strain through a fine-mesh sieve into a clean 2-cup glass measuring cup and set aside. Use immediately or place plastic wrap directly on the surface of the sauce (to prevent a skin from forming) and cool to room temperature. (The sauce can be refrigerated for up to 2 days.)

3. FOR THE PUFF PASTRY POCKETS: Whisk 6 of the eggs, salt, and pepper together in a medium bowl. Melt the butter in a 12-inch nonstick skillet over high heat, swirling

the pan to evenly coat the bottom and sides, until the foam begins to subside. Pour in the eggs and, using a spatula or wooden spoon, slowly push them from one side of the pan to the other until they are set but remain shiny and wet, 2½ to 3 minutes. Transfer the eggs to a rimmed baking sheet lined with foil and refrigerate until cool, about 30 minutes. (Alternatively, place in the freezer until cool, about 10 minutes.)

4. Working with one sheet of pastry at a time, unfold the puff pastry on a lightly floured work surface. Dust the top of the pastry lightly with flour and, using a 9-inch plate or cake pan as a guide, cut out a 9-inch circle of pastry using a sharp paring knife. Discard the pastry scraps. Repeat with the remaining 2 sheets of pastry. You should have three 9-inch circles. Use a dry pastry brush to remove any excess flour.

5. Lightly beat the remaining egg in a small bowl. Working with 1 pastry round at a time, use a pastry brush to brush egg lightly over half of the pastry. Following the illustrations on the right, place one third of the scrambled egg evenly over the egg-brushed half of the pastry, leaving a ½-inch border at the edge. Arrange 1 teaspoon of the shallot, ½ cup of the cheese, and 2 slices of the ham on top of the egg. Fold the pastry into a half-moon shape and press the edges together firmly to seal. Transfer to a rimmed baking sheet and set aside. Repeat with the remaining pastry and transfer to the baking sheet. Refrigerate for 30 minutes. Reserve the remaining beaten egg.

6. Adjust an oven rack to the middle position and heat the oven to 400 degrees. Remove the pastries from the refrigerator, brush the tops with the remaining egg, and bake until golden brown, 25 to 30 minutes. Cool on a wire rack for 5 minutes. Meanwhile, reheat the cream sauce over low heat. Transfer the pastries to a cutting board and, using a serrated knife, cut each into 4 pie-shaped wedges. Spoon ¼ cup of the cream sauce on each of 6 individual plates, if desired. Place 1 wedge of pastry in the center of each sauced plate and lean a second wedge up against it. Garnish with the scallions and serve immediately.

SHAPING PASTRY POCKETS

1. Using a rubber spatula, place one third of the scrambled egg in an even layer across the bottom half of the pastry round, leaving a ½-inch border uncovered. Arrange the shallot, cheese, and ham over the egg, maintaining the ½-inch border.

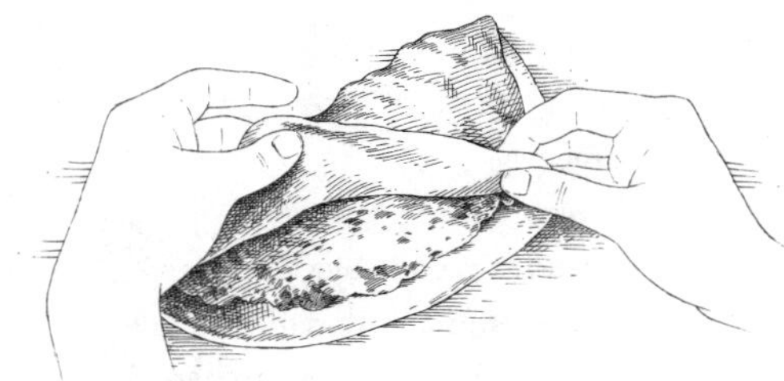

2. Brush the uncovered edges with the egg and fold over the top half of the pastry to form a half-moon and press the edges together to seal.

Smoked Salmon Hash

Adapted from Smoked Salmon Hash

The Heathman Hotel, Portland, Oregon

"HASHED" TOGETHER IN A SKILLET WITH some onions and butter, hash is traditionally the humble reincarnation of leftover scraps from the previous night's meat and potatoes supper. At the Heathman Hotel in Portland, Oregon, however, the leftover scraps are a bit fancier—smoked salmon and capers along with horseradish and whole-grain mustard to enliven the dish. The humbleness of this particular version lies in the chef's choice of frozen hash browns for leftover potatoes, which, frankly, seemed altogether too humble for us in the test kitchen—until we tasted the dish. Surprisingly, the frozen potatoes cooked up crisp and full of potato flavor.

The method for cooking salmon hash is uncomplicated. The potatoes are cooked until brown and crisp, then tossed with the other ingredients, which require no cooking other than being heated through. To accustom ourselves to frozen hash browns, we purchased several brands and found little difference. They are all shredded, partially cooked, and then frozen. Learning how to use them, however, was a challenge.

We used a nonstick skillet, since the hash browns had a tendency to stick to a traditional one, and noted the importance of using a fair amount of butter. Getting the hash browns crisp takes more patience than anything else. After the frozen hash browns are tossed with melted butter in the hot skillet, they must be lightly packed into a cohesive, skillet-size cake. After the first side is crisp, the hash brown should then be flipped over (with the aid of a large plate) and returned to a freshly buttered skillet so that the second side can crisp. Although it is tempting to try to rush the process with constant stirring, we found this prevented the potatoes from crisping at all. When the potato cake is well browned on both sides, it is then broken up slightly with a wooden spoon and tossed with the remaining ingredients. Using store-bought smoked salmon, we just had to warm it through rather than cook it. Served with a dollop of sour cream alongside, this fancy hash is far more sophisticated than what you'll find at your local diner.

Smoked Salmon Hash

SERVES 4

Choose the presliced salmon lined with the least amount of visible fat, otherwise it will be unpleasantly chewy.

- **6 ounces sliced smoked salmon, cut into 1-inch-wide strips**
- **1/2 cup minced red onion**
- **1 tablespoon drained capers**
- **2 tablespoons prepared horseradish**

- 1 tablespoon whole-grain Dijon mustard
- 6 tablespoons sour cream
- 1/8 teaspoon ground black pepper
- 5 tablespoons (1/2 stick plus 1 tablespoon) unsalted butter
- 1 pound frozen hash brown potatoes (not thawed)

1. Toss the salmon, onion, capers, horseradish, mustard, 2 tablespoons of the sour cream, and pepper together in a medium bowl and set aside

2. Melt 3 tablespoons of the butter in a 12-inch nonstick skillet over medium-high heat until the foaming subsides. Add the hash browns and toss to coat with the butter. Using the back of a wooden spoon, press the hash browns into a flat, cohesive cake and cook until the first side is golden brown and crisp, 10 to 12 minutes.

3. Remove the pan from the heat. Invert a large plate over the skillet and flip the hash brown cake out of the pan onto the plate, golden-side up. Melt the remaining 2 tablespoons butter in the pan off the heat. Return the skillet to medium heat and slide the hash brown cake back into the pan, golden-side up. Cook until the second side is golden brown and crisp, 10 to 12 minutes.

4. Using the wooden spoon, break the hash brown cake into bite-size pieces. Sprinkle the salmon mixture evenly over the hash browns and toss to incorporate. Cook until the salmon is heated through, about 1 minute.

5. Transfer the hash to a large serving platter or 4 individual plates and dollop with the remaining 4 tablespoons sour cream. Serve immediately.

EQUIPMENT: Inexpensive Nonstick Skillets

Although you could spend $100 or more on a nonstick skillet, most cooks would rather buy a cheaper pan. To find the best pan for the job, we rounded up eight inexpensive nonstick skillets, all purchased for no more than $50 apiece.

All of our pans turned in reasonable-to-good cooking performances. Most pans produced evenly cooked omelets and released them with ease. We also tested both traits in a purposefully abusive manner by burning oatmeal in the pan over high heat for 45 minutes. That kind of test would trash a traditional pan, but the scorched cereal slid out of our nonstick pans.

Of course, construction quality is also a concern with any piece of cookware but especially with inexpensive models. Will the thing hold up, or will you have to replace it in six months? Based on our experience, you may well sacrifice a measure of construction quality with a budget pan. Pans with handles that were welded or riveted to the pan body felt solid and permanent, but heat-resistant plastic handles that were not riveted in place came loose during testing.

THE BEST INEXPENSIVE NONSTICK SKILLET

The Farberware Millennium 18/10 Stainless Steel 12-Inch Nonstick Skillet costs about $30, and it delivered superior results in our tests. It was heavier than the other inexpensive pans we tested and had the most solid construction.

Green Eggs & Ham

Adapted from Green Eggs and Ham

The Friendly Toast, Portsmouth, New Hampshire

IT WAS BOUND TO APPEAR ON A MENU somewhere—Dr. Seuss's idea of "green eggs and ham" is just too good to remain intangible. But unlike the story, wherein "Sam I am" has trouble getting his friend to taste them, these eggs are regularly scarfed down at the funky New Hampshire diner called The Friendly Toast. Luckily, the green is a creamy herb sauce poured over two poached eggs, some sautéed ham, and a thick slice of toasted cornmeal and molasses-flavored anadama bread.

To start, we found it necessary to make our own anadama bread, since it is nearly impossible to find, even at good bakeries. Although making a loaf of bread for breakfast the next day is a bit over the top for the home cook, we found that the bread was incredibly easy to prepare, and worth the effort (see the recipe on page 329). In a pinch, any sweet, wheaty, unsliced loaf will suffice.

The sauce is a breeze to make in the blender with some mayonnaise and herbs, and the ham is thick-sliced Virginia ham from the deli given a quick sauté to heat it through and add color. The real trick to making this recipe at home, we found, is correctly poaching the eggs. Poaching eggs can be tricky, and mere seconds can make the difference between perfect and overcooked yolks. Also, we wanted to find a way to poach all the eggs at the same time. For a six-person breakfast, that means poaching 12 eggs at once.

To start, we traded in the standard saucepan for a shallow, wide skillet. Not only did this pan make it easier to add and retrieve the delicate eggs without breaking the yolks, but its wide surface area brought the water to a boil faster. Adding vinegar to the water helps the egg whites coagulate (cook) faster and prevents those annoying, wandering egg white trails. We found that 3 tablespoons of white vinegar (for six eggs) was enough to accomplish this without flavoring the eggs. We also found it necessary to add salt to the water or else the eggs tasted bland. Contrary to the usual interpretation of poaching, we also thought we'd try to limit the eggs' exposure to rapidly boiling water, which can cause them to disintegrate. We brought the water up to a full boil before adding the eggs, then turned off the heat once they were in the pan, letting the residual heat in the water cook them. It worked like a charm; large eggs cooked through in only four minutes. To retrieve them from the pan, we found that a slotted spoon easily drains the water while carefully cradling the egg, preventing it from sloshing around. The flat, slippery surface of a skimmer or the coarser texture of a wire-mesh spider, on the other hand, doesn't work as well.

Trying to poach all 12 eggs in one skillet was a disaster. There were just too many eggs for the relatively small amount of water, and the result looked like a really bad soup. We tried cooking them in batches, keeping the first batch warm in the oven while the second cooked, but this didn't work either. The first batch overcooked while waiting for the second, even when we purposefully undercooked them. We then tried poaching all the eggs at the same time using two separate skillets. Not only were the eggs easy to monitor, but the slightly staggered cooking time between the pans made it easy to cook them all to a tee. We found it best to crack the eggs into small cups with handles (two per cup) and then slip them into the water. While the eggs cook, there is just enough time to arrange the toast and ham on individual plates. This way, the eggs can be drained and plated straightaway. Topped with the green herb sauce, these green eggs and ham look less dramatic than they sound, but are a welcome break from boring breakfasts.

Green Eggs and Ham

SERVES 6

If poaching medium eggs, reduce the cooking time to 3 minutes; if using extra-large or jumbo eggs, increase the poaching time to 4½ minutes. We found it easiest to have all the components cooked, warm, and waiting for the eggs, which can then can be plated immediately after emerging from the poaching water.

- **½ cup mayonnaise**
- **1 tablespoon minced fresh basil leaves**
- **1 tablespoon minced fresh cilantro leaves**
- **1 tablespoon minced fresh dill**
- **2 tablespoons vegetable oil**
- **Salt and ground black pepper**
- **6 (¼-inch-thick) slices Virginia ham**
- **12 large eggs**
- **6 tablespoons distilled white vinegar**
- **6 (½-inch-thick) slices Anadama Bread (page 329) or any slightly sweet wheat bread, toasted**

1. Adjust an oven rack to the middle position and heat the oven to 200 degrees. Process the mayonnaise, basil, cilantro, dill, 3 tablespoons cold water, and 1 tablespoon of the vegetable oil in a blender until smooth and green. Transfer to a medium bowl, season with salt and pepper to taste, and set aside.

2. Heat ½ tablespoon of the remaining oil in a 12-inch nonstick skillet over medium-high heat until just smoking. Add 3 slices of the ham, not overlapping, and sauté until golden brown, about 1 minute. Flip the ham and sauté until golden on the second side, about 1 minute longer. Transfer the ham to a clean plate and place in the oven to keep warm. Heat the remaining ½ tablespoon oil in the skillet until just smoking and repeat with the remaining ham. Transfer the ham to the warm plate in the oven.

3. Fill two 10- or 12-inch skillets nearly to the rim with water. Add 1½ teaspoons salt and 3 tablespoons vinegar to each skillet and bring to a boil over high heat. Crack 6 eggs into 3 small cups with handles, 2 per cup. Working with just one skillet, gently lower the lips of all the cups into the water at the same time. Tip the eggs into the boiling water, cover, and remove the pan from the heat. Poach until the yolks are loose, exactly 4 minutes. Repeat with the remaining eggs in the second skillet of boiling water.

4. Meanwhile, place a piece of toast in the center of each of 6 individual plates and top with a slice of sautéed ham. Using a slotted spoon, carefully lift and drain 2 eggs over the skillet. Season to taste with salt and pepper and place on a piece of toast. Pour 2 tablespoons of green sauce over each serving of eggs. Serve immediately.

Fried Potatoes & Eggs *with* Chile Sauce

Adapted from MM's Papas Fritas

Café Pasqual, Santa Fe, New Mexico

CAFÉ PASQUAL IS WELL KNOWN FOR inspired southwestern cooking. Its rendition of the classic fried potato dish *papas fritas* is just that: a heaping pile of crisp-fried potatoes topped with eggs and smothered with a spicy red chile sauce, cheese, sour cream, and scallions. Flavorful and filling, it's a versatile dish, perfect for breakfast, brunch, or dinner. Without altering the recipe's flavor in the least, we put our own spin on the cooking technique for an easier approach.

Potatoes and eggs may be the prime components of papas fritas, but the red chile sauce steals the show. A staple condiment of the Southwest and many regions of Mexico, the sauce is a mixture of dried chiles, herbs, and spices that is slathered on everything from eggs to enchiladas. Café Pasqual's version is a blend of three distinctive chiles: guajillo for sweetness, ancho for rich fruit flavor, and arbol for intense heat. Onion, garlic, a splash of red wine vinegar, and Mexican oregano—a potent relative of Mediterranean oregano—round out the sauce. All the ingredients are simmered until soft, pureed, and then "fried," a Mexican technique in which sauces are added to a fiery hot skillet to concentrate and combine flavors. We have found that most larger markets nationwide carry a fair selection of dried chiles, but Latino specialty stores are a sure bet. Mexican oregano can be tricky to find outside the specialty stores, but it's worth looking for in the supermarket since some major brands sell it. If you can't find it, it's no big deal: conventional Mediterranean oregano is a more than adequate replacement. Do, however, try to find each of the chiles, since we found the trio important to the sauce's balanced flavor.

The potatoes for this dish are little more than home fries. At the café, the chefs cook Red Bliss potatoes whole and slice them thin before frying, but this took a significant amount of time. It's a valid technique because it prevents the potatoes from absorbing too much moisture as they boil (which is why we boil our potatoes whole for mashed potatoes), but in this dish we had little problem with moisture. Presliced potatoes boiled and fried just fine. We did find that they browned most successfully if cooled before frying, which we accomplished by spreading the blanched slices out on a rimmed baking sheet and refrigerating them for about 15 minutes (though longer—even overnight—didn't hurt). One caveat: sliced potatoes take more careful monitoring when boiling than whole potatoes, since they will overcook quickly.

Bitter and browned or gelatinous and runny, fried eggs are rarely what they should be: creamy white, soft, and flavorful. We've had our fair share of bad eggs and have spent many hours in the test kitchen rectifying the problem. Café Pasqual's instructions were minimal, so we applied our own technique, honed through much experimentation in the test kitchen.

The number one technical problem with fried eggs is heat. The pan is either too hot and the egg white browns, or too cold and the egg white spreads all over the pan. A proper preheat circumvents either extreme. After experimenting with a variety of temperatures, we found that heating a skillet on the lowest setting for five minutes puts it in the ideal temperature range. For a visual cue, a tablespoon of butter added to the pan will swirl easily and foam. If it browns within a minute, the pan is too hot. Picky timing, yes, but the method produces perfect eggs every time.

For this recipe, which requires a dozen fried eggs, a 12-inch nonstick skillet is absolutely necessary, since six eggs may be fried at one go—two batches total. But cracking six eggs at one time without breaking a yolk? A seasoned breakfast cook could do it, but nobody in the test kitchen had such skills. Our solution? Precrack the eggs into bowls, then gently pour the eggs into the hot skillet. Three eggs per bowl, poured into the skillet from opposite sides, spread the eggs out evenly. Once fried, it was easy to slide them out whole onto a plate and then fry the remaining six eggs.

To grace the mountain of potatoes, eggs, and red chile sauce, Café Pasqual adds Monterey Jack cheese, sour cream, and a sprinkle of sliced scallions. We liked all three, though some tasters felt the sour cream was overkill. We leave that up to you, but by no means skip the scallions—they add a much-appreciated sharp note.

Fried Potatoes and Eggs with Chile Sauce

SERVES 6

If you have trouble locating the dried chiles, a Latin specialty store will definitely stock them, or check the Internet—there are numerous mail-order resources. The sauce is also delicious on burritos and enchiladas. Café Pasqual serves this dish with fresh, hot tortillas; we recommend the same. The sauce may be prepared up to 3 days ahead and refrigerated in an airtight container. The potatoes may be parboiled a day ahead of time, but are best fried just before serving.

- **6** large Red Bliss potatoes (about 2 pounds), sliced 1/8 inch thick
- Salt
- **4** dried guajillo chiles, stemmed and seeded
- **3** dried ancho chiles, stemmed and seeded
- **1** de arbol chile, stemmed and seeded
- **1/2** small onion, chopped coarse
- **1** medium garlic clove, peeled
- **1/2** teaspoon dried oregano (preferably Mexican)
- **1 1/2** teaspoons red wine vinegar
- **2** tablespoons vegetable oil
- **5** tablespoons (1/2 stick plus 1 tablespoon) unsalted butter
- Ground black pepper
- **12** large eggs
- **4** ounces Monterey Jack cheese, shredded (1 cup)
- **6** tablespoons sour cream (optional)
- **6** scallions, sliced thin

1. Bring the potatoes, 2 teaspoons salt, and enough water to cover the potatoes by 1 inch to a boil in a large saucepan over medium-high heat. Simmer until just tender, about 5

minutes. Drain, transfer to a rimmed baking sheet, and spread out in a single layer. Refrigerate until slightly cooled, about 15 minutes.

2. Bring the chiles, onion, garlic, oregano, 1 teaspoon salt, 2 cups water, and red wine vinegar to a boil in a medium saucepan over medium-high heat. Remove from the heat and cool for 5 minutes, then process in a blender until smooth, about 30 seconds. Strain the sauce into a medium bowl, pushing on the solids to extract all the liquid.

3. Heat the vegetable oil in a large saucepan over medium-high heat until shimmering. Carefully pour in the sauce. Reduce the heat to medium. Stirring frequently and scraping the pan bottom with a wooden spatula, cook until slightly thickened and darkened in color, 5 to 6 minutes. Remove from the heat and adjust the seasoning with salt. Cover and keep warm.

4. Heat 3 tablespoons of the butter in a large skillet over medium-high heat until the foam subsides. Add the potatoes and cook, stirring occasionally, until cooked through and most slices are lightly browned, about 10 minutes. Season with salt and pepper to taste, cover, and set aside.

5. Heat a 12-inch heavy-bottomed nonstick skillet over low heat for 5 minutes. Meanwhile, crack 3 of the eggs into a small cup or bowl; crack 3 more eggs into a second cup. Melt the remaining 2 tablespoons butter in the skillet. When the foam subsides (this process should take about 1 minute; if the butter browns in 1 minute, the pan is too hot), swirl to coat the pan.

6. Working quickly, pour one cup of eggs on one side of the pan and the second cup on the other side. Season with salt and pepper to taste, then cover and cook for about 2½ minutes for runny yolks, 3 minutes for soft but set yolks, and 3½ minutes for firmly set yolks. Transfer the eggs to a warmed plate and cover with foil to keep warm. Repeat the process with the remaining eggs, skipping the preheating step.

7. Divide the potatoes evenly among 6 warmed plates and top with 2 eggs apiece. Drizzle ¼ cup of the sauce over each portion and garnish with the cheese, sour cream (if desired), and scallions. Serve immediately.

INGREDIENTS: Chiles

The pungent members of the genus Capsicum contain capsaicin, the compound responsible for the mouth-burning, nose-running, sweat-inducing sensations associated with hot peppers. The level of capsaicin in chiles is measured in Scoville units on a scale from a mild zero to a fiery 500,000.

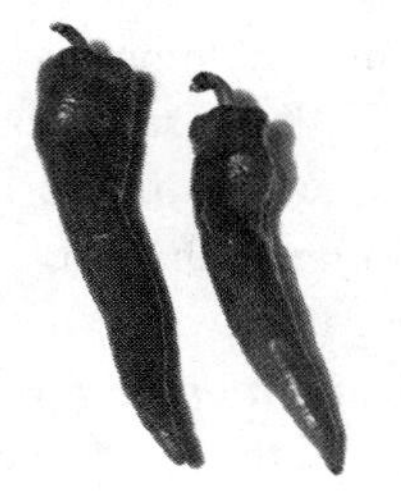

ANAHEIM

Scoville Rating: 2,500 to 5,000

Named after the California city, these pale to medium green peppers are also called California Green when young. At maturation, the chiles turn red and may then be referred to as California Red or Chile Colorado. Because of their sweet, simple flavor and mild heat level, they are often stuffed for chiles rellenos and used in salsas. They are long and narrow—typically 6 to 8 inches long by 1 to 2 inches wide—and have a tough skin that peels off easily when the chile is roasted.

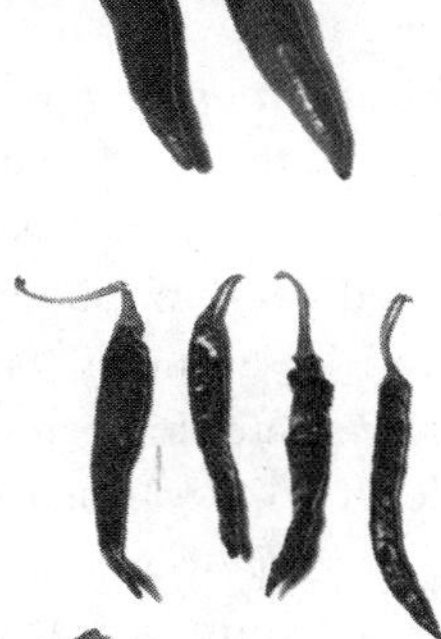

CHILE DE ARBOL

Scoville Rating: 15,000 to 30,000

De Arbol is Spanish for "small tree"—presumably a reference to the small trees on which these chiles grow in Mexico. Depending on maturity, the chiles range in color from green to bright red. Average specimens are 2 to 3 inches long and 1/4 inch in diameter. Chiles de Arbol have thin flesh, thin skin, and a searing, acidic heat. They are often dried and used sparingly in stir-fries.

GUAJILLO

Scoville Rating: 2,000 to 4,500

Grown in Mexico, these chiles are green when young and become a burnished brown-orange-red at maturity. They are relatively long and pointy, measuring about 4 inches by 1 inch. Their fruity flavor and mild heat level make them ideal for moles. Guajillos are also typically stuffed, roasted, or fried.

HABANERO

Scoville Rating: 100,000 to 500,000 units

These chiles have a fierce, intense heat—30 to 60 times hotter than jalapeños. We find these chiles very close in heat level and flavor to Scotch Bonnet chiles. A classic habanero is roughly 2 inches long, 1 to 1 1/2 inches wide, and is shaped like a lantern with a pointed end. When ripe, the color ranges from orange to orange-red to red. Habaneros are native to the Caribbean, the Yucatán, and the north coast of South America.

JALAPEÑO/CHIPOTLE

Scoville Rating: 3,000 to 8,000 units

Named after Jalapa, the capital of Veracruz, jalapeños are one of best known and most widely used chiles in the United States. They have a distinct vegetal flavor when raw, and their heat level varies from mild to moderate. Jalapeños are used fresh, pickled, and dried. Fairly short and stubby, the thick-fleshed chiles are usually

2 to 3 inches long by 1 ½ inches wide. Chipotles are dried, smoked jalapeños. You can find them dried (and reconstitute them yourself), but it's easier to buy them canned, in adobo—a tomato, vinegar, and herb paste.

PIQUILLO

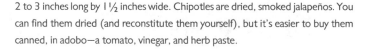

Scoville Rating: 500 to 1,000

These extremely mild, slightly sweet chili peppers (piquillo means "little beak" in Spanish) are grown in the Navarra region of northern Spain. The green or red peppers are typically picked, washed, roasted over wood fires, and then peeled and packed in brine. Jarred piquillo peppers can be found in specialty food shops and from mail-order sources.

POBLANO/ANCHO

Scoville Rating: 2,500 to 3,000

Poblanos have a mild, fruity, smoky (rather than hot) flavor. The blackish green, heart-shaped peppers turn red when fully mature and measure 4 to 7 inches long by 2 ½ to 3 inches wide. Their thick flesh makes them ideal for stuffing. Dried poblano chiles are called ancho chiles.

SCOTCH BONNET

Scoville Rating: 100,000 to 500,000 units

Scotch Bonnet chiles are very close in heat and flavor to habaneros. They hail from Jamaica and are popular throughout the Caribbean. The chiles are wider than they are long, measuring approximately 1 to 1 ½ inches long and 2 to 2 ½ inches wide, and are green, yellow, and orange. The name Scotch Bonnet refers to the pepper's relatively flat, wide shape, which resembles the beret-like Scottish cap called a tam-o'-shanter.

SERRANO

Scoville Rating: 7,000 to 25,000

Highly acidic serranos are a staple of Mexican and Latino cooking—they are considered an all-purpose hot pepper in those cuisines. Narrow and elongated with thin flesh, these chiles typically measure 1 ½ to 3 inches long and ½ inch in diameter. As they mature, serranos turn from bright greenish yellow to red. Dried serranos are known as chiles *secos.*

THAI

Scoville Rating: about 60,000

Used fresh and dried, spicy Thai chiles are referred to as bird chiles or bird peppers when dried. Some sources say they are so named because during drying the chiles curve into the shape of a bird's beak; other sources claim that birds enjoy eating the chiles. Tiny and potent, the cone-shaped chiles measure 1 to 1 ½ inches long by ¼ inch in diameter and have thin flesh and thin skin. The chiles are red when ripe and green when immature.

Spinach-&-Feta-Stuffed Chicken Rolls

Adapted from Chicken Roulades

Café Unicorn, Reading, Pennsylvania

CAFÉ UNICORN'S RECIPE REVIVES PAN-fried chicken breasts, a dish that is too often bland, boring, and overcooked. Here, a flavorful feta and spinach filling is rolled in flattened chicken breasts, coated in bread crumbs, and pan-fried until the coating is light and crispy and the chicken is moist and tender. Served sliced into medallions and arranged over a bed of wilted spinach, the roulades form colorful spirals that elevate chicken breasts to a new level.

To make these roulades, the chicken breasts must be pounded thin. For this recipe, we used a disk-style pounder with a handle in the center (see the illustration on page 163). A rubber mallet found at any hardware store is an inexpensive option. With a heavy head and great leverage, a rubber mallet takes the work out of pounding chicken breasts. Whatever implement you choose, place the chicken breast between two sheets of plastic wrap and, starting in the center of the breast, pound evenly out toward the edges. Pound firmly but gently, taking care not to tear the flesh of the chicken. If you do accidentally tear the flesh, use the toothpicks creatively to secure the breasts once rolled. After cooking, carefully remove the toothpicks and no one will know the difference.

You can use homemade or commercial bread crumbs. In the test kitchen, we typically use panko (Japanese-style bread crumbs), owing to their light, crisp texture and toasty, wheaty flavor. If you can't find panko at your market, try our Homemade Panko, on page 17. Once a crisp crust has formed on the skillet-cooked chicken, place the roulades on a wire rack set over a rimmed baking sheet and place the whole thing in the oven to finish cooking the breasts. This way, the extra fat and moisture will drip away from the breasts into the pan and won't make the crusts soggy.

This recipe calls for two different kinds of spinach. The flat-leaf spinach typically sold in bundles works best in the salad, where its leaves wilt slightly when tossed with the warm vinaigrette. The dark green, crinkly variety sold in plastic bags is used in the roulade filling, where its large, dark green leaves soften when cooked, but retain their shape. Be sure to wash the leaves thoroughly to remove the dirt that stubbornly adheres to them.

Like many recipes with both sautéed and fried ingredients, this recipe calls for two kinds of oil. First, the spinach is cooked in extra-virgin olive oil, while later the stuffed chicken roulades are cooked in vegetable oil.

The reason behind this is a matter of taste and smoke point. Extra-virgin olive oil is rich in taste and, when heated, works best over low to medium heat. We used canola oil to fry the roulades. Canola oil, made from rapeseed, has little flavor of its own and has a relatively high smoke point.

Spinach-and-Feta-Stuffed Chicken Rolls

SERVES 6

When trimming the excess fat and the tenderloins from the chicken breasts, be sure to use a sharp chef's or boning knife. Dull knives are dangerous and will make sloppy, imprecise cuts. It is a good practice to dry the chicken breasts with paper towels prior to trimming. A good drying will keep the meat from slipping around on the cutting board.

The chicken breasts can be pounded, filled, and rolled in advance, then refrigerated for up to 24 hours. Coat them with the flour, egg mixture, and bread crumbs when ready to cook.

- **2 tablespoons plus 1/4 cup extra-virgin olive oil**
- **2 (10-ounce) bags crinkly-leaf spinach, stemmed, washed, and dried**
- **6 medium boneless, skinless chicken breasts (6–8 ounces each), tenderloins removed and reserved for another use, trimmed of excess fat**
- **Salt and ground black pepper**
- **9 ounces feta cheese, crumbled (about 1 1/2 cups)**
- **1 1/2 cups unbleached all-purpose flour**
- **3 large eggs**
- **1 cup canola oil**
- **2 1/2 cups panko (Japanese-style bread crumbs) or Homemade Panko (page 17)**
- **1 pound flat-leaf spinach (1 bunch), stemmed, washed, and dried**
- **2 medium garlic cloves, minced or pressed through a garlic press**
- **1/4 teaspoon dried oregano**
- **2 tablespoons juice from 1 lemon**
- **Toothpicks, for securing the chicken rolls**

1. Adjust an oven rack to the middle position and heat the oven to 400 degrees. Heat 1 tablespoon of the olive oil in a 12-inch nonstick skillet over medium heat until shimmering. Add half of the crinkly-leaf spinach and cook, tossing constantly with tongs, until slightly wilted, about 2 minutes.

EQUIPMENT: Meat Pounder

In the test kitchen, we tried several pounding gadgets—makeshift as well as purchased—and found that the best chicken breast pounders were relatively lightweight, with large flat surfaces. A disk-style pounder with a handle in the center was our favorite. As long as we pounded lightly, its relatively large, round surface quickly and efficiently transformed breasts into cutlets. If you don't have this kind of pounder, we suggest pounding gently with what you have on hand, which is likely heavier than our disk-style pounder. A rubber mallet or rolling pin would be our second choice, but the bottom of a small saucepan will work in a pinch.

THE BEST MEAT POUNDER
We tested several styles of meat pounders and found that a disk-style pounder with a handle in the center is the gentlest on delicate chicken cutlets; it is our top choice.

Transfer to a medium bowl and repeat with 1 tablespoon of the remaining olive oil and the remaining crinkly-leaf spinach.

2. Pound the chicken breasts, following the illustration below. Working with 1 piece of chicken at a time, place the breasts, smooth-side down, on a work surface covered with plastic wrap. Season the breasts with salt and pepper. Place ¼ cup lightly packed wilted spinach leaves on the tapered end of each breast, layer ¼ cup lightly packed feta on the spinach, and then top with an additional ¼ cup wilted spinach. Roll up the breast and secure with a toothpick. Transfer the roulade to a clean plate. Repeat with the remaining chicken.

3. Spread the flour in a shallow dish or pie plate. Whisk the eggs with ¼ cup of the canola oil in a separate shallow dish. Spread the panko in a third dish. Position the flour, egg, and panko plates in a row. Roll a roulade in the flour and pat it to remove any excess. Then, using tongs, dip it into the egg mixture, turning to coat well, and allow the excess to drip off. Place the roulade in the panko and press the crumbs lightly to adhere. Place the roulade on a wire rack set over a rimmed baking sheet. Repeat with the remaining roulades.

4. Heat the remaining ¾ cup canola oil in a 12-inch nonstick skillet over medium-high heat until it shimmers. Add 3 of the roulades seam-side down and cook until medium golden brown, about 4 minutes. Turn each roulade and cook until medium golden brown on all sides, 3 to 5 minutes longer. Return the roulades seam-side down to the rack set over the baking sheet. Repeat with the 3 remaining roulades.

5. Place the baking sheet in the oven and bake until the roulades are deep golden brown and an instant-read thermometer inserted into the center of each roll registers 160 degrees, 10 to 15 minutes. Remove from the oven and allow to rest for 5 minutes. Carefully remove the toothpicks from the roulades.

6. Meanwhile, place the flat-leaf spinach in a large bowl and set aside. Heat the remaining ¼ cup olive oil, garlic, and oregano in a small saucepan over low heat, stirring frequently, until warm, about 1½ minutes. Remove the pan from the heat, swirl in the lemon juice, and season with salt and pepper to taste. Pour the warm vinaigrette over the flat-leaf spinach and toss to wilt slightly.

7. Divide the flat-leaf spinach among 6 individual plates. Slice each roulade crosswise on the bias into 5 medallions. Arrange the slices over the flat-leaf spinach. Serve immediately.

POUNDING CHICKEN FOR CUTLETS

Place the breasts, smooth-side down, on a large sheet of plastic wrap. Cover with a second sheet of plastic and pound gently. The cutlets should already be thin; you simply want to make sure that they have the same thickness from end to end.

Grilled Lime Chicken *with* Black Bean Rice & Pumpkin Seed Guacamole

Adapted from Key Lime Chicken with Black Bean Rice and Pepita Guacamole

Nava, Atlanta, Georgia

NAVA USES THE SWEET-TART, EXOTIC FLAVOR and perfumed aroma of Key limes on the savory side of the menu as well as the sweet. Its Key lime chicken is a finely balanced and complexly flavored dish, redolent of spicy arbol chiles, pungent cilantro, and cooling lime. All the components of the dish spell work for the cook, but with some time-saving steps we were able to move it from the restaurant realm to the home kitchen.

We found that the best way to prepare the dish was to make the components that held best first, and finish with the chicken. The arbol chile–vinegar sauce, a sweet and spicy blend of arbol chiles, roasted red bell peppers, garlic, shallots, sugar, and champagne vinegar, gives the dish much of its heat. Arbol chiles are smallish red chiles popular in the Southwest that pack a heat level and flavor similar to cayenne pepper. Hot, but not incendiary, they provide a fruity punch. Normally toasted and ground to a powder, in this dish the chiles instead are simmered with the other ingredients and, once soft, pureed and strained. We were able to trim some work from the original recipe by replacing fresh-roasted bell peppers with jarred roasted peppers—tasters couldn't detect much of a difference. A little sauce goes a long way; we halved the recipe sent by Nava and still had plenty left over to pass at the table and slather on quesadillas the following day.

For the black bean rice, Nava simply folds black beans into rice seasoned with garlic and jalapeño, but there's a surprise: the rice is cooked in the liquid left over from cooking the beans. The starchy water turns the rice an inky shade of blue and imbues it with a mildly beany flavor. The rice tasted great and we were suitably impressed with the method, which we had never come across before. But there was a problem in that we hoped to substitute canned beans for the dried to trim time from the already labor-intensive recipe. We tried adding that sludgy goo the beans come packed in to the rice, but that accomplished little except negatively affecting the rice's texture. On a whim, we pureed a portion of the beans with enough water to cook the rice in. The results were very thick, but akin to the leftover bean water. A few tests and we found the ideal ratio: ¾ cup beans to 2½ cups water.

Nava's guacamole is pretty standard, outside of the inclusion of pepitas, or toasted pumpkin seeds. The seeds add a pleasing crunch and nuttiness that works well with the rest of the dish. Most natural food stores sell them in bulk bins. The amount of lime juice added makes the guacamole surprisingly tart, but when tasted against the dish as a whole, the sharpness mitigated the sweetness of the beans and rice and intensified the chicken's flavor.

With all the components prepared, we finally tackled the chicken. At Nava, the chefs marinate the chicken breasts in a sweet-tart blend of Key lime juice, sugar, arbol chiles, garlic, shallots, and cilantro prior to grilling. Key limes lend the marinade an inimitable flavor, but, unfortunately, can be hard to find. Some markets stock fresh Key limes, but bottled juice is the norm. If Key lime juice—fresh or bottled—proves too difficult to locate, conventional lime juice, we found, is an adequate substitute.

The restaurant grills the chicken for flavor and color, and then finishes it in the oven to prevent the meat from drying out. We chose to start and finish the chicken on the grill, using a technique we developed that guarantees moist chicken. We make a two-level fire and start the chicken on the high-heat side, then, once it is grill-streaked, we transfer it to the lower heat to finish, covered with a disposable aluminum roasting pan. The results were moist and flavorful, but, surprisingly, the marinade flavor was fleeting, even after hours of marination. We decided to change tack completely and apply the marinade almost as a glaze once the chicken was cooked. The flavors stayed bright and the aroma pungent—much more so than when the chicken was coated prior to cooking.

BUILDING A MODIFIED TWO-LEVEL FIRE

Pile all the lit coals into half the grill. Leave the remaining portion of the grill empty. Some heat from the coals will still cook foods placed over the empty part of the grill, but the heat is very gentle and no browning will occur here.

Grilled Lime Chicken with Black Bean Rice and Pumpkin Seed Guacamole

SERVES 6

If firing up the grill is too much effort, a grill pan can lend a similar smoky flavor and grill-streaked appearance. Brush the pan with vegetable oil and heat it over high heat until smoking. Cook the breasts until grill-marked on each side, then finish them on a baking sheet in a 350-degree oven. If you can find only salted pepitas (pumpkin seeds), do not season the guacamole until the pepitas are added; otherwise it may be too salty. This dish can easily serve 8 if more chicken breasts are cooked (there should be enough marinade). If you can find Key lime juice for this recipe, by all means use it, but regular lime juice (from Persian limes) will work just as well.

ARBOL CHILE–VINEGAR SAUCE

- 3/4 cup champagne vinegar
- 3/4 cup sugar
- 3/4 cup coarsely chopped jarred roasted red bell peppers
- 4 arbol chiles, stemmed and seeded (or 1 1/2 teaspoons red pepper flakes)
- 1 medium shallot, sliced thin
- 2 medium garlic cloves, chopped coarse
- 1/2 teaspoon salt

BLACK BEAN RICE

- 2 (15-ounce) cans black beans, well rinsed
- 1 tablespoon vegetable oil
- 1 small jalapeño pepper, seeded, ribs removed, and minced
- 2 medium garlic cloves, minced or pressed through a garlic press (about 2 teaspoons)
- 2 cups long-grain white rice, rinsed well
- 1/2 teaspoon salt
- 1/4 cup chopped fresh cilantro leaves

PUMPKIN SEED GUACAMOLE

- 2 ripe avocados, halved, pitted, flesh scooped from the skin, and coarsely mashed
- 1/4 cup minced red onion
- 1/4 cup chopped fresh cilantro leaves
- 1/4 cup toasted pumpkin seeds (pepitas)
- 1/2 teaspoon salt
- 2 tablespoons juice from 1 lime

LIME CHICKEN

- 1/4 cup sugar
- 4 arbol chiles, stemmed and seeded (or 1 1/2 teaspoons red pepper flakes)
- 3 medium garlic cloves, chopped coarse
- 1 small shallot, sliced
- Salt
- 1/4 cup lime juice from 2 limes (or 1/4 cup juice from 4–5 Key limes)
- 1 bunch fresh cilantro (including stems), washed and chopped coarse (about 1 1/2 cups)
- 3/4 cup vegetable oil
- 6 8 to 10-ounce bone-in, skin-on chicken breasts, patted dry with paper towels
- Ground black pepper

1. FOR THE ARBOL CHILE–VINEGAR SAUCE: Bring all the ingredients and ¼ cup water to a boil in a small saucepan over medium-high heat. Reduce the heat to medium and cook until slightly thickened and the chiles have softened, 10 to 12 minutes. Transfer the mixture to a blender and process until smooth, about 1 minute. Strain the mixture through a wire-mesh strainer over a small saucepan, cover to keep warm, and set aside. The sauce can be kept, refrigerated, in a covered container for up to 2 weeks.

2. FOR THE BLACK BEAN RICE: Process ¾ cup of the black beans and 2½ cups water in a blender until smooth, about 30 seconds. Strain the mixture through a clean wire-mesh strainer over a medium bowl. You should have 3 cups liquid (add more water if necessary). Heat the vegetable oil in a medium saucepan over medium-high heat until shimmering. Add the jalapeño and garlic and cook until very fragrant, about 30 seconds. Add the rice and salt and cook, stirring constantly, until the grains are coated with oil, about 1 minute. Add the bean liquid and bring to a boil. Stir the rice to release any adhered grains, then reduce the heat to low and cover the pot. Cook until the rice is tender and the liquid is fully absorbed, 17 to 18 minutes. Using a large fork, gently stir in the remaining beans and cilantro. Cover the pot again, sandwiching a double layer of paper

towels between the lid and the pot to absorb moisture, and set aside.

3. For the guacamole: Mix all the ingredients in a medium bowl until just combined. Cover with plastic wrap and set aside.

4. For the chicken: Process the sugar, chiles, garlic, shallot, and 1 teaspoon salt in a food processor until coarsely combined, about 20 seconds. Add the lime juice and cilantro and process until smooth, about 30 seconds, scraping down the sides of the workbowl as necessary using a rubber spatula. With the machine running, slowly pour in the vegetable oil through the feed tube. Transfer to a small bowl and set aside.

5. Light 5 quarts charcoal (1 chimney starter heaped full) and allow to burn until the flames have died down and all the charcoal is covered with a layer of fine, gray ash. Spread the coals out over half of the grill bottom, leaving the other half with no coals. Set the cooking grate in place and let it heat up for 5 minutes. Scrape the grate clean.

6. Season the chicken breasts generously with salt and pepper. Place the chicken skin-side down on the grill rack directly over the coals and grill until well browned, 2 to 3 minutes per side. Move the chicken to the area with no fire and cover with a disposable aluminum roasting pan. Cook skin-side up for 10 minutes. Turn and cook for 5 minutes longer. To test for doneness, either peek into the thickest part of the chicken with the tip of a small knife (you should see no redness near the bone) or check the internal temperature at the thickest part with an instant-read thermometer, which should register 160 degrees. Immediately transfer the chicken to a large bowl and toss with the lime mixture. Tent the bowl with aluminum foil and allow to rest for 5 minutes.

7. Divide the black bean rice evenly among the centers of 6 large plates. Remove the chicken from the lime mixture; discard the lime mixture. Lean a chicken breast against the pile of rice and drizzle the arbol chile–vinegar sauce around it. Place a dollop of the guacamole on top of the chicken. Serve immediately, accompanied by any remaining sauce and guacamole.

Rosemary Roasted Split Chicken

Adapted from Rosemary Roasted Split Chicken
Lambert's American Kitchen, Austin, Texas

LAMBERT'S AMERICAN KITCHEN MAKES A roasted split chicken that's golden on the outside, with tender and juicy white meat and dark meat close to falling off the bone, all subtly spiced with the piney flavor of rosemary. Cooking a split chicken at home to resemble the crisp-skinned, herb-infused comfort food that is easily come by in a restaurant would seem a simple task. Alas, most home-cooked chickens are either grossly overcooked, with dry, tasteless, stringy meat, or baked at an oven temperature so low that the possibility of crunchy, golden skin is nonexistent.

In our first test, we followed the instructions given, which were to split the bird, season it well, and roast it at 450 degrees for 20 minutes. At that point, the chicken was removed from the oven, cut into pieces, and returned to a 350-degree oven for an additional 15 minutes. What resulted was not the crisp, tender bird we were hoping for, and we were fairly sure we knew why. Most restaurants are equipped with convection ovens that circulate the heat around the food, thereby reducing the overall cooking time and delivering that crackling crust we knew would be difficult to achieve at home without a bit of kitchen ingenuity.

To begin with, we noticed that when we cut up the chicken after the initial roasting, we lost valuable juices to our cutting board. We decided to save a step (and the juices) and postpone the portioning until the bird was completely cooked and rested. To coax the skin into crispness, we used another restaurant technique, in which the chicken is browned skin-side down in a hot skillet on top of the stove, then slid into a hot oven skin-side up to finish cooking. The results were what we were hoping for: crisp, golden skin and moist, juicy chicken throughout.

Infusing sufficient rosemary flavor into the chicken proved to be our next challenge. Rubbing the herb onto the skin prior to browning in the skillet resulted in burned, bitter twigs, while rosemary placed under the skin steamed and imparted a medicinal flavor. We found that steeping the rosemary leaves (along with some black pepper) in the olive oil, then brushing the mixture on the chicken prior to oven-roasting, eliminated any off flavors, with the added benefit of keeping the bird moist and flavorful. Allowing the chicken to rest for 10 minutes assures moist meat by allowing the juices to be redistributed.

Rosemary Roasted Split Chicken

SERVES 4

Sharp poultry shears make light work of splitting the chicken. Alternatively, chicken can be purchased split, or ask your butcher to split it for you.

- **1 whole chicken, 3–3 1/2 pounds**
- **Salt and ground black pepper**
- **1 teaspoon vegetable oil**
- **1/4 cup extra-virgin olive oil**
- **1/2 teaspoon minced fresh rosemary**
- **2 tablespoons juice from 1 lemon**

1. Following the illustrations below, place the chicken breast-side down with the tail facing you, and use poultry shears to cut along the entire length of one side of the backbone. With the breast-side still down, turn the neck end to face you, cut along the other side of the backbone, and remove it. Using a sharp knife, cut the chicken in half by cutting down the middle of the breast. Pat the chicken dry with paper towels. Season with salt and pepper to taste.

2. Adjust an oven rack to the lowest position and heat the oven to 450 degrees. Heat the vegetable oil in a 12-inch heavy-bottomed ovenproof skillet over medium-high heat until just smoking. Swirl the skillet to coat evenly with the oil. Place the chicken skin-side down in the hot pan and reduce the heat to medium. Cook until evenly browned, 20 to 25 minutes. After 20 minutes, the skin should be crisp and golden. If it is not, increase the heat to medium-high and cook until well browned.

3. Meanwhile, mix the olive oil, 2 teaspoons pepper, and rosemary together in a small microwave-safe bowl and cover. Heat on high power for 1 minute and set aside.

4. Using tongs, carefully flip the chicken skin-side up. (If more that 3 tablespoons fat have accumulated in the skillet, transfer the chicken to a clean plate and pour most of the fat out of the skillet. Return the chicken to the skillet skin-side up and continue.) Brush the skin with the olive oil mixture and place the skillet in the oven. Roast until the thickest part of the breast registers 160 degrees on an instant-read thermometer and the thickest part of the thigh registers 170 degrees, 7 to 10 minutes. Transfer the chicken to a platter and let rest for 5 to 10 minutes. Carve, drizzle the lemon juice over the chicken, and serve.

REMOVING THE BACKBONE FROM A CHICKEN

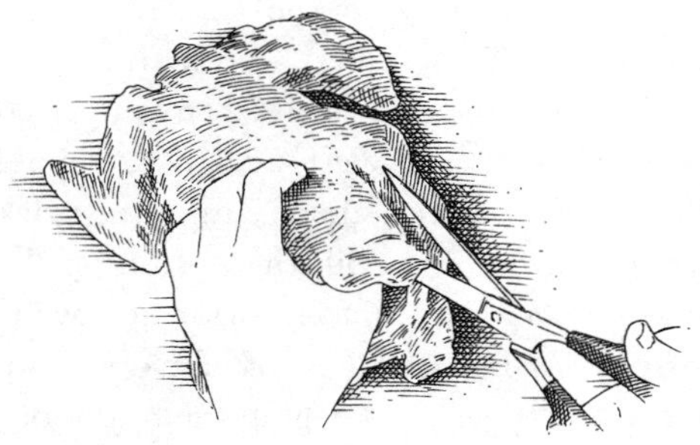

1. With the breast-side down and the tail of the chicken facing you, use poultry shears to cut along one side of the backbone down its entire length.

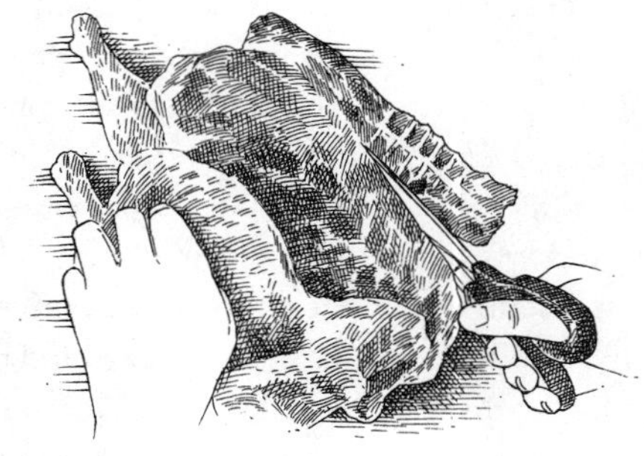

2. With the breast-side still down, turn the neck end to face you and cut along the other side of the backbone to remove it.

Sautéed Quail & Watercress Salad *with* Citrus Vinaigrette

Adapted from Quail with Orange Lime Reduction

Town, New York, New York

PEOPLE SEEM TO SHY AWAY FROM COOKING game birds such as quail, squab, and pheasant at home. Thinking that they need special handling or intricate cooking methods, most will leave these fowl to the professionals and enjoy them in a restaurant. But this intriguingly flavored quail recipe from Town will quickly dispel any such thoughts.

At Town, the meaty quail is seasoned with an exotically flavored spice rub redolent of orange and coriander. Sautéed until the skin is crisp, the quail is served on a bed of peppery watercress, which has been dressed with a citrus vinaigrette. As it stood, this recipe was very good. We did, however, make several modifications to streamline it.

With regard to the marinade, the original recipe included a procedure for making orange powder, which entailed blanching orange zest in sugar water, then air-drying it overnight. This slightly candied zest was then ground in a spice grinder and mixed with several other spices to make a dry rub–like marinade. While we liked the intense orange flavor this lent the quail, we had to consider the fact that this process was a significant investment of time and that most home cooks don't have a spice grinder. We searched for alternatives. Much to our surprise, we found that McCormick, a national spice maker, produces dried orange peel. Preparing the dish again, this time substituting the orange peel for the orange powder, we found the results similar, except the quail tasted slightly bitter. It was obvious that the store-bought orange peel lacked the sweetness that the original recipe had gained from the blanching in sugar water. To rectify this, we added a small amount of sugar to the marinade and found that when tasted side by side, the two marinades tasted virtually the same.

The salad the quail was served on also needed tweaking. While the salad was flavorful, the recipe, which called for four bunches of watercress and a scant ½ cup of dressing, was a tad on the dry side and made too much salad for four servings. Thinking we could just reduce the amount of watercress, we tried making the dish again using only two bunches of watercress. This test produced less salad, but we felt that it lacked punch. Given that watercress is fairly hearty and spicy, we sought a dressing that was more acidic. The recipe, which reduced citrus juices before making the vinaigrette, had intense flavor, but the juices lost some of their acidity during the cooking, making it a more subtly flavored dressing. So instead of making the vinaigrette with reduced citrus juices, we felt it was better to leave them in their raw state. The dressing had a more pronounced and livelier flavor, and the preparation time was significantly reduced.

The presentation of this dish, like the recipe itself, is straightforward. The crisp quail is perched atop a mound of watercress and then drizzled with leftover vinaigrette, producing an understated but elegant dish that can be prepared with ease by any home cook.

Sautéed Quail and Watercress Salad with Citrus Vinaigrette

SERVES 4

Ask your butcher for "sleeved" quail, which means that the ribs and backbones have been removed. There are two advantages to using these quail: they cook more evenly and they are easier to eat.

CITRUS VINAIGRETTE

- **1/4 cup olive oil**
- **2 tablespoons juice from 1 orange**
- **1 tablespoon juice from 1 lemon**
- **1 small shallot, minced (about 2 tablespoons)**
- **Salt and ground black pepper**

QUAIL

- **2 teaspoons fresh thyme leaves**
- **1 1/2 teaspoons dried orange peel (such as McCormick)**
- **1 teaspoon ground coriander**
- **1/4 teaspoon sugar**
- **1/2 teaspoon ground black pepper**
- **4 semiboneless (sleeved) quail (about 5 ounces each), rinsed and patted dry**
- **2 tablespoons olive oil**
- **2 tablespoons unsalted butter**
- **2 large bunches watercress, washed, dried, and large stems removed (about 6 lightly packed cups)**

1. FOR THE VINAIGRETTE: Whisk together the olive oil, orange juice, lemon juice, and shallot. Season with salt and pepper to taste. Set aside.

2. FOR THE QUAIL: Combine the thyme, orange peel, coriander, sugar, and pepper in a small bowl. Sprinkle both sides of the quail liberally with spice mixture.

3. Heat the olive oil and butter in a 12-inch skillet over medium-high heat until the foam subsides. Add the quail breast-side down and sauté until golden brown, about 4 minutes. Reduce the heat to medium and, using tongs, turn the quail and sauté until golden brown on the second side, 3 to 4 minutes longer. Transfer to a clean plate, cover loosely with foil, and let rest for 5 minutes.

4. Rewhisk the vinaigrette to combine. Toss the watercress with 4 tablespoons of the vinaigrette in a large bowl. Place a mound of watercress in the center of each of 4 plates. Cut the quail in half lengthwise and arrange over the watercress. Drizzle the quail with the remaining vinaigrette. Serve immediately.

Swedish Meatballs *with* Mashed Potatoes, Cranberry Sauce, & Pickled Cucumbers

Adapted from Swedish Meatballs with Mashed Potatoes, Cranberry Sauce, and Pickled Cucumbers

AQUAVIT, NEW YORK, NEW YORK

ONE DOESN'T USUALLY THINK OF SWEDISH meatballs as a restaurant dish, unless, that is, you're dining at the upscale Scandinavian restaurant Aquavit. Tasters in the test kitchen became quickly enamored with these rich, tender meatballs served with crisp, sweet, pickled cucumbers, ultrarich mashed potatoes, and cranberry sauce. (The restaurant serves the dish with the traditional lingonberry when it's available.) The multicomponent dish seems like a lot for the home cook to tackle, but the results are so festive that the preparation will be worth the effort for a special occasion.

For the meatballs, we had no trouble preparing them exactly as the restaurant instructed. Far richer than everyday meatballs, this recipe contains the standard mixture of ground beef, pork, and veal but is enriched with heavy cream, which enhances the meat's tenderness, along with honey, for a slight, earthy sweetness. We found that a 1½-inch ice cream scoop makes meatball-shaping a breeze and guarantees a consistent size and shape. To keep the meatballs light and tender, avoid compacting them with the scoop, which will turn them hard and dense.

The potatoes are light in texture and made extraordinarily rich with cream, milk, olive oil, and butter. Using a ricer or a food mill produces very smooth mashed potatoes. Be careful not to overcook the potatoes, because the starch cells will break down and create a sticky mass. Cook just until a thin-bladed knife inserted in the potatoes meets little resistance.

The recipe specifies an unusual and intriguing method of making cranberry sauce. Raw cranberries and sugar are combined in the bowl of a standing mixer and mixed on low speed for 40 minutes. According to Aquavit's chef, Marcus Samuelsson, this method approximates the traditional Swedish method of making the sauce wherein berries are spread out on a large tray, sprinkled with sugar, left at room temperature, and mixed by hand about every 20 minutes over the course of a day. At the end of the day, the sugar has dissolved and combined with the juices of the ruptured berries to produce a rich, deep red, syrupy sauce.

Ever the skeptics and always eager to simplify steps, we wondered if the food processor might produce the same results in significantly less time. The results were disappointing. The food processor shredded the cranberry skins into tiny strips, losing the lovely texture of the sauce. We also tried making the sauce in the standing mixer set on a high speed. At high speeds, the mixer aerated the syrup created from the cranberry juices and the sugar. The resulting sauce was lighter in color and frothy, with a carbonated mouthfeel. Finally, we took a look at traditional American holiday cranberry sauce, which is typically a cooked mixture of cranberries, water, and sugar. The two sauces, we discovered, are simply too different to use interchangeably. American holiday cranberry sauce should have the texture of a soft gel. Heat releases the berries' natural pectin, which acts as a thickening agent. The Swedish version, on the other hand, is not cooked and therefore its texture is syrupy but not gelatinous. Our conclusion: follow the restaurant's instructions for a deep red, syrupy sauce. After all, the mixer would be doing the work for us—and we'd be free to proceed with the recipe.

The only real work we had to tackle with the pickled cucumbers was in slicing them. If you have a mandoline or plastic vegetable slicer, by all means use it. (See page 8 for more information on these tools.) If not, use the slicing disk of a food processor—the slices won't be consistently thin, but they will be close. The pickling liquid in which the cucumber slices soak is a mixture of vermouth, sugar, and allspice berries—new to us in the test kitchen, but very tasty, resulting in pickles with a sweet, slightly spicy, boozy flavor.

We used the skillet in which the meatballs are cooked to make a simple, flavorful pan sauce. A quick combination of chicken broth, cream, some of the cranberry sauce, and a bit of the liquid used to pickle the cucumbers unifies all of the flavors in the dish. The meatballs are then added to the skillet and reheated. Served family style or plated, the combination of colors, flavors, and textures in this dish uplifts the mundane meatball to star status.

Swedish Meatballs with Mashed Potatoes, Cranberry Sauce, and Pickled Cucumbers

SERVES 6 TO 8
(MAKES 36 MEATBALLS)

Start the pickles the day before you plan to serve this dish. Using a mandoline or plastic vegetable slicer makes quick work of the cucumber slicing.

PICKLED CUCUMBERS

- 1 cup dry vermouth or white wine
- 2 cups sugar
- 1 bay leaf
- 2 allspice berries
- 1 English cucumber, sliced as thin as possible

CRANBERRY SAUCE

- 8 ounces (about 2 cups) fresh or frozen cranberries, thawed if using frozen
- 3/4 cup sugar

MEATBALLS

- 1/2 cup plus 1 tablespoon vegetable oil
- 1 medium onion, minced (about 1 cup)
- 1 1/2 cups dried bread crumbs (about 2 1/2 ounces)
- 2 1/2 cups heavy cream
- 12 ounces ground beef

- **12 ounces ground veal**
- **12 ounces ground pork**
- **2 large eggs, lightly beaten**
- **3 tablespoons honey**
- **Salt and ground black pepper**
- **2 cups low-sodium chicken broth**

MASHED POTATOES

- **8 medium Yukon Gold potatoes (about 3 pounds), peeled and cut into 2-inch pieces**
- **Salt**
- **4 tablespoons (1/2 stick) unsalted butter**
- **1 cup milk**
- **1/2 cup heavy cream**
- **1/2 cup olive oil**
- **1/2 teaspoon ground nutmeg**
- **Ground black pepper**

1. FOR THE PICKLED CUCUMBERS: Bring 3 cups water, vermouth, sugar, bay leaf, and allspice berries to a boil in a medium saucepan over high heat. Remove the pan from the heat and cool the mixture, about 30 minutes. Place the cucumber slices in a large plastic container with a lid. Pour the cooled pickling mixture over the slices, cover, and refrigerate for at least 12 hours. Drain, reserving ¼ cup of the pickling liquid in a separate bowl. Place the drained cucumbers in a serving bowl and refrigerate until ready to serve.

2. FOR THE CRANBERRY SAUCE: In the bowl of a standing mixer fitted with the paddle attachment, mix the cranberries and sugar on low until the cranberry skins have burst and the sauce is slightly thick and syrupy, about 40 minutes. Transfer ½ cup of the sauce to a separate bowl and set aside. Place the remaining cranberry sauce in a small serving bowl and set aside until ready to serve.

3. FOR THE MEATBALLS: Heat 1 tablespoon of the vegetable oil in a small sauté pan over medium heat until the oil shimmers. Add the onion and cook, stirring occasionally, until softened but not browned, about 5 minutes. Remove the pan from the heat and set aside to cool. Combine the bread crumbs and 1½ cups of the heavy cream in a medium bowl. Stir the mixture with a fork until smooth. Combine the beef, veal, pork, sautéed onion, eggs, and honey in a large bowl. Add the bread crumb mixture, 2 teaspoons salt, and ½ teaspoon pepper to the meat mixture and mix until fully incorporated. Using a 1½-inch ice cream scoop, lightly shape about 1 ounce, or 3 tablespoons, of the meat mixture into a round meatball the size of a golf ball without compacting the meat. Transfer to a rimmed baking sheet lined with parchment paper. You should have about 36 meatballs.

4. Heat the remaining ½ cup vegetable oil in a 12-inch nonstick skillet over medium-high heat until the edge of a meatball dipped in the oil sizzles. Add half the meatballs in a single layer and cook, adjusting the heat as needed to keep the oil sizzling but not smoking, until well browned on all sides, about 5 minutes, turning as needed. Using a slotted spoon, transfer the meatballs to a plate lined with several layers of paper towels. Repeat with the remaining meatballs. Set the meatballs and the skillet aside.

5. FOR THE MASHED POTATOES: While the meatballs are cooking, bring the potatoes, ½ teaspoon salt, and enough water to cover the potatoes by 2 inches to a boil in a large saucepan over high heat. Reduce the heat to medium-low and simmer until a paring knife slipped into the centers of the potatoes meets very little resistance, 15 to 20 minutes.

6. About 5 minutes before the potatoes are done, melt 2 tablespoons of the butter in a small heavy-bottomed saucepan over medium heat. Cook, swirling the pan frequently, until the butter turns light brown

and fragrant, about 4 minutes. Remove the pan from the heat and set aside. Combine the milk and cream in a medium, microwave-proof bowl and microwave on low until warm to the touch, 15 to 30 seconds. Set aside.

7. Drain the potatoes. Set a food mill or potato ricer over the now empty but still warm pan. Working in batches, drop the potatoes into the food mill or ricer and process the potatoes into the pan. Using a wooden spoon, stir in the browned butter, remaining 2 tablespoons butter, and olive oil until incorporated. Gently whisk in the milk mixture, add the nutmeg, and season with salt and pepper to taste. Transfer the mashed potatoes to a bowl that fits snugly over a saucepan containing about 3 inches barely simmering water. Cover with a pot lid or aluminum foil. Remove from heat. Set aside.

8. TO FINISH THE MEATBALLS: Pour off all the fat from the skillet and return to medium-high heat. Add the chicken broth, remaining 1 cup cream, reserved ½ cup cranberry sauce, and reserved ¼ cup pickling liquid. Simmer, scraping the browned bits off the pan bottom, until the mixture thickens slightly and is reduced to 1½ cups, about 20 minutes. Return the meatballs to the skillet and simmer until they are cooked through, 1 to 2 minutes

9. TO SERVE: Divide the mashed potatoes among individual plates. Divide the meatballs evenly among the plates, placing them on top of the mashed potatoes, and pour about ¼ cup of the sauce over the top. Serve immediately, accompanied by the pickled cucumbers and cranberry sauce.

EQUIPMENT: Food Mills

A food mill is no longer a fixture in the American kitchen, but it is a terrific tool to have on hand. Think of it as part food processor (because it refines soft foods to a puree) and part sieve (because it separates waste such as peels, seeds, cores, and fiber from the puree as you go). And it accomplishes all of this with a simple turn of the crank, which rotates a gently angled, curved blade that catches the food and forces it down through the holes of a perforated disk at the bottom of the mill. The separation of unwanted material from the puree is the food mill's raison d'être, but another benefit is that it does not aerate the food as it purees, as do electric mixers, food processors, and blenders, so you are able to avoid an overly whipped texture.

Seeing that you can spend as little as $15 and as much as $90 on a food mill, we wondered if some were better than others. Of the five models tested, the top performer was the Cuisipro (top), but it costs $90. The $15 Moulinex (bottom) did nearly as well, so it became the pick of the pack for its combination of price and performance. The plastic is surely not as strong as the Cuisipro's stainless steel, but for occasional use it works just fine.

THE BEST FOOD MILLS
Price may determine your choice of the top performers in our foodmill testing. The stainless steel Cuispro (top) costs $90. The plastic Moulinex (bottom) performed nearly as well and costs just $15.

Grilled Skirt Steak *with* Kimchee

Adapted from Grilled Skirt Steak with Kimchee
THE BLUE ROOM, CAMBRIDGE, MASSACHUSETTS

KIMCHEE, A NATIONAL DISH OF KOREA, IS usually eaten as a condiment at every Korean meal. Consisting mainly of fermented cabbage, it is akin to German sauerkraut. Made by a form of pickling, kimchee is usually buried in jars in the ground, where it is allowed to ferment and build its strong and spicy flavor. While the Blue Room doesn't bury its kimchee, it is nonetheless very tasty. By pairing kimchee with grilled steak in this recipe, the Blue Room has hit upon an unbeatable flavor combination.

The Blue Room's recipe for kimchee required a lengthy three-day preparation process. While this method was quick compared with the traditional way of making kimchee, we wondered if it was possible to shorten the preparation time. The initial step in making the Blue Room's kimchee was to "cure" the cabbage in kosher salt. This was done by tossing the cabbage with a copious amount of salt and then letting it sit covered in the refrigerator for two days while it wilted. This wilted cabbage was then combined with other vegetables and tossed with an intensely flavored, brine-like liquid after which it sat for another 24-hour period, giving the flavors time to meld. (We also found it necessary to use a container with a tight-fitting lid so as not to let the strong odors permeate the refrigerator.)

While we know that it takes time to make kimchee properly, we sought to consolidate and shorten the process. We looked first to the method of curing and tried varying the time that the cabbage spent curing with the salt. After many tests, we found that the cabbage needs to spend at least 24 hours with the salt. Anything less and the cabbage didn't wilt enough or achieve the slightly fermented flavor that we associate with kimchee. Cabbage that spent over 24 hours curing had a more pronounced fermented flavor, but the change was so slight that we felt the extra time wasn't worth it.

We next addressed the "pickling" of the cabbage. The pickling liquid, used to both flavor and preserve the cabbage, begins with a paste made by pureeing chili-garlic sauce, dried shrimp, and fish sauce until smooth. The paste is then added to a hot mixture of garlic, ginger, and sugar and simmered to blend the flavors. Fish sauce and dried shrimp are distinctly Asian ingredients that some American palates may find too potent on their own, but blended in this mixture they lend the kimchee a hard-to-beat depth of flavor.

Because the liquid contained so many

flavorful ingredients, we agreed that time would be needed for the flavors to meld. We just wondered whether it needed a full 24 hours to do so. As we did with the curing process, we tried varying the amount of time the kimchee sat before we served it. Like most foods, we figured that the longer the kimchee sat, the more the flavors would develop. Surprisingly, though, after numerous trials, we found that at four hours the ingredients of the kimchee had sufficiently mingled and developed deep flavors.

With a balance of hot, salty, sour, and sweet flavors in the kimchee, we focused next on the steak portion of the dish. Skirt steak was the cut of meat that the recipe specified. A rarity at most meat counters, skirt steak is an unusually shaped cut taken from the flank. Long and thin (under one inch thick), it's richly marbled with fat and thus juicy and full-flavored. Leaner flank steak is the more common choice these health-conscious days and can be substituted, but for this recipe, we highly recommend tracking down skirt steak for its full, beefy flavor and authenticity. Adding to the depth of flavor of this dish, the steak is dusted with a spice rub before being grilled. As well as providing the steak with a lot of flavor, the spice rub acts as a link between the kimchee and the steak and puts the finishing touches on a harmonious and mouthwatering combination.

INGREDIENTS: Fish Sauce

Just as Chinese and Japanese cooking relies on soy sauce, Southeast Asian cooking depends on salty fish sauce. Fish sauce is a clear, brownish liquid that is pressed from salted and fermented fish, usually anchovies. It has a strong fishy flavor that can be off-putting straight from the bottle. However, the fish flavor fades when cooked, and this sauce adds unusual (and irreplaceable) depth to countless dishes. If shopping in Asian foods stores, look for products labeled *nuoc mam* (Vietnamese) or *nam pla* (Thai). In recent years, fish sauce has become a staple in many American supermarkets.

THE EIGHT PRIMAL CUTS OF BEEF

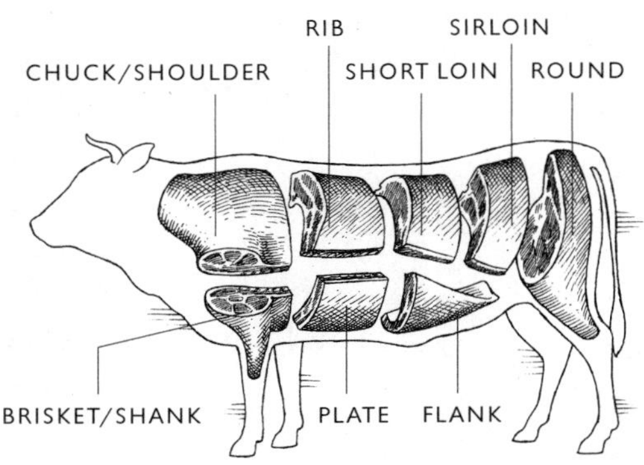

Grilled Skirt Steak with Kimchee

SERVES 6

Flank steak can be substituted for the skirt steak. Fish sauce can be found in Asian markets and many supermarkets and once opened keeps in the refrigerator for several months. Dried shrimp, which also has a long shelf life, is sold in cellophane packets in Asian markets.

KIMCHEE

- 1 large head napa cabbage, quartered, cored, and cut crosswise into 1/4-inch slices (about 12 cups)
- Kosher salt
- 1 red bell pepper, seeded and cut into matchsticks
- 1 large carrot, shredded
- 1 small daikon radish, shredded
- 4 scallions, white and green parts, cut into 1/4-inch slices

- 1 serrano chile, stemmed, seeded, and sliced into thin rings
- 3 tablespoons chili-garlic sauce
- 2 tablespoons fish sauce
- 1 1/2 tablespoons dried shrimp (optional)
- 1/4 cup minced fresh ginger
- 6 medium garlic cloves, minced or pressed through a garlic press (about 2 tablespoons)
- 2 tablespoons sugar
- 1/2 cup juice from 4–5 limes

STEAK

- 2 teaspoons dried orange peel (such as McCormick)
- 2 teaspoons ground coriander
- 1 teaspoon ground ginger
- 1 teaspoon salt
- 1/4 teaspoon red pepper flakes
- 2 1/2 pounds skirt steak, trimmed of excess fat
- 1 lime, cut into wedges

1. FOR THE KIMCHEE: Combine the cabbage and ¼ cup kosher salt in a large bowl. Transfer to a large container with a tight-fitting lid, cover, and refrigerate for 24 hours.

2. Transfer the cabbage to a colander and rinse well. Working with a handful of cabbage at a time, squeeze out any excess liquid and transfer back to the clean container. Add the bell pepper, carrot, daikon, scallions, and chile to the cabbage and set aside.

3. Process the chili-garlic sauce, fish sauce, and dried shrimp in a food processor until it is a uniform paste, about ten 1-second pulses. Set aside. Bring the ginger, garlic, sugar, and 1 cup water to a boil in a medium saucepan over medium heat. Add the chili-garlic mixture to the pan, reduce the heat to low, and simmer until the flavors have melded, 20 minutes. Pour the mixture over the vegetables, add the lime juice, and toss to combine. Refrigerate until cool before serving, at least 4 hours.

4. FOR THE STEAK: Light 5 quarts charcoal (1 chimney starter heaped full) and allow to burn until the flames have died down and all the charcoal is covered with a layer of fine gray ash. Spread the coals out over half the grill bottom, leaving the other half with no coals. Set the cooking grate in place and let it heat up for 5 minutes. Scrape the grate clean.

5. Meanwhile, combine the orange peel, coriander, ginger, salt, and red pepper flakes in a small bowl. Generously sprinkle both sides of the steak with the spice mixture. Grill the steak over the coals until well seared and dark brown on the first side, about 4 minutes. Flip the steak using tongs and grill until the interior of the meat is slightly less done than you want it to be when you eat it, 2 to 4 minutes for medium-rare (depending on the thickness of the steak and the heat of the fire).

6. Transfer the meat to a cutting board, cover loosely with foil, and let rest for 5 minutes. Arrange a portion of kimchee in the center of each of 6 plates. Slice the steak very thinly on the bias against the grain and arrange the steak over the kimchee. Serve immediately, accompanied by the lime wedges.

Grilled Skirt Steak Tacos *with* Roasted Poblanos (Rajas)

Adapted from Grilled Skirt Steak Tacos with Roasted Poblanos (Rajas)
Frontera Grill, Chicago, Illinois

UNLIKE MOST MEXICAN RESTAURANTS, which load up their tacos with an excess of messy, rich condiments, Frontera Grill—the home base of die-hard Mexican traditionalist Rick Bayless—proudly serves up spartan marinated-steak-and-pepper soft tacos. Unencumbered with competing flavors, the tacos are deliciously to the point: the grilled beef is rich and smoky, perfectly complemented by the sweet-hot peppers and piquant onions. Authentic to a fault, they just happen to be easy to prepare—the perfect recipe with which the home cook can comfortably explore traditional Mexican cooking.

All told, the recipe has few ingredients, many of which you may already have in your kitchen. Two of the ingredients, however, may be new to you: skirt steak and poblano peppers. If your market doesn't regularly stock skirt steak, it should be able to special-order it for you, or you may substitute another cut of meat, such as flank steak. Coming from the same area of the cow (see the illustration on page 178), flank steak has some of the same characteristics we like about skirt steak. Following the recipe, but replacing the skirt steak with a flank steak, we found that the cooking times and temperatures were virtually the same but that because flank steak is leaner than skirt steak, it ended up being slightly less flavorful and a little chewier. Flank steak is an acceptable substitution for skirt steak in this recipe, but skirt steak is preferred.

Poblano peppers are thin-skinned, glossy, forest green peppers quite common in Mexican cooking. They are sweeter and fuller tasting than green bell peppers, and while generally mild, they can pack a punch. During testing, we found that most of the peppers we tasted were mellow, but a few were quite spicy—a little game of culinary roulette. When roasted, peeled, seeded, and cut into strips, poblano chiles are called rajas. Rajas are used throughout Mexican cooking in tostadas, quesadillas, and grilled seafood dishes. In the tacos, the sweet-hot peppers amplify the meat's smoky, rich flavor.

As far as cooking the tacos, everything is done over very hot coals on the grill. The peppers are grilled first, followed by the onions, and finally the meat. Roasting the peppers on the grill with a hot fire—as the recipe recommends—proved a faultless method: the skin blistered and blackened quickly, leaving the flesh relatively unscathed. Do pay keen attention as you grill the peppers, checking them often to prevent burning—there's a fine line between blackened and burned. If you see any gray patches, the peppers have burned. Immediately place the peppers in a bowl and cover with aluminum foil so that the heat is contained. The resulting steam makes for easy peeling later on.

The original recipe called for marinating the meat before grilling in a combination of lime juice, garlic, cumin, and white onion. The marinade tasted good—sharp and piquant—but it proved problematic. Even after the recommended maximum eight hours of marination, the grilled meat possessed little of the marinade's flavor. We decided to take a slightly different approach—one we have used often in other grilled meat recipes—and coat the meat with the marinade after grilling, while it rested (the time allotted post-cooking to allow the juices to recirculate throughout the meat). The marinade's flavors were much more apparent. Unconventional, yes, but successful in a case like this, in which the marinade does little to tenderize the meat. And it saves hours; the marinade can be prepared just 30 minutes before dinner instead of 8 hours ahead.

For the most tender texture, skirt steak must be cut against the grain. Granted, this is true for most meat, but with skirt steaks it means slicing parallel to the long side. Considering that some of the steaks we cooked were upward of a foot long, this posed some problems. The best method we found was to cut the steaks into smaller (roughly four- to six-inch) lengths, and then slice them thinly crosswise. The smaller strips were quite tender and easily fit into small tortillas.

For a hint of additional smokiness, we briefly warmed the tortillas over the grill before wrapping them in a damp towel as the recipe specified. In a matter of seconds, the tortillas picked up light grill markings and improved flavor. If left unwrapped, they dry out quickly, leading to cracking.

Grilled Skirt Steak Tacos with Roasted Poblanos (Rajas)

SERVES 6

If you can't find skirt steak, substitute flank steak, although the meat will be a bit more chewy. This is at its best served family-style in communal bowls so that people can assemble their own tacos. While not specified in Frontera's recipe, the tacos can be served with sour cream. Leftovers make great sandwich fillings, with a spritz of lime and a little mayonnaise.

- **4 medium white onions, 3 peeled and sliced crosswise into ½-inch-thick rounds, 1 chopped coarse**
- **1 tablespoon vegetable oil**
- **Salt and ground black pepper**
- **3 medium garlic cloves, coarsely chopped (about 1 tablespoon)**
- **½ teaspoon ground cumin**
- **6 tablespoons juice from 3 limes**
- **1½ pounds poblano chiles**
- **2 pounds skirt steak, trimmed of excess fat**
- **18–24 small corn tortillas**
- **1 lime, cut into wedges**

1. Adjust an oven rack to the middle position and heat the oven to 200 degrees. Following the illustration on page 182, skewer the onion slices with bamboo skewers. Brush both sides of each onion slice with the vegetable oil and season generously with salt and pepper. Set aside.

2. Process the chopped onion, garlic, 1 teaspoon salt, cumin, and lime juice in a food processor until smooth, about 30 seconds, scraping down the sides of the bowl

with a rubber spatula as necessary. Transfer to a large, shallow baking dish and set aside.

3. Light 5 quarts charcoal (1 chimney starter heaped full) and allow to burn until the flames have died down and all the charcoal is covered with a layer of fine gray ash. Spread the coals out over half the grill bottom, leaving the other half with no coals. Set the cooking grate in place and let it heat up for 5 minutes. Scrape the grate clean.

4. Place the poblano chiles in the center of the grill rack and cook until the skin is blistered and blackened, but not gray, 3 to 4 minutes. Turn and blacken the next side. Repeat the process until all the chiles are blackened on all sides.

5. Meanwhile, place the onion slices around the chiles on the grill and cook until streaked with dark grill marks, about 6 minutes. Using tongs, turn and cook the second side until marked. Transfer to an oven-safe dish and slide the slices off the skewers. Separate the slices into individual rings and keep warm in the oven.

6. Transfer the chiles to a bowl and cover with aluminum foil for 5 minutes. Rub the blackened skin off the outside of the chiles, then remove the stems and seeds. Slice into thin strips and add to the baking dish with the onions. Cover and keep warm in the oven.

7. Grill the steak over the coals until well seared and browned on the first side, about 4 minutes. Flip the steak using tongs and grill until the interior of the meat is slightly less done than you want it to be when you eat it, 2 to 4 minutes for medium-rare (depending on the thickness of the steak and the heat of the fire). Remove the steak from the grill and coat with the onion puree. Cover the dish with aluminum foil and let rest for at least 5 minutes.

8. Spread the tortillas out on the grill rack and grill until lightly marked, 15 to 30 seconds. Using tongs, flip the tortillas and grill on the second side until marked, 10 to 15 seconds longer. Wrap the tortillas in a clean, damp dish towel on a baking sheet and keep warm in the oven.

9. Remove the chiles and onions from the oven. Remove the excess marinade from the steak and slice the steak into 4- to 6-inch lengths. Cutting across the grain, slice the meat thin and place in a serving bowl. Serve immediately, accompanied by the poblano and onion mixture, tortillas, and lime wedges.

GRILLING ONIONS

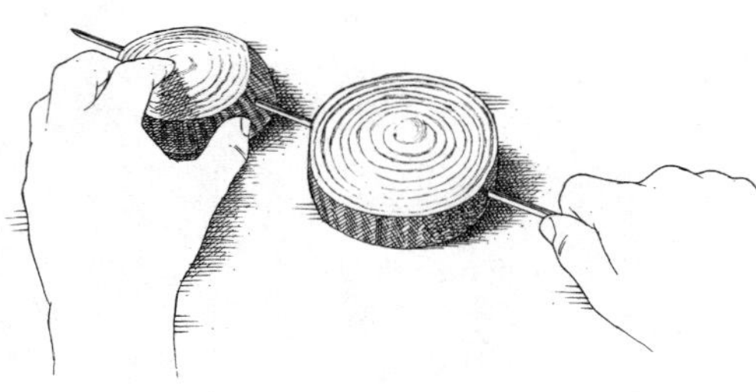

Slide the onion slice onto a thin bamboo skewer. (If using long skewers, thread 2 slices onto each skewer.) The skewered onion slices will remain intact as they grill, so no rings will fall onto the coals. Best of all, the onions can be easily flipped using tongs.

BEEF TOURNEDOS *with* BLUE CHEESE MASHED POTATOES

Adapted from Tournedos of Beef with Maytag Whipped Potatoes

KING LOUIE'S, ST. LOUIS, MISSOURI

TOURNEDOS ARE A THROWBACK TO THE time when French cooking in America was at its peak. Nothing more than medallions (thick, boneless rounds) cut from the beef tenderloin, the lean cuts of steak were typically served with heavy, cream-laden sauces. But with this updated version from King Louie's, it's worth reviving tournedos for the present-day palate.

A flavorful and multifaceted dish, the unbeatable combination of steak and mashed potatoes was improved upon with the addition to the potatoes of tangy blue cheese and with a sweet-tart sauce made with honey and balsamic vinegar for the beef (instead of the traditional cream sauce). While most of the flavors were spot on in this recipe, the potatoes weren't quite as rich as we'd like, and we thought the sauce could use some streamlining for the home cook.

We turned first to the mashed potatoes. King Louie's recipe called for one-half cup of cream and one-quarter cup of butter for four pounds of potatoes. But after making the potatoes this way, we found they lacked the richness we were looking for. They also made enough for eight servings rather than the four we needed. The next time we prepared the potatoes, we reduced the amount of potatoes by half (to two pounds) and mixed in the same amount of cream and butter. Although the amount of potatoes this batch made was more along the lines of what we were looking for, they still lacked richness. So we made the mashed potatoes again, this time slowly increasing the butter and cream one tablespoon at a time until we reached the desired consistency. In the end, three-quarters cup of cream and six tablespoons of butter to two pounds of potatoes proved to be the best ratio.

The sauce was an element of the dish we felt needed streamlining. The original recipe called for making a reduction consisting of balsamic vinegar, honey, and demi-glace (partially reduced veal stock). This reduction, along with red wine, was then used to deglaze the pan in which the steaks were cooked, forming the sauce for the dish. While this technique simplifies the task of making a pan sauce in a restaurant kitchen, for the home cook it usually means more work and more dirty pans. Wanting to keep the same flavors but forgo making a separate reduction, we prepared the recipe several more times using different techniques.

We explored the four ingredients in the sauce separately in order to determine the best ratio. First, we experimented with the stock. The King Louie's recipe called for demi-glace. Unsuccessful in our attempts to find a demi-glace worth using, we opted to use equal amounts of beef and chicken broth. Since these broths were less intense in flavor than the demi-glace, we had to reduce the 1½ cups of broth to mimic the flavor and body of the demi-glace. Next, we tested the vinegar. The original reduction used three-quarters cup, but it was obvious that this would be too much for our purposes. We tried using one-quarter cup in our first attempt, but this amount proved to be slightly acidic, masking the other flavors in the sauce. Even with successively smaller amounts, we found that this problem persisted. In the end, we found that by finishing the sauce with 2 tablespoons of vinegar right before serving in lieu of mixing it into the sauce in advance, the sauce had a clear, bright acidity and the other flavors were able to shine through. Not wanting to compound the acidity of the vinegar, we found it necessary to reduce the amount of red wine from one cup to one-half cup. And considering that we had reduced the amount of vinegar significantly, we also needed to reduce the amount of honey. After several tests, we found that one tablespoon of honey did the job, without making the sauce too sweet or floral.

Beef Tournedos with Blue Cheese Mashed Potatoes

SERVES 4

It's important to use steaks that are thick enough not to overcook, but small enough in diameter so that they don't crowd the pan. Steaks cut from the center portion of the tenderloin, also known as the Châteaubriand, are perfect for this recipe.

MASHED POTATOES

- **2 pounds Yukon Gold potatoes, peeled, halved, and cut into ½-inch pieces**
- **Salt**
- **¾ cup heavy cream**
- **6 tablespoons (¾ stick) unsalted butter, softened**
- **Ground black pepper**
- **¼ cup crumbled Maytag blue cheese**

TOURNEDOS

- **3 tablespoons olive oil**
- **8 (4-ounce) filets mignons, at least 1 inch thick**
- **Salt and ground black pepper**
- **4 ounces white mushrooms, sliced ⅛ inch thick**
- **¾ cup low-sodium beef broth**
- **¾ cup low-sodium chicken broth**
- **½ cup dry red wine**
- **1 tablespoon honey**
- **2 tablespoons balsamic vinegar**

1. FOR THE POTATOES: Bring the potatoes, 1 teaspoon salt, and enough water to cover the potatoes by 1 inch to a boil in a large saucepan over high heat. Reduce the heat to medium-low and simmer until a paring knife can be slipped into and out of the center of the potatoes with very little resistance, 10 to 13 minutes. Drain thoroughly.

2. FOR THE TOURNEDOS: Meanwhile, heat 2 tablespoons of the olive oil in a 12-inch skillet over high heat until smoking. Season the beef with salt and pepper to taste. Place the beef in the skillet and cook without disturbing until well browned on the first side, about 3 minutes. Using tongs, flip the steaks and cook for 2 minutes longer for rare, 3 minutes for medium-rare, and 4 minutes for medium. Transfer the beef to a platter and cover with foil to keep warm.

3. Reduce the heat to medium-high and

heat the remaining 1 tablespoon olive oil until shimmering. Add the mushrooms and cook, stirring frequently, until tender and golden, about 2½ minutes. Transfer to a medium bowl and set aside.

4. Add the broths, wine, and honey to the pan and bring to a boil, scraping up the browned bits on the pan bottom using a wooden spoon. Boil until the liquid is reduced to 1 cup, 5 to 6 minutes. Stir in the vinegar and any accumulated juices from the steaks and cook for 1½ minutes to allow the flavors to blend. Add the mushrooms to the sauce and remove from the heat. Season with salt and pepper to taste and transfer to a liquid measuring cup; cover with plastic wrap to keep warm.

5. To FINISH THE POTATOES: Place a food mill or ricer over the now empty but still warm saucepan. Process or rice the potatoes into the saucepan. Stir in the cream and butter until smooth. Season with salt and pepper to taste. Rewarm if necessary.

6. Stir the blue cheese into the mashed potatoes, then divide the potatoes evenly among the centers of 4 warmed dinner plates. Place 2 tournedos, overlapping slightly, on top of the potatoes on each plate. Drizzle the pan sauce over the steaks and around the edge of the potatoes. Serve immediately.

INGREDIENTS: Filet Mignon

When we discovered that some less-than-honorable restaurants and butchers serve and sell cheaper cuts masquerading as expensive filet mignon, we immediately consulted our knowledgeable local butcher. He told us that the two most likely impostors are the chuck tender, which comes from the animal's shoulder, and the top butt, which originates between the loin and round at the animal's posterior. Both may be priced as much as 80 percent less than a real filet. But questions remained. How would they taste in comparison? Wouldn't even a semiconscious diner be able to tell the difference? To answer these questions, we held a blind taste test pitting the two cheap cuts against the expensive filet.

Real filet has a very fine grain and a buttery texture that all tasters identified without fail. By comparison, the chuck tender had a fine to medium grain, more marbling, and noticeable connective tissue. Tasters denounced the chuck tender for being gristly, rubbery, and tough. The top butt steak had a coarser, slightly stringy grain, giving it a texture that tasters rejected as tough, stringy, and chalky. So we were still left with the question. How could anyone get away with this obvious fraud? Apparently, the perpetrators are counting on the fact that most diners eat filet infrequently and/or will chalk up any tough steaks to improper cooking.

Although some unscrupulous restaurateurs and butchers may try to pass off cheaper cuts, such as chuck tender and top butt, as filet mignon, our tasters had no trouble picking out these tough "faux" filets in a blind tasting. Real filets have no connective tissue (the large streaks of white or gray visible in the impostors) and very little marbling (seen as fine white lines in the fake filets).

FILET MIGNON

CHUCK TENDER

TOP BUTT

German-Style Pot Roast

Adapted from Rheinisher Sauerbraten

The Heidelberg, Naples, Florida

SAUERBRATEN, OR SOUR ROAST, IS A TRADItional German dish that consists of a beef roast marinated in a sweet-and-sour liquid for two to three days before being simmered in the same marinade for several hours. The liquid, which normally contains red wine and red wine vinegar, is usually highly seasoned with herbs and spices, including juniper berries, bay leaves, and allspice. All said, this dish is hearty and flavorful, as demonstrated by the Heidelberg's recipe.

Chuck roast makes the most flavorful and tender meat for sauerbraten. The intramuscular fat and connective tissue in chuck make it well suited for the long, slow, moist cooking that is stewing. The first question that occurred to us even before preparing this dish was whether the meat actually needed to spend three days in the marinade before cooking, or if we could shorten this soaking period. Interested in comparing the differences in varying soaking times, we soaked three different roasts over a span of three days, varying the soaking time of each. On the fourth day, we cooked all three roasts in the same fashion and tasted them side by side. The beef that sat for the longest (all three days) was the unanimous winner. Tasters agreed that the roast that marinated for three days was by far the most tender and had the deepest flavor of the three. Those that sat for only two days or one day just didn't measure up. Unable to save any time on this end, we looked at other aspects of the dish to see if they could be made more efficient.

We next looked at the cooking of the roast. While there was not much we could do about the cooking time, we figured we could shorten the process of thickening the sauce and finishing the dish, which originally required two steps. In the first step, beef broth was added to the strained cooking liquid and then simmered for 15 minutes. It was then thickened with a combination of flour and cornstarch. This second step took an additional 15 minutes. Feeling that perhaps we could consolidate these two steps, we added the beef broth to the beef before we started to cook, rather than waiting until the end. By doing so, we were able to avoid the first step. We also decided to forgo the thickening of the sauce with the flour mixture, opting instead to reduce the sauce by boiling it. In addition to taking less time than the original recipe's thickening step, this new version of the sauce was lighter and more intensely flavored.

While the sauce was reducing, we had time to slice the sauerbraten and arrange it on a large serving platter. Although the Heidelberg didn't supply us with a recipe for potato dumplings, we agree with its recommendation that they would be the perfect accompaniment to this roast.

German-Style Pot Roast

SERVES 6 TO 8

It's possible to substitute ½ cup of pickling spice for all the spices below, but considering that most pickling spices contain cinnamon, expect the finished dish to have a slightly sweeter flavor. You'll have 3½ cups sauce left over after saucing the meat—plenty for passing at the table to pour over mashed potatoes or potato dumplings, as well as leftovers.

- 2 medium onions, cut into ¼-inch-thick slices
- 3 medium carrots, cut into ¼-inch-thick slices
- 8 bay leaves
- 1 tablespoon juniper berries
- 1 tablespoon whole black peppercorns
- 1 tablespoon yellow mustard seeds
- ½ teaspoon caraway seeds
- 8 allspice berries
- 4 whole cloves
- 2 cups red wine vinegar
- 2 cups dry red wine
- 1 (3-pound) boneless beef chuck roast
- 1 cup low-sodium beef broth
- 1 cup low-sodium chicken broth
- 1½ teaspoons salt
- 2 tablespoons light brown sugar
- Ground black pepper

1. Combine the onions, carrots, bay leaves, juniper berries, peppercorns, mustard seeds, caraway seeds, allspice, cloves, vinegar, wine, and 3 cups water in a 1-gallon, non-reactive container. Submerge the roast in the liquid, cover, and marinate in the refrigerator for 3 days, turning every 12 hours.

2. Adjust an oven rack to the lower-middle position and heat the oven to 325 degrees. Transfer the roast to a large plate and set aside. Bring the marinade, beef broth, chicken broth, and salt to a simmer in a large heavy-bottomed Dutch oven over high heat, skimming any foam that rises to the top. Add the roast and return to a simmer. Cover and transfer to the oven. Cook, turning every 30 minutes, until fully tender and a sharp knife easily slips in and out of the roast, 3 to 3½ hours.

3. Transfer the roast to a cutting board and tent with foil to keep warm. Strain the liquid through a fine-mesh sieve into a large bowl and allow it to settle for 5 minutes. With a ladle or wide spoon, skim the fat from the surface. Return the liquid to the Dutch oven, add the brown sugar, and bring to a boil over high heat. Boil until the liquid is reduced to 4 cups, 12 to 15 minutes. Season with salt and pepper to taste.

4. Using a chef's or carving knife, cut the roast into ½-inch-thick slices. Transfer the slices to a serving platter and pour ½ cup of the sauce over it. Serve, passing the remaining sauce separately.

Short Rib Pot Roast *with* Pennsylvania Dutch Black Vinegar Sauce

Adapted from Zinfandel Pot Roast with Pennsylvania Dutch Black Vinegar

West Town Tavern, Chicago, Illinois

APTLY DESCRIBED AS "WHAT SUNDAY DINNER would have been if my mother had gone to culinary school" by Indiana food and wine writer Doug Pendelton, this upscale pot roast is one of the few that not only tastes good, but looks a bit refined as well. Because the West Town Tavern's recipe calls for portion-size pieces of boneless short ribs instead of a huge roast, the meat is easy to slice in attractive pieces when tender. Topped with a tangy black vinegar sauce that hails from the German-friendly parts of Pennsylvania, this pot roast is hard to beat.

Following the directions and ingredient amounts as originally written, we found they required no alterations beyond increasing the meat so that it could serve six people rather than four. We did this because the recipe is worth making for company or for having left-overs to be incorporated into hash or reheated as a sandwich filling. The cooking technique is a braise—the meat is seared, aromatics and liquid are added, and then the roast is cooked in a 325-degree oven until tender. And the unusual sauce—vinegar, sugar, and raisins—we found, was a perfect match for the beef.

INGREDIENTS: Short Ribs

English-style short ribs are butchered with the bone, so that each piece has a single length of bone surrounded by meat. Flanken-style short ribs are butchered across the ribs so that each piece has roughly three cross-sectioned slices of bone with meat in between.

In braising the two, flanken style was favored by most tasters because the relatively thin, across-the-grain cut made the meat more pleasant to eat; the English style ribs were a bit stringier because they contained longer segments of "grain." Both types were equally tender and good, but considering that the flanken costs almost twice that of the English style, look to your wallet for guidance.

ENGLISH STYLE

FLANKEN STYLE

Short Rib Pot Roast with Pennsylvania Dutch Black Vinegar Sauce

SERVES 6

The meat can be cooked up to 2 days in advance. (For information on selecting the preferred English-style short ribs, see page 188.) Cool the meat in its braising liquid and refrigerate. To reheat, bring the meat in its braising liquid to a simmer over medium-low heat, being careful not to break the meat into smaller pieces. The sauce can also be made in advance and reheated in the microwave or in a saucepan over medium-low heat. Since the braising liquid is not used beyond cooking the beef, it can be strained and kept in the refrigerator to be used in other applications, such as soup, or in place of beef broth. Serve this dish, as the restaurant does, with your favorite mashed potatoes.

SHORT RIBS

- 6 boneless, square-cut short ribs (English-style short ribs) (about 9 ounces each), trimmed of excess fat
- Salt and ground black pepper
- 1 tablespoon vegetable oil
- 1 small red onion, cut into 1/2-inch pieces (about 1 cup)
- 2 medium carrots, cut into 1/2-inch pieces (about 1/2 cup)
- 1 large celery rib, cut into 1/2-inch pieces (about 1/2 cup)
- 5 sprigs fresh parsley
- 2 bay leaves
- 2 cups low-sodium beef broth
- 1 cup red Zinfandel wine

BLACK VINEGAR SAUCE

- 4 cups good-quality red wine vinegar, preferably Zinfandel vinegar
- 1 1/2 cups packed dark brown sugar
- 3/4 cup dark raisins

1. FOR THE SHORT RIBS: Adjust an oven rack to the middle position and heat the oven to 325 degrees. Season the short ribs liberally with salt and pepper. Heat the vegetable oil in a large Dutch oven over medium-high heat until just smoking. Add the ribs and sauté, turning as necessary, until well browned on all sides, about 6 minutes.

2. Add the onion, carrots, celery, parsley, bay leaves, beef broth, and wine and bring to a boil, scraping up the browned bits from the bottom of the pot. Cover and transfer to the oven. Cook until the short ribs are tender, 2 to 2½ hours hours. (The meat can be cooled in its braising liquid at this point and refrigerated.)

3. FOR THE BLACK VINEGAR SAUCE: When the meat has about 30 minutes of braising time left, bring the vinegar and brown sugar to a boil in a medium saucepan over medium-high heat. Boil until the liquid is reduces to 2½ cups, about 25 minutes. Add the raisins and boil, stirring frequently, until the sauce is black and glossy and measures about 2 cups, about 5 minutes longer. Remove from the heat and set aside. (The sauce can be cooled at this point and refrigerated.)

4. To serve, remove the beef from its braising liquid and cut into ½-inch-thick slices. (Strain and reserve the flavorful braising liquid for another use, using it as you would beef broth.) Briefly reheat the vinegar sauce if necessary. Arrange the sliced meat on 6 individual plates or a serving platter and pour the warm vinegar sauce over it, letting the raisins garnish the top. Serve immediately.

Braised Short Ribs over Creamy Polenta

Adapted from Braised Short Ribs over Polenta with Truffle Oil

Mockingbird Bistro, Houston, Texas

HEARTY AND SATISFYING ON A COLD day, beef short ribs are like pot roast for company. The braised meat is falling off the bones—literally—and these ribs look beautiful and require no messy, postbraise slicing. The problem with short ribs, however, is that they are fatty and sometimes hard to shop for.

To start, Mockingbird Bistro's recipe called for four short ribs. At the supermarket, we found that short ribs come in two distinctly different cuts (see page 188). Both types were equally tender and good, but considering that the flanken costs almost twice that of the English-style, we suggest the latter.

Using a standard braising procedure—the meat is seared, aromatics are sautéed, then all is combined with liquid and simmered until the meat is tender—the interesting part of this recipe is the addition of orange zest and the substitution of white wine for the more traditional red. Simmered for just over two hours, the ribs emerged lightly scented with orange and with a fragrant sauce far more lithe than the dark, brooding sauces that usually accompany short ribs. However, the recipe called for veal stock, for which we found it necessary to substitute a combination of canned low-sodium chicken and beef broths, compensating for lost flavor by adding extra herbs including thyme, parsley, and bay leaves. Since short ribs are incredibly fatty, we found it necessary to let the braising liquid, which eventually becomes the sauce, sit for a few minutes to allow the rendered fat to surface so that it can be easily removed. Increasing the yield from four to six people, this is exactly the type of winter dish that is perfect for company.

Mockingbird serves the short ribs with baby vegetables: easy to do if you're located in an area with a warm climate, in this case, Texas, but not so for many folks. Rather than replace the otherwise seasonal vegetables, we omitted them and recommend serving these short ribs with a vegetable side dish.

The polenta, made with a combination of chicken broth and milk and finished with truffle oil, overwhelmed tasters with its flavor and richness, especially when paired with the short ribs. Wanting to simplify the ingredient list and highlight the marvelous short rib flavor, we found it necessary to take the polenta down a few notches. Tasters loved the balance of the complex-tasting ribs over perfectly cooked polenta finished with chopped parsley.

Braised Short Ribs over Creamy Polenta

SERVES 6

For smooth polenta, be sure to stir it thoroughly every 5 minutes.

SHORT RIBS

- **1** teaspoon vegetable oil
- **6** pounds bone-in English-style short ribs (see page 188), trimmed of excess fat
- Salt and ground black pepper
- **1** large onion, cut into 1/4-inch dice
- **2** medium carrots, cut into 1/4-inch dice
- **2** celery ribs, cut into 1/4-inch dice
- **1/4** cup tomato paste
- **2** cups dry white wine or vermouth
- **4 1/2** cups low-sodium chicken broth
- **1 3/4** cups low-sodium beef broth
- **2** tablespoons grated orange zest
- **3** sprigs fresh thyme
- **3** sprigs fresh parsley
- **3** bay leaves

CREAMY POLENTA

- **1** cup whole milk
- Salt
- **1 1/2** cups medium-grind cornmeal, preferably stone ground
- Ground black pepper

- **2** tablespoons minced fresh parsley

1. For the short ribs: Adjust an oven rack to the middle position and heat the oven to 325 degrees. Heat the oil in a large Dutch oven over medium-high heat until shimmering. Season the ribs with salt and pepper. Add half the ribs and sauté, turning as necessary, until well browned on all sides, about 6 minutes. Transfer the ribs to a clean plate and set aside. Pour off all but 1 teaspoon fat from the pot and return to medium-high heat. Repeat with the remaining ribs and transfer to the plate.

2. Pour off all but 1 tablespoon fat from the pot and return it to medium heat. Add the onion, carrots, celery, and ¼ teaspoon salt and cook until the vegetables begin to soften, about 5 minutes. Stir in the tomato paste and cook until the vegetables are soft, about 2 minutes longer. Stir in the wine, chicken broth, beef broth, orange zest, thyme, parsley, and bay leaves and bring to a boil. Return the ribs to the pot, submerging them in the liquid, and return to a boil. Cover and transfer to the oven. Cook until the meat is tender and falling off the bones, 2½ to 3½ hours.

3. Remove the pot from the oven and reduce the oven temperature to 200 degrees. Transfer the ribs to a clean, ovenproof plate, cover with foil, and return to the oven to keep warm. Cool the braising liquid slightly so the fat will rise to the top. Skim off the fat using a ladle or spoon. Remove and discard the bay leaves and thyme and parsley sprigs. Bring the braising liquid to a simmer over medium-high heat and cook until it has thickened, about 10 minutes. Remove from the heat.

4. For the polenta: About 45 minutes before serving, bring 5 cups water and the milk to a boil in a medium saucepan over medium-high heat. Add 1 teaspoon salt and pour the cornmeal into the water in a very slow stream while stirring constantly with a wooden spoon. Reduce the heat to the lowest possible setting and cook, stirring vigorously every 5 minutes and making sure to scrape clean the bottom and sides of the pot, until the polenta is smooth and tender, about 30 minutes. Remove the polenta from the heat and season with salt and pepper to taste.

5. Divide the polenta among 6 bowls. Nestle a rib in the center of each, standing it upright. Drizzle the sauce over the ribs and sprinkle with the parsley. Serve immediately.

Braised Oxtails *with* Fresh Pasta & Tomato Gremolata

Adapted from Braised Oxtails with Fresh Pasta and Tomato Gremolata

Lark Creek Inn, Larkspur, California

TODAY, OXTAILS ARE GENERALLY THOUGHT of as a specialty cut of meat, finding their way onto the menus at the finest restaurants. But in the past, when meat was a luxury, oxtails enjoyed a much more widespread popularity as an inexpensive way to make a meaty, flavorful dish. While not containing a lot of meat, oxtails produce an intensely rich stock, which can form the base of a very savory dish, as exemplified in this recipe from Lark Creek Inn.

Producing a wonderfully comforting and homey dish, this recipe was a quintessential example of braised oxtails: a deeply meaty broth flavored with just the right amount of sweet vegetables, tart tomatoes, and a hint of smoky bacon. As a twist, the rich oxtails were paired with wheaty homemade noodles and tomato gremolata (a Mediterranean-style salsa), which provided a lively, fresh finish. In addition to being tasty, the recipe required very little modification in order to make it accessible to the home cook.

The main details we focused on were the cooking time and temperature of the oxtails. The original recipe called for cooking the oxtails in a 350-degree oven for about 2½ hours. Following these guidelines, we found the oxtails to be perfectly tender in a little over two hours, but the resulting broth was cloying and a bit greasy. Wondering if the oven temperature was perhaps a little too high, we tried the recipe again, this time cooking the meat at 325 degrees. Because the broth simmered less vigorously at this temperature, it ended up less oily. We nevertheless found that we had to strain the broth and let it stand for 5 minutes in order to remove the excess fat from the dish before serving.

The other recipe item we explored was the fresh noodles. While we enjoyed the fresh pasta, we needed to consider the fact that most cooks don't have a pasta machine or the time needed to make fresh pasta. Wanting to find a suitable substitute, we tried serving the dish with several store-bought alternatives—fresh pasta, dried egg noodles, and dried fettuccine. The fresh pasta was a little thicker and chewier than the pasta that we made ourselves, but was a suitable substitute. We also found that the dried egg noodles paired well with the oxtails, but (as expected) they didn't have the fresh egg flavor or the substantial texture of the fresh egg pasta. The dried fettuccine was a miss altogether, disliked for its gumminess and lack of flavor.

Other than the cooking process for the oxtails and the question of which pasta to use, the only other changes that we made were minor. Although the recipe called for using whole, peeled plum tomatoes in the braise, preparing the tomatoes this way was time-consuming, and their large chunks were oddly out of place in the final dish. We opted to use canned diced tomatoes instead, which achieved a consistent and more attractive result. Also from an aesthetic point of view, we felt it was better to reduce the size of the vegetable dice from one inch to one-half inch, giving the dish a refined, rather than rustic appearance.

Braised Oxtails with Fresh Pasta and Tomato Gremolata

SERVES 4

When buying the oxtails, ask your butcher for the larger pieces that are cut from the base of the tail rather than the tip—you'll find that there is more meat in relation to bone. A 9-ounce package of fresh fettuccine can be substituted for the homemade pasta in this recipe.

OXTAILS

- 3 tablespoons unbleached all-purpose flour
- Salt and ground black pepper
- 2 pounds oxtails, cut into 1-inch rounds, trimmed of excess fat
- 12 sprigs fresh parsley
- 4 sprigs fresh thyme
- 1 bay leaf
- 2 tablespoons olive oil
- 2 ounces slab bacon, chopped fine
- 3 medium carrots, cut into ½-inch pieces
- 2 celery ribs, cut into ½-inch pieces
- 1 medium onion, cut into ½-inch pieces
- 1 medium leek, white part only, quartered and cut into ½-inch pieces
- 1 (14.5 ounce) can diced tomatoes, drained
- 1 garlic clove, crushed
- 1 cup low-sodium chicken broth, plus more if needed
- 1 cup dry red wine
- 2 tablespoons red wine vinegar

PASTA

- 1 cup (5 ounces) unbleached all-purpose flour
- Salt
- 1 large egg
- 1 teaspoon olive oil
- 2 tablespoons unsalted butter

TOMATO GREMOLATA

- 1 medium plum tomato, seeded and diced
- ¼ cup chopped fresh parsley
- 1 small shallot, minced (about 1 tablespoon)
- 1 medium garlic clove, minced or pressed through a garlic press (about 1 teaspoon)
- 2 teaspoons grated lemon zest from 1 lemon
- ½ teaspoon olive oil
- ½ teaspoon red wine vinegar

1. For the oxtails: Adjust an oven rack to the middle position and heat the oven to 325 degrees. Combine the flour, 1 teaspoon salt, and ¼ teaspoon black pepper in a shallow dish or pie plate. Dredge the oxtails in the flour, shake off the excess, and set aside. Tie the parsley and thyme sprigs and bay leaf together with a 4-inch length of string. Set aside.

2. Heat the oil and bacon in a heavy-bottomed Dutch oven over medium-high heat. Cook the bacon until browned and most of its fat has rendered, about 6 minutes. Using a slotted spoon, transfer the bacon to a plate lined with several layers of paper towels. Add the oxtails in a single layer and sauté until golden brown on one side, about 3 minutes. Using tongs, flip the oxtails and sauté on the second side until golden, about 2 minutes longer. Transfer the oxtails to a clean plate. Pour off all but 2 tablespoons fat from the pan and return it to medium-high heat. Add the carrots, celery, onion, and leek and sauté until softened and lightly browned, 6 to 7 minutes.

3. Add the oxtails, bacon, tomatoes, herb bundle, garlic, ½ teaspoon salt, ¾ teaspoon pepper, chicken broth, wine, and vinegar to the pan and bring to a simmer. Cover and transfer to the oven. Cook the oxtails until the meat is very tender, 2 to 2½ hours.

4. For the pasta: Pulse the flour and ½ teaspoon salt in the workbowl of a food processor to distribute it evenly and aerate it. Add the egg, oil, and 2 teaspoons water and process until the dough forms a rough ball, about 30

ROLLING PASTA DOUGH

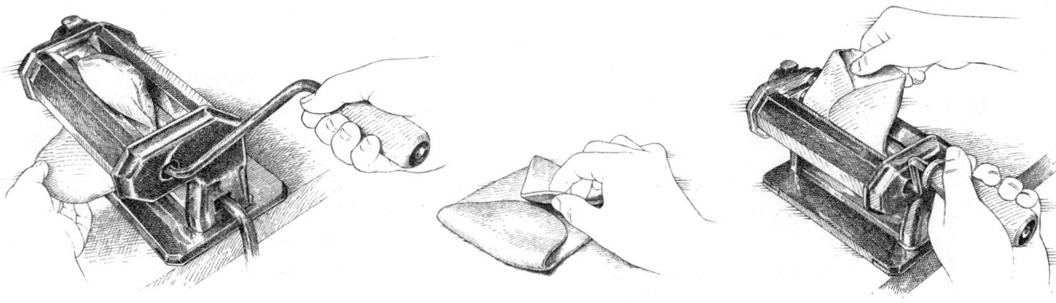

1. Run the dough rectangle through the rollers set to the widest position.

2. Bring the ends of dough toward the middle and press down to seal.

3. Feed the open side of the pasta through the rollers. Repeat steps 1 and 2.

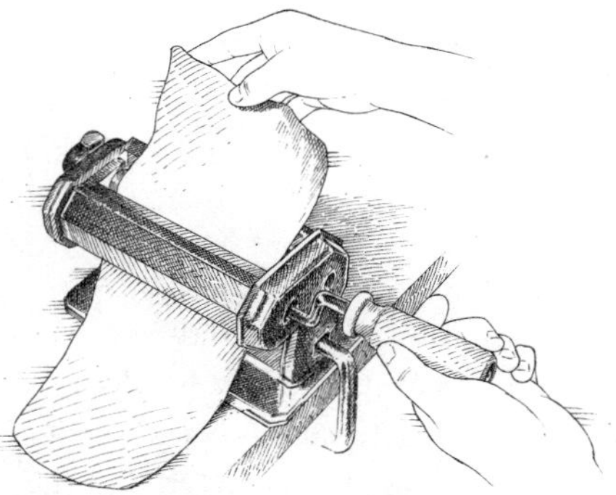

4. Without folding again, run the pasta through the widest setting twice, or until the dough is smooth. If the dough is at all sticky, lightly dust it with flour.

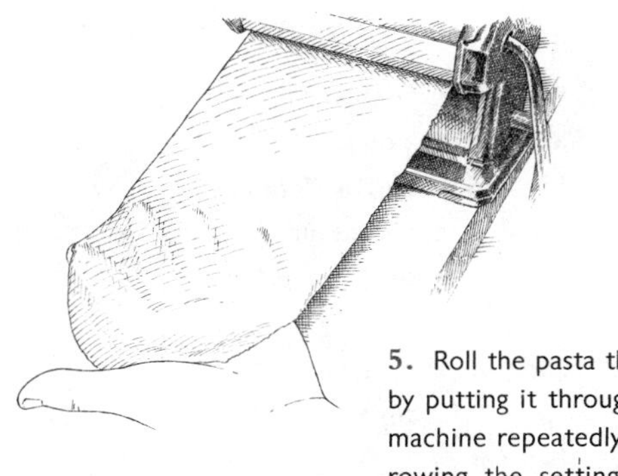

5. Roll the pasta thinner by putting it through the machine repeatedly, narrowing the setting each time. Roll until the dough is thin and satiny. You should be able to see the outline of your hand through the pasta. Repeat with the other pieces of dough.

seconds. (If the dough resembles small pebbles, add water, ½ teaspoon at a time; if the dough sticks to the side of the workbowl, add flour, 1 tablespoon at a time, and process until the dough forms a rough ball.)

5. Turn out the dough ball and small bits on a dry work surface; knead until the dough is smooth, 1 to 2 minutes. Form the dough into a flat square, wrap tightly with plastic wrap, and set aside to rest for 1 hour.

6. Unwrap the dough and cut it in half. Working with one piece at a time, keeping the remaining dough covered with plastic wrap so it doesn't dry out, slowly process the dough through a pasta machine following the manufacturer's instructions (see the illustrations on page 194), until the dough is very thin but not translucent. Lay the rolled dough on lightly floured work surface and cut into 12-inch lengths. Dry the pasta for 4 minutes, flipping once, before processing through widest cutting roller. Lay the cut pasta on a rimmed baking sheet lined with floured parchment paper and cover with plastic wrap. Repeat with the remaining dough. Set aside in the refrigerator.

7. For the gremolata: Combine all the ingredients in a small bowl. Set aside.

8. To assemble: Bring 4 quarts water to a boil in a large pot. Add 1 tablespoon salt and the pasta and boil until al dente, about 3 minutes. Drain thoroughly and return to the pot. Add the butter and stir to coat.

COLLECTING ZEST NEATLY

To prevent citrus zest from flying off the zester and all over your work surface, try this solution. Turn the zester upside down, so that the teeth face down and the fruit is under the zester rather than above it. The shavings collect right in the trough of the zester.

9. Meanwhile, remove the oxtails from the oven. Transfer the oxtails to a clean plate and cover with foil. Strain the broth, reserving the vegetables, through a coarse sieve into a 4-cup glass measure. Let the broth stand for 5 minutes. Skim off the fat that has risen to the top. Add enough chicken broth to measure 1 cup.

10. Place the pasta in 4 warmed pasta bowls. Divide the oxtails and vegetables among the bowls. Pour ¼ cup of the broth over each serving and sprinkle with the tomato gremolata. Serve immediately.

Stuffed Osso Buco

Adapted from Osso Buco

Hoku's, Kahala Mandarin Oriental Hotel, Honolulu, Hawaii

WE NEVER WOULD HAVE EXPECTED SUCH a hearty, winter-friendly dish as osso buco to be prepared with such finesse at a restaurant situated on the sunny shore of Honolulu. At Hoku's, the upscale restaurant in the Kahala Mandarin Oriental Hotel, the chef prepares a stellar version of the northern Italian dish of braised veal shanks, but replaces the traditional gremolata garnish (a combination of minced lemon zest, garlic, and parsley) with a stuffing enriched with prosciutto and marrow garnished with North African preserved lemon. We tend to be skeptical of modern flourishes applied to standards, but in this case the touches are stylish and flavorful, not frivolous or distracting. By its very nature, osso buco takes a good deal of time to cook—from preparation to hours of slow simmering—so time and effort are necessary. Finessing Hoku's restaurant-style recipe, however, we could do.

Osso buco is braised, the cooking method in which inexpensive cuts of tough meat are rendered buttery soft via slow, moist cooking. For osso buco, the veal shanks are browned, then simmered with aromatics (vegetables and herbs) over low heat until the meat is "fork tender," or easily pierced by the tines of a fork. The liquid is strained and used as a sauce to grace the meat and a starch, usually risotto (flavored with saffron) or polenta. For osso buco, we favor a size in which each shank serves as a single serving, roughly eight to ten ounces each. Shanks of this size tend to be 1½ to 2 inches in height. Be careful when shopping, though, since we found they are often poorly cut and packages can contain a hodgepodge of different sizes. To keep the meat on the bone as it cooks, it's crucial to bind the shanks with butcher's twine. Otherwise, as the connective tissue breaks down, the meat will fall from the bones and the dish will look more like a stew than a braise. The recipe calls for dredging the meat, or lightly dusting it with seasoned flour, before browning. From previous experience, we knew that dredging can yield mixed results. The flour thickens the broth, but it prevents the meat from effectively browning and thus has an impact on the overall flavor of the dish. In the end, we decided to eschew dredging in favor of attaining a deep and flavorful sear on the meat.

For aromatics, Hoku's employs a standard combination: onion, carrot, celery, leek, and garlic. The garlic is left as a whole, unpeeled head, with the top third lopped off to expose the cloves. By the time the meat is tender, the cloves have fully softened and blend well with the braising liquid when it's strained. Little effort and big flavor—a combination we like. Once the vegetables are well browned and very soft, the tomatoes (we replaced the original recipe's fresh tomatoes with canned diced tomatoes) and bay leaves are added. In another technique new to us, Hoku's adds a potato to the braising liquid for its thickening ability. The garlic (which lends some thickening power to the sauce when it's mashed during straining), potato, and the marrow leached from the veal bones provided the braising broth with an unctuous smoothness that didn't need reduction to thicken it, as most do.

EQUIPMENT: Dutch Ovens

We find that a Dutch oven (also called a lidded casserole) is almost essential to making stews and braises, such as osso buco. A Dutch oven is nothing more than a wide, deep pot with a cover. It was originally manufactured with ears on the side (small round tabs used to pick up the pot) and a top that had a lip around the edge. The latter design element was important because a Dutch oven was heated by coals placed both underneath and on top of the pot. The lip kept the coals on the lid from falling off. One could bake biscuits, cobblers, beans, and stews in this pot. It was, in the full sense of the word, an oven. This oven was a key feature of chuck wagons and essential in many Colonial American households, where all cooking occurred in the fireplace. This useful pot supposedly came to be called "Dutch" because at some point the best cast iron came from Holland.

Now that everyone in the United States has an oven, the Dutch oven is no longer used to bake biscuits or cobblers. However, it is essential for dishes that start on top of the stove and finish in the oven, as many stews do. To make recommendations about buying a modern Dutch oven, we tested 12 models from leading makers of cookware.

We found that a Dutch oven should have a capacity of at least six quarts to be useful. Eight quarts is even better. As we cooked in the pots, we came to prefer wider, shallower Dutch ovens because it's easier to see and reach inside them, and they offer more bottom surface area to accommodate large batches of meat for browning. This reduces the number of batches required to brown a given quantity of meat and, with it, the chances of burning the flavorful pan drippings. Ideally, the diameter of a Dutch oven is twice as great as its height.

We also preferred pots with a light-colored interior finish, such as stainless steel or enameled cast iron. It is easier to judge the caramelization of the drippings at a glance in these pots. Dark finishes can mask the color of the drippings, which may burn before you realize it. See our favorite Dutch ovens below.

THE BEST DUTCH OVENS

Our favorite pot is the eight-quart All-Clad Stainless Stockpot (left). Despite the name, this pot is a Dutch oven. Expect to spend nearly $200 for this piece of cookware. A less expensive alternative is the seven-quart Lodge Dutch Oven (about $45; right), which is made from cast iron. This pot is extremely heavy, making it a bit hard to maneuver; it must be seasoned (wiped with oil) regularly; and the dark interior finish is not ideal, but it does brown food quite well.

As far as the cooking method, Hoku's broke with tradition and cooked the shanks at 400 degrees—significantly higher than most other recipes we have tried. Granted, the meat was ready relatively quickly, but the flavor was less developed and the meat drier than that of shanks braised at a lower temperature. Our ex–restaurant line cooks in the test kitchen suggested that the high temperature was most likely due to the exigencies of a restaurant kitchen; oven thermostats are generally fixed at a high temperature so that a variety of items can cook simultaneously. We reduced the temperature to a mellower 325 degrees—a pretty standard braising temperature—and within two hours the meat was tender and very flavorful. The slight increase in cooking time was well worth it for the better flavor and texture.

To finish the dish, it was a simple matter of straining the braising liquid and preparing the filling. A fine-mesh strainer produces the smoothest broth, though it requires a bit of elbow grease. It's important to work the solids back and forth against the strainer's bottom to extract as much liquid as possible and force some of the vegetables through to thicken the broth. The stuffing took a matter of minutes, since the vegetables needed to be sautéed only briefly; the prosciutto is at its best mixed in off the heat. To save on laborious knife work, we chopped the vegetables in a food processor until almost paste-like. Mixed with the prosciutto, bread crumbs, and herbs, the unevenness was impossible to see.

Preserved lemon, a staple condiment of the North African table, has become a hot restaurant ingredient in the past few years. It's bright and citrusy tasting, but briny too. You'll find preserved lemon in specialty markets, but if you can't locate it, grated lemon zest will suffice.

Stuffed Osso Buco

SERVES 6

For the best results, braise the osso buco (through step 3) a day ahead of time: the flavor only improves and it will be easier to skim any excess fat from the broth. If you prefer a thicker broth, feel free to reduce it to the desired consistency over medium heat. Minced preserved lemon rind can be found at specialty markets. Hoku's serves the osso buco with risotto, but we found it just as delicious over a bed of plain polenta.

OSSO BUCO

- 6 tablespoons olive oil
- 6 veal shanks (8–10 ounces each), about 1 1/2 inches thick, patted dry with paper towels and tied around the equator with butcher's twine
- Salt and ground black pepper
- 2 cups dry white wine
- 2 medium onions, cut into medium dice
- 2 medium celery ribs, cut into medium dice
- 1 medium carrot, cut into medium dice
- 1 large leek, white part only, cut into medium dice
- 1 head garlic, top third cut off and discarded, loose outer skin removed and discarded
- 1 medium russet potato, peeled and cut into medium dice
- 1 (14.5-ounce) can diced tomatoes, drained
- 2 bay leaves
- 1 teaspoon whole black peppercorns, lightly crushed
- 2 cups low-sodium chicken broth
- 6 sprigs fresh thyme
- 1 sprig fresh rosemary

STUFFING

- 1 small carrot, chopped coarse
- 1 medium celery rib, chopped coarse
- 1 medium onion, chopped coarse
- 4 medium garlic cloves, chopped coarse
- 2 tablespoons unsalted butter
- 1/4 pound prosciutto, chopped fine
- 1 cup panko (Japanese-style bread crumbs) or Homemade Panko (page 17)
- 1 tablespoon minced fresh parsley leaves
- 1 teaspoon minced fresh thyme leaves
- Salt and ground black pepper
- 1 tablespoon finely minced preserved lemon rind (or 2 teaspoons finely grated lemon zest from 1 lemon)

1. FOR THE OSSO BUCO: Adjust an oven rack to the lower-middle position and heat the oven to 325 degrees. Heat 2 tablespoons of the olive oil in a Dutch oven over medium-high heat until shimmering. Sprinkle both sides of the shanks generously with salt and pepper. Swirl to coat the pan bottom with the oil. Place 3 of the shanks in a single layer in the pan and cook until golden brown on the first side, about 5 minutes. Using tongs, flip the shanks and cook on the second side until golden brown, about 5 minutes longer. Transfer the shanks to a bowl and set aside. Off the heat, add ½ cup of the wine to the pot, scraping the bottom with a wooden spoon to loosen any browned bits. Pour the liquid into the bowl with the browned shanks. Return the pot to medium-high heat, add 2 tablespoons of the remaining olive oil, and heat until shimmering. Repeat with the 3 remaining shanks. Transfer the shanks and liquid to the bowl with the other shanks.

2. Add the remaining 2 tablespoons olive oil, onions, celery, carrot, leek, garlic head, 1 teaspoon salt, and ¼ cup water to the pan. Cook, stirring frequently, until the vegetables are soft and lightly browned, about 10 minutes. Add the shanks and their accumulated juices, potato, tomatoes, bay leaves, peppercorns, chicken broth, the remaining 1½ cups wine, and just enough water to cover the shanks and bring to a simmer. Cover and transfer to the oven. After 1½ hours, add the thyme and rosemary sprigs to the braising liquid. Cook the shanks until the meat can be easily pierced with a fork but is not falling off the bone, about 30 minutes longer. Carefully transfer the meat to a large plate and tent with foil to keep warm.

3. Strain the braising liquid through a fine-mesh strainer into a small saucepan, pushing on the solids to extract as much liquid as possible; discard the solids. Adjust the seasoning with salt and pepper and keep warm over low heat.

4. FOR THE STUFFING: Finely chop the carrot, celery, onion, and garlic in a food processor, about ten 1-second pulses. Melt the butter in a large skillet over medium-high heat until the foam subsides. Add the vegetables and cook, stirring frequently, until softened, 3 to 4 minutes. Remove from the heat and stir in the prosciutto, panko, parsley, and thyme. Season with salt and pepper to taste.

5. Adjust an oven rack so it is 6 inches away from the broiler element and heat the broiler. Using a narrow-bowled spoon, scoop out the marrow from the veal bones. Coarsely chop it and mix it into the stuffing. Carefully transfer the shanks to a rimmed baking sheet and cover them with the stuffing, packing it into the holes as well (about ¼ cup per shank). Broil until the stuffing is browned, 1 to 2 minutes. Sprinkle the preserved lemon rind over the top. Serve the shanks with the starch of your choice and a ladleful of braising liquid.

Pan-Seared Veal Chops *with* Porcini Risotto & White Truffle Oil

Adapted from Milk-Fed Veal Chops over Creamy Porcini Risotto and Foie Gras Demi-Glace

The Baricelli Inn, Cleveland, Ohio

THE BARICELLI INN'S MENU IS LOADED with luxurious main courses epitomizing high-end dining, such as these veal chops. From the fancy chops to the foie gras (not to mention the truffle oil generously drizzled over the risotto), this is a restaurant dish through and through—delicious, but packed with hard-to-find, expensive ingredients and labor-intensive preparation. For some recipes in this book we've trimmed steps, and in other recipes ingredients, but in this instance, we needed to do a little of both to bring it into the realm of the home kitchen. After tasting the restaurant's recipe, we decided that the veal and risotto tasted great on their own and that, while delicious, the foie gras demi-glace sauce was gilding on the lily and could be omitted for the sake of convenience. Even sans sauce, we had our work cut out for us in the kitchen.

Between the hard-to-find ingredients and the vagaries of risotto making, the inn's porcini risotto was a stiff challenge. The first step was finding the ingredients; technique would follow. We were off to a foreboding start when we found out that fresh porcini mushrooms were nearly impossible to find anywhere but specialty stores or mail-order mushroom purveyors (and then only seasonally). But their flavor—a robustly funky, woodsy flavor just shy of truffles—is irreplaceable. The inn suggested frozen porcini if fresh were unavailable, but we found these almost as difficult to come by. Luckily, dried porcini, common to most markets, pack all the flavor of their fresh counterparts at a fraction of the cost. Bulked up with sautéed fresh cremini mushrooms, the dish would come close to the original.

There are two ways to incorporate dried mushrooms into dishes: rehydrated in hot liquid and ground to powder. We commonly use the former method, but the latter is more common in restaurants, so we chose to give it a whirl. Once cleaned (by rubbing the mushrooms together in a fine-mesh strainer), the whole, dried mushrooms quickly turned to a fine powder in a spice grinder (we recommend a coffee grinder as an inexpensive choice). When we added the powder to the risotto, we were impressed by the intense flavor and deep brown hue the powder lent the rice.

For stock, the inn's recipe specified veal stock. Veal stock may be a classic ingredient in traditional French cooking, but it is virtually nonexistent in most markets (some do stock it, or an ersatz concentrated version). We found that mixing equal parts of chicken broth and beef broth proved a passable substitute—perfectly adequate for a risotto in which it is merely a supporting flavor.

Risotto must be made from a medium-grain rice naturally high in amylopectin, a simple starch that lends risotto its characteristic creaminess. Almost always, an Italian medium-grain rice is used, Arborio being the most common variety. The Baricelli Inn, however, specifies a less common variety called Vialone Nano. In a side-by-side tasting in the test kitchen, tasters found the texture of Vialone soft and a little pasty, preferring instead the firmness of standard Arborio and another variety called Carnaroli. Most stores carry Arborio rice, though be wary of packages that look old and of rice in bulk bins, since age has a negative impact on risotto's texture.

While the inn employs a traditional technique for preparing the risotto—adding the liquid in limited amounts to the sautéed shallots and rice and constantly stirring—we have found that there's a simpler method. We add about one third of the liquid and let the rice simmer freely—stirring occasionally—until the liquid is absorbed, about 10 minutes. Then we add the liquid a little bit at a time until the rice is completely tender. While the technique doesn't expedite the process, it does save some effort and debunks the "constant stirring" myth.

To finish the risotto, the inn employs two classic restaurant techniques: whipped heavy cream and truffle oil. Strictly untraditional to Italian recipes, whipped cream lends risotto an unctuous, full mouthfeel—and plenty of extra fat. In fact, some tasters in the kitchen felt it was "over-the-top rich." But we were able to appease everyone by scaling back the amount specified by the inn by half. And, surprisingly, we found it unnecessary to whip the cream: unwhipped cream yielded nearly identical results. As for the truffle oil, a little goes a long way. The lightest drizzle over each portion imbued the rice with an earthy fragrance and intensified the mushroom flavor. From a taste test (see page 95), we knew to use white truffle oil.

With the risotto under our belt, we felt ready to tackle the veal chops. "Milk-fed" veal chops are just that: the calves have been fed only a milk formula, and consequently the meat possesses a mild flavor and creamy texture. But it doesn't come cheap: milk-fed veal is very expensive due to high production costs. The inn's

INGREDIENTS: Rib versus Loin Veal Chops

The best veal chops come from the rib area and the loin. (We find that the shoulder chops can be tough and are best braised or cut off the bone and used in stews.) A loin chop looks like a T-bone steak, with the bone running down the center and meat on both sides. We find that rib chops are juicier and more flavorful than loin chops. The bone runs along the edge of a rib chop, with all the meat on one side.

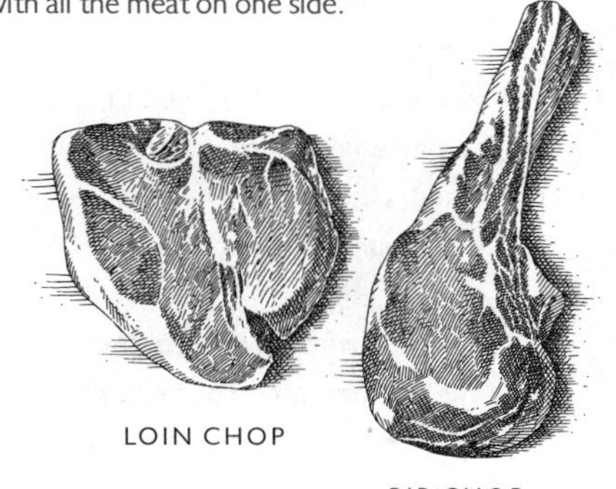

recipe recommends veal from Provimi, a high-end veal producer whose products are popular in restaurants and available in some specialty markets. If you can find it, great, but it's not essential to the dish's success: any good-quality veal chops will fit the bill. However, do make sure that they are bone-in rib chops since they have the most flavor and the bone protects the meat from drying out. If the price is too steep, loin chops are our next choice.

The recipe calls for "frenching" the veal chops, a butchering technique in which the bone protruding beyond the meat is trimmed clean, rendering it stark and white. It's a matter of aesthetics more than anything else, since frenching doesn't affect the manner in which the chop cooks. Either whole or "frenched" is fine by us, though we shy away from the premium price that "frenched" chops command.

As far as cooking the veal chops, the original instructions were scant, so we chose to apply our own. For proper searing, heat's the key: if the pan isn't hot enough, the chop won't develop that dark brown, flavorful sear across the surface—the signature of restaurant-cooked meat. To ensure such high heat, we slick a heavy-bottomed skillet with a minimum of vegetable oil (which has a high smoke point and a neutral flavor) and wait for wisps of smoke to drift upward. Only then is the pan ready. And once the meat—generously seasoned with salt and pepper—is in the skillet, resist the urge to peek, because moving the chops will disrupt the browning process. When the first side is cooked, we reduce the temperature to medium to prevent burning. And like any cut of meat, the chop needs to rest for at least five minutes before serving so that the juices may be redistributed through the meat.

Pan-Seared Veal Chops with Porcini Risotto and White Truffle Oil

SERVES 4

Keep the presentation simple: spoon the risotto into the middle of a large plate and lean the chop against the side, bone pointing upward. The Parmesan curls and chopped thyme garnish are plenty of adornment. If you can't find dried porcini mushrooms, look for cèpes, their French name.

PORCINI RISOTTO

- 1/2 ounce dried porcini mushrooms
- 4 sprigs fresh thyme
- 2 cups low-sodium chicken broth
- 2 cups low-sodium beef broth
- 6 tablespoons (3/4 stick) unsalted butter
- 2 pounds cremini mushrooms, stem bottoms trimmed, each cut into 6 wedges
- 3 medium shallots, diced fine (about 3/4 cup)
- Salt
- 2 cups Arborio rice
- 1/2 cup dry white wine
- Ground black pepper
- 2 tablespoons heavy cream
- White truffle oil, for drizzling

VEAL CHOPS

- 2 teaspoons vegetable oil
- 4 bone-in rib veal chops, 1–1 1/4 inches thick, trimmed of excess fat and patted dry with paper towels (frenched, if desired)
- Salt and ground black pepper

- Shavings of Parmesan cheese, for garnish (see the illustration on page 203)
- 1 teaspoon chopped fresh thyme leaves, for garnish

1. FOR THE RISOTTO: Place the dried porcini in a fine-mesh wire strainer and, over a sink, rub the mushrooms back and forth to remove any grit. Transfer the mushrooms to a spice grinder and process until finely ground. Transfer to a small bowl and set aside. Tie the thyme sprigs together with string. Bring the chicken broth, beef broth, 1½ cups water, and the thyme bundle to a simmer in a medium saucepan over medium-high heat. Reduce the heat to the lowest possible setting to keep the broth warm.

2. Heat 3 tablespoons of the butter in a large skillet over medium-high heat until the foam subsides. Add the cremini mushrooms, one third of the shallots, and ½ teaspoon salt and cook, stirring frequently, until the mushrooms are well browned around the edges, 10 to 11 minutes. Off the heat, add ¼ cup of the warm broth and scrape with a wooden spoon to loosen any browned bits from the bottom of the pan. Cover and set aside.

3. Melt the remaining 3 tablespoons butter in a large saucepan over medium heat until the foam subsides. Add the remaining shallots and ½ teaspoon salt and cook, stirring occasionally, until the shallots are very soft and translucent, about 3 minutes. Add the rice and cook, stirring frequently, until the edges of the grains are transparent, about 4 minutes. Stir in the porcini powder. Add the wine and cook, stirring frequently, until it is completely absorbed by the rice, about 30 seconds. Add 2 cups of the warm broth and simmer, stirring occasionally (about every 3 minutes), until the liquid is absorbed and the bottom of the pan is dry, 10 to 12 minutes.

4. Add more broth, ½ cup at a time, as needed to keep the pan bottom from drying out (every 3 to 4 minutes). Cook, stirring frequently, until the grains of rice are cooked through, but still somewhat firm in the center, 10 to 12 minutes. Stir in the cremini mushroom mixture and season with salt and pepper to taste. Remove from the heat, stir in the heavy cream, and cover to keep warm. Drizzle with the truffle oil just before serving.

5. FOR THE CHOPS: Meanwhile, heat the vegetable oil in a large skillet over medium-high heat until smoking. Season the chops generously with salt and pepper. Lay the chops in the pan and cook without disturbing until well browned, about 3 minutes. Using tongs, flip the chops. Reduce the heat to medium. Cook for 5 to 6 minutes longer for medium (130 degrees on an instant-read thermometer). Transfer the chops to a large plate, tent with foil, and let rest for 5 minutes. Serve on large, warmed plates accompanied by the risotto and garnished with the Parmesan shavings and chopped thyme.

SHAVING PARMESAN

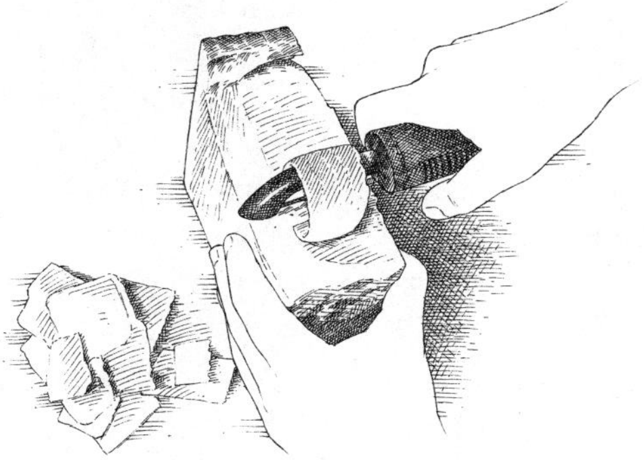

Run a vegetable peeler over a block of Parmesan. Use a light touch for thin shavings.

Pork Chops *with* Rice, Eggs, Onions, & Gravy

Adapted from Pork Chops Loco Moco

Sam Choy's, Honolulu, Hawaii

Pork Chops Loco Moco is Sam Choy's uptown version of Hawaii's roadside diner classic, Loco Moco. Traditionally consisting of rice topped with hamburger, fried egg, and brown gravy, the restaurant replaces the hamburger with a pork chop, the fried egg with a scrambled one, and the brown gravy with a shiitake cream sauce. To top it off, it's garnished with fried onions. Sounding crazy to us, we were nothing but skeptical from the get-go. Yet it took just one bite of this off-the-wall concoction for us to get hooked.

The most difficult aspect of the recipe was juggling its five components. The rice, eggs, pork chops, gravy, and fried onions are all crucial elements of the dish, and we needed to organize their preparation in a manner that made sense for a home cook. Unlike at the restaurant, where loads of rice, gravy, and fried onions are prepared earlier in the day and are on hand during service, each of these items needed to be made from scratch.

To start, we found it best to fry the onions and cook the rice. Of the five components, these two have the longest staying power and require little attention after they're cooked. Wanting the fried onions to be golden and crisp, we found it necessary to slice them very thinly. Difficult to do by hand, we found that the slicing disk of a food processor worked well, yet a mandoline worked better and produced far more consistent slices (see page 8 for information on mandolines). We then dredged the onion slices in flour seasoned with salt and pepper and fried them in 350-degree vegetable oil until crisp and brown.

For the rice, we liked the flavor of rice that has first been lightly toasted in a small saucepan with a little oil. Adding just enough water to cook the rice without turning it mushy or sticky, we found it best to use 1½ cups water to 1 cup rice as opposed to the classic 2-to-1 ratio. We also found it beneficial to drape a clean dish towel or paper towel over the mouth of the pot, underneath the lid, as the rice finished cooking to prevent any condensation from dripping back onto the rice and turning it sticky. We then set aside the covered rice while we cooked the remaining components.

Made with shiitake mushrooms and cream, the gravy is flavored with soy sauce and oyster sauce and thickened slightly with cornstarch. In order to make a smaller batch than the original gallon-yielding recipe, we found it necessary to treat the mushrooms a little differently. For a large batch, the numerous mushrooms are cooked together, their combined weight forcing the moisture and flavor out of one another. Yet when making a smaller batch, we found the mushrooms seared quickly and held onto their moisture. To encourage the mushrooms to release their flavor, we turned the heat down and covered the pot. Known as "sweating," this technique worked like a charm and took only a few minutes.

Last, we turned our attention to the eggs and pork chops. Wanting to streamline any further pan usage, we decided it would be best to scramble the eggs in a nonstick pan, then wipe it out and fry the pork chops. We then seared the pork chops at a higher temperature, using vegetable oil instead of butter, which we found just burned. Trying Pork Chops Loco Moco with bone-in thick and thin pork chops, we found thick chops were overwhelming on the already crowded plate. Thin chops, on the other hand, offered the perfect ratio of meat to loco moco.

STEAMING RICE

After the rice absorbs the liquid, remove the pan from the heat. Cover the pan with a clean dish towel and then the lid; allow the rice to sit for 15 minutes. The towel absorbs moisture and helps produce dry, fluffy rice.

Pork Chops with Rice, Eggs, Onions, and Gravy

SERVES 4

This hearty, traditional Hawaiian diner dish is good for breakfast, lunch, or dinner.

FRIED ONIONS

- 3 cups vegetable oil
- 1/2 cup all-purpose flour
- 1 teaspoon salt
- 1/2 tablespoon ground black pepper
- 1 small yellow onion, halved and sliced thin on a mandoline (see page 8) or in a food processor

RICE

- 2 teaspoons vegetable oil
- 1 cup long-grain white rice
- 1/2 teaspoon salt

SAUCE

- 1 teaspoon cornstarch
- 1 tablespoon vegetable oil
- 4 ounces fresh shiitake mushrooms, stemmed and sliced thin
- 1 cup heavy cream
- 2 teaspoons soy sauce
- 1 teaspoon oyster sauce
- Salt and ground black pepper

EGGS

- 4 large eggs
- 1/4 cup whole milk
- 1/4 teaspoon salt
- Pinch ground black pepper
- 1 tablespoon unsalted butter

PORK CHOPS

- 1 tablespoon vegetable oil
- 4 thin bone-in center-cut loin pork chops, about 1/2 inch thick
- Salt and ground black pepper

1. For the fried onions: Heat the vegetable oil in a Dutch oven over medium-high heat until it reaches 350 degrees. (Use an instant-read thermometer that registers high temperatures or clip a candy/deep-fat thermometer onto the side of the pan before turning on the heat.) Meanwhile, mix the flour, salt, and pepper together in a large bowl. Add the onion to the flour mixture and toss thoroughly to coat. Transfer the floured onion to a large strainer (or colander) set over another large bowl (or the sink) and shake vigorously to remove the excess flour. Add the onion to the oil and fry until golden brown, 2 to 2½ minutes, adjusting the heat as necessary to maintain the cooking temperature. Remove the onion from the oil using a spider (see page 9) or slotted spoon, tapping the handle several times on the rim of the pot to drain any excess oil, then transfer to a large plate lined with several layers of paper towels. Set aside.

2. For the rice: Heat the vegetable oil in a small saucepan over medium heat until shimmering. Add the rice and cook, stirring constantly, until transparent, 2 to 3 minutes. Add 1½ cups water and the salt. Bring to a boil, swirling the pan to blend the ingredients. Reduce the heat to low, cover tightly, and cook until the liquid is absorbed, about 15 minutes. Remove from the heat and cover the pan with a clean dish towel and then the lid (see page 205). Let the rice stand, covered, to finish cooking, about 15 minutes longer. Fluff with a fork and set aside.

3. For the sauce: Mix the cornstarch and 1 teaspoon water together in a small bowl and set aside. Heat the vegetable oil in a large saucepan over medium-high heat until shimmering. Stir in the shiitakes, cover, and reduce the heat to low. Cook until the mushrooms release their moisture and begin to brown, about 5 minutes. Stir in the cream, soy sauce, and oyster sauce, increase the heat to medium-high, and bring to a boil. Whisk in the cornstarch mixture and return to a boil, whisking constantly. Cook, whisking constantly, until the sauce is slightly thickened, about 30 seconds. Remove the sauce from the heat and season with salt and pepper to taste. Transfer the sauce to a liquid measuring cup, cover tightly with plastic wrap, and set aside.

4. For the eggs: Crack the eggs into a medium bowl and add the milk, salt, and pepper. Beat with a fork until the streaks are gone and the color is pure yellow; stop beating while the bubbles are still large. Melt the butter in a 12-inch nonstick skillet over high heat until foaming, swirling it around and up the sides of the pan. Before the foam completely subsides, pour in the beaten eggs. Using a heatproof spatula, push the eggs from one side of the pan to the other, slowly but deliberately lifting and folding the eggs as they form curds, until the eggs are nicely clumped into a single mound but remain shiny and wet, about 2 minutes. Transfer to a medium bowl and cover to keep warm.

5. For the pork chops: Wipe the nonstick skillet clean with a wad of paper towels. Add the vegetable oil and heat over high heat until smoking. Season the pork chops generously with salt and pepper. Lay the pork chops in a single layer in the skillet and cook until golden brown, 2 to 3 minutes. Turn and cook on the second side until lightly brown and cooked through, 1 to 2 minutes longer.

6. To serve: Divide the rice among 4 individual plates. Lay a pork chop on top of the rice and top with equal portions of scrambled eggs. Pour about 3 tablespoons of the sauce over the egg and pork on each plate, and sprinkle with the fried onions. Serve immediately.

Kimchee Fried Rice

Adapted from Kimchee Fried Rice
Big City Diner, Kaimuki, Hawaii

FRIED RICE IS OFTEN A GREASY CONCOCtion of rice, pork, and overcooked vegetables. The Big City Diner, however, reinvents this tired takeout staple with the addition of kimchee (zesty Korean pickled cabbage) and two varieties of spicy sausage. This fried rice is ideal served with eggs for breakfast, or straight up for dinner.

Our most difficult challenge in making over this recipe for the home kitchen was finding enough leftover rice to make a full batch. In a restaurant, leftover rice is a given, and fried rice is merely its thrifty reincarnation. Requiring six cups of cold rice to make a batch that serves four people for dinner (or six to eight people as a side dish), we found that we had to cook and cool the rice on purpose. Although Big City Diner uses a combination of two parts white rice and one part brown rice, we didn't want to cook both, and decided to use just white. Testing steamed rice against boiled rice (boiled like pasta), we noted that the boiled rice was better and faster. Cutting the cooking time down by about 15 minutes, the abundant amount of cooking water actually washed the excess starch off the rice, producing a fluffier, less clumpy texture. We spread the rice on a rimmed baking sheet immediately after cooking, then chilled it in the refrigerator. When not cooled, the resulting fried rice was a huge, starchy mess. However, if you do have day-old rice, use it. It is much drier and fries up into lovely, separate grains.

Beyond the rice, the difficulty in making this dish was neither the cooking nor the prep work, but rather the shopping. The recipe called for Chinese barbecued pork (known as *char sui*). We found it necessary to visit an Asian grocery store that actually cooks the barbecued pork on the premises—usually found hanging next to the Peking duck. Kimchee is also found in Asian grocery stores, in jars in the refrigerator case (or see our homemade version on page 177). The only preparation required for the ready-made kimchee was a quick drain of its excess liquid. The recipe also called for spicy Portuguese sausage, a popular Hawaiian ingredient that we could not find, for which we substituted linguiça, a readily available Portuguese sausage.

Cooking everything in a large, nonstick skillet with some sesame oil is simple when only a few ingredients are added at a time. We were skeptical because sesame oil is generally not used for cooking—but it works here. Finished with a quick sauce made by mixing equal parts soy sauce and oyster sauce, and sprinkled with more kimchee, this Hawaiian-style fried rice is worth boiling rice for.

Kimchee Fried Rice

SERVES 4 AS A MAIN COURSE,
6 TO 8 AS A SIDE DISH

If you don't have 6 cups of leftover white rice, cook 1½ cups of long-grain white rice in 4 quarts of boiling water with 1½ teaspoons of salt until tender but not soft, about 15 minutes. Drain the rice in a large, fine-mesh strainer, spread on a foil-lined rimmed baking sheet, and refrigerate until cold. Kimchee is sold both canned and jarred, but we prefer the jarred version found in the refrigerator section of Asian markets and some supermarkets. To make homemade kimchee, see Grilled Skirt Steak with Kimchee on page 177.

- 3 tablespoons oyster sauce
- 3 tablespoons soy sauce
- 2 teaspoons toasted sesame oil
- 4 large eggs, lightly beaten
- 8 ounces Chinese barbecued pork (*char sui*), cut into ½-inch pieces
- 6 ounces linguiça sausage, cut into ½-inch pieces
- 4 ounces thick-sliced deli ham, cut into ½-inch pieces
- ½ small onion, minced
- ¼ cup frozen peas, thawed
- 6 cups cold cooked long-grain white rice, large clumps broken up
- 1 cup kimchee, drained

1. Combine the oyster sauce and soy sauce in a small bowl and set aside

2. Heat a 12-inch nonstick skillet over medium-high heat. Add 1 teaspoon of the sesame oil and swirl to coat the pan bottom. Add the eggs and cook, without stirring, until they just begin to set, about 30 seconds, then scramble and break into small pieces with a wooden spoon. Cook, stirring constantly, until the eggs are cooked through but not browned, about 1 minute longer. Transfer the eggs to a medium bowl and set aside.

3. Add the remaining 1 teaspoon sesame oil to the skillet and heat until shimmering. Add the pork, sausage, ham, and onion and cook, stirring constantly, until the onion is translucent, about 2 minutes. Stir in the peas, scrambled eggs, and rice. Add the oyster sauce mixture and cook, stirring constantly and breaking up the rice clumps, until heated through, about 2 minutes. Stir in ¾ cup of the kimchee. Transfer the rice to a serving platter and sprinkle the remaining kimchee over the top. Serve immediately.

Pork Tenderloin *with* Rhubarb Sauce

Adapted from Pork with Rhubarb

Parker's New American Bistro, Cleveland, Ohio

AT PARKER'S NEW AMERICAN BISTRO, ingredients are shopped for early in the morning at the farmers market, then pulled together for the night's menu by Chef Parker Bosley. It is in such a restaurant that a dish like sautéed pork tenderloin would be paired successfully with an unlikely rhubarb sauce.

Cutting the pork tenderloin into small steaks to be sautéed, we found that three small tenderloins served six people. Sautéed in two batches, the pork was then set aside in a warm oven to rest while we made the sauce. Using the classic method for making a pan sauce, we deglazed the browned bits left in the pan, known as *fond,* with wine and broth and then simmered them into a sauce. The interesting thing about this sauce, however, is that rather than finishing it with the traditional butter, Chef Bosley finishes it with rhubarb that has been previously cooked with some sugar. Although we thought this technique sounded a bit odd, we found it to be spot on, and the resulting flavor out of this world. The rhubarb not only added a slightly tart, perfumed flavor to the sauce, but its lightly starchy texture rounded out the butterless sauce. Cooking the rhubarb with sugar until tender, as the original recipe directed, was a breeze. Although there might be a way to re-create the recipe using frozen rhubarb, the flavor of the sauce would suffer dramatically. Much like at the restaurant, this dish should be made only when fresh, local rhubarb is in season.

Pork Tenderloin with Rhubarb Sauce

SERVES 6

The cooking time for the rhubarb depends on the age and size of the stalks. Cook until the pieces are tender but have not lost their shape. Braised greens, such as chard, make a nice accompaniment to this dish.

- 6 large rhubarb stalks, cut into ½-inch dice (about 4 cups)
- ¾ cup sugar
- 3 small pork tenderloins (12–16 ounces each, for a total of 2 ½–3 pounds), trimmed of silver skin and excess fat
- Salt and ground black pepper
- 2 tablespoons vegetable oil
- ½ cup ruby port
- 1 cup low-sodium chicken broth

1. Cook the rhubarb and sugar together in a medium, heavy-bottomed saucepan over low heat until the rhubarb has softened but still retains its shape, 25 to 35 minutes.

Transfer to a medium bowl and set aside.

2. Following the illustrations below, cut each pork tenderloin crosswise into six 2-inch-thick slices. With a cut side facing up, lightly pound each slice into a round ¾-inch-thick medallion. Season the medallions generously with salt and pepper.

3. Adjust an oven rack to the middle position and heat the oven to 200 degrees. Heat 1 tablespoon of the vegetable oil in a 12-inch skillet (not nonstick) over medium-high heat until just smoking. Lay 9 medallions in the pan and cook until lightly browned, 3 to 4 minutes. Flip the medallions and cook on the second side until lightly browned and nearly cooked through, 3 to 4 minutes longer. Transfer to a clean plate and keep warm in the oven. Add the remaining 1 tablespoon vegetable oil to the skillet and repeat with the remaining 9 medallions. Transfer to the plate in the oven.

4. Add the port and bring to a simmer. Simmer until the port is thick and syrupy, about 2 minutes. Stir in the broth and any accumulated rhubarb juices and return to a simmer. Simmer until the mixture is thick and has reduced to about ½ cup, about 12 minutes. Stir in the rhubarb mixture and any accumulated juices from the pork medallions and heat through, about 30 seconds. Season with salt and pepper to taste. Arrange 3 pork medallions on each of 6 individual plates and spoon about ¼ cup of the rhubarb sauce over the top. Serve immediately.

CUTTING A PORK TENDERLOIN INTO SIX SLICES

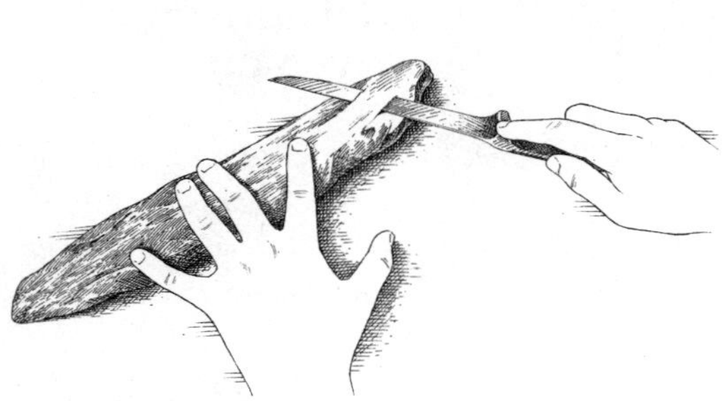

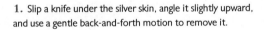

1. Slip a knife under the silver skin, angle it slightly upward, and use a gentle back-and-forth motion to remove it.

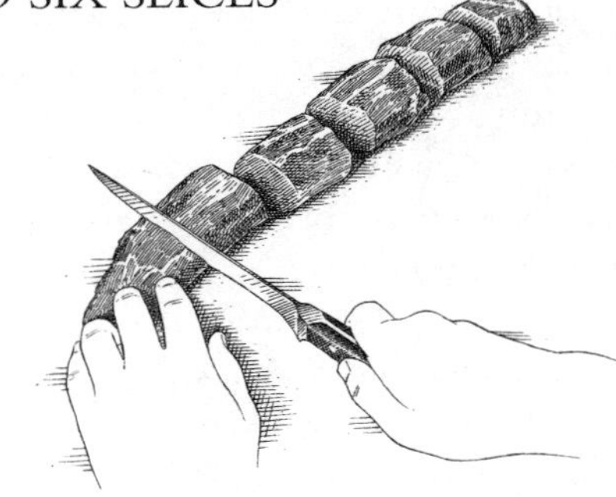

2. Cut the tenderloin crosswise into six equal pieces, including the tapered tail end.

3. Stand one piece of tenderloin on its cut side on a piece of plastic or parchment, cover with a second piece, and pound very gently with a mallet or meat pounder to an even thickness of ¾ inch.

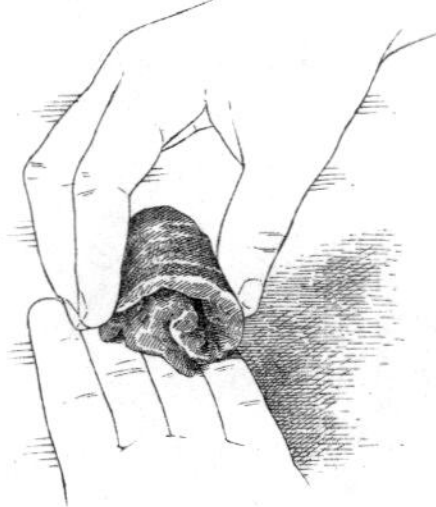

4. The thin piece of tenderloin requires extra care to produce a cutlet. Fold the tip of the tail under the cut side before using the heel of your hand to press each slice into ¾-inch-thick medallions.

FRIED GREEN TOMATOES WITH GOAT CHEESE **PAGE 15**

TUNA TARTARE WITH SWEET POTATO CRISPS **PAGE 40**

CRAB TOWERS WITH AVOCADO & GAZPACHO SALSAS **PAGE 58**

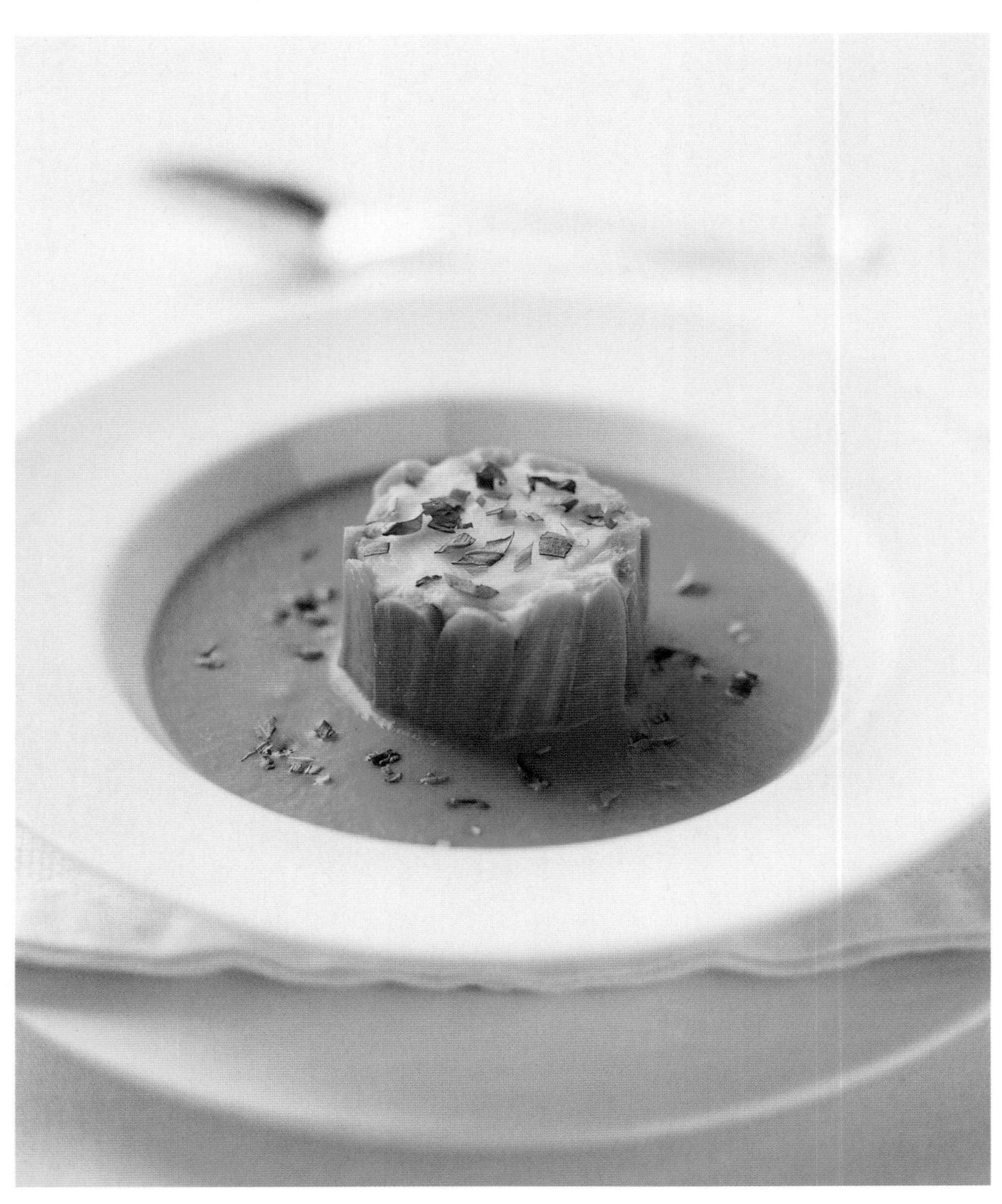

CARROT SOUP WITH ROOT VEGETABLE CHARLOTTE **PAGE 71**

BLUE CHEESE POTATO CROQUETTES **PAGE 320**

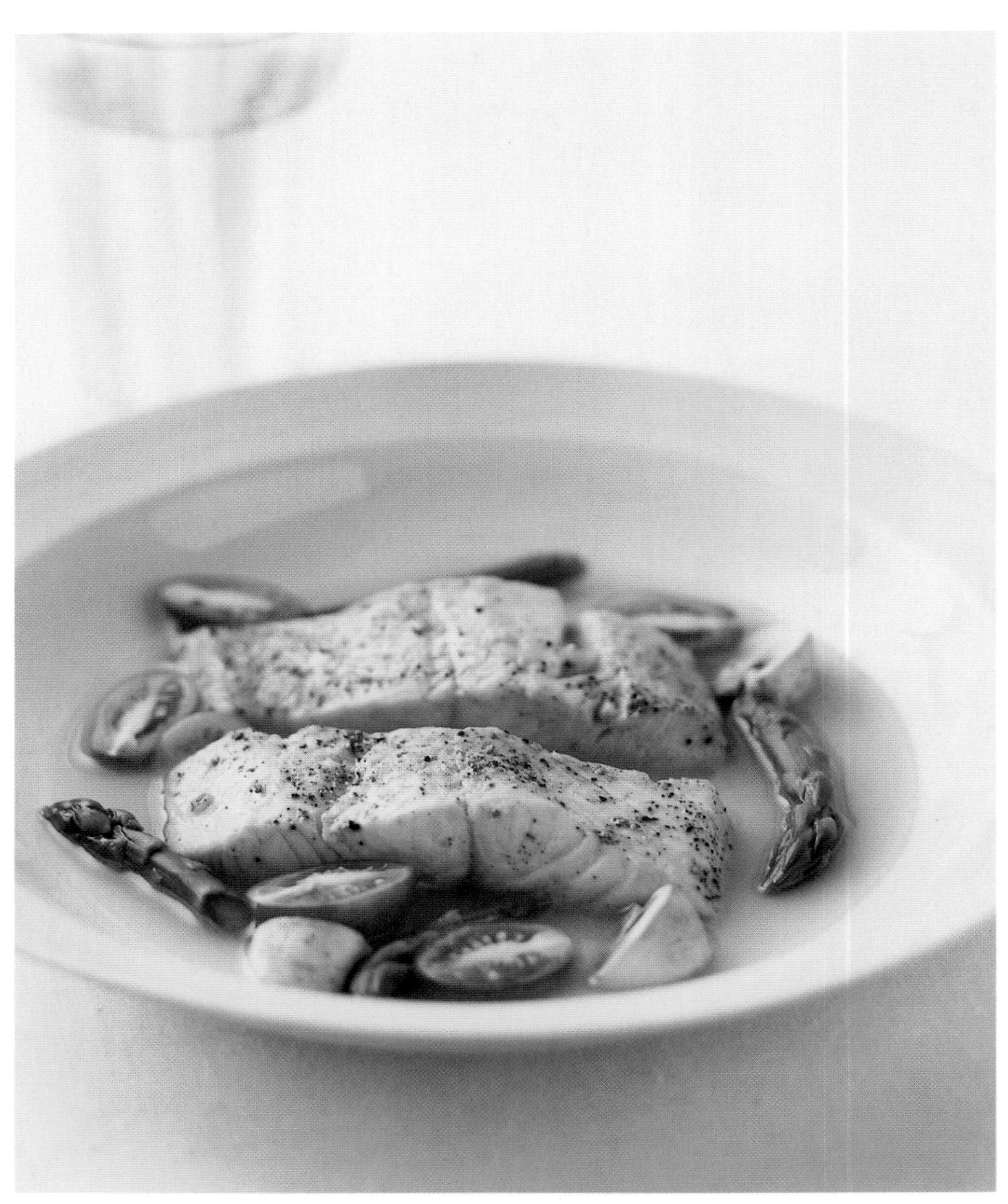

SALMON CONFIT WITH LEMON GRASS BROTH & SPRING VEGETABLES **PAGE 277**

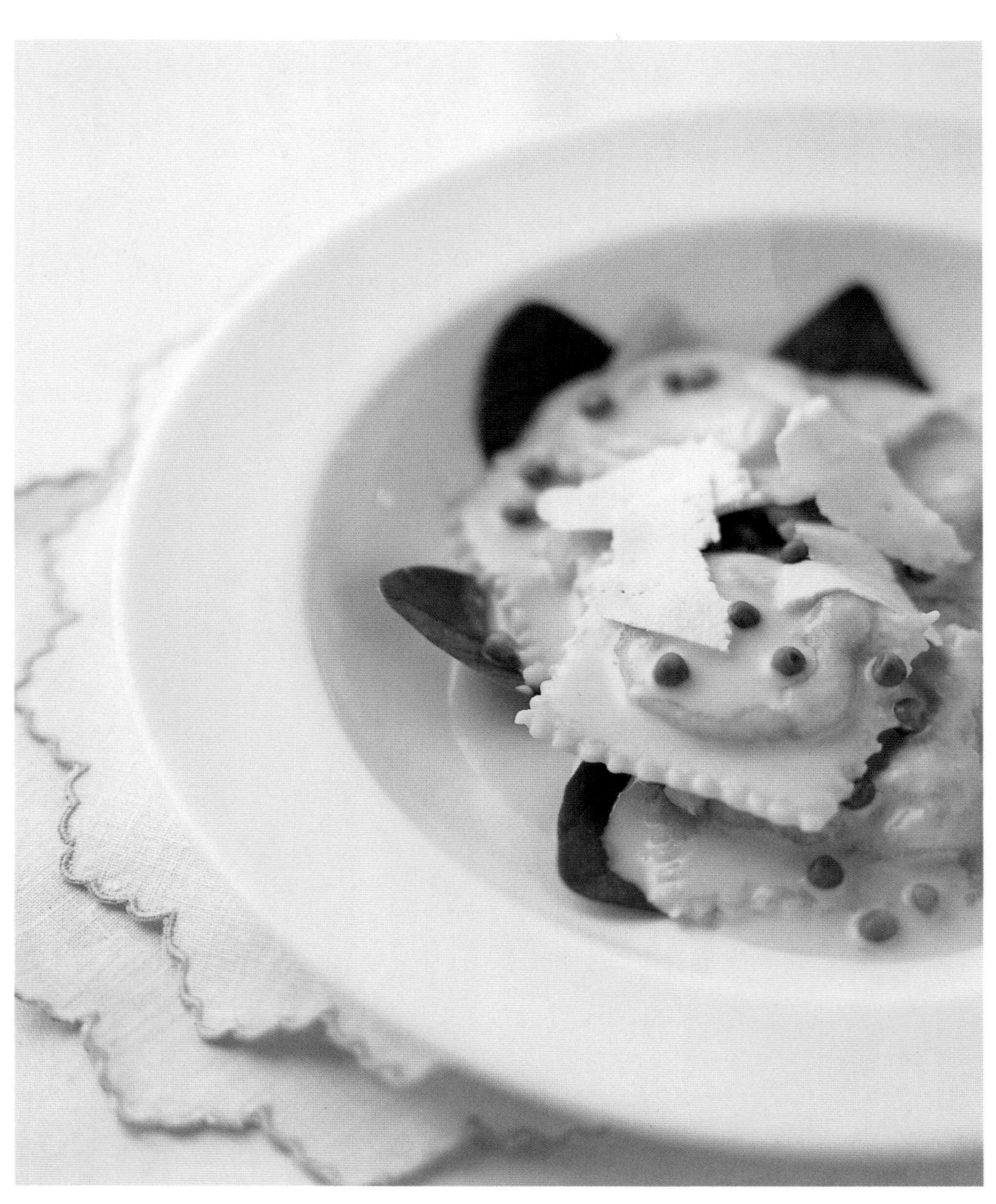

WHITE TRUFFLE–SCENTED RAVIOLI WITH MASCARPONE & PEAS **PAGE 131**

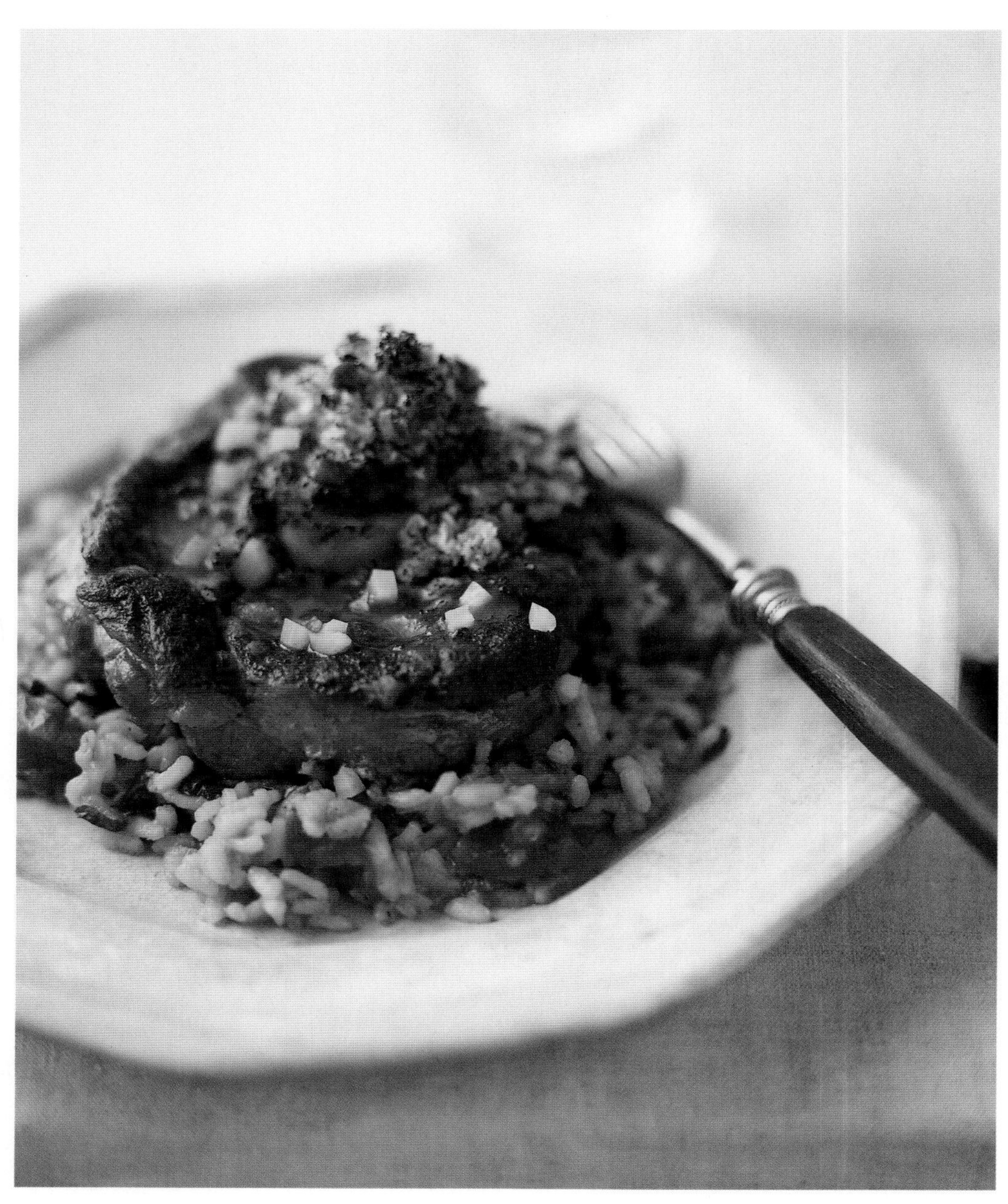

STUFFED OSSO BUCO **PAGE 196**

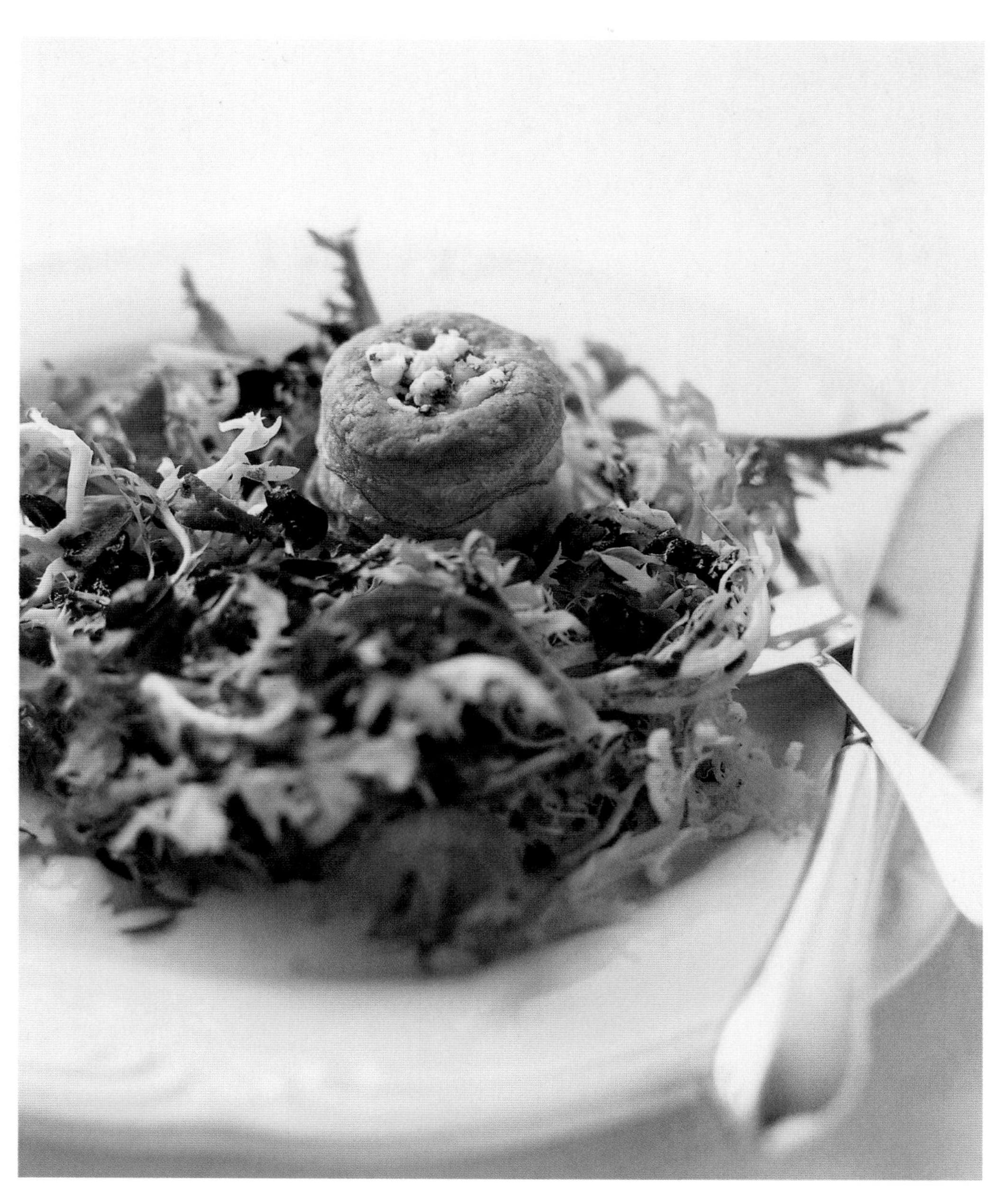

FRISÉE SALAD WITH CRANBERRY-BACON VINAIGRETTE & BLUE CHEESE PASTRIES

PAGE 103

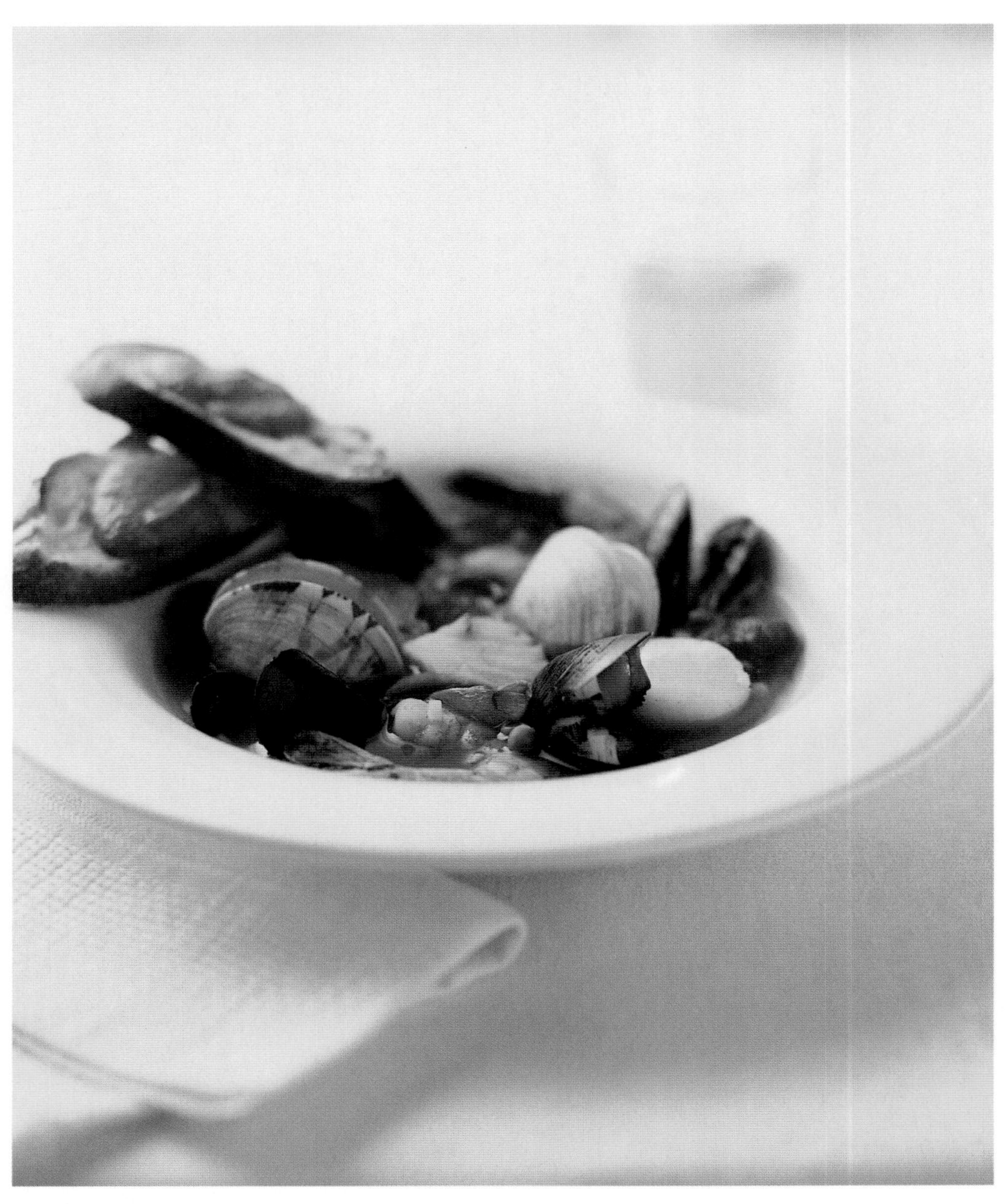

BAJA BOUILLABAISSE **PAGE 298**

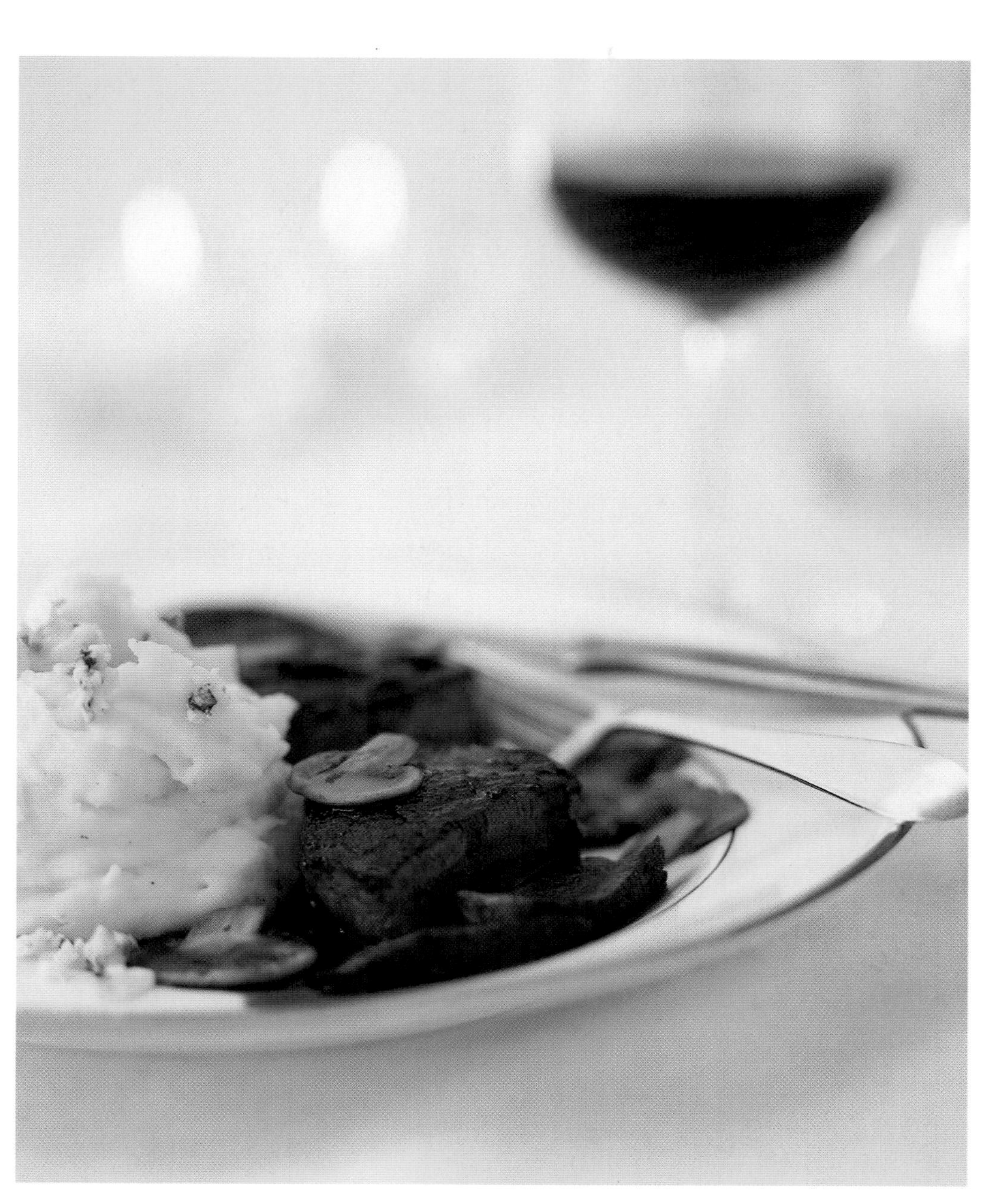

BEEF TOURNEDOS WITH BLUE CHEESE MASHED POTATOES **PAGE 183**

PORK TENDERLOIN WITH RHUBARB SAUCE **PAGE 209**

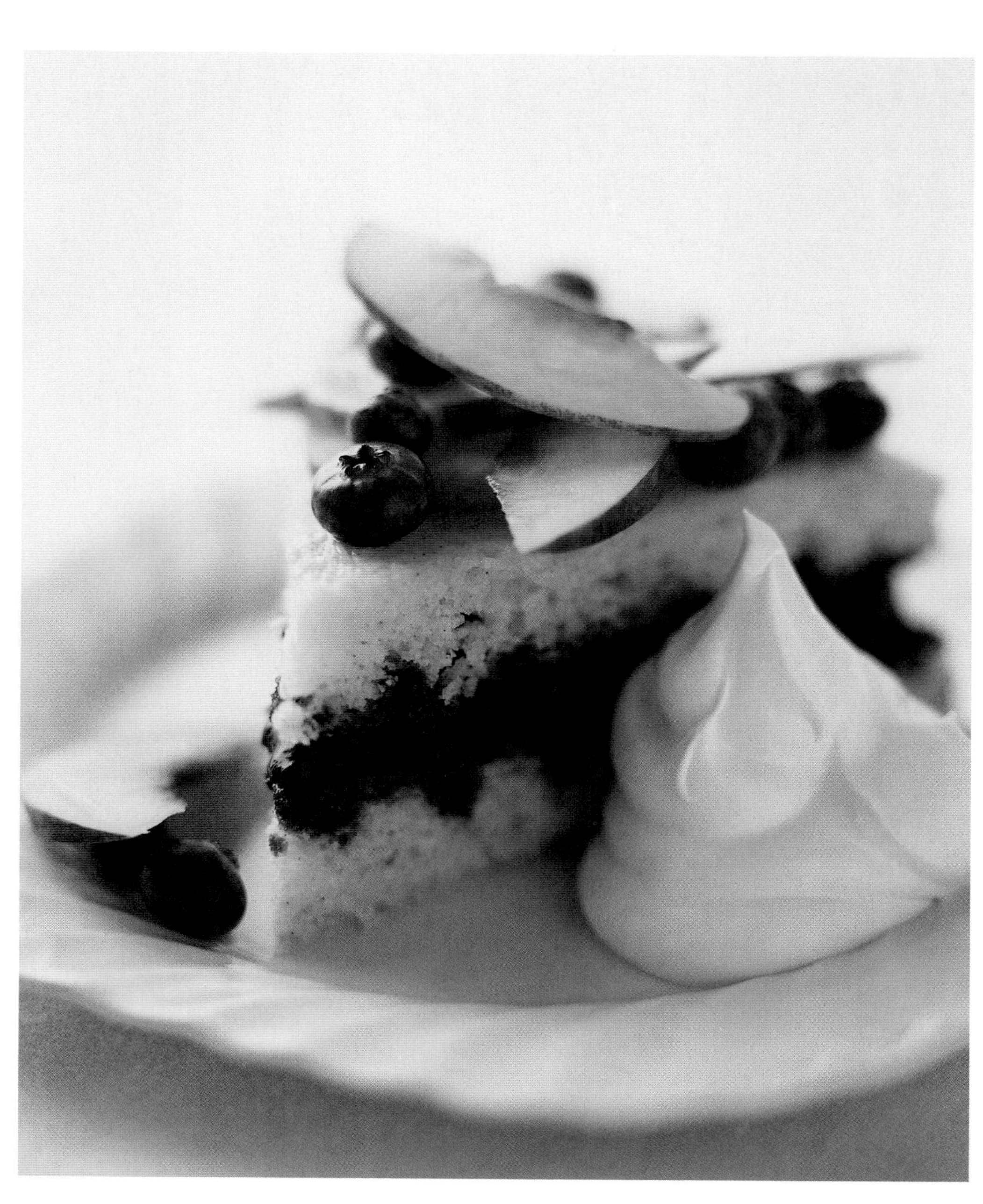

VANILLA CAKE WITH ROASTED PEACHES & BLUEBERRIES **PAGE 361**

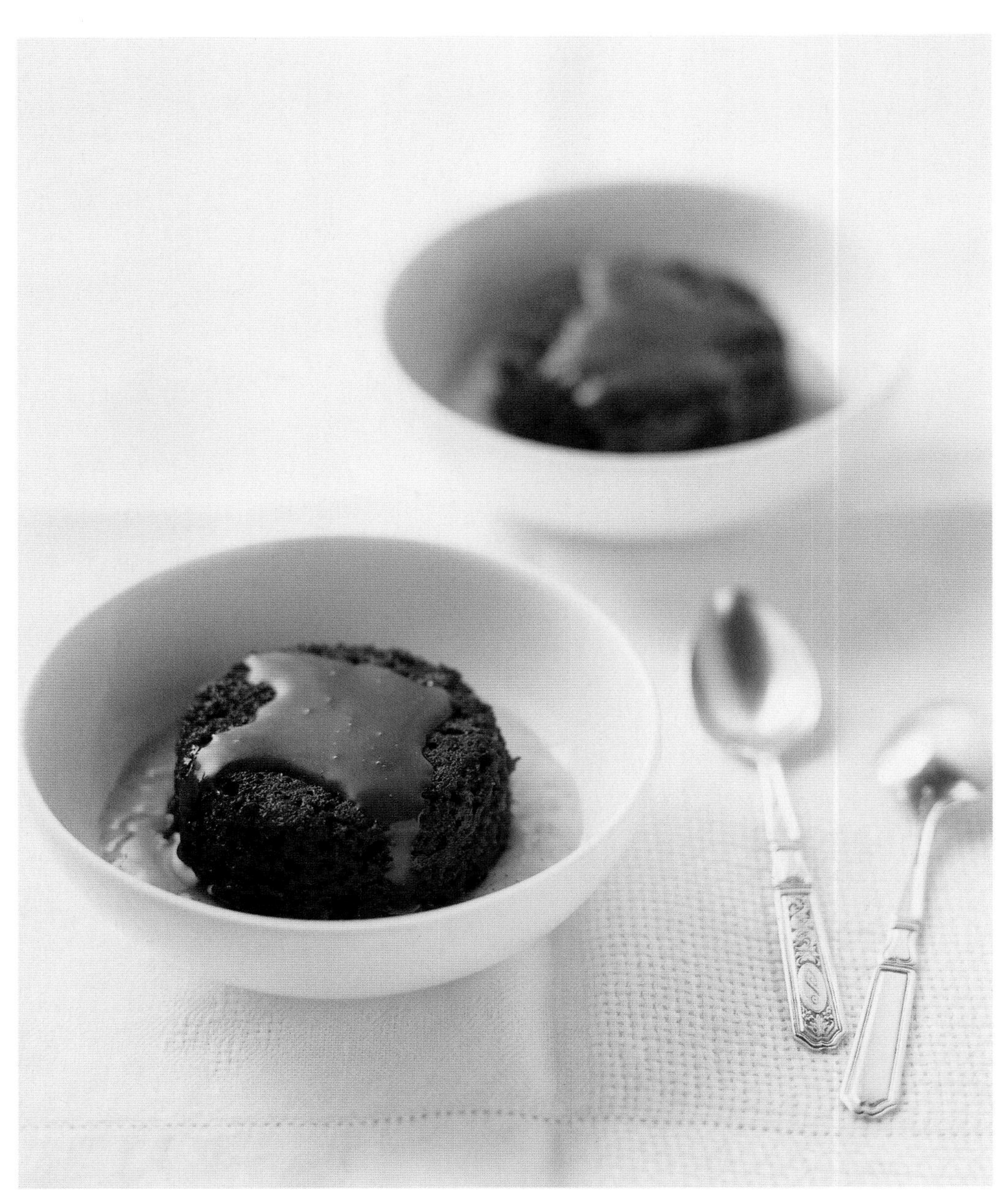

STICKY TOFFEE PUDDING **PAGE 377**

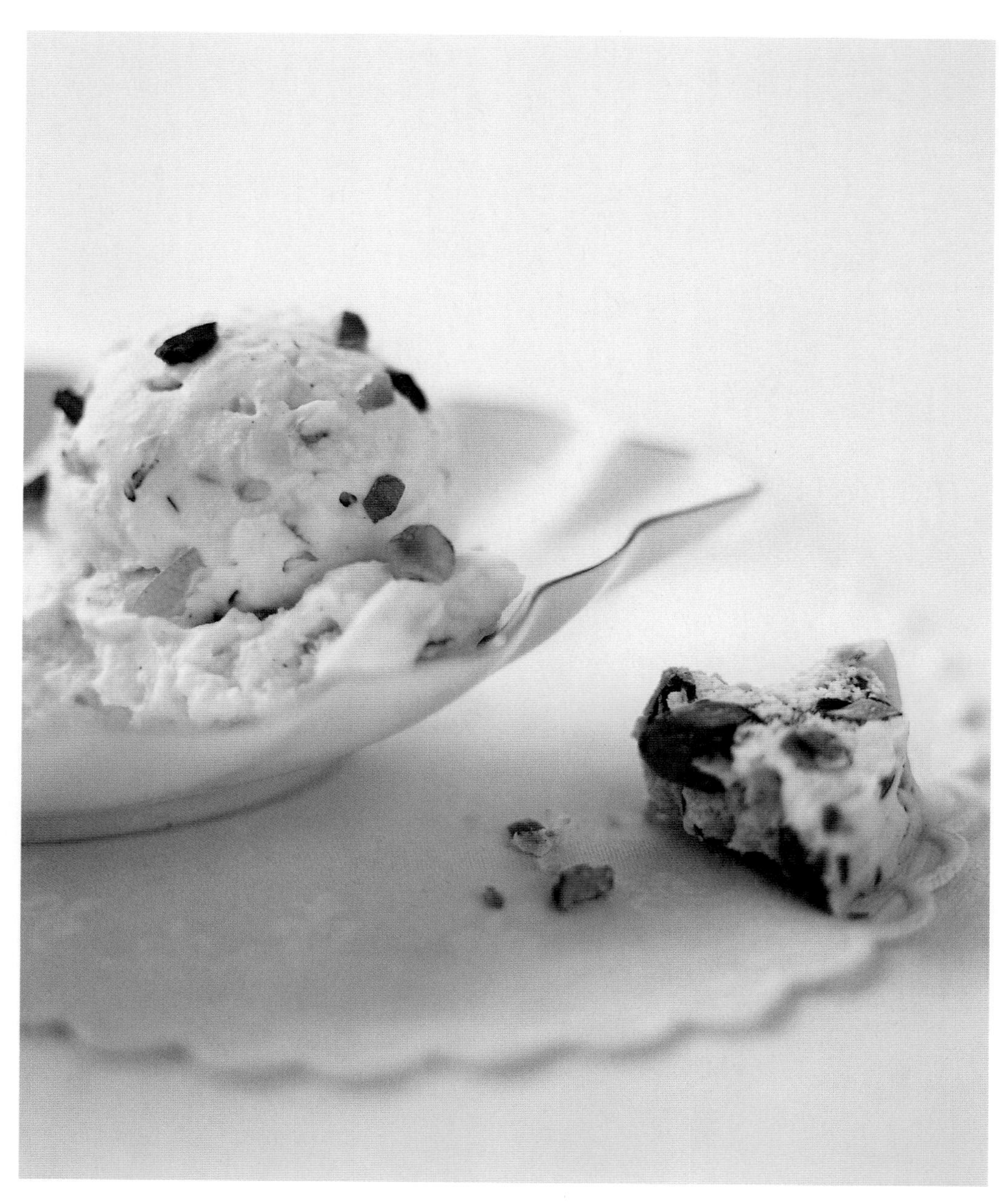

CANNOLI GELATO **PAGE 401**

INDIVIDUAL GERMAN CHOCOLATE CAKES **PAGE 349**

Grill-Smoked Pork Chops *with* Apple Chutney

Adapted from Smoked Pork Loin with Apple Chutney

Wente Vineyards, Livermore, California

THE RATHER OBVIOUS THEORY BEHIND the restaurant at Wente Vineyards is to have good, simple food that will show off the wine. Yet with a year-round garden attached to the kitchen (complete with a gardener) and chef Elisabeth Schwarz at the helm, the "simple" food draws as much attention as the wine. Case in point is the signature dish of smoked pork loin with apple chutney. The recipe reads as nothing more than thick grilled pork chops and a quick chutney, but it yields incredibly tender chops with a delicately perfumed smoke flavor that, when paired with the spicy-sweet chutney, had us drooling in the test kitchen.

The key to this dish's success is the grilling technique. The theory behind the technique is to cook the 14-ounce center-cut pork chops slowly on the cool side of the grill (opposite the fire), and maximize their exposure to the flavorful smoke. Getting the temperature of the grill just right is therefore crucial. If you start with a grill that is too cool, the pork chops will take too long to cook through and wind up incredibly dry and overly smoky. Yet at the other extreme, a grill that is too hot will cook the chops too quickly, denying them exposure to the smoke. The original recipe just said to make "a small fire and let it burn down to embers" in either a smoker or kettle-type grill. Realizing that most people don't own a smoker, we figured out how to produce tender, flavorful pork chops using either a charcoal or gas grill. Starting with a charcoal grill, we fiddled with various amounts of fuel and determined that half a large chimney full of briquettes (about 45 briquettes), banked to one side of the grill was just right, bringing the initial temperature of the grill to roughly 350 degrees. Moving over to the gas grill, we found it necessary to heat up the grill initially by turning all the burners to high, but then turning off all but one to cook the chops. For good smoky flavor, it is necessary to add to the grill wood chunks or chips that have been presoaked in water. If not soaked, they will only burn rather than "smoke." Soaked wood *chunks* can be tossed onto the hot coals of a charcoal grill, but wood *chips* require a foil packet or foil tray before being added to a charcoal or gas grill (see illustrations on page 230).

The recipe recommends that the chops be brought to room temperature before being grilled. Although sounding a bit odd, we found this small step helped them cook more evenly, and they came off the grill tender and juicy. Placing the pork chops on the grill correctly is another crucial step. They should be placed on the opposite side of the fire, bone-side down so that they stand upright. This ensures that the meat of each chop has full exposure to the flavoring smoke. Last, we noted it was important to cover the grill with the lid vents opposite the fire (over the chops) to help draw the smoke through the grill. The chops took roughly 35 minutes to reach 145 degrees, at which point we removed them from the grill. Allowing the chops to rest for 10 minutes before serving, we noted their temperature rose to 155 degrees. The meat will have a slightly pink tinge, but it will be far juicier than chops cooked to an internal temperature just 10 degrees higher. (A temperature of 155 degrees is high enough to kill the parasite that causes trichinosis. However, the U.S. Department of Agriculture recommends cooking all meat to an internal temperature of 160 degrees to kill bacteria such as salmonella. If safety is your primary concern, follow the USDA's guidelines.)

While the pork chops are grilling, there is plenty of time to make the apple chutney. The base of the chutney is a quickly simmered brown sugar and cider vinegar mixture flavored with onions, garlic, ginger, red bell pepper, and several spices including cayenne. The apples are sautéed separately in a skillet, then added to the sugar-vinegar base after it has cooled off a bit. This dual-pot method ensures that the chutney is well seasoned and has the correct consistency, yet the apples retain just a little of their crunch. The winery suggests Pinot Noir as the perfect accompaniment to this smoky pork chop topped with a sweet, vinegary, cayenne-laced chutney. However, we found its flavor actually paired perfectly with, we daresay, a cold beer.

Grill-Smoked Pork Chops with Apple Chutney

SERVES 6

At the winery, this is served with polenta, but you could also serve it with roasted potatoes or the Roasted Root Vegetable Gratin on page 312. If using wood chips rather than chunks, see the illustrations on page 263 for information about wrapping them in a foil packet. The chutney can be made a day ahead, kept refrigerated, and reheated in a small heavy-bottomed saucepan over low heat.

PORK CHOPS

- 2 (3-inch) wood chunks or 2 cups wood chips
- 6 (14-ounce) center-cut pork chops, about 2 inches thick
- Salt and ground black pepper

CHUTNEY

- 3 tablespoons vegetable oil
- 1 medium red bell pepper, seeded and cut into 1/2-inch dice
- 1/2 small onion, minced (about 1/4 cup)
- 2 tablespoons minced or grated fresh ginger
- 2 garlic cloves, minced or pressed through a garlic press (about 2 teaspoons)
- 1 cup apple cider vinegar
- 1 cup packed light brown sugar
- 1 tablespoon mustard seeds
- 1/2 teaspoon ground allspice
- 1/8 teaspoon cayenne pepper
- 3 Granny Smith apples, peeled, cored, and cut into 1/2-inch dice

1. FOR THE PORK CHOPS: Soak the wood chunks in cold water to cover for 1 hour and drain, or place wood chips on an 18-inch square of aluminum foil, seal to

GRILLING PORK CHOPS

To ensure that the smoke evenly surrounds the pork chops, place them bone-side down on the grill, about 2 inches apart.

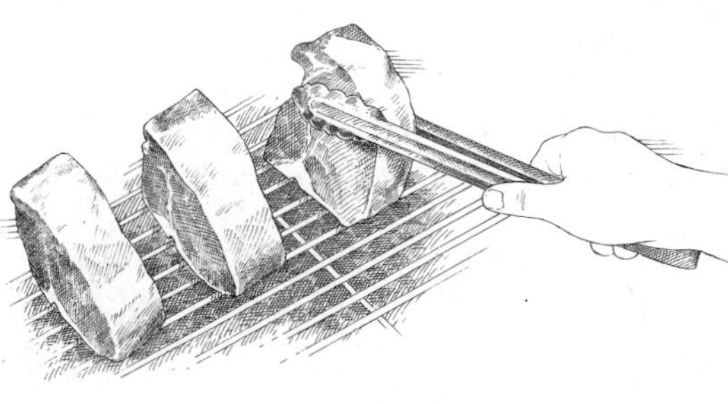

make a packet, and use a fork to create about 6 holes to allow smoke to escape (see the illustration on page 263). Meanwhile, allow the pork chops to come to room temperature, about 1 hour.

2. Open the bottom vents on the grill. Ignite half a large chimney-full of charcoal (about 45 briquettes) and allow to burn until the flames have died down and the charcoal is covered with a layer of fine gray ash. Spread coals out over half the grill bottom, piling them 2 or 3 briquettes high, leaving the other half with no coals. Place the soaked wood chunks (or wood chip packet) on top of the coals. Set the cooking grate in place and let it heat up for 5 minutes. Scrape the grate clean. Cover the grill and open the lid vents two thirds of the way.

3. Season the chops generously with salt and pepper. Arrange them bone-side down (see the illustration above) on the cool side of the grill parallel to the fire. Cover the grill, positioning the lid so that the vents are opposite the wood chunks to draw the smoke through the grill (the grill temperature should register about 350 degrees on a grill thermometer, but will soon start dropping). Cook until an instant-read thermometer inserted in the side of a chop away from the bone registers 145 degrees, 30 to 45 minutes.

4. For the chutney: While the pork chops are on the grill, heat 1 tablespoon of the vegetable oil in a medium saucepan over medium-high heat until shimmering. Add the bell pepper, onion, ginger, and garlic. Cover, reduce the heat to medium, and cook until the vegetables have softened, about 5 minutes. Stir in the vinegar, sugar, mustard seeds, allspice, and cayenne and bring to a simmer over medium-high heat. Cook, adjusting the heat as necessary to maintain a simmer, until the mixture is thick and syrupy and has reduced to 1¼ cups, about 10 minutes. Remove from the heat, transfer to a medium bowl, and cool.

5. Heat 1 tablespoon of the remaining vegetable oil in a 12-inch nonstick skillet over medium-high heat until just smoking. Add half of the apples and cook, stirring frequently, until golden brown on all sides, about 4 minutes. Transfer to the bowl with the syrupy vinegar reduction. Repeat with the remaining 1 tablespoon vegetable oil and the remaining apples. Toss the chutney gently to combine. Serve with the pork chops.

➢ VARIATION

Gas Grill–Smoked Pork Chops with Apple Chutney

If you're using a gas grill, leaving one burner on and turning off the other(s) mimics the indirect-heat method on a charcoal grill. Use wood chips instead of wood chunks and an aluminum foil pan to hold them (see the illustrations on page 230).

Follow the recipe for Grill-Smoked Pork Chops with Apple Chutney, making the following changes: Cover 2 cups wood chips with water and soak for 1 hour, then drain. Meanwhile, make a tray out of aluminum foil following the illustrations below. Place the soaked wood chips in the small aluminum tray and set the tray over the burner that will remain on. Turn all the burners to high, close the lid, and heat the grill until the chips smoke heavily, about 20 minutes. (If the chips ignite, extinguish the flames with water from a squirt bottle.) Turn off the burner(s) without the wood chips. Arrange the pork chops bone side down (see the illustration on page 229) on the cool side of grill and cover (the grill temperature should register about 275 degrees on a grill thermometer). Cook until an instant-read thermometer inserted in the side of a chop away from the bone registers 145 degrees, 30 to 45 minutes.

USING WOOD CHIPS ON A GAS GRILL

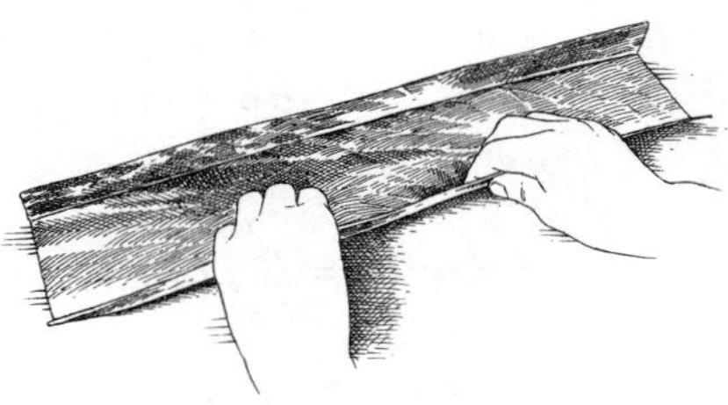

1. Start with a 12 by 18-inch piece of heavy-duty aluminum foil. Make a 1-inch fold on one long side. Repeat 3 more times, then turn the fold up to create a sturdy side that measures about 1 inch high. Repeat the process on the other side.

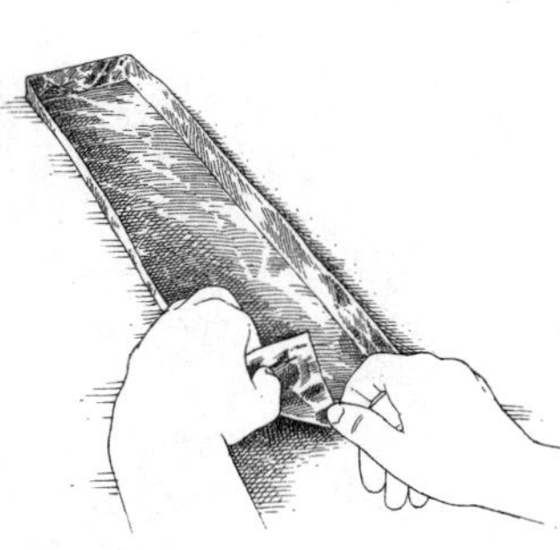

2. With a short side facing you, fold in both corners as if wrapping a gift.

3. Turn up the inside inch or so of each triangular fold to match the rim on the long sides of the foil tray.

4. Lift the pointed end of the triangle over the rim of the foil and fold down to seal. Repeat the process on the other short side.

5. Fill the tray with wood chips and place it on the grill over the burner.

Caldo

Adapted from Caldo

Lon's at the Hermosa, Paradise Valley, Arizona

THIS RECIPE'S SIMPLE NAME, CALDO, WHICH means soup or stew in both Spanish and Portuguese—belies its intense and complex flavor. Sweet and spicy, this hearty one-pot meal unites different Latin-American flavors into a rich and satisfying dish.

The recipe preparation begins with grilling tomatoes and a poblano chile. This important step concentrates the flavor of the vegetables, intensifies the sweetness of the tomatoes, and gives the dish an earthy, rich taste that contrasts with the brighter flavors of the lime juice, cilantro, carrots, and corn. Restaurants like Lon's at the Hermosa are well equipped with powerful ventilating systems that make indoor grilling possible. Few home kitchens, however, have range-top grills and external exhaust systems. We were unwilling to omit the smoky depth of the vegetables, but wanted to forgo grilling outside. The broiler gave us just what we were hoping for: concentrated flavor and smoky depth. Of course, if you have an outdoor grill and the weather permits, feel free to grill the tomatoes and poblano chile. Otherwise, use the broiler. Once roasted or grilled, the tomato and chile skins separate from the flesh and can be easily removed.

The recipe next calls for browning chicken thighs and country-style pork ribs. The meats are removed from the pan and the fat is discarded, and then the remaining ingredients are added to build the stew's layers of flavor. Carrots and corn add a pleasing sweetness; mushrooms and garlic, along with the chicken, pork, and roasted tomatoes, add depth and richness. Chorizo sausages and the poblano add spice. The recipe also calls for Mexican oregano, a slightly stronger herb than Mediterranean oregano, typically used in the spicier foods of Mexico and Latin America. Although the two herbs come from unrelated plants, we found that they can be used interchangeably in this recipe. Finally, lime juice and chopped fresh cilantro leaves brighten the deep roasted flavors of the stew. Serve the caldo, accompanied by salsa, hot sauce, and tortillas, if desired, over rice in wide, shallow soup bowls.

Caldo

SERVES 6 TO 8

Mexican oregano imparts a slightly stronger flavor than the Mediterranean oregano. However, if you are unable to find Mexican oregano, you may substitute Mediterranean, but use a little less.

- **1 pound tomatoes, cored and halved crosswise**
- **1 medium poblano chile**
- **6 bone-in chicken thighs**
- **6 country-style pork ribs**
- **Salt and ground black pepper**

- **2** tablespoons vegetable oil
- **4** ounces bacon, chopped fine
- **1** medium white onion, chopped (about 1 cup)
- **8** ounces mushrooms, halved
- **2** medium carrots, cut into 2-inch lengths
- **2** garlic cloves, minced or pressed through a garlic press
- **2** cups low-sodium chicken broth
- **3** tablespoons tomato puree
- **3** chorizo sausages (about 1 ½ pounds), cut into 2-inch pieces
- **2** bay leaves
- **½** teaspoon dried Mexican oregano
- **3** ears corn, husks and silk removed, halved crosswise
- **¼** cup juice from 2 limes
- **1** cup chopped fresh cilantro leaves

1. Adjust an oven rack so it is 6 inches away from the broiler element and heat the broiler. Arrange the tomatoes cut-side down and the chile on a rimmed baking sheet lined with aluminum foil. Broil until the tomato skins begin to retract, about 4 minutes. Transfer the tomatoes to a plate, remove and discard the skins, and set aside the flesh. Continue to broil the chile, turning it several times, until its skin is blackened, about 6 minutes longer. Transfer the poblano to a small bowl and cover tightly with plastic wrap until softened and cooled, about 10 minutes. Using the edge of a paring knife, scrape off and discard the charred skin. Stem and seed the chile. Slice it lengthwise into ⅛-inch-thick slices and set aside.

2. Season the chicken thighs and pork ribs generously with salt and pepper. Heat the vegetable oil in a Dutch oven over medium-high heat until shimmering. Add the chicken skin-side down and cook until golden, about 4 minutes. Turn the chicken and cook until the second side is golden, about 2 minutes longer. Transfer the chicken to a plate. Using paper towels, pull the skin off the chicken and discard it.

3. Drain all but 2 tablespoons fat from the pot and return the pot to high heat. When the fat shimmers, add the pork ribs and brown on each side, about 2 minutes per side. Transfer the pork ribs to a plate and set aside.

4. Pour off all the fat from the pan and discard it. Return the pot to medium heat, add the bacon, and cook until the bacon is crisp and the fat is rendered, about 5 minutes. Using a slotted spoon, transfer the bacon to a plate lined with several layers of paper towels and set aside. Heat the bacon fat until shimmering and add the onion and 1 teaspoon salt. Cook until the onion starts to color around the edges, about 2 minutes. Add the mushrooms, carrots, and garlic and cook just until the mushrooms begin to release their juices, about 2 minutes. Stir in the chicken broth and tomato puree, then add the chicken, ribs, bacon, chorizo, bay leaves, and oregano. Increase the heat to high and bring to a boil. Reduce the heat to low, skim off any foam that has risen to the surface, remove the bay leaves, and add the corn. Cover and simmer gently until the chicken is cooked through, about 25 minutes.

5. Add the reserved tomatoes (which will be quite soft from roasting) and chile and simmer, uncovered, until heated through, about 5 minutes. Remove the pot from the heat. Stir in the lime juice and cilantro, and season with salt and pepper to taste. Serve immediately.

Choucroute Garnie

Adapted from Choucroute Garnie

Brasserie Jo,
Chicago, Illinois, and Boston, Massachusetts

TRADITIONAL ALSATIAN CHOUCROUTE is a dish as rich in history as it is in flavor. Nearly synonymous with the French restaurants in which it is served, choucroute (spiced sauerkraut) gained popularity with the rise of the brasserie in Paris in the late nineteenth century. Alsatian refugees from the Franco-Prussian war founded informal brasseries where they served food and drink particular to the northeastern region of France, such as sausages, onion tarts, sauerkraut, beer, Gewürztraminer, and Riesling. At Brasserie Jo, Chef Jean Joho has brought the traditional French brasserie to Chicago and Boston. Choucroute is served family-style on a large oval platter of potatoes, sausages, pork loin, and smoked pork chops along with delicately spiced sauerkraut, or choucroute. A dollop of grainy mustard and a glass of Alsatian beer or Riesling complete the meal.

Traditional choucroute is remarkably easy to prepare in the home kitchen. We made few changes to Brasserie Jo's restaurant method in order to adapt the recipe for the home cook. The recipe originally called for infusing spices and garlic into the sauerkraut by wrapping a head of garlic, bay leaves, whole juniper berries, coriander seeds, and cloves in a bundle of cheesecloth and submerging it in the sauerkraut during cooking. Although this method works well when making large quantities of choucroute in a restaurant kitchen, we found that a different method worked better for the smaller portion made in the home kitchen. We discarded the cheesecloth and added the bay leaves, coriander seeds, and juniper berries directly to the pot. Instead of adding whole cloves and an entire head of garlic, we added a pinch of ground cloves and three minced garlic cloves. This method imparted the lightly spiced flavor tasters were anticipating, and the flecks of juniper berries and coriander seeds added visual interest to the dish. The whole coriander seeds also contributed a pleasant crunch to the sauerkraut. One cautionary note, however: although the juniper berries impart a necessary and distinctive depth and pungency to the flavor of the dish, many find juniper berries too astringent and bitter to eat. Move them to the side of your plate as you would a hot chile or bay leaf.

The recipe also originally called for cooking the onions in goose fat. Because goose fat is not readily available, we looked for an alternative. We considered using vegetable oil and lard, but finally chose bacon fat. Four slices of bacon rendered the right amount of fat and heightened the pork flavor characteristic of the dish. While we wanted the bacon flavor, we did not want slices of bacon lacing the sauerkraut. We knew that by the time the dish was finished, the bacon would be soft and soggy. We considered removing the bacon once it had rendered its fat and saving the crisp pieces for another use. Finally, however, we landed upon a clever technique. We processed the bacon in the food processor until it was finely ground. Then we cooked the ground bacon and left the tiny pieces in the dish. This approach supplied the requisite flavor and fat to the dish. It also prevented the soggy bacon problem and did not interfere with the dish's texture. However, if you do have access to goose fat and prefer to use it, feel free to omit the bacon and heat one-quarter cup of goose fat over medium heat until it shimmers before adding the onions.

Use the fresh sauerkraut sold at delicatessens or in vacuum-sealed packages in the refrigerator case, rather than canned or jarred cooked sauerkraut for this dish. In our first attempt at this recipe, we did not rinse or drain the sauerkraut before adding it to pot. The sour notes of the sauerkraut dominated the resulting choucroute and overwhelmed the subtle and delicately pungent depth of the herbs and spices and the smoky richness of the meats. We found that rinsing the sauerkraut under cool running water and squeezing out the excess moisture dramatically improved the flavor of the dish. This important step reduced the sourness of the sauerkraut and removed excess moisture, allowing the sauerkraut to absorb the flavors of the herbs, spices, and meats more readily.

Finally, although choucroute is traditionally served with peeled boiled potatoes, tasters preferred the color, flavor, and texture of unpeeled red potatoes.

Choucroute Garnie

SERVES 8

When looking for the sausages, choose subtly flavored German-style sausages, like knockwurst and kielbasa. (Avoid breakfast-style, Italian, or other heavily seasoned sausages whose flavors won't blend with this dish.) Choose fresh sauerkraut sold at the delicatessen or in vacuum-sealed packages rather than canned or jarred cooked sauerkraut. Also, avoid eating the juniper berries. They impart a distinctive pungency to the dish but are too bitter to eat whole. Simply move them to the side of your plate as you eat.

- 4 slices bacon (about 4 ounces)
- 3 small yellow onions, cut into 1/4-inch dice (about 2 cups)
- Salt
- 3 garlic cloves, minced or pressed through a garlic press (about 1 tablespoon)
- 3 1/2 pounds fresh sauerkraut, rinsed in a colander under cool running water, drained, and squeezed dry
- 2 1/4 cups Alsace Riesling wine or another dry Riesling
- 2 bay leaves
- 12 whole juniper berries
- 12 whole coriander seeds
- Pinch ground cloves
- Ground black pepper
- 1 1/2 pounds boneless pork loin
- 1 tablespoon vegetable oil
- 6 fresh pork sausages or pork and beef sausages, such as knockwurst
- 3 smoked pork sausages, such as kielbasa
- 12 medium red potatoes, such as Red Bliss (about 4 pounds)
- 3 smoked pork loin chops
- Whole-grain mustard, for accompaniment

1. Adjust an oven rack to the lower-middle position and heat the oven to 350 degrees. Process the bacon in a food processor until finely ground, about 10 seconds. Transfer the bacon to a large Dutch oven and cook over medium-high heat until the fat is rendered and the bacon is crisp, about 8 minutes. Add the onions and ½ teaspoon salt and cook, stirring occasionally, until the onions are soft and light brown around the edges, about 10 minutes. Add the garlic and cook, stirring frequently, for 1 minute. Add the sauerkraut and cook, stirring frequently until it is wilted and steaming, about 10 minutes. Add the wine, bay leaves, juniper berries, coriander seeds, cloves, ½ teaspoon salt, and ¼ teaspoon pepper and bring to a boil. Nestle the pork loin in the sauerkraut in the center of the pot. Cover the pot and transfer it to the oven. Cook until the pork is cooked through yet still tender and registers 145 to 150 degrees on an instant-read thermometer, about 50 minutes.

2. Meanwhile, prepare the sausages. Heat the vegetable oil in a nonstick skillet over medium-high heat until shimmering. Add the fresh pork sausages and cook until well browned on all sides, about 8 minutes (they will not be cooked through). Transfer the sausages to a plate and set aside. Add the smoked sausages to the skillet and cook until well browned on all sides, about 8 minutes. Transfer to a separate plate and set aside.

3. While the sausages are cooking, bring the potatoes, ½ teaspoon salt, and enough water to cover the potatoes by 1 inch to a boil in a large pot over high heat. Reduce the heat and simmer until a paring knife can be slipped into and out of the centers of the potatoes with very little resistance, 20 to 25 minutes. Drain the potatoes, return them to the pot, cover, and set aside.

4. About 20 minutes before the sauerkraut and pork loin are done, nestle the browned, fresh pork sausages in the Dutch oven to finish cooking.

5. About 10 minutes before the sauerkraut and pork loin are done, nestle the browned smoked pork sausages and the smoked pork loin chops into the Dutch oven to finish cooking. Remove and discard the bay leaves.

6. Heap the sauerkraut onto a large oval serving platter. Place the potatoes around the perimeter of the sauerkraut. Arrange the sausages on top of the sauerkraut. Slice the pork loin and smoked pork chops and arrange them on top of the sauerkraut as well. Serve immediately, accompanied by the mustard.

Cassoulet Toulousian

Adapted from Cassoulet Toulousian

Les Halles, New York, New York

WE LOVED THE RICH, HEARTY FLAVORS OF this traditional southern French pork and bean casserole from chef Anthony Bourdain of the restaurant Les Halles, known for its well-executed classic French cuisine. Served in a large Dutch oven and topped with a crisp crust of homemade bread crumbs browned under the broiler, this dish brings the flavors of the Languedoc region of France to life. The relative humbleness of cassoulet belies the high esteem with which cassoulet connoisseurs regard this dish. Aficionados debate the origin and composition of authentic cassoulet. Consensus is rarely achieved, since different regions in southern France produce slightly different variations of the dish depending upon the types of meat particular to their region. Despite its pedigree, cassoulet is essentially a pork and beans dish, albeit not the kind traditionally served in Boston on Saturday nights.

Cassoulet is one of those dishes that takes days to prepare. Such lengthy preparation was fine years ago, when families weren't pressed to have dinner on the table in under an hour. So it's not so surprising that today cassoulet has headed into the restaurant kitchen, where a well-stocked pantry, specialty kitchen equipment, and many professionally trained hands can handle this classic, laborious dish. Our goal was to find a way to help the home cook pull it together without days of shopping and preparation time.

At Les Halles, Bourdain bases his recipe on the Toulousian version, which typically includes some kind of duck or goose. He embellishes the dish with duck foie gras sausage, garlic and pork sausage (often referred to as *saucisson de Toulouse*), duck legs and duck giblets preserved in duck fat (called confit), and fresh pork skin. Although we were eager to replicate this recipe, the cooks in the test kitchen had difficulty finding some of the specialty meats it called for, so we decided to trim our shopping list. We kept the salt pork and fresh garlic and pork sausages, since they were easily found at the local supermarket. Duck confit legs can be purchased through mail order (D'Artagnan, www.dartagnan.com, or Grimaud Farms, www.grimaud.com). Including the duck giblets confit seemed superfluous, since we were keeping the duck legs confit, so they were nixed. Although local supermarkets, specialty butcher shops, and mail-order companies all make some form of duck sausage, none had duck and foie gras sausage available at the time of our inquiries, so we doubled the amount of fresh garlic and pork sausage.

The specialty meats and sausages clearly stand out in cassoulet, but the dish's foundation is the beans. True connoisseurs of cassoulet from Toulouse would demand the inclusion of dried Tarbais beans, as chef

Bourdain did in the original recipe. A specialty of the Tarbe plain of southwestern France, Tarbais beans are similar to great Northern beans in size and appearance, but are less starchy in texture, and their thinner skins are more readily digested. If you are able to find these beans at specialty food shops or online specialty food purveyors, by all means use them. We used flageolet beans, but great Northern beans can also be substituted. Both work exceptionally well. Never substitute canned beans—they'd become a pasty mass in this long-cooking stew.

As for the method of preparing the beans, it's fairly simple, but we found in the test kitchen that cooking the beans to the correct texture can be fairly tricky. If they are improperly cooked, even the rich meats cannot make up for mushy or crunchy beans. There are two methods of rehydrating dried beans: overnight soaking and the quick-soak method. In the first, the beans are covered in cool water and allowed to soak at least 6 hours or up to 20 hours. In the quick-soak method, the dried beans are briefly boiled in water and then allowed to soak for 2 hours. In the test kitchen, we compared a cassoulet made with beans that had been soaked overnight with one made with beans given the quick-soak method. Although the quick-soaked beans were palatable, tasters preferred the texture of the beans soaked in water overnight.

Given the awe usually reserved for this dish, you might expect a sophisticated presentation. Yet cassoulet is essentially a rustic dish with humble origins. It is traditionally served in France in a *cassole,* an earthenware casserole dish made specifically for the purpose of serving cassoulet. Bring the cassoulet to the table in the Dutch oven in which it was cooked and ladle portions onto individual plates.

Cassoulet Toulousian

SERVES 6

If flageolet beans aren't available, use great Northern beans or other small white beans. You may have to modify the cooking times slightly to account for differences in the size of the beans. Avoid using canned beans—their flavor and texture will pale in comparison to properly cooked dried beans. Leave the salt pork skin in the cassoulet when serving. Although it is not eaten, it imparts flavor to the dish and should be left in the pot.

- 1 pound dried flageolet beans, washed, picked over, covered with 10 cups water, and soaked overnight (6 hours or longer)
- 8 sprigs fresh parsley
- 4 sprigs fresh thyme
- 2 bay leaves
- 4 ounces salt pork, skin removed and reserved, meat cut into 1/2-inch pieces
- 1 large white onion, diced (about 1 cup)
- 1 large carrot, diced (about 1 cup)
- 1 cup canned whole peeled tomatoes, drained
- 3 medium garlic cloves, smashed
- Salt
- 6–8 cups low-sodium chicken broth
- 8 fresh garlic and pork sausages (about 1 1/4 pounds)
- 1 large baguette (about 12 ounces), crust removed, cut into 1-inch pieces
- 3 duck confit legs, thighs and drumsticks separated
- Ground black pepper

1. Drain the beans, place them in a medium bowl, and set aside. Tie the parsley stems, thyme sprigs, and bay leaves into a bundle with kitchen twine. Set aside.

2. Cook the salt pork skin and meat in a Dutch oven over low heat until most of their

fat has rendered, about 20 minutes. Increase the heat to medium and add the onion, carrot, tomatoes, garlic, and 1 teaspoon salt. Cook until the onion is tender, about 10 minutes.

3. Stir in the drained beans, herb bundle, and 6 cups of the broth. Increase the heat to high and bring to a boil. Reduce the heat to medium and skim any foam from the surface. Add the sausages and reduce the heat to low. Cover and simmer gently until the sausages are cooked through, about 15 minutes.

4. Using tongs, transfer the sausages to a plate and cool. Cut the sausages into 2-inch-thick pieces. Set aside. Simmer the beans until they are almost tender, 45 to 55 minutes longer.

5. Meanwhile, process the baguette into coarse crumbs in a food processor, about five 1-second pulses. Set aside.

6. Adjust an oven rack to the middle position and heat the oven to 425 degrees. Remove and discard the herb bundle from the beans. Return the sliced sausages to the beans and gently stir in the duck confit drumsticks and thighs. Simmer over low heat until the duck confit is heated through and the beans are tender, about 5 minutes. Remove the pot from the heat and season with salt and pepper to taste. Sprinkle the bread crumbs evenly over the bean mixture and transfer the pot to the oven. Bake until the bread crumbs have turned a deep golden color and the cassoulet is bubbling, about 10 minutes. Serve immediately.

Shepherd's Pie

Adapted from Shepherd's Pie

Scuttlebutt's Pub, Nutley, New Jersey

A TRADITIONAL SAVORY DISH OF GROUND lamb and chopped vegetables topped with mashed potatoes, shepherd's pie is easy to make, hearty, and perfect for a cold winter's evening meal. In a unique twist, Scuttlebutt's Pub enhances the dish's rustic qualities with the addition of the earthy flavors of nutmeg, cinnamon, and allspice and the rich, slightly bitter flavor of Guinness stout.

This recipe originally called for lamb or beef demi-glace sauce to be added to the meat mixture. Demi-glace is a traditional French sauce that requires a relatively complex and time-consuming series of steps to produce; it is a rich, smooth, velvety sauce with deep, concentrated flavor. Restaurants typically have the time and resources to produce this sauce in large quantities. For home cooks, on the other hand, making the sauce requires careful planning and skillful selection of ingredients. Because the inclusion of demi-glace in this recipe transforms the dish from an easy weeknight meal into a special weekend production, we decided to omit the demi-glace and substitute a mixture of beef broth, chicken broth, tomato paste, and fresh herbs. We found that this mixture produces a rich sauce with a depth of flavor comparable to that of demi-glace. The recipe also calls for adding Guinness, instead of wine or another acid. Tasters in the test kitchen were surprised to find that, in addition to the characteristic slightly bitter flavor of Guinness, the beer also contributed a rich texture that mimicked the velvety texture of demi-glace.

In the test kitchen, we typically force potatoes through a ricer to make our mashed potatoes light and fluffy. In keeping with this dish's rustic quality, however, tasters preferred chunkier mashed potatoes. Using a potato masher instead of a ricer or food mill produces slightly chunky mashed potatoes.

Shepherd's Pie

SERVES 6

To prevent the mashed potatoes from turning sticky or gummy, be careful not to overcook the potatoes and to drain them well.

- **1 teaspoon olive oil or vegetable oil**
- **2 pounds ground lamb**
- **2 celery ribs, cut into 1/2-inch dice (about 1 1/2 cups)**
- **2 medium carrots, cut into 1/2-inch dice (about 1 cup)**
- **2 medium onions, cut into 1/2-inch dice (about 1 cup)**
- **Salt**
- **2 tablespoons tomato paste**
- **4 garlic cloves, minced or pressed through a garlic press (about 4 teaspoons)**
- **1 teaspoon ground cinnamon**

- 1/2 teaspoon ground nutmeg
- 1/2 teaspoon ground allspice
- 2 tablespoons all-purpose flour
- 1 (14.5-ounce) can Guinness stout
- 1 cup low-sodium chicken broth
- 1 cup low-sodium beef broth
- 6 sprigs fresh parsley
- 4 sprigs fresh thyme
- 2 bay leaves
- 1/2 cup frozen peas
- Ground black pepper
- 4 large russet potatoes (about 2 1/2 pounds), peeled and cut into 2-inch pieces
- 2 tablespoons unsalted butter, cut into 2 pieces
- 1/3 cup heavy cream, warmed
- 1 large egg

1. Heat the oil in a large Dutch oven over medium-high heat until just smoking. Add the lamb and cook, stirring frequently, until well browned and the fat has rendered, about 4 minutes. Using a slotted spoon, transfer the lamb to a large bowl and set aside.

2. Pour off all but 2 tablespoons fat from the Dutch oven and return the pot to medium-high heat. Add the celery, carrots, onions, and 1 teaspoon salt and cook, stirring occasionally, until the vegetables are softened and beginning to brown around the edges, about 10 minutes. Stir in the tomato paste, garlic, cinnamon, nutmeg, and allspice and sauté until fragrant, 15 to 20 seconds. Stir in the flour and cook until it begins to dissolve, about 30 seconds. Add the Guinness and bring to a simmer. Simmer, stirring frequently, until the liquid thickens, about 5 minutes. Return the lamb to the pot and stir in the chicken broth, beef broth, parsley sprigs, thyme sprigs, and bay leaves. Return to a simmer and cook until the mixture is thick but still saucy and has reduced to about 6 cups, about 10 minutes. Remove the pan from the heat and discard the parsley sprigs, thyme sprigs, and bay leaves. Stir in the peas and season with salt and pepper to taste. Set aside.

3. Meanwhile, bring the potatoes, ½ teaspoon salt, and enough water to cover the potatoes by 1 inch to a boil in a large saucepan over high heat. Reduce the heat to medium-low and simmer until a paring knife can be slipped into and out of the centers of the potatoes with very little resistance, 15 to 20 minutes. Drain the potatoes and return them to the saucepan. Add the butter and mash using a potato masher until no large chunks of potato remain. Stir in the warm cream and season with salt and pepper to taste.

4. Adjust an oven rack so it is 6 inches away from the broiler element and heat the broiler. Whisk the egg with 1 tablespoon water. Transfer the meat mixture to a 13 by 9-inch baking dish. Spread the mashed potatoes evenly over the meat mixture. Brush the potatoes with the egg. Broil until the potatoes are lightly browned, 2 to 3 minutes. Serve immediately.

Broiled Lamb Chops *with* Sautéed Spinach & Feta

Adapted from Luigi's Lamb Chops

Luigi's, Harrison Township, Mississippi

It's usually a good rule to order only pizza in a pizza joint, but ordering the house special lamb chops at Luigi's is an exception. Lightly seasoned with garlic, basil, and oregano, the chops are broiled to medium-rare and served with sautéed spinach with toasted garlic and feta.

At first, we were suspicious of Luigi's use of dry seasonings on $17-per-pound lamb chops. Using granulated garlic or garlic powder (not garlic salt), dried oregano, and dried basil, we were surprised to find that when used in correct amounts, they tasted surprisingly fresh. The original recipe gave general directions, so we tested various amounts per chop. In the end, we came up with a rub made with granulated garlic, dried oregano, dried basil, salt, and black pepper, using one-half teaspoon of the rub per chop. We found that three 3-ounce rib chops were enough for one portion, with a total of 18 chops to serve six. We also found that broiling them on a rack six inches from the broiling element was key. The close proximity allowed the chops to brown without overcooking, taking only seven minutes to cook to medium-rare. We found it best to let the cooked chops rest underneath loosely tented foil for 10 minutes before serving them.

At Luigi's, the lamb chops are accompanied by crinkly-leaf spinach that has been wilted in a hot skillet with oil, garlic, and fresh tomatoes. We found, however, that in order to cook six portions of spinach at once we needed to change the cooking method slightly. First, we upgraded the relatively small skillet to a Dutch oven. Because the spinach wilted down to a fraction of its original volume, we noted that three 10-ounce bags were required to serve six people. To help the spinach wilt, we found it best to dry the spinach only partially after washing it. The droplets of water that clung to the leaves helped create necessary steam during cooking. Although the spinach is cooked with the garlic at Luigi's, our larger batch took longer to wilt and, in turn, burned the garlic. Instead, we toasted the garlic in the Dutch oven first and removed it before adding the spinach, using it later as a garnish. Last, we noted that this large amount of spinach turned somewhat watery after it was cooked. To prevent this water from leaching out onto the plate, we squeezed the excess moisture out of the cooked spinach using tongs and a colander set over the sink. Finished with a sprinkling of feta, this lamb and spinach dish takes less than half an hour to prepare from start to finish (and tastes much better than your standard pizza).

Broiled Lamb Chops with Sautéed Spinach and Feta

SERVES 6

Do not heat the oil before adding the garlic when making the spinach; heating them together over gentle heat helps reduce the risk of burnt, bitter garlic. To accommodate the bulky spinach when raw, use the largest Dutch oven—or even stockpot—that you have. Stir several times as the leaves wilt so that they cook evenly.

- Salt and ground black pepper
- 1 1/2 teaspoons dried oregano
- 1 1/2 teaspoons dried basil
- 1/2 teaspoon granulated garlic or 1/4 teaspoon garlic powder
- 18 rib lamb chops (3–4 ounces each), about 1 inch thick
- 3 tablespoons olive oil
- 6 garlic cloves, sliced very thin (about 1/4 cup)
- 3 (10-ounce) bags crinkly-leaf spinach, stemmed, washed thoroughly, and partially dried, with some water left clinging to the leaves
- 3 plum tomatoes, cored, seeded, and cut into 1/2-inch pieces
- 2 ounces feta cheese, crumbled (about 1/2 cup)

1. Adjust an oven rack so it is 6 inches away from the broiler element and heat the broiler. Mix 1½ tablespoons salt, 1½ teaspoons pepper, oregano, basil, and granulated garlic together in a small bowl. Sprinkle each lamb chop with ½ teaspoon of the spice mixture (¼ teaspoon per side). Lay in a single layer, not overlapping, on a slotted broiler pan top set over a broiler pan bottom lined with aluminum foil. Broil until browned, about 5 minutes. Flip the chops and broil until an instant-read thermometer reads 120 degrees, about 2 minutes longer. Transfer the chops to a cutting board and tent loosely with foil.

2. Meanwhile, heat the oil and sliced garlic together in a large Dutch oven or stockpot over medium heat. Cook, stirring occasionally, until the garlic is golden and very crisp, 8 to 10 minutes. Using a slotted spoon, transfer the garlic chips to a plate lined with several layers of paper towels. Add the spinach and tomatoes and toss to coat with the oil. Cover, increase the heat to medium-high, and cook, stirring occasionally, until the spinach is tender and wilted but still bright green, 3 to 5 minutes. Remove the pan from the heat. Using tongs, transfer the spinach to a colander set in the sink and gently squeeze the spinach with the tongs to release any excess juices. Return the spinach to the pot and season with salt and pepper to taste.

3. Divide the spinach among 6 individual plates and sprinkle with the feta and garlic chips. Lean 3 chops up against the spinach on each plate. Serve immediately.

Tapenade-Encrusted Lamb Shanks

Adapted from Tapenade-Encrusted Lamb Shanks
ZuZu's Petals, Kirkwood, Missouri

BRAISING IS THE METHOD OF COOKING in which a relatively tough cut of meat is first browned and then cooked slowly in a tightly covered pot with a small amount of liquid, usually a combination of wine and stock. This slow method of cooking tenderizes meat by breaking down its connective tissue while also developing and concentrating flavor. This recipe for lamb shanks from ZuZu's was a textbook example of braising. With meltingly tender lamb shanks topped with a briny olive tapenade and served with chunks of vegetables, all swimming in a flavorful red wine broth, this recipe left little else to be desired.

The recipe was straightforward, in terms of both ingredients and technique. For the most part, it didn't need any modifications in order to be used by the home cook. There were, however, several items that we wanted to explore in hopes of making this recipe even more streamlined.

The first area we explored was the red wine reduction that formed the base of the braising liquid. The original recipe called for reducing five cups of red wine by half before adding it to the other ingredients in the braising liquid. In our first test, it took almost 15 minutes to reduce the liquid to this stage, and we wondered if this process was truly necessary. We made the next batch of lamb shanks using two cups of red wine, forgoing the reduction process. To our surprise, we found that the two batches tasted almost identical.

We also experimented with the amount of beef broth used in the braising liquid. We felt that a gallon of stock, which the initial recipe called for, was far more than necessary and added time to the cooking process. Given that a restaurant chef cooks in much larger batches, with pans that dwarf even the largest of the home cook's collection, we assumed that there was room to reduce the proportions in this recipe. And so in our next test, we tried reducing the amount of stock to less than a quart. By adding just enough liquid to come halfway up the sides of the lamb, we found that we shaved about 15 minutes off the cooking time and had a much more flavorful broth.

In addition to changing the amount of liquid the shanks were cooked in, we also found it necessary to change the type of stock used. ZuZu's recipe used beef stock. But considering that a home cook doesn't usually have beef stock on hand, we used canned beef broth instead. However, the resulting sauce tasted a little overpowering, so we found it necessary to use a mixture of chicken and beef broths.

The finishing component of this dish was tapenade, a Mediterranean-style puree of olives, anchovies, garlic, capers, and olive oil, which was a perfect complement to the rich lamb. But to the traditional tapenade ingredients, ZuZu's added bread crumbs, which gave the dish an interesting textural contrast and also helped the tapenade stick to the lamb shanks, forming an attractive and delicious exterior.

Tapenade-Encrusted Lamb Shanks

SERVES 8

Mashed potatoes or soft polenta make a nice accompaniment to the lamb. Make sure to let the broth stand for the full 5 minutes before skimming the excess fat from the top. Shortcutting this step will result in an overly greasy and unpleasant sauce.

- 8 lamb shanks (about 1 pound each), trimmed of excess fat and connective tissue
- Salt and ground black pepper
- 4 tablespoons olive oil
- 6 large carrots, diced (about 2 cups)
- 2 large onions, diced (about 2 cups)
- 2 celery ribs, diced (about 1 cup)
- 1/4 cup tomato paste
- 2 cups dry red wine
- 1 3/4 cups low-sodium chicken broth
- 1 3/4 cups low-sodium beef broth
- 1 3/4 cups (about 1/2 pound) Kalamata olives, pitted
- 1/2 cup panko (Japanese-style bread crumbs) or Homemade Panko (page 17)
- 3 tablespoons capers, rinsed
- 6 anchovy fillets, minced
- 2 medium garlic cloves, chopped
- 3 tablespoons extra-virgin olive oil

1. Adjust an oven rack to the lower-middle position and heat the oven to 325 degrees. Season the lamb shanks generously with salt and pepper. Heat 2 tablespoons of the olive oil in a 12-inch skillet over medium-high heat until shimmering. Add 4 of the lamb shanks and cook, turning, until browned on all sides, about 7 minutes. Transfer the browned shanks to a large roasting pan. Repeat with the remaining 2 tablespoons olive oil and the remaining 4 lamb shanks.

2. Drain all but 2 tablespoons fat from the pan and return it to medium-high heat. Add the carrots, onions, and celery and sauté until slightly softened, about 4 minutes. Transfer to the roasting pan with the lamb shanks. Bring the tomato paste, wine, chicken broth, and beef broth to a simmer in the skillet. Pour into the roasting pan with the lamb and vegetables. Cover the pan with foil and transfer to the oven. Cook until the lamb is tender and almost falling off the bones, about 2½ hours.

3. Meanwhile, process the olives, panko, capers, anchovies, garlic, and extra-virgin olive oil in a food processor until it forms a paste, about fifteen 1-second pulses. Transfer to a medium bowl and set aside.

4. Transfer the cooked lamb shanks to a rimmed baking sheet. Strain the braising liquid into a large bowl; transfer the vegetables to another large bowl and set aside. Let the braising liquid stand for 5 minutes. Meanwhile, spread an even layer of the tapenade over the lamb shanks. Transfer the shanks to 8 plates. Arrange a portion of the vegetables, which will be quite soft, around each shank. Skim all the fat from the braising liquid and adjust the seasoning with salt and pepper. Spoon some braising liquid over each shank and serve.

Braised Lamb Shanks *with* Lentils

Adapted from Braised Lamb Shanks with Ale and Rosemary

Kaspar's, Seattle, Washington

POSSIBLY ONE OF THE MOST IMPORTANT traits of a chef is the ability to transform a tough cut of meat into one that is falling-off-the-bone tender and full of flavor. While this ability does not require magical powers, it does require time, patience, and good technique. Oftentimes, without invoking these qualities, a home cook meets with lackluster results. But with this recipe from Kaspar's, we were moving in the right direction.

After our first stab at this recipe, the results left us with mixed feelings. We were enthusiastic about the wonderful flavors of the dish—the tender, rich lamb and nutty lentils were perfectly paired with a mixture of sweet vegetables, aromatic rosemary, and a hint of malty beer. But the cooking method left us perplexed. We ended up cooking the dish for a lot longer than the recipe called for in order to cook the lamb, and as a result the lentils were overcooked before the lamb was done. While tasty, it just didn't look appetizing. Thinking that a more traditional approach might produce a more consistent and uniform result, while keeping the same intense and unusual flavors, we set off to explore our options.

Focusing solely on the cooking method, we addressed several steps of the process. The first was the browning of the shanks. The recipe instructed us to roast the lamb shanks in a 450-degree oven for one hour, or until they were browned. Although this method is invaluable in a restaurant kitchen when preparing many lamb shanks at once, we found that our lamb shanks failed to achieve a well-caramelized exterior. Considering that the restaurant might be using a convection oven, which would better brown the shanks, however, we felt that searing the shanks in a pot on the stovetop was our best option for a couple of reasons. The first is that we were able to caramelize the exterior of the shanks well, which in turn translated to deeper flavor. Second, this method created a flavorful *fond* (the crusty bits that remain from searing the meat on the bottom of the pan), which, when deglazed and incorporated into the broth, allowed us to coax out even more lamb flavor.

Now we needed to figure the best time to add the lentils to the pot in order for both the lamb and the lentils to be fully cooked at the same time. This coordination turned out to be very challenging. From our first test, we estimated that the lentils required about 30 minutes to be fully cooked and that the lamb needed roughly 1½ to 2 hours. So we tried cooking the lamb for three different time periods before adding the lentils. We cooked the lamb, covered, for 1 hour, 1½ hours, and 2 hours and then added the lentils, taking the entire dish off the heat when the lentils were tender. The 1-hour and 2-hour tests were disappointing. In the former, the lamb was underdone by the time the lentils were cooked through. In the latter, the lamb was falling off the bone excessively and difficult to handle when the lentils were finally tender. So we settled on the middle, adding the lentils after 1½ hours.

Finalizing these searing and timing issues led us to stumble into a different problem with the dish. Many tasters felt that the dish was incredibly rich, bordering on greasy. Since we were adding the lentils to the lamb without removing any of the fat that the lamb had shed during cooking, the lentils absorbed this fat and became overly rich. To counter this, before adding the lentils and vegetables we strained the broth of the aromatics, ridding it of pesky bay leaves and rosemary stems, and then let it stand for 5 minutes. After this short rest, the fat had risen to the top and we were able to skim it off. At this time, we could also add a little extra liquid to the broth to make sure the lentils had a sufficient amount in which to cook.

Another question arose during these trials. After the lentils had been added, was it better to cook the lamb covered or uncovered? By cooking the dish covered, the lentils cooked more quickly and the finished broth was soupier. But with the uncovered version, the lamb shanks acquired a beautiful mahogany appearance. In order to have it both ways, we found it best to cook the lentils covered for a portion of the time, then remove the lid to allow the shanks to brown and the lentils to finish cooking.

Braised Lamb Shanks with Lentils

SERVES 4

While this dish is satisfying as is, the chef of Kaspar's recommends serving the lamb shanks with mashed potatoes, polenta, or risotto. The chef also recommends, and we concur, that Le Puy lentils are best suited for this dish because they hold their shape and don't become mushy.

- 1 tablespoon vegetable oil
- 4 lamb shanks (about 1 pound each), trimmed of excess fat and connective tissue
- Salt and ground black pepper
- 1 medium onion, chopped fine (about 1 cup)
- 6 garlic cloves, peeled
- 1 sprig fresh rosemary
- 2 bay leaves
- ½ teaspoon crushed black peppercorns
- 1 (12-ounce) bottle amber ale, such as Sierra Nevada
- 1½ cups low-sodium chicken broth, plus more if needed
- 1 medium leek, white part only, chopped fine (about 1 cup)
- 2 celery ribs, chopped fine (about 1 cup)
- 1 medium parsnip, chopped fine (about ¾ cup)
- 1 medium carrot, chopped fine (about ½ cup)
- ¾ cup French green (Le Puy) lentils
- 1 cup baby spinach leaves
- 1 tablespoon chopped fresh parsley leaves

1. Adjust an oven rack to the middle position and heat the oven to 350 degrees. Heat the vegetable oil in a Dutch oven over medium-high heat until shimmering. Season the shanks generously with salt and pepper.

Add the shanks in a single layer and cook, turning, until they are well browned on all sides, about 7 minutes. Transfer the shanks to a plate and set aside.

2. Drain all but 1 tablespoon fat from the pot. Add onion, garlic, rosemary, bay leaves, peppercorns, and a light sprinkling of salt and cook until the onion softens slightly, 2 to 3 minutes. Add the beer and chicken broth and bring to a simmer, scraping up the browned bits from the bottom of the pan. Add the shanks, cover, and transfer the pot to the oven.

3. Braise the shanks for 1½ hours. Remove the pot from the oven and transfer the lamb shanks to a clean plate. Strain the broth into a 4-cup glass measure and discard the solids. Let the broth stand for 5 minutes. Skim off the fat that has risen to the top and discard. Add more chicken broth, if necessary, to make 3½ cups. Return the liquid to the pot. Add the leek, celery, parsnip, carrot, lentils, and ¼ teaspoon salt and bring to a simmer over high heat. Return the shanks to the pot. Cover, return to the oven, and braise for 15 minutes.

4. Remove the lid from the pot and cook until the lentils are fully cooked and the shanks are browned and fork-tender, about 20 minutes longer.

5. Transfer the shanks to a serving platter. Skim off any excess fat from the braising liquid. Add the spinach leaves and stir until wilted, about 30 seconds. Adjust the seasoning with salt and pepper. Ladle the lentils and sauce around the shanks, sprinkle with the parsley, and serve immediately.

EQUIPMENT: Chef's Knives

A good chef's knife is probably the most useful tool any cook owns. Besides chopping vegetables, it can be used for myriad tasks, including cutting up poultry, mincing herbs, and slicing fruit. So what separates a good knife from an inferior one? To understand the answer to this question, it helps to know something about how knives are constructed.

Until recently, all knives were hot drop forged—that is, the steel was heated to 2,000 degrees, dropped into a mold, given four or five shots with a hammer, and then tempered (cooled and heated several times to build strength). This process is labor intensive (many steps must be done by hand), which explains why many chef's knives cost almost $100.

A second manufacturing process feeds long sheets of steel through a press that punches out knife after knife, much the way a cookie cutter slices through dough. Called stamped blades, these knives require some hand finishing but are much cheaper to produce because a machine does most of the work.

While experts have long argued that forged knives are better than stamped ones, our testing did not fully support this position. We liked some forged knives and did not like others. Likewise, we liked some stamped knives and did not like others. The weight and shape of the handle (it must be comfortable to hold and substantial but not too heavy), the ability of the blade to take an edge, and the shape of the blade (we like a slightly curved blade, which is better suited to the rocking motion often used to mince herbs or garlic, better than a straight blade) are all key factors in choosing a knife.

When shopping, pick up the knife and see how it feels in your hand. Is it easy to grip? Does the weight seem properly distributed between the handle and the blade? The Henckels Four Star and Wüsthof-Trident Grand Prix are top choices, but expect to spend about $80 for one of these knives. The Forschner (Victorinox) Fibrox is lighter but still solid and costs just $30.

Buying a good knife is only half the challenge. You must keep the edge sharp. To that end, we recommend buying an electric knife sharpener. Steels are best for modest corrections, but all knives will require more substantial sharpening at least several times a year, if not more often if you cook a lot. An electric knife sharpener (we like models made by Chef's Choice) takes the guesswork out of sharpening and allows you to keep edges sharp and effective.

Blackened Fish Tacos *with* Spicy Mayonnaise & Tropical Fruit Salsa

Adapted from Blackened Rockfish Tacos with Tropical Fruit Salsa

Anthony's Homeport Restaurant, Tacoma, Washington

NEARLY EVERYONE HAS EXPERIENCED tacos, but rarely are they associated with fish. Born in the Baja region of Mexico, fish tacos have become a standard fast food in Mexico and southern California. Consisting most often of batter-fried fish wrapped in a corn tortilla with a mayonnaise-based sauce, we found this version from Anthony's Homeport to be an unusual spin on this popular street food. The restaurant replaces the batter coating with Cajun spices.

Anthony's relies on the abundance of Alaskan rockfish (also known as rockcod or Pacific red snapper) available on the West Coast. We here in Boston were hard-pressed to find a true rockfish, but we discovered that any firm-fleshed white fish will do, including haddock or, our favorite, halibut.

Blackening fish became popular with the upsurge of Cajun cooking. In the blackening process, the fish is coated with a Cajun spice mixture and cooked in a preheated, searing-hot pan (traditionally cast iron). While we tested oiling the hot pan first, we found that by dipping the fish in oil first, then in the seasoning mixture, and then cooking it in a dry, hot pan, we were able to achieve a better crust, with more of the spice mixture sticking to the fish, not the pan. This searing process creates fish that is highly seasoned on the outside, while still moist on the inside. An effective ventilation system is also necessary, since the cooking produces a great deal of smoke.

There are two "sauces" for this taco: a salsa mayonnaise and a tropical fruit salsa. The addition of chiles, tomatillo, and fresh cilantro adds character and heat to the typical mayonnaise base. The fruit salsa offsets the heat of the salsa mayonnaise and the spiciness of the blackened fish with fresh pineapple, mango, and lime. The finely shredded red and green cabbage in the taco add a refreshing crunch. We found the combination had the perfect balance of color, taste, and textures.

Although most fish tacos rely on corn tortillas as their wrap, this recipe specified eight-inch flour tortillas to blanket the fish and salsa without masking their flavors. They may be heated in a variety of ways, but our favorite method is in a hot skillet one at a time. They bubble and puff up slightly, becoming soft and pliant.

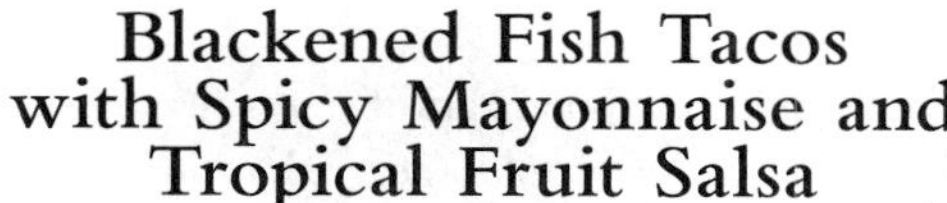

Blackened Fish Tacos with Spicy Mayonnaise and Tropical Fruit Salsa

SERVES 6

Canned diced green chiles can be found in the Mexican food aisle of most supermarkets. If you can't find tomatillos, increase the amount of tomato. Blackening spice is a Cajun spice mixture found in the spice aisle.

SPICY MAYONNAISE

- 1 plum tomato, seeded and diced (about 1/3 cup)
- 1/2 small onion, minced
- 2 tablespoons minced fresh cilantro leaves
- 2 jalapeño chiles, stemmed, seeded, and minced
- 1 tablespoon canned diced green chiles
- 1 tomatillo, husk removed and diced
- 3 tablespoons juice from 1–2 limes
- 1 cup mayonnaise
- Salt and ground black pepper

TROPICAL FRUIT SALSA

- 1 cup fresh pineapple cut into 1/2-inch cubes
- 1 medium red bell pepper, stemmed, seeded, and minced
- 1 mango, peeled, pitted, and cut into 1/2-inch pieces
- 1 kiwi, peeled and diced
- 2 tablespoons juice from 1 lime
- Salt and ground black pepper

FISH TACOS

- 12 (8-inch) flour tortillas
- 1/2 cup vegetable oil
- 1 (2-ounce) jar Cajun blackening spice (such as Chef Paul Prudhomme's Blackened Redfish Magic)
- 1 1/2 pounds sturdy white fish fillets (such as halibut, snapper, cod, or haddock), skinned if necessary and cut into 4 by 1-inch pieces
- 1 cup finely shredded green cabbage (about 1/4 small head)
- 1 cup finely shredded red cabbage (about 1/4 small head)

1. FOR THE SPICY MAYONNAISE: Combine the tomato, onion, cilantro, jalapeños, green chiles, and tomatillo in a medium bowl. Stir in the lime juice and mayonnaise. Season with salt and pepper to taste. Set aside.

2. FOR THE TROPICAL FRUIT SALSA: Combine the pineapple, bell pepper, mango, kiwi, and lime juice in a medium bowl. Season with salt and pepper to taste. Set aside.

3. FOR THE TACOS: Toast the tortillas one at a time in a 12-inch heavy-bottomed skillet over medium-high heat until softened and speckled with brown, 10 to 15 seconds per side. Wrap the tortillas in a slightly moistened dish towel to keep warm and soft.

4. Return the skillet to medium-high heat. Pour the oil into a medium bowl. Place the blackening spice in another medium bowl. Working with one piece at a time, coat the fish with the oil, then dredge in the blackening mixture, shaking off the excess. Add to the hot pan and cook until the fish is a deep brown, 3 to 5 minutes depending of the type of fish used. Using tongs, turn the fish over and cook on the second side until cooked through, 3 to 5 minutes more. Transfer the fish to a warm serving plate.

5. TO SERVE: At the table, spread 2 to 3 tablespoons of the salsa mayonnaise on each tortilla. Top with green and red cabbage and 2 or 3 pieces of fish. Top with tropical fruit salsa to taste. Fold and serve immediately.

TECHNIQUE: Presenting Food Like a Chef—at Home

Plating

IT SHOULD GO WITHOUT SAYING THAT HOT food deserves to be served on heated plates, especially during the cold winter months. To warm plates, platters, or bowls for serving, we recommend two methods: Turn your oven to the lowest heat and place the serving dishes directly on the oven rack for about 10 minutes. If your oven is already heated, turn it off and place the dishes inside. The residual heat inside the oven will heat the plates quickly. Be sure to use oven mitts when removing the hot plates and always be sure to let diners know when the dish in front of them is very hot. Or, try this method: run them through the dishwasher on the dry cycle.

Likewise, be sure to serve chilled soups and salads in ice cold bowls and plates—about 15 minutes in the freezer should do it. Serving dishes for frozen confections (ice cream, sorbet, etc.) should also be chilled in the freezer before serving.

If you're making an elaborate dinner for a large group, it is often helpful to plate the courses assembly-line style. Elicit the help of one or two of your guests and assign tasks. One person can arrange sliced beef on each plate, another can artfully drizzle on a sauce (poured from a liquid measuring cup for control), and a third can top the dish with frizzled leeks, for example. For very complicated garnish schemes, restaurant chefs may create a sample plate for their sous chefs to re-create and ask a cook (called an expeditor) to check each plate. Expeditors usually also clean the rim of each plate with a towel dipped in a solution of equals parts vinegar and water, followed by a quick wipe with a dry, clean towel to ensure spotless edges.

The arrangement of food on a serving plate can affect significant differences in presentation. For example, rather than just serving a fillet of salmon with a pile of greens alongside, plate the greens first and then put the salmon on top for more drama. Also pay attention to the way meats are presented—cutting on the bias or fanning meat not only makes for a prettier presentation but also creates the illusion of larger portion sizes.

Tongs are an excellent tool for placing meats and vegetables exactly where you want them on the plate. When serving soups, hold a plate under the ladle to prevent drips from marring the edges of the soup dishes. For salad, the most effective tool is your own hands. First, be sure your hands are scrupulously clean (or slip on a pair of plastic gloves to avoid soiling shirt cuffs). To coat the salad greens, gently toss the greens in a large bowl with the dressing, being sure to use a light tough to avoid bruising the greens. For plating the salad, use your hands to transfer the greens to the center of salad plates and gently pile and fluff the greens into an attractive mound.

A plastic squeeze bottle is the perfect receptacle for savory and sweet sauces. The bottle allows just the right amount of control when drizzling a plate or creating an elaborate design—and in the cases of a sauce meant to be served warm, like caramel or chocolate, the plastic bottles can be kept warm by partially submerging them in hot water.

Garnishing

GARNISHES SHOULD ADD COMPLEMENTARY or contrasting flavors, textures, and colors to a dish. To garnish or not to garnish? For most home cooks, the answer to that question balances on the stem of a parsley sprig. Parsley cleanses the palate and perfumes the breath—it is a worthwhile addition to many plates. For restaurant chefs, on the other hand, the answer—almost always in the affirmative—includes a range of decorative food flourishes, from the ubiquitous and somewhat tiresome parsley sprig or radish rose to elaborate and often architectural affairs.

In classic French cooking, garnishes played an important role on the plate. Strict guidelines were established and definitions imposed. In his influential *Complete Guide to the Art of Modern Cookery,* the famous French chef Escoffier devotes an entire chapter to the topic and lists 132 garnishes, each categorized, defined, named, and alphabetized—from Garnish à l'Algérienne to Garnish à la Zingara. Escoffier uses the term *garnish* broadly. Nearly all vegetables that accompany meat are considered garnishes.

However elaborate his garnishes seem to us today, Escoffier imposed general guidelines that professional chefs and home cooks still follow. Lest an inspired chef consider pairing that sprig of parsley with a chocolate tart, Escoffier warns that the composition of garnishes "should always be in direct keeping with the item or piece that they will accompany. All fanciful outlandish ideas should be rigorously avoided." Be sensible and pair the parsley with a red potato salad or a pot-au-feu.

HERE ARE OUR FAVORITE GARNISHING IDEAS:

- When grilling meat, fish, poultry, or vegetables, throw a few whole scallions on the grill toward the end of the cooking time for a quick flourish. Grilled fruit (apples, pears, bananas, pineapple, peaches, plums, or mangoes) enhances grilled beef, pork, and chicken with sweetness and color.

- Some dishes are greatly improved by a drizzle of white truffle oil or high-quality extra-virgin olive oil.

- A very fine dice (brunoise) or julienne of a vegetable used in the dish, either raw or cooked, may serve as a colorful accent.

- Fresh herbs can be minced, cut into chiffonade, or left whole on the stem for garnishing. Herb leaves are also delicious when deep-fried, especially sage or parsley. To give whole basil leaves extra sheen, rub them with a small amount of olive oil.

- Deep-fry finely julienned ginger or leeks until golden brown and crispy for a frizzled embellishment.

- Although some chefs demand plates with spotless rims, others prefer to dress them up a bit. To do so, rub the rim of a serving plate lightly with oil so a dusting of complementary herbs, spices, or finely minced chiles will adhere.

- For simple pan-fried or grilled steak, a sprinkle of fancy sea salt, especially one with large crystals, serves as an effortless, luxurious garnish.

- When the flavors are appropriate, chopped nuts, olives, or cornichons can serve as no-cook garnishes.

- Edible flowers are available in many supermarkets and make a summery, fragrant addition to both savory dishes and desserts.

- Desserts can also be finished with chocolate shavings (made by scraping a chocolate bar with a vegetable peeler), a dusting of confectioners' sugar or cocoa powder (using a small, fine-mesh strainer), fresh berries, or candied citrus peel.

Braised Monkfish *with* Pistachio Gremolata

Adapted from Braised Monkfish with Pistachio Gremolata

Rialto, Cambridge, Massachusetts

RIALTO'S BRAISED MONKFISH WITH PIStachio Gremolata has one of those fashionably brief, minimalist titles that belies the dish's complexity. A stew of sorts, tender monkfish is served in a style the French call *à la nage:* swimming in an orange-and-anise-flavored, vegetable-studded broth with mussels, cherry tomatoes, and a garnish of gremolata. Refined yet rustic at heart, it's archetypal of Rialto's menu. Despite the restaurant pedigree, we found the dish relatively easy for the home cook, and quick to boot—an easy one-hour prep-to-table dish.

Most of the cooking takes place in the oven, outside of sautéing the vegetables for the broth. And while the monkfish braises, the mussels, tomatoes, and gremolata may be prepared. Don't be put off by the seemingly long ingredient list: very little preparation is necessary. The vegetables that flavor the broth—carrot, celery, and onion—are just sliced—no arduous dicing here. The broth involves opening a couple of bottles, and the monkfish comes pan-ready from the market. The knife work required for the gremolata is the most labor-intensive part of the dish, but that's only a matter of mincing.

As for unique ingredients, many home cooks might be new to monkfish and Pernod, a prime flavoring agent in the dish. While always popular in Europe, monkfish (aka anglerfish) was once deemed a "trash fish" by American fishermen because of its hideous appearance (the head, which is normally discarded at sea, is over half the fish, an almost entirely gaping maw picketed with sharp teeth). But in recent years, it's become quite popular for its firm, sweet flesh akin to lobster, but at a fraction of the crustacean's stiff price. In fact, monkfish is often colloquially referred to as the "poor man's lobster." The fish's firm-textured flesh means that it can be used in a variety of preparations, just as long as it's cooked through, since monkfish can be rubbery and bland if undercooked. Braising, then, makes perfect sense: the slow, moist cooking method gently cooks the fish, imbuing it with the flavor of the broth. Monkfish is sold in slightly cylindrical fillets—each fillet being half a tail. Big or small, size has little effect on flavor. It does alter cooking time, however, and it's a good idea to purchase fillets similar in size.

Pernod, the liquor Rialto specifies to flavor the broth, is one of several anise-flavored liquors produced in France. Generally consumed as an aperitif (thinned with water, which turns it milky white), it also finds its way into many dishes in the kitchen. Pernod is a brand name; but other anisette liquors work just as well, as does Greek ouzo or Turkish arrack. Rialto's recipe specifies a tablespoon, which we found perfect—any more, and the anise overpowered the dish's other flavors.

If you're unfamiliar with gremolata, it's a garnish of Italian derivation, most commonly served with osso buco. Classically, it's equal parts minced parsley, lemon zest, and garlic, but Rialto adds a unique touch with chopped pistachios, which pair surprisingly well with the fish's flavor and provide interesting textural contrast with its buttery softness.

While the dish was easily and quickly prepared following Rialto's instructions, we found that we could simplify Rialto's cooking method by trimming the number of pans employed. In the original recipe, the vegetables are sautéed and the broth built in a large skillet, then transferred to a baking dish to braise the fish. Once the fish is tender, the broth is transferred—yet again—to a saucepan to simmer the mussels and tomatoes. We found that we could limit the recipe to just one pan: a large, ovensafe skillet with a lid. Once the broth was ready, we slipped the fish into the pan and transferred it to the oven. Our cooking time and temperature were consistent with Rialto's recipe, despite the pan change; at 275 degrees, the monkfish took about 30 minutes to cook fully—flipped at the midpoint. To finish the dish, we transferred the fish from the skillet to a plate, returned the skillet to the range over medium-high heat, and added the mussels and tomatoes. Within three to four minutes, the mussels had opened and dinner was ready.

For serving, position the monkfish in the center of a large, shallow soup bowl and ladle the broth and mussels around the outside. Sprinkle the gremolata over the top. It's also quite attractive served family-style in a large tureen. Whatever presentation you choose, be sure to serve plenty of crusty bread to soak up the flavorful broth.

Braised Monkfish with Pistachio Gremolata

SERVES 6

Try to purchase monkfish fillets that are similar in size for the most even cooking. Monkfish is often sold with a membranous gray coating attached that, if you ask, will be removed by the fishmonger. Otherwise, a thin, sharp knife will easily remove the coating. If you can't find monkfish, halibut would make an acceptable substitute. Closely monitor the mussels—they are ready to eat as soon as they open.

PISTACHIO GREMOLATA

- **½ cup shelled pistachios, chopped coarse**
- **¼ cup chopped fresh parsley leaves**
- **3 medium garlic cloves, minced or pressed through a garlic press (about 1 tablespoon)**
- **1 teaspoon grated lemon zest from 1 lemon**

BRAISED MONKFISH

- **2 tablespoons vegetable oil**
- **1 small onion, halved and sliced thin**
- **1 small carrot, sliced thin**
- **1 medium celery rib, sliced thin**
- **Salt**
- **1 cup dry white wine or dry vermouth**
- **1 cup bottled clam juice**
- **1 tablespoon Pernod (or other anise-flavored liquor)**
- **1 teaspoon grated orange zest from 1 orange**

- 1 teaspoon chopped fresh tarragon leaves
- 1 teaspoon chopped fresh thyme leaves
- 1 ½ pounds monkfish fillets, trimmed of membrane and cut into 6 pieces
- Ground black pepper
- 1 pound mussels, scrubbed and debearded
- 1 pint cherry tomatoes, halved

1. FOR THE GREMOLATA: Combine the pistachios, parsley, garlic, and lemon zest in a small bowl. Set aside.

2. FOR THE MONKFISH: Adjust an oven rack to the middle position and heat the oven to 275 degrees. Heat the oil in a large ovenproof skillet over medium-high heat until shimmering. Add the onion, carrot, celery, and ½ teaspoon salt and cook, stirring frequently, until softened and beginning to brown, 5 to 6 minutes. Add the wine and simmer until reduced by half, about 3 minutes. Add the clam juice, Pernod, orange zest, tarragon, and thyme and bring to a boil. Remove from the heat. Season the monkfish with salt and pepper and arrange it in a single layer in the skillet. Cover and bake for 15 minutes. Using tongs or a spatula, turn each monkfish fillet over. Bake, still covered, until the fish is cooked through, 12 to 15 minutes longer.

3. Transfer the fish to a plate and tent with aluminum foil to keep warm. Set the skillet over medium-high heat, add the mussels and tomatoes, cover, and cook until all the mussels have opened, 3 to 4 minutes (discard any mussels that haven't opened). Adjust the broth's seasoning with salt and pepper.

4. Divide the monkfish among 6 warmed shallow bowls and ladle the mussels, tomatoes, and broth on top. Sprinkle the gremolata over the top and serve immediately.

Layers of Sole & Ratatouille *with* Roasted Red Pepper Vinaigrette

Adapted from Layer Cake of Sole

Park Avenue Café, New York, New York

THE PRESENTATION OF THIS MEDITERRANEAN-inspired dish from Park Avenue Café looks complicated: layers of delicate broiled sole and sautéed ratatouille are lightly drizzled with a roasted red pepper vinaigrette and garnished with calamari. The secret, however, is that it is a breeze to make. Not only are all of the components simple, but they are cooked independently of one another, making it a cinch to organize your time in the kitchen. Although the method may sound equipment-heavy, it requires only a skillet, a saucepan, a baking sheet, and a food processor. To simplify the dish further, we decided to omit the poached calamari. We found it was unnecessarily complicated, especially for the home cook, and the dish was still delicious without it.

The most difficult part of transforming this dish into an approachable recipe wasn't the cooking, but rather the shopping. The original recipe called for eight-ounce fillets of lemon sole (actually a type of flounder), which we had trouble locating. After consulting with several fishmongers, we gave up on the lemon sole and substituted a more readily available fish, gray sole. Its clean, delicate, slightly sweet flavor paired well with the other components; the only complication we ran into was the smaller, three-ounce size of the gray sole fillets. Luckily, the layered design of the dish made this an easy problem to solve. Originally, the recipe trimmed and cut the eight-ounce fillets of lemon sole into four-ounce portions, using one piece for each layer. Substituting gray sole, we used one small fillet for each layer, using eight small fillets in all. As for cooking the sole, we noted that broiling the fish on an oiled baking sheet was not only easy and foolproof, but conveniently left the 12-inch skillet (most home kitchens have only one) free for cooking the ratatouille.

The restaurant's method for cooking ratatouille is again surprisingly simple. Using medium heat and a 12-inch skillet with a lid, the vegetables are partly sautéed, partly steamed, rendering them tender in minutes without losing any of their festive colors. Wanting to make just enough ratatouille for four servings without omitting any of the seven vegetables, we found it necessary to buy the smallest (sometimes baby) versions of each. The interesting part of this ratatouille, however, was the addition of a very thick tomato sauce, known as "tomato fondue." Not only does this sauce give the otherwise quick ratatouille heft and flavor, but it lightly binds the loose, sautéed vegetables together into a cohesive mixture.

Although the recipe for tomato fondue is easy—canned tomatoes are simmered with some aromatics down to a thick paste, then pureed—it takes several hours to cook and produces nearly five cups. We pared down the ingredients and cooking time without losing any of its complex, tomato-flavored punch.

The minimal ingredients in the roasted red pepper vinaigrette allowed the sweet flavor of the peppers to shine through, and we made no changes to the original recipe. We did, however, include the test kitchen's favorite way to roast bell peppers at home—under the broiler. Layering the fillets of sole between layers of ratatouille turned out to be a straightforward procedure. When drizzled with the bright red vinaigrette, the layers look incredibly impressive.

Layers of Sole and Ratatouille with Roasted Red Pepper Vinaigrette

SERVES 4

In our experience, the fish takes longer to cook under a gas broiler than an electric one, which is why the cooking times in the recipe range widely. Because each plate has to be assembled, we found it better to work with warm plates, which help to ensure the food will still be hot when served. (See the methods for warming plates on page 250.)

RED PEPPER VINAIGRETTE

2 medium red bell peppers
6 tablespoons olive oil
2 tablespoons red wine vinegar
Salt and ground black pepper

SOLE AND RATATOUILLE

1 (14.5-ounce) can diced tomatoes, drained, juice reserved
9 tablespoons olive oil
4 large garlic cloves, minced or pressed through a garlic press (about 4 teaspoons)
Salt and ground black pepper
1 small onion, chopped fine
1 small red bell pepper, seeded and cut into 1/2-inch dice
1 small yellow bell pepper, seeded and cut into 1/2-inch dice
1 baby eggplant (about 6 ounces), peeled and cut into 1/2-inch dice
1 small zucchini (about 6 ounces), halved lengthwise, seeded, and cut into 1/2-inch dice
1 small yellow summer squash (about 6 ounces), halved lengthwise, seeded, and cut into 1/2-inch dice
1/2 cup plus 2 tablespoons minced fresh basil leaves
8 (3-ounce) gray sole fillets

1. FOR THE VINAIGRETTE: Adjust an oven rack so that it is 6 inches away from the broiler element and heat the broiler. Meanwhile, cut ¼ inch off the tops and bottoms of the bell peppers and remove the seeds. Slice through one side of each of the two peppers so they lay flat, and trim away the white ribs (following the illustrations on page 148). Lay the bell peppers skin-side up on a rimmed baking sheet lined with heavy-duty foil and broil until the skin is charred and puffed but the flesh is still firm, 8 to 10

minutes, turning the pan around halfway through. Remove the pan from the oven, cover with foil, and allow the peppers to steam for 5 minutes. Peel and discard the skins and pat dry with paper towels. Cut the roasted peppers into large pieces and puree with 1 tablespoon of the olive oil in a food processor. Combine the puree with the remaining 5 tablespoons olive oil and vinegar in a medium bowl. Season with salt and pepper to taste. Set aside. Wash the processor's workbowl and blade.

2. FOR THE SOLE AND RATATOUILLE: Measure ½ cup of the diced tomatoes into a small bowl and set aside. Puree the remaining diced tomatoes and their reserved juices in the food processor, about 5 seconds. Heat 1 tablespoon of the olive oil and half the garlic together in a medium saucepan over medium heat until the garlic is sizzling, about 1 minute. Stir in the pureed tomatoes and bring to a simmer. Simmer, uncovered, until the sauce is very thick and has reduced to ½ cup, about 15 minutes. Remove from the heat and season with salt and pepper to taste. Set aside.

3. Heat the broiler, leaving the oven rack in the same position as in step 1. Heat 2 tablespoons of the remaining olive oil in a large skillet over medium heat until shimmering. Add the remaining garlic, onion, and red and yellow bell peppers and cook, stirring frequently, until tender, about 5 minutes. Transfer to a medium bowl and set aside. Return the pan to medium heat, add 4 tablespoons of the remaining olive oil and heat until shimmering. Add the eggplant, zucchini, and squash, cover, and cook until tender, about 5 minutes. Stir in the reserved diced tomatoes, tomato sauce, onion mixture, and ½ cup of the basil. Cook, uncovered, until the flavors have melded, 1 to 2 minutes.

4. Meanwhile, brush a baking sheet with 1 tablespoon of the remaining olive oil and lay the fish on it in a single layer. Brush the fish with the remaining 1 tablespoon olive oil and season generously with salt and pepper. Broil until the fish is cooked through, 2 to 5 minutes.

5. To arrange the layer cake, use a soupspoon to spread about ½ cup of the ratatouille across the plate in a straight line. Using a long, metal spatula, remove a large fillet from the baking sheet and lay it on top of the ratatouille. Spread another ½ cup of the ratatouille on top of the fish and lay a second, smaller fillet over the top. Drizzle with the roasted red pepper vinaigrette and sprinkle with some basil. Repeat with the remaining ratatouille, sole, vinaigrette, and basil. Serve immediately.

Whole Grilled Striped Bass *with* Chard

Adapted from Whole Grilled Sea Bass

Kokkari, San Francisco, California

BEYOND FUNKY PLATE DESIGNS AND exotic ingredients, the real test of a good restaurant is in the execution of simple dishes, such as a whole grilled fish. With no unique flavors or glamorous towers to hide behind, the quality of the ingredients and the knowledge of proper cooking methods speak volumes about the level of expertise behind those kitchen doors. At Kokkari, sea bass is seasoned with olive oil, salt, and pepper and grilled whole, preserving its fresh flavor and tender texture. To be successful, however, it is imperative that the fish be as fresh as possible, then be grilled within a turn.

Finding whole striped bass isn't too hard, yet finding freshly caught whole striped bass might be. When shopping, look for fish with clear eyes and clean-smelling bellies. Cloudy eyes and overly fishy aromas are the easiest ways to detect old fish. Ask your fishmonger to scale and gut the fish. Before grilling the fish, it is necessary to season it with salt and pepper and brush it with some olive oil. The oil not only helps the skin from sticking to the grill, but it adds flavor and keeps the inner cavity of the fish moist as it grills. Also, we found it beneficial to slash the skin several times using a sharp knife. This allows the heat easy access to the flesh so that it grills evenly, and also makes it easy to check for doneness. With the fish cooking through in only 15 to 20 minutes, we found a medium-hot fire (achieved by using a chimney starter three quarters full of charcoal) was perfect.

The biggest problem with grilling whole fish is that the skin often sticks to the grill grate. To lessen the chances of this happening, in addition to brushing the fish with oil, it helps to clean the grill grate thoroughly and heat it up for 10 minutes, as opposed to the traditional 5 minutes. Cooking the fish for roughly 8 to 12 minutes per side, we noted that turning the fish was another point at which good technique is required. Try to position the fish on the grill initially so that it can be turned by rolling. (Make sure that you can reach the fish with a spatula and that when you roll the fish, it rolls onto an area with the same intensity of heat.) Lifting the whole fish off the grill is risky because the fish can snap in half. When turning the fish, lift it gently at first to make sure it is not sticking to the grill. If the fish is sticking, gently pull it up, working the sticking skin off the grill grate. The skin may still break, but at least you won't split the fish in half. To remove the fish from the grill once it's done, two metal spatulas provide proper support and greatly reduce the risk of breaking the fish in half on the way to a platter. Ask someone to hold the platter right next to the grill for an easy transfer.

Kokkari serves the whole fish on a bed of sautéed greens, such as kale, collards, or Swiss chard. We liked chard because it isn't as tough as the kale or collards, so it doesn't require blanching (quick cooking in boiling water) to turn it tender and less bitter. The chard stems can be diced and sautéed as well. Sautéed with a little olive oil and garlic, then tossed with lemon juice, as Kokkari's recipe described, the chard is another example of how to cook a simple ingredient perfectly. Served on a large platter with wedges of fresh lemon and a small ramekin of lemon-herb vinaigrette to be drizzled over the fish, this dinner tastes complicated, but it's not.

Whole Grilled Striped Bass with Chard

SERVES 4

When shopping for whole, fresh fish, look for clear eyes and a clean-smelling cavity. Flare-ups may occur because some of the oil rubbed onto the fish may drip onto the coals, so be ready to spray any flames with water.

VINAIGRETTE

- 1/4 cup extra-virgin olive oil
- 2 tablespoons juice from 1 large lemon
- 1 small shallot, minced
- 1 1/2 teaspoons minced fresh parsley leaves
- 1/2 teaspoon minced fresh oregano leaves
- Salt and ground black pepper

FISH

- 2 whole striped bass (about 2 pounds each), scaled, gutted, and skin slashed on both sides following the illustration on page 260
- 1/4 cup extra-virgin olive oil
- Salt and ground black pepper
- Vegetable oil, for grill rack

CHARD

- 1 tablespoon extra-virgin olive oil
- 1 pound Swiss chard, stems and leaves separated (see the illustration on page 88), stems chopped medium, leaves sliced thin (about 4 heaping cups)
- 4 medium garlic cloves, thinly sliced
- 1 tablespoon juice from 1 lemon
- Salt and ground black pepper
- 1 lemon, cut into wedges

1. FOR THE VINAIGRETTE: Whisk the oil, lemon juice, shallot, parsley, and oregano together in a small bowl. Season with salt and pepper to taste. Set aside.

2. FOR THE FISH: Light a large chimney starter three quarters full of charcoal and allow to burn until the flames have died down and all the charcoal is covered with a layer of fine gray ash. When the coals are medium-hot (you can hold your hand 5 inches above the surface of the grill for no more than 2 to 3 seconds), spread the coals evenly over the bottom of the grill. Set the grill grate in place,

OILING THE COOKING GRATE

Dip a small wad of paper towels in vegetable oil, grab the wad with tongs, and wipe the grill grate thoroughly to lubricate it. This extra step also removes any remaining residue on the grate, which might mar the delicate flavor of the fish.

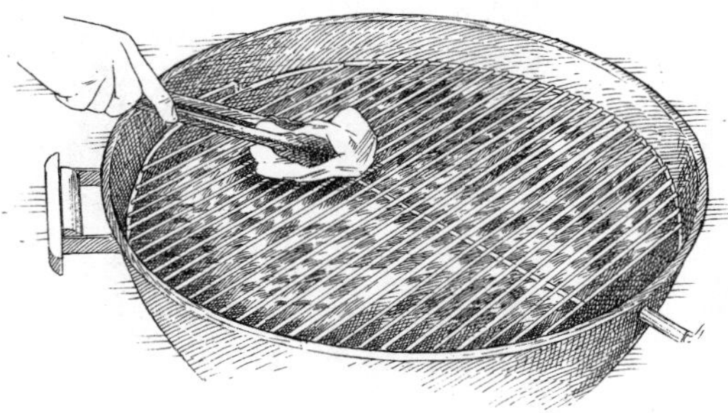

cover the grill with the lid, and let the rack heat up for 10 minutes. Use a wire brush to scrape clean the cooking grate.

3. Rub the fish inside and out with the olive oil and season generously with salt and pepper.

4. Lightly dip a small wad of paper towels in the vegetable oil. Holding the wad with tongs, wipe the grill grate. Grill the fish, uncovered and without disturbing, until the first side is browned and crisp, 8 to 10 minutes. (Use a squirt bottle filled with water to extinguish any flare-ups.) Gently roll the fish over using two spatulas and cook until the flesh is no longer translucent at the center and the skin on both sides of each fish is blistered and crisp, 8 to 12 minutes longer. (To check for doneness, peek into the slashed flesh or the interior through the opened bottom area of each fish.) Use two metal spatulas to transfer the fish to a nearby platter.

5. FOR THE CHARD: Heat the olive oil in a large skillet over medium-high heat until shimmering. Add the chard stems and cook until tender, 3 to 5 minutes. Stir in the garlic and cook until fragrant, about 30 seconds. Add the chard leaves and cook until completely wilted and glossy, 1½ to 2 minutes. Remove the pan from the heat and toss the chard with the lemon juice and season with salt and pepper. Arrange the chard and lemon wedges on the platter around the fish. Serve immediately, passing the vinaigrette separately.

VARIATIONS

Gas Grill Variation

Heat the gas grill with all burners set to high and the lid down until very hot, about 15 minutes. Meanwhile, prepare the fish as directed. Use a wire brush to scrape clean the cooking rack. Lightly dip a small wad of paper towels in the vegetable oil. Holding the wad with tongs, wipe the grill grate. Grill the fish, covered, as directed.

SLASHING THE SKIN

Once the fish is scaled and gutted, use a sharp knife to make shallow diagonal slashes every 2 inches along both sides of the fish from top to bottom, beginning just behind the dorsal fin. This helps to ensure even cooking and also allows the cook to peek into the flesh to see if it's done.

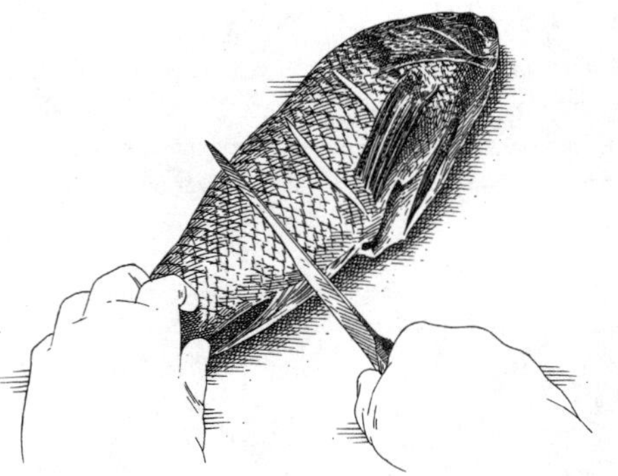

REMOVING FISH FROM THE GRILL

Once the fish is done, slide two metal spatulas under the belly to give it proper support, lifting gently to make sure the skin is not sticking to the grill. Quickly lift the fish and place it on a nearby platter.

Grill-Roasted Trout *with* Tarragon Vinaigrette

Adapted from Wood-Roasted Trout with Chervil Vinaigrette

Beacon, New York, New York

IN RECENT YEARS, CHEFS IN MANY RESTAURANTS have moved away from traditional gas-fired cooking equipment toward wood-fired equipment. The trend of cooking with wood grills, ovens, and rotisseries has changed the face of American cooking. This style of cooking has a rustic feel, reminiscent of cooking over a campfire and reminding us of days when all meals were cooked with wood due to necessity. This recipe from Beacon is exemplary of wood-fired cooking.

As far as preparation goes, the only item that needed any, other than the fish, was the vinaigrette, which is used as a marinade and a sauce for the fish. Made by processing the ingredients in a blender, this step was very easy. But we did have one concern: the use of chervil. Related to parsley, chervil has a subtle, anise-like flavor and can be hard to find. Concerned that most home cooks would be unable to find chervil, we sought alternatives. But considering chervil's anise flavor, our choices were limited. The most promising substitute seemed to be tarragon. Preparing the vinaigrette the same way as before, substituting an equal amount of tarragon for the chervil, we found that the sauce had lost its subtleness. To counteract this, we reduced the amount of tarragon and increased the amount of parsley in the vinaigrette, and found that we had a reasonable replacement.

The other step we tested was the cooking method for the trout. Finding the most efficient way to reproduce the flavors of wood-roasting at home proved to be a challenge. While the recipe from Beacon gave us adequate instructions on how to grill-roast the fish, we felt that some of the information was ill-adapted to the home cook.

We worked first to address the question of the temperature of the fire and the best way to introduce the woodsy smoke aroma. In the past, we found that a single-level fire spread over the bottom of the grill was best for cooking whole fish. In this case, however, where we were trying to introduce a smoky flavor, the fish cooked too quickly and charred too much, prohibiting it from picking up a significant smoke flavor. We next considered cooking the fish with a traditional grill-roasting method: a banked fire and indirect heat. This technique worked much better. Because the fish wasn't over direct heat, it didn't char excessively. This way, too, the fish could spend more time on the grill soaking up the smoke flavor. The recipe also suggested lining that part of the grill where the trout would be placed with foil that had been coated with nonstick cooking spray. This proved to be invaluable. By following this tip, we no longer had to worry about flipping the trout or having it stick to the grill grates—two problems that commonly plague home cooks when preparing fish on the grill.

Now that the structure of the fire had been decided, we could address the most efficient way of adding the wood smoke flavor to the fish. Our options were hardwood chunks or hardwood chips, both of which came in a wide variety of types of wood, from apple to mesquite. We quickly ruled out hardwood chunks, which came in fist-sized pieces, because they took too long to heat up. By the time the hardwood chunks started to smoke, the trout was fully cooked. We set those aside for long-cooking applications and turned to the hardwood chips. In our first attempt, we spread the chips over the hot coals, but found that they quickly burst into flames and didn't give off much smoke. Next we tried soaking the chips in water for half an hour first, but found that they quickly dried out and still burst into flame. It was apparent that we needed something to protect the chips while still allowing them to smoke. Enclosing the chips in a foil packet proved to be the perfect solution. The chips didn't catch fire and provided plenty of heavy smoke to flavor the fish. Another advantage of using this foil packet was that we didn't have to soak the wood chips in water, saving prep time.

The trout, which can be presented together on a large platter or individually on plates, was finished with the remaining vinaigrette. And while the recipe didn't specify what to serve with the fish, we couldn't imagine anything better than whole steamed baby potatoes and wilted spinach to round out this rustic dish.

Grill-Roasted Trout with Tarragon Vinaigrette

SERVES 4

There are many types of hardwood chips available, so feel free to use whatever wood is available or one that you particularly like.

- **1 cup extra-virgin olive oil**
- **2 tablespoons champagne vinegar**
- **½ cup fresh tarragon leaves**
- **¾ cup fresh parsley leaves**
- **1 large shallot, chopped rough**
- **Salt and ground black pepper**
- **4 boned freshwater trout, skin on, heads removed (about 10 ounces each)**
- **2 cups hardwood chips**
- **Vegetable oil spray**

1. Process the olive oil, vinegar, tarragon, parsley, shallot, ½ teaspoon salt, and ¼ teaspoon pepper in a blender until uniformly smooth, about 30 seconds. Transfer half the vinaigrette to a small bowl and set aside. Place the trout in a shallow dish and season the inside of the fish with salt and pepper. Spoon the remaining vinaigrette over the fish, evenly coating them inside and out. Cover loosely with plastic wrap and refrigerate for 30 minutes.

2. Place the wood chips on an 18-inch square of aluminum foil, seal to make a packet, and use a fork to create about 6 holes to allow the smoke to escape (see the illustrations on page 263). Spray one side of another 18-inch square piece of foil with vegetable oil spray and set aside.

3. Meanwhile, light a large chimney starter full of charcoal and allow to burn until the flames have died down and all the charcoal is covered with a layer of fine gray ash, about

30 minutes. Transfer the coals to one side of the grill, piling them up in a mound. Keep the bottom vents open. Place the wood chip packet on top of the coals. Set the cooking grate in place, open the grill lid vents fully, and cover the grill with the lid. Let the grate heat up for 2 minutes.

4. Cover the side of the grill with no coals underneath with the greased square of aluminum foil, greased side up. Place the fish on the foil with the thickest part of the fish closest to the hot coals. Grill the trout, covered, until the flesh is no longer translucent at the center and the skin is starting to blister slightly, about 10 minutes. (To check for doneness, peek into the interior through the opened bottom area of each fish.) Use two metal spatulas to transfer the fish to a nearby serving platter. Serve immediately, topped with the remaining vinaigrette.

USING WOOD CHIPS ON A CHARCOAL GRILL

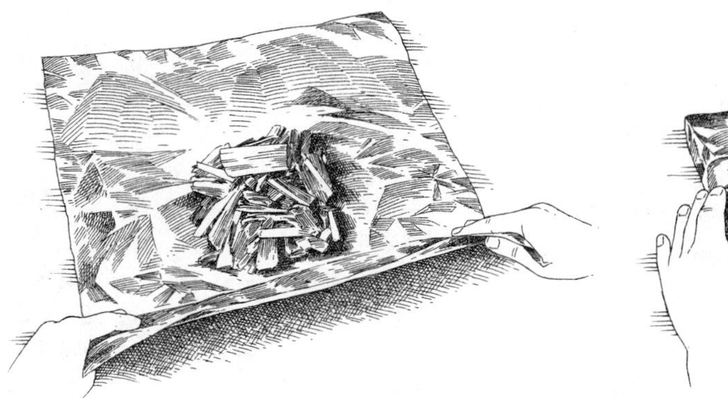

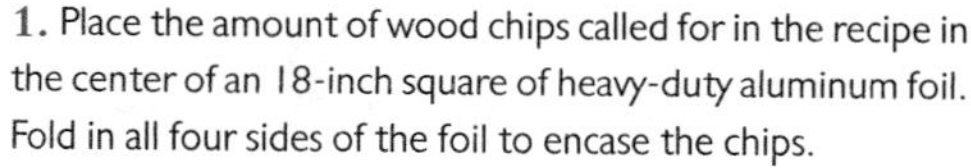

1. Place the amount of wood chips called for in the recipe in the center of an 18-inch square of heavy-duty aluminum foil. Fold in all four sides of the foil to encase the chips.

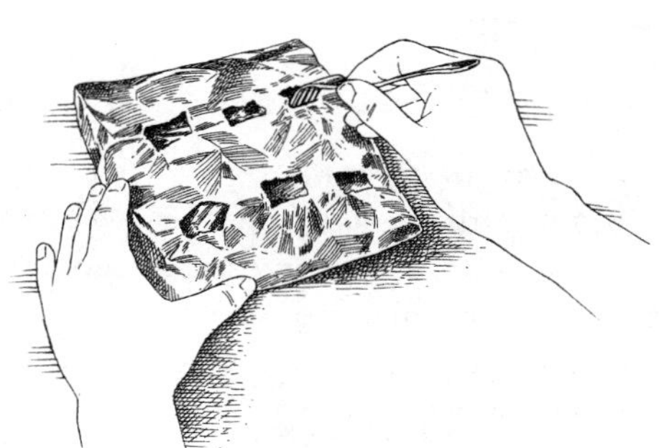

2. Turn the foil packet over. Poke about six large holes (each the size of a quarter) through the top of the foil packet with a fork to allow smoke to escape. Place the packet hole-side up directly on the pile of lit charcoal.

Sesame-Crusted Tuna *with* Asian Vegetables & Sticky Jasmine Rice

Adapted from Sesame-Crusted Tuna with Asian Vegetables and Sticky Jasmine Rice

Canal Street Pub and Restaurant, Reading, Pennsylvania

THIS ASIAN-INSPIRED DISH WAS AN IMMEDIATE hit in the test kitchen. Rich, red tuna is coated with sweet, nutty sesame seeds and served with jasmine rice flavored with cilantro and ginger, and colorful vegetables coated in a salty-sweet sauce.

The rice and vegetables in this recipe are easy to prepare. However, a couple of guidelines developed in the test kitchen guarantee lightly crisp vegetables and perfectly textured rice. Chopping the vegetables into uniform pieces ensures that they will cook evenly in the short time in the skillet. The addition of vinegar, sugar, and vegetable oil to the rice makes it pleasantly sticky. The idea here is to have neither fluffy rice with separate grains, nor mushy rice. To avoid a starchy mass, do not stir the rice while it cooks. Wait until the rice has absorbed the cooking water before gently stirring in the vinegar, sugar, and oil. Wait a bit longer, until the rice cools slightly, before adding the chopped cilantro. If the rice is too hot, the cilantro will turn brown.

Good-quality tuna is essential for this dish. Be sure to choose firm tuna steaks at least one inch thick with bright red flesh. Cooking the steaks in a nonstick skillet prevents the sesame seeds from scorching and sticking to the pan. Most members of the test kitchen staff prefer their tuna steaks rare to medium-rare; the cooking times given in the recipe are for steaks cooked to these two degrees of doneness. For those who prefer their tuna steaks cooked to medium, observe the timing for medium-rare, then tent the steaks loosely with foil for 5 minutes before slicing them. If you prefer tuna steaks cooked so rare they are still cold in the center, try to purchase steaks that are 1½ inches thick and cook them according to the timing suggestions on page 266. Bear in mind, though, that the cooking times are estimates; check for doneness by nicking the fish with a paring knife.

Garnishing the plates with Sriracha sauce and wasabi paste and adding ponzu sauce to the vegetables heightens the meal's Asian flavors. Made from the root of the wasabi plant, wasabi is readily available in powder and paste form in the international section of the supermarket. Often referred to as Japanese horseradish and used in sushi and sashimi preparations, wasabi imparts a very strong and spicy note to foods and should be used sparingly. Sriracha sauce is a Thai-style hot sauce made from a mixture of red chile peppers and garlic. It too is easily found in the international section of supermarkets. Ponzu sauce, made fresh in this recipe, is typically a citrus-based Japanese sauce that is also served with sashimi. This recipe, however, omits the citrus and sweetens the sauce with honey.

Use a quick restaurant trick when serving this dish: Warm the serving dishes in the oven on low heat for a couple of minutes before plating the meal. Use oven mitts to deliver the colorful, flavorful, and warm dishes to the table.

Sesame-Crusted Tuna with Asian Vegetables and Sticky Jasmine Rice

SERVES 6

Add the chopped fresh cilantro to the cooked rice just before serving, after the rice has cooled a bit. If added while the rice is still very hot, the cilantro will turn brown. If you prefer tuna cooked to rare, purchase steaks 1½ inches thick. Whichever your preference, rare or medium-rare, the tuna will not be hot when served.

PONZU SAUCE

- 1 tablespoon toasted sesame oil
- 1 tablespoon olive oil
- 1 tablespoon honey
- 1 tablespoon soy sauce
- ½ teaspoon fish sauce
- Pinch dried parsley flakes
- Pinch ground black pepper

RICE

- 2 cups jasmine rice
- 2 tablespoons grated fresh ginger
- 1½ teaspoons salt
- ½ cup rice vinegar
- 2 teaspoons sugar
- 2 tablespoons vegetable oil
- 1 cup minced fresh cilantro leaves
- Ground black pepper

TUNA

- ½ cup white sesame seeds
- ½ cup black sesame seeds
- 6 (8-ounce) tuna steaks, about 1 inch thick
- 4 tablespoons olive oil
- Salt and ground black pepper

VEGETABLES

- 1 tablespoon olive oil
- 2 cups 1-inch pieces savoy cabbage
- 2 cups 1-inch pieces bok choy
- 2 cups 1-inch pieces napa cabbage
- ½ cup 1-inch pieces radicchio
- 1 medium carrot, cut into matchstick-size pieces (about ½ cup)

GARNISH

- 6 tablespoons thin strips pickled ginger (about 3 ounces)
- 1 tablespoon wasabi paste made by mixing 4 teaspoons wasabi powder with 2 teaspoons water
- 6 tablespoons Sriracha sauce

1. FOR THE PONZU SAUCE: Whisk the sesame oil, olive oil, honey, soy sauce, fish sauce, parsley flakes, and pepper together in a small bowl. Set aside.

2. FOR THE RICE: Bring the rice, ginger, salt, and 3½ cups water to a boil in a medium saucepan over medium-high heat, without stirring. Reduce the heat to low, cover, and

simmer until all the liquid is absorbed, 15 to 17 minutes. Remove the rice from the heat. Whisk the rice vinegar and sugar together in a small bowl until the sugar dissolves. Add the vinegar mixture to the rice and stir gently to combine. Add the vegetable oil and stir gently to combine. Cover and set aside.

3. For the tuna: Combine the white and black sesame seeds in a shallow dish or pie plate. Pat the tuna steaks dry with paper towels. Rub both sides of the tuna with 2 tablespoons of the olive oil and season with salt and pepper. Drop the tuna steaks into the sesame seeds and shake to coat. Using your fingers, press the sesame seeds onto both sides of the tuna.

4. Heat 1 tablespoon of the remaining olive oil in a 12-inch nonstick skillet over high heat until just smoking, swirling the pan to coat with the oil. Add 3 of the tuna steaks and cook for 30 seconds without disturbing. Reduce the heat to medium-high and cook until the white sesame seeds are golden brown, about 1½ minutes. Using tongs, carefully turn the tuna steaks over and cook, without disturbing, until golden brown on the second side, about 1½ minutes longer for rare (opaque at the perimeter and translucent red and cool in the center when checked with the tip of a knife) or 2 to 2½ minutes for medium-rare (opaque at the perimeter and reddish pink in the center). Remove the pan from the heat. Transfer the steaks to a cutting board and immediately cut them into ¼-inch-thick slices. Using a wad of paper towels, carefully wipe away and discard any sesame seeds left in the skillet. Return the pan to high heat, add the remaining 1 tablespoon olive oil, and heat until just smoking. Repeat with the remaining 3 tuna steaks.

5. For the vegetables: Using a wad of paper towels, carefully wipe away and

INGREDIENTS: Wasabi

While you might think that little green mound served beside your sushi is wasabi, the truth is most people haven't ever tasted true wasabi. Surprised? So were we. Perplexed, we examined several of the packages of "wasabi" powders we had in the kitchen. Lo and behold, it's true: not one of them contained wasabi. What we believed to be wasabi was actually a mixture of horseradish and mustard, together with other ingredients ranging from cornstarch to spirulina and colored with FD&C Yellow #5.

True wasabi, or Japanese horseradish, until recently was grown only in the loose, gravelly soil of Japanese mountain streams, fed by the cold, nutrient-rich waters. In the past 10 years, farmers in the Pacific Northwest have started to cultivate this precious rhizome, but even with increased production wasabi fetches exorbitant sums of money, and can rarely be found in its whole state in the United States.

Curious to determine whether there was a true difference between wasabi and these wasabi impostors, we conducted a blind taste test (much to the dismay of the test kitchen staff). We pitted several faux-wasabi powders and pastes against true wasabi in three forms: powdered, paste, and the real McCoy—a freshly grated wasabi rhizome.

The results were very interesting. The three forms of the real wasabi all rated almost identically, and far better than the other powders and pastes. Most tasters agreed that the heat of the wasabi "grew in intensity," and then "dissipates quickly" ending with a "sweet," "grassy" flavor. The impostors were described as "boring," "stale," "metallic," and "fiery."

But the price of real wasabi is not cheap. The fresh piece we ordered through a local food purveyor cost $119 per pound. While the pastes we mail-ordered from Pacific farms were less expensive (six 1.5-ounce tubes for $25), we would just as soon use Hime Brand powdered wasabi, which costs $3.99, and spend our money on sushi. It was nearly as good as the wasabi paste and fresh wasabi and far better than the impostors.

discard any sesame seeds left in the skillet. Return the skillet to medium heat, add the olive oil, and heat until shimmering. Add the savoy cabbage, bok choy, napa cabbage, radicchio, and carrot and cook, stirring constantly, until the vegetables begin to wilt, about 1 minute. Rewhisk the ponzu sauce to combine, pour over the vegetables, and toss to coat. Cook over medium heat, stirring constantly, until the vegetables are tender, about 2 minutes longer. Remove the pan from the heat and set aside.

6. TO SERVE: Stir the cilantro into the rice and season with pepper to taste. Divide the rice among 6 dinner plates. Using tongs, arrange the stir-fried vegetables next to the rice. Using a spatula, fan the tuna steak slices over the vegetables. Arrange 1 tablespoon of pickled ginger over each serving of rice. Garnish the rim of each plate with ½ teaspoon wasabi and 1 tablespoon Sriracha sauce. Serve immediately.

PAN-SEARED TUNA STEAKS

COOKED MEDIUM

COOKED RARE

A tuna steak cooked to medium will be opaque from the edges through the center. A steak cooked to rare will have a seared crust, opaque edges, and a translucent red center. Because tuna steaks continue to cook after they are removed from the pan, slice them immediately to release the internal heat.

Five-Spice Tuna *with* Asian Ginger Slaw & Fried Noodles

Adapted from Five-Spice Tuna with Asian Ginger Slaw and Fried Noodles

Bexley's Monk Restaurant and Grill, Columbus, Ohio

THIS STYLIZED TUNA DISH FROM BEXLEY'S Monk epitomizes the plate presentations achieved by skilled restaurant chefs. Crispy fried rice noodles form a nest for a colorful Asian-style slaw. Sliced grilled yellowfin tuna leans against the slaw, and a pale green wasabi vinaigrette flows down the pale pink slices. More often than not, restaurants' flair for flash takes precedence over flavor. This dish, however, is an exception. It not only looks impressive, its flavors and textures rival its eye-catching appeal.

The original recipe had four components: an Asian glaze, fried rice vermicelli, Asian ginger slaw with wasabi vinaigrette, and grilled yellowfin tuna.

We began with the Asian glaze that was to serve as the final "plate art," painted from a squirt bottle onto the noodle nest. Hoisin sauce, a thick, sweet-spicy mixture of soybeans, garlic, chiles, and spices, forms the base of the glaze, with the flavors of ginger, sherry, rice vinegar, and fresh cilantro balancing the sweetness of the hoisin. The recipe for the glaze, made in restaurant proportions, used a cornstarch and water mixture (called a slurry) for body, stability, and its capacity to thicken. When we adjusted the recipe for the home kitchen, we found that simmering for a short period of time reduced the sauce to the desired quantity and consistency (negating the need for the slurry). The result was an intensely flavored, rich, reddish brown sauce that accented the crispy fried rice noodles perfectly.

For the noodle nest, the recipe specified rice vermicelli (also called rice sticks or mai fun noodles), which are then deep fried. They are very thin, similar to angel hair pasta, and brittle, with a tendency to shatter and fly all over the kitchen when an attempt is made at breaking them apart. Restaurant kitchens equipped with large deep-fryers wouldn't give a second thought to frying these noodles. But at home, deep-frying can seem an intimidating task. When the rice noodles hit the hot oil, they puff and swell with surprising speed, taking mere seconds to cook. While most recipes call for dropping the dry noodles into the hot oil, we found a method that suggested a quick dip in water and a 30-minute air-dry. This softened the noodles just enough so that we were able pull them apart without the usual flying noodle mess. We were a little skeptical about taking this extra step, so we first tried to break apart the noodles (they did indeed fly all over the counter) and drop them in the hot oil dry, without the prior soaking. Next we tried the soaking method prior to frying. We were able to separate them without too much breakage, and without rice sticks flying around the kitchen. The brief soaking also seemed to produce fluffier fried noodles than those not soaked.

With the preparation settled, our focus turned to the frying itself. As with most deep-frying preparations, proper oil temperature is crucial. Too low a temperature and the noodles sank to the bottom of the pot, absorbing large quantities of oil. Once they did manage to struggle to the surface, they weren't fully puffed. When the oil was too hot, it overbrowned the delicate noodles just as soon as they touched the oil. After much trial and error, we found that 360 degrees was the magic number for producing crisp, puffed, delicate white noodles. You can be assured of the proper temperature only by using an instant-read thermometer or a clamp-on deep-fat thermometer.

Satisfied with two of our make-ahead components, we moved on to the Asian ginger slaw. The vegetables in this slaw form a rainbow of colors, but for home purposes we knew it would be best to adjust the variety. While the original called for both red and green cabbage, tasters felt that one cabbage, napa in particular, might be better suited to the slaw. The result was a tender, delicate slaw more in keeping with the Asian theme. The dressing for the slaw (and for the tuna) is a wasabi vinaigrette. Wasabi powder is made from dried Japanese horseradish root and frequently added ingredients such as cornstarch, spirulina (algae), and color. When mixed with water into a paste, it is often used as an accompaniment to sushi. In this dish, it pairs well with the rare tuna. When used sparingly, wasabi paste (see page 266) adds a pungent, pleasant heat to a dish. Because this vinaigrette was to serve dual roles—as a dressing for the slaw and as a sauce for the tuna—we needed to create a balance among the wasabi, the vinegar, and the oil that would complement the slaw without overpowering the tuna. We settled on two tablespoons of the wasabi paste and balanced that with canola oil, rice vinegar, and fresh cilantro. The resulting vinaigrette has a decidedly sharp bite that adds a unique flavor and delicate color contrast to the final plate.

Yellowfin (or ahi) tuna can vary from pink to deep red. When selecting tuna for grilling, choose the deeper red flesh. Its relatively high fat content helps prevent it from drying out on the grill. The tuna is seasoned with Chinese five-spice powder, whose intensity and ingredients we found varied from brand to brand. Its ancient creation is believed to have been an attempt to encompass all of the five elements of Chinese cooking—sour, bitter, sweet, pungent, and salty—in one blend. The traditional mixture includes cinnamon, cloves, fennel, star anise, and Sichuan peppercorns. Good-quality prepared mixtures are readily available in Asian markets. We tried varying proportions of the powder on the tuna and concluded that the best way to avoid concentrating too much of the powder on one spot on the fish was to combine it with salt in a small bowl and season the fish prior to grilling.

We tried several different ways to present this dish, starting with the slaw on the bottom, then the grilled tuna sliced and fanned out, and the fried rice noodles on top.

While this gave great height to the plate, we decided that the fried noodles resembled a nest of sorts, and therefore belonged on the bottom of the stack. We formed a ring of noodles on the plate, placed the slaw inside the ring of noodles, thinly sliced the beautiful pink tuna and fanned it out alongside the slaw, and ladled a spoonful of the vinaigrette at the top of the tuna fan. This presentation gave the restaurant-style plate the height we were looking for, and still gave equal billing to all of the components of the dish. The glaze for the noodles can be applied artistically with a squirt bottle, as Bexley's does, but we found a spoon worked perfectly well for the job. Be generous with the sauce, since the noodles have great crunch and visual appeal, but little flavor on their own.

Five-Spice Tuna with Asian Ginger Slaw and Fried Noodles

SERVES 6

This recipe has many components, all of which can easily be prepared in advance, with the exception of the tuna. The noodles can be fried and set aside, and the slaw, wasabi vinaigrette, and glaze can be made ahead as well. Rice vermicelli noodles are commonly sold in six-ounce packages. Although prepared wasabi paste is acceptable, we prefer making our own wasabi paste by mixing wasabi powder with warm water (proportions are given on the can).

ASIAN GLAZE

- 1 tablespoon toasted sesame oil
- 1 (2-inch) piece fresh ginger, peeled and coarsely grated (about 2 tablespoons)
- 6 garlic cloves, minced or pressed through a garlic press (about 2 tablespoons)
- 1 tablespoon chili-garlic sauce
- 1 cup dry sherry
- 3/4 cup hoisin sauce
- 1/2 cup rice vinegar
- 2 tablespoons chopped fresh cilantro leaves

ASIAN GINGER SLAW

- 1 small head napa cabbage, finely shredded (about 4 cups)
- 1 red bell pepper, seeded and cut into 1/4-inch strips
- 1 cup mung bean sprouts
- 1 medium carrot, shredded
- 2 ounces snow peas, trimmed and cut into 1/4-inch strips
- 1 (2-inch) piece fresh ginger, peeled and finely grated (about 2 tablespoons)

WASABI VINAIGRETTE

- 5 tablespoons rice vinegar
- 2 tablespoons wasabi paste, made by mixing 8 teaspoons wasabi powder with 4 teaspoons water
- 2 tablespoons minced fresh cilantro leaves
- 3/4 cup canola oil
- Salt and ground black pepper

FRIED RICE NOODLES

- 3 ounces rice vermicelli (also called rice sticks or mai fun noodles)
- 4 cups vegetable or canola oil

TUNA

- 1 teaspoon Chinese five-spice powder
- 1/2 teaspoon salt
- 6 (4-ounce) tuna steaks, about 1 1/2 inches thick
- 1/4 cup extra-virgin olive oil
- Ground black pepper
- Vegetable oil, for grill rack

1. FOR THE GLAZE: Heat the sesame oil in a medium saucepan over medium heat until shimmering. Add the ginger and garlic and cook, stirring constantly, until fragrant, about 30 seconds. Add the chili-garlic sauce and cook, stirring constantly, for 1 minute. Add the sherry, bring to a boil, and simmer until reduced by half, 5 to 7 minutes. Add the hoisin sauce and rice vinegar, return to a simmer, and cook until slightly thickened and reduced to about 1 cup, about 2 minutes. Remove from the heat, strain through a fine-mesh sieve into a medium bowl, and stir in the cilantro. Set aside to cool. The glaze can be made up to 3 days ahead and refrigerated in an airtight container.

2. FOR THE SLAW: Toss the napa cabbage, bell pepper, bean sprouts, carrot, snow peas, and ginger together in a medium bowl. Set aside.

3. FOR THE VINAIGRETTE: Combine the rice vinegar, wasabi paste, and cilantro in a blender. With the machine running, slowly drizzle in the canola oil and process until emulsified, about 20 seconds. Season with salt and pepper to taste. Transfer to a small bowl and set aside.

4. FOR THE RICE NOODLES: Dip the vermicelli in a bowl of cold water for 10 seconds, drain, and transfer to a rimmed baking sheet lined with several layers of paper towels. Dry for 30 minutes, separating the noodles after 15 minutes. Heat the vegetable oil in a Dutch oven over medium-high heat until it reaches 360 degrees. (Use an instant-read thermometer that registers high temperatures or clip a candy/deep-fat thermometer onto the side of the pan before turning on the heat.) Working in batches, drop a handful of noodles into the hot oil. (The noodles will immediately puff and swell. They will not color, but will remain white.) Turn the noodles over and cook until puffed and crispy, about 10 seconds. Using a slotted spoon or spider, transfer the noodles to a rimmed baking sheet lined with several layers of paper towels. Repeat with the remaining noodles. Set aside.

5. FOR THE TUNA: Light a large chimney starter full of hardwood charcoal (about 2½ pounds) and allow to burn until the flames have died down and all the charcoal is covered with a layer of fine gray ash. Spread the coals evenly over the bottom of the grill. Set the cooking grate in place and let it heat up for 5 minutes. Scrape the grate clean.

6. Combine the five-spice powder and salt in a small bowl. Brush the tuna with the olive oil, then sprinkle it generously with the five-spice mixture and pepper.

7. Lightly dip a small wad of paper towels in vegetable oil. Holding the wad with tongs, wipe the grill grate. (See the illustration on page 259.) Grill the tuna, uncovered, turning once using a metal spatula, to the desired doneness, 4 to 5 minutes for rare or 6 to 7 minutes for medium-rare.

8. TO SERVE: Grab a handful of fried noodles and form a ring around the perimeter of each of 6 plates. Drizzle the glaze over the fried noodles. Drizzle ½ cup of the vinaigrette onto the slaw and toss to combine. Divide the slaw equally among the centers of the noodle rings. Slice the tuna and fan it over the slaw. Drizzle each serving of tuna with 2 tablespoons of the vinaigrette. Serve immediately.

Red Chile–Rubbed Salmon *with* Smoked Yellow Pepper Sauce

Adapted from Red Chile–Rubbed Salmon with Smoked Yellow Pepper Sauce

Ivar's Acres of Clams, Seattle, Washington

A fixture on Seattle's waterfront since 1946, Ivar's Acres of Clams has always had a reputation for quality fish dishes, though that reputation was once secondary to Ivar's promotional antics and outsized character. In this recipe from current executive chef Ray Espinoza, the Pacific Northwest's favorite fish is flavored with southwestern spices and a smoky roasted pepper sauce. Easy to make and dramatic on the plate, it is a restaurant dish that we found needed only minor adjustments to make it as foolproof for home cooks as for the restaurant.

In contrast to many restaurant dishes constructed from a long list of ingredients, this recipe contains few, relying instead on the rich flavor of salmon, a spice rub, and a finely balanced sauce. And best of all, it requires no special techniques or equipment: a blender is the most exotic tool necessary. The sauce's rich, full flavor belies its short ingredient list. The original recipe yielded a prodigious amount, so our job was to scale it back to just four servings.

The first step was to roast the yellow peppers. The method employed by Ivar's was well suited to large amounts of peppers, but not so effective for the small amount we needed. Instead, we employed our method in which the peppers are cut into flat "planks" and quickly roasted on a baking sheet set close to the broiler. Thoroughly blackened, the peppers are wrapped in foil for a few minutes to steam the skins loose from the pepper's flesh.

Once the peppers were roasted, it was quick work to puree them with the other sauce components. For body and piquancy, Ivar's includes raw red onion, for which we substituted a small shallot with success (owing to the smaller yield of sauce, it seemed excessive to require just a tablespoon from a whole red onion). Lime juice added a fruity tang, and salt, pepper, and sugar balanced the sauce's sweetness and acidity. Chipotle chile had the biggest impact, its fiery heat and full, smoky flavor rounding out the otherwise mild sauce. Chipotle chiles are smoked jalapeño peppers that are available either dried or rehydrated and packed in a thick tomato-based sauce called adobo. For this recipe, the latter are preferred, since the adobo sauce lends its own particular flavor. The cans are available at many markets.

The final step was to blend in olive oil for richness and body. Ivar's uses a high proportion of oil to pepper puree that, for the sake of healthfulness, we reduced (many restaurant dishes contain very high amounts of fat). The sauce possessed the same rich mouthfeel and full flavor, but with a fraction of the oil. At first, we were surprised that Ivar's didn't use extra-virgin olive oil for the sauce, but we quickly found out why: extra-virgin olive oil lent an unpleasant bitterness.

The red chile spice rub was an effective blend of ancho chile powder, ground cumin, salt, and pepper. Ancho chiles are dried poblano chiles with an earthy, subtly smoky sweetness. Ancho chile powder may be found at many specialty stores and through a variety of mail-order companies, but whole dried ancho chiles are common in many supermarkets and are easily ground at home. They should be lightly toasted in a 350-degree oven until fragrant and puffed, about six minutes. Next, the stem and seeds must be removed. Then the chiles can be ground in a spice mill until powdery. Sifting the powder through a fine-mesh sieve is a good idea to remove any coarse, unground pieces.

To finish the dish, Ivar's pan-sears the spice-rubbed salmon. Pan-seared fish is a mainstay of restaurants, since it guarantees a crisp crust and moist flesh with little effort, but many home cooks are intimidated by the technique. The only secret to speak of is a very hot pan glazed with a minimum of oil. Once the oil smokes, the pan is ready. While we normally sear fish skin-side down first and flip it midway through—after about four minutes—the spice rub (and Ivar's recipe) necessitated searing the fish flesh-side down first. We quickly found that the spice rub burned if cooked too long—this is not a Cajun-style blackened dish. A scant minute proved ideal, yielding a brick red, fully flavored crust. The fish then finished skin-side down, cooking for about six minutes more.

Red Chile–Rubbed Salmon with Smoked Yellow Pepper Sauce

SERVES 4

If you prefer skinless salmon (the skin tastes great in this recipe, since it's crisp-fried), remove the crisped skin after cooking, not before, so it can protect the flesh from overcooking. The bright colors of the fish and sauce present many options for presentation. At Ivar's, Chef Espinoza drizzles the salmon with the sauce, which is attractive. We also pooled the sauce under the fillet for maximum color impact. Side dishes may include green beans, sautéed spinach, or a green salad. This is a great dish for entertaining, because the sauce and spice rub may be prepared well ahead of time and the dish completed just before serving.

SMOKED YELLOW PEPPER SAUCE

- 2 large yellow bell peppers
- 1 small shallot, roughly chopped (about 1 tablespoon)
- 1/2 canned chipotle chile (about 2 teaspoons)
- 1 teaspoon sugar
- Salt
- 2 tablespoons juice from 1 lime
- 1/4 cup olive oil (not extra-virgin)
- Ground black pepper

RED CHILE–RUBBED SALMON

- 1 tablespoon ancho chile powder
- 1/2 teaspoon ground cumin
- 1/2 teaspoon salt
- 1 teaspoon ground black pepper
- 1 tablespoon vegetable oil
- 4 center-cut salmon fillets (6–8 ounces each), 1 to 1 1/4 inches thick, blotted dry with paper towels

1. For the sauce: Adjust an oven rack so it is 6 inches away from the broiler element and heat the broiler. Cut ¼ inch off the tops and bottoms of the bell peppers and remove the seeds. Slice through one side of each pepper so they lay flat, and trim away the white ribs (following the illustrations on page 148). Lay the bell peppers skin-side up on a rimmed baking sheet lined with heavy-duty foil. Broil until the skin is charred and puffed but the flesh is still firm, 8 to 10 minutes, turning the pan around halfway through. Remove the pan from the oven, cover with foil, and allow the peppers to steam for 5 minutes. Peel and discard the skins. Roughly chop the peppers and transfer to a blender. Add the shallot, chipotle, sugar, ½ teaspoon salt, and lime juice and process until smooth, about 30 seconds. With the machine running, slowly add the olive oil until emulsified, about 30 seconds. Adjust the seasoning with salt and pepper. Set aside.

2. For the salmon: Combine the ancho chile powder, cumin, salt, and pepper in a small bowl. Heat the vegetable oil in a large nonstick skillet over medium-high heat until smoking. Meanwhile, rub the top of each salmon fillet with about 1¼ teaspoons of the spice rub. Add the salmon flesh-side down and cook until a well-browned crust forms, about 1 minute. Using tongs and a spatula, turn the fillets over and cook until the fish is just firm to the touch, 5 to 6 minutes longer. Serve immediately, either drizzling each fillet with the sauce or positioning the fillets on small pools of sauce.

Pan-Seared Salmon *with* Lemon-Lime Aïoli

Adapted from Pan-Seared Salmon with Lemon-Lime Aïoli

Restaurant 155, Wichita, Kansas

CRISP-SKINNED AND GOLDEN BROWN, PAN-seared salmon is a restaurant staple, popular for its full flavor and healthful omega-3 fatty acids, not to mention its seductive, silky texture. Such a piece of fish needs little adornment: a spritz of bright citrus perhaps, or something rich to carry the flavor. Restaurant 155 has paired the fish with an especially fitting complement: lemon-lime aïoli (the French name for a garlicky mayonnaise popular in Provence). Simultaneously tart and rich—subtly spiced, too—the aïoli is perfect along with the fish. Between the seared salmon and aïoli, this is definitely a restaurant-style dish, but one you can easily replicate at home—even on a fever-pitch work night.

A garlic-and-oil-based sauce once made with a mortar and pestle and traditional to southern France, aïoli has been modernized and is now synonymous with mayonnaise—albeit souped-up mayonnaise flavored with garlic and lemon. At Restaurant 155, lime and seasonings are added to the mix for a unique rendition.

While mayonnaise can easily be made by hand with the aid of a whisk and sturdy wrists, we much prefer a food processor. Because of the high speed of the blade, there is less chance of the mayonnaise "breaking"—the mess of separated egg and oil that occurs when oil is added more rapidly than the egg mixture can absorb it. All of the ingredients except for the oil are blended, and then the oil is added in a slow, steady trickle through the feed tube (that pinprick of a hole in the feed-tube plunger of some models is designed for making mayonnaise, though we never use it). At Restaurant 155, the chefs surprisingly add a little water to the finished mayonnaise, which we noted made for a light and creamy texture.

We've addressed the mechanics of pan-searing salmon previously in Red Chile–Rubbed Salmon with Smoked Yellow Pepper Sauce (page 272), but to reiterate, the principles are simple. For the richest, most flavorful crust, we have found that the fillets must be dried and the pan must be extremely hot—oil slicked across the surface will smoke. And once the fish is in the skillet—flesh-side down and generously coated with salt and pepper—resist the urge to move the fillets for at least two minutes. Any movement will have a negative impact on the crust development. For flipping the fish, we favor a flexible metal spatula (some companies market fish-specific spatulas).

Rigid spatulas can break the fillets, which will mar the presentation. Unlike meat, fish should be served immediately—no resting required.

Pan-Seared Salmon with Lemon-Lime Aïoli

SERVES 4

There will most likely be a little aïoli left over, but it tastes great slathered on sandwiches, vegetables, or even other seafood, such as poached shrimp or fried calamari. Store leftover aïoli in an airtight container for up to 2 days. Please note that this recipe contains raw eggs yolks, which may pose health concerns for some readers.

LEMON-LIME AÏOLI

- 2 large egg yolks
- 1 tablespoon juice plus 1/4 teaspoon grated zest from 1 medium lemon
- 1 tablespoon juice plus 1/4 teaspoon grated zest from 1 medium lime
- 2 medium garlic cloves, minced or pressed through a garlic press (about 2 teaspoons)
- 1 teaspoon Old Bay Seasoning
- Salt
- 1 cup olive oil
- Ground black pepper

PAN-SEARED SALMON

- 2 teaspoons olive oil
- 4 center-cut salmon fillets (6–8 ounces each), 1 to 1 1/4 inches thick, blotted dry with paper towels
- Salt and ground black pepper

1. For the Aïoli: Process the egg yolks, lemon zest and juice, lime zest and juice, garlic, Old Bay Seasoning, and ¼ teaspoon salt in a food processor until combined, about 20 seconds. With the machine running, slowly pour the oil through the feed tube in a thin, steady stream until completely incorporated. With the machine still running, slowly pour in 2 tablespoons water. Adjust the seasoning with salt and pepper. Transfer to a small bowl and set aside.

2. For the Salmon: Heat the olive oil in a large nonstick skillet over medium-high heat until smoking. Season the salmon generously with salt and pepper. Place the fillets in the skillet flesh-side down and cook, without disturbing, until well browned, 2½ to 3 minutes. Using tongs and a spatula, turn the fillets over and cook until the fish is opaque and just firm to the touch, 2½ to 3 minutes longer. Serve immediately, accompanied by a dollop of the aïoli.

Salmon Confit *with* Lemon Grass Broth & Spring Vegetables

Adapted from Salmon Confit in Extra-Virgin Olive Oil, Lemon Grass Broth of Button Mushrooms, Pear Tomatoes, and Asparagus

Padovani's Restaurant and Wine Bar, Honolulu, Hawaii

THIS ELEGANT SALMON DISH IS REMARKable for its juxtaposition of eye-catching colors and complementary flavors, as well as its unorthodox cooking method. Here tender pink salmon fillets swim in an aromatic, lightly acidic broth dotted with green asparagus, red and yellow tomatoes, and white mushrooms. Instead of poaching the salmon in the classic fashion, Padovani's adapts the confit method of cooking meat in its own fat to fish. This unusual preparation produces salmon fillets that tasters in the test kitchen found exceptionally moist and flavorful.

Cooking salmon fillets for a brief period of time in boiling liquid—usually water and wine—is a classic restaurant preparation. Once cooked, the fish is removed from the broth and then served warm or cold, often accompanied by a sauce made from a portion of the poaching medium. The confit preparation, on the other hand, is a classic restaurant method that involves cooking and preserving meat—traditionally although not exclusively duck and goose—submerged in rendered fat. In this recipe, Chef Padovani submerges the salmon fillets in a roasting pan filled with very warm extra-virgin olive oil and cooks them in a warm oven for a brief period of time. Once cooked, the fillets are drained and served in a wide soup bowl along with the separately prepared broth. Given the need to completely submerge the fillets in the extra-virgin olive oil, a large quantity of oil is required. In the test kitchen, tasters preferred a mild-flavored, delicate extra-virgin olive oil for this recipe. Avoid the expensive artisanal brands and stick with the supermarket brands for this recipe. (See page 278 for the results of our taste test of supermarket extra-virgin olive oils.)

Although the method is quite simple, our initial attempts at adapting it for the home kitchen hit a roadblock. The recipe originally called for heating the oil in a saucepan on the stove and then pouring it into a larger pan, adding the salmon fillets, and transferring the pan to a 200-degree oven to cook for two to three minutes. Although this worked well when we tried the recipe with two

INGREDIENTS: Supermarket Extra-Virgin Olive Oils

When you purchase an artisanal oil in a high-end shop, certain informational perks are expected (and paid for). These typically include written explanations of the character and nuances of the particular oil as well as the assistance of knowledgeable staff. But in a supermarket, it's just you and a price tag (usually $8 to $10 per liter). How do you know which supermarket extra-virgin oil best suits your needs? To provide some guidance, we decided to hold a blind tasting of the nine best-selling extra-virgin oils typically available in American supermarkets.

The label extra-virgin denotes the highest quality of olive oil, with the most delicate and prized flavor. (The three other grades are virgin, pure, and olive pomace. Pure oil, often labeled simply "olive oil," is the most commonly available.) To be tagged as "extra-virgin," an oil must meet three basic criteria. First, it must contain less than 1 percent oleic free fatty acids per 100 grams of oil. Second, the oil must not have been treated with any solvents or heat. (Heat is used to reduce strong acidity in some nonvirgin olive oils to make them palatable. This is where the term ***cold-pressed*** comes into play, meaning that the olives are pressed into a paste using mechanical wheels or hammers and are then kneaded to separate the oil from the fruit.) Third, it must pass taste and aroma standards as defined by groups such as the International Olive Oil Council (IOOC), a Madrid-based intergovernmental olive oil regulatory committee that sets the bar for its member countries.

Tasting extra-virgin olive oil is much like tasting wine. The flavors of these oils range from citrusy to herbal, musty to floral, with every possibility in between. And what one taster finds particularly attractive—a slight briny flavor, for example—another might find unappealing. Also like wine, the flavor of a particular brand of olive oil can change from year to year, depending on the quality of the harvest and the olives' place of origin.

We chose to taste extra-virgin olive oil in its most pure and unadulterated state: raw. Tasters were given the option of sampling the oil from a spoon or on neutral-flavored French bread and were asked to eat a slice of green apple—for its acidity—to cleanse the palate between oils. The olive oils were evaluated for color, clarity, viscosity, bouquet, depth of flavor, and lingering of flavor.

Whereas, in a typical tasting, we are able to identify a clear winner and loser, in this case we could not. In fact, the panel seemed to divide itself quickly into those who liked a gutsy olive oil with bold flavor and those who preferred a milder, more mellow approach. Nonetheless, in both camps, one oil clearly had more of a following than any other—the all-Italian-olive Davinci brand. Praised for its rounded and buttery flavor, it was the only olive oil we tasted that seemed to garner across-the-board approval with olive oil experts and in-house staff alike. Among tasters who preferred full-bodied, bold oils, Colavita and Filippo Berio also earned high marks. Tasters in the mild and delicate camp gave high scores to Pompeian and Whole Foods oils.

THE BEST ALL-PURPOSE OIL

Davinci Extra-Virgin Olive Oil was the favorite in our tasting of leading supermarket brands. It was described as "very ripe," "buttery," and "complex."

THE BEST FULL-BODIED OIL

Colavita Extra-Virgin Olive Oil was the favorite among tasters who preferred a bold, full-bodied oil. It was described as "heavy," "complex," and "briny."

THE BEST MILD OIL

Pompeian Extra-Virgin Olive Oil was the favorite among tasters who preferred a milder, more delicate oil. It was described as "clean," "round," and "sunny."

three-ounce fillets, the amount the restaurant would cook to order, we had problems when we cooked all 12 three-ounce fillets at the same time. The temperature of the oil dropped when it was poured into the roasting pan and dropped even further when all of the cool salmon fillets were added to the pan. The oil temperature by this point was so low that the oven-cooking time increased substantially. After 15 minutes in the oven, the fillets were finally cooked through, but by then the oil had permeated the fillets to such an extent that they had an unpleasant oily texture.

After several experiments in the test kitchen, we found a method of cooking all the fillets quickly to preserve their delicate texture. Allow the fillets to come to room temperature before adding them to the oil. Pour the oil into a large roasting pan and heat the pan on the stove before adding the fillets. Heating the oil in the roasting pan, instead of in a saucepan, prevents the cooling that occurs when the oil is transferred from the saucepan to the roasting pan. Finally, heat the oil to 250 degrees, slide a long, wide metal spatula under several fillets, and transfer them to the pan at the same time. Adding several fillets at once reduces the oil temperature enough so that the fillets won't fry but will cook quickly once the pan is placed in the oven.

Once cooked, the salmon fillets are placed in large, shallow soup bowls with a delicate broth. Chicken broth forms the base of the broth, with the additional flavors of aromatics, white wine, lemon juice, and lemon grass providing a slightly Asian influence. Dotted with tomatoes, mushrooms, and asparagus, the broth looks as refined as it tastes.

Salmon Confit with Lemon Grass Broth and Spring Vegetables

SERVES 6

Bring the salmon fillets to room temperature about 30 minutes before cooking to avoid prolonging the cooking time. Cooking the asparagus separately gives you control over the tenderness of the spears and prevents overcooking once they are added to the broth. Avoid using expensive extra-virgin olive oil for poaching the fish, since there's no discernible difference in flavor between it and less expensive varieties in this dish.

LEMON GRASS BROTH

- 2 tablespoons unsalted butter
- 1 large carrot, cut into 1/4-inch dice (about 1 cup)
- 1 small onion, cut into 1/4-inch dice (about 1/2 cup)
- 3 garlic cloves, smashed
- Salt
- 1 cup dry white wine
- 1 1/2 cups low-sodium chicken broth
- 1 tablespoon juice from 1 lemon
- 1 large stalk lemon grass, trimmed and minced
- 12 sprigs fresh parsley
- 1 sprig fresh thyme
- 4 whole cloves
- 2 bay leaves
- Ground white pepper
- Pinch cayenne pepper

VEGETABLES

- 1 bunch asparagus (about 1 pound), ends trimmed
- 4 ounces button mushrooms, cut into sixths (about 1 1/2 cups)
- 12 yellow pear tomatoes, halved
- 12 red pear tomatoes, halved
- 1 teaspoon chopped fresh thyme leaves

- **3 tablespoons minced fresh chives**
- **1 tablespoon roughly chopped fresh tarragon leaves**

SALMON

- **6 (6-ounce) salmon fillets, 1 to 1 1/4 inches thick, cut in half, at room temperature**
- **Salt and ground black pepper**
- **8 cups extra-virgin olive oil (see headnote)**

1. FOR THE BROTH: Melt the butter in a medium saucepan over medium heat until the foam subsides. Add the carrot, onion, garlic, and ½ teaspoon salt and cook, stirring frequently, until the onion softens and turns light brown around the edges, about 10 minutes.

2. Add the wine, bring to a simmer, and cook until reduced to ½ cup, about 5 minutes. Add the chicken broth, 1½ cups water, lemon juice, lemon grass, parsley sprigs, thyme sprig, cloves, bay leaves, a pinch of white pepper, and cayenne. Increase the heat to high and bring to a boil. Reduce the heat to medium-low and simmer until the liquid is reduced to 3 cups, about 5 minutes. Remove the pan from the heat and strain the broth through a fine-mesh sieve into a medium bowl. Return the strained broth to the saucepan. Set aside.

3. FOR THE ASPARAGUS: Fill a medium bowl with ice water. Bring 2 cups water to a boil in a large skillet over high heat. Add the asparagus and cook until just tender, about 1 minute. Turn off the heat. Using tongs, immediately transfer the asparagus to the ice water. Cool for 1 minute, then drain the asparagus, pat it dry with paper towels, and cut the spears into 2-inch lengths. Set aside.

4. FOR THE SALMON: Adjust an oven rack to the middle position and heat the oven to 200 degrees. Season the salmon fillets on both sides with salt and pepper. Heat the olive oil in a large roasting pan over medium-high heat until the temperature of the oil reaches 250 degrees on an instant-read thermometer. Using a large, metal spatula, and adding several fillets at once, submerge the salmon in the warm oil in a single layer. Transfer the pan to the oven. Cook the fillets, turning halfway through cooking, until the center of the thickest part of the fillets changes from bright to pale pink, about 6 minutes total.

5. Remove the salmon from the oven. Transfer the fillets to a wire rack set over a rimmed baking sheet, placing them on their sides. (Discard the oil.) Using your fingers and the tip of a paring knife, peel the skin from the fillets. Discard the skin and set aside the fillets on the wire rack.

6. TO FINISH THE VEGETABLES: Bring the lemon grass broth to a simmer over medium-high heat. Add the mushrooms, tomatoes, and chopped thyme and stir gently to combine. Add the asparagus and simmer for 30 seconds. Remove the broth from the heat and stir in the chopped chives and tarragon. Adjust the seasoning with salt and white pepper.

7. TO SERVE: Place two salmon fillets in the center of each of 6 large soup bowls and pour ½ cup of the lemon grass broth over the salmon in each plate. Using a soupspoon, arrange the vegetables around the salmon. Serve immediately.

Seared Scallops *with* Buttered Artichokes & Mashed Yukon Gold Potatoes

Adapted from Seared Scallops with Buttered Artichokes and Truffled Potatoes

Lulou's, Reno, Nevada

One of the attractions of dining out is eating things that you normally wouldn't prepare at home. Admittedly, a chef has more manpower and resources than a home cook, but that difference doesn't necessarily mean that the end result will differ. The home cook willing to expend a little effort can easily prepare a restaurant-quality meal, like this dish from Lulou's.

After cooking this dish once, we were impressed by its subtle and varied flavors. The sweet scallops were complemented perfectly by the earthiness of the artichokes and truffle oil, while a rich bed of mashed potatoes provided a base for these flavors and acted as a unifying component. Still, there were some issues that we wanted to address. Our first concern was that the dish, especially the potatoes, called for a shockingly high amount of butter and oil. While some of this fat was needed for flavor, we felt that the recipe could do with less of it. Our second concern was the preparation of the artichokes. The recipe's preparation, which required a long, two-step process, was better suited for a restaurant kitchen. We wondered if there was a way to make it easier for the home cook.

The original recipe called for first roasting slices of artichoke hearts, covered, with copious amounts of butter for 30 minutes. After roasting, the artichokes were browned in additional butter with shallots until the shallots became slightly crisp. We tried consolidating the two steps into one, but because the lengthy roasting time of the artichokes intensified their flavor and ensured that they were not stringy, we decided against a different cooking method. Instead, we wanted to see if we could forgo the sautéing step. We started roasting the artichokes as we had originally, but instead of keeping them covered for the full 30 minutes, we uncovered them after 15 minutes, then added the shallots and continued to roast them. This technique yielded the same flavor and browning that had taken place originally, but with fewer steps (and pans)—a sure time-saver for the home cook.

As for the potatoes, the recipe required cooking them whole in their skins (our preferred method), but also required adding a whopping two sticks of butter. While we agree that potatoes are best with butter, this amount seemed a little extreme. We tried it again, this time reducing the butter by half. This way, the potatoes still had the rich, buttery flavor we loved, but they were less heavy. Addressing the use of buttermilk in the recipe, we knew we liked the tanginess that buttermilk added to the potatoes, but we considered substituting either half-and-half or milk, thinking the home cook was more likely to have these ingredients on hand. Tasting two batches of potatoes side by side, one with milk and the other with half-and-half, we found that tasters preferred the potatoes made with the half-and-half, saying they had more depth of flavor. Indeed, the milk had a tendency to make the potatoes taste "thin." And since we used only a cup of half-and-half to achieve the flavor we sought, and since we had reduced the amount of butter significantly, we didn't have to worry about adding too much fat to the potatoes. In the end, we decided to remove the truffle oil from the mashed potatoes and save it for drizzling over the scallops, where the truffle flavor would be better appreciated. This also meant that we could use less of the expensive truffle oil without sacrificing the intended truffle flavor, something that makes sense for the home cook.

PREPARING ARTICHOKES FOR ROASTING

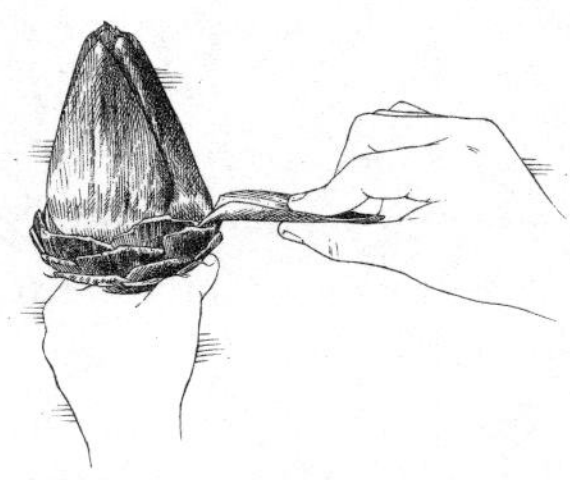

1. Holding the artichoke by the stem, bend back and snap off the thick outer leaves, keeping the bottom portion of each leaf attached. Continue snapping off the leaves until you reach the light yellow cone at the center.

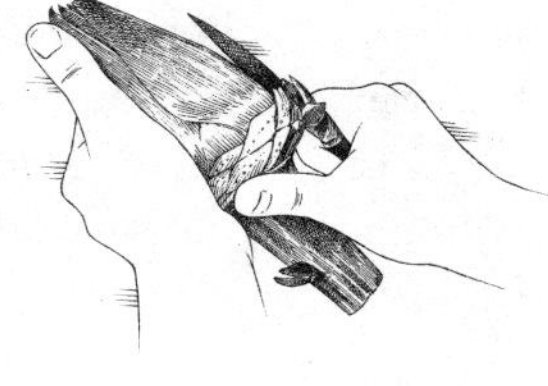

2. With a paring knife, trim off the dark outer layer from the bottom—this is the base of the leaves you've already snapped off.

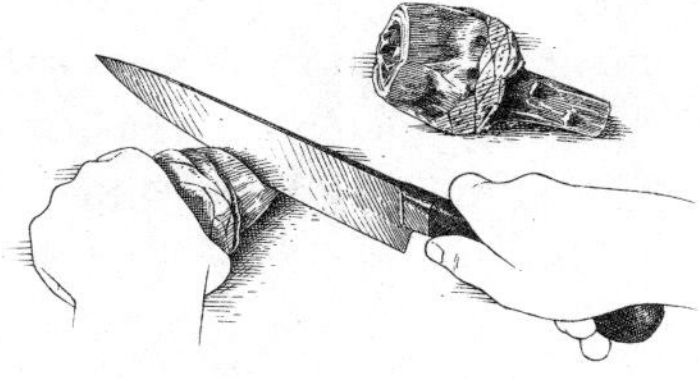

3. Cut off the dark, purplish tip from the yellow cone of artichoke leaves.

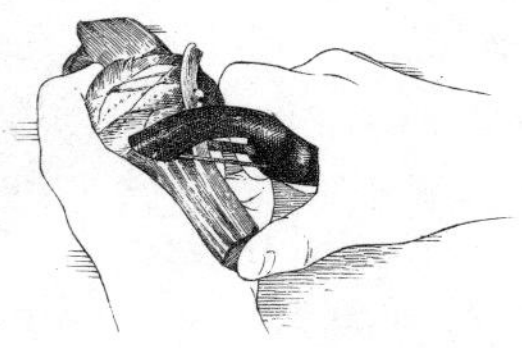

4. With a vegetable peeler, peel off the fibrous, dark green exterior of the stem. Once peeled, cut off the bottom $^{1}/_{2}$ inch of stem.

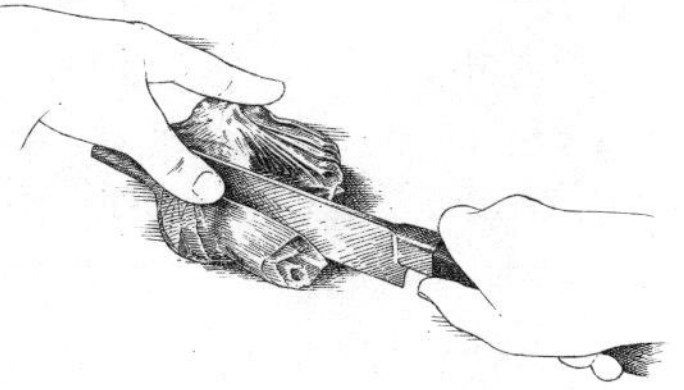

5. Cut the artichoke in half, slicing from tip to stem.

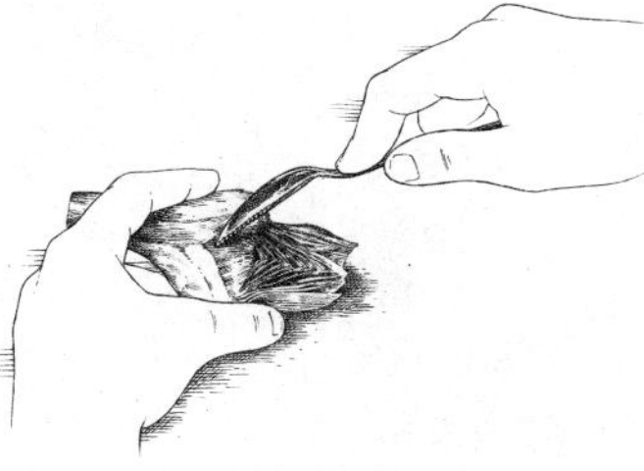

6. Scrape out the small purple leaves and the fuzzy choke with a grapefruit spoon or tomato corer. Cut the artichoke into $^{1}/_{2}$-inch slices.

Seared Scallops with Buttered Artichokes and Mashed Yukon Gold Potatoes

SERVES 4

Be sure to use dry scallops, which have not been chemically treated, in this recipe. (See the note to the recipe on page 285 for details.)

MASHED POTATOES

- **2 pounds Yukon Gold potatoes, unpeeled**
- **Salt**
- **8 tablespoons (1 stick) unsalted butter, melted**
- **1 cup half-and-half, warmed**
- **Ground black pepper**

ARTICHOKES

- **4 large artichokes, rinsed, trimmed to the heart, and cut into 1/2-inch slices (see the illustrations on page 282)**
- **4 tablespoons (1/2 stick) unsalted butter, melted**
- **1/4 teaspoon salt**
- **1/4 teaspoon ground black pepper**
- **1 medium shallot, sliced thin**

SCALLOPS

- **2 tablespoons olive oil**
- **24 large sea scallops (about 1 1/2 pounds), tendons removed (see the illustration on page 64)**
- **Salt and ground black pepper**
- **2 tablespoons white truffle oil (see page 95 for buying information)**
- **2 tablespoons chopped fresh chives**

1. FOR THE POTATOES: Bring the potatoes, 1 tablespoon salt, and enough water to cover the potatoes by 1 inch to a boil in a large saucepan over high heat. Reduce the heat to medium-low and simmer until a paring knife can be slipped into and out of the center of the potatoes with very little resistance, 20 to 30 minutes. Drain.

2. Set a food mill or ricer over the empty but still warm saucepan. Spear the potatoes with a fork, then peel back the skin with a paring knife. Working in batches, cut the peeled potatoes into rough chunks and drop into the food mill. Process or rice the potatoes into the saucepan. Stir in the butter until incorporated. Gently stir in the warm half-and-half and salt and pepper to taste.

3. FOR THE ARTICHOKES: Meanwhile, adjust an oven rack to the middle position and heat the oven to 400 degrees. Toss the artichokes with the melted butter, salt, and pepper in a medium bowl. Lay the artichokes on a rimmed baking sheet lined with parchment paper and cover the artichokes with foil. Roast for 15 minutes. Remove the foil from the baking sheet and discard. Toss the shallot with the artichokes and return the pan to the oven. Roast until the shallot is browned and the artichokes are tender, 15 to 17 minutes longer.

4. FOR THE SCALLOPS: Heat the olive oil in a 12-inch skillet over medium-high heat until smoking. Season the scallops with salt and pepper on both sides. Add the scallops flat-side down and cook until well browned, about 2½ minutes. Using tongs, turn the scallops over, one at a time. Cook until medium-rare (the sides have firmed up and all but the middle third of the scallop is opaque), about 30 seconds longer.

5. TO SERVE: Divide the mashed potatoes evenly among the centers of 4 plates. Nestle the artichokes in the mashed potatoes. Arrange the scallops in a ring around the outside of the potatoes. Drizzle the dish with the truffle oil and sprinkle with the chopped chives. Serve immediately.

Pan-Seared Sea Scallops *with* Bean Fricassee & Pistou

Adapted from Roasted Sea Scallops with Bean Fricassee and Pistou Broth

Daniel, New York, New York

ROASTED SEA SCALLOPS WITH BEAN FRICASSEE and Pistou Broth, from New York's esteemed Daniel, is four-star dining at its best. Crispy, seared scallops sit atop a complexly flavored, beautifully prepared mosaic of al dente vegetables. None of the ingredients in the dish is too exotic or exorbitantly priced—unique ingredient combinations and meticulous preparation are indicative of its restaurant roots. If you've got the time and the urge to hone your knife skills, a close approximation of Daniel's scallops can be made at home.

There are three components to the dish: pistou sauce, bean fricassee, and scallops. *Pistou* is the French name applied to pesto, the Italian sauce of basil, nuts, garlic, Parmesan, and olive oil. Daniel blanches the basil prior to grinding the ingredients together in a food processor, which makes for a surprisingly bright-colored sauce. We're long accustomed to the muddied olive hue pesto normally turns as the basil oxidizes after processing. At Daniel, the chefs thin the pistou with rich chicken stock prior to drizzling it over the scallops, but we preferred to leave it full strength and placed a small dollop on top of each scallop. It saved a little effort, and the change didn't harm the dish's flavor.

By classic definition, a fricassee is a chunky stew of meat usually flavored with wine. Daniel takes some liberties by substituting seafood for the meat and excluding the wine, though not to the dish's detriment. A variety of precisely sliced beans and assertive seasonings lubricated with chicken broth and butter sounded good to us. Three varieties of beans are specified for the fricassee: haricots verts, wax beans, and Romano beans. While the results were stellar—visually, texturally, and flavor-wise—it involved a lot of preparation. And finding a market that stocks all three varieties? Fat chance. We took a minimalist approach and scaled the beans back to just two varieties. Standard green beans replaced the more delicate haricots verts (which are both hard to find and expensive) and we kept the wax beans. Romano beans proved hard to find and almost identical in color and flavor to the wax beans, though feel free to substitute them for the wax beans if you desire.

Once the beans are blanched until tender (and shocked in ice water to set their color and texture), the fricassee is assembled in a skillet. Pearl onions are sautéed—fresh ones, since frozen lacked the same texture and flavor—and then the beans and remaining ingredients, including diced olives, tomatoes, basil, parsley, sliced almonds, and, our favorite touch, finely diced lemon. Adding lemon juice just before serving is a common restaurant trick that brightens flavors, but bits of lemon were a whole other story. Instead of a generalized, intensified brightness, there are tiny bursts of surprising sharpness.

Despite the name of the original dish, the scallops are not roasted: they are pan-seared on the stovetop. With their creamy, full flavor and tender texture, scallops signify luxury. Restaurants receive the cream of the crop when it comes to scallops, including diver scallops, which are harvested individually by scuba-tanked fishermen (for a very stiff price). But your local market should stock a fine selection. Use the largest you can find for both ease of preparation and aesthetics.

In a unique step, Daniel coats one side of each scallop in rice flakes, a product new to us but common throughout India. Looking more like oatmeal than rice, rice flakes go by many names, including *poha, aval,* and *chiwda.* For this dish, they add crunchy texture to the otherwise creamy, smooth scallops. Unless you have access to an Indian specialty store, you might be hard-pressed to find rice flakes. But we found that panko (Japanese-style bread crumbs) are a more than adequate substitute. Seared for just two minutes on the breaded side and a minute or so on the second side in a minimum of shimmering-hot oil (not smoking-hot, as we normally prefer when searing meat and fish), the bread crumbs turned golden brown and the scallops retained their trademark buttery texture.

Pan-Seared Sea Scallops with Bean Fricassee and Pistou

SERVES 6

Make sure to ask your fishmonger for "dry" scallops, or those that have not been soaked in a chemical preservative compound. "Dry" scallops will be creamier looking, as opposed to the stark white of "wet" scallops. And don't try to substitute small bay scallops; they will be messy to bread and are difficult to sear. Dicing a lemon is easier than it sounds. Using a very sharp paring knife, shave off the peel, including all the pith, then proceed as you would with any fruit or vegetable. However, be wary of seeds and remove them as you dice. Since this dish is somewhat soupy, we recommend serving it in shallow soup bowls, the scallops propped atop the fricassee and dolloped with a thimbleful of pistou.

PISTOU

- Salt
- 4 cups loosely packed fresh basil leaves
- 1 tablespoon grated Parmesan cheese
- 2 teaspoons pine nuts, lightly toasted
- 1 small garlic clove, coarsely chopped (about 1 teaspoon)
- 1/2 cup extra-virgin olive oil
- Ground black pepper

BEAN FRICASSEE

- 1/2 pound wax beans, trimmed and cut into 1-inch lengths
- 3/4 pound green beans, trimmed and cut into 1-inch lengths
- 2 tablespoons extra-virgin olive oil
- 16 pearl onions, peeled, root end trimmed, and quartered
- 1 cup low-sodium chicken broth
- 2 medium garlic cloves, minced or pressed through a garlic press (about 1 teaspoon)

- 1 tablespoon unsalted butter
- 2 medium beefsteak tomatoes (about 8 ounces each), cored, seeded, and diced fine
- 1 medium lemon, peeled, seeded, and diced fine
- 1/4 cup pitted and finely chopped Kalamata olives
- 2 tablespoons sliced almonds
- 2 tablespoons finely chopped fresh basil leaves
- 2 tablespoons finely chopped fresh parsley leaves
- Salt and ground black pepper

SCALLOPS

- 1/2 cup all-purpose flour
- Salt and ground black pepper
- 1 large egg
- 1 cup panko (Japanese-style bread crumbs) or Homemade Panko (page 17)
- 24 large "dry" (see headnote) sea scallops (1 1/2–2 pounds), patted dry with paper towels, tendons removed (see the illustration on page 64)
- 3 tablespoons vegetable oil

1. For the pistou: Bring 1 gallon water and 1 tablespoon salt to a boil in a large pot over high heat. Fill a large bowl with ice water. Add the basil to the boiling water and blanch for 2 minutes. Using a wire-mesh strainer or tongs, transfer the basil to the ice water (leaving the water on the stove to boil). Using your hands, squeeze out as much liquid as possible from the basil. Transfer the basil, Parmesan, pine nuts, garlic, and olive oil to a food processor and process until smooth, about 1 minute. Season with salt and pepper to taste. Transfer to a small bowl. Set aside.

2. For the bean fricassee: Add the wax beans to the boiling water and cook until just tender, 5 to 6 minutes. Using a wire-mesh strainer, transfer the beans to the ice water. Add the greens beans to the boiling water and cook until just tender, 5 to 6 minutes. Transfer to the ice water and cool. Drain the beans and set aside.

3. Heat the olive oil in a large skillet over medium-high heat until just shimmering. Add the pearl onions and cook, stirring frequently, until just translucent, 2 to 3 minutes. Add the chicken broth and cook until reduced by half, about 4 minutes. Add the beans, garlic, and butter and cook until lightly glazed, 1 to 2 minutes. Gently stir in the tomatoes, lemon, olives, almonds, basil, and parsley. Adjust the seasoning with salt and pepper. Cover and set aside.

4. For the scallops: Spread the flour in a shallow dish or pie plate and season with salt and pepper to taste. Lightly beat the egg in a second shallow dish. Spread the panko in a third dish. Working with one scallop at a time, dredge one side in the flour, shaking off the excess. Carefully dip the floured side of the scallop into the egg mixture, allowing the excess to drip off. Finally dip the floured and egged side of the scallop into the panko, and press the crumbs lightly to adhere. Place the breaded scallops on a large plate in a single layer.

5. Heat the vegetable oil in a large skillet over medium-high heat until shimmering. Add half the scallops, breading-side down, and cook until golden brown, 2 to 2½ minutes. Using tongs, flip the scallops and cook the second side until lightly browned, 1 to 2 minutes. Transfer to a large, clean plate and tent with foil to keep warm. Repeat the process with the remaining scallops.

6. To serve: Divide the fricassee equally among 6 warmed shallow bowls and place the scallops on top, breading-side up. Top each scallop with a small dollop of pistou and serve immediately.

Jambalaya

Adapted from Seafood Jambalaya

Tim Schafer's Cooking with Passion, Morristown, New Jersey

JAMBALAYA IS USUALLY A ONE-POT DISH that includes rice, shrimp, chicken, sausage, tomatoes, and Cajun spices. Giving his own twist to this classic New Orleans dish, Chef Schafer leaves the rice off to the side and makes the jambalaya more like a spicy Cajun stew. Still employing just one pot, the success of this recipe depends on knowing both how the ingredients are prepared and when to add them to the pot.

The ingredient preparation is unusual for jambalaya in that most of them are minced, diced, or sliced, which cuts even the main characters of chicken, tasso (a highly spiced pork shoulder), and andouille down to a fork-friendly size. Not only does this make the jambalaya easy to eat, but it helps standardize the cooking time.

Taking a closer look at the ingredient list, we made just a few changes. Originally, the recipe started off rendering one pound of bacon for both fat and flavor. The dirty little secret of most restaurants is that they cook with far more fat than home cooks (that's why they cook behind closed doors). Although Schafer's version is tasty, we trimmed the bacon back to half a pound with no negative effect on the flavor. The original recipe also called for one cup each of tomato puree and crushed tomatoes—easy enough in a restaurant, where both are readily available, but at home this would require opening two cans, then using only a small portion of each. Instead, we found it easy to use all crushed tomatoes. The problem with crushed tomatoes, however, is that their consistency can range dramatically from chunky to smooth depending on the brand. To standardize their consistency, we pulsed the crushed tomatoes in a food processor until fairly smooth, simulating the texture of partly crushed, partly pureed tomatoes.

Now on to the second crucial aspect of this one-pot meal: when to add the various ingredients to the pot. Not only do some of the ingredients have small windows of time between raw and overcooked (such as chicken and shrimp), but some ingredients taste far better if they have seen dry heat. Bacon, for example, is an ingredient that requires being cooked in a dry, hot pan, rather than being simmered with the crushed tomatoes and broth. Lining the ingredients up into an efficient queue, it is important to note whether dry or moist heat is required. After rendering the bacon, we added the minced vegetables, salt, and spices. Coated lightly with bacon fat, the vegetables sauté and get a little brown around the edges, adding depth of flavor. The spices also taste deeper and fuller when allowed to toast in the hot fat. Many spices are oil-soluble (as opposed to water-soluble) and therefore release more of their flavorful compounds when cooked first in oil.

Adding the salt early in the cooking process (often called "preloading") ensures that all the ingredients will taste well seasoned and encourages the vegetables to release their moisture and flavor into the pot.

Next, the tasso and chicken are added and given a few minutes to heat through and become coated by the spicy, flavorful fat. Then the tomato paste and flour are stirred into the pot. It is important for the tomato paste and flour to see dry heat, so that the paste can lose its tinny, canned flavor and the flour can mix with the bacon fat to make a thickening paste (known as a roux). Finally, the crushed tomatoes and some chicken broth are added and the mixture is brought to a simmer. Wanting the flavors to meld without overcooking the chicken, we found a simmering time of 15 minutes was just right. Finally, we added andouille and shrimp, neither of which require dry heat, but just a brief cooking time before serving. Seasoned with Worcestershire sauce, Tabasco, and black pepper, this jambalaya is knock-your-socks-off spicy, so be sure to serve it with a bowl of plain white rice and a large pitcher of iced tea.

Jambalaya

SERVES 12

Several brands of Cajun seasoning can be found in the spice aisle at the supermarket. Crushed tomatoes, depending on the brand, can vary in consistency from smooth to chunky. Pulse the tomatoes in a food processor to achieve a smooth consistency.

- **½ pound (about 8 slices) bacon, sliced crosswise into ¼-inch-wide pieces**
- **1 large onion, minced**
- **1 large carrot, minced**
- **2 medium celery ribs, minced**
- **1 small red bell pepper, seeded and minced**
- **1 small green pepper, seeded and minced**
- **6 garlic cloves, minced or pressed through a garlic press (about 2 tablespoons)**
- **1 tablespoon Cajun seasoning**
- **Salt**
- **½ pound tasso, cut into ¾-inch dice**
- **1 pound boneless skinless chicken breasts, cut into ¾-inch dice**
- **1 tablespoon all-purpose flour**
- **2 tablespoons tomato paste**
- **1 (14-ounce) can crushed tomatoes (see headnote)**
- **1 cup low-sodium chicken broth**
- **1 pound medium shrimp (41–50 per pound), peeled and deveined**
- **8 ounces andouille sausage, cut into ¼-inch-thick rounds**
- **1 teaspoon Worcestershire sauce**
- **Tabasco sauce**
- **Ground black pepper**

1. Cook the bacon in a Dutch oven over medium heat until crisp and brown, 6 to 8 minutes. Stir in the onion, carrot, celery, red bell pepper, green bell pepper, garlic, Cajun seasoning, and ¼ teaspoon salt and cook until the vegetables are softened, about 8 minutes. Stir in the tasso and chicken and cook until the chicken begins to turn white, about 3 minutes. Stir in the flour and tomato paste and cook until the flour has dissolved, about 30 seconds. Add the crushed tomatoes and chicken broth, increase the heat to medium-high, and bring to a simmer. Reduce the heat to low and simmer until the chicken is cooked through, about 15 minutes longer.

2. Stir in the shrimp and andouille and cook until the shrimp are pink and curled, about 5 minutes. Season with Worcestershire, Tabasco, and salt and pepper to taste. Serve immediately.

Barbecued Shrimp *with* Corn & Goat Cheese Torta

Adapted from "Criolla Mama" BBQ Shrimp with Corn and Goat Cheese Torta

Norman's, Miami, Florida

SOMETIMES A RESTAURANT MEAL IS WORTH every penny—the culinary expertise and exhaustive preparation are writ large across the plate. A case in point is a dish devised by Norman van Aken called "Criolla Mama" BBQ Shrimp with Corn and Goat Cheese Torta. It's a showstopper of a dish: gargantuan shrimp are tossed in a fiery tomato-and-pepper–based sauce, which is then draped around a tall stack of fresh corn griddle cakes sandwiching a goat cheese and corn filling. The spicy, multiflavored complements up the shrimp's sweet, briny flavor, and the mild torta soothes the sauce's burn. And the combination of textures—chewy shrimp, tender cakes, and unctuous goat cheese—is as finely balanced as the flavors. Our goal was to pare down the recipe's exhaustive ingredient list and exacting method to make it accessible to the home cook, who usually lacks a batterie of prep cooks and a full-time dishwasher.

First things first, we broke the dish down into its three components: the "criolla mama" sauce; the corn griddle cakes, sandwiched three-high with a mixture of corn kernels and goat cheese; and the shrimp. As the sauce was the most time-consuming element, we decided it was the best place to start. Literally translated, *criolla* means "native," but it is used more loosely to refer to Caribbean Creole-style cooking, which is clearly an influence in this dish. The sauce is built on a base of rendered bacon, onion, garlic, chile, bell pepper, and celery—the classic ingredients of a sofrito (the sautéed ingredients that start off most Latin American sauces). The restaurant then rounds out the sauce with a variety of other ingredients that we sensed could be pared down for the home cook without seriously compromising the flavor. For example, the recipe calls for three sources of chile heat: Scotch bonnet chiles (a close relative of the habanero, with which they can be substituted), ground cayenne pepper, and Tabasco sauce. Admittedly, each ingredient added a slightly different flavor and degree of "heat," but we found that the Scotch bonnets, with the seeds included, provided enough kick to make the cayenne and Tabasco redundant. For herbs, we omitted basil for a simpler combination of thyme and oregano—tasters felt the basil contributed the least. And instead of laboriously picking and mincing the leaves, we favored a bouquet garni, a bundle of the herbs simmered in the sauce and removed prior to serving: the flavors were just as intense, but with none of the labor.

Our last two alterations to the sauce were

for stock and tomatoes. Van Aken originally requested "sea creature" stock, a shellfish-based stock of his own creation that we found to be too time-consuming. Bottled clam juice lent the proper briny maritime depth to the sauce. As for tomatoes, the recipe specified "tomato concassé," a classical cooking term for peeled, seeded, and roughly chopped fresh tomatoes. Concassé is laborious, so we favored canned diced tomatoes, which possessed all of the flavor without the work. With such minor adjustments, an all-day project was now reduced to a more manageable two hours.

With the sauce simmering away, we tackled the torta, which is composed of two parts: cakes and filling. The cakes themselves are little more than silver-dollar pancakes flavored with cornmeal and fresh corn. As fresh corn is available only during summer's high months, we opted to use frozen corn. A standout technique in this recipe was pureeing a portion of the corn into the pancake's liquid ingredients, which suffused the pancake with a sweet corn flavor. To reinforce the flavor and add texture, we then whisked in whole corn kernels. Chemical leavener—baking powder, in this instance—was kept to a minimum, as much of the "lift" was provided by whipped egg whites.

The filling for the cakes is nothing but fresh goat cheese blended with sautéed corn and flavored with garlic. Once again, we replaced the fresh corn with frozen to little detriment. The only other minor adjustment was replacing a dash of heavy cream with milk to minimize the ingredient list—the flavor difference went unnoticed by tasters.

Finishing the dish was a simple matter of cooking the shrimp and assembling the tortas. The original recipe called for sautéing the shrimp with shallots before tossing them in the sauce. We found that the sauce was flavorful enough without the shallots or the sautéing step and so we excluded them. The flavor differences were slight when compared with the original recipe, and our method had saved on labor, cooking time, and dishes—everything we had hoped to accomplish.

Barbecued Shrimp with Corn and Goat Cheese Torta

SERVES 4

To plate this dish, the restaurant sets a torta in the center and positions the shrimp around the periphery, spooning the sauce over the shrimp. The sauce can be prepared up to three days ahead of time and stored in an airtight container, but the pancakes, torta filling, and shrimp are all best prepared on the same day the dish is served. If time is short, the restaurant suggests substituting white rice for the tortas.

SPICY SAUCE

- **6 sprigs fresh thyme**
- **2 sprigs fresh oregano**
- **2 ounces bacon (about 2 slices), diced fine**
- **1 tablespoon olive oil**
- **1 small Scotch bonnet (or habanero) chile, stemmed and minced (including seeds)**
- **3 medium garlic cloves, minced or pressed through a garlic press**
- **1 small red onion, diced medium**
- **1 teaspoon sugar**
- **1 large celery rib, diced medium**
- **1 small yellow (or red) bell pepper, cored, seeded, and diced medium**
- **Salt and ground black pepper**
- **4 teaspoons sherry vinegar**
- **2 cups bottled clam juice**
- **1 1/2 cups canned diced tomatoes, well drained (about one and one-half 14.5-ounce cans)**

CORN CAKES, FILLING, AND SHRIMP

- 1/4 cup fine yellow cornmeal
- 1/4 cup all-purpose flour
- 1/4 teaspoon baking powder
- 1/4 teaspoon sugar
- Salt
- 1/4 cup plus 2 tablespoons whole milk
- 2 cups frozen corn kernels
- 3 eggs, 2 of the eggs separated
- 4 tablespoons unsalted butter, 3 tablespoons melted
- 1 tablespoon olive oil, plus more as necessary
- 2 medium garlic cloves, minced or pressed through a garlic press
- 4 ounces goat cheese (about 1/2 cup), softened
- Ground black pepper
- 1 1/2 pounds jumbo shrimp (16 to 20 per pound), peeled and deveined

1. For the sauce: With a 4-inch piece of kitchen twine, tie together the thyme and oregano sprigs; set aside. Heat the bacon and olive oil in a large heavy-bottomed saucepan over medium-high heat and cook, stirring occasionally, until most of the fat is rendered, about 4 to 5 minutes. Add the Scotch bonnet, garlic, and red onion and, stirring frequently, cook until the onion is softened and beginning to brown, about 3 to 4 minutes. Add the sugar, celery, bell pepper, ½ teaspoon salt, and ½ teaspoon ground black pepper and cook, continuing to stir frequently, until the peppers begin to soften, about 5 minutes. Add the vinegar and cook until evaporated, about 30 seconds. Add the bundled herbs and 1 cup of the clam juice and cook until the liquid is almost evaporated, about 10 minutes. Reduce the heat to medium, add the tomatoes and the remaining clam juice, and simmer until the sauce is reduced to 2½ cups, about 25 minutes. Adjust seasonings with salt and pepper, cover, and keep warm.

2. For the corn cakes: Adjust an oven rack to the middle position and heat the oven to 200 degrees. Combine the cornmeal, flour, baking powder, sugar, and ½ teaspoon salt in a mixing bowl; set aside. Combine ¼ cup of the milk and ½ cup of the corn kernels in a blender and process until smooth, about 30 seconds; set aside.

3. In a medium mixing bowl, gently whisk together the whole egg and the 2 yolks. Stir in the creamed corn mixture, another ½ cup corn kernels, and the 3 tablespoons melted

PEELING SHRIMP

1. Holding the tail end of the shrimp with one hand and the opposite end with the other, bend the shrimp side to side to split the shell.

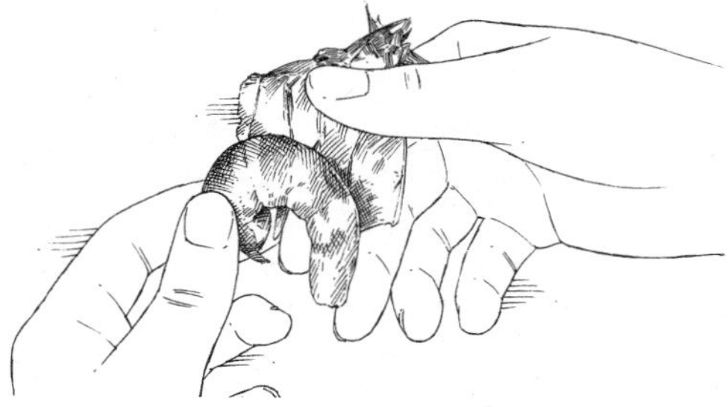

2. Lift off the tail portion of the shell, then slide your thumb under the legs of the remaining portion and lift it off as well.

butter; mix in the dry ingredients until just combined. In a separate bowl, beat the egg whites until stiff. Fold the whipped whites into the corn mixture.

4. Heat 1 tablespoon oil in a large nonstick skillet over medium-high heat for 2 minutes and swirl the oil to coat the pan. Add 2 tablespoons of batter per cake and cook until golden brown, about 30 to 45 seconds. Using a thin spatula, flip the cakes and cook the second side until browned, about 30 seconds. Transfer to a wire cooling rack set over a rimmed baking sheet and keep warm in the oven. Repeat the process, adding more oil as necessary, until all of the batter is cooked (there should be 12 cakes).

5. FOR THE FILLING: Heat the remaining 1 tablespoon butter in a large nonstick skillet over medium-high heat until foaming subsides and add the garlic and remaining 1 cup corn. Cook, stirring frequently, until the corn begins to brown, about 1½ minutes. Add the remaining 2 tablespoons milk and transfer the mixture to a bowl. Mix in the goat cheese and season to taste with salt and ground pepper.

6. TO ASSEMBLE THE TORTAS: Spread 2 tablespoons of the filling on one corn cake and top with a second; spread another 2 tablespoons of filling on this layer and top with a third cake; set aside. Repeat the process with the remaining corn cakes and filling to make 4 tortas total. Keep warm while you cook the shrimp.

7. TO SERVE: Add the shrimp to the sauce over medium-high heat and cook, stirring frequently, until the shrimp have turned pink and firm, about 3 to 5 minutes. Position one torta in the center of each of 4 large plates and arrange the shrimp around the perimeter of each torta. Divide the sauce evenly among the 4 plates and serve immediately.

Shrimp & Grits

Adapted from Shrimp and Grits

Loretta's, Mobile, Alabama

THE COMBINATION OF SHRIMP AND GRITS is a classic in the South, and Loretta's in downtown Mobile is the place to eat it. Although the recipe is fairly short, it came with ample text explaining the proper way to make grits. Since *Cook's Illustrated* is based in Boston and most of us are native Yankees, we knew better than to take any liberties with this authentic grits recipe.

This recipe calls for coarse-ground grits and includes explicit instructions not to use instant grits. Although we found only one type of noninstant grits in our northern supermarkets, Quaker, we were able to track down coarse-ground grits sold in bulk in a natural food store. Grits, which look very much like polenta, are actually ground hominy—corn from which the hull and germ have been removed, either mechanically or chemically. Comparing the coarse, natural-food-store grits to the less coarse Quaker, tasters preferred the coarse, but were not offended by the Quaker.

The key to making grits, as Loretta's described, is cooking them in a double boiler, which eliminates any possibility of scorching. Using a combination of water and milk, the grits are cooked much like polenta. Liquid is brought to a boil and seasoned, then the grits are slowly poured amidst constant stirring to prevent any lumps. The grits are then simmered until tender, additional liquid being added along the way to prevent them from drying out. Before serving, we found it necessary to adjust their consistency with additional hot water, since the grits have the ability to soak up seemingly endless amounts of liquid.

With the grits held warm in the double boiler off the heat, we moved on to the shrimp. Flavored with bacon and garlic, the shrimp are sautéed and finished with a sherry-and-cream-based pan sauce. At Loretta's, of course, the chefs cook only one serving of shrimp at a time. However, we needed to change the method slightly to accommodate the larger batch. Cooking the bacon first, we then used the bacon grease to cook the shrimp. After sautéing the shrimp until tender, we removed them from the pan to make the pan sauce. The recipe called for sherry and heavy cream to be reduced together, and we found that the fresh, cream flavor got lost in the longer simmering time necessary for the larger batch. We found it better to reduce the sherry on its own and finish it with a fresh splash of cream. After returning the shrimp and their accumulated juices to the pan, we tossed the shrimp with the sauce to coat. Garnished with the light onion flavor of chives, the grits and shrimp are surprisingly hearty and make for a nearly complete meal.

Shrimp and Grits

SERVES 6

Grits are sold in three textures: fine, medium, and coarse. Although this recipe calls for coarse grits, fine or medium will work if coarse are not available. If a double boiler is not available, use a large metal bowl set over a large pot filled with boiling water.

- **4 cups boiling water**
- **Salt**
- **2 cups coarse-ground grits (not instant)**
- **2 cups whole milk, plus more if needed**
- **4 slices bacon, cut into ¼-inch pieces**
- **2 pounds extra-large shrimp (21–25 per pound), peeled and deveined**
- **2 garlic cloves, minced or pressed through a garlic press (about 2 teaspoons)**
- **2 cups dry sherry**
- **¼ cup heavy cream**
- **Ground black pepper**
- **2 tablespoons minced fresh chives**

1. Bring 2 inches of water to a boil in the bottom of a double boiler over high heat. Insert the top of the double boiler. Add the 4 cups boiling water and ½ teaspoon salt to the pan. Slowly pour in the grits, whisking constantly, until all are incorporated. Cook, adding the milk as necessary to prevent the grits from drying out, about ¼ cup at a time until the grits are fully cooked and tender, about 45 minutes. Finish with milk or water to reach the desired consistency. Remove the double boiler from the heat, cover tightly with foil, and set aside.

2. Cook the bacon in a 12-inch nonstick skillet over medium-high heat until crisp, about 5 minutes. Transfer the bacon to a plate lined with several layers of paper towels and set aside. Pour off all but 1 tablespoon fat from the skillet. Return the skillet to medium-high heat, add the shrimp, and sauté until almost cooked through, about 2 minutes. Add the garlic and sauté until fragrant, about 30 seconds. Transfer the shrimp to a clean bowl.

3. Return the skillet to medium-high heat, add the sherry, and simmer, scraping up the browned bits from the bottom of the pan, until it has reduced to about ¼ cup, about 12 minutes. Stir in the cream and simmer until slightly thickened, about 1 minute. Season with salt and pepper to taste. Return the shrimp to the pan and toss to coat and warm through, about 30 seconds. Remove the pan from the heat.

4. Stir the grits and add hot water, ¼ cup at a time, to adjust their consistency. Divide the grits among 6 individual bowls and top with the shrimp and sauce. Garnish with the bacon and chives. Serve immediately.

Flambéed Pan-Roasted Lobster

Adapted from Pan-Roasted Lobster

The Summer Shack, Cambridge, Massachusetts

WHEN IT COMES TO LOBSTER, MOST PEOPLE follow the tried-and-true and boil it, serving the whole crustacean with a side of drawn butter and a bib. Not that there's anything wrong with tradition, but Jasper White, the renowned New England–based chef, has long applied another practice that we think—at the risk of sounding heretical—produces tastier results. White "pan-roasts" his lobster, employing a combination of high-heat stovetop cooking, the broiler, and flambéing. The intense heat yields very rich-flavored, succulent lobster meat—nothing rubbery or bland here. And to replace the side of butter, White whips up a quick pan sauce from the lobster drippings, shallots, bourbon, and tomalley—the lobster's liver. Everything's feasible for the home cook, and we highly recommend that lobster lovers give this dish a whirl, though be forewarned: the bravura cooking method takes some steely nerves and kitchen confidence.

Progress no further if you are unwilling to kill a live lobster. Some people—even a few pacifists in the test kitchen—are unwilling to commit the deed, so we fully understand any reticence. The first step in preparing the dish is halving the lobster lengthwise and quartering it—separating the head from the tail and the claws from the body. The head doesn't contain much meat, but it does lend flavor to the dish, so we include it. The best tool for the job is a large heavy-duty chef's knife or cleaver, which can easily puncture the hard shell without damage to the blade. Center the blade on the lobster's upper portion (that is, the head) and give it a sturdy whack with the mallet. The blade should cleanly cleave the lobster in two. If the knife's blade is short, you may need to finish splitting the tail. The halved lobster may twitch a bit, but it's strictly reflexive—by no means is it alive at this point. The claws can be easily cut at their narrow junction with the body. The legs should be left attached; they don't have much meat inside, but they're great to nibble on.

The lobsters are now ready for cooking. The original recipe specifies heating the skillet on the stovetop over high heat for upward of five minutes before adding the peanut oil and segmented lobsters, but we found this a little dangerous for the home kitchen. Instead, we preferred to heat the oil in the skillet over high heat until smoking. The lobsters are added to the pan shell-side down; otherwise the meat overcooks. The high heat effectively roasts the shells, which imbues the meat with an intense, almost nutty flavor. When the shells are flame red and lightly speckled with browned or blackened spots, the pan is transferred to the broiler to cook the exposed meat.

Now the recipe starts getting really interesting. The skillet is removed from the broiler, returned to the stovetop, and the lobster is flambéed with a shot of bourbon or cognac. For those who have never flambéed before, it's a little intimidating, but fun, too. And it's for more than just show: in a side-by-side taste test using shrimp and bourbon, we found the flambéed shrimp more fully flavored than those in which the bourbon had just been reduced. In a restaurant kitchen, there's little worry about setting things alight, but the home kitchen presents a different story. White specifies one-quarter cup of bourbon, enough to send a two-foot curtain of flames skyward when ignited—way too dangerous for the home kitchen. For a safer method, we allow the bourbon to reduce for 10 seconds prior to ignition. The flames are lower and the flavor the same. A long fireplace or grill match is the safest bet for lighting the alcohol.

After the lobster is flambéed, it is removed from the pan and what is essentially a classic pan sauce is quickly "built" in the skillet. Shallots are sautéed and the reserved tomalley and a splash of white wine are added. Despite its unappetizing hue, the tomalley packs an intense flavor and is important to the end result. But if the tomalley leaves you cold, exclude it—the sauce will still taste fine. Drizzled with the sauce, the lobster makes for messy eating (and still requires a bib), but it's well worth it.

Flambéed Pan-Roasted Lobster

SERVES 2

If you want to prepare more than two lobsters, we suggest that you engage some help. This dish requires close attention, and managing multiple extremely hot pans can be tricky. Before flambéing, make sure to roll up long shirtsleeves, tie back long hair, turn off the exhaust fan (otherwise the fan may pull up the flames), and turn off any lit burners (this is critical if you have a gas stove). For equipment, you will need a large ovensafe skillet, oven mitts, a pair of tongs, and long fireplace or grill matches.

- **2 live lobsters, 1 1/2–2 pounds each**
- **2 tablespoons peanut or canola oil**
- **1/4 cup bourbon or cognac**
- **6 tablespoons (3/4 stick) unsalted butter, cut into 6 pieces**
- **2 medium shallots, minced**
- **3 tablespoons dry white wine**
- **1 teaspoon minced fresh tarragon**
- **1 tablespoon minced fresh chives**
- **Salt and ground black pepper**
- **1 lemon, cut into wedges (optional)**

1. To quarter the lobsters: Using a large, heavy-duty chef's knife or cleaver, which can easily puncture the hard shell without damage to the blade, center the blade lengthwise on the lobster's upper portion (its head) and give it a sturdy whack with a mallet. Then split again in half to quarter. Break the claws free from the head and, using a spoon, remove and reserve the green tomalley, if desired. Keep the split lobsters shell-side down. (Don't be put off if the lobsters continue to twitch a little after quartering: it's a reflexive movement.)

2. Adjust an oven rack so it is 6 inches from the broiler element and heat the broiler.

Heat the peanut oil in a large ovensafe skillet over high heat until smoking. Add the lobster pieces shell-side down in a single layer and cook, without disturbing, until the shells are bright red and lightly browned, 2 to 3 minutes. Transfer the skillet to the broiler and cook until the tail meat is just opaque, about 2 minutes.

3. Remove the pan from the oven and return it to the stovetop. Off the heat, pour the bourbon over the lobsters. Wait for 10 seconds, then light a long match and wave it over the skillet until the bourbon ignites. Return the pan to medium-high heat and shake it until the flames subside. Transfer the lobster pieces to a warmed serving bowl and tent with foil to keep warm.

4. Using tongs, remove any congealed albumen (white substance) from the skillet and add 2 tablespoons of the butter and the shallots. Cook, stirring constantly, until the shallots are softened and lightly browned, 1 to 2 minutes. Add the tomalley and white wine and stir until completely combined. Remove the skillet from the heat and add the tarragon and chives. Stirring constantly, add the remaining 4 tablespoons butter, 1 piece at a time, until fully emulsified. Season with salt and pepper to taste. Pour the sauce over the lobster pieces. Serve immediately, accompanied by the lemon wedges, if desired.

Baja Bouillabaisse

Adapted from Baja Bouillabaisse

Janos, Tucson, Arizona

THE FUSION FOOD FAD SEEMS TO HAVE spread rapidly in the past decade. While this mixing of cultures and foodstuffs often leads to interesting and innovative dishes, in the hands of the inexperienced it can lead to disaster. This recipe from Janos thankfully fits into the first category. The chef deftly puts a new spin on the quintessential Mediterranean stew, bouillabaisse, giving it a southwestern flair. While we were impressed with the fresh approach to this classic, the recipe required some adaptation to make it accessible to the home cook.

In order to address the issues we had with this recipe, we broke it down into its different components: the broth, the fish, the garnishes, and the rouille. As for the broth, Janos's recipe called for the use of fish stock to form its base. Considering that we were trying to simplify the recipe, we didn't think it worth investing the time making fish stock. We instead experimented with bottled clam juice, which worked admirably and provided the broth with just the right amount of briny ocean flavor. We also examined the recipe's use of peeled, seeded, and diced tomatoes in the broth. Again, we felt we could save time if we substituted canned diced tomatoes for fresh, which in the end gave the broth the same flavor.

Next up was the fish. Like most bouillabaisse, the recipe called for a mixture of different sea creatures. Janos's recipe called for several types of fish that we were concerned would not be available to all home cooks. For example, the recipe called for guaymas shrimp and cabrilla, which are found in the waters surrounding Baja. Both were easily replaced with regular shrimp and monkfish, readily available in most fish markets.

Instead of simmering the fish and shellfish in the broth, like most bouillabaisse, Janos's recipe suggests cooking the scallops, shrimp, and fish separately on the grill. While we liked this idea, and it certainly made the dish different, we felt this step was too laborious for the everyday cook. For a restaurant, where the grill is indoors and an essential feature of the kitchen, this isn't a problem. But for the home cook, this grilling step presents an unnecessary difficulty.

The bouillabaisse garnishes, which consisted of a small dice of squash and red pepper, peas, and roasted Anaheim chiles, gave the finished dish dramatic color and added substance. The roasted Anaheim chiles also gave the bouillabaisse its southwestern flair and a spicy punch—so much so that we had to decrease the number of chiles from 16 to 6 for those less heat tolerant. We also chose to omit the red pepper dice, feeling that it was superfluous, especially with the addition of the rouille. We also opted to use frozen peas, an invaluable time-saver that didn't sacrifice quality.

All that was left to do now was to focus on the rouille and croutons. Rouille, the classic accompaniment to bouillabaisse, is made by emulsifying olive oil into a mixture of red pepper, bread, and garlic. Having the consistency of mayonnaise, rouille is often placed on a slice of garlic toast, which is then floated on top of the bouillabaisse. Janos made its rouille in the traditional manner, except for using a raw red pepper in place of a roasted one. While we liked the flavor of the rouille, leaving the skins on the pepper gave it an off-putting consistency. Considering that we were already roasting the Anaheim chiles, we decided to roast the red peppers as well. We then used the peeled red peppers to make the rouille, and found that we no longer disliked the consistency. Also, the subtle smokiness of the roasted peppers heightened the flavor of the chiles.

The original recipe called for garlic toast to be served with the bouillabaisse. Given that the broiler was already on from roasting the peppers, it occurred to us that we could easily toast slices of bread brushed with oil and garlic. In testing this procedure, we also found that we regularly had leftover bread, which was easily utilized in the rouille. And that was one less ingredient for the home cook to worry about.

Baja Bouillabaisse

SERVES 6

The monkfish's firm flesh makes it perfect for bouillabaisse. Just make sure that the dark outer membrane has been removed before cooking, something that your fishmonger will be happy to do.

- **2 medium red bell peppers**
- **6 Anaheim chiles**
- **4 cups bottled clam juice**
- **1 cup dry white wine**
- **2 tablespoons brandy**
- **1 (14.5-ounce) can diced tomatoes in juice**
- **1/4 teaspoon saffron threads**
- **3/4 cup olive oil**
- **3 large garlic cloves, minced or pressed through a garlic press (about 3 teaspoons)**
- **1 baguette, cut into twelve 1/2-inch-thick slices, the remaining bread trimmed of crust and cut into small cubes (about 1 cup)**
- **Salt and ground black pepper**
- **1 1/2 pounds firm-fleshed fish, such as monkfish or halibut, cut into 1 1/2-inch cubes**
- **18 mussels (about 1 pound), scrubbed and debearded**
- **12 littleneck clams (about 1 pound), scrubbed**
- **12 extra-large shrimp (21–25 per pound), peeled and deveined**
- **12 large sea scallops, tendons removed**
- **1 zucchini, cut into 1/8-inch dice (about 1 cup)**
- **1 yellow summer squash, cut into 1/8-inch dice (about 1 cup)**
- **1/2 cup frozen peas**

1. Adjust an oven rack so it is 6 inches away from the broiler element and heat the broiler. Cut ¼ inch off both the tops and bottoms of the bell and Anaheim peppers and remove the seeds. Slice through one side of each pepper so they lay flat, and trim away the white ribs. Lay the peppers skin-side up on a rimmed baking sheet lined with heavy-duty foil. Broil the peppers until the skin is charred and puffed but the flesh is still firm, 8 to 10 minutes,

turning the pan around halfway through. Remove the pan from the oven without turning off the broiler, cover with foil, and allow the peppers to steam for 5 minutes. Peel and discard the skins. Set aside the red bell peppers for the rouille. Cut the Anaheim chiles into ¼-inch-wide strips and set aside.

2. Bring the clam juice, wine, brandy, tomatoes, and saffron to a boil in a Dutch oven over medium-high heat. Reduce the heat to medium-low and simmer until the flavors are melded, about 5 minutes.

3. Meanwhile, combine ¼ cup of the olive oil and 1 teaspoon of the garlic in a small bowl. Place the bread slices in a single layer on a rimmed baking sheet. Brush both sides with the olive oil mixture and broil until lightly toasted, about 1½ minutes. Flip the slices and broil until lightly toasted on the second side, about 1½ minutes. Set aside.

4. Process the roasted red bell peppers, bread cubes, remaining 2 teaspoons garlic, ¼ teaspoon salt, and ¼ teaspoon pepper in a food processor until smooth, about 30 seconds. With the machine running, slowly drizzle in the remaining ½ cup olive oil and process until all the oil is incorporated and the rouille is thick. Set aside.

5. Add the fish, mussels, clams, shrimp, scallops, zucchini, and squash to the clam juice mixture and return to a simmer. Simmer for 5 minutes, stirring occasionally. Remove the pot from heat, add the peas and roasted Anaheim chiles. Let stand, covered, until the fish is cooked through and the mussels and clams have opened, about 3 minutes. (Discard any mussels or clams that have not opened by this time.) Season with salt and pepper to taste.

6. Ladle the bouillabaisse into 6 bowls and float 2 croutons topped with rouille onto each serving. Serve immediately.

INGREDIENTS: Canned Tomatoes

Canned whole tomatoes are the closest product to fresh. Whole tomatoes, either plum or round, are steamed to remove their skins and then packed in tomato juice or puree. We prefer tomatoes that are packed in juice; they generally have a fresher, livelier flavor than tomatoes packed in puree, which has a cooked tomato flavor that imparts a slightly stale, tired taste to the whole can.

To find the best canned whole tomatoes, we tasted eight brands, both straight from the can and in a simple tomato sauce. Muir Glen (an organic brand available in most supermarkets and natural food stores) finished at the head of the pack. S&W "Ready-Cut" (a West Coast brand) and Redpack (Redgold on the West Coast) also rated well and are recommended.

Diced tomatoes are simply whole tomatoes that have been roughly chopped during processing and then packed with juice. For most recipes, we prefer diced tomatoes to whole tomatoes because they save time and effort. Why chop canned tomatoes (a messy proposition at best) if you don't have to? Unless otherwise indicated, use the entire contents of the can (both the diced tomatoes and the juice) in recipes.

THE BEST CANNED TOMATOES

Muir Glen diced tomatoes have a fresh, lively flavor (they are packed in juice, not puree) and are recipe ready.

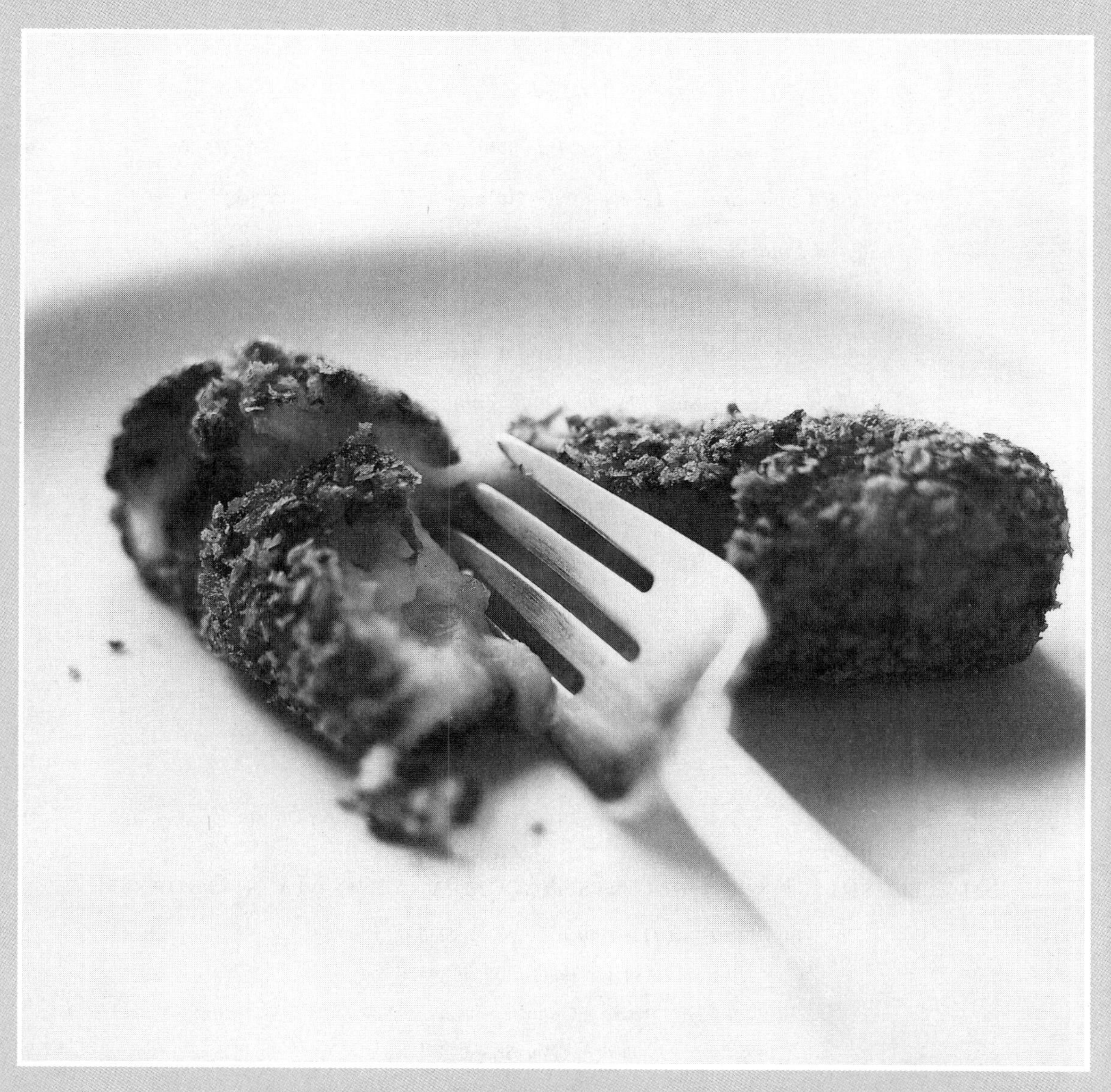

3 SIDE DISHES

Side Dishes

Sides Dishes & Condiments Accompanying Main Courses

Spicy Chile-Fried Edamame

Adapted from Wok-Charred Soybeans with Garlic and Chiles

Alan Wong's, The Pineapple Room, Honolulu, Hawaii

Edamame are a specialty variety of immature, green soybean that are sold either in their pods or shelled. The fuzzy pods contain two or three beans that are sweet and buttery, with a firm texture that can be likened to a cross between a sweet pea and a lima bean. Edamame are a traditional Japanese bar food. The pods are blanched and sprinkled with salt. The beans are then squeezed from the pods, and eaten as we would eat peanuts—and are just as addictive. This version from Alan Wong's elevates the lowly bean to a delicious side dish that's easy to prepare and fun to eat.

By its nature, stir-frying is quick. This side dish recipe is quicker than most, with little advance preparation necessary. Edamame are most commonly available frozen in one-pound bags, so that's what we used when testing this recipe. In our first test, we thawed the pods, then proceeded with the stir-fry. We unanimously came to the conclusion that although the edamame are blanched prior to freezing, a quick stir-fry was not enough to cook the inner bean thoroughly. We then tried boiling the pods in salted water for six to eight minutes and found that was enough to yield a tender bean.

Next we proceeded to the stir-frying. Woks are the ideal tool for stir-frying on a restaurant stove, where intense flames lick the bottom and sides of the pan, heating the whole surface to an extremely high temperature. Stir-frying in a wok at home can be frustrating, though, with the bottom of the wok getting hot and the sides, having no direct contact with the heat, getting barely warm. For this reason, we recommend a large nonstick skillet (at least 12 inches in diameter) for the job, set over high heat. The flat bottom of the skillet will absorb enough heat to stir-fry adequately, without steaming the vegetables in question.

The cooked edamame are stir-fried with a spicy-sweet-salty sauce consisting of serrano chiles, garlic, ginger, soy sauce, and oyster-flavored sauce.

Spicy Chile-Fried Edamame

SERVES 4 TO 6

While the pod itself is inedible, in this dish that's where all the flavor is, which makes eating the edamame a two-step process. The idea is to get the tasty sauce off the outside of the pod as you squeeze the silky beans into your mouth. You can either hold the pod by the tip and remove the beans with your teeth, as you would eat an artichoke leaf, or eat it as the Japanese do, by holding the pod at both ends and pressing the outside seam of the bean against your lips to pop the beans into your mouth. Serve with plenty of napkins and cold beer.

- **1 pound frozen edamame (green soybeans) in their pods**
- **1 tablespoon salt**
- **4 tablespoons peanut oil**
- **2 serrano chiles, seeded and minced**
- **1 (2-inch) piece fresh ginger, peeled and minced (about 2 tablespoons)**
- **2 garlic cloves, minced or pressed through a garlic press (about 2 teaspoons)**
- **3 tablespoons soy sauce**
- **1 tablespoon oyster-flavored sauce**
- **½ teaspoon toasted sesame oil**

1. Bring 4 quarts of water to a boil in a Dutch oven over high heat. Add the edamame and salt, return to a boil, and cook for 6 to 8 minutes, or until the beans inside the pods are tender. Drain and refresh with cold water to stop the cooking.

2. Heat 2 tablespoons of the peanut oil in a 12-inch nonstick skillet over high heat until shimmering. Add the edamame and cook, stirring constantly, until the beans are heated through, 2 to 3 minutes. Push the beans to one side of the pan. Add the remaining 2 tablespoons peanut oil and chiles and cook for 30 seconds, stirring constantly. Add the ginger and garlic and cook, stirring constantly, until fragrant and golden, about 1 minute. Add the soy sauce, oyster-flavored sauce, and sesame oil and cook, stirring constantly, until the liquid has evaporated, about 30 seconds. Serve immediately.

MINCING GINGER

1. Slice the peeled knob of ginger into thin rounds, then fan the rounds out and cut them into thin, matchstick-like strips.

2. Chop the matchsticks crosswise into a fine mince.

Sautéed Spinach *with* Hazelnuts & Crunchy Chickpeas

Adapted from Didi's Spinach, Hazelnuts, and Crunchy Chickpeas

Veggie Planet, Cambridge, Massachusetts

SAUTÉED SPINACH WITH NUTS AND RAISINS is a staple Mediterranean side dish, found in one form or another from Spain to Greece. At Veggie Planet, Chef Didi Emmons puts an updated spin on the dish with the addition of oven-roasted chickpeas and tomatoes. It's hard to imagine how such seemingly disparate ingredients combine, but they do to great effect. The piquancy of the capers intensifies the sweetness of the spinach, and the raisins lend a deep, earthy body to the dish. The tomatoes serve as a splash of fruity flavor and vibrant color—this dish is as visually appealing as it is delicious.

The chickpeas should be the first ingredient prepared; everything else can completed as they cook. Roasting the beans—a technique new to us, though used in Middle Eastern and Indian cooking—intensifies their flavor and renders them slightly crunchy. Using canned chickpeas makes this dish quick and convenient. In fact, we generally find canned chickpeas a suitable substitute for dried, since chickpeas survive the canning process better than any other legume, retaining a firm texture and full, nutty flavor. Before roasting, they need to be thoroughly rinsed, because the liquid the beans are packed in is often quite salty, which will concentrate during roasting to an unpalatable salinity.

Similar in appearance to the chickpeas, hazelnuts lend a sweet richness and crunchy bite to the dish. Like most nuts, hazelnuts benefit from a bit of toasting, which is also the easiest method to remove their tenacious, papery skins. While we normally roast nuts at a lower temperature, we found that, in this instance, they could toast at the same time as the chickpeas (on a separate pan). Within 10 minutes, the nuts were golden and their flavor intensified. Burnt hazelnuts are intensely bitter, so keep a close eye on them. To remove the skin, use friction. When the nuts are cool enough to handle, bundle them in a kitchen towel and vigorously rub them back and forth; they will readily slough their skins (see the illustrations on page 306).

As for the other ingredients, preparation takes little effort at all. The spinach—mature bunched spinach—needs a wash and a quick whirl in a salad spinner. The tomatoes must be seeded; otherwise we found the dish too watery. The raisins benefit from a soak in hot water to soften their leathery exterior. The original recipe suggests adding a portion of the soaking water to the dish, but we found it unnecessary since there was more than enough liquid in the dish between the spinach and the tomatoes' juices. A garlic press makes quick work of the garlic, though hand chopping is only nominally slower.

There's no special technique involved in cooking this dish. We did opt to start the olive oil and minced garlic in a cold pan to reduce the chance of the minced garlic burning and tasting acrid. Once the garlic shows signs of coloring, the raisins, spinach, tomatoes, and capers are added and cooked until the spinach is completely wilted, though not overcooked. It should be a glossy emerald green, not dark olive. Usually, when cooking spinach, the exuded moisture is nothing but a liability, but in this case it blends with the juices exuded by the tomatoes to form a thin sauce that naps the chickpeas. A final touch is a spritz of lemon, courtesy of lemon wedges served alongside. There was little consensus among tasters about how much lemon juice to add to the finished dish, so we left the choice to the diner.

TOASTING AND SKINNING HAZELNUTS

1. Spread the hazelnuts on a rimmed baking sheet and toast until fragrant, about 10 minutes. Transfer the toasted nuts to the center of a clean dish towel.

2. When the nuts are cool enough to handle, bring up the sides of the towel and twist it closed to seal in the nuts.

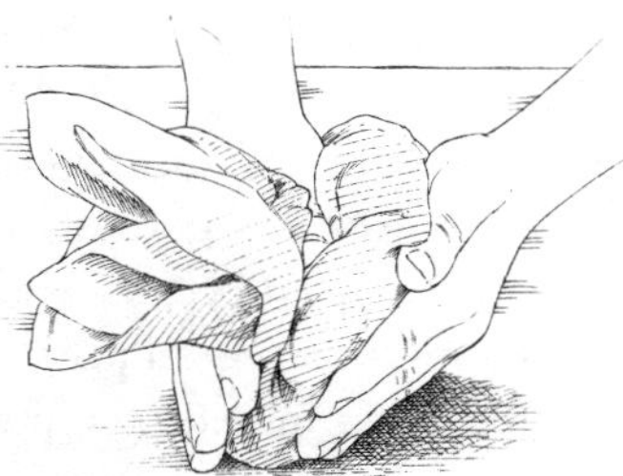

3. Rub the nuts together in the towel, scraping off as much of the brown skin as possible to reveal the light-colored nutmeats. It's fine if patches of skin remain.

4. Carefully open the towel on a flat surface. Gently roll the nuts away from the skins.

Sautéed Spinach with Hazelnuts and Crunchy Chickpeas

SERVES 4 AS A SIDE DISH, 2 AS A LIGHT MAIN COURSE

Resist seasoning the dish until the chickpeas are added, since they can be salty. Serve this dish with roasted chicken or grilled salmon, or serve it with a side of bruschetta or polenta for a light vegetarian meal. Tossed with salt, pepper, and a pinch of paprika or cayenne pepper, the chickpeas can be served on their own as a unique tapas *or cocktail snack.*

- 1 (15-ounce) can chickpeas, rinsed and drained
- 1/4 cup hazelnuts
- 2 tablespoons dark raisins
- 1/2 cup boiling water
- 2 tablespoons extra-virgin olive oil
- 2 large garlic cloves, minced or pressed through a garlic press (about 2 teaspoons)
- 1 bunch flat-leaf spinach (about 10 ounces), stems removed, leaves washed and dried
- 3 large plum tomatoes, cored, seeded, and cut into medium dice
- 2 tablespoons capers, drained
- Salt and ground black pepper
- 1 lemon, cut into wedges

1. Adjust an oven rack to the middle position and heat the oven to 400 degrees. Spread the chickpeas in a single layer on a rimmed baking sheet and bake until lightly browned and crunchy, about 30 minutes. Meanwhile, on a small rimmed baking sheet or in a pie plate, roast the hazelnuts until golden underneath the skin, about 10 minutes.

2. Once the hazelnuts are cool enough to handle, wrap them in a dish towel and rub them vigorously to remove the skins (see the illustrations on page 306). Coarsely chop them and set aside. Steep the raisins in the boiling water for 10 minutes, then drain and set aside.

3. Heat the oil and garlic together in a 12-inch skillet over medium-high heat, stirring frequently, until the garlic is fragrant and just beginning to color, about 1 ½ minutes. Stir in the spinach, tomatoes, capers, and ¼ teaspoon salt. Cook, stirring frequently, until the spinach is completely wilted and half of the liquid in the pan has evaporated, 3 to 4 minutes. Stir in the chickpeas and season with salt and pepper to taste. Sprinkle the hazelnuts over the top and serve immediately, accompanied by the lemon wedges.

Stewed Pinto Beans *with* Bacon, Tomatoes, & Cilantro

Adapted from Frijoles Borrachos

Picante Grill, San Antonio, Texas

FRIJOLES BORRACHOS, OR "DRUNKEN BEANS," are a longstanding northern Mexican staple that's more like a stew than a soup. Other than being "drunk" from the addition of beer, or sometimes tequila, frijoles borrachos usually contain bacon, tomatoes, chiles, and cilantro. All these ingredients combine to make a flavorful and hearty side dish. This version from Picante Grill is not truly drunk, since it doesn't contain any alcohol. Perhaps sensitive to the fact that not all people want to ingest alcohol, the restaurant omitted the beer. It nevertheless created a flavorful bean dish with all the flavor and texture we expect from drunken beans: creamy smooth pinto beans; smoky, meaty bacon; the spicy bite of chiles; tangy tomatoes; and fresh cilantro. With all these great flavors, there was no reason to add beer. This version of frijoles borrachos was as good as any we'd ever had.

First, it's important to use dried beans for this dish for the best bean flavor. Canned beans just won't cut it. The restaurant doesn't soak the beans overnight, but rather cooks them through with plenty of liquid—in this case salted water with garlic—so they don't dry out. (This is a method we favor in the test kitchen as well.)

Next, bacon is cooked in a Dutch oven until crisp, some of the fat is drained out, and onion is added to the pan along with plum tomatoes and jalapeño chiles. The drained beans and some of their cooking liquid are added to the skillet and cooked to allow the beans to reheat and the flavors to blend. A sprinkling of cilantro garnishes the dish, which gives the beans a welcome freshness.

Stewed Pinto Beans with Bacon, Tomatoes, and Cilantro

SERVES 10 TO 12

Some cooks may prefer to soak the beans overnight. If you choose to soak the beans overnight, reduce the amount of water the beans are cooked in to 9 cups and shorten the cooking time to about 45 minutes. These beans are the perfect accompaniment to the Grilled Skirt Steak Tacos with Roasted Poblanos (page 180) or any other Mexican-inspired dish.

- 1 ½ cups dried pinto beans, picked over and rinsed
- 4 medium garlic cloves, minced or pressed through a garlic press
- Salt
- 4 ounces thick-sliced bacon (about 3 slices)
- 1 small onion, cut into ¼-inch dice (about 1 cup)
- 3 plum tomatoes, seeded and cut into ¼-inch dice (about 1 cup)
- 2 jalapeño chiles, stemmed, seeded, and minced
- ½ cup chopped fresh cilantro leaves
- Ground black pepper

1. Bring the beans and 11 cups water to a boil in a Dutch oven over medium-high heat. Add the garlic and 1 teaspoon salt and reduce the heat to a simmer. Simmer, partially covered, until the beans are tender, about 1 hour and 10 minutes. Drain the beans, reserving the liquid. Set aside.

2. Heat the bacon in a Dutch oven over medium heat. Cook, stirring occasionally, until browned and crisp, about 10 minutes. Remove the pan from the heat. Drain all but 3 tablespoons fat from the pan, leaving the bacon in the pan.

3. Return the pan to medium heat. Add the onion and cook, stirring frequently, until softened and golden, about 3 minutes. Add the tomatoes and jalapeños and cook until the tomatoes have cooked down and lost their shape, about 10 minutes.

4. Add the drained beans and 4 cups of the reserved cooking liquid to the pan and bring to a simmer. Cook for 5 minutes to blend the flavors. The beans should be quite soupy; add additional cooking liquid if necessary.

5. Stir in the cilantro and season with salt and pepper. Serve in small, deep bowls.

INGREDIENTS: Bacon

We tested a range of bacons, including nine leading supermarket brands, a preservative-free "natural" brand, and two premium mail-order brands. Tasters were asked to rate all 12 brands based on flavor, balance of lean to fat, and overall quality. Our tasting showed that both the flavor of the meat itself and the flavors provided by the curing process were crucial factors in judging bacon.

We found a surprising difference in the "pork" flavor of the brands tested. Different manufacturers use different parts of the pork belly to make their bacon. Once the spareribs have been removed, the entire remaining belly can be used for bacon, but the best bacon comes from the center of the belly. The top portion of the belly is quite lean, while the bottom portion is very fatty.

In terms of flavors provided by curing, tasters preferred a strong balance of salt and sugar. We found that most bacons have only a mild smoky flavor, no doubt because the smoking process in most modern processing plants takes just six to eight hours. The one bacon with a real smoked flavor was one of the mail-order varieties. This bacon was smoked for 24 hours and was clearly in a class by itself. Among supermarket brands, Oscar Mayer took top honors, followed by John Morrell and Hillshire Farm. The one brand cured without preservatives landed at the bottom of the rankings owing to its rubbery texture and excessive sweetness.

Creamed Spinach

Adapted from Creamed Spinach

Ruth's Chris Steak House, Metairie, Louisiana,
and throughout the United States

CREAMED SPINACH IS A TRIED-AND-TRUE traditional side dish in steakhouses across America, nestled next to fluffy baked potatoes and perfectly grilled, thick, juicy steaks. Ruth's Chris is an internationally known restaurant chain, renowned for its midwestern beef as well as its superlative side dishes. Its creamed spinach is at the top of the list of diners' perennial favorites.

The béchamel sauce—a creamy white sauce thickened with flour—is flavored with clove, bay leaf, and onion and serves as the binder for the spinach. It provides richness, body, and delicate flavor to the deep green mound of tender spinach. Ruth's Chris calls for either half-and-half or milk for this classic sauce, and we found the richer half-and-half unnecessary since the final dish also contains eight tablespoons of butter. The sauce made with whole milk was silky and smooth without being overwhelmingly thick and cloying.

Spinach appears in many forms in the supermarket, ranging from tiny baby spinach leaves to the plastic-bagged, dark green, crinkly-leaf variety, with the flat-leaf bunched spinach in between. We chose the latter for its tenderness as well as its easy cleaning properties (there are fewer cracks and crevices to hold the stubborn dirt that takes three or four washings to remove). We experimented with different ways to cook the spinach, striving for the most spinach flavor possible from the delicate leaves. We started with blanching whole leaves in boiling water, then chilling them in ice water and squeezing out the liquid (as directed in the original recipe). Next we sweated coarsely chopped spinach in a Dutch oven, then pressed out the liquid with the back of a spoon. While both methods achieved the same purpose, the former yielded more control over the moisture content of the spinach. Squeezing cold spinach is much easier than trying to extract moisture from hot spinach, and although the flavor was slightly more pronounced in the leaves that were not dunked in water, we opted for the standard blanching and shocking method.

The texture of the cooked spinach for this venerable side dish was one we felt warranted some experimentation. We tested spinach that had been coarsely hand-chopped as well as spinach that had been roughly chopped in the food processor. While hand chopping gave the most control over the final product, we found that pulsing the spinach briefly in the food processor delivered an end product that was comparable to the hand-chopped spinach, and a bit faster. One disconcerting trait of spinach is its bewildering ability to shrink to a fraction of its former self. We found that two pounds of leaf spinach (which sounds like an awful lot, and yields enough fluffy leaves to fill an eight-quart mixing bowl) shrinks down to a mere two cups of cooked spinach. While prepping this much spinach for so little reward may seem like a lesson in futility, all of the work can be done in advance, so that when you at long last sit down to enjoy your steakhouse-style creamed spinach, you will be able to appreciate it for its rich, delicate flavor and silky texture and feel justly rewarded for your time and effort.

Creamed Spinach

SERVES 6

This classic steakhouse side dish features two components that are both easily prepared in advance. Though spinach can be a chore to clean, prewashed flat-leaf spinach is widely available. We suggest going the traditional route with this side dish and serving it alongside juicy steak, such as Beef Tournedos with Blue Cheese Mashed Potatoes (page 183).

BÉCHAMEL SAUCE

- 3 cups whole milk
- 1 whole clove
- 1 bay leaf
- 6 tablespoons (3/4 stick) unsalted butter
- 3 tablespoons minced onion
- 4 tablespoons all-purpose flour
- Salt and ground black pepper

SPINACH

- 2 pounds (about 2 bunches) flat-leaf fresh spinach, stemmed and washed
- Salt
- 2 tablespoons unsalted butter
- Ground black pepper

1. FOR THE BÉCHAMEL SAUCE: Heat the milk, clove, and bay leaf in a medium saucepan over medium heat until just below the boiling point. (Alternatively, the milk, clove, and bay leaf can be microwaved in a large glass measuring cup until hot, 2 to 2½ minutes.) Remove from the heat and cover.

2. Melt the butter in a separate medium saucepan over medium-high heat until foamy. Add the onion and cook, stirring constantly, until translucent, about 2 minutes. Add the flour and cook, stirring constantly, for 2 minutes.

3. Discard the clove and bay leaf and whisk the hot milk into the flour and butter mixture, stirring constantly, until the sauce comes to a simmer and thickens. Reduce the heat to low and simmer, whisking constantly, for 5 minutes. Season with salt and pepper to taste. Strain through a sieve into a medium bowl, cover, and set aside.

4. FOR THE SPINACH: Bring 4 quarts water to a boil in a Dutch oven. Add the spinach and 1 tablespoon salt and cook until the spinach is tender, 1 to 2 minutes. Drain in a colander and immediately rinse with cold water to stop the cooking. Squeeze the spinach until very dry. You should have about 2 cups. Transfer the spinach to a food processor and pulse 2 or 3 times, or until coarsely chopped. Alternatively, you can hand-chop the spinach on a cutting board.

5. Return the Dutch oven to medium heat. Add the béchamel sauce and spinach, and cook, stirring constantly, until combined and heated through, about 2 minutes. Remove from the heat, stir in the butter, and season with salt and pepper to taste. Serve immediately.

Root Vegetable Gratin

Adapted from Root Vegetable Gratin
Jay's, Dayton, Ohio

WITH THE ADDITION OF CARROTS AND parsnips and three distinctive cheeses—Parmesan, mozzarella, and blue—this recipe from Jay's elevates the ubiquitous potato gratin to a new level. The distinctive flavors of three ordinary and, at least in the case of parsnips, often maligned root vegetables meld into a refined and cohesive whole. In the test kitchen, tasters who typically shun parsnips or avoid blue cheese asked for second samples of this dish.

This recipe is easily followed, but does require attention to a couple of important details to ensure its success. We found that using a mandoline or other vegetable slicer facilitates cutting the root vegetables into uniform one-eighth-inch-thick slices. (See page 8 for more information on mandolines.) If the vegetables are not sliced thinly and evenly, the thinner slices will cook more quickly than thicker slices and the cooking time will vary from the one specified in the recipe. After slicing the potatoes, submerge them in a bowl of water to keep them from discoloring. The enzymes and substrates released once potatoes are peeled and sliced react with oxygen and cause the potato flesh to turn an unpalatable, dull color. Restaurants that typically peel and cut large amounts of potatoes before cooking them depend on this handy trick to keep the potato flesh creamy white. Before adding the slices to the gratin, drain them well, shaking the colander gently to remove excess water. The drops of water that continue to cling to the potato slices lighten the cream in the gratin and contribute to the sauce of the dish.

Some tasters in the test kitchen were skeptical of the addition of blue cheese, especially in combination with the sweetness of carrots. To ensure that the tanginess of the blue cheese did not overwhelm the other flavors, we carefully crumbled it into small pieces so that it was evenly dispersed throughout the gratin. If you prefer a subtle blue cheese flavor, choose mild supermarket brands such as Stella. If you enjoy a strong blue cheese flavor, look for a stronger-flavored cheese, such as Spanish Cabrales or Roquefort. Once baked for over an hour, however, tasters found that the distinctive blue cheese flavor supported rather than dominated the other, more subtle flavors of the dish.

The recipe calls for layering vegetables, cheeses, seasonings, cream, and bread crumbs in a particular order. The most complicated part of this step is unwittingly leaving out one of the layers. Be sure to have all your ingredients prepared, available, and visible when you begin to assemble the dish. Don't skip a layer because the ingredient was hidden behind the paper towel roll on the counter.

The term *gratin* refers to both a dish topped with bread crumbs and/or the cheese that is browned in the oven and the actual dish in which the gratin is served. In the test kitchen, we learned that it is important to use the right size gratin dish for the recipe you are making. The gratin should fill the dish right to the top, and the topping should be arranged in a thin, even layer. A thick coating of bread crumbs may be crisp on top, but will be soggy underneath. For this dish, we recommend an 8-inch-square glass baking dish. If you use a larger, shallower dish, you will need to reduce the cooking time to account for the larger surface area of the thinner gratin.

Root Vegetable Gratin

SERVES 6

Submerging the sliced potatoes in water serves two purposes: the water keeps the slices from turning gray, and the residual water that clings to the drained potatoes contributes to the saucy consistency of the finished gratin. If you don't have a mandoline (see page 8) for slicing the vegetables, you can use the slicing disk of a food processor or slice them by hand with a very sharp knife.

This rich and hearty side dish goes well with the Rosemary Roasted Split Chicken (page 169) or Pork Tenderloin with Rhubarb Sauce (page 209).

- **3 large russet potatoes (about 1 3/4 pounds), peeled**
- **2 medium parsnips (about 8 ounces), peeled**
- **2 medium carrots (about 8 ounces), peeled**
- **Vegetable oil spray**
- **Salt and ground black pepper**
- **1 3/4 ounces Parmesan cheese, grated (about 3/4 cup)**
- **1 3/4 ounces mozzarella cheese, grated (about 1/2 cup)**
- **1 3/4 ounces finely crumbled mild blue cheese (about 1/2 cup)**
- **1 cup heavy cream**
- **1 cup panko (Japanese-style bread crumbs) or Homemade Panko (page 17)**
- **2 tablespoons unsalted butter, melted**

1. Adjust an oven rack to the middle position and heat the oven to 350 degrees. Using a mandoline or other vegetable slicer, cut the potatoes into ⅛-inch-thick slices. Place the potato slices in a medium bowl and cover with water. Set aside.

2. Using the mandoline, cut the parsnips into ⅛-inch-thick slices. Place the parsnips in a small bowl and set aside. Using the mandoline, cut the carrots into ⅛-inch-thick slices. Place the carrots in another small bowl and set aside.

3. Coat an 8-inch square glass baking dish with vegetable oil spray. Drain the potatoes in a colander, shaking to remove excess water. Layer half the potatoes evenly over the bottom of the dish. Spread half the carrots over the potatoes and follow with half the parsnips. Season with ½ teaspoon salt and ¼ teaspoon pepper. Sprinkle half the Parmesan, mozzarella, and blue cheese over the vegetables. Repeat the layering of the potatoes, carrots, parsnips, salt, pepper, and cheeses once more.

4. Pour the cream over the vegetables. Combine the bread crumbs and melted butter in a small bowl and toss to coat well. Sprinkle the bread crumbs evenly over the gratin.

5. Cover the pan with aluminum foil and bake until the vegetables are tender, about 1 hour and 20 minutes. Remove the foil and bake until the bread crumbs are golden, about 10 minutes more. Cool for 5 minutes before serving.

Mashed Sweet Potatoes *with* Vanilla

Adapted from Sweet Potatoes with Vanilla Bean Cream

Emily's, Northville, Mississippi

A REGULAR AT THE HOLIDAY TABLE, mashed sweet potatoes always seem to receive shoddy treatment. Often suffering from being oversweetened and covered with marshmallows, they are better left on the kids' table. This recipe from Emily's skips the candy-like treatment and produces more sophisticated mashed sweet potatoes that are smooth and creamy, with a rich, buttery flavor. As an interesting variation, Emily's adds a vanilla bean to the cream. The complex floral overtones of the vanilla perfume the dish and heighten the earthy sweetness of the potatoes. Although the recipe produced a praiseworthy dish, it was definitely geared toward restaurant use. With half a gallon of cream, a pound of butter, and six quarts of potatoes, we figured this wasn't a recipe for home unless you were cooking for 20. So our first task was to scale down the amount of ingredients to a more suitable proportions for the home cook.

Wanting enough to serve six people, we started by cooking six potatoes. Cooking and mashing this amount resulted in about two quarts of mashed potatoes, which was one third of the potatoes called for in the recipe. Paring down the rest of the recipe by one third, we were surprised to find that the potatoes had an overpowering vanilla flavor and were rather watery. As with a lot of recipes, it can be hard to divide or multiply the amounts and achieve the same results. After numerous tests, we found that half a vanilla bean, instead of a whole one, infused in the cream gave us a subtler vanilla flavor. Also, the step of simmering the cream to reduce it slightly intensified the richness of the potatoes without making them too watery. Along with the reduced cream, the addition of four tablespoons of butter gave us the consistency we were looking for.

With the ratio of ingredients established, we wanted to test the method of cooking the potatoes. The recipe instructed us to bake the potatoes at 400 degrees until soft, which took about 70 minutes. Wondering if we could save ourselves some time using a quicker cooking method, we prepared the recipe several times varying only the cooking technique. We first tried boiling the potatoes, but found that the resulting mash was slightly bland and watery. Steaming the potatoes, while better than boiling because of the use of less water, still produced potatoes that were much milder in flavor and wetter than those in our initial tests. We decided we were willing to sacrifice some time in an effort to maximize flavor, so we opted to stay with baking the potatoes, which produced the best results.

Mashed Sweet Potatoes with Vanilla

SERVES 6 TO 8

It is important to choose potatoes that are about the same size so that they cook at the same rate. If you don't have a food mill, a potato masher will work just fine; however, the finished puree will be slightly chunkier. The natural sweetness of these mashed potatoes makes them an ideal accompaniment to poultry and pork dishes, such as the Pork Tenderloin with Rhubarb Sauce (page 209).

- **6** **large sweet potatoes (about 4 ½ pounds), washed, dried, and lightly pricked with a fork in 3 places**
- **1** **cup heavy cream**
- **½** **vanilla bean, split in half lengthwise**
- **4** **tablespoons (½ stick) unsalted butter, softened**
- **Salt and ground black pepper**

1. Adjust an oven rack to the middle position and heat the oven to 400 degrees. Bake the sweet potatoes on a rimmed baking sheet lined with foil until a knife slips easily into the centers of the potatoes, about 1 hour and 10 minutes. Remove from the oven and cool slightly.

2. Meanwhile, pour the cream into a large saucepan. Using a paring knife, scrape the vanilla seeds into the cream, then add the pod to the cream. Bring to a simmer over medium-high heat. Reduce the heat to medium-low and simmer until reduced to ¾ cup, about 4 minutes. Remove the vanilla pod and discard. Cover to keep warm and set aside.

3. Once the sweet potatoes are cool enough to handle, peel and process them through a food mill or ricer into a large bowl. Stir in the vanilla cream and butter. Season with salt and pepper to taste. Serve immediately.

REMOVING SEEDS FROM A VANILLA BEAN

1. Use a small sharp knife to cut the vanilla bean in half lengthwise.

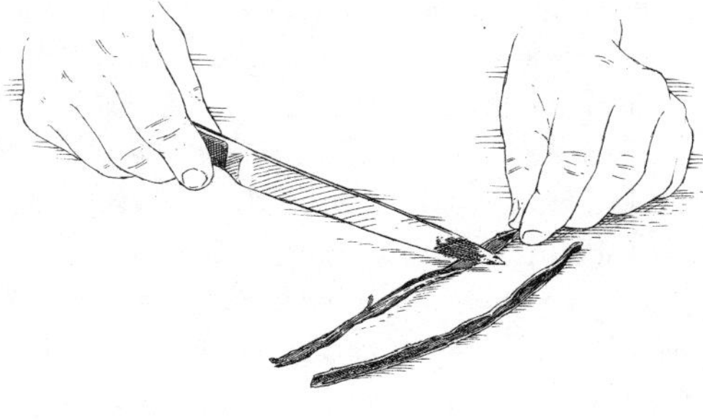

2. Place the knife at one end of one bean half and press down to flatten the bean as you move the knife away from you and catch the seeds on the edge of the blade.

Sweet Potato Chips

Adapted from Sweet Potato Chips

Juban's, Baton Rouge, Louisiana

FEW CAN RESIST THE ALLURE OF CRUNCHY sweet potato chips. This recipe from Juban's produced delicate, crisp wafers. The challenge was not in reproducing the flavorful chips, but in finding the best way for the home cook to prepare them.

Considering that the difference between frying at home and in a restaurant is drastic, it can sometimes be difficult to translate a restaurant recipe requiring deep frying into one designed for the home cook. Therefore, our testing focused mainly on the cooking of the sweet potatoes. The original recipe called for frying the chips at 350 degrees. After frying several batches at this temperature, however, we found that the sweet potato slices took a long time to cook, resulting in chips that were both greasy and undercooked. We figured that these undesirable characteristics were due to the fact that the chips were cooling down the oil in which they were being cooked, making the cooled oil unable to cook the chips quickly enough. A commercial fryer avoids this problem with the capacity both for more oil and intense heat. Absent the availability of a commercial fryer, it was obvious that we were going to have to make some adjustments in this recipe.

We had several options. We could increase the amount of oil, but that seemed wasteful in light of the two quarts we were already using. The other option was to increase the temperature of the oil. Increasing the temperature in increments of 10 degrees, we found that a starting temperature of 375 to 380 degrees was ideal. The chips browned quickly enough so that they didn't become greasy, and they cooked evenly enough so that we didn't have a problem with undercooked, chewy spots.

As you add the potatoes to the oil, the temperature will drop, so it is important to increase the temperature of the flame underneath the pot. The higher flame allowed us to maintain a high constant temperature, and the oil overcame the initial heat loss from the added sweet potatoes. In following this method, we were able to prepare consistently browned and flavorful chips, one batch after another.

As an interesting finish, Juban's dusted its fried and cooled chips with confectioners' sugar. At first, we thought that this dish was some sort of dessert accompaniment. But after trying our first batch of chips prepared in this way, we were surprised to find the confectioners' sugar brought out the natural sweetness of the potatoes without making the overall flavor too sweet. Coupled with a light sprinkling of salt, these chips were not only a very pleasurable mix of sweet and salty flavors, but a very addictive snack.

Sweet Potato Chips

SERVES 6

These chips can be served with any fish or meat entrée or on their own as a snack. It is important to cut the potatoes just 1/16 inch thick, a task easily done by a mandoline (see page 8). If you don't have a mandoline, the slicing blade of a food processor will suffice, although it won't achieve quite the right thickness, so you may need to increase the cooking time to ensure crisp chips. Because the oil will bubble up when you add the chips, be sure you have at least 3 inches of room at the top of the pot.

- 2 quarts canola oil
- 4 large sweet potatoes (about 3 pounds), peeled and cut into 1/16-inch-thick slices
- Salt
- Confectioners' sugar

1. Heat the canola oil in a Dutch oven over medium heat until it reaches 375 degrees. (Use an instant-read thermometer that registers high temperatures or clip a candy/deep-fat thermometer onto the side of the pan before turning on the heat.) Carefully add one sixth of the sweet potatoes and fry until lightly browned, 2½ to 3 minutes, increasing the heat to medium-high, or as necessary to maintain the cooking temperature. Using a slotted spoon or spider (see page 9), transfer the chips to a rimmed baking sheet lined with several layers of paper towels and sprinkle them lightly with salt. Fry the remaining batches, letting the oil come back to 375 degrees after each batch, adding them to the baking sheet, and salting them.

2. Let the sweet potato chips cool completely. Dust them with confectioners' sugar and serve.

EQUIPMENT: Vegetable Peelers

You might imagine that all vegetable peelers are pretty much the same. Not so. In our research, we turned up 25 peelers, many with quite novel features. The major differences were the fixture of the blade, either stationary or swiveling; the material of the blade, carbon stainless steel, stainless steel, or ceramic; and the orientation of the blade to the handle, either straight in line with the body or perpendicular to it. The last arrangement, with the blade perpendicular to the handle, is called a harp, or Y, peeler because the frame looks like the body of a harp or the letter Y.

To test the peelers, we recruited several cooks and asked them to peel carrots, potatoes, lemons, butternut squash, and celery root. In most cases, testers preferred the Oxo Good Grips peeler with a sharp stainless steel blade that swivels. Peelers with stationary blades are fine for peeling carrots, but they have trouble hugging the curves on potatoes. As for blade material, we found peelers made from stainless steel, carbon steel, and ceramic that were both sharp and dull. We concluded that sharpness is a factor of quality control during the manufacturing process and not blade material.

The Y-shaped peelers tested well, although they removed more flesh along with the skin on potatoes, lemons, and carrots and therefore did not rate as well as the Oxo Good Grips. The one case where this liability turned into an asset was with butternut squash, where these Y-shaped peelers took off the skin as well as the greenish-tinged flesh right below the skin in one pass. With the Oxo Good Grips, it was necessary to go over the peeled flesh once the skin had been removed. Among Y-shaped peelers, the Kuhn Rikon was preferred by testers. Because both the Oxo Good Grips and Kuhn Rikon peelers can be had for less than $10, we recommend that you purchase both.

THE BEST VEGETABLE PEELERS
The sharp, comfortable Oxo Good Grips Peeler (right) was the best overall peeler we tested. The Kuhn Rikon Peeler (left) takes off very wide, thick strips of peel, making it especially good on winter squash or celery root.

Hand-Cut Fries *with* Whole-Grain Mustard Aïoli

Adapted from Hand-Cut Fries with Whole-Grain Mustard Aïoli

Paley's Place, Portland, Oregon

PERFECTLY COOKED FRENCH FRIES ARE irresistible, like this version from Paley's Place. The lightly salted exterior is crisp and golden brown, while inside the potato is tender, moist, and creamy. In a welcome shift away from the ubiquitous ketchup accompaniment, the restaurant pairs these superior fries with a mustard-spiked aïoli (garlicky mayonnaise of Provençal origin).

The restaurant uses russet potatoes, and we can't argue with that, since that's what we use when frying potatoes in the test kitchen. Russet potatoes have a high starch content, which helps them hold up well during the frying process.

To start, there were a couple of issues we needed to address for the home cook regarding the fries. Russets are generally sold individually or in five-pound bags. We found that bagged potatoes vary dramatically in size and were consequently difficult to cut into uniform strips. Buying russets individually allows you to choose potatoes of equal size that can be cut into uniform strips for more consistent cooking. And a ruler helps to ensure that the strips are the correct width.

Avoid leaving the strips exposed to the air for too long. Peeling and cutting potatoes releases enzymes and substrates that react with oxygen and cause the potato to discolor. To circumvent this problem, first rinse the raw potatoes under several changes of cool water to remove excess starch from the surface, which will help them crisp nicely when frying. Then place the strips in ice water and refrigerate. (It's very important to drain the potatoes well and pat them dry before adding them to the hot oil; excess water will cause the hot oil to splatter.)

One dip in hot oil, however, is not sufficient to produce fries with both crisp exteriors and tender interiors. A single extended bath in frying oil produces wooden and overcooked fries. To avoid this, first fry the chilled potato strips at a relatively low temperature to cook them through without much browning. Then give them a brief rest to cool off before refrying them quickly at a higher temperature until nicely browned.

This recipe suggested duck fat for cooking the fries, so we tried it. Surprisingly, duck fat produced mediocre results in our tests. Expensive and not easy to find, it just didn't seem worth the bother. Corn and peanut oils produced better results. Corn oil offered a clean flavor and rebounded well from temperature fluctuations. Peanut oil, we found, produced light fries, rich but not dense, with an earthy flavor, which tasters felt gave it a slight edge.

Perfectly cooked, the fries are served with mustard aïoli. At the restaurant, the chefs make their own—not a difficult process, but one that we thought the home cook could skip. We found that spiking good-quality mayonnaise with the flavorings recommended by the restaurant—garlic, fresh lemon juice, mustard, and a dash of pepper—turned out a good aïoli, and with much less effort.

Hand-Cut Fries with Whole-Grain Mustard Aïoli

SERVES 4

Because the oil will bubble up when you add the fries, be sure you have at least 3 inches of room at the top of the pot. Also, be aware that cooking times can vary widely depending on the starch content of the potatoes. Pay particular attention to visual cues to achieve the proper doneness—cooked fries will be a deep golden brown.

WHOLE-GRAIN MUSTARD AÏOLI

- **3/4 cup prepared mayonnaise**
- **3 tablespoons whole-grain mustard**
- **1 small garlic clove, minced or pressed through a garlic press (about 1/2 teaspoon)**
- **1/8 teaspoon ground black pepper**
- **1 tablespoon juice from 1 lemon**

HAND-CUT FRIES

- **4 large russet potatoes (2 1/2–3 pounds)**
- **2 quarts peanut oil**
- **Salt and ground black pepper**

1. FOR THE AÏOLI: Combine the mayonnaise, mustard, garlic, pepper, and lemon juice in a small bowl. Cover with plastic wrap and refrigerate for at least 1 hour.

2. FOR THE FRIES: Trim the ends and sides of the potatoes and cut lengthwise into ½-inch-thick slices. Cut each slice lengthwise into ½-inch-thick strips. Place the potato strips in a large bowl and rinse in several changes of cool water until the milky potato starch is removed and the water is clear. Cover the potato strips with cold water and then top with ice cubes. Cover with plastic wrap and refrigerate for at least 30 minutes or for up to 3 days.

3. Heat the peanut oil in a Dutch oven over medium-low heat until it reaches 325 degrees. (Use an instant-read thermometer that registers high temperatures or clip a candy/deep-fat thermometer onto the side of the pan before turning on the heat.) Pour off the ice and water from the potatoes, quickly wrap them in a clean kitchen towel, and thoroughly pat dry. Increase the heat to medium-high and add half the potatoes, a handful at a time, to the hot oil. Fry, stirring with a large-holed slotted spoon or spider (see page 9), until the fries are limp and soft, 4 to 8 minutes. (The oil temperature will drop 50 to 60 degrees during this frying, and the potatoes will not color.) Transfer the fries to a rimmed baking sheet lined with several layers of paper towels and let rest for at least 10 minutes. Repeat with the remaining potatoes, replacing the paper towels with fresh ones. (The fries can stand at room temperature for up to 2 hours.)

4. When ready to serve the fries, reheat the oil over medium heat until it reaches 350 degrees. Line another rimmed baking sheet with several layers of paper towels. Add half the fries and fry, stirring almost constantly, until medium brown and puffed, 5 to 10 minutes. Transfer the fries to the baking sheet to drain. Repeat with the remaining fries, replacing the paper towels as necessary. Season with salt and pepper to taste. Serve immediately, accompanied by the aïoli.

Blue Cheese Potato Croquettes

Adapted from Blue Cheese Potato Croquettes

The Kaufman House, Zelienople, Pennsylvania

TO MANY, THE WORD "CROQUETTES" conjures images of 1950s diner food—grease-laden and breaded meat patties served with a pasty white cream sauce. Or worse, something that appeared weekly on the school cafeteria menu. But today croquettes have become more sophisticated and often contain a wide variety of fillings—from smoked salmon to rice and, in this case, potatoes. These croquettes have a crisp and light exterior that surrounds creamy, rich mashed potatoes spiked with Gorgonzola, an Italian blue cheese. Shaped into finger-length cakes and rolled in crunchy panko (Japanese-style) bread crumbs before being fried, these croquettes are more like sophisticated Tater Tots.

The recipe needed very little modification for the home cook. We did, however, have one concern about the potatoes. The mashed potatoes, which formed the base of the croquettes, were prepared with the skin on. Worried that the consistency might seem a little odd, we tried making the croquettes with potatoes that had been peeled before cooking. Much to our surprise, we found that the croquettes had far less flavor and lost the earthy character that we had enjoyed in the first batch. We also noted that the skins were crucial in providing a textural contrast in the croquettes.

We turned next to frying the croquettes, but ran into a roadblock. On more than one occasion, when we added the croquettes to the hot oil, they burst through their bread crumb coating and the potatoes oozed into the oil—creating an inedible disaster. At the restaurant, the chefs no doubt fry the croquettes in a piece of equipment not available to the home cook: a commercial deep fryer whose temperature is easily regulated. In our initial batches, we found that when using a quart of oil to fry the croquettes, they didn't become fully submerged and needed turning halfway through the cooking time in order for the entire surface to brown. We also noticed that the croquettes were bursting, after we turned them, at the point that was above the oil level. Curious to see if an increase in oil would rectify this problem, we increased the amount of oil by several cups. As we expected, with the croquettes fully submerged throughout the cooking process, we no longer had any "eruptions." This produced a light and delicate croquette, best served immediately.

Blue Cheese Potato Croquettes

SERVES 4 TO 6

Serve these croquettes with the Rosemary Roasted Split Chicken (page 169) or in place of the blue cheese mashed potatoes in Beef Tournedos (page 183).

- **1 ½ pounds Yukon Gold potatoes, scrubbed and cut into quarters**
- **Salt**
- **3 tablespoons unsalted butter, melted**
- **3 tablespoons heavy cream**
- **Ground black pepper**
- **½ cup plus 2 tablespoons all-purpose flour**
- **3 large eggs**
- **1 ½ ounces Gorgonzola (or another assertively flavored blue cheese, such as Roquefort), crumbled (about ¼ cup)**
- **Pinch ground nutmeg**
- **6 cups plus 1 tablespoon canola oil**
- **2 cups panko (Japanese-style bread crumbs) or Homemade Panko (page 17)**

1. Bring the potatoes, 1 teaspoon salt, and enough water to cover the potatoes by 1 inch to a boil in a medium saucepan over high heat. Reduce the heat to medium-low and simmer until a paring knife can be slipped into and out of the center of the potatoes with very little resistance, 10 to 12 minutes. Drain thoroughly. Mash the potatoes with a potato masher. Add the butter, cream, ½ teaspoon salt, and ¼ teaspoon pepper, and mix with a wooden spoon until smooth. Spread the potatoes on a large plate or rimmed baking sheet, place in the freezer, and chill thoroughly, about 10 minutes.

2. Transfer the chilled potatoes to a large bowl. Stir in 2 tablespoons of the flour, 1 of the eggs, the cheese, and the nutmeg. To form the croquettes, scoop ¼ cup potato mixture into the palm of one hand and gently roll the dough back and forth between your palms until the croquette is 3 inches long. Repeat with the remaining potato mixture. You should have 12 croquettes. Place the croquettes on a baking sheet and refrigerate for at least 1 hour.

3. Spread the remaining ½ cup flour in a shallow dish or pie plate. Lightly whisk the remaining 2 eggs, 1 tablespoon of the canola oil, 1 teaspoon salt, and ½ teaspoon pepper together in a separate shallow dish. Spread the panko in a third dish. Working with several croquettes at a time, drop them into the flour and gently shake the dish to coat. Shake the excess flour from each croquette, then, using tongs, dip the croquettes into the egg mixture, turning to coat well, and allow the excess to drip off. Place the croquettes in the panko, rolling and pressing the crumbs lightly to adhere. Shake off any excess panko and place the breaded croquettes on a wire rack set over a rimmed baking sheet. Repeat with the remaining croquettes.

4. Heat the remaining 6 cups canola oil in a Dutch oven over medium-high heat until it reaches 350 degrees. (Use an instant-read thermometer that registers high temperatures or clip a candy/deep-fat thermometer onto the side of the pan before turning on the heat.) Using a slotted spoon or spider, gently place half the croquettes in the oil and fry until golden brown and crisp, about 2½ minutes, adjusting the heat as necessary to maintain the cooking temperature. Using tongs, carefully transfer the croquettes to a rimmed baking sheet lined with several layers of paper towels. Repeat with the remaining croquettes. Serve immediately.

Pumpkin Risotto

Adapted from Pumpkin Risotto

Union Square Café, New York, New York

THERE IS NOTHING REVOLUTIONARY about pumpkin risotto, a standard rendition of the Italian rice dish, but securing a full-barreled, pumpkin presence takes some skill. In too many versions we have tasted, the pumpkin lends little but color and the faintest flavor. The Union Square Café makes a robust version seasoned with sage, warm spices, and peppery arugula and enriched with Parmesan and mozzarella cheeses. The flavors are exciting and full, especially that often elusive pumpkin flavor. So what's the restaurant's secret? The chefs cook the rice in a spiced pumpkin broth and stud the risotto with diced winter squash. It's an intelligent method for flavoring the dish—an approach we had never seen before.

Union Square preloads most of the risotto's flavoring into the broth. The rice itself has no aromatics in it—a real deviation from tradition. Into the broth go carrots, onions, leeks, and celery, as well as pumpkin puree and warm spices, including cinnamon, nutmeg, and allspice. Slowly simmered, the flavors meld and the puree thickens the broth. A splash of maple syrup provides sweetness to round out the pumpkin's flavor. Quite frankly, we were skeptical that warm spices and maple syrup could pair amicably with the sage, arugula, and Parmesan in the risotto. But we were wrong: the spices are virtually unnoticeable, outside of their buttressing of the pumpkin's flavor. Our only alteration to the restaurant's recipe was to withhold the nutmeg until the risotto was finished (and to reduce the amount accordingly). Freshly grated and bright tasting, the nutmeg tasted better to us this way.

Once the broth is simmered and strained, the risotto pulls together quickly. The rice is sautéed with winter squash, and then the liquid is added in small amounts until the rice is al dente and the squash tender. The arugula, sage, and cheeses are then stirred in and the dish served immediately—risotto is always best fresh from the pot. To make the dish a little easier to prepare, we applied our simplified risotto method to the dish and added half the liquid at once and allowed the rice to simmer freely. Because of the thickness of the broth—pureed pumpkin adds a certain viscosity—the rice had a strong tendency to stick to the pan's bottom, so stirring is important.

The restaurant's recipe allows any winter squash for the risotto. We favored butternut squash, but acorn, kabocha, not to mention pumpkin itself, all taste fine, too. Choose wisely, however, since many pumpkins—like your basic carving pumpkin—won't do. Look for the small, fine-textured, firm-fleshed sugar pumpkins.

To finish the risotto, Union Square stirs in butter, grated Parmesan cheese, and cubes of creamy fresh mozzarella. Most tasters thought the latter was overkill, making for a gooey, sinfully decadent dish. Our revised approach was to include the mozzarella as an optional garnish. The stark white lent visual contrast to the amber-colored risotto and didn't turn quite so stringy as quickly. It was possible to take bites of barely melted cheese with the risotto—a textural contrast appreciated by tasters.

Pumpkin Risotto

SERVES 6

The broth may be made a day or two ahead of time and refrigerated in an airtight container, but the risotto should be made just before serving. If you can't find arugula, substitute fresh baby spinach. If you use all the broth before the rice is tender, add water. The risotto's slightly sweet flavor pairs especially well with pork or poultry. It's also rich enough to serve as the center of a vegetable-based meal, served alongside braised hearty greens and broccoli or cauliflower.

PUMPKIN BROTH

- **1 tablespoon unsalted butter**
- **1 medium onion, sliced thin**
- **2 medium carrots, sliced thin**
- **1 medium celery rib (including leaves if any), sliced thin**
- **1 medium leek, white part only, cleaned thoroughly and sliced thin**
- **Salt**
- **1 (16-ounce) can pumpkin puree**
- **1 bay leaf**
- **1 (1-inch) length cinnamon stick**
- **½ teaspoon whole black peppercorns**
- **4 allspice berries**
- **8 cups low-sodium chicken broth**
- **2 tablespoons maple syrup**
- **Ground black pepper**

RISOTTO

- **¼ cup olive oil**
- **1 ¾ cups Arborio rice**
- **1 ½ cups peeled, seeded, and medium-diced winter squash (butternut, sugar pumpkin, acorn, or kabocha)**
- **½ cup dry white wine**
- **2 cups loosely packed arugula leaves, coarsely chopped**
- **1 tablespoon minced fresh sage leaves**
- **1 ½ ounces finely grated Parmesan cheese (about ¾ cup)**
- **1 tablespoon unsalted butter**
- **Pinch freshly grated nutmeg**
- **Salt and ground black pepper**
- **4 ounces fresh mozzarella cheese, cut into ½-inch dice (optional)**

1. FOR THE BROTH: Melt the butter in a large saucepan over medium heat until the foam subsides. Add the onion, carrots, celery, leek, and ½ teaspoon salt. Cook, stirring occasionally, until the vegetables are softened but not browned, 8 to 9 minutes. Add the pumpkin puree, bay leaf, cinnamon stick, peppercorns, allspice, broth, and maple syrup. Increase the heat to medium-high and bring to a boil. Reduce the heat to low and simmer until the flavors have combined, about 45 minutes. Strain the broth through a fine-mesh strainer into a medium saucepan, gently pressing on the solids to extract as much liquid as possible. Season with salt and pepper to taste. Keep warm over low heat.

2. FOR THE RISOTTO: Heat the olive oil in a large saucepan over medium heat until just shimmering. Add the rice and squash and cook, stirring frequently, until the edges of the rice grains are translucent, 3 to 4 minutes. Add the wine and cook, stirring

frequently, until it is completely absorbed by the rice, about 30 seconds. Add 3½ cups of the warm broth and simmer, stirring occasionally (every 2 to 3 minutes), until the liquid is absorbed and the bottom of the pan is dry, 8 to 10 minutes.

3. Add more broth, ½ cup at a time, as needed to keep the pan bottom from drying out (every 2 to 3 minutes), until the grains of rice are cooked through, but still somewhat firm in the center, 10 to 12 minutes. Stir in the arugula and sage, then the Parmesan, butter, and nutmeg. Adjust the seasoning with salt and pepper. Serve immediately in 6 warmed, shallow bowls, garnished with diced mozzarella, if desired.

CUTTING WINTER SQUASH

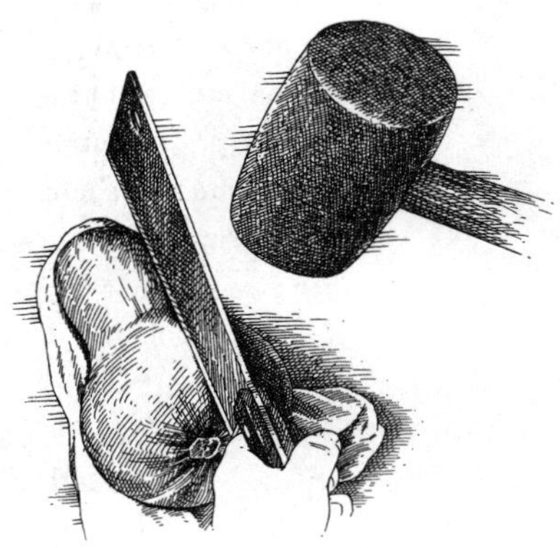

1. Set the squash on a damp kitchen towel to hold it in place. Position a cleaver on the skin of the squash.

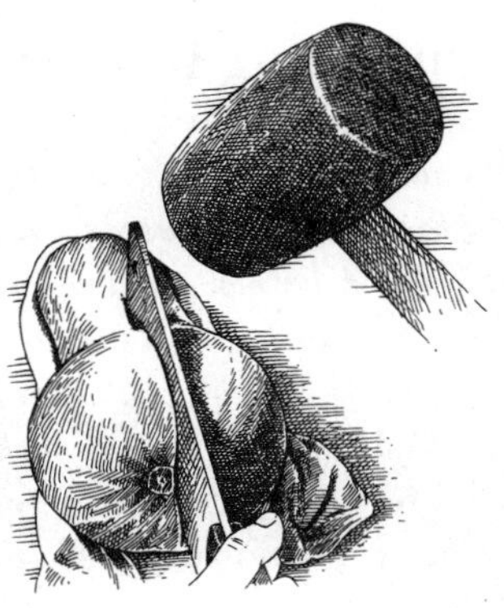

2. Strike the back of the cleaver with a mallet to drive the cleaver deep into the squash. Continue to hit the cleaver with the mallet until the cleaver cuts through the squash and opens it up.

Soft & Sexy Grits

Adapted from Soft and Sexy Grits
Sazerac, Seattle, Washington

SOFT, YES, BUT CAN COOKED GRITS BE sexy? Surprisingly, tasters in the test kitchen found these grits so creamy and alluring that they earned their appellation. Enriched with whole milk, cream, and butter, these grits are also flavored with garlic and hot sauce—a far cry from traditional southern-style grits that are essential breakfast fare. Sazerac, however, serves these grits for dinner with robust pork chops, pickled cabbage, and gravy. In the test kitchen, we found the recipe so tempting and easy to make that tasters thought they might very well make them for breakfast, lunch, or dinner.

Grits are ground hominy (dried white or yellow corn kernels that have been soaked in lye or lime to remove the germ and hull). The process of soaking corn in an alkaline substance was vital for early North American civilizations. Soaking made it easier to remove the kernels' hulls and had the added benefit of improving the corn's nutritional value. Although machines now remove the hulls and the processed corn is chemically enriched, the practice of soaking the corn in an alkaline substance remains. The resulting hominy is ground to different sizes—coarse, medium, or fine—and boiled, like oatmeal, in a relatively large amount of liquid.

Like oats, grits are available in "quick" versions that require less liquid and reduced cooking time. Our previous tests of instant oats produced mediocre results at best, so we were skeptical of the quick grits called for in this recipe. Surprisingly, however, the quick grits work wonderfully. Their delicate texture in combination with the cream and milk called for here give the grits their rich, seductive creaminess.

The ingredient list for this dish is short, and the method is easily followed. In the test kitchen, we discovered a trick essential to achieving smoothly textured grits. Stir the milk and cream mixture constantly while adding the grits in a slow, steady stream—much like polenta. This step allows each piece of ground hominy to be coated

CLEANING A GARLIC PRESS

Garlic presses make quick work of garlic but are notoriously hard to clean. Recycle an old toothbrush with a worn brush for this job. The bristles will clear bits of garlic from the press and are easy to rinse clean.

and penetrated by the hot cream mixture, preventing the starch granules from clumping together to form a sticky mass. Once the grits have been incorporated, reduce the heat and stir occasionally while they cook. Season with salt and white pepper and add a couple shakes of Tabasco for a pleasing kick.

Soft and Sexy Grits

SERVES 8 TO 10

Be sure to stir constantly while adding the grits so that they do not clump and stick to the bottom of the pan. Also, be sure to use white pepper instead of black pepper. The milder flavor of white pepper works well with the creamy grits, whereas the sharper flavor—and color—of ground black pepper stands out.

- **2 tablespoons unsalted butter**
- **2 garlic cloves, minced or pressed through a garlic press**
- **4 cups low-sodium chicken broth**
- **2 cups whole milk**
- **2 cups heavy cream**
- **2 cups quick grits**
- **Hot pepper sauce, such as Tabasco**
- **Salt and ground white pepper**

1. Melt the butter in a large saucepan over medium heat. Add the garlic and cook until softened and fragrant, about 30 seconds. Increase the heat to medium-high, add the broth, milk, and cream, and bring just to a boil.

2. Reduce the heat to low and, stirring constantly with a wooden spoon, slowly add the grits. Simmer, stirring occasionally, until the grits are smooth and creamy, 8 to 10 minutes. Season with Tabasco and salt and pepper to taste. Serve immediately, or cover the pan to keep the grits warm and serve within 15 minutes. (You should not need to add any more liquid.)

SUN-DRIED TOMATO POLENTA

Adapted from Sun-Dried Tomato Polenta

SILVER PEAK RESTAURANT AND BREWERY, RENO, NEVADA

POLENTA IS A TIME-HONORED NORTHERN Italian staple made from dried ground corn and cooked in a liquid, usually water or stock. It can be served in a soft, porridge-like consistency, or cooled until firm and then grilled, baked, or sautéed. Restaurants often choose the latter method, allowing for advance preparation of large quantities that are a perfect foil for a variety of cheeses, herbs, and sauces. Polenta has the added advantage of making do as an appetizer, a side dish (as at Silver Peak), or on its own as a vegetarian entrée.

The secret to good polenta is the cornmeal, which comes in a wide variety of textures and grinds, ranging from powdery, overprocessed corn with little flavor, to stone-ground meals that retain their natural germ. Large commercial mills use steel rollers to grind corn into meal. Some smaller mills grind with millstones, producing a coarser, more flavorful meal. The difference is like that between granulated sugar (which is a tiny bit coarse) and table salt (which is smooth and fine). In our tests, we found that the texture of polenta made with stone-ground meal was more substantial than polenta made with mass-produced cornmeal, and the corn flavor stood out rather than being masked by the flavors of the sun-dried tomatoes and cheese.

With the choice of cornmeal settled, we moved on to the ideal liquid to use and the best way to cook the polenta, which is traditionally a labor-intensive proposition. We tried using chicken broth and cream for our first batch of polenta and found that the broth overpowered the delicate corn flavor and the cream seemed to keep the polenta from solidifying when cooled. We then substituted water for some of the broth and finished the polenta with cream, rather than cooking it with the cornmeal. This yielded a smooth polenta that was firm enough to set up for cutting, yet still rich in flavor. Many traditional recipes require constant stirring and monitoring until the polenta thickens and loses its raw flavor, which can take more than 40 minutes. The method employed by Silver Peak—finishing the polenta in the oven after stirring in the cornmeal—required little babysitting and yielded perfectly cooked polenta with a creamy texture.

Polenta can easily serve as a backdrop for a multitude of flavor enhancements, such as fresh herbs, cheeses, and, in this case, the earthy flavor of sun-dried tomatoes, which lend taste, color, and texture to the polenta. Sun-dried tomatoes come either dried or rehydrated and packed in olive oil. When we tested the dried tomatoes rehydrated in hot water, the result was a fibrous texture that tasters found unappetizing. The oil-packed tomatoes were more tender, required less work, and pureed to a smoother texture than their dried counterpart. The next flavoring components were the two cheeses, Asiago and fontina, which were to top the polenta. Asiago is a sharp, nutty flavored, hard cheese similar to Parmesan or pecorino. We decided to streamline the process by stirring the firmer of the two cheeses, the Asiago, into the polenta before it was set. The polenta is then poured into a baking dish and refrigerated, where it will firm up sufficiently to be cut into shapes. The restaurant suggests half-moons, but we found that triangles were more efficient, leaving little waste and requiring no special cutting tools. The polenta is topped with fontina cheese and baked until the cheese reaches a golden, bubbly brown. The restaurant serves the polenta with a simple tomato sauce that can be made in a matter of minutes, although tasters in the test kitchen found the polenta just as good without the sauce—we leave the choice up to you.

Sun-Dried Tomato Polenta

SERVES 6 TO 8

Serve this polenta dish alongside grilled Italian sausages, or pair it with a hearty green salad for a vegetarian meal. We found that medium-grind, stone-ground cornmeal produced the most interesting texture and most pronounced corn flavor.

- 2 tablespoons extra-virgin olive oil
- 1 small onion, minced
- 2 garlic cloves, minced or pressed through a garlic press (about 2 teaspoons)
- 4 cups low-sodium chicken broth
- 2 1/4 cups medium-grind cornmeal, preferably stone-ground
- 1 (8-ounce) jar oil-packed sun-dried tomatoes, drained (oil reserved), and tomatoes chopped and patted dry with paper towels
- 1 tablespoon unsalted butter
- 1/2 cup heavy cream
- 8 ounces Asiago cheese, grated (4 cups)
- Salt and ground black pepper
- Vegetable oil spray
- 8 ounces fontina cheese, grated (about 4 cups)
- Simple Tomato Sauce (page 13) (optional)

1. Adjust the oven rack to the middle position and heat the oven to 350 degrees. Heat the olive oil in a Dutch oven over medium-high heat until shimmering. Add the onion and garlic and cook, stirring constantly, until the garlic is golden, about 1 minute. Add the broth and 3½ cups water and bring to a simmer. Stirring constantly in a circular motion with a whisk, pour the cornmeal into the broth in a very slow stream from a measuring cup. Whisk until thoroughly combined. Cover, transfer to the oven, and bake for 40 to 45 minutes, or until the polenta is very thick.

2. Lightly oil a 13 by 9-inch baking dish with 1 teaspoon of the reserved oil from the sun-dried tomatoes. Remove the polenta from the oven. Stir in the sun-dried tomatoes, butter, cream, and Asiago cheese and pour it into the prepared baking dish. Refrigerate for at least 3 hours or up to 3 days.

3. Heat the oven to 450 degrees, with the oven rack still in the middle position. Trim ½ inch off the long ends of the polenta. Cut the polenta into twelve 3-inch squares. Cut each square diagonally into triangles. Place the triangles ½ inch apart on a rimmed baking sheet lightly sprayed with vegetable oil. Evenly sprinkle each triangle with the fontina cheese. Bake until the cheese is melted and golden brown, 8 to 10 minutes. Let cool for 5 minutes. Serve with the Simple Tomato Sauce, if desired.

Anadama Bread

Adapted from Anadama Bread
The Friendly Toast, Portsmouth, New Hampshire

AN IMPORTANT COMPONENT OF THE Friendly Toast's famous Green Eggs and Ham (see page 155), anadama is an eccentric name for what amounts to sandwich bread enriched with cornmeal and molasses. Most sources attribute the unique name to an ornery New England farmer "damning" his wife "Anna" for the unwavering diet of cornmeal mush she provided for him. True or not, anadama bread has deep roots in New England cookery.

Starting with the Friendly Toast's original recipe, we found it made three large loaves, requiring nearly 12 cups of flour. Paring down the recipe to make a single loaf, we found it necessary to rearrange the method slightly to make it easier for the home cook.

At the Friendly Toast, the chefs place all the liquid ingredients in a mixer, then add flour until the dough reaches the right consistency. We decided to go with a more standard bread dough–making method. Figuring out the ratio of wet to dry ingredients ahead of time, we placed the flour in the mixing bowl and, with the mixer running, slowly added the liquid to make a dough. Knowing that roughly four cups of flour make a good-size loaf, we broke out appropriate measurements of all the dry ingredients. The restaurant mixes a small percentage of whole wheat flour with the all-purpose flour, and we determined that 3¼ cups of all-purpose flour, ¼ cup of whole wheat flour, and ¾ cup of cornmeal produced a well-balanced loaf. To this amount of dry ingredients, we added adjusted amounts of all the wet ingredients—the milk, melted butter, eggs, molasses, and sugar (which is always calculated as a liquid ingredient when baking).

Although we now had a well-proportioned dough that was easy to put together, we found the raw cornmeal discernibly gritty and lacking in flavor. In order to soften it, we microwaved it with some of the milk for two minutes on high, also throwing the butter into the mix so that it would melt. Coming out of the microwave a bit hot, we whisked in the remaining cold milk, molasses, and eggs to cool it down before making the dough.

We tried various types of cornmeal using this method, and tasters unanimously favored coarse, stone-ground cornmeal over finer cornmeal. Even after baking, the coarser meal retained a deep corn flavor and pleasing texture. Fine commercial cornmeal disappeared behind the strong flavor of the molasses. We tried different coarse cornmeals, both local and nationally available, and they all worked well. As far as molasses, dark, or "robust"-flavored, molasses (not to be confused with the extremely potent blackstrap molasses) was the winner, adding depth and a little mild bitterness that complemented the sweet corn flavor. The dark molasses also lent the loaf a rich ebony color reminiscent of gingerbread.

Anadama Bread

MAKES 1 LOAF

This bread is toasted in the Green Eggs and Ham recipe (see page 156), but it also makes a good accompaniment to soups and stews.

- **1 cup whole milk**
- **2 tablespoons unsalted butter, cut into 4 pieces**
- **3/4 cup (4 1/4 ounces) coarse-grind cornmeal, preferably stone-ground**
- **1/4 cup dark molasses (also called robust)**
- **2 large eggs**
- **3 1/4 cups (16 1/4 ounces) unbleached all-purpose flour**
- **1/4 cup (1 1/2 ounces) whole wheat flour**
- **1/4 cup sugar**
- **1 package instant yeast (about 2 1/2 teaspoons)**
- **1 1/2 teaspoons salt**
- **Vegetable oil spray**

1. Adjust an oven rack to the lowest position and heat the oven to 200 degrees. Once the oven reaches 200 degrees, maintain the heat for 10 minutes, then turn off the heat. Stir together ½ cup of the milk, the butter, and the cornmeal in a medium, microwave-proof bowl and microwave on high power, stirring occasionally, until the butter has melted and the cornmeal has expanded, 1 to 2 minutes. Whisk in the remaining ½ cup milk, the molasses, and the eggs and set aside to cool slightly.

2. Meanwhile, combine the all-purpose flour, whole wheat flour, sugar, yeast, and salt in the bowl of a standing mixer fitted with the dough hook. Turn the mixer on low and add the egg mixture in a slow, steady stream. Knead on low, scraping down the sides of the bowl as necessary, until a rough dough forms, about 2 minutes. Turn the mixer to medium-low and knead until the dough is taut but still sticky, about 8 minutes.

3. Turn the dough out onto a lightly floured work surface and knead to form a smooth, round ball, 15 to 30 seconds. Transfer to a large bowl very lightly coated with vegetable oil spray. Cover the bowl with plastic wrap and let rise in the warmed oven until doubled in size, about 1½ hours.

4. Grease a 9 by 5-inch loaf pan. Gently press the dough into a rectangle 1 inch thick and no longer than 9 inches. With a long side facing you, roll the dough firmly into a cylinder, pressing with your fingers to make sure the dough sticks to itself. Place the dough in the prepared pan and press gently so it touches all four sides of the pan. Loosely cover with plastic wrap and set aside in a warm place until the dough rises about 1½ inches above the rim of the pan, about 1½ hours.

5. Adjust an oven rack to the middle position and heat the oven to 350 degrees. Bake until an instant-read thermometer inserted at an angle just above the pan rim into the center of the loaf reads 195 degrees, 40 to 45 minutes. Remove the bread from the pan, transfer to a wire rack, and cool to room temperature. Slice and serve.

TAKING THE TEMPERATURE OF BREAD

Insert the thermometer from the side, just above the edge of the loaf pan, directing it at a downward angle toward the center of the loaf.

4 DESSERTS

Desserts

Brown Sugar Shortbread

Adapted from Brown Sugar Shortbread

Nola, New Orleans, Louisiana

RECIPE TITLES CAN OFTEN BE MISLEADING, as was the case with this recipe from Nola. Our expectations of shortbread were traditional: a cookie—buttery, sweet, with a "sandy" texture. Although this shortbread was certainly buttery and sweet, it lacked the crumbly, sandy texture and was instead candy-like—crisp and chewy, no doubt due to the substitution of brown sugar for the traditional granulated sugar. Before being baked, the shortbread cookies are sprinkled with a light coating of granulated sugar and cinnamon—another departure from tradition, but considering how good they were, we had no complaints.

The ease of this recipe and the short ingredient list left very few issues for us. Our goal was to fill in some blanks in order to ensure that a home cook could produce a consistently flavored and textured version of this shortbread cookie.

As the recipe stood, we felt that the procedure for creaming the butter and sugar was unclear. Without definitive times and visual cues, we were concerned that results could vary greatly, and in fact the results of our tests ranged widely. The creaming process in the original recipe was done in two stages. The butter was first whipped in a bowl, then the sugar was added and the mixture was beaten further. The recipe did not give us a time frame in which to cream the butter and sugar, however, so we made batch after batch varying the creaming times of each, to see what the best time was. After numerous batches, we found that whipping the butter on medium speed for 1½ minutes and then the butter and sugar for 1 minute longer resulted in a nicely textured cookie—crisp, yet chewy. Any longer and too much air was incorporated into the dough, which resulted in the shortbread becoming puffy and having an airy texture. Creaming for less time, we found, left the shortbread slightly denser and a little greasy.

The baking time was another issue that we worked to refine. The recipe called for baking the shortbread for a total of 30 to 40 minutes. Baking our initial shortbreads for 40 minutes, which matched the visual cues given in the recipe, we found that the center of the shortbread was slightly raw. This discrepancy was no doubt due to the fact that most restaurant kitchens are equipped with convection ovens that circulate the heat, thus speeding up the baking process. Increasing the baking time on subsequent tests by five minutes each time, we found that the shortbreads baked for 55 to 60 minutes were fully baked.

One final point we addressed was the pan in which the shortbread was baked. While most shortbread recipes call for a round cake pan, Nola chose to use a springform pan. Curious as to why, we tried baking Nola's recipe in a round cake pan. While the shortbread baked in the cake pan was similar in all aspects to the one baked in the springform pan, removing the shortbread from the round cake pan proved to be very difficult, with the cookie cracking all over during removal. Although we favored the springform pan, we did find it necessary to bake the shortbread on a baking sheet in order to keep excess butter from dripping onto the bottom of the oven and burning. Like traditional shortbread, this version did adhere to the method of scoring the cookies before they're baked. Just out of the oven, it's necessary to cut the cookies along the scores. (Don't wait until they're fully cooled, otherwise the shortbread will be impossible to cut.) Like most cookies with a high-butter content, these shortbreads will keep for just three days in an airtight container at room temperature.

EQUIPMENT: Digital Scales

Every serious cook needs an accurate scale for weighing fruits, vegetables, and meats. When making bread, a scale is even more critical. Professional bakers know that measuring flour by volume can be problematic. A cup of flour can weigh between 4 and 6 ounces, depending on the type of flour, the humidity, whether or not the flour has been sifted, and the way the flour has been put into the cup. Weight is a much more accurate way to measure flour.

There are essentially two types of kitchen scales. Mechanical scales operate on a spring and lever system. When an item is placed on the scale, internal springs are compressed. The springs are attached to levers, which move a needle on the scale's display (a ruler with lines and numbers printed on a piece of paper and glued to the scale). The more the springs are compressed, the farther the needle moves along the ruler.

Electronic, or digital, scales have two plates that are clamped at a fixed distance. The bottom plate is stationary, the top plate is not. When food is placed on the platform attached to the top plate, the distance between the plates changes slightly. The movement of the top plate (no more than one thousandth of an inch) causes a change in the flow of electricity through the scale's circuitry. This change is translated into a weight and expressed in numbers displayed on the face of the scale.

We tested 10 electronic scales and 9 mechanical scales. As a group, the electronic scales were vastly preferred. Their digital displays are much easier to read than the measures on most mechanical scales, where the lines on the ruler are so closely spaced it's impossible to nail down the precise weight within half an ounce. Also, many mechanical scales could weigh items only within a limited range—usually between 1 ounce and 5 pounds. What's the point of owning a scale that can't weigh a large chicken or roast? Most electronic scales can handle items that weigh as much as 10 pounds and as little as ¼ ounce. Among the electronic scales we tested, we found that several features make the difference between a good electronic scale and a great one. Readability is a must. The displayed numbers should be large. Also, the displayed numbers should be steeply angled and as far from the weighing platform as possible. If the display is too close to the platform, the numbers can hide beneath the rim of a dinner plate or cake pan.

An automatic shut-off feature will save battery life, but this feature can be annoying, especially if the shut-off cycle kicks in at under two minutes. A scale that shuts off automatically after five minutes or more is easier to use. A large weighing platform (that detaches for easy cleaning) is another plus. Last, we preferred electronic scales that display weight increments in decimals rather than fractions. The former are more accurate and easier to work with when scaling a recipe up or down.

Brown Sugar Shortbread

MAKES 12

While delicious on their own, these cookies are the perfect accompaniment to ice cream or afternoon tea.

- Vegetable oil spray
- 16 tablespoons (2 sticks) unsalted butter, softened
- 1 cup packed (7 ounces) light brown sugar
- 2 cups (10 ounces) unbleached all-purpose flour
- ¼ teaspoon salt
- 1 tablespoon granulated sugar
- ¼ teaspoon ground cinnamon

1. Adjust an oven rack to the middle position and heat the oven to 350 degrees. Lightly spray the bottom and sides of a 9-inch springform pan with vegetable oil spray.

2. In the bowl of a standing mixer fitted with the paddle attachment, beat the butter on medium speed until light and pale yellow, about 1½ minutes. Add the brown sugar and mix on medium speed until fluffy, about 1 minute. Add the flour and salt and mix on low speed until just incorporated. Empty the mixture into the prepared pan and, following the illustrations at the right, press it evenly into the bottom of the pan.

3. Combine the sugar and cinnamon in a small bowl and sprinkle evenly over the surface of the shortbread. Using a paring knife, score the shortbread into 12 even wedges.

4. Place the springform pan on a rimmed baking sheet. Bake until the shortbread is golden brown and firm at the edges, yet slightly soft in the center, 55 to 60 minutes. Transfer to a wire rack, remove the springform pan sides, and cool for 10 minutes. Slide the shortbread onto a cutting board and recut the wedges along the existing lines. Let the cookies cool completely before serving, about 3 hours. (The shortbread may be stored in an airtight container at room temperature for up to 3 days.)

PRESSING THE DOUGH INTO THE PAN

1. Use the bottom of a ramekin or drinking glass to press the dough into the bottom of the prepared pan. Press the dough as far as possible into the edges of the pan.

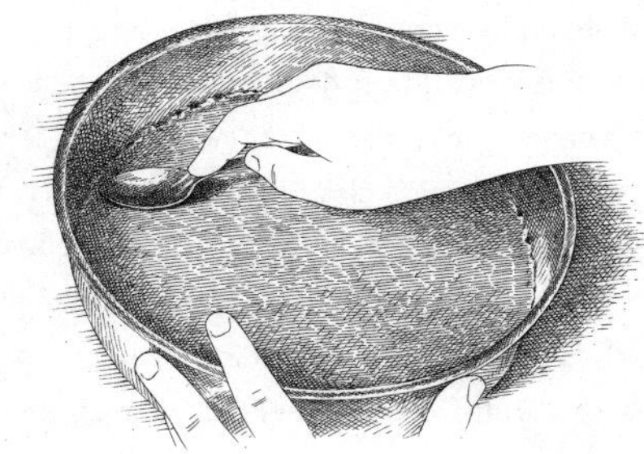

2. Use a teaspoon to press the dough neatly into the corners of the pan to create a clean edge.

Fig Bars

Adapted from Emma's Fig Bars

Olga's Cup and Saucer, Providence, Rhode Island

BEARING LITTLE RESEMBLANCE TO THE prepackaged fig bars of childhood, these pastries from Olga's Cup and Saucer are a grown-up treat better suited to a cup of tea than a glass of milk. A puree of dried Turkish figs plumped in apple juice is sandwiched between layers of buttery oatmeal crust. The result is chewy, rich, and homey—the definitive bar cookie.

The ease of these bars lies in the crust, which does double duty as the base and the topping. Many recipes for fruit bars call for mixing dry ingredients, then adding cold butter to make a sandy-looking dough. Emma's recipe beats the butter with the brown sugar, then adds the combined dry ingredients, resulting in an unusually light dough that complements the dense fig filling without weighing down the bar. Quick and rolled oats are the most widely available, and we wondered if they could be used interchangeably in this recipe. After baking one batch of bars with rolled oats, and one with quick oats (not instant), we concluded that the differences were noticeable, but neither produced a bad bar. The rolled oats yielded a bar with good chew (not a bad thing) with discernable oat pieces. The bars made with quick oats were a bit softer and more delicate, with oat pieces that were less visible—still a perfectly acceptable bar.

Although many varieties of dried figs are available, the restaurant specifies Turkish figs for this recipe, and we naturally wondered why. To answer our question, we made purees of four of the varieties available in local markets: organic Black Mission, organic Calimyrna, Turkish, and organic Turkish. Three of the figs tested made an acceptable puree that would serve the bars well. Calimyrna were well liked, but tasters preferred the Turkish figs for their sweetness and earthy flavor (the Black Mission, one of the most common varieties, yielded an unattractive color and an off-putting, medicinal flavor). If Turkish figs are unavailable, the Calimyrna variety makes a perfectly acceptable substitute.

We were curious as to what the effects of baking the bars in an eight-inch pan would be if the specified nine-inch pan could not be found. As it turned out, the one-inch difference produced dramatically different results. The bars baked in the smaller pan had a hefty fig filling, nearly an inch thick. Those from the larger pan had a more moderate layer of fruit that made the bar easier to cut while still a bit warm. Both sizes had their fans, the bottom line being how much of a fig fanatic you are. Duly noted was the fact that the thinner bars made for easier portability, with less filling to ooze out the sides. Whatever your preference, thick or thin, crumbly or chewy, this bar cookie is a toothsome treat.

Fig Bars

MAKES 36

Note that a glass baking dish will yield a browner bottom crust than a metal pan. If you prefer a bar with more chew, choose the rolled oats over the quick oats. When buying figs, look for either Turkish or Calimyrna figs that are plump and soft.

- 1 pound dried Turkish or Calimyrna figs, stems removed
- 2 1/2–3 cups apple juice
- Vegetable oil spray
- 1 3/4 cups (8 3/4 ounces) unbleached all-purpose flour
- 1 1/2 cups rolled or quick oats (see headnote)
- 1 teaspoon ground cinnamon
- 1/2 teaspoon baking soda
- 1/2 teaspoon salt
- 16 tablespoons (2 sticks) unsalted butter, softened
- 1 cup packed (7 ounces) light brown sugar
- 2 teaspoons vanilla extract

1. Bring the figs and 2½ cups of the apple juice to a simmer in a medium saucepan over medium heat. Cook, stirring occasionally, adding more juice as necessary, ¼ cup at a time, until the figs are puffed and soft and most of the liquid has been absorbed and the remaining liquid is thick and syrupy, 30 to 40 minutes. Transfer the figs and the remaining apple juice to a food processor and puree until very smooth, about 1 minute, scraping down the sides of the bowl with a rubber spatula as necessary. Transfer to a medium bowl and set aside at room temperature until completely cool, about 45 minutes.

2. Adjust an oven rack to the lower-middle position and heat the oven to 350 degrees. Spray a 9-inch square baking pan with vegetable oil spray. Following the illustrations below, fit one sheet of foil or parchment (large enough to overhang the sides of the pan) into the bottom of the greased pan, pushing it into the corners and up the sides of the pan (the overhang will help in the removal of the baked bars). Fit the second sheet in the pan in the same manner, perpendicular to the first sheet. Spray the foil with vegetable oil spray.

3. Whisk the flour, oats, cinnamon, baking soda, and salt together in a medium bowl and set aside. In the bowl of a standing mixer

EASY BAR COOKIE REMOVAL

1. Place two sheets of aluminum foil or parchment perpendicular to each other in the pan. Transfer half of the crumb mixture into the pan, pressing it evenly onto the bottom, reaching all corners. Spread the crust with the fig puree and sprinkle with the remaining crumb mixture.

2. After the bars have baked and cooled, use the foil or parchment to transfer them to a cutting board, then slice into individual portions.

fitted with the paddle attachment, beat the butter, brown sugar, and vanilla on medium speed until light and fluffy, about 3 minutes. Turn the mixer to low speed, add the dry ingredients, and beat until the mixture is well combined and resembles moist sand, about 2 minutes. Transfer half of the mixture to the prepared pan and use your hands to press the crumbs evenly into the bottom. Using a rubber spatula, spread the cooled fig puree evenly over the bottom crust. Sprinkle the remaining crumbs evenly over the puree and press lightly to adhere.

4. Bake until the fig puree bubbles around the edges and the top is golden brown, 40 to 50 minutes, rotating the pan from front to back halfway through the baking time. Cool on a wire rack to room temperature, about 2 hours. Remove the bars from the pan using the foil handles (see illustration 2 on page 338) and transfer to a cutting board. Cut into 1½-inch squares and serve.

GAUGING PROPERLY SOFTENED BUTTER

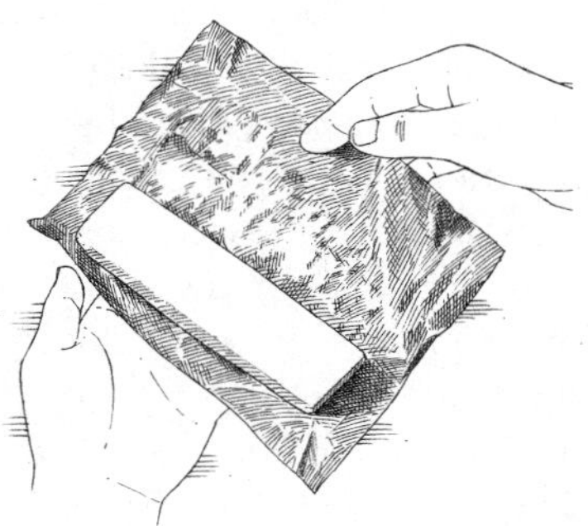

1. When you unwrap the butter, the wrapping should have a creamy residue on the inside. If there's no residue, the butter is probably too cold.

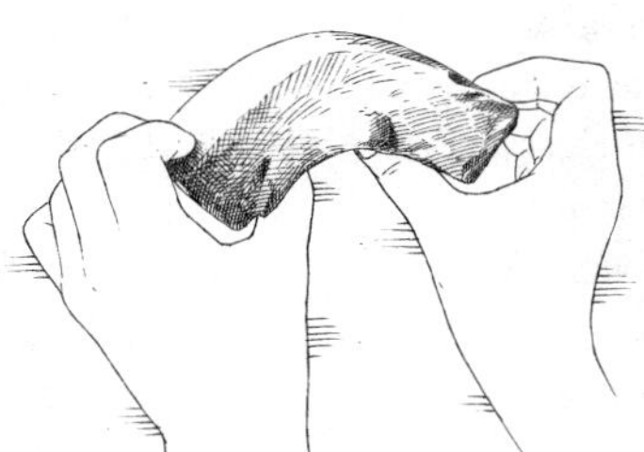

2. The butter should bend with little resistance and without cracking or breaking.

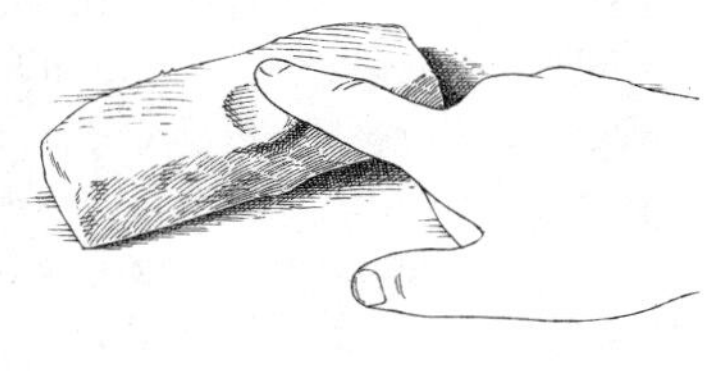

3. The butter should give slightly when pressed but still hold its shape.

Raspberry-Filled Pocket Tarts

Adapted from Raspberry-Filled Pop Tarts

Flour Bakery & Café, Boston, Massachusetts

AT FIRST GLANCE, THESE TARTS MIGHT seem familiar to those who grew up thinking that tarts needed to be "popped" into the toaster before eating—but be assured that the comparisons end there. These treats from Flour Bakery & Café consist of rich, buttery pastry encasing a thin layer of tart raspberry jam. Brushed with a shiny, white glaze, they make for a sweet breakfast, fun snack, or whimsical dessert.

Made with lots of butter and enriched with egg yolks and milk, the texture of the tart crust is a cross between shortbread, pie dough, and puff pastry. Like most commercial bakeries, the bakers make this rich dough in a large-capacity commercial standing mixer to accommodate huge batches. Most home cooks, however, make doughs in a food processor or household standing mixer. Giving both the food processor and standing mixer a whirl, we found the mixer actually worked far better. Rather than having the blades of the processor cut the butter into the flour, the paddle of the standing mixer smeared the butter into the flour, simulating a French technique called *fraisage.* The resulting texture was unique—it crumbled apart into short flakes after being baked.

Because of its high proportion of butter, the dough is quite soft and more difficult to manipulate than a pie dough. The bakery is lucky enough to have an expensive machine called a sheeter—a long conveyor belt that runs dough back and forth between a set of rolling pins to help roll out the dough quickly without using a lot of excess flour (which makes the dough tough). To approximate the action of a sheeter, we rolled the dough out between two pieces of floured parchment paper. We also noted that it was important to keep the dough chilled and firm to prevent it from falling apart. Rather than rolling, trimming, forming, and cutting both crusts at the same time, we worked with one at a time while letting the other chill in the refrigerator.

When assembling the tarts, we found it easiest to use the bakery's efficient all-at-once method rather than assembling them individually. After laying an entire sheet of pastry on the counter, a ruler is used to outline the edges. Egg wash is brushed over the entire surface of the crust, then small spoonfuls of jam are placed in the center of each outlined tart. The second crust is then laid over the top and pressed tightly to seal around the pockets of jam. The tarts are then cut apart from one another and frozen before being baked. Although the freezing is done for reasons of efficiency in the bakery, we found that the frozen tarts baked more evenly and leaked less in the oven than unfrozen ones (a little leakage of jam is to be expected). The cooled tarts are finished with a sweet glaze that is a traditional combination of water mixed with confectioners' sugar.

Raspberry-Filled Pocket Tarts

MAKES 9

The dough may be made through step 2 and then wrapped tightly in plastic wrap and refrigerated for up to 2 days or frozen for up to 2 months. Thaw the frozen dough in the refrigerator for 1 day before you plan to bake it.

- **2** large egg yolks
- **¼** cup whole milk
- **2½** cups (12½ ounces) unbleached all-purpose flour
- **4** teaspoons granulated sugar
- **½** teaspoon salt
- **16** tablespoons (2 sticks) very cold unsalted butter, cut into ¼-inch cubes
- **1** large egg, lightly beaten
- **4½** tablespoons raspberry jam (seedless, if desired)
- **1** cup confectioners' sugar

1. Whisk the egg yolks and milk together in a small bowl and set aside. In the bowl of a standing mixer fitted with the paddle attachment, mix the flour, sugar, and salt on low until combined, about 10 seconds. Add the butter and mix on low until the flour is no longer white and the butter pieces are the size of lentils, about 1½ minutes. Add the yolk mixture and mix on low just until the dough comes together, about 20 seconds.

2. Transfer the dough to a work surface. Using your hands, press the dough into a 6-inch square about 1 inch thick. Cut the dough into two smaller rectangles, each about 6 by 3 inches. Wrap tightly with plastic wrap and refrigerate for at least 30 minutes or up to 2 days.

3. If the dough has been refrigerated for longer than 30 minutes, let it stand at room temperature until malleable. Working with one piece of dough at a time, roll out into a 12½ by 9½-inch rectangle about ⅛ inch thick between two large, lightly floured sheets of parchment paper. (If the dough begins to soften before it is completely rolled out, transfer it to a baking sheet and refrigerate until firm enough to continue.) Using the edges of the parchment as handles, slide the crusts onto a baking sheet and refrigerate until firm, about 5 minutes.

4. Working with one crust at a time, transfer to a cutting board and remove the top layer of parchment. Following illustration 1 on page 342, use a ruler and a pizza cutter to trim the crust into a tidy 12 by 9-inch rectangle. Replace the top layer of parchment and return to the baking sheet in the refrigerator. Refrigerate the trimmed crusts until very firm, about 10 minutes.

5. Transfer one of the crusts to a cutting board and remove the top piece of parchment. Following illustrations 2 through 5 on page 342, use a pizza cutter to score the crust gently, without cutting through it, into thirds both lengthwise and widthwise, outlining nine 4 by 3-inch rectangles. Brush the crust with the beaten egg. Place 1½ teaspoons of the jam in the middle of each scored rectangle. Remove the second crust from the refrigerator. Remove both pieces of parchment paper and lay the second crust directly over the first crust. (If the crust feels too feels soft, gently drape it over a rolling pin to make the transfer easier.) Use your

fingertips to press the crusts together firmly around the pockets of jam to seal tightly. Cut the dough evenly between the jam pockets into 9 individual tarts and transfer to a rimmed baking sheet lined with parchment paper. Freeze until very hard, about 1 hour. (You can also wrap the pockets in plastic wrap and freeze for up to 1 month.)

6. Meanwhile, adjust an oven rack to the middle position and heat the oven to 350 degrees. Bake the tarts straight from the freezer until the tops are golden brown, 40 to 45 minutes. Transfer the tarts to a wire rack and cool to room temperature, about 30 minutes.

7. Whisk the confectioners' sugar and 2 tablespoons water together in a small bowl to make a thick glaze. Using a pastry brush or the back of a soup spoon, gently spread the glaze over the tops of the cooled tarts. Let the glaze harden, about 5 minutes. The tarts are best when eaten the same day they are baked.

ASSEMBLING THE TARTS

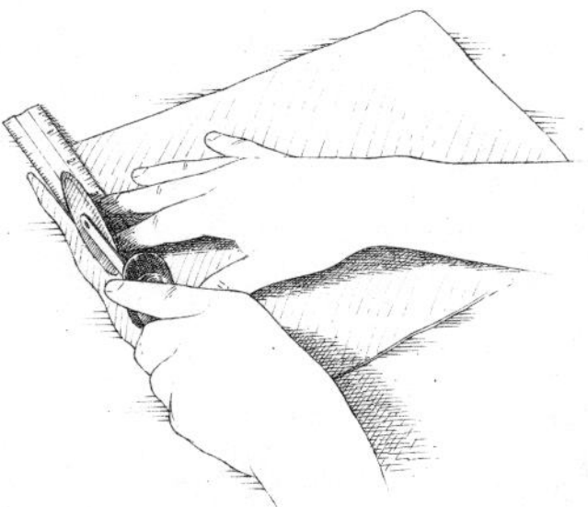

1. After rolling both pieces of dough into 12½ by 9½-inch rectangles, use a ruler and a pizza cutter to trim the crusts into tidy 12 by 9-inch rectangles. Return both to the refrigerator to chill for 10 minutes.

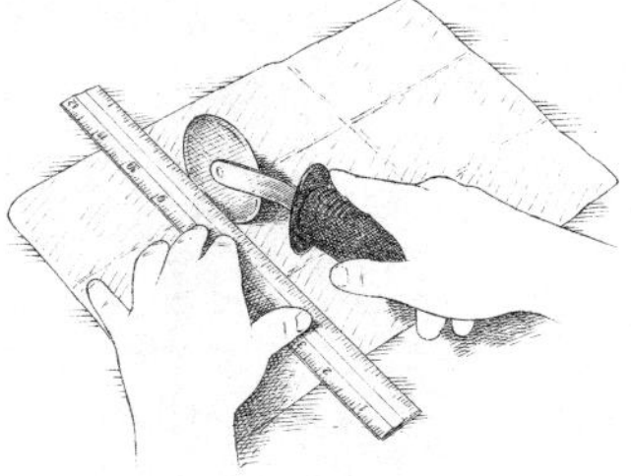

2. Transfer one crust to a cutting board and remove the top piece of parchment. Using a pizza cutter, gently score (do not cut through) the dough into thirds both lengthwise and widthwise, outlining nine 4 by 3-inch rectangles.

3. After brushing the sheet with the beaten egg, place 1½ teaspoons of the jam in the middle of each scored rectangle.

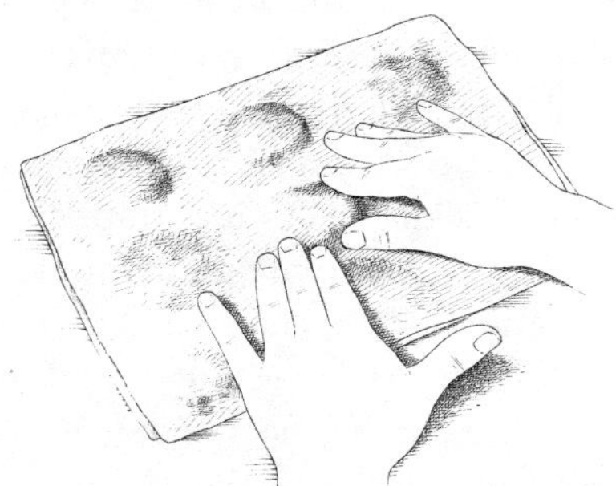

4. Remove the other crust from the refrigerator and remove both pieces of parchment. Gently lay the top crust directly over the bottom crust. (If the dough feels soft, gently drape it over a rolling pin to make the transfer easier.) Using your fingertips, press firmly around each pocket of jam, sealing the dough tightly.

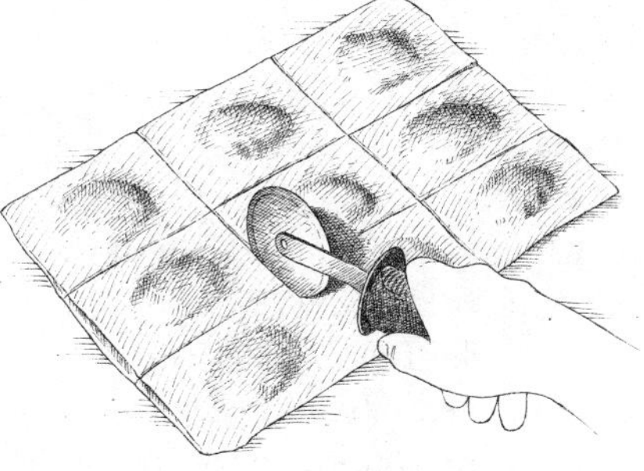

5. Use the pizza cutter to cut the tarts apart and arrange them 1 inch apart on a rimmed baking sheet lined with parchment paper. Freeze for 1 hour.

CHICAGO-STYLE CHEESECAKE

Adapted from Eli's Cheesecake

ELI'S THE PLACE FOR STEAK, CHICAGO, ILLINOIS

ELI'S THE PLACE FOR STEAK IS A RESTAURANT with deep roots in Chicago, known as much for its cheesecake and celebrity following as its steaks. Dense, creamy, and lightly flavored with vanilla and sour cream, this Chicago cheesecake, we daresay, easily rivals its New York cousin.

Beginning with Eli's signature cookie crust, we made just one alteration in the method. The original recipe makes the crust much as you would a pie crust: making and chilling a large batch of crumbly dough, then rolling it out and trimming it to fit the bottom of the cheesecake pan (a springform pan). Instead, we found it easier to scale back the amount of cookie dough and press it immediately into the bottom of the pan. We chilled this pressed crust (in its pan) for 30 minutes to ensure that it wouldn't shrink as it baked. The key to making a crisp cheesecake crust that doesn't turn soggy is baking it separately before adding the cheesecake filling (known as blind baking). The original recipe blind-bakes the crust at two different temperatures (to prevent shrinkage), but our method requires only about 20 minutes at 350 degrees. Finding that the crust bakes very little after it's filled, it is best to blind-bake the crust until it is completely golden and crisp.

Made in a standing mixer, the cheesecake filling is easy to put together, requiring only a small amount of patience and an agile rubber spatula. The trick here is to incorporate the ingredients into the dense cream cheese slowly, scraping down the bowl and beater repeatedly, so that the final batter is smooth and consistent. In addition to cream cheese, sour cream, sugar, and vanilla, Eli's uses a combination of flour, whole eggs, and an egg yolk for structure and flavor. Some cheesecakes are baked in a water bath, which ensures slow, steady heat, giving the cakes a light, almost custardy texture. This cheesecake is dense and creamy, much like a New York–style cheesecake, and doesn't require this extra step. The springform pan is placed on a rimmed baking sheet to help catch any drips or spills.

The original recipe calls for baking the cake at 360 degrees, which might make sense when using fancy, expensive, and insanely accurate professional ovens, but is somewhat awkward on a dial-style, home oven. Baking it at 350 degrees, we found, worked just as well, taking 50 to 60 minutes. To tell when it's done, we found it easiest to use an instant-read thermometer. Reaching an internal temperature of 150 degrees, the center of the cake should jiggle just slightly when done. Cool the cheesecake on the counter and then in the refrigerator for several hours—the flavor is so incredible, it's worth the wait.

Chicago-Style Cheesecake

SERVES 8

When cutting the cake, have a pitcher of hot tap water ready; dipping the blade of the knife into the water and wiping it after each slice helps make clean slices.

CRUST

- **6 tablespoons (3/4 stick) unsalted butter, cut into 1-inch pieces, softened**
- **1/4 cup (1 ounce) confectioners' sugar**
- **1/8 teaspoon vanilla extract**
- **3/4 cup (3 3/4 ounces) unbleached all-purpose flour**
- **Pinch salt**

FILLING

- **1 1/2 pounds cream cheese, softened**
- **3/4 cup (5 1/4 ounces) granulated sugar**
- **1 tablespoon unbleached all-purpose flour**
- **1/8 teaspoon salt**
- **1/2 cup sour cream**
- **1 teaspoon vanilla extract**
- **1 large egg yolk**
- **2 large eggs**
- **Melted unsalted butter, for greasing pan**

1. FOR THE CRUST: In a standing mixer fitted with the paddle attachment, beat the butter and confectioners' sugar together on medium speed until light and fluffy, about 3 minutes, scraping down the sides of the bowl with a rubber spatula as needed. Add the vanilla and mix until combined, about 30 seconds. Add the flour and salt and beat on low speed until just combined, about 30 seconds.

2. Empty the mixture into an 8-inch springform pan and, following illustrations 1 and 2 on page 336, press it evenly into the bottom of the pan. Refrigerate until firm, about 30 minutes. Wash the mixer bowl and paddle.

3. Meanwhile, adjust an oven rack to the lower-middle position and heat the oven to 350 degrees. Prick the chilled crust several times with a fork and bake until golden, about 20 minutes. Transfer to a wire rack and cool completely. Adjust the oven rack to the middle position, maintaining the oven temperature to 350 degrees

4. FOR THE FILLING: In a standing mixer fitted with the paddle attachment, beat the cream cheese on medium-low speed to break it up and soften it slightly, about 1 minute. Scrape the paddle and bowl well with a rubber spatula. Add half the sugar and beat on medium-low speed until combined, about 1 minute. Scrape the bowl. Beat in the remaining sugar, flour, and salt until combined, about 1 minute. Scrape the bowl. Add the sour cream and vanilla and beat on low speed until combined, about 1 minute. Scrape the bowl. Add the egg yolk and beat on medium-low speed until thoroughly combined, about 1 minute. Scrape the bowl. Add the eggs, 1 at a time, and beat after each addition until thoroughly combined, about 1 minute.

5. Brush the sides of the cooled springform pan with melted butter. Set the pan on a rimmed baking sheet to catch any spills or leaks. Pour the filling onto the cooled crust and bake until the cheesecake is firm around the edges, jiggles slightly in the center, and an instant-read thermometer inserted into the center registers about 150 degrees, 50 to 60 minutes. Transfer to a wire rack and cool for 3 hours. Wrap tightly in plastic wrap and refrigerate until cold, at least 3 hours. (The cheesecake can be refrigerated for up to 4 days.)

6. To unmold the cheesecake, remove the sides of the pan. Slide a thin, metal spatula between the crust and pan bottom to loosen, then slide the cake onto a serving plate. Let the cheesecake stand at room temperature for about 30 minutes, then cut into wedges and serve.

Asian Five-Spice Chocolate Cake

Adapted from Asian Five-Spice Chocolate Cake
Asia Nora, Washington, D.C.

AN ASIAN CHOCOLATE DESSERT? TO THOSE who miss a chocolate finale to an Asian meal—where fruit and sweetened rice desserts usually prevail—Asia Nora offers this deceptively light, moist chocolate cake infused with a homemade version of Asian five-spice powder. The cake looks somewhat like a brownie, but when sliced reveals a texture that lies somewhere between a chocolate mousse cake and a molten chocolate cake. Served alongside the cake is a delicate whipped cream flecked with candied ginger, which heightens the cake's Asian flavors and complements its chocolatey richness.

A traditional seasoning used in Chinese cooking, five-spice powder adds a pungent, aromatic depth to foods. Commercial blends typically contain five or more of the following in varying ratios: cinnamon, star anise, Sichuan peppercorns, cloves, fennel seeds, anise seeds, ground ginger, and dried orange peel. Because the types of spices and their ratios are not standard, different brands of the spice mixture produce dramatically different results when used in the same recipe. Fortunately, Chef Haidar Karoum includes his own eight-spice version of the blend with this chocolate cake recipe. His blend contains the usual suspects, but replaces the anise seeds and dried orange peel with coriander seeds and black peppercorns.

Berries from the native Asian prickly ash tree, Sichuan peppercorns are characteristic of Chinese five-spice powders. Unfortunately, packaged separately, they can be difficult to find outside of specialty food shops and Asian markets. Do not try substituting black peppercorns for Sichuan peppercorns. Although similar in name, the two spices are unrelated and impart different flavors to a dish. If you have trouble finding Sichuan peppercorns, you may add two additional star anise pods and ¼ teaspoon ground white pepper to achieve a similar woodsy flavor and piquancy.

We were skeptical of commercial five-spice blends for this recipe, but were curious enough in the test kitchen to compare the cake made with Chef Karoum's blend and one made with a widely available commercial brand. The results could not have been more dramatic. Tasters found the store-bought blend too strong for this cake. The restaurant's blend was much more delicate. It added a pleasing warmth that rounded out the cake's intense chocolate flavor.

This cake depends on whole eggs

whipped with sugar to give it structure. Whole-egg foams are created by emulsifying water and air in much the same way that vinaigrettes are made by combining oil and vinegar. Like oil and vinegar, air and water are incompatible and will not mix unless forced to combine by the mechanical action of mixing and the emulsifying agents present in egg yolks. When you beat the eggs, air and the water present in the egg whites become suspended in the eggs and the mixture increases substantially in volume.

Since the structure of the cake depends on the strength of the emulsion, pay careful attention to the process of beating the whole eggs. In kitchen tests, we discovered a couple of important guidelines to ensure that the eggs are properly beaten. Cold eggs will not achieve the same volume when whipped as eggs at room temperature, so before whipping the eggs bring them to room temperature by covering them, still in their shells, with warm water while you prepare the other ingredients. Beat the eggs and sugar on medium-high speed until the eggs have tripled in volume and are a very pale, slightly dull yellow with tiny, uniform bubbles, but are not dry. When the whisk is lifted, a thick, billowy strand of beaten eggs will fall back into the bowl and rest for about 10 seconds on top of the eggs before dissolving into the mixture. The amount of time required to beat the eggs depends on the type of equipment you use. Using a balloon whisk will take much more energy and effort than using either a standing mixer or a hand mixer. Typically, a hand mixer will take a couple minutes longer to whip the eggs and sugar properly than a standing mixer. If not using a standing mixer, rely more on visual cues than on time estimates to determine when to stop mixing.

Finally, cooking the cake in a water bath allows the fragile whole-egg foam to cook slowly and evenly so that the cake's structure does not collapse. Make sure that you add simmering water, rather than cold water, to the roasting pan so that the cake will cook in the time specified in this recipe.

Asian Five-Spice Chocolate Cake

SERVES 12 TO 16

The Asian spice blend makes about ¼ cup of powder—more than you will need for one cake. Save the extra powder in an airtight container for the next time you make this cake or use it in a savory preparation that calls for Chinese five-spice powder, such as Five-Spice Tuna with Asian Ginger Slaw and Fried Noodles (page 268). The cake is baked in a bain-marie, or hot water bath. To prevent water from leaking into the cake during baking, the springform pan is wrapped in a double layer of foil.

- 10 tablespoons (1 ¼ sticks) unsalted butter, cut into ½-inch pieces, plus more for greasing the pan
- 5 whole star anise pods
- 1 tablespoon fennel seeds
- 1 tablespoon Sichuan peppercorns
- 1 ½ teaspoons coriander seeds
- 15 whole black peppercorns
- 6 whole cloves
- ¼ teaspoon ground cinnamon
- ⅛ teaspoon ground ginger
- 1 ¼ cups (8 ¾ ounces) sugar
- 7 ounces unsweetened chocolate, finely chopped
- 6 ounces bittersweet chocolate, finely chopped
- 6 large eggs, at room temperature
- ¼ teaspoon salt
- Candied Ginger Whipped Cream (page 348)

1. Adjust an oven rack to the lower-middle position and heat the oven to 350 degrees. Wrap the outside of a 9-inch springform pan with two 18-inch squares of heavy-duty foil. Butter the sides and bottom of the pan. Line the bottom of the pan with a circle of parchment paper and butter the paper.

2. Finely grind the star anise, fennel seeds, Sichuan peppercorns, coriander seeds, black peppercorns, and cloves in a spice grinder, about 1 minute. Transfer the spice mixture to a small bowl, stir in the cinnamon and ginger, and set aside.

3. Bring ½ cup water, 1 cup of the sugar, and 1 tablespoon of the spice mixture to a boil in a medium saucepan over high heat. Remove the pan from the heat, cover, and steep for 5 minutes.

4. Place the unsweetened and bittersweet chocolates and remaining 10 tablespoons butter in a large, heatproof bowl. Strain the warm, steeped water through a fine-mesh strainer into the bowl of chocolate. Warm the bowl over a saucepan filled with 2 quarts simmering water, stirring frequently, until the chocolate is completely melted and the mixture is smooth. Remove the bowl from the heat and set the simmering water aside.

5. In a standing mixer fitted with the whisk attachment, beat the eggs, salt, and remaining ¼ cup sugar on medium-high speed until the eggs have tripled in volume,

UNMOLDING THE CAKE

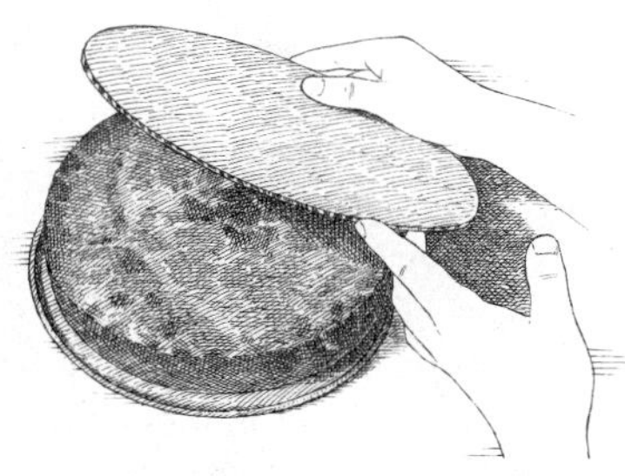

1. After removing the sides of the springform pan, lay a cardboard cake round (or large, flat plate) on top of the cake.

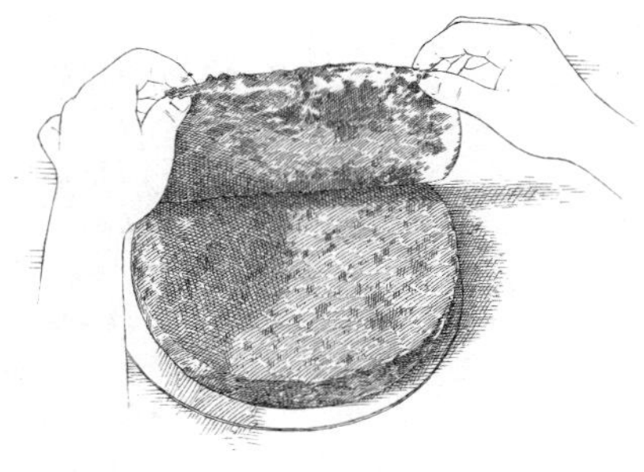

2. Pressing the cake pan bottom and cardboard round together firmly, flip the cake upside down onto the cardboard. Carefully remove the springform pan bottom and parchment paper from the cake bottom.

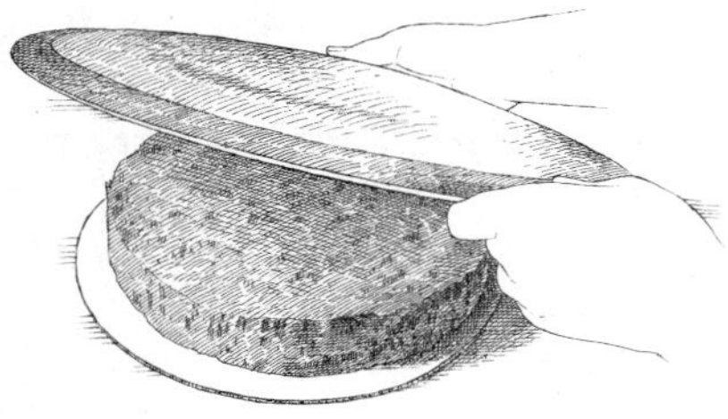

3. Invert a large, flat cake platter over the upside-down cake.

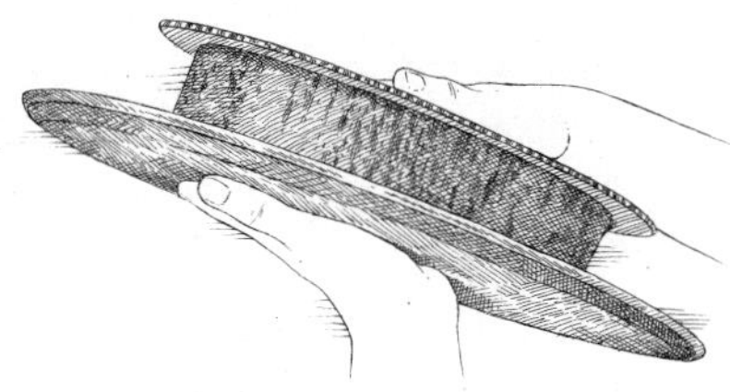

4. Pressing the cake round and platter firmly together, flip the cake right-side up onto the platter and remove the cardboard round.

turned pale yellow, and leave a thick ribbon when the beaters are raised, about 7 minutes. Using a whisk, stir about one-quarter of the beaten eggs into the chocolate mixture to lighten it. Gently fold in the remaining eggs using a whisk until no streaks remain.

6. Gently scrape the batter into the prepared pan. Place the springform pan into a roasting pan, then pour the hot water from the saucepan into the roasting pan to a depth of 1½ inches. Carefully slide the roasting pan into the oven and bake until the cake has risen, is firm around the edges, just set in the center, and registers 165 degrees on an instant-read thermometer, 40 to 45 minutes. Remove the cake from the water bath, remove the foil, and cool completely on a wire rack, about 2 hours.

7. To unmold the cake, run a paring knife around the edge of the cake to loosen, and remove the sides of the springform pan. Following illustrations 1 through 4 on page 347, invert the cake onto a cardboard cake round (or flat plate) and remove the pan bottom and parchment paper. Invert the cake right-side up onto a serving platter. (The cake can be made up to 2 days ahead, wrapped tightly in plastic wrap, and refrigerated. Bring to room temperature before serving.) To serve, cut with a sharp, thin-bladed knife, dipping it into a pitcher of hot water and wiping the blade before each cut. Serve with Candied Ginger Whipped Cream.

Whipped Cream

MAKES ABOUT 2 CUPS

Many sources suggest sweetening whipped cream with confectioners' sugar to ensure that the sugar dissolves. In our tests of lightly sweetened whipped cream, regular granulated sugar dissolved just as well as long as it was added before beating, not after. When making a highly sweetened whipped cream topping (with more than 2 tablespoons of sugar per cup of heavy cream), it is best to use fine confectioners' sugar to prevent the possibility of grittiness.

- **1 cup heavy cream, chilled, preferably pasteurized (not ultrapasteurized) or pasteurized organic**
- **1 tablespoon sugar**
- **1 teaspoon vanilla extract**

1. Chill a deep, nonreactive, 1- to 1½-quart bowl and beaters for a hand mixer in the freezer for at least 20 minutes.

2. Add the cream, sugar, and vanilla to the chilled bowl. Beat on low speed until small bubbles form, about 30 seconds. Increase the speed to medium and beat until the beaters leave a trail, about 30 seconds. Increase the speed to high and beat until the cream is smooth, thick, and nearly doubled in volume, about 20 seconds for soft peaks or about 30 seconds for stiff peaks. If necessary, finish beating by hand to adjust the consistency. Serve immediately or spoon into a fine sieve or strainer set over a medium bowl and refrigerate for up to 8 hours.

VARIATION

Candied Ginger Whipped Cream

Follow the recipe for Whipped Cream, omitting the vanilla extract. Fold 1 tablespoon (about 1 ounce) finely chopped candied ginger into the whipped cream. Serve immediately.

Individual German Chocolate Cakes

Adapted from German Truffle Layer Cake

Syrah, Naples, Florida

MOST GERMAN CHOCOLATE CAKES LOOK downright homey, dripping with copious amounts of gooey, coconut frosting. At Syrah, however, they've managed to turn this sweet, sticky mess into elegant, individual desserts. Large rounds are stamped from a chocolate sheet cake, then sliced in half and layered with just enough coconut filling to deserve its name. Served on a plate decorated with both chocolate and caramel sauces and garnished with a thin, curly, flower-shaped cookie (called a tuile), its inside-out presentation is a far cry from homey.

Focusing on the cake first, we were pleasantly surprised to find it was based on an easy technique known as a simple, two-step method. This method mixes the liquid ingredients and the dry ingredients separately, combining them just briefly before being poured in a cake pan and baked. The wet ingredients include milk, water, eggs, vegetable oil, and vinegar. Chocolate cakes of this type classically use buttermilk for its tang and leavening properties (in conjunction with either baking soda or baking powder). However, the restaurant's substitution of whole milk and vinegar is far more pantry-friendly. Most cakes also use melted butter as opposed to vegetable oil. However, we found that the flavorless oil made the cake taste clean and delicate.

The dry ingredients include all-purpose flour, Dutch-processed cocoa, sugar, and baking powder. After reducing the cake's overall yield by a third, we found it necessary to add salt and increase the percentage of cocoa to bring out the chocolate flavor. Testing the difference between baking powder and the more traditional baking soda (usually used in cakes like this), we found that soda simply didn't work. Baking powder produced cakes that were dark and even, while baking soda produced odd, orange-hued cakes so uneven they looked as though they had been baked aboard a rocking sailboat. The soda, as it turned out, was just too powerful for the delicate cake, which preferred a slow, even rise with baking powder.

Cutting rounds out of a large sheet cake may make sense in a restaurant where the leftover scraps can be used for other things (such as cake crumbs, or bribing the chef for a night off), but such a technique at home is just wasteful. We baked the cake in an eight-inch square cake pan, then cut it into nine tidy, individual squares after being cooled. Because none of the cake will be trimmed, it is crucial that the rise be impeccably even, and that the cake is easy to remove from the pan. By greasing the pan and then dusting it with cocoa (which doesn't show up on a chocolate cake like flour), the cake is able to "climb" up the pan's sides evenly, while lining the pan bottom with parchment paper ensures a quick and easy release.

The sweet, gooey filling is a mixture of sweetened coconut, pecans, condensed milk, vanilla, and melted butter. Finding no reason to change any ingredient proportions here, we reduced the overall amount to accommodate our smaller yield. Two tablespoons of this incredibly sweet, rich filling was plenty between the layers of cake, with a small dollop on top of each cake to anchor the tuile.

Admittedly a bit fussy, tuiles are a dramatic restaurant flourish worth reproducing at home and requiring only quick hands and a little patience. Tuiles are made from a thick batter that is spread thinly over a stencil on an upside-down, greased baking sheet and then baked (see the illustrations on page 351). They are bendable for several seconds after they emerge from the oven, and can be quickly draped over a rolling pin to curl them. Baking the cookies in batches, we found it easiest to remove them from the oven one at a time (working quickly with the oven door open), so that each can be curled before turning brittle. The keys to making tuiles are to use a good stencil (see the illustration on page 351), spread the batter evenly, and work quickly when they are ready to be curled.

Since Syrah offered no recipe for the accompanying chocolate and caramel sauces, we used our own. Both sauces, the cake, the filling, and the tuiles can be made up to two days ahead, and can even be plated an hour or two before serving, making it an easy addition to a dinner-party menu.

Individual German Chocolate Cakes

SERVES 9

The cake, filling, and tuiles can be made up to 2 days in advance. The cake and filling should be refrigerated, while the tuiles should be left at room temperature. The Bittersweet Chocolate Sauce and the Caramel Sauce yield more than you'll need for this recipe.

CAKE

- **Vegetable oil spray**
- **1/2 cup packed Dutch-processed cocoa powder, plus more for dusting the pan**
- **1 cup (7 ounces) granulated sugar**
- **3/4 cup (3 3/4 ounces) unbleached all-purpose flour**
- **2 teaspoons baking powder**
- **1/8 teaspoon salt**
- **1/2 cup whole milk**
- **2 large eggs, lightly beaten**
- **1/4 cup vegetable oil**
- **1 tablespoon white vinegar**

FILLING

- **3/4 cup sweetened condensed milk**
- **2 1/2 tablespoons unsalted butter, melted**
- **1/8 teaspoon vanilla extract**
- **4 ounces sweetened shredded coconut (about 1 1/2 cups)**
- **3 ounces pecans, chopped (generous 3/4 cup)**

TUILES

- **4 tablespoons (1/2 stick) unsalted butter, softened, plus more for greasing the pan**
- **1/2 cup (2 ounces) confectioners' sugar**
- **2 large egg whites**
- **1/4 teaspoon vanilla extract**
- **1/2 cup (2 ounces) plain cake flour**
- **Bittersweet Chocolate Sauce (page 398)**
- **Caramel Sauce (page 352)**

1. FOR THE CAKE: Adjust the oven rack to the middle position and heat the oven to 350 degrees. Spray an 8-inch square cake pan with vegetable oil spray and dust it lightly with cocoa powder. Line the pan bottom with parchment paper and set aside.

2. Sift the sugar, flour, remaining ½ cup cocoa powder, baking powder, and salt together in a large bowl and set aside. Whisk ½ cup room-temperature water, milk, eggs, vegetable oil, and vinegar together in a medium bowl. Pour the milk mixture into the flour mixture and stir slowly with a whisk to combine. Pour the batter into the prepared cake pan and bake until a toothpick inserted in the center of the cake comes out clean, 30 to 40 minutes. Transfer the cake to a wire rack to cool completely. Leave the oven on.

3. FOR THE FILLING: Mix the condensed milk, melted butter, vanilla, coconut, and pecans together in a small bowl until uniform. Cover with plastic wrap and refrigerate. Remove from the refrigerator 15 minutes before assembling the cakes.

MAKING TUILES

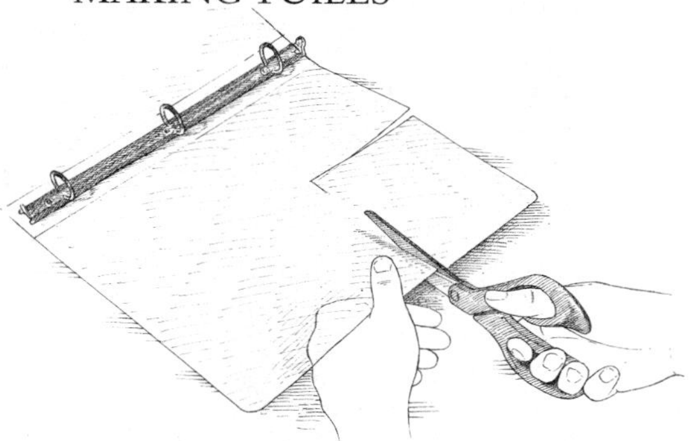

1. Using either the plastic top of a food canister or a thin, plastic, three-ring binder, cut out a 5-inch square of flat, bendable plastic.

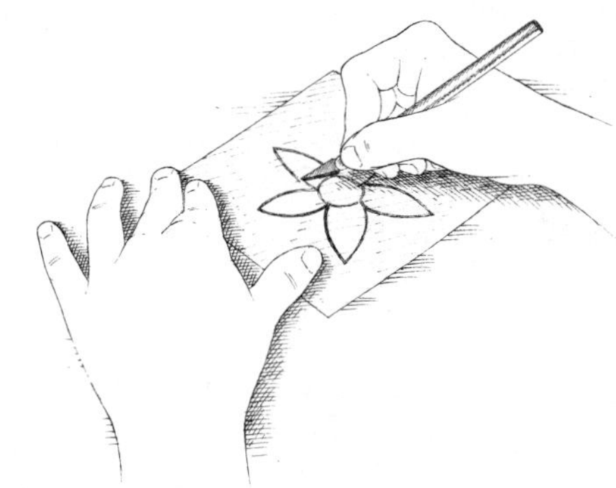

2. Outline a 3 to 4-inch shape with a marker and, using a sharp X-Acto knife, carefully cut it from the plastic to make a stencil.

3. Lay the stencil flat on the upside-down, greased baking sheet. Using an offset spatula, spread the tuile batter in a thin layer evenly inside the stencil.

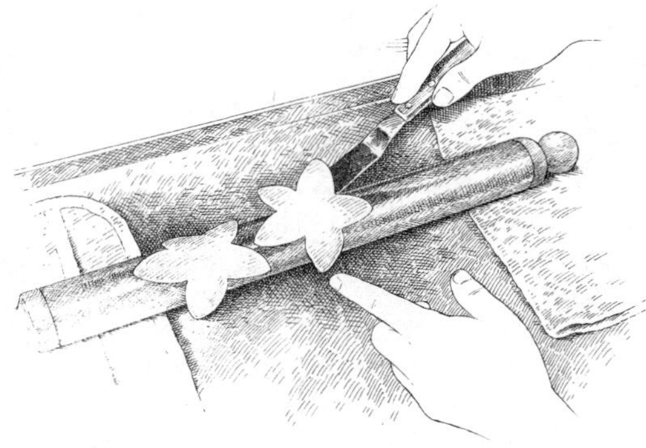

4. After baking the tuiles, leave them in the oven with the oven door open. Working quickly, lift each tuile off the pan with a spatula and drape it over a large, steadied rolling pin or wine bottle and cool.

4. For the tuiles: In a standing mixer fitted with the paddle attachment, beat the butter and confectioners' sugar on medium-high speed until light and fluffy, about 2 minutes. Reduce the speed to medium-low and add the egg whites, 1 at a time, beating after each addition until thoroughly combined and scraping the bowl as necessary. Add the vanilla and mix thoroughly. Reduce the speed to the lowest setting, add the flour, and beat until just incorporated, about 30 seconds. Give the dough a final stir with a rubber spatula to ensure that no pockets of flour remain on the bottom.

5. Following illustrations on page 351, make a tuile stencil. Turn a rimmed baking sheet upside down and grease the bottom with butter. Using a small, offset spatula and the stencil, spread the batter evenly inside the stencil on the prepared baking sheet. Bake until lightly golden, 5 to 8 minutes. Open the oven door but do not remove the tuiles from the oven. Using a small offset metal spatula, remove one tuile from the oven and drape it over a large, steadied rolling pin or wine bottle, using your fingers to wrap it around the pin. Repeat with the remaining tuiles. Gently transfer the tuiles to a plate and set aside.

6. To serve: Invert the cooled cake onto a cutting board and peel back the parchment. Flip the cake right side up. Cut the cake into nine 2⅔-inch squares. Slice each square horizontally through the middle into two layers. Spread 2 tablespoons filling over each bottom slice. Replace the top cake layers on top of the filling and transfer to individual plates. Dollop 2 teaspoons of the remaining filling on top of each cake. Gently adhere a tuile to the filling. Drizzle each plate attractively with the chocolate and caramel sauces.

Caramel Sauce

MAKES ABOUT 1½ CUPS

If you make the caramel sauce ahead, reheat it in the microwave or in a small saucepan over low heat until warm and fluid. When the hot cream mixture is added in step 3, the hot sugar syrup will bubble vigorously (and dangerously), so don't use a smaller saucepan.

- **1 cup (7 ounces) granulated sugar**
- **1 cup heavy cream**
- **⅛ teaspoon salt**
- **½ teaspoon vanilla extract**
- **½ teaspoon juice from 1 lemon**

1. Measure ½ cup water into a heavy-bottomed 2-quart saucepan. Pour the sugar in the center of the pan, taking care not to let sugar crystals adhere to the sides. Cover and bring to a boil over high heat. Once boiling, uncover and boil until the syrup is thick, straw-colored, and registers 300 degrees on a candy thermometer, about 7 minutes. Reduce the heat to medium and cook until the syrup is deep amber and registers 350 degrees, 1 to 2 minutes.

2. Meanwhile, bring the cream and salt to a simmer in a small saucepan over high heat. (If the cream boils before the sugar reaches a deep amber color, remove the cream from the heat and cover to keep warm.)

3. Remove the sugar syrup from the heat, then very carefully pour about one quarter of the hot cream into it (the mixture will bubble vigorously). Let the bubbling subside. Add the remaining cream, vanilla, and lemon juice and whisk until the sauce is smooth. (The sauce can be cooled and refrigerated in an airtight container for up to 2 weeks.)

CHOCOLATE VOLCANO CAKES *with* ESPRESSO ICE CREAM

Adapted from Chocolate Volcano Cakes with Espresso Ice Cream Bombes

IXORA, WHITEHOUSE STATION, NEW JERSEY

RESTAURANT MENUS OFTEN OFFER A molten chocolate cake, but the test kitchen staff, who've had their share of bad molten cakes (either raw-tasting and soggy or reheated and stale), were impressed with this version. Served straight out of the oven with a hot, rich, liquidy center, Ixora tempers its intensely flavored cake by serving a tiny, chocolate-coated, ice cream bombe alongside. The dramatic range in temperatures, powerful chocolate punch, and visual appeal make this dessert appear far more difficult and time-consuming than it really is. Using a durable cake batter and a minimal number of ingredients, one of the best things about this dessert is that it can largely be prepared up to 24 hours in advance.

Combining the features of a both a brownie and a fallen chocolate cake, the exterior walls of the individual cakes are toothsome and sturdy, while the centers are smooth and creamy and the tops become shiny and appealingly cracked as they bake. The batter has a high proportion of sugar and chocolate, like a fudgy brownie, yet the cake gets its basic structure from eggs and egg yolks, much like a fallen chocolate cake. Flavored with a little Grand Marnier, the real star of this cake is the concentrated chocolate flavor. The original recipe called for extra-bittersweet chocolate, which is somewhat difficult to find. We approximated the intense flavor by using both a supermarket bittersweet chocolate and a few ounces of unsweetened chocolate. With a little cornstarch to stabilize the chocolate and a complete absence of both chemical leavening (such as baking powder or soda) and whipped eggs (which could deflate over time), this batter has been engineered to be unfailingly successful regardless of how hot, hectic, or harried the restaurant's kitchen might get.

We found it easiest to portion the batter into individual ramekins as soon as it was mixed. The cakes can then either be baked right away or wrapped tightly with plastic wrap, refrigerated, and baked straight from the refrigerator at a moment's notice. Although the cakes could be served right in their ramekins, we preferred to unmold them onto individual plates so they could nuzzle up to the ice cream. To help the cakes fall right out of the hot ramekins without a struggle, we found it helpful to butter and sugar the ramekins before pouring in the batter.

Offering bites of relief from the intense, lava-hot cakes, the ice cream bombes are small domes of espresso ice cream coated with a thin shell of hardened chocolate—like a bonbon. After attempting to replicate these morsels on several occasions, however, we realized that this is one task best left to professionals. In order to thinly coat the ice cream, we found it took multiple dips into chocolate that was melted to a very specific temperature. If done any other way, the chocolate coating became either too thick and hearty or slid right off the ice cream. Instead, we liked a scoop of the espresso ice placed on the plate next to the hot cake.

The restaurant makes its own espresso ice cream, but in the spirit of home cooking, we found it just as satisfying to mix finely ground espresso beans into coffee-flavored ice cream. Softening the ice cream on the counter for a few minutes, the ground espresso can be folded in using a rubber spatula. Lastly, we noted that a sprinkling of confectioners' sugar over the cake and plate not only helped prevent the scoop of ice cream from sliding around, but also made the dessert look truly impressive.

Chocolate Volcano Cakes with Espresso Ice Cream

SERVES 8

Use a bittersweet bar chocolate in this recipe, not chips—the chips include emulsifiers that will alter the cakes' texture. The cake batter can be mixed and portioned into the ramekins, wrapped tightly with plastic wrap, and refrigerated up to 24 hours in advance. The cold cake batter should be baked straight from the refrigerator.

ESPRESSO ICE CREAM

- **2** pints coffee ice cream, softened
- **1 1/2** tablespoons finely ground espresso beans

CAKES

- **10** tablespoons (1 stick plus 2 tablespoons) unsalted butter, cut into 1/2-inch pieces, plus more for buttering the ramekins
- **1 1/2** cups (10 1/2 ounces) sugar, plus more for dusting the ramekins
- **8** ounces bittersweet chocolate, finely chopped
- **2** ounces unsweetened chocolate, finely chopped
- **2** tablespoons cornstarch
- **3** large eggs, at room temperature
- **4** large egg yolks, at room temperature
- **2** teaspoons Grand Marnier (or other orange-flavored liqueur)
- Confectioners' sugar, for dusting the cakes

1. For the ice cream: Transfer the ice cream to a medium bowl and, using a rubber spatula, fold in the ground espresso until incorporated. Press a sheet of plastic wrap flush against the ice cream (see the illustration on page 397) to prevent freezer burn and return it to the freezer. (The ice cream can be prepared up to 24 hours ahead.)

2. For the cake: Lightly coat eight 4-ounce ramekins with butter. Dust with sugar, tapping out any excess, and set aside.

3. Melt the bittersweet and unsweetened chocolates and remaining 10 tablespoons butter in a medium bowl over a medium saucepan of simmering water, stirring occasionally, until the chocolate mixture is smooth. In a large bowl, whisk the remaining 1½ cups sugar and cornstarch together. Add the chocolate mixture and stir to combine. Add the eggs, egg yolks, and Grand Marnier and whisk until fully combined. Scoop ½ cup of the batter into each of the prepared ramekins. (The ramekins can be covered tightly with plastic wrap and refrigerated for up to 24 hours.)

4. Adjust an oven rack to the middle position and heat the oven to 375 degrees. Place the filled ramekins on a rimmed baking sheet and bake until the tops of the cakes are set,

have formed shiny crusts, and are beginning to crack, 16 to 20 minutes.

5. Transfer the ramekins to a wire rack and cool slightly, about 2 minutes. Run a paring knife around the edge of each cake. Using a towel to protect your hand from the hot ramekins, invert each cake onto a small plate, then immediately invert again right-side up onto 8 individual plates. Sift confectioners' sugar over each cake and the area of the plate where the ice cream will be placed. Remove the ice cream from the freezer and scoop a portion on top of the confectioners' sugar, next to the cake. Serve immediately.

EQUIPMENT: Ice Cream Scoops

We've all struggled with an intractable pint of rock-hard ice cream. That's where a good ice cream scoop comes in handy; it can release even hard-frozen ice cream from bondage. We gathered ten readily available scoops and dipped our way through twenty pints of vanilla ice cream to find the best. We tested three basic types of scoops: classic, mechanical-release (or spring-loaded), and spade-shaped. Prices ranged from $3.99 to $22.

Classic ice cream scoops sport a thick handle and curved bowl. They can be used by lefties and righties with equal comfort. There are a few variations on the theme; of the four classic scoops we purchased, one had a pointed "beak" scoop, another offered a "comfort grip" rubber handle, and another contained a self-defrosting liquid. Testers were unanimous in assigning first place—in both its own category and overall—to the Zeroll Classic Ice Cream Scoop ($22). Its thick handle was comfortable for large and small hands, and its nonstick coating and self-defrosting liquid (which responds to heat from the user's hand) contributed to perfect release, leaving only traces of melted cream inside the scoop. The defrosting fluid and the elegantly curved bowl allowed the scoop to take purchase immediately, curling a perfect scoop with minimal effort. Only one caveat: Don't run this scoop through the dishwasher, as it will lose its magical defrosting properties.

Coming in second among the other classic scoops tested was the Oxo Beak Scoop ($11.99). The beak point dug into ice cream with ease, and the ice cream curled up nicely. Our only minor quibble was the short handle, which forced testers with larger hands to choke up close to the head. If price is a concern, you might consider this model.

Mechanical-release scoops come in various sizes and operate with a spring-loaded, squeezable handle (or thumb trigger) that connects to a curved steel lever inside the scoop. When the handle or lever is released, the ice cream pops out in a perfectly round ball. Although we frequently use a mechanical-release scoop to measure even portions of cookie dough and muffin batter, we found this type less than ideal when it came to ice cream. The scoops are designed for right-handed users only, and their thin, straight-edged handles were distinctly uncomfortable when considerable pressure was applied. Of the four models we tested, none was worthy of recommendation.

Spades, with their flat, paddle-type heads, are useful when you need to scoop a lot of ice cream quickly—say, for an ice cream cake or sandwiches—but they are too big to fit into pint containers. If you make frozen desserts frequently or need to work your way through multiple gallon-sized containers of ice cream, a spade might be for you. Our preferred model, made by the same manufacturer as our overall winning scoop, is the Zeroll Nonstick Ice Cream Spade ($19.60).

THE BEST ICE CREAM SCOOPS
The Zeroll Classic Ice Cream Scoop (left) was the favorite model tested. If you need to scoop a lot of ice cream for an ice cream cake, you might consider the Zeroll Nonstick Ice Cream Spade (right), but this tool is too big to fit into pint containers.

Chocolate-Ricotta Mousse Parfaits

Adapted from Chocolate-Ricotta Mousse Parfaits

Pauli's Restaurant, Melrose, Massachusetts

As busy home cooks would probably agree, quickly prepared desserts that actually taste good are worth their weight in gold to a busy restaurant. Requiring zero cooking and just a few minutes to assemble, this chocolate-ricotta parfait studded with chewy bits of brownie and layered attractively into a parfait glass with whipped cream is the epitome of easy.

Although simple to prepare, we were disappointed with the results of our first attempt. The chocolate-ricotta mousse, made by blending whole-milk ricotta and melted chocolate in a food processor, turned out incredibly grainy. Taking a closer look at both ingredients, it dawned on us that the restaurant probably stocks authentic, Italian ricotta rather than the supermarket version we were using. Knowing that a true Italian ricotta would yield a rich flavor and a creamy, smooth texture, we were further disappointed when we had trouble tracking any down. Yet rather than running around town for a rare ingredient in this otherwise effortless dessert, we focused our attention on doctoring the ricotta we could easily get at the supermarket. We tried pureeing it longer, and heating it briefly in the microwave, but what finally worked was smoothing it out with some heavy cream. Adding tablespoon after tablespoon of cream to the ricotta as it pureed in the food processor, we found that its dry, mealy texture turned smooth and luscious when no less than half a cup of heavy cream was incorporated.

Pureeing melted chocolate with the cream-enriched ricotta was straightforward, and we strongly preferred the sweeter flavor of semisweet chocolate over

TECHNIQUE: How to Melt Chocolate in a Microwave Oven

Melting chocolate in the microwave is fast and easy. Note that the chocolate will hold its shape even when melted so be sure to stir the chocolate to gauge its temperature. Because fats, such as butter, cream, or shortening heat more quickly than chocolate, add them during the first stirring rather than at the beginning. Use the times given as a guideline. For larger quantities of chocolate, increase the microwave times.

Put the chopped chocolate in a 2-cup Pyrex measuring cup. Microwave at 50 percent power to melt partially, about 1 ½ minutes for 4 ounces.

Stir with a rubber spatula; continue to microwave at 50 percent power until fully melted, about 1 minute longer. Stir until perfectly smooth.

bittersweet, since the rest of the dessert has very little sugar. Layering the chocolate-ricotta mousse alternately with whipped cream in a parfait glass, we found the small bits of broken brownie nestled in the center of the glass a welcome change in texture. The original recipe called for chocolate brownies, which restaurants no doubt always have on hand. Rather than bake our own brownies, we merely crumbled some plain, unfrosted brownies we found in the baked goods section of the supermarket. Assembled in less than 10 minutes, the best part of this simple yet incredibly satisfying dessert is that it can be made up to six hours in advance and stored in the refrigerator until dessert time.

Chocolate-Ricotta Mousse Parfaits

SERVES 4

Serve in clear martini or parfait glasses so that the alternating layers of cream and chocolate-ricotta mousse will be visible. The assembled parfaits can be served immediately or covered tightly with plastic wrap and refrigerated for up to 6 hours. Allow them to soften at room temperature for 15 minutes before serving.

- **8 ounces semisweet chocolate, chopped, or 8 ounces semisweet chocolate chips**
- **1 (15-ounce) container whole-milk ricotta cheese**
- **½ cup heavy cream**
- **½ recipe (1 cup) Whipped Cream (page 348)**
- **4 plain store-bought brownies**

1. Melt the chocolate in a medium, heat-proof bowl set over a saucepan of barely simmering water, stirring occasionally, until smooth. Remove from the heat and cool until barely warm, about 20 minutes.

2. Process the ricotta and heavy cream in the workbowl of a food processor fitted with a steel blade until smooth and creamy, about 1½ minutes, stopping the machine and scraping down the sides of the bowl with a rubber spatula as needed. With the machine running, pour the melted chocolate through the feed tube and process until incorporated, about 15 seconds. Scrape down the bowl and process for 5 seconds longer. Set aside.

3. To SERVE: Divide half the chocolate-ricotta mousse among 4 stemmed martini or parfait glasses or clear bowls. Top each portion with about 2 tablespoons of the Whipped Cream. Crumble 1 brownie into each glass. Repeat the layers with the remaining chocolate-ricotta mousse and whipped cream. Serve immediately or wrap tightly with plastic wrap and refrigerate for up to 6 hours. (If made in advance and refrigerated, soften at room temperature for 15 minutes before serving.)

Floating Islands

Adapted from Floating Islands

LAFITTE'S LANDING, NEW ORLEANS, LOUISIANA

AT FIRST GLANCE, FLOATING ISLANDS might seem a little odd. This classic French dessert consists of small scoops of whipped egg whites, which are poached and then served "floating" in a generous amount of vanilla custard sauce (crème anglaise). Considering its French origins, it wasn't surprising to find that this recipe from the New Orleans–based Lafitte's Landing was an archetypical *îles flottantes* (floating islands), sometimes referred to as *oeufs à la neige* (snow eggs).

Our first test of Lafitte's recipe yielded positive results. The light-as-air meringues were tender and moist, the sauce was rich and eggy with a hint of vanilla, and the two combined were beguiling. Yet although this dish turned out well for us, we understood that the technique might be too advanced for some novice cooks. Wanting to make the recipe more accessible for those less experienced, we looked to simplify the process.

The meringues are the trickiest part of this dish, and therefore were the focus of most of our attention. Whipping the egg whites to a stiff meringue was simple enough. The key here is to whip the meringues to the right consistency (see the photographs below). Underwhipped whites will not hold their shape, while overwhipped ones will have an unappealing, choppy texture. Once properly whipped, we found the easiest way to shape the meringue into attractive quenelles (football shapes) is to use two serving spoons.

DISCERNING PROPERLY BEATEN EGG WHITES

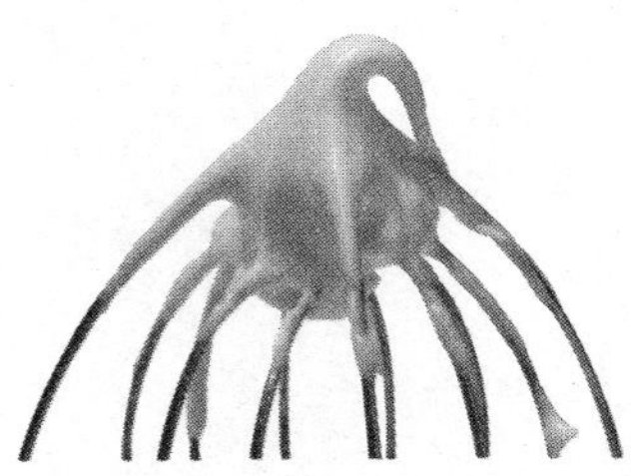

A. Underbeaten egg whites are foamy and soft. They will collapse when poached.

B. Overbeaten egg whites will look dry and grainy and will begin to separate.

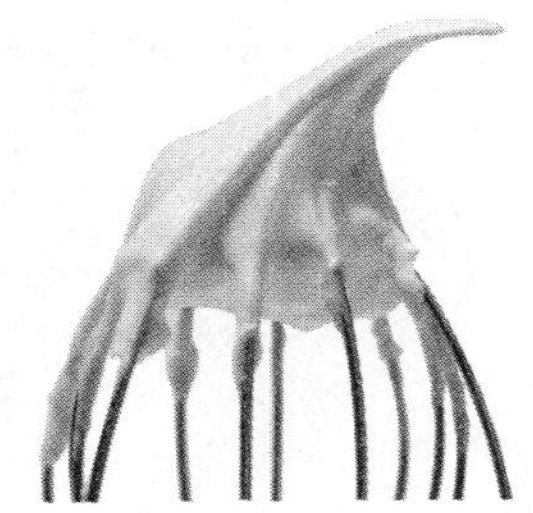

C. Properly beaten egg whites will look creamy and glossy. They will hold a stiff peak and they will hold their shape when poached.

Scraping the meringue back and forth between the spoons, the sticky, malleable meringue is quickly forced into a quenelle shape without much effort (see illustration 1 on page 360). Very often this shaping technique is done at the stove, right next to the poaching liquid, so that each meringue can be cooked immediately upon being shaped. Finding this time-frame a bit harried and intense (not to mention that workspace right next to the stove is often quite limited), we scraped each meringue onto a baking sheet to hold until they were all formed.

Classically, the meringues are poached in warm milk, which is then used to make the accompanying crème anglaise sauce. This makes for a complicated timing sequence, which the restaurant skirts by poaching in water. Wanting to find a large, shallow vessel commonly found in a home kitchen that could poach all the meringues at one time, we landed on a roasting pan, which worked like a charm. The only issue we had was monitoring the temperature of the poaching water. Set over just one burner, the water boiled in some areas, tearing the fragile meringues apart. Straddling the pan over two burners (much like when making a pan gravy), we found it easy to moderate the temperature (see illustration 3 on page 360). Bringing the water to an initial simmer over medium-high heat, we then reduced the temperature to medium-low after adding all the meringues so they could cook through evenly. Perfectly poached to a tender, creamy texture in four minutes, we had found a way to make good-looking "islands" without all of the fuss.

Lafitte's recipe for crème anglaise, like most traditional recipes, consists of heavy cream flavored with sugar and vanilla and thickened with egg yolks. It's an easy recipe that produces a wonderfully sweet, smooth, and luscious sauce, and the only change we made was to reduce the yield to serve six people. As for the presentation, a shallow soup bowl is necessary for the meringues to "float" properly. There is some debate about the temperature at which floating islands should be served. While most traditional recipes call for serving room-temperature meringues on top of warm sauce, we found that the dish was more flavorful when both the meringue and sauce were at room temperature.

Floating Islands

SERVES 6

If you don't have a large roasting pan, the "islands" can be cooked in batches in a large skillet following the same technique.

CRÈME ANGLAISE

- **2 cups heavy cream**
- **4 large egg yolks**
- **1/2 cup (3 1/2 ounces) sugar**
- **1/2 teaspoon cornstarch**
- **Pinch ground cinnamon**
- **Pinch ground nutmeg**
- **1/2 teaspoon vanilla extract**

MERINGUES

- **6 large egg whites**
- **1/8 teaspoon salt**
- **1/2 cup (3 1/2 ounces) sugar**

1. FOR THE CRÈME ANGLAISE: Bring the cream to a simmer in a medium saucepan over medium-high heat. When the cream reaches a simmer, reduce the heat to low. Whisk the egg yolks, sugar, cornstarch, cinnamon, and nutmeg together in a medium bowl. Slowly whisk ½ cup of the hot cream into the yolk mixture, then slowly whisk the tempered yolk mixture

FORMING AND POACHING MERINGUES

1. Working over a parchment-lined baking sheet, gently scrape ½ cup of the meringue back and forth between two serving spoons until it forms a 3½-inch football-shaped oval.

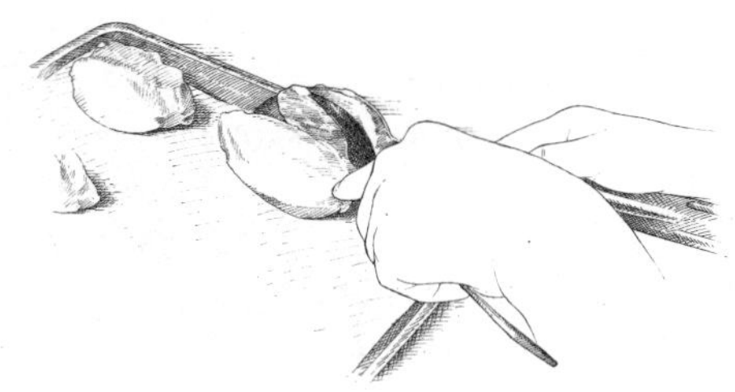

2. Gently nudge the shaped meringue onto the baking sheet with tip of the second spoon.

3. Using a spoon, carefully transfer the shaped meringues into the simmering water one at a time.

into the hot cream. Cook, whisking constantly, until the sauce has thickened (lightly coats the back of a spoon) and reaches 165 degrees on an instant-read thermometer, about 2 minutes.

2. Immediately pour the crème anglaise through a fine-mesh strainer into a medium bowl. Stir in the vanilla. Press plastic wrap directly against the surface of the sauce to prevent a skin from forming, and set aside to cool at room temperature.

3. For the meringues: In the bowl of a standing mixer fitted with the whisk attachment, beat the egg whites on medium speed until they are light, shiny, and start to hold a peak, 3 to 5 minutes. Add the salt and gradually add the sugar, beating until incorporated. Beat on high speed until the whites are glossy and hold a stiff peak, about 1½ minutes. Following illustrations 1 and 2 at the left, use two large serving spoons to shape ½ cup of the egg-white mixture into a football shape and transfer to a rimmed baking sheet lined with parchment paper. Repeat with the remaining egg-white mixture. You should have 12 meringues.

4. Bring 1½ inches (about 5 quarts) water to a simmer in a large roasting pan set over 2 burners over medium-high heat. Following illustration 3, use a spoon to transfer the meringues to the water. Reduce the heat to medium-low and gently simmer the meringues until they are firm, about 4 minutes, flipping them over halfway through the cooking time.

5. Meanwhile, ladle ½ cup of the cooled crème anglaise into 6 shallow soup bowls. Using a slotted spoon, transfer 2 meringues from the simmering water into each bowl. Drizzle the meringues with the remaining crème anglaise. Serve immediately.

Vanilla Cake *with* Roasted Peaches & Blueberries

Adapted from Vanilla Cake with Roasted Peaches and Blueberries

Beacon, New York, New York

"Cook's desserts" are a fast-and-loose category of desserts that fall outside the rigid rules of classic pastry arts. Driven more by flavor and less by technique, they tend to be somewhat casual in appearance, more likely created by a tinkering chef than a methodical pâtissier. This vanilla cake with roasted peaches and blueberries is a case in point. Roasting, a cooking method firmly planted on the savory side of the menu, is employed to intensify the fruits' flavors and render a sauce from the "pan" juices. The vanilla cake is a simple affair, playing the humble role of a starch to soak up flavor. This cake is wickedly easy to make and gorgeous to boot, a surefire midsummer winner for a backyard barbecue.

In essence, the dessert is a riff on a classic British dessert called "summer pudding" (cake or bread packed into a mold with berries), but modernized with the addition of roasted fruit. Roasting fruit concentrates its flavor by evaporating the fruit's moisture. Even fruit of questionable pedigree can taste great when subjected to blazing temperatures. The restaurant's recipe tosses the fruit together with sugar, lemon juice, and vanilla bean pods (the more flavorful seeds are reserved for the cake). Roasted at 400 degrees, the mixture bubbles vigorously, the peaches brown a bit, and the blueberries render to a jammy spread. After roasting, the fruit is cooled and drained, the juices reserved as a sauce for the finished cake.

A portion of the raw fruit is reserved to lend both color and brightness to the dish. At Beacon, the chefs use this fruit as a garnish on the plate, but we chose to top the cake with it. The blues and oranges of the fruit pop vividly against the pale yellow base of the cake.

The vanilla cake is essentially a basic yellow cake, but made sturdier than most to resist the fruits' juices and weight. The sturdiness spells simplicity as far as preparation: the ingredients are combined in the workbowl of a mixer and blended until just combined. The only issues we found were warming the eggs and butter sufficiently so that they wouldn't curdle—baking basics, but important to remember nonetheless. To bring eggs quickly to room temperature, steep them in a bowl of warm water for 10 minutes. For butter, the microwave works wonders—just be careful with the timing, which will vary depending on the microwave's wattage. We generally use the defrost setting, which is a lower power. However, not all microwaves have defrost settings. Cutting the butter into small pieces can also expedite matters. If you don't have a microwave, seal the butter in a plastic bag and submerge it alongside the eggs in the warm water. The butter should be checked often: there's a big difference between softened butter and melted butter.

Once both the fruit and cake are sufficiently cooled, the dessert is assembled into a layer cake, the fruit sandwiched in the middle. Beacon splits the cake into three even layers, but we found this pretty difficult to do, requiring a steady hand and a very long, serrated knife. We chose to limit ourselves to just two layers. The flavor was unaffected. The drained fruit is placed between the cake layers, and then the cake is wrapped tightly in plastic wrap and packed into a cake pan to chill for at least eight hours or overnight. We had trouble waiting that long, but eight hours proved to be the absolute minimum for the fullest flavor and best texture. The refrigerated cake isn't much to look at, but when unwrapped and topped with the reserved raw fruit, it's deliciously homespun, packing all the casual insouciance of summer. Garnish with a fat dollop of whipped cream.

Vanilla Cake with Roasted Peaches and Blueberries

SERVES 8

If you don't have a vanilla bean, add an additional teaspoon of vanilla extract to the cake. While not quite the same, the extract will fill some of the bean's role. If you like, add the restaurant touch of a mint garnish when plating.

6 **large peaches, pitted and cut into ½-inch-thick wedges**
6 **cups fresh blueberries**
1½ **cups (10½ ounces) sugar**
½ **vanilla bean, split in half lengthwise, seeds removed, seeds and pod reserved (see the illustrations on page 315)**
¼ **cup juice from 1–2 lemons**
8 **tablespoons (1 stick) unsalted butter, softened, plus more for greasing the pan**
1 **cup (5 ounces) unbleached all-purpose flour, plus more for dusting the pan**
1½ **teaspoons baking powder**
½ **teaspoon salt**
2 **large eggs, at room temperature**
1 **teaspoon vanilla extract**
½ **cup whole milk**
Whipped Cream (page 348)

1. Adjust an oven rack to the middle position and heat the oven to 400 degrees. Toss the peaches, blueberries, 1 cup of the sugar, vanilla bean pod (not the reserved seeds), and lemon juice together in a large bowl. Measure 2½ cups of the fruit into a medium bowl, cover, and refrigerate until needed. Spread the remaining fruit evenly in a 13 by 9-inch glass baking dish. Dot the top evenly with 4 tablespoons of the butter. Bake until the peaches are spotty brown and about half the blueberries have burst, about 30 minutes, stirring with a wooden spoon halfway through the baking time. Transfer the dish to a wire rack and cool slightly. Drain the fruit in a fine-mesh strainer set over a medium bowl, reserving the juices. Cool the fruit to room temperature. Refrigerate the juices until needed.

2. Reduce the oven temperature to 350 degrees. Grease a 9-inch round cake pan with butter and dust with flour. Combine the 1 cup flour, baking powder, and salt in a medium bowl. In the bowl of a standing mixer fitted with the paddle attachment, beat the remaining 4 tablespoons butter and remaining ½ cup sugar on medium speed until light and fluffy, about 3 minutes. Add

the eggs, vanilla extract, and vanilla seeds and mix, scraping down the sides of the bowl as necessary, until smooth and creamy, 1 to 2 minutes. With the mixer on low speed, add the flour mixture and milk alternately in 2 batches and beat until the batter is smooth and homogenized.

3. Scrape the batter into the prepared cake pan and smooth into an even layer using a metal spatula. Bake until the top is light golden brown and a toothpick inserted in the center comes out clean, 23 to 25 minutes. Transfer to a wire rack and cool to room temperature.

4. Gently invert the cake out of the pan onto a plate, then invert again (right-side up) onto a cutting board. Following illustrations 1 through 6 below, slice and reassemble the cake with the cooled, baked fruit in a clean, 9-inch cake pan lined with plastic wrap. Refrigerate for at least 8 and up to 24 hours.

5. TO SERVE: Unwrap the cake and, using the edges of the plastic wrap as handles, transfer to a serving platter. Holding the cake and platter steady, gently pull the plastic wrap out from under the cake and discard. Spread the reserved raw fruit over the top of the cake. Slice the cake into 8 pieces. Serve immediately, with the reserved fruit juices and whipped cream.

ASSEMBLING THE CAKE

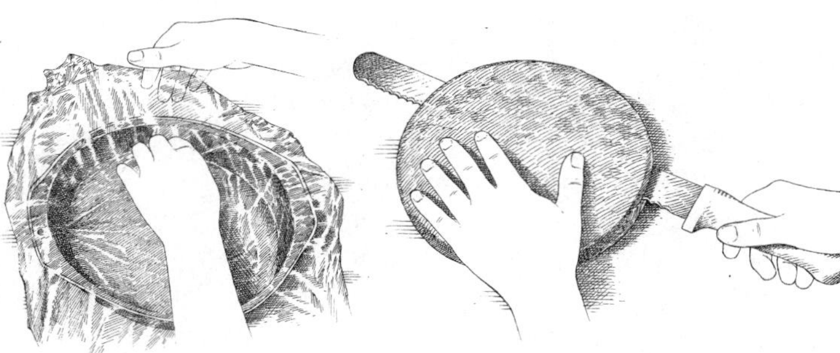

1. Line a clean 9-inch-round cake pan with enough plastic wrap so that the excess hangs over the edges.

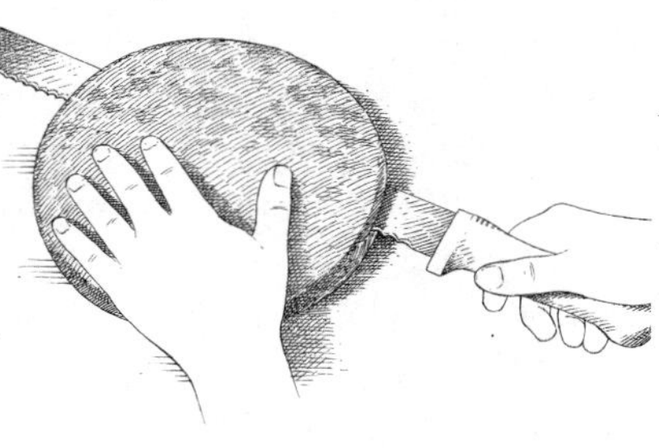

2. Using a long, serrated knife, slice the cake into 2 even layers.

3. Place the bottom layer of cake cut-side up in the plastic wrap–lined pan.

4. Spread all of the drained, cooked fruit evenly over the bottom layer of cake.

5. Lay the top layer of the cake cut-side down over the fruit and press gently to adhere.

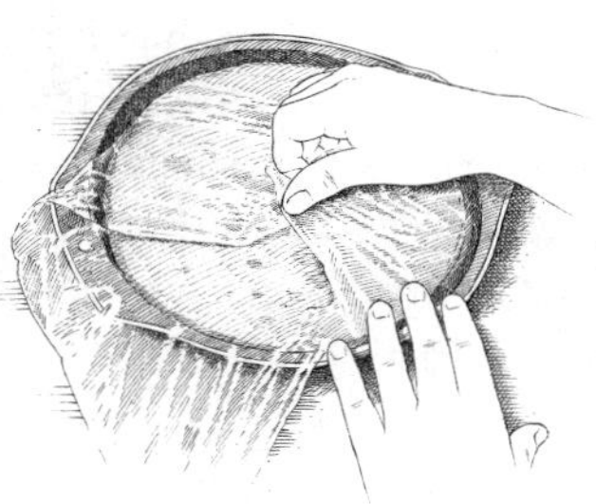

6. Pull the edges of the plastic wrap up over the cake to cover. Refrigerate for at least 8 hours and up to 24 hours.

Strawberry Shortcake

Adapted from Strawberry Shortcake

Pastiche, Providence, Rhode Island

GOOD, OLD-FASHIONED STRAWBERRY shortcake is hard to beat. But somehow, over time, this classic dessert has changed into a cloying combination of syrupy frozen strawberries served over circles of spongy yellow cake—a far cry from the classic dessert that strawberry shortcake can be. Happily, the café Pastiche adheres to the old ways. Consisting of loads of juicy strawberries sandwiched between large, tender, real shortcake biscuits, this recipe was one of the best renditions we've tasted. Although the results were exemplary, for the home cook, the recipe needed some adjustments.

The first component of the dish we focused on was the shortcakes. Made in the traditional way of cutting butter into dry ingredients and then adding liquid (in this case, heavy cream) to form a dough, we found the dough very easy to make. But we ran into problems when it came to portioning the dough into shortcakes. The recipe called for using a half-cup scoop to drop portions of dough onto the baking sheet, but much of the dough stubbornly stuck to our measuring cup. We found that a light coating of vegetable oil spray was all that was needed to help release the dough quickly and completely. The resulting biscuits had the uneven, rustic shape we were looking for, but, more important, this method limited the handling of the dough, making sure the shortcakes stayed light and tender.

The next issue we addressed was the baking time of the shortcakes. Since Pastiche's baking times were based on using a convection oven, where the heat is constantly circulated from all sides of the oven's interior, thus cooking faster and more evenly, we had to find the proper baking times and temperatures using a conventional oven. We tried baking the biscuits in our conventional oven at temperatures of 350, 375, and 400 degrees. The shortcakes baked at 350 degrees, which was too cool, were dry and quite flat. The shortcakes baked at 400, while puffy, were slightly doughy in the center. Baking at 375 avoided these undesirable characteristics and turned out perfectly baked shortcakes.

The other major component of the dish was, of course, the strawberries. Pastiche prepared its strawberries by quartering about two-thirds of the fruit. They pureed the remaining third with a little bit of sugar, then tossed the puree with the quartered strawberries. We initially thought that making the puree might be a time-consuming step that could be omitted. So on a subsequent trial we tried making the shortcake with quartered strawberries tossed with sugar, as most recipes do. Surprisingly, we found that we much preferred the strawberries with the puree, feeling that the sauce gave the dessert more body since it wasn't immediately absorbed by the shortcakes, as happens with the strawberries without the puree. By making the filling first and letting it sit for 45 minutes—roughly the time it takes to make the shortcakes—we got just the final texture we were seeking.

Presentation is simple: Spoon the strawberries over the bottom half of the shortcake, follow with a spoonful of whipped cream, and replace the top of the biscuit—not the architectural triumph of some restaurants, but when something tastes as good as this, who needs dazzling presentation?

Strawberry Shortcake

SERVES 6

Prepare the strawberries first so that they can sit and become syrupy while the shortcakes are prepared. This recipe can be easily doubled to serve 12.

FILLING

- **3 pounds (about 6 pints) fresh strawberries, cleaned, dried, and hulled, with 2 of the pounds cut into quarters (sixths, if large)**
- **1/4 cup (1 3/4 ounces) sugar**

SHORTCAKES

- **1 cup heavy cream, plus more if needed**
- **1 large egg yolk**
- **1/2 teaspoon vanilla extract**
- **2 1/2 cups (12 1/2 ounces) unbleached all-purpose flour**
- **7 tablespoons sugar**
- **1 tablespoon baking powder**
- **1/2 teaspoon salt**
- **1/4 teaspoon grated lemon zest from 1 lemon**
- **6 tablespoons (3/4 stick) very cold unsalted butter, cut into 1/4-inch pieces**
- **Vegetable oil spray**
- **1 large egg, lightly beaten**
- **Whipped Cream (page 348)**

1. FOR THE FILLING: Puree 1 pound of the whole strawberries with the sugar in a food processor until smooth, about 20 seconds. Toss the puree and remaining 2 pounds cut strawberries together in a large bowl. Set aside.

2. FOR THE SHORTCAKES: Adjust an oven rack to the middle position and heat the oven to 375 degrees. Whisk 1 cup cream, egg yolk, and vanilla together in a medium bowl. Pulse the flour, 6 tablespoons of the sugar, baking powder, salt, and lemon zest in a food processor until combined, about three 1-second pulses. Sprinkle the butter evenly over the mixture and pulse until the mixture resembles coarse cornmeal, about twelve 1-second pulses. Transfer the crumbs to a large bowl. Using a wooden spoon or rubber spatula, stir the cream mixture into the flour mixture until it forms a cohesive ball. (If the dough does not form a ball, add up to 4 tablespoons more heavy cream, 1 tablespoon at a time, until the dough is tacky but not wet.)

3. Spray the inside of a ½-cup measuring cup with vegetable oil spray and lightly pack with dough. Invert the cup, shaking gently, to remove the shaped shortcake, and transfer to a baking sheet lined with parchment paper. Brush the biscuit tops with the beaten egg and sprinkle with the remaining 1 tablespoon sugar. Bake until the shortcakes are golden brown, about 25 minutes. Transfer the biscuits to a wire rack and cool for at least 15 minutes before serving.

4. TO SERVE: Split each cake horizontally into two even layers using a serrated knife. Spoon a generous ¾ cup of the berries and then a dollop of whipped cream over each shortcake bottom. Cap with the shortcake tops. Serve immediately.

Rhubarb Galette

Adapted from Rhubarb Galette

Bluehour Restaurant, Portland, Oregon

THE APPEARANCE OF RHUBARB IN LOCAL markets is a sure sign that spring has officially arrived. In season from early April to September, rhubarb is a versatile plant with tender, pinkish red stalks and a tart, delicate flavor that makes it ideal for both sweet and savory dishes. Considered a fruit by many culinary enthusiasts because of its adaptability to pies, cakes, breads, and puddings, rhubarb is in fact a vegetable; it looks somewhat like a blushing celery stalk. The Bluehour Restaurant transforms this sour stalk into a rustic, free-formed fruit tart (also known as a galette) with just the right amount of sweetness, then accentuates the vibrant red hue with a syrup made from the rhubarb juices, served on the side.

Traditional galette dough is very rich, often containing cream cheese, making it flavorful but soft and a bit tricky to roll out. This dough, however, is unique in structure, texture, and flavor. The cornmeal in the dough adds a bite to the crust and gives added support to the flour, which is necessary to contain the fruit filling and accumulating juices. The addition of buttermilk in place of cream cheese lends an unusual tang that pairs well with the rhubarb.

Outwardly sturdy, rhubarb is in reality a very delicate fruit (sorry, vegetable), with a high water content that requires a minimum amount of cooking to soften and become edible. The problem that arises is the quantity of liquid that leaches out when the rhubarb is heated. Many recipes use excessive amounts of cornstarch to compensate, resulting in a viscous, gluey mess that masks the delicate rhubarb flavor. In the process of heating the cornstarch enough to thicken the juice, you run into the prospect of overcooking the rhubarb, leaving you with a stringy pulp that has lost all color and flavor. What we liked about this recipe was the method for preparing the rhubarb filling. The rhubarb is cooked in a hot skillet with sugar and lemon zest for a mere three minutes. The rhubarb releases juices to the pan that are reserved and reduced to serve alongside the tart. This step removes excess moisture from the finished tart and intensifies the rhubarb's flavor and color. Spreading the rhubarb out on a baking sheet to cool helps to preserve the color and prevent overcooking. A small amount of cornstarch is then added to the slightly cooked rhubarb, along with butter for richness. The filling is encased in the sturdy dough and baked until the rhubarb has thickened, and the crust is golden brown. The fruit retains its structural integrity and, devoid of excess juice, the crust holds up well.

We found that baking the dessert on a rimless baking sheet lined with parchment paper made serving a snap, since the rather large galette can be easily slid onto a cutting board and cut into wedges. Serve with vanilla ice cream or a dollop of fluffy whipped cream to add a decadent finish to this springtime dessert.

Rhubarb Galette

SERVES 8

Choose rhubarb that is pink to deep red. Avoid limp, brown, or slightly green stalks, since their flavor will not be as intense. It may seem unusual not to peel the rhubarb, but because it's cooked twice in this recipe, peeling is unnecessary. This tart is not very sweet, and tastes best when served with either sweetened whipped cream or vanilla ice cream.

CRUST

- 1/4 **cup cold buttermilk**
- 2 **large egg yolks**
- 2 **cups (10 ounces) unbleached all-purpose flour**
- 1/2 **cup fine-grind cornmeal**
- 3 **tablespoons confectioners' sugar**
- 1/2 **teaspoon salt**
- 16 **tablespoons (2 sticks) very cold unsalted butter, cut into 1/4-inch dice**

FILLING

- 2 **pounds rhubarb, washed, tops and bottoms trimmed, and cut into 1/2-inch dice (about 6 cups)**
- 3/4 **cup (5 1/4 ounces) granulated sugar**
- 1 **tablespoon finely grated lemon zest from 1 lemon**
- 1 **vanilla bean, split in half lengthwise, seeds removed, seeds and pod reserved (see the illustrations on page 315)**
- 2 **tablespoons cornstarch**
- 2 **tablespoons unsalted butter, cut into 1/4-inch dice**
- 4 **tablespoons granulated sugar**
- 2 **tablespoons whole milk**
- **Whipped Cream (page 348) or 2 pints vanilla ice cream**

1. FOR THE CRUST: Whisk the buttermilk, egg yolks, and 1 tablespoon water together in a medium bowl. Set aside. In the bowl of a standing mixer fitted with the paddle attachment, combine the flour, cornmeal, confectioners' sugar, and salt. Add the butter and mix on low speed until the mixture resembles coarse crumbs with pieces of butter the size of Grape-Nuts cereal, about 1 minute. With the mixer running on low speed, slowly add the buttermilk mixture. Mix on low until the dough comes together, about 20 seconds (do not overmix). Remove the dough from the mixer, form into an 8-inch disk, cover with plastic wrap, and refrigerate until firm, about 1 hour.

MEASURING FLOUR

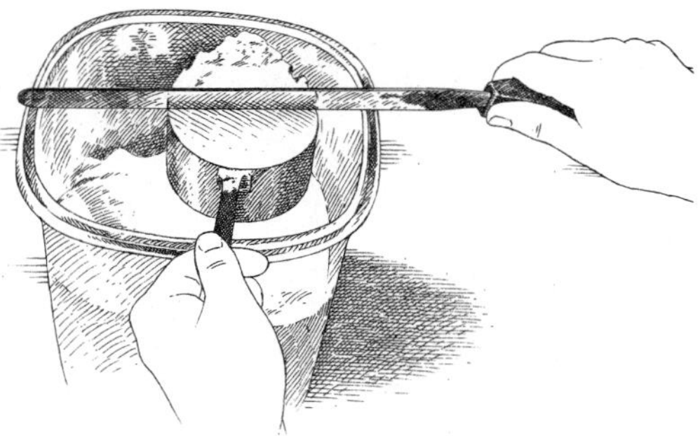

No matter the type or brand, we measure all flour by the dip-and-sweep method. Dip a metal or plastic dry measure into a bag of flour so that the cup is overflowing. Then use the flat side of a knife or an icing spatula to level off the flour, sweeping the excess back into the bag. Short of weighing flour (which is what professional bakers do), this measuring method is your best guarantee of using the right amount of flour. Spooning the flour into the measuring cup aerates it, and you might end up with as much as 25 percent less flour by weight.

2. For the filling: Cook the rhubarb, sugar, lemon zest, and vanilla seeds and pod in a 12-inch skillet over high heat, stirring frequently, until the rhubarb releases its juices, about 3 minutes. Discard the vanilla pod and drain the mixture in a fine-mesh sieve set over a medium bowl, reserving the juices. Transfer the drained rhubarb to a rimmed baking sheet and cool completely at room temperature, about 30 minutes. Transfer the cooled rhubarb to a medium bowl, stir in the cornstarch and butter, and set aside.

3. Meanwhile, simmer the reserved rhubarb juices in a small saucepan over medium-high heat until syrupy and reduced to ½ cup, 3 to 5 minutes. Transfer to a small bowl and cool at room temperature.

4. To assemble the galette: Adjust an oven rack to the middle position and heat the oven to 350 degrees. Roll the dough out on a lightly floured work surface to a 16-inch round, about ¼ inch thick, trimming and discarding any excess dough. Transfer the dough to a rimless baking sheet (or an inverted rimmed baking sheet) lined with parchment paper. Evenly sprinkle 2 tablespoons of the sugar over the crust, leaving a 3-inch border. Carefully spread the filling evenly over the sugar, leaving the 3-inch border uncovered. Fold the border of dough up over the rhubarb in overlapping folds, pleating at equal intervals. Brush the top crust with the milk and sprinkle with the remaining 2 tablespoons sugar. Bake until the crust is golden and the rhubarb filling is bubbling, 45 to 55 minutes. Cool the galette on the baking sheet for 30 minutes.

5. To serve: Slide the galette onto a cutting board, removing the parchment paper, and slice into 8 wedges. Serve immediately, with the cooled rhubarb syrup and the Whipped Cream or vanilla ice cream.

Butterscotch-Banana Pie

Adapted from Butterscotch-Banana Pie

Bayona, New Orleans, Louisiana

PIES ARE THE ALL-AMERICAN DESSERT. Bayona's recipe creates a pie with a smooth, creamy filling that packs a rich caramel flavor and boozy kick from Scotch, along with sweet chunks of banana. Topped with whipped cream and served in a flaky and tender crust, this pie was a blue-ribbon candidate. Although the recipe produced a good pie, it required three pans and four laborious steps. In hopes that we could develop a streamlined version, we set to work.

We focused on the filling component as a time-saver. While we thought the flavor and texture of the filling were just right, we felt that the multiple-step process used to make it could be significantly shortened. We attributed the many steps to the fact that the restaurant made the pie with components already prepared and on hand. Ingredients like pastry cream and caramel sauce, which are common restaurant staples, were combined with several other ingredients to create a new dessert. But when translated into a recipe for the home cook, each of these components had to be made individually and consecutively, making the recipe very complicated and time-consuming.

Pastry cream, a workhorse in many restaurants, is often used as the base for pies and tarts. Bayona's recipe started by making a vanilla pastry cream in one pan, followed by a caramel sauce in a second pan, to later be added to the pastry cream. The filling was then further thickened with the addition of gelatin, which required the use of a third pan.

Using the same ingredients, we consolidated the process into one pan with virtually the same results in less time. Here's how we did it. Instead of making the pastry cream first and folding in the other ingredients, we started off by making the caramel sauce. We then added the pastry cream ingredients to the same pan containing the caramel sauce and proceeded to cook the pastry cream as usual, essentially making a caramel pastry cream. We also decided to forgo the use of gelatin to thicken the filling further, feeling that this was most likely done in the restaurant to elongate the shelf life of the pie and was therefore unnecessary for the home cook. Last, we noted it was important for the filling to be just the right temperature when poured into the crust. If the filling is too warm, the crust will turn soggy, yet if too cool the filling will become too thick to pour. Allowing the filling to cool on the counter for 30 minutes worked perfectly—it was warm enough to pour but cool enough to keep the crust crisp.

With a flavorful and now streamlined filling, we focused last on the crust. Considering that the crust was flaky and tender and melded perfectly with the butterscotch filling, our modification to this recipe was minimal. We found that chilling the pie crust for an additional 20 minutes in the freezer made the finished crust even flakier than before. Using pie weights is important to keep the crust from slipping down the sides of the pan and bubbling up on the bottom. Unlike most recipes, which remove the pie weights partway through baking, we found no reason to do this and left the pie weights on the crust for the entire baking time.

Butterscotch-Banana Pie

SERVES 8

The crust for this pie can be made up to 24 hours in advance. If you don't have ceramic pie weights, you can substitute pennies. Once cooled, wrap the crust with plastic wrap. Making the filling and assembling the pie should be done on the same day the pie is served. If the pie is filled too far in advance, the crust will become soggy.

CRUST

- 1 1/4 cups (6 1/4 ounces) unbleached all-purpose flour
- 1/2 teaspoon salt
- 3 tablespoons cold vegetable shortening
- 4 tablespoons (1/2 stick) very cold unsalted butter, cut into 1/4-inch pieces
- 4–5 tablespoons ice water

FILLING

- 1/4 cup (1 ounce) cornstarch
- 1/4 cup packed (1 3/4 ounces) light brown sugar
- 1/4 teaspoon salt
- 1 1/4 cups whole milk
- 2 large egg yolks
- 1 large egg
- 1 cup (7 ounces) granulated sugar
- 1 1/4 cups heavy cream
- 2 tablespoons unsalted butter
- 3 tablespoons Scotch
- 2 teaspoons vanilla extract
- 3 firm, ripe bananas

1. FOR THE CRUST: Pulse the flour and salt in a food processor to combine. Add the shortening and process until the mixture has the texture of coarse sand, about 10 seconds. Sprinkle the butter pieces over the flour mixture and pulse until the mixture is pale yellow and resembles coarse crumbs, with butter pieces no larger than small peas, about ten 1-second pulses. Transfer the mixture to a medium bowl.

2. Sprinkle 4 tablespoons of the ice water over the flour mixture. Using a rubber spatula, use a folding motion to mix. Press down on the mixture with the broad side of the spatula until the dough sticks together, adding another tablespoon of ice water if it will not come together. Shape the dough into a ball, squeezing two or three times with your hands until it is cohesive, then flatten it into a 4-inch disk. Dust lightly with flour, wrap in plastic wrap, and refrigerate for at least 1 hour or up to 2 days before rolling.

3. If the dough has been refrigerated for longer than 1 hour, let it stand at room temperature until malleable before rolling. Following illustrations 1 through 3 on page 371, roll the dough out and fit it into a pie plate. Using a fork, prick the entire surface of the dough. Refrigerate the crust for 30 minutes and then freeze it for 20 minutes.

4. Meanwhile, adjust an oven rack to the middle position and heat the oven to 375 degrees. Press a doubled 12-inch square of aluminum foil inside the crust, then evenly distribute 1 cup ceramic or metal pie weights over the foil. Bake until light golden brown, about 30 minutes, leaving the foil and weights in place. Transfer to a wire rack, carefully remove the foil and weights, and cool completely.

5. FOR THE FILLING: Dissolve the cornstarch, brown sugar, and salt in ½ cup of the

milk in a medium bowl. Whisk in the egg yolks and egg and set aside.

6. Pour ½ cup water into a medium heavy-bottomed saucepan. Pour the granulated sugar into the center of the pan, taking care not to let the crystals adhere to the sides. Cover and bring to a boil over high heat. Once boiling, uncover and boil until the syrup is thick, straw-colored, and registers 300 degrees on an instant-read or candy thermometer, 8 to 9 minutes. Reduce the heat to medium and boil until the syrup is light amber and registers 350 degrees, about 1½ minutes.

7. Remove the pan from the heat and gradually whisk in ½ cup of the cream to prevent it from bubbling over. Add the cornstarch mixture and whisk until smooth. Whisk in the remaining ¾ cup milk. Return the pan to medium heat and cook, stirring constantly, until thick and boiling, about 2½ minutes. Remove from the heat and stir in the butter, Scotch, and vanilla. Scrape into a shallow bowl and press plastic wrap directly against the surface of the filling to prevent a skin from forming. Cool at room temperature until just slightly warm but still fluid, about 30 minutes.

8. Meanwhile, slice 2 of the bananas into ¼-inch-thick rounds and spread evenly over the bottom of the cooled pie shell. Pour the slightly warm filling over the bananas and press plastic wrap directly against the surface of the filling. Refrigerate until completely chilled, at least 3 and up to 6 hours.

9. Beat the remaining ¾ cup heavy cream using an electric mixer on medium speed until stiff peaks form. Spread the whipped cream over the surface of the pie. Cut the remaining banana into thin slices and arrange decoratively on top of the whipped cream. Serve immediately.

FITTING DOUGH INTO THE PIE PLATE

1. To make sure that you've rolled the dough to the right size, place the pie plate you are using upside down on top of it; the diameter of the dough should be 2 inches greater than that of the pie plate.

2. When the dough has reached the correct size, fold it into quarters. Place the folded dough in the empty pie plate, with the folded point of the dough in the center of the plate. Unfold gently.

3. Lift the edge of the dough with one hand and ease the pastry along the bottom into the corners with the other hand; continue around the circumference of the pan. Do not stretch the dough. Trim the dough edges to extend about ½ inch beyond the rim of the pan, fold the overhang under itself, and either flute the dough or press the tines of a fork against the dough to flatten it against the rim of the pie plate.

Crème Brûlée

Adapted from Crème Brûlée
Le Cirque, New York, New York

A properly made crème brûlée should be a study in contrasts. A warm, crisp, bittersweet sugar shell concealing a silky smooth custard is a perfect balance of egginess, creaminess, and sweetness. When this dessert is right on, as it always is at Le Cirque, it can't be beat.

The first component we looked at was the custard base of the brûlée. Le Cirque flavors a quart of heavy cream with half a cup of sugar along with the seeds and pod of a single vanilla bean. Quickly warmed on the stove to dissolve the sugar and infuse the cream with vanilla, the mixture is then thickened with eight egg yolks. Strained through a fine-mesh strainer to remove the vanilla pod and any overlooked pieces of eggshell, the tiny vanilla seeds pass through the mesh into the final custard—a visible sign that an actual vanilla bean, rather than extract, was used.

Finding no fault with the custard itself, we noted the first sign of trouble with this recipe when we tried to bake it in individual ramekins. Baked in a 200-degree oven for one hour and 15 minutes (according to the recipe), the custard was still completely soupy. We continued to bake for an additional two hours, but the custard never set up fully and we had to dump it down the drain. A quick call to the pastry chef identified our problem—200 degrees works only in a convection oven. Since convection ovens are expensive and rare in home kitchens, we went about adapting this cooking technique to a regular home oven. Convection ovens push the hot air around with fans, creating a gentle and even heat. To approximate this in a regular oven, we found it necessary to increase the temperature to 300 degrees and bake the ramekins in a water bath. Hot water is carefully poured around the ramekins (which sit in a baking dish), tempering the heat of the oven. Baked for 35 to 40 minutes, the custards then need to be cooled slowly—on the counter at first (so as not to shock the custard into clumping), then in the refrigerator until well chilled, at least two hours and up to four days. The result is cold, creamy, velvety smooth crème brûlées comparable to the convection-cooked desserts for which Le Cirque is known.

While reconfiguring the baking technique, we discovered several tips that further ensure the custard's success. The first was the use of an instant-read thermometer. When dealing with an egg yolk–thickened mixture, there is a fine line between perfect and overcooked (see the photos on page 373). Monitoring the custard's temperature as it bakes eliminates the guesswork completely, so you know exactly when to remove it from the oven. We also found it far easier to use a roasting pan for the water bath instead of a rimmed baking sheet, as instructed in the original recipe, which didn't use a water bath. Home quantities are more suited to the easier-to-handle roasting pan. The taller sides of the roasting pan work better at preventing spills of the hot water onto the floor (and your shoes). Also, the roasting pan's handles make it much easier to move the custards in and out of the oven. Finally, lining the bottom of the pan with a kitchen towel proved invaluable. It protects the bottom of the custards from the higher heat of the regular oven, while preventing the custard from sloshing around and becoming contaminated with water.

With the custards completed, we could focus on brûléeing the top. Le Cirque uses light brown sugar that has been dried at room temperature for three hours, then passed though a sieve to remove any clumps. When we tried this method, we ran into more home-cooking issues. First, we found the process of drying, then sieving, the brown sugar to be both time-consuming and a pain. We also noted that unless you are an experienced hand at brûléeing, the tiny granules of brown sugar are easy to scorch into unattractive patches of burnt sugar. Looking for an alternative, we experimented with two other types of sugar—white granulated sugar and turbinado sugar (known to most of us as Sugar in the Raw). Although both sugars caramelized successfully, the coarser turbinado sugar was far more forgiving to a less-experienced hand, producing an even, slightly thicker coating. Tasters also felt the turbinado sugar had a better caramel flavor than the white granulated sugar, which was somewhat cloying.

All that was left was to determine the best technique for brûléeing the sugar. Le Cirque's suggested method was using the broiler. While this method might work in a restaurant kitchen—usually equipped with a superhot broiler called a salamander, or "sally"—the weak, uneven heat of a home-kitchen broiler didn't provide such pleasing results. Some ramekins were left with pockets of raw sugar crystals, others with custards that became warm and soupy, having heated through completely. Instead, we opted to use a torch. Coming in a variety of sizes and flame intensities (see page 374), we found that propane torches not only worked better but also made for a dramatic after-dinner show.

CURDLED VERSUS CREAMY CUSTARD

The difference between an overcooked, curdled custard (top) and a smooth, creamy custard (bottom) can be a matter of a few minutes in the oven.

Crème Brûlée

SERVES 8

If you cannot find a vanilla bean, whisk 2 teaspoons of vanilla extract into the egg yolks in step 3. The cooking time of the custards will depend on their shape and depth—shallow dishes will bake faster. The custards can be baked, chilled, then wrapped tightly in plastic wrap and refrigerated for up to 4 days. The large crystals of turbinado sugar are easier to brûlée into an attractive, even-colored shell, but if it's not available, granulated sugar can be used as a substitute.

- 4 cups heavy cream
- ½ cup (3 ½ ounces) granulated sugar
- 1 vanilla bean, split in half lengthwise, seeds removed, seeds and pod reserved (see the illustrations on page 315)
- Pinch salt
- 8 large egg yolks
- 8–12 teaspoons turbinado sugar

1. Adjust an oven rack to the lower-middle position and heat the oven to 300 degrees. Place a clean kitchen towel in the bottom of a large roasting pan and arrange eight 4- or 5-ounce ramekins on the towel.

2. Heat the cream, granulated sugar, vanilla seeds and pod, and salt in a medium saucepan over medium-high heat, stirring frequently, until the sugar dissolves and bubbles cluster around the edge of the pan, about 3 minutes. Remove the pan from the heat and set aside

3. Twist a damp towel into a nest on the counter. Anchor a large bowl in the center of the towel nest. Add the egg yolks and whisk until broken up and combined. Gradually pour the warm cream mixture into the egg yolks, whisking constantly, until the mixture is smooth and homogenous. Strain though a fine-mesh strainer into a 2-quart measuring cup or pitcher, discarding the solids left in the strainer. Pour the mixture into the ramekins, stirring as necessary to distribute the vanilla seeds evenly.

4. Carefully place the roasting pan with the ramekins on the oven rack. Pour hot tap water around the ramekins, taking care not to splash it into the custard, until the water reaches two thirds up the sides of the ramekins. Bake until the centers of the custards are barely set (they should jiggle and shake rather than slosh) and an instant-read thermometer inserted in the centers registers 185 to 190 degrees, about 40 minutes (35 minutes for shallow dishes). Begin checking the temperature about 5 minutes before the recommended time.

5. Transfer the ramekins to a wire rack. Cool to room temperature, about 30 minutes. Set the ramekins on a rimmed baking sheet, cover tightly with plastic wrap, and refrigerate until cold, at least 2 hours and up to 4 days.

6. Uncover the ramekins. If condensation has collected on the custards, place a paper towel on the surface to soak up the moisture. Sprinkle each with about 1 teaspoon of the turbinado sugar (1½ teaspoons for shallow ramekins). Tilt and tap the ramekins for even coverage. Ignite the torch and, working from the edge of the ramekin inward, run the blue flame over the custard to caramelize the sugar. Serve immediately.

EQUIPMENT: Pass the Torch

Fire up a torch to caramelize the sugar on your crème brûlée—it's the best way to put the crowning glory of a crust on the custard. We tested a hardware-store propane torch (right) against a petite kitchen torch (left) fueled by butane. The propane torch, with its powerful flame, caramelized the sugar quickly and easily, but, admittedly, it's not the for the fainthearted. The butane torch was less intimidating, but its puny flame did the job slowly. If you are looking to buy a propane torch, look for one with a built-in ignition trigger that does not need to be held down for the torch to remain lit. If a kitchen torch is more your speed, purchase a can of butane along with it—otherwise you'll have more luck "brûléeing" with a book of matches.

Souffléed Lemon Custard

Adapted from Souffléed Lemon Custard

Hamersley's Bistro, Boston, Massachusetts

SOUFFLÉS AND CUSTARDS STRIKE TREPIDAtion in the hearts of even the most seasoned home cooks. The fear is that towering soufflés will fall if someone bangs a door shut and creamy custards will curdle if given a wayward glance. Unwilling to endure such disappointment, cooks too often abandon all attempts at home and leave soufflés and custards to pastry chefs. Fortunately, help is on the way in the form of a souffléed lemon custard from Hamersley's Bistro that will ease any apprehension in the home cook. Combining the best of soufflés and custards in one easy-to-follow recipe, the dessert tops a soft, creamy custard with a lightly browned, ethereal soufflé. Stabilized with flour and served when cooled to room temperature, the dessert erases concerns over collapsing soufflés and broken custards. Perhaps best of all, there is no need to assemble a dozen small ramekins or specialty soufflé pans. One large cake pan is all that is required.

The recipe begins with a creamed butter-and-sugar mixture enriched with egg yolks. Flour, lemon juice, lemon zest, cream, and milk are then added to form a custard batter. Finally, beaten egg whites are folded into the batter to lighten it. The result is a delicate, smooth, and uniform batter. In the oven, however, the uniform mixture forms two texturally distinct layers: the bottom is a rich, smooth custard while the top is a delicate meringue with a lightly browned crust. Use a large serving spoon to scoop both layers onto each dessert plate. The textural contrast between the layers, combined with the bright lemon flavor, brings together the best of a custard and a soufflé.

Be sure to have the ingredients at the specified temperature before you begin. Eggs at room temperature and softened butter incorporate air and combine with other ingredients more easily than when cold. To soften butter quickly, cut a cold stick of butter into ½-inch pieces and set aside for five minutes. To bring eggs to room temperature quickly, cover the eggs, still in their shells, in a bowl of hot tap water for two minutes. A 10-inch cake pan is essential for the amount of batter in this recipe. If you use a smaller pan, you will have extra batter and will need to adjust the cooking time significantly. Allow the souffléed custard to come to room temperature before serving. In the time it takes to cool, the bottom layer of the dessert will set up properly.

Souffléed Lemon Custard

SERVES 8

Because this dessert is best served at room temperature, you may make the souffléed custard well ahead of time, but do note that you will need to serve the custard the same day it's made.

- **8 tablespoons (1 stick) unsalted butter, softened**
- **1 1/2 cups (10 1/2 ounces) sugar**
- **6 large egg yolks, at room temperature**
- **1 teaspoon grated zest and 1 cup juice from 4 lemons**
- **2/3 cup (3 1/3 ounces) unbleached all-purpose flour, sifted**
- **1/8 teaspoon salt**
- **2 cups whole milk**
- **1 cup heavy cream**
- **6 large egg whites, at room temperature**
- **1/4 teaspoon cream of tartar**
- **1 pint fresh berries (such as blueberries or raspberries)**
- **8 sprigs fresh mint, for garnish (optional)**

1. Adjust an oven rack to the lower-middle position and heat the oven to 350 degrees. Set a 10-inch cake pan inside a roasting pan and set aside.

2. In the bowl of a standing mixer fitted with the paddle attachment, beat the butter and all but 1 tablespoon of the sugar on medium speed until fluffy, about 3 minutes. Reduce the speed to medium-low and add the egg yolks, one at a time, beating for 20 seconds after each addition. Add the lemon zest, juice, flour, and salt and beat until combined, about 10 seconds, scraping the bowl as necessary. Remove the bowl from the standing mixer and gently whisk in the milk and cream until smooth. Transfer the lemon custard to a large bowl and set aside.

3. Bring 8 cups water to a boil in a medium saucepan and set aside. Wash and dry the bowl of the standing mixer and return to the mixer fitted with the whisk attachment. Beat the egg whites, remaining 1 tablespoon sugar, and cream of tartar on medium-high until light and shiny and beginning to hold a soft peak, 1½ to 2 minutes.

4. Using a spatula, stir one third of the egg whites into the lemon custard to lighten it. Fold the remaining egg whites into the custard mixture until just combined. Pour the mixture into the prepared cake pan. Pour the hot water into the roasting pan until it comes halfway up the sides of the cake pan. Bake until the custard is light brown and just set in the middle, about 45 minutes, turning the pan around halfway through the baking time, so that it browns evenly. It will not rise very much, and the top will be fairly sturdy, much like a cake.

5. Remove the cake pan from the water bath and cool on a wire rack to room temperature. To serve, spoon the custard onto 8 individual dessert plates or into bowls and garnish with the berries and mint, if using.

Sticky Toffee Pudding

Adapted from Sticky Toffee Pudding

Biga on the Banks, San Antonio, Texas

TRADITIONALLY FLAVORED WITH TREACLE (sometimes called golden syrup) and dates, steamed sticky toffee pudding is decidedly English. Serving it hot with an ice-cold vanilla sauce and a steaming-hot toffee sauce, Biga on the Banks (in Texas, of all places) makes a stellar version of this classic "pud," trading the treacle for American molasses and "steaming" them in individual ramekins.

Beginning with the pudding, we pared down the original yield from 14 ramekins to 6. The method for preparing the puddings, luckily, was incredibly straightforward and required zero streamlining. Key to the recipe's success is letting the dates soak in hot water laced with baking soda for several minutes before adding them to the batter. The alkalinity of the baking soda helps render the dates and their tough skins tender. The batter, which is a standard mixture of creamed butter and dark brown sugar, as well as soaked dates, molasses, egg, vanilla, flour, and baking powder, is then poured into buttered ramekins and "steamed" in a foil-covered water bath in a 325-degree oven. The puddings are served warm, either straight from the oven or after being reheated in the microwave. Rather than serve them in their ramekins, however, Biga unmolds them into individual bowls. To make the unmolding easier, we found it best to line the bottoms of the ramekins with small rounds of parchment paper.

A splash of cold vanilla sauce (also known as crème anglaise) is poured around the hot pudding just before serving. We reduced the sauce recipe, which originally made more than a quart, to yield enough for six servings. To match the texture of the pudding, Biga on the Banks makes the crème anglaise on the thicker side by using a higher than usual ratio of yolks (the thickening agent) to liquid. The restaurant also makes the sauce with whole milk as opposed to cream, preventing the dessert from becoming overwhelmingly rich. Flavored with the traditional vanilla bean and nontraditional honey, the trick to making this sauce smooth (as with all egg yolk–thickened sauces) is to temper the eggs yolks with some of the warm milk before stirring them into the pot. We found it easiest to make this sauce first, so that it has ample time to chill before serving.

Last, hot toffee sauce is poured over the pudding, making it an authentic sticky toffee pudding. Made with light brown sugar, butter, and cream, the method is quite similar to making a caramel sauce: the brown sugar and butter are cooked for a bit to deepen their flavors, then combined with cream to make a sauce. To streamline the list of ingredients, we tried making the sauce with dark brown sugar (used in the puddings), but the resulting flavor was far too sweet and potent.

Serving the pudding and the toffee sauce steaming hot, and the vanilla sauce ice cold, is key. If you are going to serve the puddings straight from the oven, then make the toffee sauce just before serving so it is hot. Both the toffee sauce and the individual puddings, however, are easy to reheat in the microwave if made ahead of time.

Sticky Toffee Pudding

SERVES 6

To reheat the toffee sauce, microwave it, covered, on 50-percent power, stirring occasionally, until hot, 3 to 6 minutes. To reheat the puddings, microwave them in their ramekins, uncovered, on 100-percent power until hot and steaming, 1 to 3 minutes. Unmold and serve the reheated puddings immediately.

CUSTARD SAUCE

- **2/3 cup whole milk**
- **1/2 vanilla bean, split in half lengthwise, seeds removed, seeds and pod reserved (see the illustrations on page 315)**
- **4 large egg yolks**
- **2 tablespoons granulated sugar**
- **Pinch salt**
- **1 teaspoon honey**

PUDDING

- **5 tablespoons (1/2 stick plus 1 tablespoon) unsalted butter, softened, plus more for greasing the ramekins**
- **1/2 pound whole pitted dates, cut crosswise into 1/4-inch-thick slices**
- **3/4 teaspoon baking soda**
- **2/3 cup boiling water, plus more for the water bath**
- **1 cup (5 ounces) unbleached all-purpose flour**
- **1/2 teaspoon baking powder**
- **1/8 teaspoon salt**
- **1/4 cup (1 3/4 ounces) dark brown sugar**
- **1/3 cup mild or light molasses**
- **3/4 teaspoon vanilla extract**
- **1 large egg**

TOFFEE SAUCE

- **2 1/3 tablespoons unsalted butter**
- **1/3 cup packed (2 1/3 ounces) light brown sugar**
- **3 tablespoons heavy cream**
- **Pinch salt**

1. For the custard sauce: Bring the milk and vanilla seeds and pod to a simmer in a medium saucepan over medium-high heat. When the milk reaches a simmer, reduce the heat to low. Whisk the egg yolks, granulated sugar, and salt together in a medium bowl. Whisk 3 tablespoons of the hot milk mixture into the yolk mixture. Slowly whisk the tempered egg yolk mixture into the simmering hot milk. Cook, whisking constantly, until the sauce is quite thick (heavily coats the back of a spoon) and registers 165 degrees on an instant-read thermometer, about 2 minutes.

CUTTING DATES

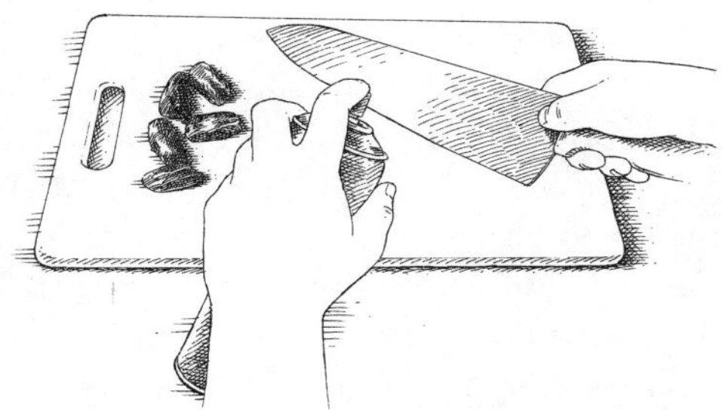

Dried fruit, like dates, very often sticks to the knife when you try to chop it. To avoid this problem, coat the blade with a thin film of vegetable oil spray just before you begin chopping it. The dates won't cling to the blade and the knife stays relatively clean.

2. Pour the mixture through a fine-mesh strainer into a clean bowl and stir in the honey. Cover with plastic wrap and refrigerate until needed (or place in the freezer to chill immediately).

3. For the pudding: Adjust an oven rack to the middle position and heat the oven 325 degrees. Grease six 4-ounce ramekins with butter and line the bottoms with small rounds of parchment paper. Arrange the ramekins in a small roasting pan lined with a clean dish towel (to prevent them from sliding around in the pan). Combine the dates, baking soda, and ⅔ cup boiling water in a medium bowl and set aside.

4. Whisk together the flour, baking powder, and salt in a small bowl. In the bowl of a standing mixer fitted with the paddle attachment, beat the remaining 5 tablespoons butter and dark brown sugar together on medium-low speed until just mixed, about 1 minute. Add the molasses and vanilla and beat until just combined. Scrape down the paddle and bowl using a rubber spatula. Resume mixing on medium-low, add the egg, and beat until just combined. Add the date mixture and mix to combine. Slowly add the flour mixture and mix until just combined.

5. Divide the batter evenly among the prepared ramekins. Fill the roasting pan with enough boiling water to come halfway up the sides of the ramekins, making sure not to splash it into the puddings. Cover the pan tightly with foil, crimping the edges to seal. Bake the puddings until they are slightly puffed and a butter knife inserted into the center of the puddings comes out clean, about 35 minutes.

6. For the toffee sauce: Meanwhile, melt the butter in a medium saucepan over medium heat. Whisk in the light brown sugar and cook, whisking occasionally, until an instant-read thermometer registers 250 degrees. Carefully whisk in the cream and salt and bring to a simmer. Remove from the heat and transfer to a glass measuring cup. Cover tightly with plastic wrap to keep warm (see the headnote for reheating instructions if necessary).

7. To serve: Transfer the hot puddings to a wire rack to cool slightly. Run a paring knife around the edges of the ramekins to loosen the puddings. Overturn the ramekins into 6 large, shallow individual bowls, releasing the puddings. Pour the cold custard sauce, as desired, around each pudding. Pour the warm toffee sauce, as desired, over the top of each pudding and serve immediately.

Praline Bread Pudding

Adapted from Praline Bread Pudding à la Louisiane

Primos, Baton Rouge, Louisiana

PRALINE BREAD PUDDING IS COMFORT food at its best. Tender layers of bread are supersaturated with a rich, sweet custard scented with vanilla and pecan and baked until all of the flavors are infused into the bread. The result is a pudding that is firm enough to cut, yet tender enough to melt in your mouth. Finished with a satiny hazelnut-butter sauce, nothing could be so simple to make, yet so satisfying to eat.

Originally a thrifty way to use up day-old bread, bread pudding can be a boon to cooks (restaurant or otherwise) finding themselves with an extra loaf, and nothing for dessert. Finding the best bread for this recipe showed us that not all breads are perfect for puddings. We tried challah (an egg bread), thinking that its richness would add flavor to the pudding, but found that it lacked the structure to support the heavy cream and egg base, yielding a soggy pudding bottom. Everyday white bread worked, but tasters felt the texture was still a bit slimy, especially at the bottom of the dish. Since this was a recipe from Louisiana, our next inclination was to use the bread that any respectable Baton Rouge restaurant most certainly serves: French bread. It was just the thing. Stale or toasted bread absorbs far more custard than fresh bread (more is definitely better), so we placed the bread, cut into cubes, on a baking sheet in the oven to dry out, then drenched it with the custard twice. In the first round, the bread soaked up the custard like a thirsty sponge. This was a good thing, but the bread looked too dry. The second addition saturated the bread with the perfect amount of custard to yield a pudding that was full of flavor and richness yet firm enough to hold its own on a plate. Adding the custard in separate batches gave the bread time to absorb the most custard possible from each addition without flooding the baking dish.

Bread puddings can serve as the perfect foil for a multitude of flavorings, and here the southern influence shines through with one of the South's premier harvests, pecans. While our original recipe sautéed the nuts in butter, we found we were able to coax more flavor out of the pecans by toasting them in the oven. The intense flavor came from the inside of the nutmeat, rather than from just a bit of browning on the outside. Praline liqueur (a pecan and vanilla–infused liqueur) was an ingredient that we were hard-pressed to find in our area. Hazelnut liqueur, such as Frangelico (suggested by the restaurant), served as a viable alternative in both the pudding and the sauce that followed.

The last question remaining for us was the most efficient way to cook the pudding. Baking puddings, and in particular custards, in a water bath (or bain-marie) is a method that is designed to protect the eggs in the custard from overcooking, or cooking at too high a temperature. It involves setting the baking dish in a larger pan and filling the larger pan with hot water before baking. In this case, we found that baking without the water bath produced a pudding that was firm and perfectly cooked, without the hassle of the water bath. The bread seemed to have an insulating effect on the eggs so that overcooking was not an issue. We also found that this is one dessert that actually benefits from advance preparation. Allowing the pudding to sit for a few hours before baking maximizes the amount of custard that is absorbed by the dry bread.

The restaurant included two sauces in its recipe for us to choose from: a praline-butter sauce and a white chocolate sauce. Tasters felt the praline-butter sauce was better suited to the pudding (the white chocolate sauce seemed to be gilding the already-rich lily). The added hit of liqueur in the sauce complements the flavors of the pudding. It is made just like a hollandaise, with egg yolks cooked over a water bath until light and fluffy, then removed from the heat and whisked constantly while a slow, steady stream of hot, melted butter is added. The resulting sauce is smooth, rich, gooey, and buttery—everything a classic southern dessert should be.

Praline Bread Pudding

SERVES 12

The pudding can be assembled in advance and refrigerated up to 12 hours ahead. Allow 1 hour for baking and at least 20 minutes for the pudding to cool. The sauce is best made while the pudding is cooling. If there happen to be any leftovers, the sauce can be reheated for 1 minute on 30-percent power, stirring halfway through heating.

PUDDING

- **12 ounces good-quality French baguette, cut into 1 1/2-inch cubes**
- **2 cups pecans**
- **6 tablespoons (3/4 stick) unsalted butter, cut into 1/2-inch pieces, plus more for greasing the pan**
- **12 large eggs**
- **2 large egg yolks**
- **3 tablespoons vanilla extract**
- **2 tablespoons hazelnut liqueur, such as Frangelico**
- **1 1/2 cups (10 1/2 ounces) sugar**
- **6 cups heavy cream**

SAUCE

- **4 large egg yolks**
- **1/2 cup (3 1/2 ounces) sugar**
- **1/4 cup hazelnut liqueur**
- **8 tablespoons (1 stick) unsalted butter**

1. For the pudding: Adjust an oven rack to the middle position and heat the oven to 250 degrees. Spread the bread cubes in a single layer on a rimmed baking sheet and bake until dry, 30 to 40 minutes. Remove from the oven, transfer to a large plate, and cool to room temperature. Increase the oven temperature to 350 degrees. Spread the nuts on the empty baking sheet and toast, shaking the pan once to turn the nuts, until fragrant, 5 to 8 minutes. Set the toasted nuts aside. Turn off the oven.

2. Grease a 13 by 9-inch baking dish with butter. Spread the dried bread cubes evenly in the baking dish. Whisk the eggs, egg yolks, vanilla, hazelnut liqueur, and sugar together in a large bowl. Whisk in the cream. Pour three quarters of the custard over the bread and sprinkle the toasted pecans over the top. Using a rubber spatula, press the bread into the custard. Cover with plastic wrap and refrigerate until the liquid is absorbed,

about 20 minutes. Pour the remaining custard evenly over the top, replace the plastic wrap, and refrigerate until most of liquid is absorbed, about 1 hour.

3. Return the oven temperature to 350 degrees. Remove the plastic wrap and dot the top of the pudding evenly with the remaining 6 tablespoons butter. Bake until the top is a deep golden brown, the center is slightly puffed, and the custard begins to climb up the sides of the baking dish, 50 to 60 minutes. Transfer to a wire rack and cool until set, about 20 minutes.

4. For the sauce: While the pudding is cooling, place the egg yolks in a medium bowl. Heat the sugar and hazelnut liqueur in another medium bowl over a medium saucepan of simmering water, whisking constantly, until the sugar is dissolved, about 5 minutes. Slowly stir the warm liqueur mixture into the egg yolks. Place the bowl of yolk mixture over the simmering water, and cook, whisking constantly, until the mixture is fluffy, pale yellow, and the whisk leaves distinct trails, about 2 minutes.

5. Melt the butter in a glass measuring cup in the microwave on high power, 1 to 2 minutes. Meanwhile, twist a damp kitchen towel into a nest on the counter. Remove the bowl of yolk mixture from the simmering water and place it in the towel nest. Slowly drizzle the hot melted butter into the yolk mixture, whisking constantly, until all of the butter is incorporated and the sauce is thick and creamy.

6. To serve: Cut the pudding into 12 squares. Use a metal spatula to transfer the portions to 12 individual plates and pour 2 tablespoons of the hot hazelnut sauce over each. Serve immediately.

Stir-Fried Fruit *with* Ginger Ice Cream & Jasmine Caramel

Adapted from Stir-Fried Fruit with Ginger Ice Cream and Jasmine Caramel

PARK AVENUE CAFÉ, NEW YORK, NEW YORK

STIR-FRIED FRUIT—AND FOR DESSERT, no less? Only a restaurant could pull it off, and the Park Avenue Café does so with panache. A colorful, multitextured mixture of fruit is quickly cooked and tossed in a jasmine tea and Grand Marnier sauce, then topped with ginger ice cream. It's subtly Asian in flavoring, but versatile enough to finish any number of meals. The dessert is also very "adult" tasting, sharpened by bitter caramel and hot, biting ginger, not to mention the boozy fullness of the Grand Marnier. To make the dessert a little more home-kitchen friendly, we chose to replace the homemade ice cream the restaurant serves with doctored store-bought ice cream. The shortcut shaves hours off the preparation time with no detriment to the flavor.

Ginger ice cream—slightly exotic but instantly recognizable—has become a restaurant staple in the past few years, though the commercial producers have yet to catch on. We found it unavailable from anyone but small-batch, boutique producers selling on a local level (Ben and Jerry's, take note). That said, we figured it couldn't be too difficult to add ginger flavoring to commercial, premium vanilla ice cream. Folding minced, candied ginger into ice cream seemed like the most direct method, but the bits of chewy ginger and crunch of the granulated sugar coating marred the ice cream's creamy texture and made it too sweet. Powdered ground ginger imparted an unpleasant dustiness.

Fresh ginger, in some form, was looking to be the best option. We grated it finely and stirred it in, but the stringy bits of ginger were unpleasant. The flavor, however, was spot on—very potent. To achieve the flavor without the fiber, we squeezed the grated ginger in a fine-mesh strainer, pressing out as much ginger juice as possible, which was then easy to stir into the softened ice cream. The ginger flavor was sharp and full, with a slight smoldering burn to cut the fruit's sweetness. Tasted vis-à-vis the restaurant's version, our doctored ice cream stood its ground. Some tasters even preferred it, finding the vanilla flavor note pleasant (the restaurant's version was flavored solely with ginger).

The jasmine caramel sauce is a mixture of double-strength jasmine tea and caramelized sugar lightened with lemon juice and honey and spiked with Grand Marnier. The slightly flowery, musty flavor of the tea accents the caramel's heavy, bittersweet flavor. For the novice, making caramel can be intimidating, since every cookbook seems to offer a different technique and plenty of warnings about the dangers of molten sugar. We agree with the warnings (so be careful and don't splash), but as far as technique, we have found a simple, foolproof method. We first add water, then sugar, to a heavy-bottomed, tall-sided saucepan and cook it, covered, unstirred, over medium-high heat until it boils. Then we remove the cover and cook the syrup until it registers 300 degrees on an instant-read or candy thermometer. Then we reduce the heat to medium and cook it until the syrup registers 350 degrees and is light amber in color. For this sauce, tasters favored a relatively light, mild-tasting caramel—"dirty blond" is probably the most apt description of its color (the darker the color of the caramel, the more robust the flavor).

Adding the tea to the caramel will "seize" it, or prevent it from further darkening. Stand back when you add the tea, since it's liable to sputter and steam, which is why we make caramel in a tall-sided saucepan. The caramel will likely partially solidify in the pan, but as the sauce reduces according to the restaurant's recipe, any hard bits will dissolve.

And finally, on to the fruit. In the "stir-fry," the restaurant includes melon, apple, pineapple, strawberries, blueberries, and raspberries, though only the hearty melon, apple, and pineapple actually see heat. Despite the dessert's title, the fruit isn't really stir-fried, but briefly sautéed to soften it and intensify its flavors. The restaurant offered sketchy instructions for this step, but it was easy to find the best method. We used a large skillet—not a wok—and slicked it with flavorless vegetable oil. Once the oil was smoking hot, we added the fruit and stirred frequently. The fruit browned lightly and glazed over within one to two minutes. Off the heat, we added the remaining fruit and sauce. The colorful fruit, pale yellow ice cream, and glossy caramel sauce make this is a showstopper of a dessert.

Stir-Fried Fruit with Ginger Ice Cream and Jasmine Caramel

SERVES 6

Prepare the ice cream quickly to prevent it from melting too much, which will impair its creamy texture. Both the ice cream and caramel may be prepared up to 2 days ahead of time, but hold off on cooking the fruit until the very last minute; texture is important to the dessert's success. If you can't find an acceptable melon, double the amount of pineapple. If Granny Smiths are unavailable, choose another tart, firm apple.

GINGER ICE CREAM

- 1 (2 1/2-inch) piece fresh ginger, scrubbed
- 1 pint premium vanilla ice cream, softened (but not melting)

JASMINE CARAMEL

- 1 jasmine tea bag
- 1/2 cup boiling water
- 1 tablespoon honey
- 1 tablespoon juice from 1 small lemon
- Pinch salt
- 1/2 cup (3 1/2 ounces) sugar
- 1/4 cup Grand Marnier (or fresh-squeezed orange juice)

STIR-FRIED FRUIT

- **1 tablespoon vegetable oil**
- **1 medium Granny Smith apple, peeled, cored, and sliced thin**
- **½ cup honeydew or cantaloupe melon, diced medium**
- **½ cup fresh pineapple, diced medium**
- **1 cup strawberries, hulled and quartered**
- **1 cup fresh blueberries**
- **1 cup fresh raspberries**
- **6 sprigs fresh mint, for garnish (optional)**

1. FOR THE ICE CREAM: Using a Microplane grater or fine-holed box grater, grate the ginger. Transfer the grated ginger to a fine-mesh strainer set over a small bowl and press firmly with a spoon to extract as much juice as possible. Place the softened ice cream in a medium bowl and, using a stiff rubber spatula, fold the ginger juice into the ice cream. Cover tightly with plastic wrap, pressing the plastic flush against the ice cream. (See the illustration on page 397.) Return the ice cream to the freezer to firm up, about 30 minutes.

2. FOR THE CARAMEL SAUCE: Steep the tea bag in the boiling water in a small bowl for 5 minutes. Remove and discard the tea bag. Stir in the honey, lemon juice, and salt until dissolved and set aside.

3. Measure ¼ cup water into a small heavy-bottomed saucepan. Pour the sugar into the center of the pan, taking care not to let the crystals adhere to the sides. Cover and bring to a boil over high heat. Once boiling, remove the cover and continue to boil until the syrup is thick, straw-colored, and registers 300 degrees on an instant-read or candy thermometer, 6 to 7 minutes. Reduce the heat to medium and cook until the syrup is light amber and registers 350 degrees, 1 to 2 minutes. Remove from the heat and very slowly stir in the tea mixture, being careful of the steam. Return the saucepan to medium-high heat and cook, stirring occasionally, until the mixture has thickened and reduced to ½ cup, about 5 minutes. Transfer to a small bowl, stir in the Grand Marnier, and set aside.

4. FOR THE STIR-FRIED FRUIT: Heat the vegetable oil in a 12-inch skillet over medium-high heat until smoking. Add the apple, melon, and pineapple and cook, stirring frequently, until the fruit is lightly browned around the edges, 1 to 1½ minutes. Remove from the heat and, using a heat-resistant rubber spatula, stir in the strawberries, blueberries, and caramel sauce. Gently fold in the raspberries.

5. TO SERVE: Divide the fruit equally among 6 individual shallow bowls and top with small scoops of the ginger ice cream. Garnish with the mint sprigs, if using. Serve immediately.

Asian Poached Pears *with* Fresh Ginger Pastry Cream & Spicy Shortbread Chopsticks

Adapted from Asian Poached Pears with Fresh Ginger Pastry Cream and Spicy Shortbread Chopsticks

The Winds Café and Bakery, Yellow Springs, Ohio

AN ELEGANT DESSERT THAT IS SURPRISingly easy to make, poached pears are a dependable, impressive finale to any meal. In an unusual twist, the Winds Café uses Asian aromatics such as fresh ginger and star anise, and pairs them with vanilla, cinnamon, and white wine for fusion flair. A pastry cream infused with fresh ginger and unexpectedly spicy, delicate shortbread "chopstick" cookies complete this picture-perfect dessert.

Unlike many fruit desserts whose success hinges on the availability and ripeness of seasonal fruit for flavor, underripe, less-than-perfect pears are actually more desirable for this dish. Pears will absorb virtually any flavoring that is added to the poaching liquid—the longer they spend in the liquid, the more flavor they absorb. The pears that we started with were as hard as rocks, with no discernable pear aroma. (Chalk it up to winter in New England.) Poaching not only softened them, it brought their natural flavors out of winter hiding with the added flavor bonus of the aromatics and wine. The pears were perfect—tender and flavorful.

Ginger pastry cream is an incredibly rich vanilla pudding flavored with fresh ginger. Our first batch of pastry cream ran into problems, and we suspected that the fresh ginger was the culprit. When steeped with milk, the enzymes in the ginger curdled it, resulting in a lumpy consistency that could not be eliminated by straining. We made the pastry cream again with half-and-half and found that the added fat seemed to protect the proteins in the liquid from enzyme breakdown, and also produced a richer cream. The resulting pastry cream was thick enough to spoon, as directed in the recipe, but some tasters felt that it was a bit too thick for this application, preferring the cream to be thinned with some of the pear-poaching liquid (it seemed a shame not to use such a flavorful brew). This afforded us a more spreadable cream on which to perch the pear, thereby eliminating the inevitable problem of the pear sliding around the plate on its poaching liquid when being served.

The spicy shortbread chopsticks piqued our curiosity, and we were eager to investigate the recipe. While the dough is quick to prepare, rolling and cutting proved to be the most difficult part of the whole dessert, particularly for the mathematically challenged. Instructed to roll the dough to three sixteenths inch thick at one end and six sixteenths inch thick at the other end (which was nearly impossible), we found that little visual appeal was lost if the dough was rolled to an even one-quarter-inch thickness. We then used a chopstick (as a one-quarter-inch template) to cut the cookies to the most realistic size possible. With the rolling and cutting settled on, it was time to bake and taste. The combination of the sweet, buttery shortbread with the slight sting of chile heat and curry warmth was a pleasant surprise. On their own, these innocent-looking cookies packed a powerful punch. To our surprise, the cold poached pear balanced the heat of the cookie and left us with a curious hot-cold sensation (kind of like a Peppermint Patty without the chocolate). When we tasted the dish with all its components, the result was an unusual, balanced dessert that was well worth making.

Asian Poached Pears with Fresh Ginger Pastry Cream and Spicy Shortbread Chopsticks

SERVES 6

All of the components for this dessert are easily prepared in advance. The shortbread chopsticks have quite a bit of heat, so cut back on the chili powder and cayenne if you prefer a milder taste. We recommend using Bosc or Bartlett pears in this recipe because they won't discolor when poached.

POACHED PEARS

- **1 1/2 cups (10 1/2 ounces) sugar**
- **1 (3-inch) piece fresh ginger, sliced into 1/4-inch coins**
- **2 whole star anise pods**
- **2 tablespoons grated zest from 2 lemons**
- **1 vanilla bean, split lengthwise**
- **1 cinnamon stick, broken into pieces**
- **4 cups dry white wine**
- **6 firm Bosc or Bartlett pears, stem on, peeled, and 1/4 inch trimmed off the bottom of each pear so it will stand upright**

PASTRY CREAM

- **2 cups half-and-half**
- **1 (1-inch) piece fresh ginger, sliced into 1/4-inch coins**
- **1 vanilla bean, split lengthwise**
- **1/8 teaspoon salt**
- **1/2 cup (3 1/2 ounces) sugar**
- **2 tablespoons cornstarch**
- **6 large egg yolks**
- **4 tablespoons (1/2 stick) cold unsalted butter, cut into 4 pieces**

SHORTBREAD CHOPSTICKS

- **1/2 cup plus 6 tablespoons (4 3/8 ounces) unbleached all-purpose flour, plus more for rolling out the dough**
- **1/2 teaspoon curry powder**
- **1/2 teaspoon turmeric**
- **1/4 teaspoon paprika**
- **1/8 teaspoon chili powder**
- **1/8 teaspoon cayenne pepper**
- **6 tablespoons (3/4 stick) unsalted butter, softened**
- **3 tablespoons sugar**

1. FOR THE POACHED PEARS: Bring the sugar, ginger, star anise, lemon zest, vanilla bean, cinnamon stick, wine, and 2 cups water to a boil in a medium saucepan over

medium-high heat. Add the pears, reduce the heat to low, and simmer, covered, until the pears are tender (a toothpick or skewer inserted into a pear should slide in and out with very little resistance) and translucent, 15 to 20 minutes. Remove the pears from the liquid and set aside to cool. Strain the poaching liquid into a nonreactive bowl and set aside to cool. Return the pears to the cooled poaching liquid, cover, and refrigerate for 3 to 4 hours. (At this point, the pears and liquid can be covered and refrigerated for up to 3 days.)

2. FOR THE PASTRY CREAM: Bring the half-and-half, ginger, vanilla bean, and salt to a simmer in a small saucepan over medium-high heat. Remove from the heat and steep for 20 minutes. Strain through a fine-mesh sieve into a medium saucepan.

3. Whisk the sugar, cornstarch, and egg yolks together in a medium bowl. Return the half-and-half mixture to a simmer over medium-high heat. Slowly whisk the warm half-and-half mixture into the yolk mixture. Return the mixture to the saucepan and cook, whisking constantly, until it thickens to the consistency of soft pudding. Remove from the heat and whisk in the butter until melted. Transfer to a medium bowl and place a piece of plastic wrap directly against the surface of the cream to prevent a skin from forming. Refrigerate until cold. (The pastry cream can be kept, refrigerated, up to 2 days.)

4. FOR THE SHORTBREAD CHOPSTICKS: Sift the flour, curry powder, turmeric, paprika, chili powder, and cayenne together into a medium bowl. In the bowl of a standing mixer fitted with the paddle attachment, cream the butter and sugar until light and fluffy, 1 to 2 minutes. Add the flour mixture and mix until well combined and the dough forms a smooth ball. Transfer the dough to a clean work surface and knead for 1 minute. Lightly dust the work surface with flour and roll the dough out into a 7 by 6-inch rectangle, about ¼ inch thick. Transfer to a rimmed baking sheet lined with parchment, cover with plastic wrap, and refrigerate until firm, about 1 hour.

5. Adjust an oven rack to the middle position and heat the oven to 350 degrees. Using a sharp knife or pizza cutter dusted with flour, cut the dough rectangle lengthwise into thin strips, about ¼ inch wide. You should have 25 to 28 strips. Separate the strips using a spatula, leaving ¼ inch in between. Bake until the strips are golden brown and quite firm, 20 to 25 minutes. Let cool on the baking sheet for 20 minutes. Carefully transfer to a cooling rack and cool completely. (The chopsticks are very delicate, so handle them as little as possible.)

6. TO SERVE: If you like your pastry cream on the thin side (it will be like pudding, as is), thin it with some of the reserved poaching liquid. Spread about ¼ cup of the pastry cream over the center of each of 6 individual plates with the back of a soupspoon. Place a pear in the center of each plate and garnish with 3 or 4 of the shortbread chopsticks. Serve immediately.

HONEY-GLAZED BANANA FRITTERS *with* SALTED PEANUT ICE CREAM

Adapted from Tempura-Fried Banana Fritters with Honey Glaze and Salted Peanut Ice Cream

TENPENH RESTAURANT, WASHINGTON, D.C.

IN THE TEST KITCHEN, TASTERS FOUND this Asian-inspired rendition of the classic American banana split impossible to resist. TenPenh Restaurant coats ripe bananas in a light tempura batter and fries them until they are a deep golden brown. Arranged in a shallow serving bowl, the tempura bananas are drizzled with honey, sprinkled with toasted sesame seeds, and topped with a scoop of salted peanut ice cream. This intriguing dessert is a study in contrasting flavors, temperatures, and textures. The ice cream melts slightly over the warm tempura bananas, whose sweet, soft interiors and crisp, light exteriors balance the salty-sweetness of the peanut ice cream. Although the dish has all the components of a complicated restaurant creation, you'll find our version of this dessert simple to make.

We began with the ice cream. We love homemade ice cream, especially this uniquely flavored version, but in an effort to streamline the recipe we decided to doctor store-bought ice cream. By folding ground, salted, roasted peanuts into softened vanilla ice cream, we were able to achieve the rich nutty flavor of the original in a fraction of the time it would have taken to make homemade. The doctored version wasn't as creamy as the original but still was satisfying.

Because we shaved time off the ice cream preparation, we prepared the bananas just as the restaurant does, with a few minor adjustments. When we were ready to fry the bananas, we toasted the sesame seeds in a small skillet and then whisked the tempura-batter ingredients together while heating 4 cups of canola oil in a Dutch oven to 370 degrees. Although the recipe originally called for heating the oil to 350 degrees, we found that the temperature of the oil drops significantly when the bananas are added, extending the cooking time. The bananas turn a deep golden brown faster at a higher temperature when cooked in such a small amount of oil. The large amounts of oil used in restaurant fryers retain heat more readily when food is added compared with the small amount of oil used on the stovetop at home.

After a quick respite on a rack lined with

paper towels to drain, the bananas are ready to be served. We found that ripe bananas provide a much more dramatic and appealing sweet contrast to the salty ice cream than firm, unripe bananas. A drizzle of honey adds a sharp sweetness to the mix, and the sprinkle of the toasted sesame seeds reinforces the ice cream's nutty flavor.

Honey-Glazed Banana Fritters with Salted Peanut Ice Cream

SERVES 6

This dessert makes a great ending to an Asian-inspired meal.

PEANUT ICE CREAM

- **1/4 cup salted roasted peanuts**
- **1 pint premium vanilla ice cream, softened (but not melting)**

BANANA FRITTERS

- **2 tablespoons sesame seeds**
- **1/2 cup (2 ounces) cornstarch**
- **6 tablespoons unbleached all-purpose flour**
- **1 1/2 teaspoons baking powder**
- **3/4 cup ice water, plus more if needed**
- **4 cups plus 1 tablespoon canola oil**
- **6 ripe medium bananas, peeled and quartered**
- **1/4 cup honey**

1. FOR THE PEANUT ICE CREAM: Process the peanuts in a food processor until finely ground and sandy, about fifteen 1-second pulses. Scoop the softened ice cream into a large bowl and, using a stiff rubber spatula, fold in the nuts. Cover the bowl with plastic wrap, pressing the plastic flush against the ice cream. (See the illustration on page 397.) Return to the freezer to firm up, at least 30 minutes, or until needed. (The peanut ice cream can be made up to 2 days ahead.)

2. FOR THE FRITTERS: Toast the sesame seeds in a small nonstick skillet over medium heat, stirring frequently, until lightly browned, about 5 minutes. Transfer to a small bowl and set aside.

3. Combine the cornstarch, flour, and baking powder in a large bowl. Slowly add the ice water and 1 tablespoon of the canola oil, whisking constantly, until the mixture is smooth and slightly thinner than pancake batter, adding more water if necessary. Set aside.

4. Heat the remaining 4 cups canola oil in a Dutch oven over medium-high heat until it reaches 370 degrees. (Use an instant-read thermometer that registers high temperatures or clip a candy/deep-fat thermometer onto the side of the pan before turning on the heat.) Drop half the bananas into the cornstarch batter and toss to coat. Use a slotted spoon or spider (see page 9) to remove the bananas from the batter, tapping the handle of the spoon against the edge of the bowl to remove the excess batter. Add the batter-coated bananas to the hot oil and fry, stirring occasionally, until deep golden brown, about 3 minutes, adjusting the heat as necessary to maintain the cooking temperature. Using a clean slotted spoon or spider, transfer the fried bananas to a rimmed baking sheet lined with several layers of paper towels. Repeat with the remaining bananas.

5. TO SERVE: Divide the fried bananas evenly among 6 individual bowls and drizzle each serving with 2 teaspoons of the honey and 1 teaspoon of the toasted sesame seeds. Top with a small scoop of the peanut ice cream. Serve immediately.

Caramelized Pears *with* Blue Cheese & Black Pepper–Caramel Sauce

Adapted from Caramelized Pears and Stilton with a Black Pepper–Caramel Sauce

Tea Tray in the Sky, Cambridge, Massachusetts

An updated version of the classic combination of pears and blue cheese, these pears are caramelized, rendering them soft and golden. Although tasty on their own, it is the rich caramel sauce surprisingly flavored with crushed black pepper that really sets this dessert apart. Served on an early menu from the café Tea Tray in the Sky, this incredible dessert sounded so delicious that we tracked down the chef and coerced the recipe from his memory.

At the café, the caramel sauce was made in advance, while the pears were cut, dipped in sugar, then seared in a hot nonstick pan to caramelize per order. This multipot method makes sense in a restaurant because it limits the amount of last-minute work during dinner service, but it doesn't make sense for the home cook. To streamline the recipe, we found it easy to cook the pears right in the caramel sauce, saving time and eliminating some dirty dishes. We brought water and sugar (the basis for caramel sauce) to a boil in a skillet and slid the pears into the hot mixture and let them cook in the slowly browning caramel. Because this method actually cooks the pears in the sauce, we found it best to use firm pears that could take the extensive amount of heat. Also, we noted it was easiest to trim the bottom of the pears so that they stand upright on the plate before being cooked, as opposed to after.

With our first batch, we tried removing the pears from the pan before finishing the caramel by stirring in the heavy cream. This didn't work so well: the pears turned unappetizingly sticky as they cooled, having been essentially cooked in sugar candy. For our next batch, we tried adding the cream to the pan around the pears as they finished caramelizing, which transformed the sticky sugar syrup into a smooth sauce that slid right off the pears. We let the pears drain for a few minutes on a wire rack set over a rimmed baking sheet before serving. After removing the pears, we were able to season the sauce left in the skillet with just the right amount of black pepper and salt.

The presentation of this elegant and

sophisticated dessert can be as dramatic or casual as the mood dictates. Whether served individually with an attractive wedge of blue cheese and a fancy swirl of sauce, or presented to the table family-style on a platter, passing the sauce and cheese separately, it is the surprising combination of flavors that makes this dessert so good.

CORING A PEAR

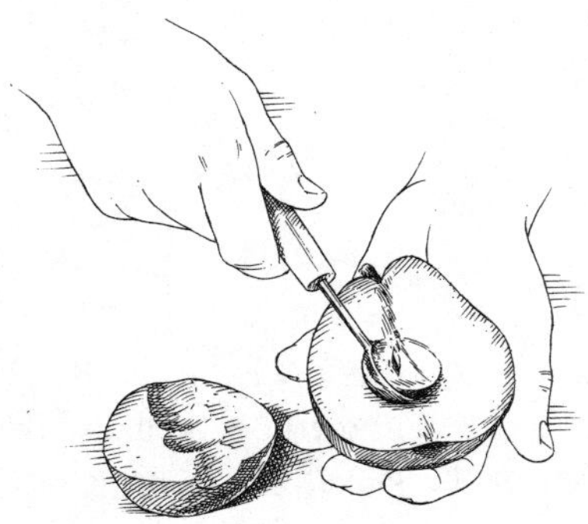

1. To core a pear, cut the fruit in half from stem to blossom end. Use a melon baller to cut around the central core with a circular motion.

2. Draw the melon baller from the central core to the top of the pear, removing the interior portion of the stem as you go.

Caramelized Pears with Blue Cheese and Black Pepper–Caramel Sauce

SERVES 6

Any type of pear can be used in this recipe, as long as it is firm.

- **2/3 cup (4 3/4 ounces) sugar**
- **3 firm pears, halved, seeds removed with a large melon baller, and 1/4 inch trimmed off the bottom of each pear half so it will stand upright**
- **2/3 cup heavy cream**
- **Salt**
- **1/4 teaspoon whole black peppercorns, roughly crushed (see the illustrations on page 393)**
- **3 ounces strong blue cheese (such as Stilton), cut into 6 attractive wedges**

1. Measure ⅓ cup water into a 12-inch nonstick skillet over high heat. Pour the sugar into the center of the pan, taking care not to let the crystals adhere to the sides of the pan. Bring to a boil over high heat, stirring occasionally, until the sugar is fully dissolved and the mixture is bubbling wildly. Add the pears to the skillet, cut-side down, cover, reduce the heat to medium-high, and cook until the pears are nearly tender (a paring knife inserted into the center of the pears feels slight resistance), 13 to 15 minutes.

2. Uncover, reduce the heat to medium, and cook until the sauce is golden brown and the cut sides of the pears are partly caramelized, 3 to 5 minutes. Pour the heavy cream around the pears and cook, shaking the pan back and forth until the sauce is a smooth, deep caramel color and the cut sides of the

pears are beautifully golden, 3 to 5 minutes.

3. Remove the pan from the heat. Using tongs, carefully remove the pears from the pan and place cut-side up on a wire rack set over a rimmed baking sheet. Cool slightly. Season the sauce left in the pan with salt to taste and the crushed black pepper, then pour it into a liquid measuring cup.

4. Carefully (the pears will still be hot) stand each pear half upright on an individual plate and arrange a wedge of the blue cheese beside it. Drizzle the plate and some of the pear with the caramel sauce. Serve immediately. (Alternatively, the pears can be stood upright on a large serving platter, passing the warm caramel sauce and the blue cheese separately.)

CRUSHING PEPPERCORNS

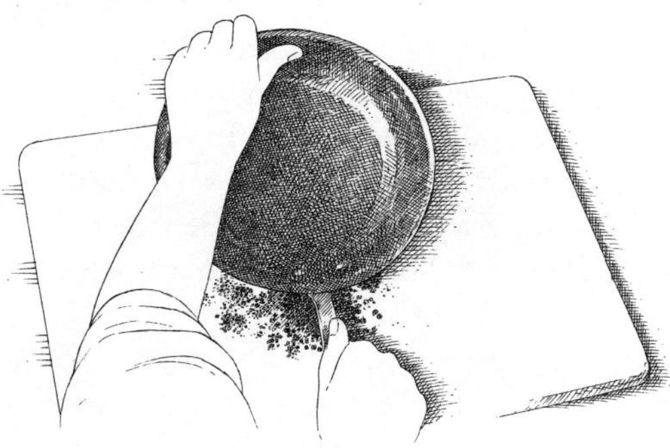

A. Chefs frequently use the back of a heavy pan and a rocking motion to grind peppercorns.

B. Or you can spread the peppercorns in an even layer in a zipper-lock plastic bag and whack them with a rolling pin or meat pounder.

Strawberry Gazpacho

Adapted from Strawberry Gazpacho

Le Relais, Great Falls, Virginia

IN OUR EXPERIENCE, ORDERING FRUIT soup in a restaurant can be disappointing. Oftentimes, you receive a thick, oversweetened concoction that is more of a dessert sauce than a soup. A fruit soup should be a light, delicate affair that focuses on the flavor of the fruit and its natural sweetness. Much to our delight, the recipe from Le Relais produced just this.

What we liked most about this recipe was its bright strawberry flavor, which was underscored by notes of floral vanilla bean, bittersweet citrus zest, earthy cumin, and rum and cognac. We also found that the texture of the soup was better than average. Instead of pureeing all the strawberries, Le Relais reserved some strawberries and diced them into small cubes, which were stirred into the soup before serving, giving it more body and a pleasing texture. Although the flavors of the soup were just right, there were several issues with the recipe that we hoped to modify for the home cook.

Our first area of concentration was the syrup, which along with the strawberries made up the base of the soup. In the original recipe, the syrup was made with a ratio of one cup sugar to two cups water with a small amount of vanilla extract. We soon found, however, that when we added the syrup to the strawberry base in the ratio called for, the soup was too sweet and cloying. No doubt this was due to the restaurant's need to prepare a much greater quantity. Using less syrup to counterbalance the sweetness made the soup too thick and viscous. In subsequent tests, we tried making syrups by increasing the ratio of water to sugar, undersweetening the syrup in hopes of finding a balance. Using one cup of sugar, we increased the amount of water by quarter-cup increments until we found a syrup that provided us with the right consistency but didn't make the soup too sugary. A final ratio of one cup sugar to three cups water was just right.

Besides changing the sugar-to-water ratio in the syrup, we also added the vanilla bean to the syrup rather than the strawberry base. As it stood, the soup gained considerable flavor from the vanilla bean, but we felt that if we were to heat the vanilla in the syrup we would gain even more flavor. In our next trial, we infused the vanilla bean into the syrup and found the flavor to be surprisingly different. As we expected, heating the vanilla had released its potency, resulting in more complex and deeper vanilla flavors.

We also worked with the diced strawberries, which were added to the soup before serving. While we felt that they were an integral part of the soup, we wondered if there was another way to prepare them other than the time-consuming small dice that the recipe called for. Trying several different types of preparation—from rough chopping by hand to pulsing the strawberries in a food processor—we found that the strawberry pieces ranged in size greatly and just didn't provide the same satisfying texture as did the small dice of berries.

The soup, presented in a shallow soup bowl, is simple yet elegant. And as a finishing touch, the soup is served with several small scoops of strawberry sorbet. The icy sorbet, a welcome addition, heightened the strawberry flavor and provided a cooling finish to this warm-weather soup.

Strawberry Gazpacho

SERVES 10

The vanilla syrup and strawberry puree can be made up to 24 hours in advance. Strawberries have a tendency to vary in their level of sweetness. So when mixing the syrup and strawberry base together, start by adding 2 cups of syrup. Taste, and add more syrup if the soup seems too tart.

- **1 cup (7 ounces) sugar**
- **1/2 vanilla bean, split in half lengthwise, seeds removed, seeds and pod reserved (see the illustrations on page 315)**
- **3 pounds (about 6 pints) strawberries, washed, dried, and hulled**
- **1/2 teaspoon grated zest from 1 lemon**
- **1/2 teaspoon grated zest from 1 orange**
- **1/8 teaspoon salt**
- **Pinch ground cumin**
- **2 tablespoons dark rum**
- **1 tablespoon cognac**
- **2 pints strawberry sorbet (or raspberry sorbet)**
- **10 sprigs fresh mint, for garnish (optional)**

1. Bring 3 cups water, sugar, and vanilla seeds and pod to a boil in a medium saucepan over medium-high heat, stirring occasionally. Pour into a large glass measuring cup. Cover tightly with plastic wrap, poke several vent holes using the tip of a paring knife, and refrigerate until needed.

2. Puree 2 pounds of the strawberries, lemon zest, orange zest, salt, cumin, rum, and cognac in a food processor until uniformly smooth, about 30 seconds. Transfer to a large container, cover, and refrigerate until chilled, about 1 hour. (The soup can be made to this point up to 24 hours in advance.)

3. Remove the vanilla pod from the cooled vanilla syrup. Stir 2 cups of the syrup into the chilled strawberry puree. Dice the remaining 1 pound strawberries into ¼-inch pieces and stir into the soup. Taste and add the remaining syrup, 1 tablespoon at a time, until the desired level of sweetness is achieved.

4. Ladle ¾ cup of the soup into each of 10 chilled, shallow soup bowls. Place 2 small scoops of strawberry sorbet in the center of each bowl. Garnish with the mint sprigs, if using. Serve immediately.

Praline Ice Cream *with* Bittersweet Chocolate Sauce

Adapted from Praline Ice Cream with Fudge Sauce

New Rivers, Providence, Rhode Island

CARAMEL, NUTS, AND VANILLA ICE CREAM wrapped into one, this praline ice cream is a whole sundae's worth of flavor in one tight package. New Rivers has kept this ice cream on its menu for over 10 years for good reason: it's a pitch-perfect combination of crowd-pleasing flavors. Spiked with dark rum and laced with caramel and crunchy almonds, the ice cream engages both the adult palate and the inner child. If you have an ice cream maker tucked away in some dark corner, now's the time to brush off the cobwebs and make some creamy homemade ice cream everyone will love.

There are three distinct components to this recipe: praline, caramel sauce, and custard base. Praline, in this instance, refers not to the brown sugar and pecan confection of New Orleans but to the classic French combination of caramelized sugar and almonds—think peanut brittle, but made with sliced almonds. Preparing the praline and caramel sauce blurs into one step since a single batch of caramel is divided—the same component put to multiple purposes in true restaurant-style efficiency. For the praline, the almonds—sliced and toasted—are arranged on a greased baking dish, over which the hot caramel will be poured. Once cool, the caramel-and-nut mixture will slide freely from the dish; if the dish is left ungreased, the caramel will hold fast. Heavy cream is added to the caramel remaining in the pot to make a caramel sauce, which will be added to the custard base as the prime flavoring agent. Adding liquids to hot caramel should always be done with close attention, since the liquid will rapidly boil and produce volumes of steam. We favor a whisk for stirring in the cream, but choose a long-handled one to keep your hands clear of the billowing steam. We also use a tall-sided saucepan to contain any bubbling.

The custard base is a standard French-style ice cream base, meaning cream and milk enriched and thickened with egg yolks, like a crème anglaise (see page 359). (American-style ice cream lacks the egg yolks, relying solely on cream for enrichment.) In a unique step, the cream—in the form of the caramel sauce—is withheld until after the custard is cooked. We found that, without the cream, the custard thickened very rapidly and required close attention and diligent stirring to prevent overcooking. Within a couple of minutes, the custard passed the classic wooden-spoon test: it covered the back of a wooden spoon in a thin but solid coating. At this point, we immediately removed the custard from the heat and strained it through a fine-mesh strainer on the off chance that any of the egg had overcooked. Then, to cool it down quickly, we stirred in the caramel sauce. The restaurant suggested cooling the custard in a bowl set over ice, but we found this step unnecessary. The final touch, prior to processing in the ice cream maker, was a hefty shot each of dark rum and vanilla extract. Being derived from molasses, rum naturally complements caramel and, in this instance, cuts the ice cream's sweetness. The vanilla rounds out the flavors, lending definition to both the cream and the caramel.

Once the ice cream has been churned, the praline is broken into small pieces and stirred in. We found little art to chopping the praline—a rolling pin worked just as well as the back of a chef's knife. Because of its high sugar and alcohol content, the ice cream will be very soft once churned and in need of several hours in the freezer before serving. Admittedly, we had trouble waiting that long before sampling some.

KEEPING ICE CREAM FRESH

To prevent ice crystals from forming on the surface of leftover ice cream, cover the portion remaining in the container with heavy-duty plastic wrap, pressing the wrap flush against the surface of the ice cream. Replace the cover and return the ice cream to the freezer. Use this tip with both homemade and store-bought ice cream.

Praline Ice Cream with Bittersweet Chocolate Sauce

MAKES ABOUT 1 QUART

The ice cream is best within a few days; otherwise the praline loses its crunchiness as it begins to melt into the ice cream. New Rivers serves the ice cream with chocolate sauce in martini glasses accompanied by a delicate cookie or two.

CARAMEL AND PRALINE

Vegetable oil spray
½ cup sliced almonds
2 cups (14 ounces) sugar
1 cup heavy cream

ICE CREAM

1 ½ cups whole milk
6 large egg yolks, lightly beaten
¼ cup (1 ¾ ounces) sugar
2 tablespoons dark rum
1 teaspoon vanilla extract
⅛ teaspoon salt

1 recipe Bittersweet Chocolate Sauce (page 398)

1. For the caramel and praline: Spray a 2-quart glass baking dish with vegetable oil spray. Toast the almonds in a medium heavy-bottomed skillet over medium heat, stirring frequently, until lightly browned, 8 to 9 minutes. Spread the toasted nuts evenly over the bottom of the prepared baking dish and set aside.

2. Measure ½ cup water into a medium heavy-bottomed saucepan. Pour the sugar into the center of the pan, taking care not to

let the crystals adhere to the sides. Cover and bring to a boil over high heat. Once boiling, uncover and boil until the syrup is thick, straw-colored, and registers 300 degrees on an instant-read or candy thermometer, 8 to 9 minutes. Reduce the heat to medium and cook until the syrup is deep amber and registers 350 degrees, 2 to 3 minutes.

3. Pour about half of the hot caramel over the almonds and set aside to cool until hardened, about 30 minutes. When the praline is cool and hard, tap the praline with the end of a wooden spoon into ¼-inch pieces and set aside.

4. Meanwhile, slowly whisk the heavy cream into the remaining hot caramel (the mixture will bubble vigorously). (If lumpy, reheat until the caramel melts and stir until smooth.) Transfer to a small bowl and set aside.

5. FOR THE ICE CREAM: Bring the milk just to a simmer in a medium saucepan over medium-high heat. Immediately remove from the heat. Whisk the eggs yolks and sugar together in a large bowl until thick. Slowly pour the hot milk mixture into the yolks, whisking constantly. Pour back into the saucepan and cook over low heat, stirring constantly with a wooden spoon, until the tiny surface bubbles disappear and the mixture is thick enough to coat the back of the spoon and registers 165 degrees on an instant-read thermometer or candy thermometer.

6. Remove the saucepan from the heat and strain the egg mixture through a fine-mesh strainer into a large bowl. Stir in the caramel-cream mixture, rum, vanilla, and salt. Place a piece of plastic wrap directly against the surface of the custard to prevent a skin from forming. (See the illustration on page 397.) Refrigerate until fully chilled, 3 to 4 hours. (The ice cream can be made to this point up to 2 days in advance.)

7. Pour the chilled mixture into an ice cream maker and process according to the manufacturer's instructions. When it reaches the consistency of soft-serve ice cream, stir in the reserved praline pieces. Scrape into a storage container and freeze until firm or up to 4 days. Serve with the chocolate sauce.

Bittersweet Chocolate Sauce

MAKES 2 CUPS

When whisking the sauce to combine, do so gently so as not to create air bubbles, which will mar its appearance. This sauce can be cooled to room temperature and refrigerated in an airtight container for up to 3 weeks. To reheat, transfer the sauce to a heatproof bowl and set over a saucepan containing 2 inches of simmering water; stir occasionally until melted and warm. Alternatively, transfer the sauce to a microwave-safe bowl and heat on 50-percent power until melted and warm, stirring once or twice, 2 to 3 minutes.

- **1–1¼ cups heavy cream**
- **¼ cup light corn syrup**
- **4 tablespoons (½ stick) unsalted butter**
- **Pinch salt**
- **8 ounces bittersweet chocolate, chopped fine**

Bring 1 cup heavy cream, corn syrup, butter, and salt to a boil in a small nonreactive saucepan over medium-high heat. Remove from the heat and add the chocolate while gently swirling the saucepan. Cover and let stand until the chocolate is melted, about 5 minutes. Uncover and whisk gently until combined. If necessary, adjust the consistency by heating up and adding the remaining ¼ cup cream.

Pear & Green Tea Sorbet

Adapted from Pear and Green Tea Sorbet

Jean Luc's Bistro, Austin, Texas

With the increasing trend toward healthful eating, sorbets for dessert have garnered immense popularity. Restaurants now offer a wide range of sorbets alongside their ice cream selections for those guests who are swearing off the fat associated with ice cream. These sorbets can be as smooth and creamy as any ice cream, satisfying the strongest urge for ice cream. The pear and green tea sorbet from Jean Luc's Bistro is a good example of these low-fat treats.

The sorbet was exceptionally creamy and smooth, and its intense pear flavor was punctuated by the floral undertones of the green tea. Overall, we found the sorbet to be light and refreshing. We did, however, feel that it was a tad too sweet. Since the sorbet consisted of only two components—a fruit puree and a sugar syrup—we hoped finding the optimal balance between the two would be a relatively easy task.

We began by looking at the sugar syrup. The syrup in the original recipe was made with a ratio of one part sugar to one part brewed green tea. While the sorbet made with this syrup had a good consistency, there were several drawbacks. One, as said already, was that the sorbet was too sweet. Second, the high amount of sugar inhibited the freezing of the sorbet such that no matter how long it spent in the freezer, it always remained slightly soupy. Keeping the amount of tea at two cups, we reduced the amount of sugar in half-cup increments with hopes of striking a balance between texture and level of sweetness. This experiment proved to be more difficult than we had expected. We found that when we had a sorbet that wasn't overly sweet, its texture was icy and granular—and vice versa, a sorbet that had a creamy, smooth texture was too sweet.

Searching for a way to rectify this problem, we did a little research and found that many sorbets contain a small amount of lemon juice to counter the sweetness of the syrup. Making the sorbet again with the addition of two tablespoons of lemon juice, we finally settled on a ratio of two parts tea to one part sugar. This syrup, in conjunction with the lemon juice, resulted in a smooth, creamy sorbet, with just the right level of sweetness.

In addition to the ratio of tea to sugar for the syrup, the ratio of syrup to pear puree was crucial to this recipe. This was so not only for texture and flavor, but in order that the sorbet would fit into our ice cream maker. Since most ice cream makers can accept only about four cups, we used this measurement as a guideline. Jean Luc's recipe instructed us to use a ratio of two parts puree to one part syrup. In our ice cream machine, however, using these proportions, the resulting sorbet was slightly icy and the pear masked the green tea flavor. We therefore increased the amount of syrup and decreased the amount of pear puree incrementally and eventually settled on a mixture of 2½ cups puree and 1½ cups syrup. This combination provided us with both smooth texture and a balance of pear and tea flavor, all while not overflowing the sides of our ice cream maker.

Somewhat surprisingly, the original recipe did not call for a specific type of pear. Making several batches of sorbet using a variety of pears, however, we, too, found that the type of pear did not make as much of a difference as the degree of ripeness. All types tasted good as long as they were superripe. Unripe pears, on the other hand, tasted awful.

Pear and Green Tea Sorbet

MAKES 1 QUART

The tea-flavored syrup can be made a day ahead of time. But don't puree the pears until you are ready to freeze the sorbet. Prolonged exposure to the air will turn the pears and the sorbet brown. Rather than calling for a specific type of pear, we found it more important to choose pears that are very ripe. Serve this sorbet with Brown Sugar Shortbread (page 334).

6 green tea bags
¾ cup (5 ¼ ounces) sugar
5 very ripe pears (about 2 pounds), peeled, cored, and cut into large chunks
2 tablespoons juice from 1 large lemon
¼ teaspoon salt

1. Bring 1½ cups water to a boil in a small saucepan over medium-high heat. Remove from the heat, add the tea bags, cover, and steep for 5 minutes. Remove and discard the tea bags and stir in the sugar. Return the pan to medium-high heat and bring to simmer, stirring to dissolve the sugar. Transfer to a medium bowl and cool to room temperature, about 1 hour.

2. Process the pears in a food processor until uniformly smooth, about 30 seconds. Transfer to a large bowl and whisk in the sugar syrup, lemon juice, and salt.

3. Pour the mixture into an ice cream maker and process according to the manufacturer's instructions. Transfer to a plastic container and place a piece of plastic directly against the surface. (See the illustration on page 397.) Freeze until firm, about 2 hours. (The sorbet can be frozen for up to 3 days.)

Cannoli Gelato

Adapted from Cannoli Gelato

Jasper's Restaurant, Kansas City, Missouri

THE TEST KITCHEN WAS INITIALLY SKEPtical of this crazy-sounding ricotta–ice cream concoction. Yet after mixing it together and rechilling it, we found ourselves readily lapping it up and realizing its full brilliance. With the addition of candied citrus peel, chocolate, and pistachios, plain old vanilla ice cream is immediately transformed into a fantastic and fairly exotic Italian dessert.

There aren't many ingredients in this recipe that can go wrong. The original recipe used both vanilla extract and cinnamon oil as flavorings; we substituted ground cinnamon for the hard-to-find oil. We also increased the amounts of chocolate and pistachios and reduced the amount of the potent lemon and orange peel. Candied citrus peels can be bought at most supermarkets in the baking aisle (they are often used in fruitcakes), as well as in Italian grocery stores. As for the vanilla ice cream, we found that using the right brand also makes a difference (see the results of our ice cream tasting on page 402).

Moving on to the method, we again found little that could go wrong. Getting the ice cream soft enough to incorporate the other ingredients without melting it, however, is key. If allowed to melt, the ice cream takes on an unappealing icy texture when it refreezes. To prevent this, we cut the ice cream from its container while quite cold, then broke it into small, evenly sized pieces in a large bowl using a wooden spoon. This way, all of the ice cream becomes soft and pliable at the same time. After folding in the other ingredients using a stiff rubber spatula, we rechilled the mixture. The interesting thing about softening and rechilling ice cream is that its volume decreases. Air that had been whipped into the ice cream when it was made, called "overrun," is removed, making the ice cream more dense, especially after being mixed with the ricotta.

The last key to this dessert's success is its texture when served—it should be soft and creamy, much like soft-serve ice cream. This is easy if it is going to be made and served immediately, since the mixture then requires only enough time in the freezer to rechill. Yet if made far in advance, attaining this soft, servable texture is more difficult because the dense mixture will freeze to a solid block. We tried letting the block sit on the counter to soften, but this didn't work. The exterior melted completely by the time the interior core had even begun to thaw. Instead, we found it best (once again) to remove the mixture from its container and break it up into smaller, evenly sized pieces that could soften quickly and evenly. But because this mixture is more dense than regular vanilla ice cream, it was necessary to upgrade the wooden spoon and bowl to

INGREDIENTS: Vanilla Ice Cream

We wondered if the many brands of vanilla ice cream on the market were very different from one another. To find out, we gathered twenty tasters to sample eight leading national brands of vanilla ice cream, made in what's known as the French, or custard, style, with egg yolks.

Many ice cream manufacturers add stabilizers—most often carrageenan gum or guar gum—to prevent heat shock, an industry term for the degradation in texture caused by the partial melting and refreezing that occurs when ice cream is subjected to extreme temperature changes during transit to the supermarket or when an ice cream case goes through its self-defrosting cycle. Gum additives stabilize ice cream by trapping water in the frozen mass and slowing the growth of ice crystals during melting and refreezing. We thought the presence of stabilizers might affect the test results. To our surprise, this was not the case. The top two brands in our tasting, Edy's Dreamery and Double Rainbow, use stabilizers.

We also expected the nature of the ice creams' vanilla flavor—artificial or natural—would affect the outcome of the test. Again, we were a bit surprised with the results. Blue Bell was the only brand in the tasting that contained artificial vanilla flavor, and it rated smack-dab in the middle, thus negating any link between natural flavor and superior flavor. In fact, tasters took greater issue with several brands made with real vanilla extract—including Häagen-Dazs, Ben and Jerry's, and Edy's Grand—for tasting "artificial" and "boozy." To help explain this odd result, we contacted Bruce Tharp, an independent ice cream consultant based in Wayne, Pennsylvania. He explained that the perceived artificial and alcohol flavors are often caused by the quantity of vanilla extract added to the ice cream—that is, the more extract, the more likely one is to taste the alcohol. Although it's impossible to confirm this theory (manufacturers won't release their recipes to the public), it was clear that the absence of stabilizers and the use of natural flavorings were not reliable indicators of quality.

Next up was the issue of butterfat, which contributes to smooth texture, rich flavor, and structure. Of the ice creams we tasted, butterfat content ranged from 10 to 16 percent and, in general, the higher the butterfat content, the higher the ice cream rated. Our two top-rated ice creams had butterfat contents of 14.5 percent (Edy's Dreamery) and 15 percent (Double Rainbow). The two lowest-rated brands had butterfat contents of 10 to 12 percent and 13 percent.

All commercial ice cream makers also add air to the mix. The air is called overrun—and without it, the ice cream would look more like an ice cube. While the top two ice creams had low overruns of 21 and 26 percent, our third favorite had a whopping overrun of 93.5 percent. Furthermore, the two last-place ice creams had very different overruns—26 percent and 100 percent, 100 percent being the legal limit. Our conclusion? In general, low overrun is preferable, although butterfat content is a better measure of quality.

The last component we researched was emulsifiers, such as mono- and diglycerides, which are used to control the behavior of fat in ice cream by keeping it from separating from the ice cream mass. Emulsifiers give an ice cream rigidity and strength. The only ice cream in our tasting with emulsifiers was also the least favored sample: Edy's Grand. So, according to our taste test, it seems that emulsifiers are not desirable.

The winner of our tasting, as mentioned above, was Edy's Dreamery, with Double Rainbow coming in second and Breyer's third. The real news, however, was the poor showing of the two best-known premium brands, Häagen-Dazs and Ben and Jerry's, which rated fourth and seventh, respectively, out of the eight brands sampled.

THE BEST VANILLA ICE CREAMS
Edy's Dreamery Vanilla (left) was the favorite of our tasters. Double Rainbow French Vanilla (middle) came in second, and Breyer's French Vanilla (right) was third.

a knife and cutting board. We cut the hard, dense mixture into one-inch pieces, which take just 10 to 20 minutes (depending on the kitchen's temperature) to soften. When soft, the small pieces can easily be mashed to a soft and creamy texture using a stiff rubber spatula. We decided that roughly a cup of this "gelato" along with a biscotti was an appropriate portion size for one person, yet duly noted that many of us in the test kitchen could happily eat more.

Cannoli Gelato

SERVES 8 TO 10

If making the dessert more than a few hours ahead of time, transfer the mixture to a plastic container lined with plastic wrap, pressing the excess wrap directly against the gelato's surface to prevent freezer burn. (See the illustration on page 397.) To serve, remove the mixture from the freezer and allow it to sit on the counter until it can be easily removed from the container. Remove the plastic wrap and cut the frozen mixture into 1-inch pieces using a serrated knife (or an electric knife) while holding it steady with a wad of paper towels. Transfer the frozen pieces to a large bowl and let soften at room temperature, mixing and mashing with a stiff rubber spatula occasionally, until soft and creamy, 10 to 20 minutes.

- **4 pints vanilla ice cream**
- **1 (15-ounce) container whole-milk ricotta cheese**
- **¼ teaspoon vanilla extract**
- **4 ounces chopped semisweet or bittersweet chocolate**
- **⅓ cup shelled pistachios, roughly chopped**
- **2 tablespoons chopped candied lemon peel**
- **2 tablespoons chopped candied orange peel**
- **⅛ teaspoon ground cinnamon**
- **10 almond biscotti**

1. Cut the ice cream from its container and transfer it to a large bowl. Using a wooden spoon, break up the ice cream into small pieces. Let the ice cream sit on the counter until it is pliable but not melted, 2 to 7 minutes. Add the ricotta and mix to incorporate using a stiff rubber spatula. Sprinkle the vanilla, chocolate, pistachios, lemon and orange peels, and cinnamon over the mixture and fold to incorporate.

2. Press a large sheet of plastic wrap directly against the surface of the mixture, wrapping the excess tightly around the bowl, and freeze until well chilled, 15 to 30 minutes. Serve immediately, accompanied by the biscotti. (For instructions on how make this dessert in advance, see the headnote.)

INDEX

NOTE: PAGE NUMBERS IN *ITALIC* REFER TO COLOR PHOTOGRAPHS.

C

D

Q

R

W

Y

Z